OUR SLAVE STATES.

A

JOURNEY

IN THE

SEABOARD SLAVE STATES,

WITH REMARKS ON THEIR ECONOMY.

BY

FREDERICK LAW OLMSTED

NEGRO UNIVERSITIES PRESS
NEW YORK

Originally published in 1856 by Dix & Edwards

Reprinted in 1968
by Negro Universities Press
A DIVISION OF GREENWOOD PUBLISHING CORP.
New York

Library of Congress Catalogue Card Number: 68-55903

Reprinted from a copy in the collections of
The New York Public Library
Astor, Lenox and Tilden Foundations;

PREFACE.

THE chief design of the author in writing this book has been, to describe what was most interesting, amusing, and instructive to himself, during the first three of fourteen months' traveling in our Slave States; using the later experience to correct the erroneous impressions of the earlier.

He is aware that it has one fault—it is too fault-finding. He is sorry for it, but it cannot now be helped; so at the outset, let the reader understand that he is invited to travel in company with an honest growler.

But growling is sometimes a duty; and the traveler might well be suspected of being a "dead head," or a sneak, who did not find frequent occasion for its performance, among the notoriously careless, make-shift, impersistent people of the South.

For the rest, the author had, at the outset of his

journey, a determination to see things for himself, as far as possible, and to see them carefully and fairly, but cheerfully and kindly. It was his disposition, also, to search for the causes and extenuating circumstances, past and present, of those phenomena which are commonly reported to the prejudice of the slaveholding community; and especially of those features which are manifestly most to be regretted in the actual condition of the older Slave States.

He protests that he has been influenced by no partisan bias; none, at least, in the smallest degree unfriendly to fair investigation, and honest reporting. At the same time, he avows himself a democrat; not in the technical and partisan, but in the primary and essential sense of that term. As a democrat he went to study the South—its institutions, and its people; more than ever a democrat, he has returned from this labor, and written the pages which follow.

SOUTH-SIDE STATEN ISLAND, Jan. 9, 1856.

CONTENTS.

CHAPTER I.

WASHINGTON.

CHAPTER II.

VIRGINIA.

CHAPTER III.

THE ECONOMY OF VIRGINIA.

CHAPTER IV.

THE POLITICAL EXPERIENCE OF VIRGINIA.

CHAPTER V.

NORTH CAROLINA.

CHAPTER VI.

SOUTH CAROLINA AND GEORGIA.

CHAPTER VII.

RICE, AND ITS CULTURE.

CHAPTER VIII.

EXPERIMENTAL POLITICAL ECONOMY OF SOUTH CAROLINA AND GEORGIA.

CHAPTER IX.

ALABAMA.

"Men are never so likely to settle a question rightly as when they discuss it freely."—*Macaulay.*

" You have among you many a purchased slave,
    Which, like your asses, and your dogs, and mules,
    You use in abject and in slavish parts,
    Because you bought them :

                "So do I answer you.
    The pound of flesh which I demand of him,
    Is dearly bought ; 'tis mine, and I will have it.
    If you deny me, fie upon your law !"—*Shylock.*

" The one idea which History exhibits as evermore developing itself into greater distinctness, is the idea of humanity, the noble endeavor to throw down all barriers erected between men by prejudice and one-sided views, and by setting aside the distinctions of religion, country, and color, to treat the whole human race as one Brotherhood, having one great object—the pure development of our spiritual nature."—*Humboldt's Cosmos.*

OUR SLAVE STATES.

CHAPTER I.

INNS AND OUTS OF WASHINGTON.

GADSBY'S HOTEL, Dec. 10.

To accomplish the purposes which brought me to Washington, it was necessary, on arriving here, to make arrangements to secure food and shelter while I remained. There are two thousand of us visitors in Washington under a similar necessity. There are a dozen or more persons who, for a consideration, undertake to provide what we want. Mr. Dexter is reported to be the best of them, and really seems a very obliging and honestly-disposed person. To Mr. Dexter, therefore, I commit myself.

I commit myself by inscribing my name in a Register. Five minutes after I have done so, Clerk No. 4, whose attention I have been unable to obtain any sooner, suddenly catches the Register by the corner, swings it round with a jerk, and throws a hieroglyphic scrawl at it, which strikes near my name. Henceforth, I figure as Boarder No. 201, (or whatever it may be). Clerk No. 4 whistles ("Boarders, away!"), and throws key, No. 201 upon the table. Turnkey No. 3 takes it, and me, and my traveling bag, up several flights of stairs, along corridors and galleries, and finally consigns me to this little square cell.

I have faith that there is a tight roof above the very much cracked ceiling; that the bed is clean; and that I shall, by-and-by, be summoned, along with hundreds of other persons, to partake, in grandly silent sobriety, of a very sumptuous dinner.

Food and shelter. Therewith should a man be content. It will enable me to accomplish my purpose in coming to Washington. But my perverse nature will not be content: will be wishing things were otherwise. They say this uneasiness—this passion for change—is a peculiarity of our diseased Northern nature. The Southern man finds Providence in all that is: Satan in all that might be. That is good; and, as I am going South, when I have accomplished my purposes at Washington, I will not here restrain the escape of my present discontent.

I have such a shockingly depraved nature that I wish the dinner was not going to be so grand. My idea is that, if it were not, Mr. Dexter would save moneys, which I would like to have him expend in other ways. I wish he had more clerks, so that they would have time to be as polite to an unknown man as I see they are to John P. Hale; and, at least, answer civil questions, when his guests ask them. I don't like such a fearful rush of business as there is down stairs. I wish there were men enough to do the work quietly.

I don't like these cracked and variegated walls; and, though the roof may be tight, I don't like this threatening aspect of the ceiling. It should be kept for people of Damoclesian ambition: I am humble.

I am humble, and I am short, and soon curried; but I am not satisfied with a quarter of a yard of toweling, having an irregular vacancy in its centre, where I am liable to insert my head. I am not proud; but I had rather have something else, or nothing, than these three yards of ragged and faded quarter-ply carpeting. I also would like a curtain to the window, and I wish the glass were not so dusty, and that the sashes did not rattle so in their casements; though, as there is no other ventilation, I suppose I ought not to complain. Of course not; but it is confoundedly cold, as well as noisy. I don't like that broken latch; I don't like this broken chair; I would prefer that this table were not so greasy in its appearance; I would rather the ashes and cinders, and the tobacco juice around the grate, had been removed before I was consigned to the cell.

I wish that less of my two dollars and a half a day went to pay for game for the dinner, and the interest of the cost of the mirrors and mahogany for the public parlors, and of marble for the halls, and more of it for providing me with a private room, which should be more than a barely habitable cell, which should *also* be a little bit tasteful, home-like, and comfortable.

SERVANTS.

I wish more of it was expended in servants' wages.

Six times I rang the bell; three several times came three different Irish lads; entered, received my demand for a fire, and retired. I was writing, shiveringly, a full hour before the fire-man came. Now he has entered, bearing on his head a hod of coal and kindling wood, without knocking. An aged negro, more familiar and more indifferent to forms of subserviency than the Irish lads, very much bent, seemingly with infirmity, an expression of impotent anger in his face, and a look of weakness, like a drunkard's. He does not look at me, but mutters unintelligibly.

"What's that you say?"

" Tink I can make a hundred fires at once ?"

" I dont want to sit an hour waiting for a fire, after I have ordered one, and you must not let me again."

"Nebber let de old nigger have no ress—hundred gemmen tink I kin mak dair fires all de same minute; all get mad at an ole nigger; I ain't a goin to stan it—nebber get no ress—up all night—haint got nautin to eat nor drink dis blessed mornin—hundred gemmen —"

" That's not my business ; Mr. Dexter should have more servants."

" So he ort ter, master, dat he had, one ole man ain't enough for all dis house, is it master? hundred gemmen —"

" Stop—here's a quarter for you; now I want you to look out that I have a good fire, and keep the hearth clean in my room as long as I stay here. And when I send for you I want you to come immediately. Do you understand?"

" I'le try, master—you jus look roun and fine me when you want yer fire; I'll be roun somewhere. You got a newspaper, Sir, I ken take for a minit ; I won't hurt it."

I gave him one; and wondered what use he could put it to, that would not hurt it. He opened it to a folio, and spread it before the grate, so the draft held it in place, and it acted as a blower. I asked if there were no blowers? "No." "But haven't you got any brush or shovel?" I inquired, seeing him get down upon his knees again and sweep the cinders and ashes he had thrown upon the floor with the sleeve of his coat, and then take them up with his hands;—no, he said, his master did not give him such things. " Are you a slave?"

" Yes, sir."

" Do you belong to Mr. Dexter?"

" No, sir, he hires me of de man dat owns me. Don't you tink I'se too ole a man for to be knock roun at dis kind of work, massa?—hundred gemmen all want dair fires made de same minute, and caus de old nigger cant do it all de same minute, ebbery one tinks dey's boun to scold him all de time; nebber no rest for him, no time."

I know the old fellow lied somewhat, for I saw another fireman in Mr. B.'s room. Was that quarter a good investment, or should I have complained at the office? No, they are too busy to listen to me, too busy, certainly, to make better arrangements.

It is time for me to call on Mr. S.; the fire has gone out, leaving a fine bituminous fragrance in the cell. I will " look round" for the fireman, as I travel the long road to the office, and, if I do not find him, leave an order, in writing, for a fire to be made before two o'clock.

A MARYLAND FARM.

WASHINGTON, Dec. 14th. Called on Mr. C., whose fine farm, from its vicinity to Washington, and its excellent management, as well as from the hospitable habits of its owner, has a national reputation. It is some two thousand acres in extent, and situated just without the District, in Maryland.

The residence is in the midst of the farm, a quarter of a mile from the high road—the private approach being judiciously carried through large pastures which are divided only by slight, but close and well-secured, wire fences. The mansion is of brick, and, as seen through the surrounding trees, has somewhat the look of an old French chateau. The kept grounds are very limited, and in simple but quiet taste; being surrounded only by wires, they merge, in effect, into the pastures. There is a fountain, an ornamental dove-cote, and ice-house, and the approach road, nicely graveled and rolled, comes up to the door with a fine sweep.

I had dismounted and was standing before the door, when I heard myself loudly hailed from a distance.

"Ef yer wants to see Master, sah, he's down thar—to the new stable."

I could see no one; and when I was tired of holding my horse, I mounted, and rode on in search of the new stable. I found it without difficulty; and in it Mr. and Mrs. C. With them were a number of servants, one of whom now took my horse with alacrity. I was taken at once to look at a very fine herd of cows, and afterwards led upon a tramp over the farm, and did not get back to the house till dinner time.

The new stable is most admirably contrived for convenience, labor-saving, and economy of space. (Full and accurate descriptions of it, with illustrations, have been given in several agricultural journals.) The cows are mainly thorough-bred Shorthorns, with a few imported Ayrshires and Alderneys, and some small black "natives." I have seldom seen a better lot of milkers; they are kept in good condition, are brisk and healthy, docile and kind, soft and pliant of skin, and give milk up to the very eve of calving; milking being never interrupted for a day. Near the time of calving the milk is given to the calves and pigs. The object is to obtain milk only, which is never converted into butter or cheese, but sent immediately to town, and for this the

Shorthorns are found to be the most profitable breed. Mr. C. believes that, for butter, the little Alderneys, from the peculiar richness of their milk, would be the most valuable. He is, probably, mistaken, though I remember that in Ireland the little black Kerry cow was found fully equal to the Ayrshire for butter, though giving much less milk.

There are extensive bottom lands on the farm, subject to be flooded in freshets, on which the cows are mainly pastured in summer. Indian corn is largely sown for fodder, and, during the driest season, the cows are regularly *soiled* with it. These bottom lands were entirely covered with heavy wood, until, a few years since, Mr. C. erected a steam saw-mill, and has lately been rapidly clearing them, and floating off the sawed timber to market by means of a small stream that runs through the farm.

The low land is much of it drained, underdrains being made of rough boards of any desired width nailed together, so that a section is represented by the inverted letter Λ. Such covered drains have lasted here twenty years without failing yet, but have only been tried where the flow of water was constant throughout the year.

The water collected by the drains can be, much of it, drawn into a reservoir, from which it is forced by a pump, driven by horse-power, to the market-garden, where it is distributed from several fountain-heads, by means of hose, and is found of great value, especially for celery. The celery trenches are arranged in concentric circles, the water-head being in the center. The water-closets and all the drainage of the house are turned to good account in the same way. Mr. C. contemplates extending his water-pipes to some of his meadow lands. Wheat and hay are the chief crops sold off the farm, and the amount of them produced is yearly increasing.

The two most interesting points of husbandry, to me, were the large and profitable use of guano and bones, and the great extent of turnip culture. Crops of one thousand and twelve hundred bushels of ruta baga to the acre have been frequent, and this year the whole crop of the farm is reckoned to be over thirty thousand bushels; all to be fed out to the neat stock between this time and the next pasture season. The soil is generally a red, stiff loam, with an occasional stratum of coarse gravel, and, therefore, not the most favorable for turnip culture. The seed is always imported, Mr. C.'s experience, in this respect, agreeing with my own:—the Ruta baga undoubtedly degenerates in our climate. Bones, guano, and ashes are used in connection with yard-dung for manure. The seed is sown from the middle to the last of July in drills, but not in ridges, in the English way. In both these respects, also, Mr. C. confirms the conclusions I have arrived at in the climate of New York; namely, that ridges are best dispensed with, and that it is better to sow in the latter part of July than in June, as has been generally recommended in our books and periodicals. Last year, turnips sown on the 20th July were larger and finer than others, sown on the same ground, on my farm, about the first of the month. This year I sowed in August, and, by forcing with superphosphate—home manufactured—and guano, obtained a fine crop; but the season was unusually favorable.

Mr. C. always secures a supply of turnips that will allow him to give at least one bushel a day to every cow while in winter quarters. The turnips are sliced, slightly salted, and commonly mixed with fodder and meal. Mr. C. finds that salting the sliced turnip, twelve hours before it is fed, effectually prevents its communicating any taste to the milk. This, so far as I know, is an original discovery of his, and is one of great value to dairymen. In certain English dairies the same result is obtained, where the cows are fed on cabbages, by the expensive process of heating the milk to a certain temperature and then adding saltpetre.

The wheat crop of this district has been immensely increased, by the use of guano, during the last four years. On this farm it has been largely used for five years; and land that had not been cultivated for forty years, and which bore only broom-sedge—a thin, worthless grass—by the application of two hundred weight of Peruvian guano, now yields thirty bushels of wheat to an acre.

Mr. C.'s practice of applying guano differs, in some particulars, from that commonly adopted here. After a deep plowing of land intended for wheat, he sows the seed and guano at the same time, and harrows both in. The common custom here is to plow in the guano, six or seven inches deep, in preparing the ground for wheat. I believe Mr. C.'s plan is the best. I have myself used guano on a variety of soils for several years with great success for wheat, and I may mention the practice I have adopted from the outset, and with which I am well satisfied. It strikes between the two systems I have mentioned, and I think is philosophically right. After preparing the ground with plow and harrow, I sow wheat and guano together, and plow them in with a gang-plow which covers to a depth, on an average, of three inches.

Clover seed is sowed in the spring following the wheat-sowing, and the year after the wheat is taken off, this—on the old sterile hills—grows luxuriantly, knee-high. It is left alone for two years, neither mown nor pastured; there it grows and there it lies, keeping the ground moist and shady, and improving it on the Gurney principle.

Mr. C. then manures with dung, bones, and guano, and with another crop of wheat lays this land down to grass. What the ultimate effect of this system will be, it is yet too early to say— but Mr. C. is pursuing it with great confidence.

SLAVE LABOR—FIRST IMPRESSIONS.

Mr. C. is a large hereditary owner of slaves, which, for ordinary field and stable-work, constitute his laboring force. He has employed several Irishmen for ditching, and for this work, and this alone, he thought he could use them to better advantage than negroes. He would not think of using Irishmen for common farm-labor, and made light of their coming in competition with slaves. Negroes at hoeing and any steady field-work, he assured me, would "do two to their one;" but his main objection to employing Irishmen was derived from his experience of their unfaithfulness—they were dishonest, would not obey explicit directions about their work, and required more personal supervision than negroes. From what he had heard and seen of Germans, he supposed they did better than Irish. He mentioned that there were several Germans who had come here as laboring men, and worked for wages several years, who had now got possession of small farms, and were reputed to be getting rich.* He was disinclined to converse on the topic of slavery, and

---

* "There is a small settlement of Germans, about three miles from me, who, a few years since (with little or nothing beyond their physical abilities to aid them), seated themselves down in a poor, miserable old field, and have, by their industry, and means obtained by working round among the neighbors, effected a change which is really surprising and pleasing to behold, and who will, I have no doubt, become wealthy, provided they remain prudent, as they have hitherto been industrious."
—F. A. CLOPPER, (Montgomery Co.), Maryland, in Patent Of. Rept., 1851.

I, therefore, made no inquiries about the condition and habits of his negroes, or his management of them.   They seemed to live in small and rude log-cabins, scattered in different parts of the farm.   Those I saw at work appeared to me to move very slowly and awkwardly, as did also those engaged in the stable.   These, also, were very stupid and dilatory in executing any orders given to them, so that Mr. C. would frequently take the duty off their hands into his own, rather than wait for them, or make them correct their blunders: they were much, in these respects, like what our farmers call *dumb Paddies*—that is, Irishmen who do not readily understand the English language, and who are still weak and stiff from the effects of the emigrating voyage.   At the entrance-gate was a porter's lodge, and, as I approached, I saw a black face peeping at me from it, but, both when I entered and left, I was obliged to dismount and open the gate myself.

Altogether, it struck me slaves coming here as they naturally did in direct comparison with free laborers, as commonly employed on my own and my neighbor's farms, in exactly similar duties— that they must be very difficult to direct efficiently, and that it must be very irksome and trying to one's patience, to have to superintend their labor.

MARKET-DAY—NEGROES AND LIVE STOCK.

WASHINGTON, Dec. 16. Visiting the market-place, early on Tuesday morning, I found myself in the midst of a throng of a very different character from any I have ever seen at the North.   The majority of the people were negroes, and, taken as a whole, they appeared inferior in the expression of their face and less well-clothed than any collection of negroes I had ever seen before.   All the negro characteristics were more clearly marked in each than they often are in any at the North. In their dress, language, manner, motions—all were distinguishable almost as much by their color, from the white people who were distributed among them, and engaged in the same occupations—chiefly selling poultry, vegetables, and small country-produce. The white men were, generally, a mean looking people, and but meanly dressed, but differently so from the negroes.

Most of the produce was in small, rickety carts, drawn by the smallest, ugliest, leanest lot of oxen and horses that I ever saw. There was but one pair of horses in over a hundred that were tolerably good—a remarkable proportion of them were maimed in some way. As for the oxen, I do not believe New England and New York together could produce a single yoke so poor as the best of them.

The very trifling quantity of articles brought in and exposed for sale by most of the market-people was noticeable; a peck of potatoes, three bunches of carrots, two cabbages, six eggs and a chicken, would be about the average stock in trade of all the dealers. Mr. F. said that an old negro woman once came to his door with a single large turkey, which she pressed him to buy. Struck with her fatigued appearance, he made some inquiries of her, and ascertained that she had been several days coming from home, had traveled mainly on foot, and had brought the turkey and nothing else with her. " Ole massa had to raise some money somehow, and he could not sell anyting else, so he tole me to catch the big gobbler, and tote um down to Washington and see wot um would fotch."

The prices of garden productions were high, compared even with New York. All the necessaries of life are very expensive in

Washington; great complaint is made of exorbitant rents, and building-lots are said to have risen in value several hundred *per cent.* within five or six years.

The population of the city is now over 50,000, and is increasing rapidly. There seems to be a deficiency of tradespeople, and I have no doubt the profits of retailers are excessive. There is one cotton factory in the District of Columbia, employing one hundred and fifty hands, male and female; a small foundry; a distillery; and two tanneries—all not giving occupation to fifty men; less than two hundred, altogether, out of a resident population of nearly 150,000, being engaged in manufactures. Very few of the remainder are engaged in *productive* occupations. There is water-power near the city, superior to that of Lowell, of which, at present, I understand that no use at all is made.

LAND AND LABOR IN THE DISTRICT.

Land may be purchased, within twenty miles of Washington, at from ten to twenty dollars an acre. Most of it has been once in cultivation, and, having been exhausted in raising tobacco, has been, for many years, abandoned, and is now covered by a forest growth. Several New Yorkers have lately speculated in the purchase of this sort of land, and, as there is a good market for wood, and the soil, by the decay of leaves upon it, and other natural causes, has been restored to moderate fertility, have made money by clearing and improving it. By deep plowing and limeing, and the judicious use of manures, it is made very productive; and, as equally cheap farms can hardly be found in any free State, in such proximity to so high markets for agricultural produce, as those of Washington and Alexandria, there are good inducements for a considerable

Northern immigration hither. It may not be long before a majority of the inhabitants will be opposed to Slavery, and desire its abolition within the District. Indeed, when Mr. Seward proposed in the Senate to allow them to decide that matter, the advocates of "popular sovereignty" made haste to vote down the motion.

There are, already, more Irish and German laborers and servants than *slaves*, and, as many of the objections which free laborers have to going further South, do not operate in Washington, the proportion of white laborers is every year increasing. The majority of servants, however, are now *free* negroes, which class constitutes one-fifth of the entire population. The slaves are one-fifteenth, but are mostly owned out of the District, and hired annually to those who require their services. In the assessment of taxable property, for 1853, the slaves, owned or hired in the District, were valued at three hundred thousand dollars.

THE NEGROES OF WASHINGTON.

The colored population voluntarily sustain several churches, schools, and mutual assistance and improvement societies, and there are evidently persons among them of no inconsiderable cultivation of mind. Among the Police Reports of the City newspapers, there was lately (April, 1855) an account of the apprehension of twenty-four "genteel colored men" (so they were described), who had been found by a watchman assembling privately in the evening, and been lodged in the watch-house. The object of their meeting appears to have been purely benevolent, and, when they were examined before a magistrate in the morning, no evidence was offered, nor does there seem

to have been any suspicion that they had any criminal purpose. On searching their persons, there were found a Bible,
a volume of *Seneca's Morals; Life in Earnest;* the printed
Constitution of a Society, the object of which was said to be
"*to relieve the sick, and bury the dead;*" and a subscription paper
to purchase the freedom of Eliza Howard, a young woman,
whom her owner was willing to sell at $650.

I can think of nothing that would speak higher for the
character of a body of poor men, servants and laborers, than
to find, by chance, in their pockets, just such things as these.
And I cannot value that man as a countryman, who does not
feel intense humiliation and indignation, when he learns that
such men may not be allowed to meet privately together, with
such laudable motives, in the capital city of the United States,
without being subject to disgraceful punishment. Washington
is, at this time, governed by the Know Nothings, and the
magistrate, in disposing of the case, was probably actuated by
a well-founded dread of secret conspiracies, inquisitions, and
persecutions. One of the prisoners, a slave named Joseph
Jones, he ordered to be flogged; four others, called in the
papers free men, and named John E. Bennett, Chester Taylor,
George Lee, and Aquila Barton, were sent to the Work-house,
and the remainder, on paying costs of court, and fines, amount-
ing, in the aggregate, to one hundred and eleven dollars, were
permitted to range loose again.

Had this happened at Naples, and had the men been Pro-
testants, what would the Protestant world have called it? Had
it happened at Havana, and the men been American citizens,
enrolling offices for volunteers would have been instantly
opened in New Orleans and New York.

CHAPTER II.

VIRGINIA.

GLIMPSES BY RAIL-ROAD.

Dec. 16th. From Washington to Richmond, Virginia, by the regular great southern route—steamboat on the Potomac to Acquia Creek, and thence direct by rail. The boat makes 55 miles in $3\frac{1}{2}$ hours, including two stoppages ($12\frac{1}{2}$ miles an hour); fare $2 ($3\cdot6$ cents a mile). Flat rail; distance, 75 miles; time, $5\frac{1}{2}$ hours (13 miles an hour); fare, $3 50 ($4\frac{2}{3}$ cents a mile).

Not more than a third of the country, visible on this route,

I should say, is cleared; the rest is mainly a pine forest. Of
the cleared land, not more than one quarter seems to have
been lately in cultivation; the rest is grown over with briars
and bushes, and a long, coarse grass of no value. But two
crops seem to be grown upon the cultivated land—maize and
wheat. The last is frequently sown in narrow beds and
carefully surface-drained, and is looking remarkably well.

A good many substantial old plantation mansions are to be
seen; generally standing in a grove of white oaks, upon some
hill-top. Most of them are constructed of wood, of two stories,
painted white, and have, perhaps, a dozen rude-looking little
log-cabins scattered around them, for the slaves. Now and
then, there is one of more pretension, with a large porch or
gallery in front, like that of Mount Vernon. These are
generally in a heavy, compact style; less often, perhaps, than
similar establishments at the North, in markedly bad, or vulgar
taste; but seldom elegant, or even neat, and almost always in
sad need of repairs.

The more common sort of habitations of the white people
are either of logs or loosely-boarded frames, a brick chimney
running up outside, at one end: everything very slovenly and
dirty about them. Swine, fox-hounds, and black and white
children, are commonly lying very promiscuously together, on
the ground about the doors.

I am struck with the close co-habitation and association of
black and white—negro women are carrying black and white
babies together in their arms; black and white children are
playing together (not going to school together); black and
white faces are constantly thrust together out of the doors, to
see the train go by.

A fine-looking, well-dressed, and well-behaved colored young man sat, together with a white man, on a seat in the cars. I suppose the man was his master; but he was much the less like a gentleman, of the two. The rail-road company advertise to take colored people only in second class trains; but servants seem to go with their masters everywhere. Once, to-day, seeing a lady entering the car at a way-station, with a family behind her, and that she was looking about to find a place where they could be seated together, I rose, and offered her my seat, which had several vacancies around it. She accepted it, without thanking me, and immediately installed in it a stout negro woman; took the adjoining seat herself, and seated the rest of her party before her. It consisted of a white girl, probably her daughter, and a bright and very pretty mulatto girl. They all talked and laughed together, and the girls munched confectionery out of the same paper, with a familiarity and closeness of intimacy that would have been noticed with astonishment, if not with manifest displeasure, in almost any chance company at the North. When the negro is definitely a slave, it would seem that the alleged natural antipathy of the white race to associate with him is lost.

I am surprised at the number of fine-looking mulattoes, or nearly white colored persons, that I see. The majority of those with whom I have come personally in contact are such. I fancy I see a peculiar expression among these—a contraction of the eyebrows and tightening of the lips—a spying, secretive, and counsel-keeping expression.

But the great mass, as they are seen at work, under overseers, in the fields, appear very dull, idiotic, and brute-like; and it requires an effort to appreciate that they are, very much more than the beasts they drive, our brethren—a part of ourselves. They are very ragged, and the women especially, who work in the field with the men, with no apparent distinction in their labor, disgustingly dirty. They seem to move very awkwardly, slowly, and undecidedly, and almost invariably stop their work while the train is passing.

One tannery and two or three saw-mills afforded the only indications I saw, in seventy-five miles of this old country—settled before any part of Massachusetts—of any industrial occupation other than corn and wheat culture, and fire-wood chopping. At Fredericksburg we passed through the streets of a rather busy, poorly-built town; but, altogether, the country seen from the rail-road, bore less signs of an active and prospering people than any I ever traveled through before, for an equal distance.

RICHMOND, AT A GLANCE.

Richmond, at a glance from adjacent high ground, through a dull cloud of bituminous smoke, upon a lowering winter's day, has a very picturesque appearance, and I was reminded of the sensation produced by a similar *coup d'œil* of Edinburg. It is somewhat similarly situated upon and among some considerable hills, but the moment it is examined at all in detail, there is but one spot, in the whole picture, upon which the eye is at all attracted to rest. This is the Capitol, an imposing Grecian edifice, standing alone, and finely placed on open and elevated ground, in the center of the town. It was built soon after the Revolution, and the model was obtained by Mr. Jefferson, then Minister to France, from the Maison Carrée.

A considerable part of the town, which contains a population of 28,000, is compactly and somewhat substantially built, but is without any pretensions to architectural merit, except in a few modern private mansions. The streets are not paved, and but few of them are provided with side-walks other than of earth or gravel. The town is lighted with gas, and furnished with excellent water by an aqueduct.

THE CAPITOL.

On a closer view of the Capitol, a bold deviation from the Grecian model is very noticeable. The southern portico is sustained upon a very high blank wall, and is as inaccessible from the exterior as if it had been intended to fortify the edifice from all ingress other than by scaling-ladders. On coming round to the west side, however, which is without a colonnade, a grand entrance, reached by a heavy buttress of stone steps, is found. This incongruity diminishes, in some degree, the usual inconvenience of the Greek temple for modern public purposes, for it gives speedy access to a small central rotunda, out of which doors open into the legislative halls and offices.

THE "PUBLIC GUARD," AND WHAT IT MEANS.

If the walling up of the legitimate entrance has caused the impression, in a stranger, that he is being led to a prison or fortress, instead of the place for transacting the public business of a free State by its chosen paid agents, it is not removed when, on approaching this side door, he sees before it an armed sentinel—a meek-looking man in a livery of many colors, embarrassed with a bright bayonetted firelock, which he hugs gently, as though the cold iron, this frosty day, chilled his arm.

He belongs to the Public Guard of Virginia, I am told; a company of a hundred men (more or less), enlisted under an Act of the State, passed in 1801, after a rebellion of the colored people, who, under one "General Gabriel," attempted to take the town, in hopes to gain the means of securing their freedom. Having been betrayed by a traitor, as insurgent slaves almost always are, they were met, on their approach, by a large body of well-armed militia, hastily called out by the Governor. For this, being armed only with scythe-blades, they were unprepared, and immediately dispersed. "General Gabriel" and the other leaders, one after another, were captured, tried, and hanged, the militia in strong force guarding them to execution. Since then, a disciplined guard, bearing the warning motto, "*Sic semper tyrannis!*"* has been kept constantly under arms in the capital, and no man can enter the legislative temple of Virginia without being reminded that "Eternal vigilance is the price of — —"

The gentleman who gave me the substance of this information, spoke of the Guard with an admiring and gratulatory tone, as "our little army." "But how is that?" I inquired; "does not our federal Constitution require that no State shall keep troops in time of peace? Is not your little army unconstitutional?"

I could get no satisfactory reply; I fear it was hardly in good taste, under the circumstances, to make such an inquiry of a Virginia democrat.

PRETENSE AND PARSIMONY.

It was not till I had passed the guard, unchallenged, and stood at the door-way, that I perceived that the imposing edifice, as I had thought it at a distance, was nothing but a cheap

---

* "So ever to tyrants," the motto on the seal of Virginia.

stuccoed building; nor would anything short of test by touch, have convinced me that the great state of Virginia would have been so long content with such a parsimonious pretense of dignity as is found in imitation granite and imitation marble.

There is an instance of parsimony, without pretense, in Richmond, which Ruskin, himself, if he were a traveler, could not be expected to applaud. The rail-road company which brings the traveler from Washington, so far from being open to the criticism of having provided edifices of a style of architecture only fitted for palaces, instead of a hall suited to conflicts with hackney-coachmen, actually has no sort of stationary accommodations for them at all, but sets them down, rain or shine, in the middle of one of the main streets. The adjoining hucksteries, barbers'-shops, and bar-rooms, are evidently all the better patronized for this fine simplicity; but I should doubt if the rail-road stock would be much advanced in value by it.

THE MODEL AMERICAN.

In the rotunda of the Capitol stands Houdon's statue of Washington. It was modeled from life, and is said to present the truest similitude of the American Great Man that is retained for posterity. The face has a lofty, serene, slightly saddened expression, as that of a strong, sensible man loaded, but not over-burdened, with cares and anxiety. A self-reliant, brave, able soul, with deep but subdued sympathies, comprehending great duties, calmly and confidently prepared to perform them. There is very little like a king, or a clergyman, or any other professional character-actor in it. In most of the portraits of Washington, he looks as if he were a great tragedian, or a high-priest; but this is a face that would satisfy and encourage one in the engine-driver of a lightning train, or the officer of the deck in a fog off Cape Race ; far-seeing, vigilant and fervid, but composed and perfectly controlled—the face of a man, wherever you found him—as a sailor, or a schoolmaster, or a judge, or a general—that you could depend upon to perform his undertakings conscientiously. The figure is not good; it struts, and has an air of nonchalance and ungentlemanly assumption. This was the fashion of the age, however, and education may have given it to the man, though his character, as seen with certainty in his face, is far superior to it.

PUBLIC GROUNDS—THE RED CEDAR.

The grounds about the Capitol are naturally admirable, and have lately been improved with neatness and taste. Their beauty and interest would be greatly increased if more of the fine native trees and shrubs of Virginia, particularly the holly and the ever-green magnolias, were planted in them. I noticed these, as well as the Irish and palmated ivy, growing, with great vigor and beauty, in the private gardens of the town. On some high, sterile lands, of which there are several thousand acres, uninclosed and uncultivated, near the town, I saw a group of exceedingly beautiful trees, having the lively green and all the lightness, gracefulness and beauty of foliage, in the Winter, of the finest deciduous trees. I could not believe, until I came near them, that they were what I found them to be—our common red cedar (*Juniperus Virginiana*). I have frequently noticed that the beauty of this tree is greatly affected by the soil it stands in ; in certain localities, on the Hudson river, for instance, and in the lower part of New Jersey, it grows in a perfectly dense, conical, cypress-like form. These, on the other hand, were square-headed, dense, flattened at the top, like the cedar of Lebanon, and with a light and slightly drooping spray, deliciously delicate and graceful, where it cut the light. They stood in a soil of small quartz gravel, slightly bound with red clay. In a soil of similar appearance at the North, cedars are usually thin, stiff, shabby, and dull in color. I notice that they are generally finer here, than we often see them under the best of circumstances; and I presume they are better suited in climate.

A NEGRO FUNERAL.

On a Sunday afternoon I met a negro funeral procession, and followed after it to the place of burial. There was a decent hearse, of the usual style, drawn by two horses; six hackney coaches followed it, and six well-dressed men, mounted on handsome saddle-horses, and riding them well, rode in the rear of these. Twenty or thirty men and women were also walking together with the procession, on the side-walk. Among all there was not a white person.

Passing out into the country, a little beyond the principal cemetery of the city (a neat, rural ground, well filled with monuments and evergreens), the hearse halted at a desolate place, where a dozen colored people were already engaged heaping the earth over the grave of a child, and singing a wild kind of chant. Another grave was already dug, immediately adjoining that of the child, both being near the foot of a hill, in a crumbling bank—the ground below being already occupied, and the graves advancing in irregular terraces up the hill-side—an arrangement which facilitated labor.

The new comers, setting the coffin—which was neatly made of stained pine—upon the ground, joined in the labor and the singing, with the preceding party, until a small mound of earth was made over the grave of the child. When this was completed, one of those who had been handling a spade, sighed deeply and said,

"Lord Jesus have marcy on us—now! you Jim—*you!* see *yar;* you jes lay dat yar shovel cross dat grave—so fash— dah—yes, dat's right."

A shovel and a hoe-handle having been laid across the unfilled grave, the coffin was brought and laid upon them, as on a trestle; after which, lines were passed under it, by which it was lowered to the bottom.

Most of the company were of a very poor appearance, rude and unintelligent, but there were several neatly-dressed and very good-looking men. One of these now stepped to the head of the grave, and, after a few sentences of prayer, held a handkerchief before him as if it were a book, and pronounced a short exhortation, as if he were reading from it. His manner was earnest, and the tone of his voice solemn and impressive, except that, occasionally, it would break into a shout or kind of howl at the close of a long sentence. I noticed several women near him, weeping, and one sobbing intensely. I was deeply influenced myself by the unaffected feeling, in connection with the simplicity, natural, rude truthfulness, and absence of all attempt at formal decorum in the crowd.

I never in my life, however, heard such ludicrous language as was sometimes uttered by the speaker. Frequently I could not guess the idea he was intending to express. Sometimes it was evident that he was trying to repeat phrases that he had heard used before, on similar occasions, but which he made absurd by some interpolation or distortion of a word;

thus, " We do not see the end here! oh no, my friends! there
will be a *putrification* of this body !" the context failing to indicate
whether he meant purification or putrefaction, and leaving it
doubtful if he attached any definite meaning to the word himself.
He quoted from the Bible several times, several times from hymns,
always introducing the latter with " in the words of the poet, my
brethren ;" he once used the same form, before a verse from the
New Testament, and once qualified his citation by saying, " I
believe the Bible says that;" in which he was right, having
repeated words of Job.

He concluded by throwing a handful of earth on the
coffin, repeating the usual words, slightly disarranged, and
then took a shovel, and, with the aid of six or seven others,
proceeded very rapidly to fill the grave. Another man had,
in the mean time, stepped into the place he had first occupied at
the head of the grave; an old negro, with a very singularly
distorted face, who raised a hymn, which soon became a confused
chant—the leader singing a few words alone, and the company
then either repeating them after him or making a response to
them, in the manner of sailors heaving at the windlass. I
could understand but very few of the words. The music was
wild and barbarous, but not without a plaintive melody. A new
leader took the place of the old man, when his breath gave out
(he had sung very hard, with much bending of the body and
gesticulation), and continued until the grave was filled, and
a mound raised over it.

A man had, in the mean time, gone into a ravine near
by, and now returned with two small branches, hung with
withered leaves, that he had broken off a beech tree ; these
were placed upright, one at the head, the other at the foot

of the grave. A few sentences of prayer were then repeated in a low voice by one of the company, and all dispersed. No one seemed to notice my presence at all. There were about fifty colored people in the assembly, and but one other white man besides myself. This man lounged against the fence, outside the crowd, an apparently indifferent spectator, and I judged he was a police officer, or some one procured to witness the funeral, in compliance with the law which requires that a white man shall always be present at any meeting, for religious exercises, of the negroes, to destroy the opportunity of their conspiring to gain their freedom.

DRESS OF THE SLAVES.

The greater part of the colored people, on Sunday, seemed to be dressed in the cast-off fine clothes of the white people, received, I suppose, as presents, or purchased of the Jews, whose shops show that there must be considerable importation of such articles, probably from the North, as there is from England into Ireland. Indeed, the lowest class, especially among the younger, remind me much, by their dress, of the "lads" of Donnybrook; and when the funeral procession came to its destination, there was a scene precisely like that you may see every day in Sackville-street, Dublin,—a dozen boys in ragged clothes, originally made for tall men, and rather folded round their bodies than worn, striving who should hold the horses of the *gentlemen* when they dismounted to attend the interment of the body. Many, who had probably come in from the farms near the town, wore clothing of coarse gray "negro-cloth," that appeared as if made by contract, without regard to the size of the particular individual to whom it had been allotted, like penitentiary uniforms. A few had a better suit of coarse blue cloth, expressly made for them evidently, for "Sunday clothes."

DANDIES.

Some were dressed with laughably foppish extravagance, and a great many in clothing of the most expensive materials, and in the latest style of fashion.   In what I suppose to be the fashionable streets, there were many more well-dressed and highly-dressed colored people than white, and among this dark gentry the finest French cloths, embroidered waistcoats, patent-leather shoes, resplendent brooches, silk hats, kid gloves, and *cau de mille fleurs*, were quite as common as among the New York " dry-goods clerks," in their Sunday promenades, in Broadway.   Nor was the fairer, or rather the softer sex, at all left in the shade of this splendor.   Many of the colored ladies were dressed not only expensively, but with good taste and effect, after the latest Parisian mode.   Many of them were quite attractive in appearance, and some would have produced a decided sensation in any Europe   drawing-room.   Their walk and carriage was more often stylish and graceful than that of the white ladies who were out.   About one quarter seemed to me to have lost all distinguishingly African peculiarity of feature, and to have acquired, in place of it, a good deal of that voluptuousness of expression which characterizes many of the women of the south of Europe. I was especially surprised to notice the frequency of thin, aquiline noses.

WHITE AND BLACK IN THE STREETS.

There was no indication of their belonging to a subject race, but that they invariably gave the way to the white people they met.   Once, when two of them, engaged in conversation and

looking at each other, had not noticed his approach, I saw a
Virginia gentleman lift his cane and push a woman aside with it.
In the evening I saw three rowdies, arm-in-arm, taking the whole
of the sidewalk, hustle a black man off it, giving him a blow, as
they passed, that sent him staggering into the middle of the
street. As he recovered himself he began to call out to, and threaten
them. Perhaps he saw me stop, and thought I should support
him, as I was certainly inclined to : " can't you find anything
else to do than to be knockin' quiet people round! You jus'
come back here, will you? Here, you! *don't care if you is
white.* You jus' come back here and I'll teach you how to
behave—knockin' people round!—don't care if I does hab to go
to der watch-house." They passed on without noticing him
further, only laughing jeeringly—and he continued : " You come
back here and I'll make you laugh ; you is jus' three white
nigger cowards, dat's what *you* be."

I observe, in the newspapers, complaints of growing insolence
and insubordination among the negroes, arising, it is thought, from
too many privileges being permitted them by their masters, and
from too merciful administration of the police laws with regard to
them. Except in this instance, however, I have seen not the
slightest evidence of any independent manliness on the part of the
negroes towards the whites. As far as I have yet observed, they
are treated very kindly and even generously as servants, but
their manner to white people is invariably either sullen, jocose, or
fawning.

The pronunciation and dialect of the negroes, here, is generally much more idiomatic and peculiar than with us. As I
write, I hear a man shouting, slowly and deliberately, meaning
to say *there : dah! dah!* DAH !

SLAVES AS MERCHANDISE.

Yesterday morning, during a cold, sleety storm, against which I was struggling, with my umbrella, to the post office, I met a comfortably-dressed negro leading three others by a rope; the first was a middle-aged man; the second a girl of, perhaps, twenty; and the last a boy, considerably younger. The arms of all three were secured before them with hand-cuffs, and the rope by which they were led passed from one to another; being made fast at each pair of hand-cuffs. They were thinly clad, the girl especially so, having only an old ragged handkerchief around her neck, over a common calico dress, and another handkerchief twisted around her head. They were dripping wet, and icicles were forming, at the time, on the awning bars.

The boy looked most dolefully, and the girl was turning around, with a very angry face, and shouting, "O pshaw! Shut up!"

"What are they?" said I, to a white man, who had also stopped, for a moment, to look at them. "What's he going to do with them?"

"Come in a canal boat, I reckon: sent down here to be sold. —That ar's a likely gall."

Our ways lay together, and I asked further explanation. He informed me that the negro-dealers had confidential servants always in attendance, on the arrival of the rail-road trains and canal packets, to take any negroes, that might have come, consigned to them, and bring them to their marts.

Nearly opposite the post office, was another singular group of negroes. They were all men and boys, and each carried a coarse, white blanket, drawn together at the corners so as to hold some articles; probably, extra clothes. They stood in a row, in lounging attitudes, and some of them, again, were quarreling, or reproving one another. A villainous-looking white man stood in front of them. Presently, a stout, respectable man, dressed in black according to the custom, and without any overcoat or umbrella, but with a large, golden-headed walking-stick, came out of the door of an office, and, without saying a word, walked briskly up the street; the negroes immediately followed, in file; the other white man bringing up the rear. They were slaves that had been sent into the town to be hired out as servants or factory hands. The gentleman in black was, probably, the broker in the business.

Near the post office, opposite a large livery and sale stable, I turned into a short, broad street, in which were a number of establishments, the signs on which indicated that they were occupied by "Slave Dealers," and that "Slaves, for Sale or to Hire," were to be found within them. They were much like Intelligence Offices, being large rooms partly occupied by ranges of forms, on which sat a few comfortably and neatly clad negroes, who appeared perfectly cheerful; each grinning obsequiously, but with a manifest interest or anxiety, when I fixed my eye on them for a moment.

In Chambers' Journal for October, 1853, there is an account of the Richmond slave marts, and the manner of conducting business in them, so graphic and evidently truthful that I omit any further narration of my own observations, to make room for it. I do this, notwithstanding its length, because I did not happen to witness, during fourteen months that I spent in the Slave States, any sale of negroes by auction. This must not be taken as an indication that negro auctions are not of frequent occurrence (I did not, so far as I now recollect, witness the sale of anything else, at auction, at the South). I saw negroes advertised to be sold at auction, very frequently.

" The exposure of ordinary goods in a store is not more open to the public than are the sales of slaves in Richmond. By consulting the local newspapers, I learned that the sales take place by auction every morning in the offices of certain brokers, who, as I understood by the terms of their advertisements, purchased or received slaves for sale on commission.

" Where the street was in which the brokers conducted their business, I did not know ; but the discovery was easily made. Rambling down the main street in the city, I found that the subject of my search was a narrow and short thoroughfare, turning off to the left, and terminating in a similar cross thoroughfare. Both streets, lined with brick-houses, were dull and silent. There was not a person to whom I could put a question. Looking about, I observed the office of a commission-agent, and into it I stepped. Conceive the idea of a large shop with two windows, and a door between ; no shelving or counters inside ; the interior a spacious, dismal apartment, not well swept ; the only furniture a desk at one of the windows, and a bench at one side of the shop, three feet high, with two steps to it from the floor. I say, conceive the idea of this dismal-looking place, with nobody in it but three negro children, who, as I entered, were playing at auctioneering each other. An intensely black little negro, of four or five years of age, was standing on the bench, or block, as it is called, with an equally black girl, about a year younger, by his side, whom he was pretending to sell by bids to another black child, who was rolling about the floor.

" My appearance did not interrupt the merriment. The little auctioneer continued his mimic play, and appeared to enjoy the joke of selling the girl, who stood demurely by his side.

" ' Fifty dolla for de gal—fifty dolla—fifty dolla—I sell dis here fine gal for fifty dolla,' was uttered with extraordinary volubility by the woolly-headed urchin, accompanied with appropriate gestures, in imitation, doubtless of the scenes he had seen enacted daily in the spot. I spoke a few words to the little creatures, but was scarcely understood ; and the fun went on as if I had not been present : so I left them, happy in rehearsing what was likely soon to be their own fate.

"At another office of a similar character, on the opposite side of the street, I was more successful. Here, on inquiry, I was respectfully informed, by a person in attendance, that the sale would take place the following morning at half-past nine o'clock.

"Next day I set out accordingly, after breakfast, for the scene of operations, in which there was now a little more life. Two or three persons were lounging about, smoking cigars; and, looking along the street, I observed that three red flags were projected from the doors of those offices in which sales were to occur. On each flag was pinned a piece of paper, notifying the articles to be sold. The number of lots was not great. On the first was the following announcement:—'Will be sold this morning, at half-past nine o'clock, a Man and a Boy.'

"It was already the appointed hour; but as no company had assembled, I entered and took a seat by the fire. The office, provided with a few deal forms and chairs, a desk at one of the windows, and a block accessible by a few steps, was tenantless, save by a gentleman who was arranging papers at the desk, and to whom I had addressed myself on the previous evening. Minute after minute passed, and still nobody entered. There was clearly no hurry in going to business. I felt almost like an intruder, and had formed the resolution of departing, in order to look into the other offices, when the person referred to left his desk, and came and seated himself opposite to me at the fire.

"'You are an Englishman,' said he, looking me steadily in the face; 'do you want to purchase?'

"'Yes,' I replied, 'I am an Englishman; but I do not intend to purchase. I am traveling about for information, and I shall feel obliged by your letting me know the prices at which negro servants are sold.'

"'I will do so with much pleasure,' was the answer; 'do you mean field-hands or house-servants?'

"'All kinds,' I replied; 'I wish to get all the information I can.'

"With much politeness, the gentleman stepped to his desk, and began to draw up a note of prices. This, however, seemed to require careful consideration; and while the note was preparing, a lanky person, in a wide-awake hat, and chewing tobacco, entered, and took the chair just vacated. He had scarcely seated himself, when, on looking towards the door, I observed the subjects of sale— the man and boy indicated by the paper on the red flag—enter together, and quietly walk to a form at the back of the shop, whence, as the day was chilly, they edged themselves towards the fire, in the corner where I was seated. I was now between the two parties— the white man on the right, and the old and young negro on the left—and I waited to see what would take place.

" The sight of the negroes at once attracted the attention of Wideawake. Chewing with vigor, he kept keenly eying the pair, as if to see what they were good for. Under this searching gaze, the man and boy were a little abashed, but said nothing. Their appearance had little of the repulsiveness we are apt to associate with the idea of slaves. They were dressed in a gray woolen coat, pants, and waistcoat, colored cotton neckcloths, clean shirts, coarse woolen stockings, and stout shoes. The man wore a black hat; the boy was bareheaded. Moved by a sudden impulse, Wide-awake left his seat, and rounding the back of my chair, began to grasp at the man's arms, as if to feel their muscular capacity. He then examined his hands and fingers ; and, last of all, told him to open his mouth and show his teeth, which he did in a submissive manner. Having finished these examinations, Wide-awake resumed his seat, and chewed on in silence as before.

" I thought it was but fair that I should now have my turn of investigation, and accordingly asked the elder negro what was his age. He said he did not know. I next inquired how old the boy was. He said he was seven years of age. On asking the man if the boy was his son, he said he was not—he was his cousin. I was going into other particulars, when the office-keeper approached, and handed me the note he had been preparing ; at the same time making the observation that the market was dull at present, and that there never could be a more favorable opportunity of buying. I thanked him for the trouble which he had taken ; and now submit a copy of his price-current :

Best Men, 18 to 25 years old, . .	1200 to 1300 dollars.	
Fair do. do. do., . .	. 950 to 1050	"
Boys, 5 feet, ...	850 to 950	"
Do., 4 feet 8 inches, . . .	. 700 to 800	"
Do., 4 feet 5 inches, . . .	500 to 600	"

Boys, 4 feet,	.	.	.	.	.	375 to 450 dollars.
Young Women,	.	.	.	.	.	800 to 1000 "
Girls, 5 feet,	.	.	.	.	.	750 to 850 "
Do., 4 feet 9 inches,	.	.	.	.	700 to 750 "
Do., 4 feet,	.	.	.	.	.	350 to 452 "

' (Signed) ————————,

Richmond, Virginia.'

" Leaving this document for future consideration, I pass on to a history of the day's proceedings. It was now ten minutes to ten o'clock, and Wide-awake and I being alike tired of waiting, we went off in quest of sales further up the street. Passing the second office, in which also nobody was to be seen, we were more fortunate at the third. Here, according to the announcement on the paper stuck to the flag, there were to be sold, ' A woman and three children ; a young woman, three men, a middle-aged woman, and a little boy.' Already a crowd had met, composed, I should think, of persons mostly from the cotton-plantations of the south. A few were seated near a fire on the right-hand side, and others stood round an iron stove in the middle of the apartment. The whole place had a dilapidated appearance. From a back-window, there was a view into a ruinous court-yard ; beyond which, in a hollow, accessible by a side-lane, stood a shabby brick-house, on which the word *Jail* was inscribed in large black letters on a white ground. I imagined it to be a dépôt for the reception of negroes.

"On my arrival, and while making these preliminary observations, the lots for sale had not made their appearance. In about five minutes afterwards they were ushered in, one after the other, under the charge of a mulatto, who seemed to act as principal assistant. I saw no whips, chains, or any other engine of force. Nor did such appear to be required. All the lots took their seats on two long forms near the stove ; none showed any signs of resistance ; nor did any one utter a word. Their manner was that of perfect humility and resignation.

" As soon as all were seated, there was a general examination of their respective merits, by feeling their arms, looking into their mouths, and investigating the quality of their hands and fingers— this last being evidently an important particular. Yet there was no abrupt rudeness in making these examinations—no coarse or domineering language was employed. The three negro men were dressed in the usual manner—in gray woolen clothing. The woman, with three children, excited my peculiar attention. She was neatly attired, with a colored handkerchief bound around her head, and wore a white apron over her gown. Her children were all girls, one of them a baby at the breast. three months old, and the others two and three years of age respectively, rigged out with clean white pinafores. There was not a tear or an emotion visible in the whole party. Everything seemed to be considered as a matter of course ; and the change of owners was possibly looked forward to with as much indifference as ordinary hired servants anticipate a removal from one employer to another.

"While intending-purchasers were proceeding with personal examinations of the several lots, I took the liberty of putting a few questions to the mother of the children. The following was our conversation :—

"'Are you a married woman ?'

"'Yes, sir.'

"'How many children have you had ?'

"'Seven.'

"'Where is your husband ?'

"'In Madison county.'

"'When did you part from him ?'

"'On Wednesday—two days ago.'

"'Were you sorry to part from him ?'

"'Yes, sir,' she replied, with a deep sigh ; 'my heart was a'most broke.'

"'Why is your master selling you ?'

"'I don't know—he wants money to buy some land—suppose he sells me for that.'

"There might not be a word of truth in these answers, for I had no means of testing their correctness ; but the woman seemed to speak unreservedly, and I am inclined to think that she said nothing but what, if necessary, could be substantiated. I spoke, also, to the young woman who was seated near her. She, like the others, was perfectly black, and appeared stout and healthy, of which some of the persons present assured themselves by feeling her arms and ankles, looking into her mouth, and causing her to stand up. She told me she had several brothers and sisters, but did not know where they were. She said she was a house-servant, and would be glad to be bought by a good master—looking at me, as if I should not be unacceptable.

"I have said that there was an entire absence of emotion in the party of men, women, and children, thus seated preparatory to being sold. This does not correspond with the ordinary accounts of slave-sales, which are represented as tearful and harrowing. My belief is, that none of the parties felt deeply on the subject, or at least that any distress they experienced was but momentary—soon passed away, and was forgotten. One of my reasons for this opinion rests on a trifling incident which occurred. While waiting for the commencement of the sale, one of the gentlemen present amused himself with a pointer-dog, which, at command, stood on its hind-legs, and took pieces of bread from his pocket. These tricks greatly entertained the row of negroes, old and young; and the poor woman, whose heart three minutes before was almost broken, now laughed as heartily as any one.

"'Sale is going to commence—this way, gentlemen,' cried a man at the door to a number of loungers outside ; and all having assembled, the mulatto assistant led the woman and her children to the block, which he helped her to mount. There she stood with her infant at the breast, and one of her girls at each side. The auctioneer, a handsome, gentlemanly personage, took his place, with one foot on an old deal chair with a broken back, and the other raised on the somewhat more elevated block. It was a striking scene.

"'Well, gentlemen,' began the salesman, 'here is a capital woman and her three children, all in good health—what do you say for them ? Give me an offer. (Nobody speaks.) I put up the whole lot at 850 dollars—850 dollars—850 dollars (speaking very fast)— 850 dollars. Will no one advance upon that ? A very extraordinary bargain, gentlemen. A fine, healthy baby. Hold it up. (Mulatto goes up the first step of the block; takes the baby from the woman's breast, and holds it aloft with one hand, so as to show that it was a veritable sucking baby.) That will do. A woman, still young, and three children, all for 850 dollars. An advance, if you please, gentlemen. (A voice bids 860.) Thank you, sir, 860; any one bids more ? (A second voice says, 870; and so on the bidding goes as far as 890 dollars, when it stops.) That won't do, gentlemen. I cannot take such a low price. (After a pause, addressing the mulatto) : She may go down.' Down from the block the woman

and her children were therefore conducted by the assistant, and, as
if nothing had occurred, they calmly resumed their seats by the
stove.

" The next lot brought forward was one of the men. The mulatto, beckoning to him with his hand, requested him to come behind a
canvas screen, of two leaves, which was standing near the back
window. The man placidly rose, and having been placed behind the
screen, was ordered to take off his clothes, which he did without a
word or look of remonstrance. About a dozen gentlemen crowded
to the spot while the poor fellow was stripping himself, and as soon
as he stood on the floor, bare from top to toe, a most rigorous scrutiny of his person was instituted. The clear black skin, back and
front, was viewed all over for sores from disease ; and there was no
part of his body left unexamined. The man was told to open and
shut his hands, asked if he could pick cotton, and every tooth in his
head was scrupulously looked at. The investigation being at an
end, he was ordered to dress himself ; and having done so, was requested to walk to the block.

The ceremony of offering him for competition was gone through
as before, but no one would bid. The other two men, after under-
going similar examinations behind the screen, were also put up, but
with the same result. Nobody would bid for them, and they were
all sent back to their seats. It seemed as if the company had conspired not to buy anything that day. Probably some imperfections
had been detected in the personal qualities of the negroes. Be this
as it may, the auctioneer, perhaps a little out of temper from his
want of success, walked off to his desk, and the affair was so far at
an end.

" 'This way, gentlemen—this way !' was heard from a voice outside, and the company immediately hived off to the second establishment. At this office there was a young woman, and also a man,
for sale. The woman was put up first at 500 dollars ; and possessing some recommendable qualities, the bidding for her was run as
high as 710 dollars, at which she was knocked down to a purchaser.
The man, after the customary examination behind the screen, was
put up at 700 dollars ; but a small imperfection having been observed in his person, no one would bid for him ; and he was ordered
down.

" 'This way, gentlemen, this way—down the street, if you please !'

was now shouted by a person in the employment of the first firm, to whose office all very willingly adjourned—one migratory company, it will be perceived, serving all the slave-auctions in the place. Mingling in the crowd, I went to see what should be the fate of the man and boy, with whom I had already had some communication.

" There the pair, the two cousins, sat by the fire, just where I had left them an hour ago. The boy was put up first.

" ' Come along, my man—jump up; there's a good boy!' said one of the partners, a bulky and respectable-looking person, with a gold chain and bunch of seals; at the same time getting on the block. With alacrity the little fellow came forward, and, mounting the steps, stood by his side. The forms in front were filled by the company; and as I seated myself, I found that my old companion, Wide-awake, was close at hand, still chewing and spitting at a great rate.

" ' Now, gentlemen,' said the auctioneer, putting his hand on the shoulder of the boy, ' here is a very fine boy, seven years of age, warranted sound—what do you say for him ? I put him up at 500 dollars—500 dollars (speaking quick, his right hand raised up, and coming down on the open palm of his left)—500 dollars. Any one say more than 500 dollars ? (560 is bid.) 560 dollars. Nonsense ! Just look at him. See how high he is. (He draws the lot in front of him, and shows that the little fellow's head comes up to his breast.) You see he is a fine, tall, healthy boy. Look at his hands.'

" Several step forward, and cause the boy to open and shut his hands—the flexibility of the small fingers, black on the one side, and whitish on the other, being well looked to. The hands, and also the mouth, having given satisfaction, an advance is made to 570, then to 580 dollars.

" ' Gentlemen, that is a very poor price for a boy of this size. (Addressing the lot)—Go down, my boy, and show them how you can run.'

" The boy, seemingly happy to do as he was bid, went down from the block, and ran smartly across the floor several times ; the eyes of every one in the room following him.

" ' Now that will do. Get up again. (Boy mounts the block, the steps being rather deep for his short legs; but the auctioneer kindly lends him a hand.) Come, gentleman, you see this is a first-rate lot. (590—600—610—620—630 dollars are bid.) I will sell him for 630 dollars. (Right hand coming down on left.) Last call. 630 dollars, once—630 dollars, twice. (A pause; hand sinks.) gone!'

"The boy having descended, the man was desired to come forward; and after the usual scrutiny behind a screen, he took his place on the block.

"'Well, now, gentlemen,' said the auctioneer, 'here is a right prime lot. Look at this man; strong, healthy, able-bodied; could not be a better hand for field-work. He can drive a wagon, or anything. What do you say for him? I offer the man at the low price of 800 dollars—he is well worth 1200 dollars. Come, make an advance, if you please. 800 dollars said for the man (a bid); thank you; 810 dollars—810 dollars—810 dollars (several bids)—820—830—850—860—going at 860—going. Gentlemen, this is far below his value. A strong-boned man, fit for any kind of heavy work. Just take a look at him. (Addressing the lot): Walk down. Lot dismounts, and walks from one side of the shop to the other. When about to reascend the block, a gentleman, who is smoking a cigar, examines his mouth with his fingers. Lot resumes his place.) Pray, gentlemen, be quick (continues the auctioneer); I must sell him, and 860 dollars are only bid for the man—860 dollars. (A fresh run of bids to 945 dollars.) 945 dollars, once, 945 dollars, twice (looking slowly round, to see if all were done), 945 dollars, going—going —(hand drops)—gone!'

"Such were a forenoon's experiences in the slave-market of Richmond. Everything is described precisely as it occurred, without passion or prejudice. It would not have been difficult to be sentimental on a subject which appeals so strongly to the feelings; but I have preferred telling the simple truth. In a subsequent chapter, I shall endeavor to offer some general views of slavery in its social and political relations.

"W. C."

A JAMES RIVER FARM.

This morning I visited a farm, some account of which will give a good idea of the more advanced mode of agriculture in Eastern Virginia. It is situated on the bank of James River, and has ready access, by water or land-carriage, to the town of Richmond.

The soil of the greater part is a red, plastic, clayey loam, of a medium or low fertility, with a large intermixture of small quartz pebbles. On the river bank is a tract of low alluvial land, varying from an eighth to a quarter of a mile in breadth. The soil of this is a sandy loam, of the very finest quality in every respect, and it has been discovered, in some places, to be over ten feet in thickness; at which depth the sound trunk of a white oak has been found, showing it to be a recent deposit. I was assured that good crops of corn, wheat, and clover, had been taken from it, without its giving any indications of "wearing out," although no manure, except an occasional dressing of lime, had ever been returned to it. Maize, wheat, and clover for two years, usually occupy the ground, in succession, both on upland and lowland, herd's-grass (red-top of New York), sometimes taking the place of the clover, or being grown with it for hay, in which case the ground remains in sward for several years. Oats are sometimes also introduced, but the yield is said to be very small.

Hay always brings a high price in Richmond, and is usually shipped to that market from the eastward. This year, however, it is but a trifle above New York prices, and the main supply is drawn from this vicinity. I notice that oats, in the straw, are brought, in considerable quantity, to Richmond, for horse-feed, from the surrounding country. It is often pressed in bales, like hay, and sells for about the same price. At present, hay, brought from New York in bales, is selling at $1 25 to $1 50 per cwt.; oats, in straw, the same; oats, by the bushel, 40 to 50 cents; maize, 66 to 70 cents; wheat straw, 75 cents per cwt.; maize leaves ("corn fodder"), 75 cents per cwt.

Wheat, notwithstanding these high prices of forage crops, is considered the most important crop of the farm. The practice is to cut the maize (which is grown on much the same plan as is usual in New York) at the root, stook it in rows upon the field, plow the lands between the rows (one way) and drill in wheat with a horse drilling machine: then remove the stooks of maize into the sown ground, and prepare the intervening lands in like manner. The maize is afterwards husked in the field, at leisure, and carted off, with the stalks, when the ground is frozen. Sometimes the seed-wheat is sown by hand on the fresh-plowed ground, and harrowed in. In the spring, clover-seed is sown by hand. The wheat is reaped by either Hussey's or M'Cormick's machine, both being used on the farm, but Hussey's rather preferred, as less liable to get out of order, and, if slightly damaged, more readily repaired by the slave blacksmith on the farm.

Lime is frequently applied, commonly at the time of wheat-sowing, at the rate of from twenty-five to fifty bushels an acre. It is brought, by sea, from Haverstraw, New York, at a cost, delivered on the farm, of $7\frac{1}{4}$ to $7\frac{1}{2}$ cents a bushel. Plaster (sulphate of lime) has been tried, with little or no perceptible effect on the crops.

Dung, largely accumulated from the farm stock, is applied almost exclusively to the maize crops. Guano is also largely used as an application for wheat. After trying greater and less quantities, the proprietor has arrived at the conclusion that 200 lbs. to the acre is most profitable. It will, hereafter, be applied, at that rate, to all the wheat grown upon the farm. It has also been used with advantage for ruta baga. For corn, it was not thought of much value; the greatest advantage had been obtained by applying it to the *poorest land of the farm, some of which was of so small fertility, and at such a distance from the cattle quarters and the river, that it could not be profitably cultivated, and had been at waste for many years. I understand this may be the case with half the land included in the large farms or plantations of this part of the country.* Two hundred weight of Peruvian guano to the acre brought fifteen bushels of wheat; and a good crop of clover was perfectly sure to follow, by which the permanent improvement of the soil could be secured. This the proprietor esteemed to be the greatest benefit he derived from guano, and he is pursuing a regular plan for bringing all his more sterile upland into the system of Convertible husbandry by its aid.

This plan is, to prepare the ground, by fallowing, for wheat; spread 200 pounds of guano, broadcast, on the harrowed surface, and turn it under, as soon as possible after the sowers, with a "two-shovel plow" (a sort of large two-shared cultivator, which could only be used, I should think, on very light, clean soils), the wheat either being sown and covered with the guano, or, immediately afterwards, drilled in with a horse-machine. In the spring, clover is sown. After the wheat is harvested, the clover is allowed to grow, without being pastured or mown, for twelve months. The ground is then limed, clover plowed in, and, in October, again guanoed, two hundred weight to the acre, and wheat sown, with clover to follow. The clover may be pastured the following year, but in the year succeeding that, it is allowed to grow unchecked until August, when it is plowed in, the ground again guanoed, and wheat sown with herd's-grass (red-top) and clover, which is to remain, for mowing and pasture, as long as the ground will profitably sustain it.

SLAVE LABOR.

The labor of this farm was entirely performed by slaves. I did not inquire their number, but I judged there were from twenty to forty. Their "quarters" lined the approach-road to the mansion, and were well-made and comfortable log cabins, about thirty feet long by twenty wide, and eight feet wall, with a high loft and shingle roof. Each, divided in the middle, and having a brick chimney outside the wall at each end, was intended to be occupied by two families. There were square windows, closed by wooden ports, having a single pane of glass in the center. The house-servants were neatly dressed, but the field-hands wore very coarse and ragged garments.

During three hours, or more, in which I was in company with the proprietor, I do not think there were ten consecutive minutes uninterrupted by some of the slaves requiring his personal direction or assistance. He was even obliged, three times, to leave the dinner-table.

"You see," said he, smiling, as he came in the last time, "a farmer's life, in this country, is no sinecure." This turning the conversation to Slavery, he observed, in answer to a remark of mine, "I only wish your philanthropists would contrive some satisfactory plan to relieve us of it; the trouble and the responsibility of properly taking care of our negroes, you may judge, from what you see yourself here, is anything but enviable. But what can we do that is better? Our free negroes—and, I believe it is the same at the North as it is here—are a miserable set of vagabonds, drunken, vicious, worse off, it is my honest opinion, than those who are retained in slavery. I am satisfied, too, that our slaves are better off, as they are, than the majority of your free laboring classes at the North."

I expressed my doubts.

"Well, they certainly are better off than the English agricultural laborers or, I believe, those of any other Christian country. Free labor might be more profitable to us: I am inclined to think it would be. The slaves are excessively careless and wasteful, and, in various ways—which, without you lived among them, you could hardly be made to understand—subject us to very annoying losses.

"To make anything by farming, here, a man has got to live a hard life. You see how constantly I am called upon—and, often, it is about as bad at night as by day. Last night I did not sleep a wink till near morning; I am quite worn out with it, and my wife's health is failing. But I cannot rid myself of it."

OVERSEERS.

I asked why he did not employ an overseer.

"Because I do not think it right to trust to such men as we have to use, if we use any, for overseers."

"Is the general character of overseers bad?"

"They are the curse of this country, sir; the worst men in the community. * * * * But lately, I had another sort of fellow offer—a fellow like a dancing-master, with kid gloves, and wrist-bands turned up over his coat-sleeves, and all so nice, that I was almost ashamed to talk to him in my old coat and slouched hat. Half a bushel of recommendations he had with him, too. Well, he was not the man for me—not half the gentleman, with all his airs, that Ned here is "—(a black servant, who was bursting with suppressed laughter, behind his chair).

"Oh, they are interesting creatures, sir," he continued, "and, with all their faults, have many beautiful traits. I can't help being attached to them, and I am sure they love us." In his own case, at least, I did not doubt it; his manner towards them was paternal—familiar and kind; and they came to him like children who have been given some task, and constantly are wanting to be encouraged and guided, simply and confidently. At dinner, he frequently addressed the servant familiarly, and drew him into our conversation as if he were a family friend, better informed, on some local and domestic points, than himself.

He informed me that able-bodied field-hands were hired out, in this vicinity, at the rate of one hundred dollars a year, and their board and clothing. Four able-bodied men, that I have employed the last year, on my farm in New York, I pay, on an average, one hundred and five dollars each, and board them; they clothe themselves at an expense, I think, of twenty dollars a year;—probably, slaves' clothing costs twice that. They constitute all the force of my farm, hired by the year (except a boy, who goes to school in Winter), and, in my absence, have no overseer except one of themselves, whom I appoint. I pay the fair wages of the market, more than any of my neighbors, I believe, and these are no lower than the average of what I have paid for the last five years. It is difficult to measure the labor performed in a day by one, with that of the other, on account of undefined differences in the soil, and in the bulk and weight of articles operated upon. But, here, I am shown tools that no man in his senses, with us, would allow a laborer, to whom he was paying wages, to be encumbered with; and the excessive weight and clumsiness of which, I would judge, would make work at least ten per cent. greater than those ordinarily used with us. And I am assured that, in the careless and clumsy way they must be used by the slaves, anything lighter or less rude could not be furnished them with good economy, and that such tools as we constantly give our laborers, and find our profit in giving them, would not last out a day in a Virginia corn-field —much lighter and more free from stones though it be than ours.

So, too, when I ask why mules are so universally substituted for horses on the farm, the first reason given, and confessedly the most conclusive one, is, that horses cannot bear the treatment that they always *must* get from negroes ; horses are always soon foundered or crippled by them, while mules will bear cudgeling, and lose a meal or two now and then, and not be materially injured, and they do not take cold or get sick if neglected or overworked. But I do not need to go further than to the window of the room in which I am writing, to see, at almost any time, treatment of cattle that would insure the immediate discharge of the driver, by almost any farmer owning them at the North.

A COAL MINE—NEGRO AND ENGLISH MINERS.

Yesterday I visited a coal-pit : the majority of the mining laborers are slaves, and uncommonly athletic and fine-looking negroes ; but a considerable number of white hands are also employed, and they occupy all the responsible posts. The slaves are, some of them, owned by the Mining Company ; but the most are hired of their owners, at from $120 to $200 a year, the company boarding and clothing them. (I have the impression that I heard it was customary to give them a certain allowance of money and let them find their own board).

The white hands are mostly English or Welchmen. One of them, with whom I conversed, told me that he had been here several years ; he had previously lived some years at the North.

He got better wages here than he had earned at the North, but he was not contented, and did not intend to remain. On pressing him for the reason of his discontent, he said, after some hesitation, that he had rather live where he could be more free ; a man had to be too "*discreet*" here : if one happened to say anything that gave offense, they thought no more of drawing a pistol or a knife upon him, than they would of kicking a dog that was in their way. Not long since, a young English fellow came to the pit, and was put to work along with a gang of negroes. One morning, about a week afterwards, twenty or thirty men called on him, and told him that they would allow him fifteen minutes to get out of sight, and if they ever saw him in those parts again, they would "give him hell." They were all armed, and there was nothing for the young fellow to do but to move "right off."

"What reason did they give him for it?"

"They did not give him any reason."

"But what had he done?"

"Why I believe they thought he had been too free with the niggers ; he wasn't used to them, you see, sir, and he talked to 'em free like, and they thought he'd make 'em think too much of themselves."

He said the slaves were very well fed, and well treated—not worked over hard. They were employed night and day, in relays.

The coal from these beds is of special value for gas manufacture, and is shipped, for that purpose, to all the large towns on the Atlantic sea-board, even to beyond Boston. It is delivered to shipping at Richmond, at fifteen cents a bushel : about thirty bushels go to a ton.

VALUABLE SERVANTS.

The hotel at which I am staying, " the American," Milberger Smith, from New York, proprietor, is a very capital one. I have never, this side the Atlantic, had my comforts provided for better, in my private room, with so little annoyance from the servants. The chamber-servants are negroes, and are accomplished in their business; (the dining-room servants are Irish). A man and a woman attend together upon a few assigned rooms, in the hall adjoining which they are constantly in waiting; your bell is answered immediately, your orders are quickly and quietly followed, and your particular personal wants anticipated as much as possible, and provided for, as well as the usual offices performed, when you are out. The man becomes your servant while you are in your room; he asks, at night, when he comes to request your boots, at what time he shall come in the morning, and then, without being very exactly punctual, he comes quietly in, makes your fire, sets the boots before it, brushes and arranges your clothes, lays out your linen, arranges your washing and dressing gear, asks if you want anything else of him before breakfast, opens the shutters, and goes off to the next room. I took occasion to speak well of him to my neighbor one day, that I might judge whether I was particularly favored.

" Oh yes," he said, " Henry was a very good boy, very— valuable servant — quite so — would be worth two thousand dollars, if he was a little younger—easy."

At dinner, a respectable looking, gray-headed man asked another:

" Niggers are going high now, aint they ?"

" Yes, sir."

" What would you consider a fair price for a woman thirty years old, with a young-one two years old?"

"Depends altogether on her physical condition, you know.
—Has she any other children?"

" *Yes; four.*"

" —— Well—I reckon about seven to eight hundred."

" I bought one yesterday—gave six hundred and fifty."

" Well, sir, if she's tolerable likely, you did well."

DRESS, AND STYLE OF PEOPLE.

What is most remarkable in the appearance of the people
of the better class, is their invariably *high-dressed* condition;
look down the opposite side of the table, even at breakfast,
and you will probably see thirty men drinking coffee, all
in full funeral dress, not an easy coat amongst them. It is the
same in the street, and the same with ladies as with gentlemen;
silk and satin, under umbrellas, rustle along the side-walk, or
skip across it between carriages and the shops, as if they were
going to a dinner-party, at eleven o'clock in the morning. The
last is only New York repeated, to be sure, but the gentlemen
carry it further than in New York, and seem never to indulge
in undress.

I have rarely seen a finer assemblage of people than filled the
theatre one night, at the benefit of the Bateman children, who
are especial favorites of the public here. As the Legislature is
in session, I presume there was a fair representation of the Virginians of all parts of the State. A remarkable proportion of
the men were very tall and of animated expression—and of the
women, fair, refined, and serene. The men, however, were very
deficient in robustness, and the women, though graceful and
attractive, had none of that dignity and stateliness for which the
dames of Virginia were formerly much distinguished.

In *manners*, I notice that, between man and man, more ceremony and form is sustained, in familiar conversation, than well-bred people commonly use at the North.

Among the people you see in the streets, full half, I should think, are more or less of negro blood, and a very decent, civil people these seem, in general, to be; more so than the laboring class of whites, among which there are many very ruffianly looking fellows. There is a considerable population of foreign origin, generally of the least valuable class; very dirty German Jews, especially, abound, and their characteristic shops (with their characteristic smells, quite as bad as in Cologne), are thickly set in the narrowest and meanest streets, which seem to be otherwise inhabited mainly by negroes.

STREET PEOPLE.

Immense wagons, drawn by six mules each, the teamster always riding on the back of the near-wheeler, are a characteristic feature of the streets. Another is the wood-carts; small trucks loaded with about a cord of pine wood, drawn by three mules or horses, one in shafts, and two others, abreast, before him; a negro always riding the shaft-horse and guiding the leaders with a single rein, one pull to turn them to the right, and two to the left, with a great deal of the whip whichever way they go. The same guiding apparatus, a single line, with branches to each bit, is used altogether upon the long wagon teams. On the canal, a long, narrow, canoe-like boat, perhaps fifty feet long and six wide, and drawing but a foot or two of water, is nearly as common as the ordinary large boats, such as are used on our canals. They come out of some of the small, narrow, crooked streams, connected with the canals, in which a difficult navigation is effected by poleing.   They are loaded with tobacco, flour, and a great variety of raw country produce.   The canal boatmen of Virginia seem to be quite as rude, insolent, and riotous a class as those of New York, and every facility is evidently afforded them, at Richmond, for indulging their peculiar appetites and tastes.   A great many low eating, and, I should think, drinking shops are frequented chiefly by the negroes.   Dancing and other amusements are carried on in these at night.

From reading the comments of Southern statesmen and news-papers on the crime and misery which sometimes result from the accumulation of poor and ignorant people, with no intelligent masters to take care of them, in our Northern towns, one might get the impression that Southern towns—especially those not demoralized by foreign commerce—were comparatively free from a low and licentious population.   From what I have seen, how-ever, I should be now led to think that there was at least. as much vice, and of what we call rowdyism, in Richmond, as in any Northern town of its size.*

The train was advertised to leave at 3.30 P. M.   At that hour the cars were crowded with passengers, and the engineer, punc-tually at the minute, gave notice that he was at his post, by a long, loud whistle of the' locomotive.   Five minutes afterwards he gave us an impatient jerk ; ten minutes afterwards we

---

* SAD PICTURE.—A gentleman informs the *Richmond* (Va.) *Dispatch* that, while taking a stroll on one of the islands in James river, not far from Mayo's Bridge, last Sunday morning, he counted as many as twenty-two boys, from ten to fifteen years of age, engaged in gaming with cards and dice for money.   In some of the parties he saw grown men and small boys playing bluff, and cursing swearing, and drinking.—*Southern Newspaper*.

advanced three rods; twelve minutes afterwards, returned to first position: continued, "backing and filling" upon the bridge over the rapids of the James river, for half an hour. At precisely four o'clock, crossed the bridge and fairly started for Petersburg.

Ran twenty miles in exactly an hour and thirty minutes, (thirteen miles an hour; mail train, especially recommended by advertisement as "fast"). Brakes on, three times, for cattle on the track; twenty minutes spent at way-stations. Flat rail. Locomotive built at Philadelphia. I am informed that most of those used on the road—perhaps all those of the *slow* trains—are made at Petersburg.

At one of the stoppages, smoke was to be seen issuing from the truck of a car. The conductor, on having his attention called to it, nodded his head sagely, took a morsel of tobacco, put his hands in his pocket, looked at the truck as if he would mesmerize it, spat upon it, and then stept upon the platform and shouted "All right! Go ahead!" At the next stoppage, the smoking was furious; conductor bent himself over it with an evidently strong exercise of his will, but not succeeding to tranquilize the subject at all, he suddenly relinquished the attempt, and, deserting Mesmer for Preisnitz, shouted, "Ho! boy! bring me some water here." A negro soon brought a quart of water in a tin vessel.

"Hain't got no oil, Columbus?"

"No, sir."

"Hum—go ask Mr. Smith for some: this yer's a screaking so, I durstn't go on. You Scott! get some salt. And look here, some of you boys, get me some more water. D'ye hear?"

Salt, oil, and water, were crowded into the box, and, after five minutes longer delay, we went on, the truck still smoking, and the water and oil boiling in the box, until we reached Petersburg. The heat was the result, I suppose, of a neglect of sufficient or timely oiling. While waiting, in a carriage, for the driver to get my baggage, I saw a negro oiling all the trucks of the train; as he proceeded from one to the other, he did not give himself the trouble to elevate the outlet of his oiler, so that a stream of oil, costing probably a dollar and a half a gallon, was poured out upon the ground the whole length of the train.

ONE OF THE LAW-GIVERS.

While on the bridge at Richmond, the car in which I was seated was over-full—several persons standing; among them, one considerably "excited," who informed the company that he was a Member of the House of Delegates, and that he would take advantage of this opportune collection of the people, to expose an atrocious attempt, on the part of the minority, to jump a Bill through the Legislature, which was not in accordance with true Democratic principles. He continued for some time to address them in most violent, absurd, profane, and meaningless language; the main point of his oration being, to demand the popular gratitude for himself, for having had the sagacity and courage to prevent the accomplishment of the nefarious design. He afterwards attempted to pass into the ladies' car, but was dissuaded from doing so by the conductor, who prevailed on a young man to give him his seat. Having taken it, he immediately lifted his feet upon the back of the seat before him, resting them upon the shoulders of its occupant. This gentleman turning his head, he begged his pardon; but, hoping it would not occasion him inconvenience, he said he would prefer to keep them there, and did so; soon afterwards falling asleep.

FREIGHT TAKEN——THE SLAVE TRADE.

There were, in the train, two first-class passenger cars, and two freight cars. The latter were occupied by about forty negroes, most of them belonging to traders, who were sending them to the cotton States to be sold. Such kind of evidence of activity in the slave trade of Virginia is to be seen every day; but particulars and statistics of it are not to be obtained by a stranger here. Most gentlemen of character seem to have a special disinclination to converse on the subject; and it is denied, with feeling, that slaves are often reared, as is supposed by the Abolitionists, with the intention of selling them to the traders. It appears to me evident, however, from the manner in which I hear the traffic spoken of incidentally, that the cash value of a slave for sale, above the cost of raising it from infancy to the age at which it commands the highest price, is generally considered among the surest elements of a planter's wealth. Such a nigger is worth such a price, and such another is too old to learn to pick cotton, and such another will bring so much, when it has grown a little more, I have frequently heard people say, in the street, or the public-houses. That a slave woman is commonly esteemed least for her laboring qualities, most for those qualities which give value to a brood-mare is, also, constantly made apparent.*

---

* A slaveholder writing to me with regard to my cautious statements on this subject, made in the *Daily Times*, says:—"In the States of Maryland, Virginia, North Carolina, Kentucky, Tennessee and Missouri, as much attention is paid to the breeding and growth of negroes as to that of horses and mules. Further South, we raise them both for use and for market. Planters command their girls and women (married or unmarried) to have children; and I have known a great many negro girls to be sold off, because they did not have children. A breeding woman is worth from one-sixth to one-fourth more than one that does not breed."

By comparing the average decennial ratio of slave increase in all the States with the difference in the number of the actual slave-population of the slave-breeding States, as ascertained by the census, it is apparent that the number of slaves exported to the cotton States is considerably more than twenty thousand a year.

While calling on a gentleman occupying an honorable official position at Richmond, I noticed upon his table a copy of Professor Johnson's Agricultural Tour in the United States. Referring to a paragraph in it, where some statistics of the value of the slaves raised and annually exported from Virginia were given, I asked if he knew how these had been obtained, and whether they were reliable. "No," he replied; "I don't know anything about it; but if they are anything unfavorable to the institution of slavery, you may be sure they are false." This is but an illustration, in extreme, of the manner in which I find a desire to obtain more correct but *definite* information, on the subject of slavery, is usually met, by gentlemen otherwise of enlarged mind and generous qualities.

A gentleman, who was a member of the "Union Safety Committee" of New York, during the excitement which attended the discussion of the Fugitive Slave Act of 1850, told me that, as he was passing through Virginia this winter, a man entered the car in which he was seated, leading in a negro girl, whose manner and expression of face indicated dread and grief. Thinking she was a criminal, he asked the man what she had done:

"Done? Nothing."

"What are you going to do with her?"

"I'm taking her down to Richmond, to be sold."

"Does she belong to you?"

"No; she belongs to ———; he raised her."

"Why does he sell her—has she done anything wrong?"

"Done anything? No: she's no fault, I reckon."

"Then, what does he want to sell for?"

"Sell her for! Why shouldn't he sell her? He sells one or two every year; wants the money for 'em, I reckon."

The irritated tone and severe stare with which this was said, my friend took as a caution not to pursue his investigation.

A gentleman, with whom I was conversing on the subject of the cost of slave labor, in answer to an inquiry—what proportion of all the stock of slaves of an old plantation might be reckoned upon to do full work?—answered, that he owned ninety-six negroes; of these, only thirty-five were field-hands, the rest being either too young or too old for hard work. He reckoned his whole force as only equal to twenty-one strong men, or "*prime* field-hands." But this proportion was somewhat smaller than usual, he added, "because his women were uncommonly good breeders; he did not suppose there was a lot of women anywhere that bred faster than his; he never heard of babies coming so fast as they did on his plantation; it was perfectly surprising; and every one of them, in his estimation, was worth two hundred dollars, as negroes were selling now, the moment it drew breath."

I asked what he thought might be the usual proportion of workers to slaves, supported on plantations, throughout the South. On the large cotton and sugar plantations of the more Southern States, it was very high, he replied; because their hands were nearly all bought and *picked for work;* he supposed, on these, it would be about one-half; but, on any old plantation, where the stock of slaves had been an inheritance, and none had been bought or sold, he thought the working force would rarely be more than one-third, at most, of the whole number.

This gentleman was out of health, and told me, with frankness, that such was the trouble and annoyance his negroes occasioned him—although he had an overseer—and so wearisome did he find the lonely life he led on his plantation, that he could not remain upon it; and, as he knew everything would go to the dogs if he did not, he was seriously contemplating to sell out, retaining only his foster-mother and a body-servant. He thought of taking them to Louisiana and Texas, for sale; but, if he should learn that there was much probability that Lower California would be made a slave State, he supposed it would pay him to wait, as probably, if that should occur, he could take them there and sell them for twice as much as they would now bring in New Orleans. He knew very well, he said, that, as they were, raising corn and tobacco, they were paying nothing at all like a fair interest on their value.*

Some of his best hands he now rented out, to work in a furnace, and for the best of these he had been offered, for next year, two hundred dollars. He did not know whether he ought to let them go, though. They were worked hard, and had too much liberty, and were acquiring bad habits. They earned money, by overwork, and spent it for whisky, and got a habit of roaming about and *taking care of themselves;* because, when they were not at work in the furnace, nobody looked out for them.

I begin to suspect that the great trouble and anxiety of Southern gentlemen is:—How, without quite destroying the capabilities

---

* Mr. Wise is reported to have stated, in his electioneering tour, when candidate for Governor, in 1855, that, if slavery were permitted in California, negroes would sell for $5,000 apiece.

of the negro for any work at all, to prevent him from learning to take care of himself.

RURAL SCENERY AND RURAL LIFE IN VIRGINIA.

PETERSBURG, Dec. 28.—It was early in a fine, mild, bright morning, like the pleasantest we ever have in March, that I alighted, from a train of cars, at a country station. Besides the shanty that stood for a station-house, there was a small, comfortable farm-house on the right, and a country store on the left, and around them, perhaps, fifty acres of cleared land, now much flooded with muddy water;—all environed by thick woods.

A few negro children, staring as fixedly and posed as lifelessly as if they were really figures "carved in ebony," stood, lay, and lounged on the sunny side of the ranks of locomotive-firewood; a white man, smoking a cigar, looked out of the door of the store, and another, chewing tobacco, leaned against a gate-post in front of the farm-house; I advanced to the latter, and asked him if I could hire a horse in the neighborhood.

"How d'ye do, sir?" he replied; "I have some horses—none on 'em very good ones, though—rather hard riders; reckon, perhaps, they wouldn't suit you very well."

"Thank you; do you think I could find anything better about here?"

"Colonel Gillin, over here to the store, 's got a right nice saddle-horse, if he'll let you take her. I'll go over there with you, and see if he will. . . . . Mornin', Colonel;—here's a gentleman that wants to go to Thomas W.'s: couldn't you let him have your saddle-horse?"

"How do you do, sir; I suppose you'd come back to-night?"

"That's my intention, but I might be detained till to-morrow, unless it would be inconvenient to you to spare your horse."

"Well, yes, sir, I reckon you can have her;—Tom!—Tom!— *Tom !* Now, has that devilish nigger gone again! Tom! *Oh,* Tom! saddle the filly for this gentleman.——Have you ever been to Mr. W.'s, sir?"

"No, I have not."

"It isn't a very easy place for strangers to go to from here; but I reckon I can direct you, so you'll have no difficulty.

He accordingly began to direct me; but, the way appeared so difficult to find, I asked him to let me make a written memorandum, and, from this memorandum, I now repeat the directions he gave me.

"You take this road here—you'll see where it's most traveled, and it's easy enough to keep on it for about a mile; then there's a fork, and you take the right; pretty soon, you'll cross a creek and turn to the right—the creek's been up a good deal lately, and there's some big trees fallen along there, and, if they ha'n't got them out of the way, you may have some difficulty in finding where the road is; but you keep bearing off to the right, where it's the most open (*i. e.*, the wood), and you'll see it again pretty soon. Then you go on, keeping along in the road—you'll see where folks have traveled before—for maybe quarter of a mile, and you'll find a cross-road; you must take that to the left; pretty soon you'll pass two cabins; one of 'em's old and all fallen in, the other one's new, and there's a white man lives into it: you can't mistake it. About a hundred yards beyond it, there's a fork, and you take the left—it turns square off, and it's fenced for a good bit; keep along by the fence, and you can't miss it. It's right straight beyond that till you come to a school-house, there's a gate opposite to it, and off there there's a big house—but I don't reckon you'll see it neither, for the woods. But somewhere, about three hundred yards beyond the school-house, you'll find a little road running off to the left through an old field; you take that and keep along in it, and in less than half a mile you'll find a path going square off to the right; you take that, and keep on it till you pass a little cabin in the woods; aint nobody lives there now: then it turns to the left, and when you come to a fence and gate, you'll see a house there, that's Mr. George Rivers' plantation—it breaks in two, and you take the right, and when you come to the end of the fence, turn the corner—don't keep on, but turn there. Then it's straight, till you come to the creek again—there's a bridge there; don't go over the bridge, but turn to the left and keep along nigh the creek, and pretty soon you'll see a meeting-house in the woods; you go to that, and you'll see a path bearing off to the right —it looks as if it was going right away from the creek, but you take it, and pretty soon it'll bring you to a saw-mill on the creek, up 'gher a piece; you just cross the creek there, and you'll find some people at the mill, and they'll put you right straight on the road to Mr. W.'s."

"How far is it all, sir?"

"I reckon it's about two hours' ride, when the roads are good, to the saw-mill. Mr. W.'s gate is only a mile or so beyond that, and then you've got another mile, or better, after you get to the gate, but you'll see some nigger-quarters—the niggers belong to Mr. W., and I reckon ther'll be some of 'em round, and they'll show you just where to go."

After reading over my memorandum, and finding it correct, and agreeing with him that I should pay two dollars a day for

the mare, we walked out, and found her saddled and waiting
for me.

I remarked that she was very good-looking.

"Yes, sir; she a'nt a bad filly; out of a mare that came of
Lady Rackett by old Lord-knows-who, the best horse we ever
had in this part of the country: I expect you have heard of him.
Oh! she's maybe a little playful, but you'll find her a pleasant
riding-horse."

The filly was just so pleasantly playful, and full of well-bred
life, as to create a joyful, healthy, sympathetic, frolicsome heedlessness in her rider—walking rapidly, and with a sometimes
irresistible inclination to dance and bound; making believe she
was frightened at all the burnt stumps, and flashes of sun-light on
the ice, and, every time a hog lifted himself up before her, starting back in the most ridiculous manner, as if she had never seen
a hog before; bounding over the fallen trees as easily as a life-
boat over a billow; and all the time gracefully playing tricks
with her feet, and her ears, and her tail, and evidently enjoying
herself just like any child in a half-holiday ramble through the
woods, yet never failing to answer to every motion of my hand
or my knees, as if she were a part of myself. In fact, there soon
came to be a real good understanding, if not even something
like a merging of identity, between Jane and me (the filly's name
was Jane Gillin); if *her* feet were not in the stirrups, I am sure
I had all the sensation of tripping it on the ground with mine,
half the time, and we both entered into each other's feelings, and
moved, and were moved, together, in a way which a two hours'
lecture, by a professor of psychology, would be insufficient, satisfactorily, to explain to people who never——but all that's of no
consequence, except that, of course, we soon lost our way.

We were walking along slowly, quietly, musingly—I was fondling her with my hand under her mane, when it suddenly came into my mind: "why Jane! it's a long time since I've thought anything about the road—I wonder where we've got to." We stopped and tried to work up our dead-reckoning.

First, we picked our way from the store down to the brook, through a deeply corrugated clay-road; then there was the swamp, with the fallen trees and thick underwood, beaten down and barked in the miry parts by wagons, making a road for themselves, no traces of which could we find in the harder, pebbly ground. At length when we came on to drier land, and among pine trees, we discovered a clear way cut through them, and a distinct road before us again; and this brought us soon to an old clearing, just beginning to be grown over with pines, in which was the old cabin of rotten logs, one or two of them falling out of rank on the door-side, and the whole concern having a dangerous lurch to one corner, as if too much whisky had been drank in it: then a more recent clearing, with a fenced field and another cabin, the residence of that white man we were told of probably. No white people, however, were to be seen, but two negroes sat in the mouth of a wigwam, husking maize, and a couple of hungry hounds came bounding over the zig-zag, gate-less fence, as if they had agreed with each other that they would wait no longer for the return of their master, but would straight-way pull down the first traveler that passed, and have something to eat before they were quite famished. They stopped short, however, when they had got within a good cart-whip's length of us, and contented themselves with dolefully *youping* as long as we continued in sight. We turned the corner, following some slight traces of a road, and shortly afterwards met a curious vehicular establishment, probably belonging to the master of the hounds. It consisted of an axle-tree and wheels, and a pair of shafts made of unbarked saplings, in which was harnessed, by attachments of raw-hide and rope, a single small black ox. There was a bit, made of telegraph-wire, in his mouth, by which he was guided, through the mediation of a pair of much knotted rope-reins, by a white man—a dignified sovereign, wearing a brimless crown—who sat upon a two-bushel sack, (of meal, I trust, for the hounds' sake,) balanced upon the axle-tree, and who saluted me with a frank "How are you?" as we came opposite each other.

Soon after this, we reached a small grove of much older and larger pines than we had seen before, with long and horizontally stretching branches, and duller and thinner foliage. In the middle of it was another log-cabin, with a door in one of the gable-ends, a stove-pipe, half-rusted away, protruding from the other, and, in the middle of one of the sides, a small square port-hole, closed by a wooden shutter. This must have been the school-house, but there were no children then about it, and no appearance of there having been any lately. Near it was a long string of fence and a gate and lane, which gave entrance, probably, to a large plantation, though there was no cultivated land within sight of the road.

I could remember hardly anything after this, except a continuation of pine trees, big, little, and medium in size, and hogs, and a black, crooked, burnt sapling, that we had made believe was a snake springing at us and had jumped away from, and then we had gone on at a trot—it must have been some time ago, that —and then I was paying attentions to Jane, and finally my thoughts had gone wool-gathering, and we must have traveled some miles out of our way and—" never mind," said Jane, lifting her head, and turning in the direction we had been going, " I don't think it's any great matter if we are lost; such a fine day— so long since I've been out; if you don't care, I'd just as lief be lost as not; let's go on and see what we shall come to."

"Very well, my dear, you know the country better than I do ; go where you like; if you'll risk your dinner, I'm quite ready to go anywhere in your company. It's quite certain we have not passed any meeting-house, or creek, or saw-mill, or negro-quarters, and, as we have been two hours on the road, it's evident we are not going straight to Mr. W.'s. ; I'll try at least to take note of what we do pass after this," and I stood up in the stirrups as we walked on, to see what the country around us was.

"Old fields"—a coarse, yellow, sandy soil, bearing scarce anything but pine trees and broom sedge. In some places, for acres, the pines would not be above five feet high—that was land that had been in cultivation, used up and " turned out," not more than six or eight years before ; then there were patches of every age ; sometimes the trees were a hundred feet high. At long intervals, there were fields in which the pine was just beginning to spring in beautiful green plumes from the ground, and was yet hardly noticeable among the dead brown grass and sassafras bushes and blackberry-vines, which nature first sends to hide the nakedness of the impoverished earth.

Of living creatures, for miles, not one was to be seen (not even a crow or a snow-bird), except hogs. These—long, lank, bony, snake-headed, hairy, wild beasts—would come dashing across our path, in packs of from three to a dozen, with short, hasty grunts, almost always at a gallop, and looking neither to right nor left, as if they were in pursuit of a fox, and were quite certain to catch him in the next hundred yards; or droves of little pigs would rise up suddenly in the sedge, and scamper off squealing into cover, while their heroic mothers would turn around and make a stand, looking fiercely at us, as if they were quite ready to fight if we advanced any further, but always breaking, as we came near, with a loud *boosch!*

Once I saw a house, across a large, new old-field, but it was far off, and there was no distinct path leading towards it out of the wagon-track we were following; so we did not go to it, but continued walking steadily on through the old-fields and pine woods for more than an hour longer.

We then arrived at a grove of tall oak trees, in the midst of which ran a brook, giving motion to a small grist-mill. Back of the mill were two log cabins, and near these a number of negroes, in holiday clothes, were standing in groups among the trees. When we stopped one of them came towards us. He wore a battered old hat, of the cylindrical fashion, stiffly starched shirt-collar, cutting his ears, a red cravat, and an old black dress coat, thread-bare and a little ragged, but adorned with new brass buttons. He knew Mr. Thomas W., certainly he did; and he reckoned I had come about four miles (he did not know but it might be eight, if I thought so) off the road I had been directed to follow. But that was of no consequence, because he could show me where to go by a straight road—a cross cut—from here, that would make it just as quick for me as if I had gone the way I had intended.

" How far is it from here ?" I asked.

" Oh, 'taint far, sar."

" How far do you think ?"

" Well, massa, I spec—I spec—(looking at my horse) I spec,

massa, ef you goes de way, sar, dat I shows you, sar, I reckon it 'll take you—"

"How far is it—how many miles?"

"How many miles, sar? ha! masser, I don 'zactly reckon I ken tell ou—not 'cisely, sar—how many miles it is, not 'zactly, 'cisely, sar."

"How is that—you don't what?"

"I don't 'zactly reckon I can give you de drection excise about de miles, sar."

"Oh! but how many miles do you think it is; is it two miles?"

"Yes, sar; as de roads is now, I tink it is just about two miles. Dey's long ones, dough, I reckon."

"Long ones? you think it's more than two miles, don't you, then?"

"Yes, sar, I reckon its four or five miles."

"Four or five! four or five long ones or short ones do you mean?"

"I don 'zactly know, sar, wedder dey is short ones or long ones, sar, but I reckon you find em middlin' long; I spec you'll be about two hours 'fore you be done gone all de way to mass W.'s."

He walked on with us a few rods upon a narrow path, until we came to a crossing of the stream; pointing to where it continued on the other side, he assured me that it went right straight to Mr. W.'s plantation. "You juss keep de straight road, master," he repeated several times, "and it'll take you right dar, sar."

He had been grinning and bowing, and constantly touching his hat, or holding it in his hand during our conversation, which

I understood to mean, that he would thank me for a dime. I gave it to him, upon which he repeated his contortions and his form of direction—"keep de straight road." I rode through the brook, and he called out again—" you keep dat road right straight and it'll take you right straight dar." I rode up the bank and entered the oak wood, and still again heard him enjoining me to " keep dat road right straight."

Within less than quarter of a mile, there was a fork in the road to the left, which seemed a good deal more traveled than the straight one ; nevertheless I kept the latter, and was soon well satisfied that I had done so. It presently led me up a slope out of the oak woods into a dark evergreen forest ; and though it was a mere bridle-path, it must have existed, I thought, before the trees began to grow, for it was free of stumps, and smooth and clean as a garden walk, and the pines grew thickly up, about four feet apart, on each side of it, their branches meeting, just clear of my head, and making a dense shade. There was an agreeable, slightly balsamic odor in the air ; the path was covered with a deep, elastic mat of pine leaves, so that our footstep could hardly be heard ; and for a time we greatly enjoyed going along at a lazy, pacing walk of Jane's. It was noon-day, and had been rather warmer than was quite agreeable on the open road, and I took my hat off, and let the living pine leaves brush my hair. But, after a while, I felt slightly chilly ; and when Jane, at the same time, gave a little sympathizing caper, I bent my head down, that the limbs might not hit me, until it nearly rested on her neck, dropped my hands and pressed my knees tightly against her. Away we bounded !

What a glorious gallop Jane had inherited from her noble grandfather !

Out of the cool, dark-green alley, at last, and soon with a more cautious step, down a steep, stony declivity, set with deciduous trees—beech, ash, oak, gum—" gum," beloved of the "minstrels." A brawling shallow brook at the bottom, into which our path descended, though on the opposite shore was a steep high bank, faced by an impenetrable brake of bush and briar.

Have we been following a path only leading to a watering-place, then? I see no continuance of it. Jane does not hesitate at all; but, as if it was the commonest thing here to take advantage of nature's engineering in this way, walking into the water, turns her head up stream.

For more than a mile we continued following up the brook, which was all the time walled in by insurmountable banks, over-hung by large trees. Sometimes it swept strongly through a deep channel, contracted by boulders; sometimes purled and tinkled over a pebbly slope; and sometimes stood in broad, silent pools, around the edges of which remained a skirt of ice, held there by bushes and long, broken water-grasses. Across the end of one of these, barring our way, a dead trunk had lately fallen. Jane walked up to it and turned her head to the right. "No," said I, "let's go over." She turned, and made a step left—"No! over," said I, drawing her back, and touching her with my heels.

Over we went, landing with such a concussion that I was nearly thrown off. I fell forward upon Jane's neck; she threw up her head, spurning my involuntary embrace; and then, with swollen nostrils and flashing eyes, walked on rapidly.

"Hope you are satisfied," said she, as I pulled my coat down; "if not, you had better spur me again."

"Why, my dear girl, what's the matter? It was nothing but leather—calf-skin—that I touched you with. I have no spurs—

don't you see?" for she was turning her head to bite my foot.
"Now, don't be foolish."

"Well, well," said she, "I'm a good tempered girl, if I am
blood; let's stop and drink."

After this, we soon came to pine woods again. Jane was
now for leaving the brook. I let her have her own way, and
she soon found a beaten track in the woods. It certainly was
not the "straight road" we had been directed to follow; but its
course was less crooked than that of the brook, and after some
time it led us out into a more open country, with young pines
and inclosed fields. Eventually we came to a gate and lane,
which we followed till we came to another cross-lane, leading
straight to a farm-house.

As soon as we turned into the cross-lane, half-a-dozen little
negro boys and girls were seen running towards the house,
to give alarm. We passed a stable, with a cattle-pen by its
side, opposite which was a vegetable garden, enclosed with split
palings; then across a running stream of water; then by a small
cabin on the right; and a corn-crib and large pen, with a
number of fatting hogs in it, on the left; then into a large,
irregular yard, in the midst of which was the farm-house, before
which were now collected three white children, six black ones,
two negro women, and an old lady with spectacles.

"How dy do, sir?" said the old lady, as we reined up,
bowed, and lifted our hat, and put our black foot foremost.

"Thank you, madam, quite well; but I have lost my way
to Mr. Thomas W.'s, and will trouble you to tell me how to
go from here to get to his house."

By this time a black man came cautiously walking in from the
field back of the house, bringing an axe; a woman, who had

been washing clothes in the brook, left her work and came up on the other side, and two more girls climbed up on to a heap of logs that had been thrown upon the ground, near the porch, for fuel.

The swine were making a great noise in their pen, as if feeding-time had come; and a flock of turkeys were gobbling so incessantly and loudly that I was not heard. The old lady ordered the turkeys to be driven away, but nobody stirred to do it, and I rode nearer and repeated my request. No better success. "Can't you shew away them turkeys?" she asked again; but nobody "shewed." A third time I endeavored to make myself understood. "Will you please direct me how to go to Mr. W.'s?"

"No, sir—not here."

"Excuse me—I asked if you would direct me to Mr. W.'s."

"If some of you niggers don't shew them turkeys, I'll have you all whipped as soon as your mass John comes home," exclaimed the old lady, now quite excited. The man with the axe, without moving towards them at all, picked up a billet of wood and threw it at the biggest cock-turkey, who immediately collapsed; and the whole flock scattered, chased by the two girls who had been on the log-heap.

"An't dat Colonel Gillen's mare, master?" asked the black man, coming up on my left.

"You want to go to Thomas W.'s?" asked the old lady.

"Yes, madam."

"It's a good many years since I have been to Thomas W.'s, and I reckon I can't tell you how to go there now."

"If master'll go over to Missy Abler's, I reckon dey ken tell 'em dah, sar."

"And how shall I go to Mrs. Abler's?"

"You want to go to Missy Abler's; you take dat path right over 'yond dem bars, dar, by de hog-pen, dat runs along by dat fence into de woods, and dat'll take you right straight dar."

"Is you come from Colonel Gillin's, massa?" asked the washwoman.

"Yes."

"Did you see a black man dar, day calls Tom, sar?"

"Yes."

"Tom's my husband, massa; if you's gwine back dah, wish you'd tell um, ef you please, sar, dat I wants to see him *particklar;* will ou, massa?"

"Yes."

"Tank you, massa."

I bowed to the old lady, and, in turning to ride off, saw two other negro boys who had come out of the woods, and were now leaning over the fence, and staring at us, as if I was a giant and Jane was a dragoness.

We trotted away, found the path, and in course of a mile had our choice of at least twenty forks to go "straight to Mrs. Abler's." At length, cleared land again, fences, stubble-fields and a lane, that took us to a little cabin, which fronted, much to my surprise, upon a broad and well-traveled road. Over the door of the cabin was a sign, done in black, upon a hogshead stave, showing that it was a " GROSERY," which, in Virginia, means the same thing as in Ireland—a dram-shop.

I hung the bridle over a rack before the door, and walked in. At one end of the interior was a range of shelves, on which were two decanters, some dirty tumblers, a box of crackers, a canister, and several packages in paper; under the shelves were a table and a barrel. At the other end of the room was a fire-place; near this, a chest, and another range of shelves, on which stood plates and cooking utensils: between these and the grocery end were a bed and a spinning-wheel. Near the spinning-wheel sat a tall, bony, sickly, sullen young woman, nursing a languishing infant. The faculty would not have discouraged either of them from trying hydropathic practice. In a corner of the fire-place sat a man, smoking a pipe. He rose, as I entered, walked across to the grocery-shelves, turned a chair round at the table, and asked me to take a seat. I excused myself, and requested him to direct me to Mr. W.'s. He had heard of such a man living somewhere about there, but he did not know where. He repeated this, with an oath, when I declined to " take " anything, and added, that he had not lived here long, and he was sorry he had ever come here. It was the worst job, for himself, ever he did, when he came here, though all he wanted was to just get a living.

I rode on till I came to another house, a very pleasant little house, with a steep, gabled roof, curving at the bottom, and extending over a little gallery, which was entered, by steps, from the road; back of it were stables and negro-cabins, and by its side was a small garden, and beyond that a peach-orchard. As I approached it, a well-dressed young man, with an intelligent and pleasant face, came out into the gallery. I asked him if he could direct me to Mr. W.'s. "Thomas W.'s?" he inquired.

"Yes, sir."

"You are not going in the right direction to go to Mr. W.'s. The shortest way you can take to go there is, to go right back to the Court House."

I told him I had just come out of the lane by the grocery on to the road. "Ah! well, I'll tell you; you had better turn round, and keep right straight upon this road till you get to the Court House, and anybody can tell you, there, how to go."

"How far is it, sir?"

"To the Court House?—not above a mile."

"And to Mr. W.'s?"

"To Mr. W.'s, I should think it was as much as ten miles, and long ones, too."

I rode to the Court House, which was a plain brick building in the centre of a small square, around which there were twenty or thirty houses, two of them being occupied as stores, one as a saddler's shop, one had the sign of "Law Office" upon it, two were occupied by physicians, one other looked as if it might be a meeting-house or school-house, or the shop of any mechanic needing much light for his work, and two were "Hotels." At one of these we stopped, to dine; Jane had "corn and fodder" (they had no oats or hay in the stable), and I had ham and eggs (they had no fresh meat in the house). I had several other things, however, that were very good, besides the company of the landlady, who sat alone with me, at the table, in a long, dining hall, and was very pretty, amiable, and talkative.

In a course of apologies, which came in the place of soup, she gave me the clue to the assemblage of negroes I had seen at the mill. It was Christmas week; all the servants thought they must go for at least, one day, to have a frolic, and to-day (as luck would have it, when I was coming,) her cook was off with some others; she did not suppose they'd be back till to-morrow, and then, likely as not, they'd be drunk. She did not think this custom, of letting servants go so, at Christmas, was a good one; niggers were not fit to be let to take care of themselves, anyhow. It was very bad for them, and she didn't think it was *right*. Providence had put the servants into our hands to be looked out for, and she didn't believe it was intended they should be let to do all sorts of wickedness, if Christmas didn't come but once a year. She wished, for her part, it did not come but once in ten years.

(The negroes, that were husking maize near the cabin where the White-man lived, were, no doubt, slaves, who had hired themselves out by the day, during the holiday-week, to earn a little money on their own account.)

In regard to the size of the dining hall, and the extent of sheds in the stable-yard, the landlady told me that though at other times they very often did not have a single guest in a day, at "Court time" they always had more than they could comfortably accommodate. I judged, also, from her manners, and the general appearance of the house, as well as from the charges, that, at such times, the company was of a rather respectable character. The appearance of the other public-house indicated that it expected a less select patronage.

When I left, my direction was to keep on the main road until I came to a fork, about four miles distant, then take the left, and keep *the best traveled road*, until I came to a certain house, which was so described that I should know it, where I was advised to ask further directions.

The sky was now clouding over; it was growing cold; and we went on, as fast as we conveniently could, until we reached the fork in the road. The direction, to keep the best traveled road, was unpleasantly prominent in my mind; it was near sunset, I reflected, and, however jolly it might be at twelve o'clock at noon, it would be quite another thing to be knocking about among those fierce hogs in the pine-forest, if I should be lost, at twelve o'clock at night. Besides, as the landlady said about her negroes, I did not think it was *right* to expose Jane to this danger, unnecessarily. A little beyond the fork, there was a large, gray, old house, with a grove of tall poplars before it; a respectable, country-gentleman-of-the-old-school look it had.— These old Virginians are proverbially hospitable.—It's rather impudent; but I hate to go back to the Court House, and I am ——I will ride on, and look it in the face, at any rate.

Zig-zag fences up to a large, square yard, growing full of Lombardy poplar sprouts, from the roots of eight or ten old trees, which were planted some fifty years ago, I suppose, in a double row, on two sides of the house. At the further end of this yard, beyond the house, a gate opened on the road, and out of this was just then coming a black man.

I inquired of him if there was a house, near by, at which I could get accommodations for the night. Reckoned his master'd take me in, if I'd ask him. Where was his master? In the house: I could go right in here (at a place where a panel of the paling had fallen over) and see him, if I wanted to. I asked him to hold my horse, and went in.

It was a simple, two-story house, very much like those built by the wealthier class of people in New England villages, from fifty to a hundred years ago, except that the chimneys were carried up outside the walls. There was a porch at the front door, and a small wing at one end, in the rear; from this wing to the other end extended a broad gallery.

A dog had been barking at me after I dismounted; and just as I reached the steps of the gallery, a vigorous, middle-aged man, with a rather sullen and suspicious expression of face, came out without any coat on, to see what had excited him.

Doubting whether he was the master of the house, I told him that I had come in to inquire if it would be convenient to allow me to spend the night with them. He asked where I came from, where I was going to, and various other questions, until I had given him an epitome of my day's wanderings and adventures; at the conclusion of which he walked to the end of the gallery to look at my horse; then, without giving me any answer, but muttering indistinctly something about servants, walked into the house, shutting the door behind him!

Well, thought I, this is not very overwhelmingly hospitable. What can it mean?

While I was considering whether he expected me to go without any further talk—his curiosity being, I judged, satisfied—he came out again, and said, " Reckon you can stay, sir, if you'll take what we'll give you." (The good man had been in to consult his wife.) I replied that I would do so, thankfully, and hoped they would not give themselves any unnecessary trouble, or alter their usual family arrangements.   I was then invited to come in, but I preferred to see my horse taken care of first. My host called for " Sam," two or three times, and then said he reckoned all his "people" had gone off, and he would attend to my horse himself.   I offered to assist him, and we walked out to the gate, where the negro, not being inclined to wait for my return, had left Jane fastened to a post.   Our host conducted us to an old square log-cabin, which had formerly been used for curing tobacco, there being no room for Jane, he said, in the stables proper.

The floor of the tobacco-house was covered with lumber, old plows, scythes and cradles, a part of which had to be removed to make room for the filly to stand.   She was then induced, with some difficulty, to enter it through a low, square door-way ; saddle and bridle were removed, and she was fastened in a corner by a piece of old plow-line.   We then went to a fodder-stack, and pulled out from it several small bundles of maize leaves. Additional feed and water were promised when "some of the niggers" came in; and, after righting up an old door that had fallen from one hinge, and setting a rail against it to keep it in its place, we returned to the house.

My host (whom I will call Mr. Newman) observed that his buildings and fences were a good deal out of order.   He had owned the place but a few years, and had not had time to make much improvement about the house yet.

Entering the mansion, he took me to a large room on the first floor, gave me a chair, went out and soon returned (now wearing a coat) with two negro girls, one bringing wood and the other some flaming brands.   A fire was made with a great deal of trouble, scolding of the girls, bringing in more brands, and blowing with the mouth. When the room had been suffocatingly filled with smoke, and at length a strong bright blaze swept steadily up the chimney, Mr. Newman again went out with the girls, and I was left alone for nearly an hour, with one interruption, when he came in and threw some more wood upon the fire, and said he hoped I would make myself comfortable.

It was a square room, with a door from the hall on one side, and two windows on each of the other sides. The lower part of the walls was wainscoted, and the upper part, with the ceiling, plastered and white-washed. The fire-place and mantle-piece were somewhat carved, and were painted black; all the other woodwork, lead color. Blue paper curtains covered the windows; the floor was uncarpeted, and the only furniture in the room was some strong plain chairs, painted yellow, and a Connecticut clock, which did not run. The house had evidently been built for a family of some wealth, and, after having been deserted by them, had been bought at a bargain by the present resident, who either had not the capital or the inclination to furnish and occupy it appropriately.

When my entertainer called again, he merely opened the door and said, in the words of an order, but in a tone of advice, "Come! get something to eat!" I followed him out into the gallery, and thence through a door at its end into a room in the wing—a family room, and a very comfortable, homely room. A most bountifully spread supper-table stood in the centre, at which was sitting a very neat, pretty little woman, of as silent habits as her husband, but neither bashful nor morose. A very nice little girl sat at her right side, and a peevish, ill-behaved, whining glutton of a boy at her left. I was requested to be seated adjoining the little girl, and the master of the house sat opposite me. The fourth side of the table was unoccupied, though a plate and chair were placed there, as if some one else had been expected.

The two negro girls waited at table, and a negro boy was in the room, who, when I asked for a glass of water, was sent to get it. An old negro woman also frequently came in from the kitchen, with hot biscuit and corn-cake. There was fried fowl, and fried bacon and eggs, and cold ham; there were preserved peaches, and preserved quinces and grapes; there was hot wheaten biscuit, and hot short-cake, and hot corn-cake, and hot griddle cakes, soaked in butter; there was coffee, and there was milk, sour or sweet, whichever I preferred to drink. I really ate more than I wanted, and extolled the corn-cake and the peach preserve, and asked how they were made; but I evidently disappointed my pretty hostess, who said she was afraid there wasn't anything that suited me,—she feared there wasn't anything on the table I could eat; and she was sorry I couldn't make out a supper. And this was about all she would say. I tried to get a free conversation started, but I have myself but poor endowments for such a purpose, and I could obtain little more than very laconic answers to my questions.

Except from the little girl at my side, whose confidence I gained by taking an opportunity, when her mother was engaged, with young hopeful t'other side the coffee-pot, to give her a great lot of quince and grape, and by several times pouring molasses very freely on her cakes and bacon; and finally by feeding Pink out of my hand. (Hopeful had done this first, and then kicked him away, when he came round to Martha and me.) She told me her name, and that she had got a kitten, and that she hated Pink; and that she went to a Sunday-school at the Court House, and

that she was going to go to an every-day school next winter—
she wasn't big enough to walk so far now, but she would be then.
But Billy said he didn't mean to go, because he didn't like to,
though Billy was bigger nor she was, a heap. She reckoned
when Billy saw Wash. Baker going past every day, and heard
how much fun he had every day with the other boys at the school,
he would want to go too, wouldn't he? etc., etc. When supper was
ended, I set back my chair to the wall, and took her on my knee;
but after she had been told twice not to trouble the gentleman,
and I had testified that she didn't do it, and after several mild
hints that I would perhaps find it pleasanter in the sitting-room—
(the chairs in the supper-room were the easiest, being country-
made, low, and seated with undressed calf-skin), she was called to,
out of the kitchen, and Mr. Newman, in the form of advice, but
with the tone of command, said—going to the door and opening
it for me—"Reckon you'd better walk into the sittin'-room, sir."

I walked out at this, and said I would go and look at the filly.
Mr. Newman called "Sam" again, and Sam, having at that
moment arrived at the kitchen-door, was ordered to go and take
care of this gentleman's horse. I followed Sam to the tobacco-
house, and gave him to know that he would be properly remembered for any attentions he could give to Jane. He watered her,
and brought her a large supply of oats in straw, and some maize
on the cob; but he could get no litter, and declared there was
no straw on the plantation, though the next morning I saw a
large quantity in a heap (not a stack), at a little greater distance
than he was willing to go for it, I suppose, at a barn on the
opposite side of the road. Having seen her rubbed clean and
apparently well contented with her quarters and her supper, I
bade her good-night, and returned to the house.

I did not venture again into the supper-room, but went to the sitting-room, where I found Miss Martha Ann and her kitten; I was having a very good time with her, when her father came in and told her she was "troubling the gentleman;" I denied it, and he took a seat by the fire with us, and I soon succeeded in drawing him into a conversation on farming, and the differences in our methods of work at the North and those he was accustomed to.

WHITE LABORING PEOPLE.

I learned that there were no white laboring men here who hired themselves out by the month. The poor white people that had to labor for their living, never would work steadily at any employment. "They mostly followed boating"—hiring as hands on the bateaus that navigate the small streams and canals, but never for a longer term at once than a single trip of a boat, whether that might be long or short. At the end of the trip they were paid by the day. Their wages were from fifty cents to a dollar, varying with the demand and individual capacities. They hardly ever worked on farms except in harvest, when they usually received a dollar a day, sometimes more. In harvest-time, most of the rural mechanics closed their shops and hired out to the farmers at a dollar a day, which would indicate that their ordinary earnings are considerably less than this. At other than harvest-time, the poor white people, who had no trade, would sometimes work for the farmers by the job; not often at any regular agricultural labor, but at getting rails or shingles, or clearing land.

He did not know that they were particular about working with negroes, but no white man would ever do certain kinds of work (such as taking care of cattle, or getting water or wood to be used in the house), and if you should ask a white man you had hired, to do such things, he would get mad and tell you he wasn't a nigger. Poor white girls never hired out to do servants' work, but they would come and help another white woman about her sewing or quilting, and take wages for it. But these girls were not very respectable generally, and it was not agreeable to have them in your house, though there were some very respectable ladies that would go out to sew. Farmers depended almost entirely upon their negroes; it was only when they were hard pushed by their crops, that they got white hands to help them any.

Negroes had commanded such high wages lately, to work on railroads and in tobacco-factories, that farmers were tempted to hire out too many of their people, and to undertake to do too much work with those they retained, and thus they were often driven to employ white men, and to give them very high wages by the day, when they found themselves getting much behind-hand with their crops. He had been driven very hard in this way this last season; he had been so unfortunate as to lose one of his best women, who died in child-bed just before harvest. The loss of the woman and her child, for the child had died also, just at that time, came very hard upon him. He would not have taken a thousand dollars of any man's money for them. He had had to hire white men to help him, but they were poor sticks and would be half the time drunk, and you never know what to depend upon with them. One fellow that he had hired, who had agreed to work for him all through harvest, got him to pay him some wages in advance, (he said it was to buy him some clothes with, so he could go to meeting, Sunday, at the

Court-House,) and went off the next day, right in the middle of harvest, and he never had seen him since. He had heard of him—he was on a boat—but he didn't reckon he should ever get his money again.

Of course, he did not see how white laborers were ever going to come into competition with negroes here, at all. You never could depend on white men, and you couldn't *drive* them any; they wouldn't stand it. Slaves were the only reliable laborers—you could command them and *make* them do what was right.

From the manner in which he always talked of the white laboring people, it was evident that, although he placed them in some sort on an equality with himself, and that in his intercourse with them he wouldn't think of asserting for himself any superior dignity, or even feel himself to be patronizing them in not doing so, yet he, all the time, recognized them as a distinct and a rather despicable class, and wanted to have as little to do with them as he conveniently could.

I have been once or twice told that the poor white people, meaning those, I suppose, who bring nothing to market to exchange for money but their labor, although they may own a cabin and a little furniture, and cultivate land enough to supply themselves with (maize) bread, are worse off in almost all respects than the slaves. They are said to be extremely ignorant and immoral, as well as indolent and unambitious. That their condition is not as unfortunate by any means as that of negroes, however, is most obvious, since from among them, men *sometimes* elevate themselves to positions and habits of usefulness, and respectability. They are said to "corrupt" the negroes, and to encourage them to steal, or to work for them at night and on Sundays, and to pay them with liquor, and also to constantly associate licentiously with them.   They seem, nevertheless, more than any other portion of the community, to hate and despise the negroes.

BED-TIME.

In the midst of our conversation, one of the black girls had come into the room and stood still with her head dropped forward, staring at me from under her brows, without saying a word.   When she had waited, in this way, perhaps two minutes, her master turned to her and asked what she wanted.

"Miss Matty says Marta Ann go to bed now."

But Martha Ann refused to budge; after being told once or twice by her father to go with Rose, she came to me and lifted up her hands, I supposed to kiss me and go, but when I reached down, she took hold of my shoulders and climbed up on to my knees.   Her father seemed to take no notice of this proceeding, but continued talking about guano; Rose went to a corner of the fire-place, dropped down upon the floor and presently was asleep, leaning her head against the wall.   In about half an hour, the other negro girl came to the door, when Mr. Newman abruptly called out, "girl! take that child to bed!" and immediately got up himself and walked out.   Rose roused herself and lifted Martha Ann out of my arms, and carried her off fast asleep.   Mr. Newman returned holding a small candle in his hand, and, without entering the room, stood at the door and said, "I'll show you your bed if you are ready, sir."   As he evidently meant, "I am ready to show you to bed if you will not refuse to go," I followed him up stairs.

Into a large room, again, with six windows, with a fire-place, in which a few brands were smoking, with some wool spread thinly upon the floor in a corner; with a dozen small bundles of tobacco leaves; with a lady's saddle ; with a deep feather-bed, covered with a bright patch-work quilt, on a maple bedstead, and without a single item of any other furniture whatever. Mr. Newman asked if I wanted the candle to undress by, I said yes, if he pleased, and waited a moment for him to set it down : as he did not do so I walked towards him, lifting my hand to take it. "No—I'll hold it," said he, and I then perceived that he had no candle-stick, but held the lean little dip in his hand : I remembered also that no candle had been brought into the "sitting-room," and that while we were at supper only one candle had stood upon the table, which had been immediately extinguished when we rose, the room being lighted only from the fire.

I very quickly undressed and hung my clothes upon a bed-post : Mr. Newman looked on in silence until I had got into bed, when, with an abrupt "good-night, sir," he went out and shut the door.

SETTLING.

It was not until after I had consulted Sam the next morning, that I ventured to consider that my entertainment might be taken as a mere business transaction, and not as "genuine planter's hospitality," though this had become rather a ridiculous view of it, after a repetition of the supper, in all respects, had been eaten for breakfast, with equal moroseness on the part of my host and equal quietness on the part of his kind-looking little wife. I was, nevertheless, amused at the promptness with which he replied to my rather hesitating inquiry—what I might pay him for the trouble I had given him—" I reckon a dollar and a quarter will be right, sir."

THE WILDERNESS.

I have described, perhaps with tedious prolixity, what adventures befell me, and what scenes I passed through in my first day's random riding, for the purpose of giving an idea of the uncultivated and unimproved—rather, sadly worn and misused—condition of some parts, and I judge, of a very large part, of all Eastern Virginia, and of the isolated, lonely, and dissociable aspect of the dwelling places of a large part of the people.

Much the same general characteristics pervade the Slave States, everywhere, except in certain rich regions, or on the banks of some rivers, or in the vicinity of some great routes of travel and transportation, which have occasioned closer settlement or stimulated public spirit. For hours and hours one has to ride through the unlimited, continual, all-shadowing, all-embracing forest, following roads, in the making of which no more labor has been given than was necessary to remove the timber which would obstruct the passage of wagons; and even for days and days he may sometimes travel, and see never two dwellings of mankind within sight of each other; only, at long distances, often several miles asunder, these isolated plantation patriarchates. If a traveler leaves the main road to go any distance, it is not to be imagined how difficult it is for him to find his way from one house to any other in particular; his only safety is in the fact that, unless there are mountains or swamps in the way, he is not likely to go many miles upon any wagon or horse track without coming to some white man's habitation.

THE MEETING-HOUSE.

The country passed through, in the early part of my second

day's ride, was very similar in general characteristics to that I have already described; only that a rather larger portion of it was cleared, and plantations were more frequent. About eleven o'clock I crossed a bridge and came to the meeting-house I had been expecting to reach by that hour the previous day. It was in the midst of the woods, and the small clearing around it was still dotted with the stumps of the trees out of whose trunks it had been built; for it was a log structure. In one end there was a single square port, closed by a sliding shutter, in the other end were two doors, both standing open. In front of the doors, a rude scaffolding had been made of poles and saplings, extending out twenty feet from the wall of the house, and this had been covered with boughs of trees, the leaves now withered; a few benches, made of split trunks of trees, slightly hewn with the axe, were arranged under this arbor, as if the religious service was sometimes conducted on the outside in preference to the interior of the edifice. Looking in, I saw that a gallery or loft extended from over the doors, across about one-third the length of the house, access to which was had by a ladder. At the opposite end was a square, unpainted pulpit, and on the floor were rows of rude benches. The house was sufficiently lighted by crevices between the upper logs.

A TOBACCO PLANTATION.

Half an hour after this I arrived at the negro-quarters—a little hamlet of ten or twelve small and dilapidated cabins. Just beyond them was a plain farm-gate, at which several negroes were standing; one of them, a well-made man, with an intelligent countenance and prompt manner, directed me how to find my way to his owner's house. It was still nearly a mile distant;

and yet, until I arrived in its immediate vicinity, I saw no cultivated field, and but one clearing. In the edge of this clearing,
a number of negroes, male and female, lay stretched out upon the
ground near a small smoking charcoal pit. Their master afterwards informed me that they were burning charcoal for the plantation blacksmith, using the time allowed them for holidays—from
Christmas to New Year's—to earn a little money for themselves
in this way. He paid them by the bushel for it. When I said
that I supposed he allowed them to take what wood they chose
for this purpose, he replied that he had five hundred acres covered with wood, which he would be very glad to have any one
burn, or clear off in any way. Cannot some Yankee contrive a
method of concentrating some of the valuable properties of this
old-field pine, so that they may be profitably brought into use in
more cultivated regions? Charcoal is now brought to New
York from Virginia; but when made from pine it is not very
valuable, and will only bear transportation from the banks of the
navigable rivers, whence it can be shipped, at one movement, to
New York. Turpentine does not flow in sufficient quantity from
this variety of the pine to be profitably collected, and for lumber
it is of very small value.

Mr. W.'s house was an old family mansion, which he had himself remodeled in the Grecian style, and furnished with a large
wooden portico. An oak forest had originally occupied the
ground where it stood; but this having been cleared and the
soil worn out in cultivation by the previous proprietors, pine
woods now surrounded it in every direction, a square of a few
acres only being kept clear immediately about it. A number of
the old oaks still stood in the rear of the house, and, until
Mr. W. commenced his improvements, there had been some

in its front. These, however, he had cut away, as interfering with the symmetry of his grounds, and in place of them had planted ailanthus trees in parallel rows.

On three sides of the outer part of the cleared square there was a row of large and comfortable-looking negro-quarters, stables, tobacco-houses, and other offices, built of logs.

Mr. W. was one of the few large planters, of his vicinity,who still made the culture of tobacco their principal business. He said there was a general prejudice against tobacco, in all the tide-water region of the State, because it was through the culture of tobacco that the once fertile soils had been impoverished; but he did not believe that, at the present value of negroes, their labor could be applied to the culture of grain, with any profit, except under peculiarly favorable circumstances. Possibly, the use of guano might make wheat a paying crop, but he still doubted. He had not used it, himself. Tobacco required fresh land, and was rapidly exhausting, but it returned more money, for the labor used upon it, than anything else; enough more, in his opinion, to pay for the wearing out of the land. If he was well-paid for it, he did not know why he should not wear out his land.

His tobacco-fields were nearly all in a distant and lower part of his plantation; land which had been neglected before his time, in a great measure, because it had been sometimes flooded, and was, much of the year, too wet for cultivation. He was draining and clearing it, and it now brought good crops.

He had had an Irish gang draining for him, by contract. He thought a negro could do twice as much work, in a day, as an Irishman. He had not stood over them and seen them at work, but judged entirely from the amount they accomplished: he thought a good gang of negroes would have got on twice as fast. He was sure they must have "trifled" a great deal, or they would have accomplished more than they had. He complained much, also, of their sprees and quarrels. I asked why he should employ Irishmen, in preference to doing the work with his own hands. "It's dangerous work (unhealthy?), and a negro's life is too valuable to be risked at it. If a negro dies, it's a considerable loss, you know."

He afterwards said that his negroes never worked so hard as to tire themselves—always were lively, and ready to go off on a frolic at night. He did not think they ever did half a fair day's work. They could not be made to work hard: they never would lay out their strength freely, and it was impossible to make them do it.

This is just what I have thought when I have seen slaves at work—they seem to go through the motions of labor without putting strength into them. They keep their powers in reserve for their own use at night, perhaps.

Mr. W. also said that he cultivated only the coarser and lower-priced sorts of tobacco, because the finer sorts required more pains-taking and discretion than it was possible to make a large gang of negroes use. "You can make a nigger work," he said, "*but you cannot make him think.*"

Although Mr. W. was very wealthy (or, at least, would be considered so anywhere at the North), and was a gentleman of education, his style of living was very farmer-like, and thoroughly Southern. On their plantations, generally, the Virginia gentlemen seem to drop their full-dress and constrained town-habits, and to live a free, rustic, shooting-jacket life. We dined in a room that extended out, rearwardly, from the house, and which, in a Northern establishment, would have been the kitchen. The cooking was done in a detached log-cabin, and the dishes brought some distance, through the open air, by the servants. The outer door was left constantly open, though there was a fire in an enormous old fire-place, large enough, if it could have been distributed sufficiently, to have lasted a New York seamstress the best part of the winter. By the door, there was indiscriminate admittance to negro-children and fox-hounds, and, on an average, there were four of these, grinning or licking their chops, on either side of of my chair, all the time I was at the table. A stout woman acted as head waitress, employing two handsome little mulatto boys as her aids in communicating with the kitchen, from which relays of hot corn-bread, of an excellence quite new to me, were brought at frequent intervals.* There was no other bread, and but one vegetable served—sweet potato, roasted in ashes, and this, I thought, was the best sweet potato, also, that I ever had eaten; but there were four preparations of swine's flesh, besides fried fowls, fried eggs, cold roast turkey, and opossum, cooked, I know not how, but it somewhat resembled baked sucking-pig. The only beverages on the table were milk and whisky.

I was pressed to stay several days with Mr. W., and should have been glad to have accepted such hospitality, had not another engagement prevented. When I was about to leave,

---

* There is probably some choice in the sort of corn used. The best corn-bread that I have eaten was made simply by wetting coarse meal with pure water, adding only a little salt, and baking in the form of a breakfast-roll. The addition of milk, butter, or eggs, damages it. I speak now from experience—having been, in my second journey in the South, often obliged to make my own bread. The only care required, except not to burn it, is to make sure, if possi-ble—which it was not, generally, in Texas—that the corn is not mouldy.

an old servant was directed to get a horse, and go with me, as guide, to the rail-road station at Col. Gillin's. He followed behind me, and I had great difficulty in inducing him to ride near enough to converse with me. I wished to ascertain from him how old the different stages of the old-field forest-growth, by the side of our road, might be; but, for a long time, he was, or pretended to be, unable to comprehend my questions. When he did so, the most accurate information he could give me was, that he reckoned such a field (in which the pines were now some sixty feet high) had been planted with tobacco the year his old master bought him. He thought he was about twenty years old then, and that now he was forty. He had every appearance of being seventy.

He frequently told me there was no need for him to go any further, and that it was a dead, straight road to the station, without any forks. As he appeared very eager to return, I was at length foolish enough to allow myself to be prevailed upon to dispense with his guidance; gave him a quarter of a dollar for his time that I had employed, and went on alone. The road, which for a short distance further was plain enough, soon began to ramify, and, in half an hour, we were stumbling along a dark wood-path, looking eagerly for a house. At length, seeing one across a large clearing, we went through a long lane, opening gates and letting down bars, until we met two negroes, riding a mule, who were going to the plantation near the school-house, which we had seen the day before. Following them thither, we knew the rest of the way (Jane gave a bound and neighed, when we struck the old road, showing that she had been lost, as well as I, up to the moment).

It was twenty minutes after the hour given in the time-table for the passage of the train, when I reached the station, but it had not arrived; nor did it make its appearance for a quarter of an hour longer; so I had plenty of time to deliver Tom's wife's message and take leave of Jane. I am sorry to say she appeared very indifferent, and seemed to think a good deal more of Tom than of me. Mr. W. had told me that the train would, probably, be half an hour behind its advertised time, and that I had no need to ride with haste, to reach it. I asked Col. Gillin if it would be safe to always calculate on the train being half an hour late: he said it would not; for, although usually that much behind the time-table, it was sometimes half an hour ahead of it. So those, who would be safe, had commonly to wait an hour. People, therefore, who wished to go not more than twenty miles from home, would find it more convenient, and equally expeditious, taking all things into account, to go in their own conveyances—there being but few who lived so near the station that they would not have to employ a horse and servant to get to it.

A FREE-LABOR FARM.

——————, ——. I have been visiting a farm, cultivated entirely by free-labor. The proprietor told me that he was first led to disuse slave-labor, not from any economical considerations, but because he had become convinced that there was an essential wrong in holding men in forced servitude with any other purpose than to benefit them alone, and because he was not willing to allow his own children to be educated as slave-masters. His father had been a large slave-holder, and he felt very strongly the bad influence it had had on his own character. He wished me to be satisfied that Jefferson uttered a great truth when he asserted that slavery was more pernicious to the white race than the black. Although, therefore, a chief part of his inheritance had been in slaves, he had liberated them all.

Most of them had, by his advice, gone to Africa. These he had frequently heard from. Except a child that had been drowned, they were, at his last account, all alive, in general good health, and satisfactorily prospering. He had lately received a letter from one of them, who told him that he was "*trying* to preach the Gospel," and who had evidently greatly improved, both intellectually and morally, since he left here. With regard to those going North, and the common opinion that they encountered much misery, and would be much better off here, he said that it entirely depended on the general character and habits of the individual: it was true of those who were badly brought up, and who had acquired indolent and vicious habits, especially if they were drunkards, but, if of some intelligence and well-trained, they generally represented themselves to be successful and contented.

He mentioned two remarkable cases, that had come under his own observation, of this kind. One was that of a man who had been free, but, by some fraud and informality of his papers, was reënslaved. He ran away, and afterwards negotiated, by correspondence, with his master, and purchased his freedom. This man he had accidentally met, fifteen years afterwards, in a Northern city; he was engaged in profitable and increasing business, and showed him, by his books, that he was possessed of property to the amount of ten thousand dollars. He was living a great deal more comfortably and wisely than ever his old master had done. The other case was that of a colored woman, who had obtained her freedom, and who became apprehensive that she also was about to be fraudulently made a slave again. She fled to Philadelphia, where she was nearly starved, at first. A little girl, who heard her begging in the streets to be allowed to work for bread, told her that her mother was wanting some washing done, and she followed her home. The mother, not knowing her, was afraid to trust her with the articles to be washed. She prayed so earnestly for the job, however—suggesting that she might be locked into a room until she had completed it—that it was given her.

So she commenced life in Philadelphia. Ten years afterwards he had accidentally met her there; she recognized him immediately, recalled herself to his recollection, manifested the greatest joy at seeing him, and asked him to come to her house, which he found a handsome three-story building, furnished really with elegance; and she pointed out to him, from the window, three houses in the vicinity that she owned and rented. She showed great anxiety to have her children well educated, and was employing the best instructors for them which she could procure in Philadelphia.

This gentleman, notwithstanding his anti-slavery sentiments, by no means favors the running away of slaves, and thinks the Abolitionists have done immense harm to the cause they have at heart. He wishes Northerners would mind their business, and leave Slavery alone, say but little about it—nothing in the present condition of affairs at the South—and never speak of it but in a kind and calm manner. He would not think it right to return a fugitive slave; but he would never assist one to escape. He has several times purchased slaves, generally such as his neighbors were obliged to sell, and who would otherwise have been taken South. This he had been led to do by the solicitation of some of their relatives. He had retained them in his possession until their labor had in some degree returned their cost to him, and he could afford to provide them with the means of going to Africa or the North, and a small means of support after their arrival. Having received some suitable training in his family, they had, without exception, been successful, and had frequently sent him money to purchase the freedom of relatives or friends they had left in slavery.

He considered the condition of slaves to have much improved since the Revolution, and very perceptibly during the last twenty years. The original stock of slaves, the imported Africans, he observed, probably required to be governed with much greater severity, and very little humanity was exercised or thought of with regard to them. The slaves of the present day are of a higher character; in fact, he did not think more than half of them were full-blooded Africans. Public sentiment condemned the man who treated his slaves with cruelty. The owners were mainly men of some cultivation, and felt a family attachment to their slaves, many of whom had been the playmates of their boyhood. Nevertheless, they were frequently punished severely, under the impulse of temporary passion, often without deliberation, and on unfounded suspicion. This was especially the case where they were left to overseers, who, though sometimes men of intelligence and piety, were more often coarse, brutal, and licentious; drinking men, wholly unfitted for the responsibility imposed on them.

He had read "Uncle Tom's Cabin;" mentioned several points in which he thought it wrong—that Uncle Tom was too highly painted, for instance; that such a character could not exist in, or spring out of Slavery, and that no gentleman of Kentucky or Virginia would have allowed himself to be in the position with a slave-dealer in which Mr. Shelby is represented—but he acknowledged that cases of cruelty and suffering, equal to any described in it, might be found. In his own neighborhood, some time ago, a man had been whipped to death; and he recollected several that had been maimed for life, by harsh and hasty punishment; but the whole community were indignant when such things occurred, and any man guilty of them would be without associates, except of similar character.

The opinions of this gentleman must not, of course, be considered as representative of those of the South in general, by any means; but as to facts, he is a competent, and, I believe, a wholly candid and unprejudiced witness. He is much respected, and on terms of friendship with all his neighbors, though they do not like his views on this subject. He told me, however, that one of them, becoming convinced of their correctness some time ago, freed his slaves, and moved to Ohio. As to " Uncle Tom," it is generally criticised very severely, and its representations of Slavery indignantly denied. I observe that it is not placarded outside the booksellers' stores, though the whole fleet of gunboats that have been launched after it show their colors bravely. It must, however, be a good deal read here, as I judge from the frequent allusions I hear made to it.

With regard to the value of slave-labor, this gentleman is confident that, at present, he has the advantage in employing freemen instead of it. It has not been so until of late, the price of slaves having much advanced within ten years, while immigration has made free white laborers more easy to be procured.

He has heretofore had some difficulty in obtaining hands when he needed them, and has suffered a good deal from the demoralizing influence of adjacent slave-labor, the men, after a few months' residence, inclining to follow the customs of the slaves with regard to the amount of work they should do in a day, or their careless mode of operation. He has had white and black Virginians, sometimes Germans, and latterly Irish. Of all these, he has found the Irish on the whole the best. The poorest have been the native white Virginians; next, the free blacks: and though there have been exceptions, he has not generally paid these as high as one hundred dollars a year, and has thought them less worth their wages than any he has had. At present, he has two white natives and two free colored men, but both the latter were brought up in his family, and are worth twenty dollars a year more than the average. The free black, he thinks, is generally worse than the slave, and so is the poor white man. He also employs, at present, four Irish hands, and is expecting two more to arrive, who have been recommended to him, and sent for by those he has. He pays the Irishmen $120 a year, and boards them. He has had them for $100; but these are all excellent men, and well worth their price. They are less given to drinking than any men he has ever had; and one of them first suggested improvements to him in his farm, that he is now carrying out with prospects of considerable advantage. House-maids, Irish girls, he pays $3 and $6 a month.

He does not apprehend that in future he shall have any difficulty in obtaining steady and reliable men, that will accomplish much more work than any slaves. There are some operations, such as carting and spreading dung, and all work with the fork, spade, or shovel, at which his Irishmen will do, he thinks, over fifty per cent. more in a day than any negroes he has ever known. On the whole, he is satisfied that at present free-labor is more profitable than slave-labor, though his success is not so evident that he would be willing to have attention particularly called to it. His farm, moreover, is now in a transition state from one system of husbandry to another, and appearances are temporarily more unfavorable on that account.

The wages paid for slaves, when they are hired for agricultural labor, do not differ at present, he says, from those which he pays for his free laborers. In both cases the hiring party boards the laborer, but, in addition to money and board, the slave-employer has to furnish clothing, and is subject, without redress, to any losses which may result from the carelessness or malevolence of the slave. He also has to lose his time if he is unwell, or when from any cause he is absent or unable to work.

The slave, if he is indisposed to work, and especially if he is not treated well, or does not like the master who has hired him, will sham sickness—even make himself sick or lame—that he need not work. But a more serious loss frequently arises, when the slave, thinking he is worked too hard, or being angered by punishment or unkind treatment, "getting the sulks," takes to "the swamp," and comes back when he has a mind to. Often this will not be till the year is up for which he is engaged, when he will return to his owner, who, glad to find his property safe, and that it has not died in the swamp, or gone to Canada, forgets to punish him, and immediately sends him for another year to a new master.

"But, meanwhile, how does the negro support life in the swamp?" I asked.

"Oh, he gets sheep and pigs and calves, and fowls and

turkeys; sometimes they will kill a small cow. We have often seen the fires, where they were cooking them, through the woods, in the swamp yonder. If it is cold, he will crawl under a fodder-stack, or go into the cabins with some of the other negroes, and in the same way, you see, he can get all the corn, or almost anything else he wants.

"He steals them from his master?"

"From any one; frequently from me. I have had many a sheep taken by them."

"It is a common thing, then?"

"Certainly, it is, very common, and the loss is sometimes exceedingly provoking. One of my neighbors here was going to build, and hired two mechanics for a year. Just as he was ready to put his house up, the two men, taking offense at something, both ran away, and did not come back at all, till their year was out, and then their owner immediately hired them out again to another man."

These negroes "in the swamp," he said, were often hunted after, but it was very difficult to find them, and, if caught, they would run again, and the other negroes would hide and assist them. Dogs to track them he had never known to be used in Virginia.

RECREATION AND LUXURY AMONG THE SLAVES.

SATURDAY, Dec. 25. From Christmas to New-Year's Day, most of the slaves, except house servants, enjoy a freedom from labor; and Christmas is especially holiday, or Saturnalia, with them. The young ones began last night firing crackers, and I do not observe that they are engaged in any other amusement to-day ; the older ones are generally getting drunk, and making business for the police. I have seen large gangs coming in from the country, and these contrast much in their general appearance with the town negroes. The latter are dressed expensively, and frequently more elegantly than the whites. They seem to be spending money freely, and I observe that they, and even the slaves that wait upon me at the hotel, often have watches, and other articles of value.

The slaves have a good many ways of obtaining " spending money," which, though in law belonging to their owner, as the property of a son under age does to his father, they are never dispossessed of, and use for their own gratification, with even less restraint than a wholesome regard for their health and moral condition may be thought to require. A Richmond paper, com- plaining of the liberty allowed to slaves in this respect, as calculated to foster an insubordinate spirit, speaks of their " champagne suppers." The police broke into a gambling cellar a few nights since, and found about twenty negroes at " high play," with all the usual accessories of a first-class " Hell." It is mentioned that, among the number taken to the watch-house, and treated with lashes the next morning, there were some who had previously enjoyed a high reputation for piety, and others of a very elegant or foppish appearance.

Passing two negroes in the street, I heard the following :

" —— Workin' in a tobacco factory all de year roun', an' come Christmas, only twenty dollars ! Workin' mighty hard, too—up to 12 o'clock o' night very often—an' then to hab a nigger oberseah !"

" A nigger !"

" Yes—dat's it, yer see. Wouldn't care if 'twarnt for dat.

Nothin' but a dirty nigger! orderin' 'round, jes' as if he was a wite man!"

It is the custom of tobacco manufacturers to hire slaves and free negroes at a certain rate of wages per year. A task of 45 lbs. per day is given them to work up, and all that they choose to do more than this they are paid for—payment being made once a fortnight; and invariably this over-wages is used by the slave for himself, and is usually spent in drinking, licentiousness and gambling. The man was grumbling that he had saved but $20 to spend at the holidays. One of the manufacturers offered to show me, by his books, that nearly all gained by overwork $5 a month, many $20, and some as much as $28.

INGENUITY OF THE NEGRO.

Sitting with a company of smokers last night, one of them, to show me the manner in which a slave of any ingenuity or cunning would manage to avoid working for his master's profit, narrated the following anecdote. He was executor of an estate in which, among other negroes, there was one very smart man, who, he knew perfectly well, ought to be earning for the estate $150 a year, and who could do it if he chose, yet whose wages for a year, being let out by the day or job, had amounted to but $18, while he had paid for medical attendance upon him $45. Having failed in every other way to make him earn anything, he proposed to him that he should purchase his freedom and go to Philadelphia, where he had a brother. He told him if he would earn a certain sum ($400 I believe), and pay it over to the estate for himself, he would give him his free papers. The man agreed to the arrangement, and by his overwork in a tobacco factory, and some assistance from his free brother, soon paid the sum agreed upon, and was sent to Philadelphia. A few weeks afterwards he met him in the street, and asked him why he had returned. "Oh, I don't like dat Philadelphy, massa; ant no chance for colored folks dere; spec' if I'd been a runaway, de wite folks dere take care o' me; but I couldn't git anythin' to do, so I jis borrow ten dollar of my broder, and cum back to old Virginny."

"But you know the law forbids your return. I wonder that you are not afraid to be seen here; I should think Mr. —— (an officer of police) would take you up."

"Oh! I look out for dat, Massr, I juss hire myself out to Mr. —— himself, ha! ha! He tink I your boy."

And so it proved, the officer, thinking that he was permitted to hire himself out, and tempted by the low wages at which he offered himself, had neglected to ask for his written permission, and had engaged him for a year. He still lived with the officer, and was an active, healthy, good servant to him.

QUALITIES AS A LABORER.

A well-informed capitalist and slave-holder remarked, that negroes could not be employed in cotton factories. I said that I understood they were so in Charleston, and some other places at the South.

"It may be so, *yet*," he answered, "but they will have to give it up."

The reason was, he said, that the negro could never be trained to exercise judgment; he cannot be made to use his mind; he always depends on machinery doing its own work, and cannot be made to watch it. He neglects it until something is broken or there is great waste. "We have tried reward and punishments, but it makes no difference. It's his nature and you cannot change it. All men are indolent and have a disinclination to labor, but this is a great deal stronger in the African race than in any other. In working niggers, we must always calculate that they will not labor at all except to avoid punishment, and they will never do more than just enough to save themselves from being punished, and no amount of punishment will prevent their working carelessly and indifferently. It always seems on the plantation as if they took pains to break all the tools and spoil all the cattle that they possibly can, even when they know they'll be directly punished for it."

As to rewards, he said, "They only want to support life, they will not work for anything more; and in this country it would be hard to prevent their getting that." I thought this opinion of the power of rewards was not exactly confirmed by the narrative we had just heard, but I said nothing. "If you could move," he continued, "all the white people from the whole seaboard district of Virginia and give it up to the negroes that are on it now, just leave them to themselves, in ten years time there would not be an acre of land cultivated, and nothing would be produced, except what grew spontaneously."

The Hon. Willoughby Newton, by the way, seems to think that if it had not been for the introduction of guano, a similar desolation would have soon occurred without the Africanization of the country. He is reported to have said:

"I look upon the introduction of guano, and the success attending its application to our barren lands, in the light of a special interposition of Divine Providence, to save the northern neck of Virginia from reverting entirely into its former state of wilderness and utter desolation. Until the discovery of guano—more valuable to us than the mines of California—

I looked upon the possibility of renovating our soil, of ever bringing it to a point capable of producing remunerating crops, as utterly hopeless.   Our up-lands were all worn out, and our bottom-lands fast failing, and if it had not been for guano, to revive our last hope, a few years more and the whole country must have been deserted by all who desired to increase their own wealth, or advance the cause of civilization by a proper cultivation of the earth."

IMPROVEMENT OF THE NEGRO IN SLAVERY.

"But are they not *improving?*" said I; "that is a point in which I am much interested, and I should be glad to know what is your observation?   Have they not, as a race, improved during the last hundred years, do you not think?"

"Oh, yes indeed, very greatly.   During my time—I can remember how they were forty years ago—they have improved *two thousand per cent.!*   Don't you think so?" he asked another gentleman?

"Yes; certainly."

"And you may find them now, on the isolated old plantations in the back country, just as I recollect them when I was a boy, stupid and moping, and with no more intelligence than when they first came from Africa.   But all about where the country is much settled their condition is vastly ameliorated.   They are treated much better, they are fed better, and they have much greater educational privileges."

EDUCATIONAL PRIVILEGES.

"Educational privileges?" I asked, in surprise.

"I mean by preaching and religious instruction.   They have

the Bible read to them a great deal, and there is preaching for them all over the country. They have preachers
of their own; right smart ones they are, too, some of
them."

"Do they?" said I. "I thought that was not allowed
by law."

"Well, it is not—that is, they are not allowed to have meetings without some white man is present. They must not preach
unless a white man hears what they say. However, they do.
On my plantation, they always have a meeting on Sundays,
and I have sometimes, when I have been there, told my
overseer,—'You must go up there to the meeting, you
know the law requires it;' and he would start as if he was
going, but would just look in and go by; he wasn't going to
wait for them."

A DISTINGUISHED DIVINE.

He then spoke of a minister, whom he owned, and described
him as a very intelligent man. He knew almost the whole
of the Bible by heart. He was a fine-looking man—a fine head
and a very large frame. He had been a sailor, and had been in
New Orleans and New York, and many foreign ports. "He
could have left me at any time for twenty years, if he had
wished to," he said. "I asked him once how he would like
to live in New York? Oh, he did not like New York at all!
niggers were not treated well there—there was more distinction
made between them and white folks than there was here. 'Oh,
dey ain't no place in de worl like Ole Virginny for niggers,
massa,' says he."

Another gentleman gave similar testimony.

HOW THEY ARE FED.

I said I supposed that they were much better off, more improved intellectually, and more kindly treated in Virginia than further South. He said I was mistaken in both respects—that in Louisiana, especially, they were more intelligent, because the amalgamation of the races was much greater, and they were treated with more familiarity by the whites; besides which, the laws of Louisiana were much more favorable to them. For instance, they required the planter to give slaves 200 pounds of pork a year: and he gave a very apt anecdote, showing the effect of this law, but which, at the same time, made it evident that a Virginian may be accustomed to neglect providing sufficient food for his force, and that they sometimes suffer greatly for want of it. I was assured, however, that this was very rare—that, generally, the slaves were well provided for—always allowed a sufficient quantity of meal, and, generally, of pork—were permitted to raise pigs and poultry, and in summer could always grow as many vegetables as they wanted. It was observed, however, that they frequently neglect to provide for themselves in this way, and live mainly on meal and bacon. If a man does not provide well for his slaves, it soon becomes known, he gets the name of a "nigger killer," and loses the respect of the community.

The general allowance of food was thought to be a peck and a half of meal, and three pounds of bacon a week. This, it was observed, is as much meal as they can eat, but they would be glad to have more bacon; sometimes they receive four pounds, but it is oftener that they get less than three. It is distributed to them on Saturday nights; or, on the better managed plantations, sometimes, on Wednesday, to prevent their using it extravagantly, or selling it for whisky on Sunday. This distribution is called the "drawing," and is made by the overseer to all the heads of families or single negroes. Except on the smallest plantations, where the cooking is done in the house of the proprietor, there is a cook-house, furnished with a large copper for boiling, and an oven. Every night the negroes take their "mess," for the next day's breakfast and dinner, to the cook, to be prepared for the next day. Custom varies as to the time it is served out to them; sometimes at morning and noon, at other times at noon and night. Each negro marks his meat by cuts, so that he shall know it from the rest, and they observe each other's rights with regard to this, punctiliously.

After breakfast has been eaten early in the cabins, at sunrise or a little before in winter, and perhaps a little later in summer, they go to the field. At noon dinner is brought to them, and, unless the work presses, they are allowed two hours' rest. Very punctually at sunset they stop work and are at liberty, except that a squad is detached once a week for shelling corn, to go to the mill for the next week's drawing of meal. Thus they work in the field about eleven hours a day on an average. Returning to the cabins, wood "ought to have been" carted for them; but if it has not been, they then go to the woods and "tote" it home for themselves. They then make a fire—a big, blazing fire at this season, for the supply of fuel is unlimited—and cook their own supper, which will be a bit of bacon fried, often with eggs, corn-bread baked in the spider after the bacon, to absorb the fat, and perhaps some sweet potatoes roasted in the ashes. Immediately after supper they go to sleep, often lying on the floor or a bench in preference to a bed. About two o'clock they very generally rouse up and cook and eat, or eat cold, what they call their "mornin' bit;" then sleep again till breakfast.

I think the slaves generally (no one denies that there are exceptions) have plenty to eat; probably are fed better than the proletarian class of any other part of the world. I think that they generally save from their ration of meal. My informant said that commonly as much as five bushels of meal was sent to town by his hands every week, to be sold for them. Upon inquiry, he almost always found that it belonged to only two or three individuals, who had traded for it with the rest; he added, that too often the exchange was for whisky, which, against his rules, they obtained of some rascally white people in the neighborhood, and kept concealed. They were very fond of whisky, and sometimes much injured themselves with it.

To show me how well they were supplied with eggs, he said that once a vessel came to anchor, becalmed, off his place, and the captain came to him and asked leave to purchase some eggs of his people. He gave him permission, and called the cook to collect them for him. The cook asked how many she should bring. "Oh, all you can get," he answered—and she returned after a time, with several boys assisting her, bringing nearly two bushels, all the property of the slaves, and which they were willing to sell at four cents a dozen.

One of the smokers explained to me that it is very bad economy, not to allow an abundant supply of food to "a man's force." The negroes are fond of good living, and, if not well provided for, know how to provide for themselves. It is, also, but simple policy to have them well lodged and clothed. If they do not have comfortable cabins and sufficient clothing, they will take cold, and be laid up. He lost a very valuable negro, once, from having neglected to provide him with shoes.

LODGINGS.

The houses of the slaves are usually log-cabins, of various degrees of comfort and commodiousness. At one end there is a great open fire-place, which is exterior to the wall of the house, being made of clay in an inclosure, about eight feet square and high, of logs. The chimney is sometimes of brick, but more commonly of lath or split sticks, laid up like log-work and plastered with mud. They enjoy great roaring fires, and, as the common fuel is pitch pine, the cabin, at night when the door is open, seen from a distance, appears like a fierce furnace. The chimneys often catch fire, and the cabin is destroyed. Very little precaution can be taken against this danger.* Several cabins are placed near together, and they are called "the quarters." On a plantation of moderate size there will be but one "quarters." The situation chosen for it has reference to convenience of obtaining water from springs and fuel from the woods. On some of the James River plantations there are larger houses, boarded and made ornamental. In these, eight families, each having a distinct sleeping-room and lock-up

---

* "AN INGENIOUS NEGRO.—In Lafayette, Miss., a few days ago, a negro, who, with his wife and three children, occupied a hut upon the plantation of Col. Peques, was very much annoyed by fleas. Believing that they congregated in great numbers beneath the house, he resolved to destroy them by fire; and accordingly, one night when his family were asleep, he raised a plank in the floor of the cabin, and, procuring an armful of shucks, scattered them on the ground beneath, and lighted them. The consequence was, that the cabin was consumed, and the whole family, with the exception of the man who lighted the fire, was burned to death."—*Journal of Commerce.*

closets, and every two having a common kitchen or living-room, are accommodated.

CLOTHING.

As to the clothing of the slaves on the plantations, they are said to be usually furnished by their owners or masters, every year, each with a coat and trousers, of a coarse woolen or woolen and cotton stuff (mostly made, especially for this purpose, in Providence, R. I.), for Winter, trousers of cotton osnaburghs for Summer, sometimes with a jacket also of the same; two pairs of strong shoes, or one pair of strong boots and one of lighter shoes for harvest; three shirts; one blanket, and one felt hat.

The women have two dresses of striped cotton, three shifts, two pairs of shoes, etc. The women lying-in are kept at knitting short sacks, from cotton which, in Southern Virginia, is usually raised, for this purpose, on the farm, and these are also given to the negroes. They also purchase clothing for themselves, and, I notice especially, are well supplied with handkerchiefs which the men frequently, and the women nearly always, wear on their heads. On Sundays and holidays they usually look very smart, but when at work, very ragged and slovenly.

At the conclusion of our bar-room session, some time after midnight, as we were retiring to our rooms, our progress up stairs and along the corridors was several times impeded, by negroes lying fast asleep, in their usual clothes only, upon the floor. I asked why they were not abed, and was answered by a gentleman, that negroes never wanted to go to bed; they always preferred to sleep upon the floor.

FRATERNITY.

As I was walking in the outskirts of the town this morning, I saw squads of negro and white boys together, pitching pennies and firing crackers in complete fraternization. The white boys manifested no superiority, or assumption of it, over the dark ones.

An old, palsied negro-woman, very thinly and very raggedly clad, met me and spoke to me. I could not, from the trembling incoherency of her voice, understand what she said, but she was evidently begging, and I never saw a more pitiable object of charity at the North. She was, perhaps, a free person, with no master and no system to provide for her.

I saw, for the first time in my life, two or three young white women smoking tobacco in clay pipes. From their manner it was evidently a well-formed habit, and one which they did not suspect there was occasion for them to practice clandestinely, or be ashamed of.

RELIGIOUS CONDITION.

With regard to the moral and religious condition of the slaves, I cannot, either from what I observe, or from what is told me, consider it in any way gratifying. They are forbidden by law to meet together for worship, or for the purpose of mutual improvement. In the cities, there are churches especially for them, in which the exercises are conducted by white clergymen. In the country, there is usually a service, after that for the whites especially, in all the churches, which, by the way, are not very thickly scattered. In one parish, about twenty miles from Richmond, I was told that the colored congregation in the afternoon is much smaller than that of the whites in the morning; and it was thought not more than one-fifth of the negroes living within a convenient distance were in the habit of attending it; and of these many came late, and many more slept through the greater part of the service.

A goodly proportion of them, I am told, "profess religion," and are received into the fellowship of the churches; but it is evident, of the greater part even of these, that their idea of religion, and the standard of morality which they deem consistent with a "profession" of it, is very degraded. That they are subject to intense excitements, often really maniacal, which they consider to be religious, is true; but as these are described, I cannot see that they indicate anything but a miserable system of superstition, the more painful that it employs some forms and words ordinarily connected with true Christianity.

A Virginia correspondent of the *N. Y. Times*, writing upon the general religious condition of the State, and of the comparative strength and usefulness of the different churches, says:

"The Baptists also number (in Eastern Virginia) 44,000 colored members. This makes a great difference. Negroes join the church —perhaps in a great majority of cases—with no ideas of religion. I have but little confidence in their religious professions. Many of them I hope are very pious; but many of them are great scoundrels— perhaps the great majority of them—regardless of their church profession as a rule of conduct. They are often baptized in great numbers, and the Baptist Church (so exemplary in so much) is to blame, I fear, in the ready admission it gives to the negroes.

"The Baptist Church generally gets the negroes—where there are no Baptists, the Methodist. *Immersion* strikes their fancy. It is a palpable, overt act, that their imagination can take hold of. The ceremony mystically impresses them, as the ceremonies of Romanism affect the devotees of that connection. They come up out of the water, and believe they see 'the Lord.' In their religion, negroes are excessively superstitious. They have all sorts of 'experiences,' and enjoy the most wonderful revelations. Visions of the supernatural are of nightly occurrence, and the most absurd circumstances are invested with some marvelous significance. I have heard that the great ordeal, in their estimation, a 'seeker' had to pass, was being *held over the infernal flames by a thread or a hair.* If the thread does not break, the suspendee is 'in the Lord.'

"It is proper, therefore, I think, to consider this circumstance, in estimating the strength of a Church, whose communicants embrace such a number of negroes. Of the Methodists, in Eastern Virginia, some six or seven thousand are colored."

This condition of the slaves is not necessarily a reproach to those whose duty it more particularly is to instruct and preach the true Gospel to them. It is, in a great degree, a necessary result of the circumstances of their existence. The possession of arbitrary power has always, the world over, tended irresistibly to destroy humane sensibility, magnanimity, and truth. Look at the sovereigns of Europe in our day. There is not one, having sovereign power, that would not, over and over again, for acts of which he is notoriously and undeniably guilty, under our laws, be confined with the most depraved of criminals. It is, I have no doubt, utterly impossible, except as a camel shall enter the eye of a needle, for a man to have the will of others habitually under his control, without its impairing his sense of justice, his power of sympathy, his respect for manhood, and his worshipful love of the Infinite Father.

But it is much more evident that involuntary subjection directly tends to turpitude and demoralization. True, it may tend also to the encouragement of some beautiful traits, to meekness, humility, and a kind of generosity and unselfishness. But where has it not ever been accompanied by the loss of the nobler virtues of manhood, especially of the noblest, the most essential of all, that without which all others avail nothing for good: TRUTH. What is the matter with the Irish? No one can rely on them—they cannot rely on one another. Though sensitive to duty, and in their way conscientious, they absolutely are not able to comprehend a rule, a law; and that a man can be fixed by his promise they have never thought. A promise with them signifies merely an expressed intention. Irishmen that have long associated with us, we can depend on, for we have their confidence; but to a stranger still, their word is not worth a farthing. They are inveterate falsifiers, on the general principle that no man can want information of them but for his own good, and that good can only exist to their injury. What is the cause of this? their religion?—that to which it is attributed in their religion is the effect of it, more than the cause. It is the subjection of generations of this people to the will of landlords, corrupted to fiendish insensibility by the long continued possession of nearly arbitrary power. The capacity of mind for truth and reliance has been all but lost, by generations of unjust subjection.

It is the same—only in some respects better, and some far worse—even already, with the African slave of the South. Every Virginian acknowledges it. Religion, to call that by the name which they do, has become subject to it. "They will lie in their very prayers to God."

I find illustrations of the trouble that this vice occasions on every hand here. I just heard this, for instance, from a lady. A house-maid, who had the reputation of being especially devout, was suspected by her mistress of having stolen from her bureau several trinkets. She was charged with the theft, and vociferously denied it. She was watched, and the articles discovered openly displayed on her person as she went to church. She still, on her return, denied having them—was searched, and they were found in her pockets. When reproached by her mistress, and lectured on the wickedness of lying and stealing, she replied with the confident air of knowing the ground she stood upon, "Law, mam, don't say I's wicked; ole Aunt Ann says it allers right for us poor colored people to 'popiate whatever of de wite folk's blessins de Lord puts in our way." Old Aunt Ann was a sort of mother in the colored Israel of the town.

It is told me as a singular fact, that everywhere on the plantations, the agrarian notion has become a fixed point of the negro system of ethics: that the result of labor belongs of right to the laborer, and on this ground, even the religious feel justified in using "Massa's" property for their own temporal benefit. This they term "taking," and it is never admitted to be a reproach to a man among them that he is charged with it, though "stealing," or taking from another than their master, and particularly from one another, is so. They almost universally pilfer from the household stores when they have a safe opportunity. Thieving, by the way, is not a national vice of the Irish, because the opportunities and temptations for it have been too small to have bred the habit.

Jefferson says of the slaves:

"Whether further observation will or will not verify the conjecture, that nature has been less bountiful to them in the endowments of the head, I believe that in those of the heart she will have done them justice. That disposition to theft, with which they have been branded, must be ascribed to their situation, and not to any depravity of the moral sense. The man in whose favor no laws of property exist, probably feels himself less bound to respect those made in favor of others.   When arguing for ourselves, we lay it down as fundamental, that laws, to be just, must give a reciprocation of right; that without this, they are mere arbitrary rules, founded in force, and not in conscience, and it is a problem which I give to the master to solve, whether the religious precepts against the violation of property were not framed for him as well as his slave? and whether the slave may not as justifiably take a little from one who has taken all from him, as he may slay one who would slay him?   That a change of the relations in which a man is placed should change his ideas of moral right and wrong, is neither new, nor peculiar to the color of the blacks.   Homer tells us it was so, 2,600 years ago :

> " ' Jove fixed it certain, that whatever day
> Makes man a slave, takes half his worth away.' "

The following is a specimen of the most careful kind of preaching, ordinarily addressed by the white clergy to the black sheep of their flocks.   It is by Bishop Meade, of the Church of England in Virginia, and is copied from a published volume of sermons, recommended by him to masters and mistresses of his diocese, for use in their households.

" And think within yourselves what a terrible thing it would be, after all your labors and sufferings in this life, to be turned into hell in the next life, and, after wearing out your bodies in service here, to go into a far worse slavery when this is over, and your poor souls be delivered over into the possession of the devil, to become his slaves forever in hell, without any hope of ever getting free from it !   If, therefore, you would be God's freemen in heaven, you must strive to be good, and serve him here on earth.   Your bodies, you know, are not your own; they are at the disposal of those you belong to; but your precious souls are still your own, which nothing can take from you, if it be not your own fault.   Consider well, then, that, if you lose your souls by leading idle, wicked lives here, you have got nothing by it in this world, and you have lost your all in the next.   For your idleness and wickedness are generally found out, and your bodies suffer for it here; and what is far worse, if you do not repent and amend, your unhappy souls will suffer for it hereafter.

"Having thus shown you the chief duties you owe to your great Master in heaven, I now come to lay before you the duties you owe to your masters and mistresses here upon earth. And for this you have one general rule, that you ought always to carry in your minds; and that is. to do all service for them as if you did it for God himself.

"Poor creatures! you little consider, when you are idle and neglectful of your masters' business, when you steal, and waste, and hurt any of their substance, when you are saucy and impudent, when you are telling them lies and deceiving them, or when you prove stubborn and sullen, and will not do the work you are set about without stripes and vexation,—you do not consider, I say, that what faults you are guilty of towards your masters and mistresses are faults done against God himself, who hath set your masters and mistresses over you in his own stead, and expects that you would do for them just as you would do for him. And pray do not think that I want to deceive you when I tell you that your masters and mistresses are God's overseers, and that, if you are faulty towards them, God himself will punish you severely for it in the next world, unless you repent of it, and strive to make amends by your faithfulness and diligence for the time to come; for God himself hath declared the same.

"And in the first place, you are to be obedient and subject to your masters in all things. * * * And Christian ministers are commanded to 'exhort servants to be obedient unto their own masters, and to please them well in all things, not answering them again, or gainsaying.' * * * You are to be faithful and honest to your masters and mistresses, not purloining or wasting their goods or substance, but showing all good fidelity in all things. * * * Do not your masters, under God, provide for you? And how shall they be able to do this, to feed and to clothe you, unless you take honest care of everything that belongs to them? Remember that God requires this of you; and if you are not afraid of suffering for it here, you cannot escape the vengeance of Almighty God, who will judge between you and your masters, and make you pay severely, in the next world, for all the injustice you do them here. And though you could manage so cunningly as to escape the eyes and hands of man, yet think what a dreadful thing it is to fall into the hands of the living God, who is able to cast both soul and body into hell."

That wicked historian, Volney, "shows up" this sort of preaching, in the following suppositious debate, which, no doubt, has often been realized in the minds of the slaves:

"Then the Spiritual Governors said: 'There is no other way. As the People is superstitious, it is necessary to frighten them by the name of God and Religion.' So they said:

"'Our dear brothers—our children! God has appointed us to govern you.'

"S. 'Show us your heavenly authority.'

"M. 'You must have faith: Reason deceives.'

"S. 'Do you rule us without Reason?'

"M. 'God wishes Peace: Religion prescribes Obedience.'

"S. 'Peace supposes Justice: Obedience wishes to know the Law.'

"M. 'One is here below only to suffer.'

"S. 'Show us an example!'

"M. 'Do you wish to live without God and without Kings?'

"S. 'We would live without Tyrants.'"

[My aunt, who, on account of my habitual carelessness—"not to suggest occasional approach to something like vulgarity"—of style, is good enough to assist me in reading proofs, thinks that I ought not to make use of a quotation from this heterodox historian, without a clearer indication of my own opinions. The Episcopalians, in the words of a certain un-eminent Southern divine, "are a high-sailin' set," and easily offended, and *The Churchman*, she thinks, will be sure to suggest doubts of my rigid orthodoxy.]

A great many bad things have been furnished with props out of Scripture, by bad men, and a great many more by mistaken men, and the venerable Virginia prelate is not infallible. Exactly what such passages as he quotes were intended to teach, it is not for me to define and limit; but that they were meant to

encourage any men, immortal and accountable, under all circumstances and forever, to submit, in acquiescent stupefaction, to
Slavery, I venture to discredit.   Because it is contrary to nature
and to common sense, and I think it takes a more hair-splitting
mind, than negroes are generally endowed with, to think otherwise.
Because it seems to me that, to do so, it is necessary that a man
should acquire a more debased condition of soul than to be a schis-
matic, a fanatic, or a murderer.   Suppose the bishop had been consigned to my cell at Gadsby's, and had found it not only wanting
in comfort, but possessed by vermin, and stenches, and damp, and
Mr. Dexter had been ready with 1 Tim. vi., 8, and ordered
him, on the strength of it, to shut up and go to bed, when he
mildly objected to the arrangements, would he have meekly
resigned himself to certain bronchitis, and a probability of acute
laryngitis and speedy transfer to the eternal mansions?   I
respect him too much to believe it.   The relation between an
impostor and one who carelessly and slothfully allows himself
to be imposed upon, is the same as that between a thief and a
receiver of stolen goods.   Indolent acquiescence in that which
is unjust and harmful to us, is as wrong as a revengeful or an
unforgiving spirit; and if the Apostles had had to travel by our
rail-roads, and rest at our hotels, and employ our hackney-
coachmen, I believe they would have said so in so many words.

The bishop seems to me to teach, by implication, the doctrine
of the Divine Right of Kings; for what else, except in name, is
this divine right of oversight with which he invests the slave's
master, and for disloyalty to which he threatens corresponding
torment eternal?   In doing so, is he not disloyal and rebellious
to his own sovereign, "the Good People of Virginia," for their
sovereignty is based in treason, and in denial of this divine right

of government of one man over another? If the bishop does
not repent, where does he expect to go to?

My aunt thinks that, before I venture to object to the preaching of a bishop, I should be ready to say what should be
preached to slaves, while the necessity of keeping them in
Slavery continues. I don't admit this; yet I may say, in
general, that I should think that it would be encouragement to
them, to so conduct and train themselves that this necessity
should be removed as rapidly as possible; the supposition
being always maintained, that this necessity rested on the
extraordinary stupidity and vicious proclivities of the slaves
themselves, and would be happily removed by their enlightenment and growth in grace.

What says the learned and pious father Gregory, bishop
of the sixth century of Christianity?

Quum redemptor noster, totius conditor creaturæ, ad
hoc propitiatus humanam voluint carnem assumere, ut
divinitatis suæ gratia, dirupto quo tenebamur captivi vin-
culo, servitatis, pristinæ nos restituerit libertati salubriter
agitur si homines quos ab initio natura liberos protulit, et
jus gentium jugo substituit servitatis, in ea qua nati sunt,
manumittentis beneficie, libertate reddantur.
                    Decret. Grat. P. 11. *Caus. XII. Quæst.* 2.*

I had an idea that a good deal was done, with some
reference to the future freedom of the slaves; but I can't hear
that such is the case, in the Episcopal or any other Chris-

* Now, as our Redeemer and the Creator of every creature, was willing to
assume a human body, in order that by the grace of his divinity he might
break the bonds of servitude, wherein we were held captive, and restore us to
our freedom; so it is a good and salutary thing when those who, by nature,
were created free, and whom the laws of men have reduced to slavery, are,
by the benefaction of manumission, restored to that liberty in which they were
born.

tian organization. The Church of England form of worship is, in my opinion, the best calculated to encourage their elevation, of any used at the South; and the slaves who habitually attend and commune in the Episcopal church are, as a general rule, much more intelligent and elevated in their religious nature than any others. The ceremony and pomp, the frequent responses and chants, in which negroes are expected and encouraged to unite, in unison with the whites, and the liturgical system of instruction in religious truth, are all favorable to the improvement in character of the negro, and admirably adapted to the idiosyncrasies of his nature.

The Baptist and Methodist clergy, when addressing negro congregations, are said to spend most of their force in arguing against each other's doctrines, and the negroes are represented to have a great taste for theological controversy.

As an illustration of the way in which a great many negroes understood a certain tenet of the Baptists, a gentleman narrated the following circumstance:

A slave, who was "a professor," plagued his master very much by his persistence in certain immoral practices, and he requested a clergyman to converse with him and try to reform him. The clergyman did so, and endeavored to bring the terrors of the law to bear upon his conscience. "Look yeah, massa," said the backslider, "don't de Scriptur say, 'Dem who believes an is baptize shall be save?'" "Certainly," the clergyman answered; and went on to explain and expound the passage: but directly the slave interrupted him again.

"Jus you tell me now, massa, don't de good book say dese word: 'Dem as believes and is baptize, shall be save;' want to know dat."

"Yes; but—"

" Dat's all I want to know, sar; now wat's de use o' talkin to me?   You aint a goin to make me bleve wat de blessed Lord says, an't so, not ef you tries forever."

The clergyman again attempted to explain, but the negro would not allow him, and as often as he got back to the judgment-day, or charging him with sin, and demanding reformation, he would interrupt him in the same way.

" De Scriptur say, if a man believe and be baptize he shall— he *shall*, be save.   Now, massa minister, I *done* believe and I *done* baptize, an *I shall be save suah*.—Dere's no use talkin, sar."

My remarks in this letter, upon the religious and moral condition of the slaves, are to be considered as my first impressions from what I see and hear.   There appears to be a great difference of opinion among those who have had better opportunities of judging than I, on the subject, and it is fair that I should say, that some assure me they have no doubt the religious character of the slaves, who are members of churches, is as high as that of the white members, and that it is better than that of the lower class of whites.   Opinions as to the general standard of morality among the slaves are strongly contradictory.   My own impression has, therefore, been derived from facts that I hear, and from general observation of the manners and conversation of the slaves.   It is true that a great deal of religious phraseology and much Scripture language is used by them; but the very levity and inappropriateness with which it is applied, shows a want of a right appreciation of it.   It is not at all improbable, however, that I shall find occasion to modify this early formed opinion, as I see and hear further.   Of the frequently elevated religious and moral as well as cultivated and refined intellectual character of the more favored household servants of many excellent families, there can be no room for doubt. I have hardly less doubt, however, of the almost heathenish condition of the slaves on many of the large plantations.

FREE NEGROES IN VIRGINIA.

"Slavery is such an atrocious debasement of human nature, that its very extirpation, if not performed with solicitous care, may sometimes open a source of serious evils."—BENJAMIN FRANKLIN.

During forty-five years, according to Howison, the number of white convicts in the Virginia penitentiaries was in the ratio of 1 to about 328 of the whole population; the number of colored convicts, 1 in 67. "The free negroes and mulattoes are, unquestionably," says this historian, "the most vicious and corrupting of the varied materials composing our social system." "The criminal law, as to free colored persons and slaves, differs widely from that applied to whites. The free negroes occupy an equivocal and most unhappy position between the whites and slaves, and the laws affecting them partake of this peculiarity. Capital punishment is inflicted on them for offenses more lightly punished in whites. They are entitled to trial by jury in cases of homicide and in all capital cases, but, for all other crimes, they are tried by justices' courts of Oyer and Terminer, who must be unanimous in order to convict. They are subjected to restraint and surveillance in points beyond number."

To show their poverty and the benevolence of providing for the race by slavery, I am told that in one county, a few years ago, an inventory and estimate of the value of their property was made by order of the magistracy. With one exception, the highest value placed upon the property of an individual was two dollars and a half, ($2 50). The person excepted owned one hundred and fifty acres of land, a cabin upon it, a mule and some implements. He had a family of nine. Of provisions for its support, there were in the house, at the time of the visit of the appraisers, a peck and a half of Indian meal and part of a herring. The man was then absent to purchase some more meal, but had no money, and was to give his promise to pay in wood, which he was to cut from his farm. And this was in winter.

That this poverty is not the result of want of facilities or security of accumulating property, is proved by the exceptional instances of considerable wealth existing among them. An account of the death of a free colored man, who devised by will property to the amount of thirty thousand dollars, has lately been in the newspapers. I am assured, by one who knew the man very well, of the general accuracy of the narration, though one somewhat important circumstance was omitted. It was stated that the man preferred that his children should continue in the condition of slaves, and gave his property to a man who was to be their master. He gave as a reason for this, that he had personally examined the condition of the free blacks in Philadelphia and Boston, as well as in Virginia, and he preferred that his children should remain slaves, knowing that their master would take better care of them than they were capable of exercising for themselves. This was substantially correct. He had been, however, for a long time before his death, in a low state of health, and it is not known how sound, or uninfluenced by others, his mind might have been. The circumstance omitted was, that these were illegitimate children, by a slave woman, and that he simply left them in the condition in which they were born, in the care of their legal owner, having himself no legal right to dispose of them in any other way. It is a general custom of white people here to leave their illegitimate children, by slaves (and they are *very* common), in slavery. The man was himself a mulatto.

A man of wealth and station, who enjoys the friendship of the best and most respected people, lately sold his own half-brother, an intelligent, and of course "valuable," young man, to the traders, to be sent South, because he had attempted to run away to the Free States. So I am informed by his neighbor and friend.

At the present rate of wages, any free colored man might accumulate property more rapidly in Virginia than almost any man, depending solely on his labor, can at the North. In the tobacco-factories in Richmond and Petersburg, slaves are, at this time, in great demand, and are paid one hundred and fifty to two hundred dollars, and all expenses, for a year. These slaves are expected to work only to a certain extent for their employers; it having been found that they could not be "driven" to do a fair day's work so easily as they could be stimulated to it by the offer of a bonus for all they would manufacture above a certain number of pounds. This quantity is so easily exceeded, that the slaves earn for themselves from five to twenty dollars a month. Freemen are paid for all they do, at rates which make their labor equally profitable, and can earn, if they give but moderate attention and diligence to the labor, very large sums. One man's wages amounted last year, as I am informed by his employer, to over nine hundred dollars; but he is supposed to have laid up none of it. Nearly all the negroes, slave and free, it is said, spend their money as fast as they receive it. And nearly all of it goes in a manner to do them injury.

Formerly, it is said, the slaves were accustomed to amuse themselves, in the evening and on holidays, a great deal in dancing, and they took great enjoyment in this exercise. It was at length, however, preached against, and the "professors" so generally induced to use their influence against it, as an immoral practice, that it has greatly gone "out of fashion," and, in place of it, the young ones have got into the habit of gambling, and worse occupations, for the pastime of their holidays and leisure hours. I have not seen any dancing during these holidays, nor any recreation engaged in by the blacks, that is not essentially gross, dissipating, or wasteful, unless I except the firing of crackers.

Improvidence is generally considered here a natural trait of African character; and by none is it more so than by the negroes themselves. I think it is a mistake. Negroes, as far as I have observed at the North, although suffering from the contamination of habits acquired by themselves or their fathers in Slavery, are more provident than whites of equal educational advantages. Much more so than the newly-arrived Irish, though the Irish, soon after their immigration, are usually infected with the desire of accumulating wealth and acquiring permanent means of comfort. This opinion is confirmed by the experience of our City Missionaries—one of whom has informed me that where the very poorest classes of New York reside, black and white in the same house, the rooms occupied by the blacks are generally much less bare of furniture and the means of subsistence than those of the whites.

I observed that the negroes themselves follow the notion of

the whites here, and look upon the people of their race as
naturally unfitted to look out for themselves far ahead. Accustomed, like children, to have all their necessary wants provided
for, their whole energies and powers of mind are habitually
given to obtaining the means of temporary ease and enjoyment.
Their masters and the poor or "mean" whites acquire somewhat of the same habits from early association with them,
calculate on it in them—do not wish to cure it—and by constant
practices encourage it. For the means of enjoying themselves
the negroes depend much on presents. Their good-natured masters (and their masters are generally very good-natured, though
capricious) like to gratify them, and are ashamed to disappoint
them—to be thought mean. So it follows that, with the free negroes, habit is upon them; the habits of their associates, slaves
make the custom of society—that strongest of agents upon weak
minds. The whites think improvidence a natural defect of
character with them, expect it of them; as they grow old, or, as
they lose easy means of gaining a livelihood, charitably furnish
it to them; expect them to pilfer; do not look upon it as a
crime, or at least consider them but slightly to blame; and
so every influence and association is unfavorable to providence,
forethought, economy.

With such influences upon them, with such a character, with
such education, with such associations, it is not surprising that
Southerners say that the condition of the slave who is subject to
some wholesome restraint, and notwithstanding his improvidence
is systematically provided for, is preferable to that of the free black.
The free black does not, in general, feel himself superior to
the slave; and the slaves of the wealthy and aristocratic families
consider themselves in a much better and more honorable position

than the free blacks. Their view of the matter is said to be expressed thus: ———" *dirty free niggers !—got nobody to take care of 'em.*"

It is for this reason that slaves of gentlemen of high character, who are treated with judicious indulgence, and who can rely with confidence on the permanence of their position, knowing that they will be kindly cared for as they grow old, and feeling their own incapacity to take care of themselves, do often voluntarily remain in slavery when freedom is offered them, whether it be at the South, or North, or in Africa. A great many slaves that have been freed and sent to the North, after remaining there for a time, are said to have returned—longing, like the faithless Israelites, for the flesh pots of Slavery—of their own accord, to Virginia, and their report of the manner in which negroes are treated there, the difficulty of earning enough to provide themselves with the luxuries to which they have been accustomed, the unkindness of the white people to them, and the want of that thoughtless liberality in payments to them which they expect here from their superiors, has not been such as to lead others to pine for the life of an outcast at the North.

A number of Mr. Randolph's slaves, it has been several times mentioned to me, have thus returned. It is well known that Mr. Randolph took a humane and democratic view of Slavery ; and his neglect to educate them for the liberty which, after his death, he bequeathed to them, may have added much to that terrible remorse which darkened his death-bed.

It is certainly true that the negroes, either slave or free, are not generally disposed to go to Liberia. It is a distant country, of which they can have but very little reliable information, and they do not like the idea, any more than other people, of emigrating from their native country. But I really think that the best reason for their not being more anxious to go there is, that they are sincerely attached, in a certain way, to the white race. At all events, they do not incline to live in communities entirely separate from the whites, and do not long for entire independence from them. They have been so long accustomed to trusting the government of all weighty matters to the whites, that they would not feel at ease where they did not have them to "take care of 'em." They do not feel inclined to take great responsibilities on themselves, and have no confidence in the talent of their race for self-government. A gentleman told me that he owned a very intelligent negro, who had acquired some property, and that he had more than once offered him his freedom, but he would always reply that he did not feel able to fall entirely upon his own resources, and preferred to have a master. He once offered him his freedom to go to Liberia, and urged him to go there. His reply was to the effect that he would have no objections if the government was in the hands of white folks, but that he had no confidence in the ability of black people to undertake the control of public affairs.

I do not wish to be understood as intimating that the slaves generally would not like to be freed and sent to the North, or that they are ever really contented or satisfied with slavery; only that having been deprived of the use of their limbs from infancy, as it were, they may not wish now suddenly to be set upon their feet, and left to shift for themselves. They may prefer to secure at least plain food and clothing, and comfortable lodging, at their owner's expense, while they will return as little for it as they can, and have only the luxuries of life to work for on their own

account. it is not easy to deprive them of the means of securing a share of these.

These luxuries, to be sure, may be of very degrading character, and such as, according to our ideas, they would be better
without; but their tastes and habits are formed to enjoy them,
and they are not likely to be content without.

But, to live either on their own means, or the charitable assistance of others, at the North, they must dispense with many of these
things. It is as much as most of them—more than some of them,
with us—can do, by their labor, to obtain the means of subsistence, such as they have been used to being provided with, without a thought of their own, at the South. And if they are known
to indulge in practices that are habitual with the race, they will
not only lose the charity, but even the custom, of most of their
philanthropic friends; and then they must turn to pilfering again,
or meet that most pitiful of all extremities—poverty from want
of work. Again: suppose them to wish to indulge in their old
habits of sensual pleasure, they can only do so by forsaking the
better class of even their own color, or by drawing them down
to their own level. In this way, Slavery, even now, day by day,
is greatly responsible for the degraded and immoral condition of
the free blacks of our cities, and especially of Philadelphia.   It
is, perhaps, necessary that I should explain that licentiousness
and almost indiscriminate sexual connection among the young is
very general, and is a necessity of the system of Slavery.   A
Northern family that employs slave-domestics, and insists upon
a life of physical chastity in its female servants, is always
greatly detested; and they frequently come to their owners and
beg to be taken away, or not hired again, though acknowledging
themselves to be kindly treated in all other respects.   A

slave-owner told me this of his own girls hired to Northern people.

That the character and condition of some is improved by coming to the North, it is impossible to deny. From a miserable, half barbarous, half brutal state they have been brought in contact with the highest civilization. From slaves they have, sometimes, come to be men of intelligence, cultivation, and refinement. There are no white men in the United States that display every attribute of a strong and good soul better than some of the freed slaves. What would Frederick Douglass have been had he failed to escape from that service which Bishop Meade dares to say is the service of God; had his spirit been once broken by that man who, Bishop Meade would have taught him, was God's chosen overseer of his body? What has he become since he dared commit the sacrilege of coming out of bondage? All the statesmanship and kind mastership of the South has done less, in fifty years, to elevate and dignify the African race, than he in ten.

PETERSBURG TO NORFOLK.

In order to be in time for the train of cars in which I was to leave Petersburg for Norfolk, I was called up at an unusual hour in the morning and provided with a very poor breakfast, on the ground that there had not been time to prepare a decent one, (though I was charged full time on the bill), advised by the landlord to hurry when I seated myself at the table, and two minutes afterwards informed that, if I remained longer, I should be too late.

Thanks to these kind precautions, I reached the station twenty minutes before the train left, and was afterwards carried with about fifty other people at the rate of ten miles an hour to City-point, where all were discharged under a dirty shed, from which a wharf projected into James river.

The train was advertised to connect here with a steamboat for Norfolk. Finding no steamboat at the wharf, I feared, at first, that the delay in leaving Petersburg and the slow speed upon the road had detained us so long that the boat had departed without us. But observing no disappointment or concern expressed by the other passengers, I concluded the boat was to call for us, and had yet to arrive. An hour passed, during which I tried to keep warm by walking up and down the wharf; rain then commenced falling, and I returned to the crowded shed and asked a young man, who was engaged in cutting the letters G. W. B., with a dirk-knife, upon the head of a tobacco-cask, what was supposed to have detained the steamboat.

"Detained her? there aint no detention to her as I know on; 'taint hardly time for her to be along yet."

Another half hour, in fact, passed, before the steamboat arrived, nor was any impatience manifested by the passengers. All seemed to take this hurrying and waiting process as the regular thing. The women sat sullenly upon trunks and pack-ing-cases, and watched their baggage and restrained their children ; the men chewed tobacco and read newspapers, lounged first on one side and then on the other, some smoked, some walked away to a distant tavern, some reclined on the heaps of freight and went to sleep, and a few conversed quietly and inter-mittingly with one another.

THE JAMES RIVER.

The shores of the James river are low and level—the scenery uninteresting; but frequent planters' mansions, often of great size and of some elegance, stand upon the bank, and sometimes these have very pretty and well-kept grounds about them—finer than any other I have seen at the South—and the plantations surrounding them are cultivated with neatness and skill. Many men distinguished in law and politics here have their homes.

I was pleased to see the appearance of enthusiasm with which some passengers, who were landed from our boat at one of these places, were received by two or three well-dressed negro servants, who had come from the house to the wharf to meet them. Black and white met with kisses, and the effort of a long-haired sophomore to maintain his supercilious dignity, was quite ineffectual to kill the kindness of a fat mulatto woman, who joyfully and pathetically shouted, as she caught him off the gang-plank, " Oh Massa George, is you come back !" Field negroes, standing by, looked on with their usual besotted expression, and neither offered nor received greetings.

NORFOLK.

I arrived in Norfolk on the eve of a terrific gale, during which vessels at anchor in the Roads went down, and the city and country were much excited by various disasters, both on shore and at sea.

JAN. 10th. Norfolk is a dirty, low, ill-arranged town, nearly divided by a morass.   It has a single creditable public building, a number of fine private residences, and the polite society is reputed to be agreeable, refined, and cultivated, receiving a character from the families of the resident naval officers.   It has all the immoral and disagreeable characteristics of a large seaport, with very few of the advantages that we should expect to find as relief to them. No lyceum or public libraries, no public gardens, no galleries of art, and though there are two "BETHELS," no "home" for its seamen; no public resorts of healthful and refining amusement, no place better than a filthy, tobacco-impregnated bar-room or a licentious dance-cellar, so far as I have been able to learn, for the stranger of high or low degree to pass the hours unoccupied by business.

Lieut. Maury has lately very well shown what advantages were originally possessed for profitable commerce at this point, in a report, the intention of which is to advocate the establishment of a line of steamers hence to Para, the port of the mouth of the Amazon. I have the best wishes for the success of the project in its important features, and the highest respect for the judgment of Lieut. Maury, but it seems to me pertinent to inquire why are the British Government steamers not sent exclusively to Halifax, the nearest port to England, instead of to the more distant and foreign port of New York? If a Government line of steamers should be established between Para and Norfolk, and should be found in the least degree commercially profitable, how long would it be before another line would be established between New York and Para, by private enterprise, and then how much business would be left for the Government steamers while they continued to end their voyage at Norfolk? So, too, with regard to a line from Antwerp to Norfolk, (a proposition to grant State aid for establishing which, was the chief topic of public discussion in Virginia, at the time of my visit). Lieut. Maury says, however:

"Norfolk is in a position to have commanded the business of the

Atlantic sea-board: it is midway the coast. It has a back country of great facility and resources; and, as to approaches to the ocean, there is no harbor from the St. Johns to the Rio Grande that has the same facilities of ingress and egress at all times and in all weathers. * * The back country of Norfolk is all that which is drained by the Chesapeake Bay—embracing a line drawn along the ridge between the Delaware and the Chesapeake, thence northerly, including all of Pennsylvania that is in the valley of the Susquehanna, all of Maryland this side of the mountains, the valleys of the Potomac, Rappahannock, York, and James rivers, with the Valley of the Roanoke, and a great part of the State of North Carolina, whose only outlet to the sea is by the way of Norfolk."

THE NEGLECTED OPPORTUNITIES OF NORFOLK.

This is a favorite theme with Lieut. Maury, who is a Virginian. In a letter to the *National Intelligencer*, Oct. 31, 1854, after describing similar advantages which the town possesses to those enumerated above, he continues:

"Its climate is delightful. It is of exactly that happy temperature where the frosts of the North bite not, and the pestilence of the South walks not. Its harbor is commodious and safe as safe can be. It is never blocked up by ice. It has the double advantage of an inner and an outer harbor. The inner harbor is as smooth as any mill-pond. In it vessels lie with perfect security, where every imaginable facility is offered for loading and unloading." * * * * "The back country, which without portage is *naturally* tributary to Norfolk, not only surpasses that which is tributary to New York in mildness of climate, in fertility of soil, and variety of production, but in geographical extent by many square miles. The proportion being as *three to one* in favor of the Virginia port." * * * "The *natural* advantages, then, in relation to the sea or the back country, are superior, *beyond comparison*, to those of New York."

There is little, if any exaggeration in this estimate; yet, if a deadly, enervating pestilence had always raged here, this Norfolk could not be a more miserable, sorry little seaport town than it is.* It was not possible to prevent the existence of some agency here, for the transhipment of goods, and for supplying the needs of vessels, compelled by exterior circumstances to take refuge in the harbor. Beyond this bare supply of a necessitous demand, and what results from the adjoining naval rendezvous of the nation, there is nothing.

Singularly simple, child-like ideas about commercial success, you find among the Virginians—even among the merchants themselves. The agency by which commodities are transferred from the producer to the consumer, they seem to look upon as a kind of swindling operation; they do not see that the merchant acts a useful part in the community, or, that his labor can be other than selfish and malevolent. They speak angrily of New York, as if it fattened on the country without doing the country any good in return. They have no idea that it is *their* business that the New Yorkers are doing, and that whatever tends to facilitate it, and make it simple and secure, is an

---

* This was written and printed long before the late sad visit of yellow fever to Norfolk. I should hardly let it stand now, if I had not previously thought and said, when in the town, that its undrained and filthy condition was such that it seemed to me incredible that its people could live in health. If the condition of the town, at the time of my visit, was not very extraordinary, this dreadful visitor certainly did not come uninvited.

Since writing this note, my attention has been called to an article in the *Boston Medical and Surgical Journal*, written by a person who had resided for two years in Norfolk, and who says the town is " destitute of sewerage, and its streets are extremely filthy, being often strewed with refuse vegetables and other garbage, which result from the immense quantity of provisions brought into the city for export. These matters become rotten, and emit a most noisome stench. The turkey-buzzard, the natural scavenger of the South, is not found in Norfolk, but his place is supplied by cows, who wander at will through the town, and gather an unhealthy subsistence from the cabbage-stalks and other substances which lie in heaps on the ground. The condition of Portsmouth is much worse than that of Norfolk. It is connected with Gosport by a causeway, nearly a mile in length, if we are not mistaken, across a swamp or flat, from which arises a powerful stench.

increase of their wealth by diminishing the costs and lessening the losses upon it.

They gravely demand why the government mail steamers should be sent to New York, when New York has so much business already, and why the nation should build costly custom-houses and post-offices, and mints, and sea defenses, and collect stores and equipments there, and not at Norfolk, and Petersburg, and Richmond, and Danville, and Lynchburg, and Smithtown, and Jones's Cross-Roads? It seems never to have occurred to them that it is because the country needs them there, because the skill, enterprise and energy of New York merchants, the confidence of capitalists in New York merchants, the various facilities for trade offered by New York merchants, enable them to do the business of the country cheaper and better than it can be done anywhere else, and that thus they can *command* commerce, and need not petition their Legislature, or appeal to mean sectional prejudices to obtain it, but all imagine it is by some shrewd Yankee trickery it is done. By the bones of their noble fathers they will set their faces against it—and their faces are not of dough—so they bully their local merchants into buying in dearer markets, and make the country tote its gold on to Philadelphia to be coined; and their conventions resolve that the world shall come to Norfolk, or Richmond, or Smithtown, and that no more cotton shall be sent to England until England will pay a price for it that shall let negroes be worth a thousand dollars a head, &c., &c., &c.

Then, if it be asked why Norfolk, with its immense natural advantages for commerce, has not been able to do their business for them as well as New York; or why Richmond, with its great natural superiority for manufacturing, has not prospered like

Glasgow, or Petersburg like Lowell—why Virginia is not like Pennsylvania, or Kentucky like Ohio?—they will perhaps answer that it is owing to the peculiar tastes they have inherited; "settled mainly (as was Virginia) by the sons of country gentlemen, who brought the love of country life with them across the Atlantic, and infused it into the mass of the population, they have ever preferred that life, and the title of country gentleman, implying the possession of landed estates, has always been esteemed more honorable than any other."* It is simply a matter of taste—an answer which reminds us of Æsop's fox.

Ask any honest stranger who has been brought into intimate intercourse for a short time with the people, why it is that here has been stagnation, and there constant, healthy progress, and he will answer that these people are less enterprising, energetic and sensible in the conduct of their affairs—that they live less in harmony with the laws that govern the accumulation of wealth than those.

Ask him how this difference of character should have arisen, and he will tell you it is not from the blood, but from the education they have received; from the institutions and circumstances they have inherited. It is the old, fettered, barbarian labor-system, in connection with which they have been brought up, against which all their enterprise must struggle, and with the chains of which all their ambition must be bound.

This conviction I find to be universal in the minds of strangers, and it is forced upon one more strongly than it is possible to make you comprehend by a mere statement of isolated facts. You could as well convey an idea of the effect of mist on a

* Dr. Little's History of Richmond.

landscape, by enumerating the number of particles of vapor that obscure it. Give Virginia blood fair play, remove it from the atmosphere of slavery, and it shows no lack of energy and good sense.

It is strange the Virginians dare not look this in the face. Strange how they bluster in their legislative debates, in their newspapers, and in their bar-rooms, about the "Yankees," and the "Yorkers," declaring that they are "swindled out of their legitimate trade," when the simple truth is, that the Northern merchants do that for them that they are unable to do for themselves. As well might the Chinese be angry with us for sending our clipper ships for their tea, because it is a business that would be more "legitimately" (however less profitably) carried on in "junks."

"LEGITIMATE" VIRGINIA SEAMANSHIP.

There's a yarn I have heard from the Staaten Island coasters, who run down to the capes of Virginia for oysters, which illustrates admirably how Virginia commerce would be "legitimately" carried on, that is, in the manner naturally resulting from her system.

Among the largest and luckiest of the Virginia merchant-marine, is the fine, fast-sailing, light-draft, putty-bottomed, packet-sloop, the Abstraction. The "old Ab" was formerly owned and commanded by Captain Jerry S., and was manned by one black boy, sixty years old, named Mopus, and commonly called Uncle Mopus. Mopus was a slave, and Captain Jerry had bought him with the sloop.

Mopus was a proper slave, patient, meek, stupid, and stubborn,—a talking donkey. He never had been taught to read or to comprehend figures. He could not understand the dial, and the binnacle-compass was a sort of fetish to him; the mystery of which he was too humble to desire to penetrate. He piously left these great things in the hands of his owner, and resigned himself to the will of that Providence which had given him a master to take care of him, who was responsible for his safety and profits, as well as the sloop's.

This resignation and faith of the good Mopus, however, often gave Captain Jerry a deal of trouble, for it obliged him to be nearly always on deck and wide awake, and he sometimes thought he might better sell Mopus, and buy a nigger that was not so good, (Captain Jerry, as I heard it, used to put in a word between so and good, and bear down on it,) but the danger that such a one would prove entirely reckless of all moral suggestions, as smart niggers are very apt to, and go and steal himself, prevented his doing so, and he tried to make the best of Mopus' muscles, and to supply the necessary brain-power for the sloop from his own private skull.

One night, Captain Jerry having been up all the previous night, and having just worked the sloop out of Hampton roads, against wind and tide, and being quite overcome with fatigue, thought he might venture to trust Mopus with the helm for a few hours, the sloop's course being now due north, up Chesapeake bay, wind light and quartering, a clear sky, and nothing in the way for fifty miles.

Mopus knew the North Star very well, as niggers generally do, and telling him to keep the bow-sprit pointing straight at it, and not to disturb him until he saw land to starboard, Captain Jerry put out the binnacle-light to save oil, and turned-in.

Captain Jerry had the habit, which small-craft men are apt to get, of consulting aloud with himself. No sooner had he closed the companion scuttle than Mopus, with head to the stove pipe, heard—"Moon fulled Thursday—slack water at six—North Star—that'll do till daylight sartain—due North—Tangier island—not afore meridian—can't go wrong till arter daylight, no how—good snooze this time—go in—off boots."

Mope was a capital helmsman; and for two hours, while the breeze held, he kept on a bee-line to the northward. Then it fell calm; and then there came little catspaws from northwest, and Mope, after giving a pull of the main-sheet, left the helm a minute to flatten the jib. While he was forward, a flaw from the northeast took him all aback. Belaying jib-sheet, he came aft, and put helm up to wear round. Just as he jibed, came another flaw from the southeast, and a pretty smart one. Mope met it, trimmed close, and seeing it was going to be steady, left the helm again, and shoved down the centre board. Then he went to the hatchway and got his coat, after which he took a pull at the scuttle-butt, and struck a light for a smoke.

All this time old Abby, with her head southeast, was shaking like a nail-mill. Mope finally hauled the jib up to port, till the mainsail filled, then took the helm again, and kept her rap full heading south, but running off to the westward, now and then, in search for the North Star, which, as he could not see it anywhere else, he thought for a long time must have got behind the mainsail.

He had smoked out two pipes before he found it, and then it was *right over the stern*, which at first struck him as a singular circumstance. There it was, "pointers and all;" he could not be mistaken. But how did it get *there?*

Mope pondered over it for two pipes more, all the while giving her a good full and nothing off. He was at first inclined to treat it as a mystery; but when, about two o'clock, the moon rose, he grew bold, knotted his eyebrows, clenched his teeth, took off his tarpaulin, and struck his reflective organs with his clenched fist.

At length the problem was solved, and his lips trembled and gathered inward and puckered back with that pleasure which niggers, in common with human beings, enjoy, when they are conscious of having acquitted themselves well of a trying and honorable responsibility. He immediately hauled the boom down close to the taffrail; he went forward, and belayed the jib to windward, lighted his pipe again, and kept a good look-out till, as day broke, he made land to starboard, just as he expected;—land to starboard and—why didn't he see it before?—a light right ahead, and not very far ahead either.

"All right," thought Mopus, "daylight, humph! let an old nigger alone to find the way to the North;" and he let the jib draw away, went aft, took the helm and called the skipper.

The skipper turned out:

"Hallo, uncle, close hauled? Wind's come out o' norrard, has it? Why, Mopus! why! what the devil—what light's that? Why, Mope! why you——Where you been taking the sloop to now, you black rascal! here's the North Star over the starn!"

"Oh yes, massa, past de Norf Star an hour ago; all right, sar, here's de land right off here to luward. Made a fine run, sar. Oh! I knows how to fotch 'em along, I does myself, ha! ha! ha! Takes old Mope arter all, don't it? ha! ha! ha!"

"Ye-es (through his teeth) mighty fine run! Old Point, by the blood of Pocahontas! just where I'd got her last night at

sunset!—you grinnin' catamount! Takes old Mope! You
bloody old cuss! I'll sell you for a chaw of tobacco to the first
white man that 'll take you off my hands."

Incidents, trifling in themselves, constantly betray to a stranger the bad economy of using enslaved servants. The catastrophe of one such occurred since I began to write this letter. I
ordered a fire to be made in my room, as I was going out this
morning. On my return, I found a grand fire—the room door
having been closed and locked upon it, and, by the way, I had
to obtain assistance to open it, the lock being "out of order."
Just now, while I was writing, down tumbled upon the floor, and
rolled away close to the valance of the bed, half a hod-full of
ignited coal, which had been so piled up on the diminutive grate,
and left without a fender or any guard, that this result was almost
inevitable. If I had not returned at the time I did, the house
would have been fired, and probably an incendiary charged with
it, while some Northern Insurance Company made good the loss
to the owner. And such carelessness of servants you have momentarily to notice.

But the constantly-occurring delays, and the waste of time
and labor that you encounter everywhere, are most annoying
and provoking to a stranger. The utter want of system and
order, almost essential, as it would appear, where slaves are your
instruments, is amazing—and when you are not in haste, often
amusing. At a hotel, for instance, you go to your room and find
no conveniences for washing; ring and ring again, and hear the
office-keeper ring again and again. At length two servants appear together at your door, get orders, and go away. A quarter of
an hour afterwards, perhaps, one returns with a pitcher of water,
but no towels; and so on. Yet as the servants are attentive and

anxious to please (expecting to be "remembered" when you leave), it only results from the want of system and order.

Until the negro is big enough for his labor to be palpably profitable to his master, he has no training to application or method, but only to idleness and carelessness. Before the children arrive at a working age, they hardly come under the notice of their owner. An inventory of them is taken on the plantation at Christmas; and a planter told me that he had sometimes had them brought in at twelve or thirteen years old, that had escaped the vigilance of the overseer up to that age. The only whipping of slaves that I have seen in Virginia, has been of these wild, lazy children, as they are being broke in to work. It is at this moment going on in the yard beneath my window. They cannot be depended upon a minute out of sight.

You will see how difficult it would be, if it were attempted, to eradicate the indolent, careless, incogitant habits so formed in youth. But it is not systematically attempted, and the influences that continue to act upon a slave in the same direction, cultivating every quality at variance with industry, precision, forethought, and providence, are innumerable.

It is impossible that the habits of the whole community should not be influenced by, and be made to accommodate to these habits of its laborers. It irresistibly affects the whole industrial character of the people. You may see it in the habits and manners of the free white mechanics and trades-people. All of these must have dealings or be in competition with slaves, and so have their standard of excellence made low, and become accustomed to, until they are content with slight, false, unsound workmanship. You notice in all classes, vagueness in ideas of cost and value, and injudicious and unnecessary expenditure of labor by a thoughtless manner of setting about work.*

I had an umbrella broken. I noticed it as I was going out from my hotel during a shower, and stepped into an adjoining locksmith's to have it repaired. He asked where he should send it when he had done it. "I intended to wait for it," I answered; "how long is it going to take you, and how much shall you charge?"

"I can't do it in less than half an hour, sir, and it will be worth a quarter."

"I shouldn't think it need take you so long, it is merely a rivet to be tightened."

"I shall have to take it all to pieces, and it will take me all of half an hour."

"I don't think you need take it to pieces."

"Yes, I shall—there's no other way to do it."

"Then, as I can't well wait so long, I will not trouble you with it;" and I went into the hotel, and with the fire-poker did the job myself, in less than a minute, as well as he could have done it in a week, and went on my way, saving half an hour and quarter of a dollar, like a "Yankee."

Virginians laugh at us for such things: but it is because they are indifferent to these fractions, or, as they say, above regarding them, that they cannot do their own business with the rest of the world, and all their commerce, as they are constantly and most absurdly complaining, only goes to enrich Northern men. A man forced to labor under their system is morally driven to indolence, carelessness, indifference to the results of

---

* A ship's officer told me that he had noticed that it took just about three times as long to have the same repairs made in Norfolk that it did in New York.

skill, heedlessness, inconstancy of purpose, improvidence, and extravagance. Precisely the opposite qualities are those which are encouraged, and inevitably developed in a man who has to make his living, and earn all his comfort by his voluntarily-directed labor. These opposite qualities are those which are essentially necessary to the success of an adventurer in commerce. The commercial success of the free states is the offspring of their voluntary labor system. The inability of the Virginians to engage in commerce is the result of their system of involuntary servitude. The condition of the laborers predetermines the condition of all the people.

GOSPORT.

Several ships were here, under orders, waiting for crews; with the rest, the Powhattan steam-frigate, among whose officers I found some acquaintances. What sort of hands they had to take, and how difficult they found the duty of efficiently commanding them, may be imagined from the disgraceful fact, that, at that time, but twelve dollars a month was allowed by Government to be paid for the best men for the national service, while merchantmen were paying twenty-five dollars for common able seamen; and yet, because, when under these circumstances, the crews obtained were not smart, clean, sober, docile, and contented, I heard officers ascribe their difficulties to the disuse of the cat and the old terrifying system of discipline.

The United States Navy should be a school of the utmost excellence of seamanship, not a refuge for irreclaimable sots, loafers, and ruffians, who cannot, or dare not, take employment elsewhere at the market rate of wages.

I, as a one-twenty-three-millionth proprietor of it, wonder if it would not be better policy to go into exactly the opposite extreme, and, by paying the best wages, get the best men—the highest priced labor in open market is usually believed to be the cheapest.

And I wonder if it would not be possible to obtain men for the labor of ships, as well as for any other labor, who would always perform the services required of them heartily, promptly and fully, as an honest return for their wages and rations; who would obey orders, not like whipped curs and cowed slaves, but as free men, and brave men, and wise men, with a republican respect for right laws, and a sensible understanding of the fit division of responsibility between them and their officers. I fear not, unless some thorough, comprehensive, and generously-directed educational department shall be adopted as a permanent, and indivisible part of our naval system.

THE DISMAL SWAMP.

The "Great Dismal Swamp," together with the smaller "Dismals" (for so the term is used here), of the same character, along the North Carolina Coast, have hitherto been of considerable commercial importance as furnishing a large amount of lumber, and especially of shingles for our Northern use as well as for exportation. The district from which this commerce proceeds is all a vast quagmire, the soil being entirely composed of decayed vegetable fibre, saturated and surcharged with water; yielding or *quaking* on the surface to the tread of a man, and a large part of it, during most of the year, half inundated with standing pools. It is divided by creeks and water-veins, and in the centre is a pond six miles long and three broad, the shores of which, strange to say, are at a higher elevation above the sea, than any other part of the swamp, and yet are of the same miry consistency.

The Great Dismal is about thirty miles long and ten miles wide on an average; its area about 200,000 acres. And the little Dismal, Aligator, Catfish, Green, and other smaller swamps, on the shores of Albemarle and Pamlico, contain over 2,000,000 acres. A considerable part of this is the property of the State of North Carolina, and the proceeds of sales from it form the chief income of the department of education of that Commonwealth.

An excellent canal, six feet in depth, passes for more than twenty miles through the swamp, giving passage not only to the lumber collected from it, but to a large fleet of coasting vessels engaged in the trade of the Albemarle and Pamlico Sounds, and making a safe outlet towards New York for all the corn, cotton, tar, turpentine, etc., produced in the greater part of the eastern section of North Carolina, which is thus brought to market without encountering the extremely hazardous passage outside, from Cape Hatteras to Cape Henry. ‾his canal is fed by the water of the pond in the centre of the swamp, its summit-level being many feet below it.*

---

* Of the main products of the country, the annual freightage on the Dismal Swamp Canal is about as.follows:

Shingles	24,000,000
Staves	6,000,000
Plank and scantling, cubic feet . .	125,000
Ship timber	40,000
Cotton bales	4,500
Shad and herring, barrels	50,000
Naval stores, barrels	30,000

Much of the larger part of the "Great Dismal" was originally covered by a heavy forest growth. All the trees indigenous to the neighboring country I found still extensively growing, and of full size within its borders. But the main production, and that which has been of the greatest value, has been of cypress and juniper; (the latter commonly known as white cedar, at the North). From these two, immense quantities of shingles have been made. The cypress also affords ship-timber, now in great demand, and a great many rough poles of the juniper, under the name of "cedar-rails," are sent to New York and other ports, as fencing material, (generally selling at seven cents a rail,) for the farms of districts that have been deprived of their own natural wood by the extension of tillage required by the wants of neighboring towns or manufactories.

The swamp belongs to a great many proprietors. Most of them own only a few acres, but some possess large tracts and use a heavy capital in the business. One, whose acquaintance I made, employed more than a hundred hands in getting out shingles alone. The value of the swamp land varies with the wood upon it, and the facility with which it can be got off, from $12\frac{1}{2}$ cents to $10 an acre. It is made passable in any desired direction in which trees grow, by

Spirits turpentine, barrels	.	.	.	.	700
Bacon, cwts.	.	.	.	.	5,000
Lard, kegs	.	.	.	.	1,300
Maize, bushels	.	.	.	.	2,000,000
Wheat, bushels	.	.	.	.	30,000
Peas, bushels	.	.	.	.	25,000

The canal was made with the assistance of the National Government and the State of Virginia, who are still the largest owners. It is admirably constructed, repairs are light, and it is a good six per cent. stock.

laying logs, cut in lengths of eight or ten feet, parallel and against each other on the surface of the soil, or "sponge," as it is called. Mules and oxen are used to some extent upon these roads, but transportation is mainly by hand to the creeks, or to ditches communicating with them or the canal.

Except by those log-roads, the swamp is scarcely passable in many parts, owing not only to the softness of the sponge, but to the obstruction caused by innumerable shrubs, vines, creepers and briars, which often take entire possession of the surface, forming a dense brake or jungle. This, however, is sometimes removed by fires, which of late years have been frequent and very destructive to the standing timber. The most common shrubs are various smooth-leafed evergreens, and their dense, bright, glossy foliage, was exceedingly beautiful in the wintry season of my visit. There is a good deal of game in the swamp—bears and wild cats are sometimes shot, raccoons and opossums are plentiful, and deer are found in the drier parts and on the outskirts. The fishing, in the interior waters, is also said to be excellent.

Nearly all the valuable trees have now been cut off from the swamp. The whole ground has been frequently gone over, the best timber selected and removed at each time, leaving the remainder standing thinly, so that the wind has more effect upon it; and much of it, from the yielding of the soft soil, is uprooted or broken off. The fires have also greatly injured it. The principal stock, now worked into shingles, is obtained *from beneath the surface*—old trunks that have been preserved by the wetness of the soil, and that are found by "sounding" with poles, and raised with hooks or pikes by the negroes.

The quarry is giving out, however, and except that lumber,

and especially shingles, have been in great demand at high prices of late, the business would be almost at an end. As it is, the principal men engaged in it are turning their attention to other and more distant supplies. A very large purchase had been made by one company in the Florida everglades, and a schooner, with a gang of hands trained in the "Dismals," was about to sail from Deep-creek, for this new field of operations.

SLAVE-LUMBERMEN.

The labor in the swamp is almost entirely done by slaves; and the way in which they are managed is interesting and instructive. They are mostly hired by their employers at a rent, perhaps of one hundred dollars a year for each, paid to their owners. They spend one or two months of the winter—when it is too wet to work in the swamp—at the residence of their master. At this period little or no work is required of them; their time is their own, and if they can get any employment, they will generally keep for themselves what they are paid for it. When it is sufficiently dry—usually early in February—they go into the swamp in gangs, each gang under a white overseer. Before leaving, they are all examined and registered at the Court-house, and " passes," good for a year, are given them, in which their features and the marks upon their persons are minutely described. Each man is furnished with a quantity of provisions and clothing, of which, as well as of all that he afterwards draws from the stock in the hands of the overseer, an exact account is kept.

LIFE IN THE SWAMP—SLAVES QUASI FREEMEN.

Arrived at their destination, a rude camp is made, huts of

logs, poles, shingles, and boughs being built, usually upon some place where shingles have been worked before, and in which the shavings have accumulated in small hillocks upon the soft surface of the ground.

The slave lumberman then lives measurably as a free man; hunts, fishes, eats, drinks, smokes and sleeps, plays and works, each when and as much as he pleases. It is only required of him that he shall have made, after half a year has passed, such a quantity of shingles as shall be worth to his master so much money as is paid to his owner for his services, and shall refund the value of the clothing and provisions he has required.

No "driving" at his work is attempted or needed. No force is used to overcome the indolence peculiar to the negro. The overseer merely takes a daily account of the number of shingles each man adds to the general stock, and employs another set of hands, with mules, to draw them to a point from which they can be shipped, and where they are, from time to time, called for by a schooner.

At the end of five months the gang returns to dry-land, and a statement of account from the overseer's book is drawn up, something like the following:

Sam Bo to John Doe, Dr.

Feb. 1. To clothing (outfit)		$5 00
Mar. 10. To clothing, as per overseer's account,		2 25
Feb. 1. To bacon and meal (outfit)		19 00
July 1. To stores drawn in swamp, as per overseer's account,		4 75
July 1. To half-yearly hire, paid his owner		50 00
		$81 00

Per Contra, Cr.

July 1. By 10,000 shingles, as per overseer's account, 10c		100 00
Balance due Sambo		$19 00

which is immediately paid him, and which, together with the
proceeds of sale of peltry which he has got while in the
swamp, he is always allowed to make use of as his own. No
liquor is sold or served to the negroes in the swamp, and, as
their first want when they come out of it is an excitement,
most of their money goes to the grog-shops.

After a short vacation, the whole gang is taken in the
schooner to spend another five months in the swamp as before.
If they are good hands and work steadily, they will commonly
be hired again, and so continuing, will spend most of their lives
at it. They almost invariably have excellent health, as do
also the white men engaged in the business. They all consider the water of "the Dismals" to have a medicinal virtue,
and quite probably it is a mild tonic. It is greenish in color,
and I thought I detected a slightly resinous taste upon first
drinking it. Upon entering the swamp also, an agreeable
resinous odor, resembling that of a hemlock forest, was
perceptible.

THE EFFECT OF PAYING WAGES TO SLAVES.

The negroes working in the swamp were more sprightly and
straight-forward in their manner and conversation than any
field-hand plantation-negroes that I saw at the South ; two or
three of their employers with whom I conversed spoke well of
them, as compared with other slaves, and made no complaints of
"rascality" or laziness.

One of those gentlemen told me of a remarkable case of
providence and good sense in a negro that he had employed in
the swamp for many years. He was so trust-worthy, that he
had once let him go to New York as cook of a lumber-schooner,

when he could, if he had chosen to remain there, have easily escaped from slavery.

Knowing that he must have accumulated considerable money, his employer suggested to him that he might *buy* his freedom, and he immediately determined to do so. But when, on applying to his owner, he was asked $500 for himself, a price which, considering he was an elderly man, he thought too much, he declined the bargain; shortly afterwards, however, he came to his employer again, and said that although he thought his owner was mean to set so high a price upon him, he had been thinking that if he was to be an old man he would rather be his own master, and if he did not live long, his money would not be of any use to him at any rate, and so he had concluded he would make the purchase.

He did so, and upon collecting the various sums that he had loaned to white people in the vicinity, he was found to have several hundred dollars more than was necessary. With the surplus, he paid for his passage to Liberia, and bought a handsome outfit. When he was about to leave, my informant had made him a present, and, in thanking him for it, the free man had said that the first thing he should do, on reaching Liberia, would be to learn to write, and, as soon as he could, he would write to him how he liked the country : he had been gone yet scarce a year, and had not been heard from.

AGRICULTURAL VALUE OF THE SWAMP LAND.

When it is no longer found profitable to get lumber out of these swamps, they will be dead property, as little or no large wood is growing to supply the place of that taken off, except in the drier parts, where pines come up, as on "old-fields." It is probable that some extensive scheme of draining and reclaiming them will eventually be adopted. I am aware of but a single attempt, as yet, to cultivate the sponge or true swamp soil. This was made by a Mr. Wallace, on the northeast border of the Great Dismal. He had, with creditable spirit and skill, reclaimed four hundred acres. Having a sufficient outfall, he cuts wide drains parallel to each other, and about one hundred and twenty-five yards apart. These serve, at first, to float away, for market, all the timber of value left on the tract, as well as to draw the water from the surface. The ground is then grubbed, as much as it is thought necessary, and the stumps and worthless logs burnt. After cultivation, the soil is almost an impalpable powder, the foot sinks to the ancle in crossing it, and it rises in clouds of dust, when disturbed in a dry season. It is, of course, easy of cultivation, and is very productive in corn and potatoes—the only crops of which Mr. W. had yet made much trial.

Mr. W. told me that he had sold, during the previous summer, two thousand one hundred barrels of potatoes, which were produced on forty acres, and were taken by contract and delivered at Norfolk, by middlemen for the New York market, at four dollars a barrel. Thus the return from forty acres was over eight thousand dollars, and this without any expenditure for manure and with very light cultivation. In New York, the potatoes sold readily, early in the season, at from five to ten dollars a barrel.

Land of this description, thus managed, can be bought, in its unreclaimed state, at from one to five dollars an acre. The success of Mr. Wallace has somewhat increased the value of it, in his neighborhood. He reckons that the cost of reclaiming and fitting it entirely, in the manner that his experience leads him to think most profitable, would be fifty dollars an acre. From this is to be deducted the value of timber obtained from it.

Persons moving here from the North, will be very subject to bilious fever during the fall months; by prudence it may be partially escaped, but the danger is a permanent one at that season. It is not often fatal, but probably has a ruinous effect upon the general constitution.

THE "TRUCK" BUSINESS OF NORFOLK.

The market-gardens at Norfolk—which have been profitably supplying New York markets with poor early vegetables, and half-hardy luxuries for several years past—do not differ at all from market-gardens elsewhere. They are situated in every direction for many miles from the city, offering a striking contrast, in all respects, to the large, old-fashioned Virginian farms, among which they are scattered.

On one of the latter, of over a thousand acres, a friend told me he had seen the negroes moving long, strawy manure with shovels, and upon inquiry found there was not a dung-fork on the place.

The soil is a poor sandy loam, and manure is brought by shipping from Baltimore, as well as from the nearer towns, to enrich it. The proprietors of the market-gardens are nearly all from New Jersey, and brought many of' their old white laborers with them. Except at picking-time, when everything possessing fingers is in demand, they do not often employ slaves.

The *Norfolk Argus* says that, from about the 20th June to

the 20th July, from 2,000 to 2,500 barrels of potatoes will be shipped daily from that city to Philadelphia and New York, together with 300 to 500 barrels of cucumbers, musk-melons, etc.

RUNAWAYS IN THE SWAMP.

While driving in a chaise from Portsmouth to Deep-river, I picked up on the road a jaded looking negro, who proved to be a very intelligent and good-natured fellow. His account of the lumber business, and of the life of the lumbermen in the swamps, in answer to my questions, was clear and precise, and was afterwards verified by information obtained from his master.

He told me that his name was Joseph, that he belonged to a church in one of the inland counties, and that he was hired out by the trustees of the church to his present master. He expressed entire contentment with his lot, but showed great unwillingness to be sold to go on to a plantation. He liked to "mind himself," as he did in the swamps. Whether he would still more prefer to be entirely his own master, I did not ask.

The Dismal Swamps are noted places of refuge for runaway negroes. They were formerly peopled in this way much more than at present; a systematic hunting of them with dogs and guns having been made by individuals who took it up as a business about ten years ago. Children were born, bred, lived and died here. Joseph Church told me he had seen skeletons, and had helped to bury bodies recently dead. There were people in the swamps still, he thought, that were the children of runaways, and who had been runaways themselves all their lives. What a life it must be; born outlaws; educated self-stealers;

trained from infancy to be constantly in dread of the approach of a white man as a thing more fearful than wild-cats or serpents, or even starvation.

There can be but few, however, if any, of these "natives" left. They cannot obtain the means of supporting life without coming often either to the outskirts to steal from the plantations, or to the neighborhood of the camps of the lumbermen. They depend much upon the charity or the wages given them by the latter. The poorer white men, owning small tracts of the swamps, will sometimes employ them, and the negroes frequently. In the hands of either they are liable to be betrayed to the negro-hunters. Joseph said that they had huts in "back places," hidden by bushes, and difficult of access; he had, apparently, been himself quite intimate with them. When the shingle negroes employed them, he told me, they made them get up logs for them, and would give them enough to eat, and some clothes, and perhaps two dollars a month in money. But some, when they owed them money, would betray them, instead of paying them.

DISMAL NIGGER HUNTING.

I asked if they were ever shot. "Oh, yes," he said, "when the hunters saw a runaway, if he tried to get from them, they would call out to him, that if he did not stop they would shoot, and if he did not, they would shoot, and sometimes kill him.

"*But some on 'em would rather be shot than be took, sir,*" he added, simply.

A farmer living near the swamp confirmed this account, and said he knew of three or four being shot in one day.

No particular breed of dogs is needed for hunting negroes:

blood-hounds, fox-hounds, bull-dogs, and curs were used,* and one white man told me how they were trained for it, as if it were a common or notorious practice. They are shut up when puppies, and never allowed to see a negro except while training to catch him. A negro is made to run from them, and they are encouraged to follow him until he gets into a tree, when meat is given them. Afterwards they learn to follow any particular negro by scent, and then a shoe or a piece of clothing is taken off a negro, and they learn to find by scent who it belongs to, and to *tree* him, etc. I don't think they are employed in the ordinary driving in the swamp, but only to overtake some particular slave, as soon as possible after it is discovered that he has fled from a plantation. Joseph said that it was easy for the drivers to tell a fugitive from a regularly employed slave in the swamps.

" How do they know them?"

" Oh, dey looks *strange.*"

" How do you mean?"

" *Skeared* like, you know, sir, and kind 'o strange, cause dey hasn't much to eat, and ain't decent [not decently clothed], like we is."

When the hunters take a negro who has not a pass, or "free papers," and they don't know whose slave he is, they confine him in jail, and advertise him. If no one claims him within a year he is sold to the highest bidder, at a public sale, and this sale gives title in law against any subsequent claimant.

The form of the advertisements used in such cases is shown by

* I have since seen a pack of negro-dogs, chained in couples, and probably going to the field. They were all of a breed, and in appearance between a Scotch stag-hound and a fox-hound.

the following, which are cut from North Carolina newspapers, published in counties adjoining the Dismals. Such advertisements are quite as common in the papers of many parts of the Slave States as those of horses or cattle " Taken up " in those of the North :

WAS TAKEN UP and committed to the Jail of Halifax County, on the 26th day of May, a dark colored boy, who says his name is JORDAN ARTIS. Said boy says he was born free, and was bound out to William Beale, near Murfreesboro', Hertford County, N. C., and is now 21 years of age. The owner is requested to come forward, prove property, pay charges, and take the said boy away, within the time prescribed by law ; otherwise he will be dealt with as the law directs.   O. P. SHELL, Jailer.
  Halifax County, N. C., June 8, 1855.

TAKEN UP,

AND COMMITTED to the Jail of New Hanover County, on the 5th of March, 1855, a Negro Man, who says his name is EDWARD LLOYD. Said negro is about 35 or 40 years old, light complected, 5 feet 9½ inches high, slim built, upper fore teeth out ; says he is a Mason by trade, that he is free, and belongs in Alexandria, Va., that he served his time at the Mason business under Mr. Wm. Stuart, of Alexandria. He was taken up and committed as a runaway. His owner is notified to come forward, prove property, pay charges, and take him away, or he will be dealt with as the law directs.   E. D. HALL, Sheriff.

In the same paper with the last are four advertisements of Runaways : two of them, as specimens, I transcribe.

$200 REWARD.

RAN AWAY from the employ of Messrs. Holmes & Brown, on Sunday night, 20th inst., a negro man named YATNEY or MEDICINE, belonging to the undersigned. Said boy is stout built, about 5 feet 4 inches high, 22 years old, and dark complected, and has the appearance, when walking slow, of one leg being a little shorter than the other. He was brought from Chapel Hill, and is probably lurking either in the neighborhood of that place, or Beatty's Bridge, in Bladen County.
  The above reward will be paid for evidence sufficient to convict any white person of harboring him, or a reward of $25 for his apprehension and confinement in any Jail in the State, so that I can get him, or for his delivery to me in Wilmington.
                              J. T. SCHONWALD.

RUNAWAY

FROM THE SUBSCRIBER, on the 27th of May, his negro boy ISOME. Said boy is about 21 years of age; rather light complexion; very coarse hair; weight about 150; hight about 5 feet 6 or 7 inches; rather pleasing countenance; quick and easy spoken; rather a downcast look. It is thought that he is trying to make his way to Franklin county, N. C., where he was hired in Jan. last, of Thomas J. Blackwell. A liberal Reward will be given for his confinement in any Jail in North or South Carolina, or to any one who will give information where he can be found.

W. H. PRIVETT,
Canwayboro', S. C.

Handbills, written or printed, offering rewards for the return of Runaway slaves, are to be constantly seen at nearly every court-house, tavern, and post-office in the Southern States. The frequency with which these losses must occur, however, on large plantations, is most strongly evidenced by the following paragraph from the domestic-news columns of the *Fayetteville Observer*. A man who would pay these prices must anticipate frequent occasion to use his purchase.

"Mr. J. L. Bryan, of Moore county, sold at public auction, on the 20th instant, a pack of ten hounds, trained for hunting runaways, for the sum of $1,540. The highest price paid for any one dog was $301; lowest price, $75; average for the ten, $154. The terms of sale were six months' credit, with approved security, and interest from date."

The newspapers of the Southwestern States frequently contain advertisements similar to the following, which is taken from the *West Tennessee Democrat:*

BLOOD-HOUNDS.—I have TWO of the FINEST DOGS for CATCHING NEGROES in the Southwest. They can take the trail TWELVE HOURS after the NEGRO HAS PASSED, and catch him with ease. I live just four miles southwest of Boliver, on the road leading from Boliver to Whitesville. I am ready at all times to catch runaway negroes.—March 2, 1853.

DAVID TURNER.

CHAPTER III.

THE ECONOMY OF VIRGINIA:

STATISTICS OF THE ELEMENTS OF WEALTH AND THE RESULTS OF LABOR.

THE *Richmond Enquirer*, a very strong and influential pro-slavery newspaper of Virginia, in advocating some rail-road projects, thus describes the progress of the State relatively to that of some of the free-states, since the Revolution. (Dec. 29, 1852.)

" Virginia, anterior to the Revolution, and up to the adoption of the Federal Constitution, contained more wealth and a larger population than any other State of this Confederacy. * * *

" Virginia, from being first in point of wealth and political power, has come down to the fifth in the former, and the fourth in the latter. New York, Pennsylvania, Massachusetts and Ohio stand above her in wealth, and all, but Massachusetts, in population and political power. Three of these States are literally chequered over with rail-roads and canals; and the fourth (Massachusetts) with rail-roads alone. * * *

" But when we find that the population of the single city of New York and its environs exceeds the whole free population of Eastern Virginia, and the valley between the Blue Ridge and Alleghany, we have cause to feel deeply for our situation. Philadelphia herself contains a population far greater than the whole free population of Eastern Virginia. The little State of Massachusetts has an aggregate wealth exceeding that of Virginia by more than one hundred and twenty-six millions of dollars—a State, too, which is incapable of subsisting its inhabitants from the production of its soil. And New York, which was as much below Massachusetts, at the adoption of the Federal Constitution, in wealth and power, as the latter was below Virginia, now exceeds the wealth of both.   While the aggregate wealth of New York, in 1850, amounted to $1,080,309,216, that of Virginia was $436,701,082—a difference in favor of the former of $643,608,134.   The unwrought mineral wealth of Virginia exceeds that of New York.   The climate and soil are better; the back country, with equal improvements, would contribute as much."

The same journal adds, on another occasion:—

" In no State of the Confederacy do the facilities for manufacturing operations exist in greater profusion than in Virginia.   Every condition essential to success in these employments is found here in prodigal abundance, and in a peculiarly convenient combination. First, we have a limitless supply of water-power —the cheapest of motors—in localities easy of access.   So abundant is this supply of water-power that no value is attached to it distinct from the adjacent lands, except in the vicinity of the larger towns.   On the Potomac and its tributaries; on the Rappahannock ; on the James and its tributaries; on the Roanoke and its tributaries ; on the Holston, the Kanawha, and other streams, numberless sites may now be found where the supply of water-power is sufficient for the purposes of a Lawrence or a Lowell.   Nor is there any want of material for building at these localities ; timber and granite are abundant; and, to complete the circle of advantages, the climate is genial and healthful, and the soil eminently productive.   *   *   *   Another advantage which Virginia possesses, for the manufacture of cotton, is the proximity of its mills to the raw material.   At the present prices of the staple, the value of this advantage is estimated at 10 per cent."

The *Lynchburg Virginian*, another newspaper of respectability, having a similar purpose in hand, namely, to induce capitalists to invest their money in enterprises that shall benefit the State, observes that—

" The coal-fields of Virginia are the most extensive in the world, and her coal is of the best and purest quality.   Her iron deposits are altogether inexhaustible, and in many instances so pure that it is malleable in its primitive state ; and many of these deposits in the immediate vicinity of extensive coal-fields. She has, too, very extensive deposits of copper, lead and gypsum. Her rivers are numerous and bold, generally with fall enough for extensive water power.

" A remarkable feature in the mining and manufacturing prospects of Virginia is, the ease and economy with which all her minerals are mined ; instead of being, as in England and elsewhere, generally imbedded deep within the bowels of the earth, from which they can be got only with great labor and at great cost, ours are found everywhere on the hills and slopes, with their ledges dipping in the direction of the plains below. Why, then, should not Virginia at once employ at least half of her labor and capital in mining and manufacturing ? Richmond could as profitably manufacture all cotton and woolen goods as Lowell, or any other town in New England. Why should not Lynchburg, with all her promised facility of getting coal and pig metal, manufacture all articles of iron and steel just as cheaply, and yet as profitably, as any portion of the northern States ? Why should not every town and village on the line of every rail-road in the State, erect their shops, in which they may manufacture a thousand articles of daily consumption, just as good and cheap as they may be made anywhere ?   *   *   *

" Dependent upon Europe and the North for almost every yard of cloth, and every coat, and boot, and hat we wear ; for our axes, scythes, tubs, and buckets—in short, for everything except our bread and meat ! It must occur to the South that if our relations with the North should ever be severed—and how soon they may be, none can know (may God avert it long !)—we would, in all the South, not be able to clothe ourselves. We could not fell our forests, plow our fields, nor mow our meadows. In fact, we would be reduced to a state more abject than we are willing to look at, even prospectively. And yet, with all these things staring us in the face, we shut our eyes, and go on blindfold."

At the Convention for the formation of the Virginia State Agricultural Society, in 1852, the draft of an address to the farmers of the State was read, approved, and once adopted by the Convention. The vote by which it was adopted was soon afterwards reconsidered, and it was again approved and adopted. A second time it was reconsidered; and finally it was rejected, on the ground that there were admissions in it that would feed the fanaticism of the abolitionists. No one argued against it on the ground of the falsity or inaccuracy of these admissions. Twenty of the most respectable proprietors in the State, immediately afterwards, believing it to contain "matter of grave import," which should not be suppressed for such a reason, united in requesting a copy of it for publication. In the note of these gentlemen to the author, they express the belief that Virginia now "possesses the richest soil, most genial climate, and cheapest labor on earth." The author of the address, in his reply, says: "Fanaticism is a fool for whose vagaries I am not responsible. I am a pro-slavery man—I believe it, at this time, impossible to abolish it, and not desirable if it were possible."

The address was accordingly published. I make the following extracts from it, not only on account of the incontrovertible facts presented in them, but to show that the ostrich-habit, of burying their heads in the ground before anything they don't like, is not universal with Virginians:

"ADDRESS TO THE FARMERS OF VIRGINIA.

"'The Southern States stand foremost in agricultural labor, though they hold but the third rank in population.' At the head of these Southern States, in production, in extent of territory, in climate, in soil, and in population, stands the Commonwealth of Virginia. She is a nation of farmers. Eight-tenths of her industry is expended upon the soil; but less than one-third of her domain is in pasturage, or under the plow."

" Out of somewhat more than thirty-nine millions of acres, she tills but little over ten millions of acres, or about twenty-six and a quarter per cent., whilst New York has subdued about forty-one per cent., or twelve and a quarter out of her twenty-nine and a half millions of acres: and Massachusetts, with her sterile soil and inhospitable climate, has reclaimed from the forest, the quarry, and the marsh, about forty-two and a half per cent., or two and one-eighth out of her little territory of five millions of acres. Yet, according to the census of 1840, only six-tenths of the labor of New York, and four-tenths of that of Massachusetts, or, relatively, one-fifth and two-fifths less than our own, is expended upon agriculture.   *   *   *

"The live stock of Virginia are worth only three dollars and thirty-one cents for every arable acre ; but in New York they are worth six dollars and seven cents, and in Massachusetts four dollars and fifty-two cents.

"The proportion of hay for the same quantity of land is, for Virginia, eighty-one pounds; for New York, six hundred and seventy-nine pounds; for Massachusetts, six hundred and eighty-four pounds.   *   *   *

"With access to the same markets, and with hundreds of mechanics of our own, who can vie with the best Northern manufacturers, we find that our implements are inferior, that the New York farmer spends upon his nearly three times as much as we do upon ours, and the Massachusetts farmer more than double.   *   *   *

"Manure is indispensable to good husbandry. Judging from the history of agriculture in all other countries, we may safely say, that farming can never attain to continued perfection where manure is not put on with an unsparing hand. By far the larger part of this can only be made by stock, which should, at the same time, be made the source of profit, at least sufficient to pay the cost of their keep, so that, *other things being equal*, it is a safe rule to estimate the condition of a farming district by the amount of live stock it may possess, and the provision made for their sustenance. Applied in this instance, we see that the New York farmer has invested in live stock two dollars and seventy-six cents, and the Massachusetts farmer one dollar and twenty-one cents per acre more than the Virginia farmer. In pasturage we cannot tell the difference. It is well, perhaps, for the honor of the State, that we cannot. But in hay, New York has five hundred and ninety-eight pounds, and Massachusetts six hundred and three pounds more per acre than we have. This, however, does not present the true state of the case. Land-locked by mountain barriers, as yet impassable for the ordinary agricultural staples, or debarred from their production by distance and prohibitory rates of transportation, most of the wealth and exports of many considerable portions of our State consists of live stock alone. What proportion these parts bear to the whole, we have been unable definitely to ascertain; but it is, no doubt, so great as to warrant us in assuming a much more considerable disparity than the statistics show in the live stock of the whole Atlantic slope, as compared with New York and Massachusetts. And we shall appreciate, still more highly, the skill of the Northern farmer, if we reflect that a readier market for every, the most trivial, product of his farm, operates a constant temptation to break up his rotation and diminish his stock.

"In the above figures, carefully calculated from the data of authentic documents,* we find no cause for self-gratulation, but some food for meditation. They are not without use to those who would improve the future by the past. They show that we have not done our part in the bringing of land into cultivation; that, notwithstanding natural advantages which greatly exceed those of the two States drawn into parallel with Virginia, we are yet behind them both— that with forty and sixty per cent. respectively of their industry devoted to other pursuits, into which it has been lured by prospects of greater gain, they have done more than we have done. * * *

"Whilst our population has increased for the last ten years, in a ratio of 11·66, that of New York has increased in a ratio of 27·52, and that of Massachusetts at the still heavier and more startling rate of 34·81. With a territorial area thirty per cent. larger than New York, we have but little more than one-third of her Congressional representation; and Massachusetts, only one-eighth our size, comes within two of our number of representatives, we being cut down to thirteen, while she rises to eleven. And thus we, who once swayed the councils of the Union, find our power gone, and our influence on the wane, at a time when both are of vital importance to our prosperity, if not to our safety. As other States accumulate the means of material greatness, and glide past us on the road to wealth and empire, we slight the warnings of dull statistics, and drive lazily along the field of ancient customs, or stop the *plow* to speed the *politician*—should we not, in too many cases, say with more propriety, the *demagogue!*

---

* Abstract of the Seventh Census, and the able work of Professor Tucker, on the "Progress of the United States in Population and Wealth."

" State pride is a good thing, it is one mode in which patriotism is manifested. But it is not always a wise one. Certainly not, when it makes us content on small grounds. And when it smothers up improvement in self-satisfaction, it is a most pernicious thing. We have much to be proud of in Virginia. In intellect and fitness to command, in personal and social qualities, in high tone and noble bearing, in loyalty, in generosity, and magnanimity, and disinterestedness, above all, in moral purity, we once stood—let us hope, still stand—preëminent among our sister States. But the possession and practice of these virtues do not comprise our whole duty as men or as citizens. The great decree which has gone forth ordaining that we shall "increase, and multiply, and replenish the earth," enjoins upon us quite other duties, which cannot be neglected with impunity; so we have found out by experience—for we *have* neglected these duties. And when we contemplate our field of labor, and the work we have done in it, we cannot but observe the sad contrast between capacity and achievement. With a wide-spread domain, with a kindly soil, with a climate whose sun radiates fertility, and whose very dews distill abundance, we find our inheritance so wasted that the eye aches to behold the prospect."

The Census of 1850 gives the following values to agricultural land in the adjoining States of Virginia and Pennsylvania.

	In Virginia.	In Pennsylvania.
No. of acres improved land in farms,	10,360,135	8,626,619
" unimproved,	15,792,176	6,294,728
Cash value of farms,	$216,401,543—$8 an acre.	$407,876,099—$25 an acre

Considering that, at the Revolution, Virginia had nearly twice the population of Pennsylvania, was in possession of much more wealth or disposable capital, and had much the best natural facilities for external commerce and internal communication, if her political and social constitution had been and had continued equally good, and her people equally industrious and enterprising with those of Pennsylvania, there is no reason why the value of her farms should not have been, at this time, at least equal to those of Pennsylvania. Were it so, it appears that Virginia, in that particular alone, would now be richer than she is by four hundred and thirty millions of dollars.

If it should be thought that this difference between the value of land in Virginia and Pennsylvania is in some degree due to more fertile soils in the latter, a similar comparison may be made with the other adjoining free State, and old State of New Jersey, the climate of which, owing to its vicinity to the ocean, differs imperceptibly from that of Virginia, while its soil is decidedly less fertile, taking both States on an average. The average value of farming-land in New Jersey is recorded at $44.

Give this value to the Virginia farms, and the difference between it and their present value would buy, at a large valuation, all the slaves now in the State, send them to Africa, provide each family of them five hundred dollars to start with when they reached there, and leave still a surplus which, divided among the present white population of the State, would give between two and three thousand dollars to each family.

Some Southern writers have lately objected to comparisons of density of population, as indications of the prosperity of communities. Between two adjoining communities, however, where there are no restrictions upon the movements of the populations, and when the people are so ready to move as both those of Pennsylvania, and New Jersey, and of Virginia have shown themselves to be, the price of land must indicate with considerable exactness the comparative value or desirableness of it, all things considered, to live upon. The Virginians do not admit, and have no occasion to do so, that Pennsylvania and New Jersey have any advantage over Virginia, in soil, in climate, or in any natural quality.

Why, then, these differences?

In intellectual productions, the same general comparative barrenness is noticeable. One or two of the richest men in material wealth in the United States, live in Virginia; but there are, also, more excessively poor men than anywhere else. The best examples of the application of science, economically to agriculture, can, I suspect, be found in Virginia; but the generally-followed system of agriculture is the worst, under the circumstances, that the ingenuity of penny-wise simpletons has yet contrived in this country. So it is with intellectual wealth: there are a few minds learned and highly cultivated, but says the *Richmond Whig*—the leading Know-nothing newspaper in the Southern States—with a provincial simplicity, the sincerity of which will hardly be credible to men of the world:

"We receive nearly all our books from Northern or foreign authors—gotten up, printed by Northern or foreign publishers— while we have among us numberless men of ripe scholarship, profound acquirements, elegant and forcible writers—men willing to devote themselves to such labor, *only a Southern book is not patronized.* The North usually scowls at it, ridicules it, or damns it with faint praise; and the South takes on a like hue and complexion and neglects it. We have printers and publishers able, willing, and competent to publish, but, such is the *apathy* on the part of Southern people, that it involves hazard to Southern publishers to put them out. Indeed, until recently, almost all the publications, even of Southern books, issued (and that was their only hope of success) from Northern houses. The last chance now of getting a Southern book sold, is to manage to secure the favorable notice of the Northern press, and then the South buys it. Our magazines and periodicals languish for support."

Mr. Howison, "the Virginia Historian," observes:

"The question might be asked, where is the literature of Virginia, and it would not be easily answered.   It is a melancholy fact, that her people have never been a reading people.   In the mass they have shown an indifference to polite literature and education in general, depressing to the mind that wishes to see them respectable and happy."

" It is with pain," says the same authority, " that we are compelled to speak of the horrible cloud of ignorance that rests on Virginia," and he computes that (1848) there are in the State 166,000 youth, between seven and sixteen years of age, and of these 126,000 attend no school at all, and receive no education except what can be imparted by poor and ignorant parents. Besides these, he reckons 449,087 slaves and 48,852 free negroes, with few exceptions, wholly uneducated.

" The policy which discourages further extension of knowledge among them is necessary : but the fact remains unchanged, that they exist among us, *a huge mass of mind, almost entirely unenlightened.* We fear that the most favorable estimates will leave, in our State, 683,000 rational beings who are destitute of the merest rudiments of knowledge."

WHAT IS NOT THE CAUSE.

What is the cause of the comparative poverty of Virginia thus asserted and described ?

This is a question often asked, and is one of direct personal interest to many at the North ; to capitalists, for instance, who are urged to invest their funds in Virginia lands, mines, and other stocks, and to creditors of the State, and of corporations and individuals in the State.   It is especially interesting to a large class of persons who would prefer to live in a milder climate than that of any of the free States, but who are withheld from immigrating to Virginia by the potent fact, that wealth has not accumulated to the people at large in that State, with anything like the ease and rapidity that it has to those of the adjoining northern States.

I am myself one of this class, and it certainly was a great temptation to me, while I was enjoying the delightful January climate of Virginia, to be offered any amount of land which I was certain could be easily made to produce, under good tillage, twenty-five or thirty bushels of wheat to the acre, within twenty-four hours of New York by rail, and forty-eight by water-carriage, at exactly one fortieth of the price, by the acre, at which I could sell my New York farm. And, since my return from the South, I have been several times consulted by persons, some of them of considerable estate, who had determined, more or less definitely, to remove to Virginia, induced thereto by such letters as the following, which are constantly addressed to Northern capitalists, farmers, and skilled laborers, or manufacturers, by Virginia land-owners. This particular one I take from the *American Agriculturist*, to the editor of which it was directed, and by whom it was published, gratis and without comment, as such advertisements usually are, in our agricultural newspapers :

"VIRGINIA—INDUCEMENTS FOR NORTHERN MEN TO INVEST CAPITAL. Why is it that capitalists do not seek for a home in Western Virginia? Why is it that manufacturers do not explore this delightful country? Is it not worth their notice? Are there no inducements offered here for the honest, industrious laborer? I will offer some reasons why men of the North should look to the South for a home for themselves and offspring. Western Virginia is, in the first place, one of the most desirable portions of the Southern States. Every facility is here offered for the investment of capital. Our mountains teem with rich ores of every kind ; our lands blossom with golden harvests. The rippling streams that gurgle down our mountain-slopes furnish every variety of water-power, easily adapted to the propelling of machinery. The States west and south furnish a ready market for the sale of manufactured articles, or agricultural products. The farmers here are dependent, notwith-standing the facilities of manufacturing, to a very great extent, upon the North for all their implements of husbandry and household articles. Suppose, then, that we had some fifty or a hundred different manufac-turing establishments in Western Virginia, it would supersede the necessity of importing such things from abroad as wagons, buggies, clocks, brooms, rakes, shoes, boots, coats, pants, etc., etc. Every mer-chant in the Southern and Western States supplies his customers with these articles from the North. Now, suppose for one moment, that our merchants can buy from the Northern manufacturers, and pay the carriage upon articles gotten up there, and sold to the Southern States at fine profit, is it not reasonable to suppose, if the article was manu-factured here, the amount now consumed in transportation would be saved to the manufacturers located here upon the spot, and make him a handsome profit?

"No man can form an adequate idea of the extent of this trade, unless he travel through the Southern States. Scarcely a broom, a clock, a boot, or shoe, or anything of the kind is used in the South that is not manufactured by Northern industry; and yet all articles used can be readily manufactured here as well as there, and, if taken hold of by some enterprising men, would be found more profitable. In fact, several Northern men have already settled in Northern Virginia, and are now pushing forward a happy and prosperous trade. The Virginia and Tennessee Rail-road will soon be completed, along the line of which an immense traffic must be conducted. Then have you no thorough-going business men, who cannot find employment at the North, and who can-not earn more than a mere livelihood? If so, I advise them to turn their faces at once toward Western Virginia, where the smiles of Pro-vidence and the rays of a Southern sun will cheer and animate them in their rapid strides to happiness and wealth."

Here is another one, ingeniously contrived for wide-awake people who read the *Tribune*, and are supposed to have pre-judices:

"The effects of Slavery in this region have only been such as to ren-der it a more profitable locality for the new settler, provided, always, he does not suffer himself to be engrafted with its spirit. This suggests to my mind another observation, taken from the experience of settlers from the North. A single family, of New England habits and tastes, settling among neighbors of the slave-holding, work-hating class, becomes, in a short time, tired of the isolation from all the friends and the habits to which they have been accustomed, and disgusted with the condition of things they find around them. The wife misses her relations and neighbors, and her Sunday-meeting, and, after a year or two of trial, declares she will stay no longer; the children want the ready companionship of more thickly populated districts; and the experiment is given up, not because it will not pay in a pecuniary sense, but for the reasons I have mentioned. Now, to obviate this difficulty, let families come and settle in groups, or let a new settler, in selecting a location, choose one in a neighborhood already occupied with small farmers or mechanics of his own class, with whom he can associate, and whose example will back him in continuing his system of working with his own hand. This plan has been adopted, as you are aware, in some of the northeastern counties of Virginia, which now contain a population of active, intelligent and prosperous farmers and mechanics, from non-slaveholding States, while single settlements in other equally favorable localities have been abandoned. The price of land in the lower counties of this State varies from three to fifty dollars an acre. In many situations, land of good quality can now be bought, covered with timber, valuable either for fuel or for ship-building, in close proximity to water-carriage, or to a line of rail-road, at eight or ten dollars an acre. The clearing of the land will often pay most or all the cost, leaving a soil of good quality, and easily cultivated, and which, from the nature of things, must rapidly enhance in value."

I have read at least a hundred such advertisements in different Northern newspapers; a dozen were printed in the *Daily Times*, cotemporaneously with my own letters from the South; and in the more pro-slavery journals they may be seen, in one form or another, almost weekly.

When Virginia gentlemen thus carefully argue the advantages which their State offers to an immigration from the free States; and when they publicly urge that Slavery is no obstacle, but the contrary, to the success of such immigrants, it seems to me they have no business to stigmatize as impertinent, Northern curiosity to learn all about the matter.

Even the condition of the slaves, moral and material, the Internal Slave Trade, tho effects of Slavery on the character of the people, I consider to be as distinctly a part of the general rural economy of the country, as legitimately connected with the value of public stocks, and as pertinent a subject of inquiry, as any of those points with regard to which every farmer in the United States was required to give information, under the head of crops and live-stock, in the census of 1850. Nor do I believe, that justice or kindness to the Slave States, or regard to tho stability of the Union, can be opposed to a thorough—so it be honest—investigation of the condition of those States, and study of the causes of that condition.

Let me frankly, and with the most respectful and friendly disposition towards those who disagree with me, state my convictions on this subject.

Very little candid, truthful, and unprejudiced public discussion has yet been had on this vexed subject of Slavery. The extremists of the South esteem their opponents as madmen, or robbers; and invariably misrepresent, misunderstand, and, consequently, entirely fail to meet their arguments. The extremists of the North esteem the slave-holders as robbers and tyrants, willfully and malevolently oppressive and cruel. But I suppose more has been done, to prevent reasonable views and judicious action, by those, both North and South, who have held moderate and more reasonable opinions, than by those of either of the extreme parties. I mean that, in the endeavor to suppress agitation, they have produced an un-

healthy distrust, and an unsound and dangerous condition of
the public mind. In the feverish effort to secure peace, they
have forgotten, as is now apparent, the easiest lessons of
history and disregarded the simplest demands of prudence.
"Men," says Macaulay, "are never so likely to settle a
question rightly, as when they discuss it freely." The principle is at the basis of free institutions. Its reverse is the
apex of despotism. The attempt to suppress discussion has
given every advantage to the unterrified partisans on both sides,
who assume to fight for truth and rights.

Since the repeal of the Missouri Compromise, I presume
no one doubts, whatever he may desire, that Slavery must
continue to be an important, if not an engrossing element in our
politics. It is impossible that it should not, while slaves are
an important article of commerce, and while their value can
be materially affected by the national legislation. Speculation
on such legislation will occur, and will be guarded against,
and there will be more or less consideration of the constitu-
tional rights of each side of the Union, according as the
people are rightly informed and honestly dealt with by
politicians.

Northern men have, at present, too little information about
the South that has not come to them in a very inexact, or in
a very suspicious form, as in novels and narratives of fugitive slaves. Northerners traveling in the South, are generally merchants, looking after their personal business; invalids
sauntering through the winter in sunny places; or wealthy
people, looking for pleasure to the society of the hospitable
wealthy. There is but little Southern literature; and what
there is is mainly imaginative or controversial. Of the

masses of the South, black and white, it is more difficult for one to obtain information, than of those of any country in Europe. I saw much more of what I had not anticipated and less of what I had, in the Slave States, than, with a somewhat extended traveling experience, in any other country I ever visited.

To return to the question of the condition of Virginia and of its causes.

The leading agriculturists of the State who are least afraid of " abolitionism," declare the conviction that not only has Virginia at this time richer soils and cheaper than the wealthier States, but also the cheapest labor in the world; the organ of the State Agricultural Society sustains the same opinion; and Mr. Ruffin, the most eminent rural economist in the State, is allowed to advocate the same opinion in a Report of the United States Patent Office.

If it is true that here are richer soils, cheaper soils, and less expensive means of developing their wealth than in Pennsylvania, New York, and Massachusetts, why is it that the immensely more abundant capital of those States is not attracted to Virginia?

Of course a question so important to the property-holders of the State cannot fail to be gravely considered, and answered according to every reflective man's sagacity. In fact, no new project of legal or social change is ever advocated, that its friends do not contend that the measure will remove either the sole cause or one of the chief causes of the decadence of Virginia. Thus seldom a day passes in the session of the Legislature, that some one does not give his judgment upon the subject. At every gathering of the people, for political purposes or for the advancement of schemes for the general benefit, some orator is almost sure to take up the topic of the poverty and slow progress of the State; and, after denouncing the fanaticism and licentiousness of any one who dares suspect that slavery has anything to do with it, to explain what, in the orator's opinion, is the real cause, and what is the right way to remove it.

Among the causes thus presented, the following are the only ones having any breadth of application, of which I can recollect to have heard.

1. The want of better education of the mass of the people, (for it is maintained that the wealthier class are better educated than any in the free States).

2. The want of more agricultural science and skill.

3. The want of more and better roads, canals, etc.

4. The want of direct commerce with Europe and elsewhere.

5. The want of manufactures.

All these alleged causes, and all others, that I have ever heard assigned for the decrepitude of the State, are reduced to the following two, by simply asking, why Virginia has these wants more than the free States:

1. The more debilitating effects of the climate upon white people; and

2. The gentle blood and the corresponding character, averse to commercial speculation, inherited by the people.

These are the only reasons that I know of, except those pointing to slavery and social aristocracy, that appear on the face worthy of a moment's consideration.

In regard to the first, the authority of those who sustain the opinion, that slavery is a blessing to the State, might be cited for the averment, that the climate of the greater part of Virginia is no less favorable to the activity of the white man than that of the more northern States. North of the country bordering upon a slave population, no similar connection between climate and prosperity is to be found; the wealth of Massachusetts is greater than that of the States lying north of her; land is of higher value in New Jersey than in Maine; the agriculture of parts of Eastern Pennsylvania is more commendable and more profitable than that of any part of New York; the manufacturing industry of New York is far greater than that of Virginia, but not so great as that of the States between her and Virginia, and between which and herself there is as great a difference of climate, and of the same nature, as that between them and Virginia. The most active, enterprising, successful and prosperous States of antiquity, were those of a climate warmer than that of States in commercial subjection to them, and warmer than that of Virginia. Any slight additional enervating effect that the climate of Virginia may possibly have upon those born and bred under it, must be more than compensated for, to the agricultural interest of the State, by the greater length of the season in which the ground is in a condition to be worked, and the greater cheapness with which cattle can be wintered; to manufacturing, mining, and commercial interests, by the smaller liability of their operations being interrupted by ice, etc.

With regard to the second reason, which is that held by the *Richmond Enquirer*, as will be inferred from the polite and modest passage extracted below,* it must be considered that

* "The relations between the North and the South are very analogous to those which subsisted between Greece and the Roman Empire after the sub-

since the earlier settlements of the American colonies, the climate and the institutions of the New World have effected important modifications in the character as well as the physique of the descendants of the settlers, why, then, with a climate so unessentially dissimilar, if it be not for the institutions which are fundamentally dissimilar, has this change been so much less favorable to material prosperity in Virginia than in the adjoining States? The people of the free States, with as great differences of origin between themselves as between the majority of them and the majority of Virginians, are now comparatively homogeneous in the elements of character which lead to prosperity. Is the difference of blood between them and those of Virginia, sufficient to account for the differences in character assumed to be found on crossing the line of freedom and slavery? But not one-tenth certainly, probably not one-thousandth, of the fathers of Virginia were of gentle blood, as those who take this ground seem to assume. The majority of them were sold and bought as laborers. There is no evidence that those who were gentle born, were less endowed with the disposition to gain wealth than their fellow-countrymen who settled New England, or the Dutch of New York, or the Swedes and Germans that

jugation of Achaia by the Consul Mummius. The dignity and energy of the Roman character, conspicuous in war and in politics, were not easily tamed and adjusted to the arts of industry and literature. The degenerate and pliant Greeks, on the contrary, excelled in the handicraft and polite professions. We learn from the vigorous invective of Juvenal, that they were the most useful and capable of servants, whether as pimps or professors of rhetoric. Obsequious, dexterous and ready, the versatile Greeks monopolized the business of teaching, publishing, and manufacturing in the Roman Empire—allowing their masters ample leisure for the service of the State, in the Senate or in the field. The people of the northern States of this Confederacy exhibit the same aptitude for the arts of industry. They excel as clerks, mechanics, and tradesmen, and they have monopolized the business of teaching, publishing, and peddling."

contributed so largely to the settlement of New Jersey and Pennsylvania—the contrary is, in fact, very obvious. That the few people of gentle blood had a paramount influence upon the character of the province, through their legislative and social power, I do not deny; indeed, I believe that through their exercise of this power and through a similar undemocratic, uneconomical and unjust, though not unpardonable, exercise of power at the present time, by a part of the people over the remainder, the character of the whole has been unfavorably affected; and to this despotism and this submission to injustice, it may not be unreasonable to attribute whatever want of prosperity there is in Virginia, when compared with the States where such causes have been wanting or have been less.

By any man whose own mind is not fettered by the system, or who is not very greatly affected by prejudice or by self-interest, in sustaining the system, it is difficult for me to believe that this cause must not be considered far more satisfactory than any other that I have ever heard suggested.

There are many gentlemen who believe, I doubt not, with perfect sincerity, Slavery to have been, and to be, a blessing to both the white and to the black people of the State; but the great reasons of their devotion to the system are, so far as I have learned them, rather prospective than otherwise, after all. They believe there are seeds, at present almost inert, of disaster at the North, against which Slavery will be their protection; indications that these are already beginning to be felt or anticipated by prophetic minds, they think they see in the demands for "Land Limitation," in the anti-rent troubles, in strikes of workmen, in the distress of emigrants at the eddies of their current, in diseased philanthropy, in radical democracy, and in the progress of socialistic ideas in general. The North, say they, has progressed under the high pressure of unlimited competition; as the population grows denser, there will be terrific explosions, disaster, and ruin, while they will ride quietly and safely at the anchor of Slavery. What they suppose to be the cause of the sad waste of natural wealth, what the necessity of the ignorance and poverty of the poor white people, what the reason that capital is not attracted by the superior soundness of their form of government and society, except it may be the stupidity of capitalists, I may very probably have failed to ascertain, because of the general disinclination they have to converse with a Northerner on this topic. The only distinct answer that I have received has been, that it is not Slavery, for nothing is more evident to them, although it may not be so to a stranger, than that Slavery is a blessing everywhere, and always (I quote, as far as convenient, the words that have been addressed to me) to the slave, in Christianizing and civilizing him; to the master, in cultivating those habits of charitable feeling which the presence of the weak, the poor, and the dependent are always suggesting, and in cherishing in him that commanding elevation of character and administrative power which is claimed to have always distinguished the owners of slaves, and the value of which they deem to have always been apparent in our national statesmanship. An institution which they know has such good influences, and which is so favorable to political success, they cannot believe to be destructive to industrial energy and effective of commercial dependence. There is nothing essentially productive in competition; on the contrary, it is evident that the work of many laborers must be more profitable when directed by one controlling mind, than when independent and uncombined; therefore, say they, slave-labor must be cheaper than free-labor. In every way, they are convinced that Slavery is, or should be, and can be made, a great advantage and blessing to them, and, therefore, by God's grace, they are determined to maintain and defend it as their fathers did, and to bequeath it, as their fathers did to them, to their children, unimpaired and unmitigated, an inheritance forever.

Having confidence myself that all the fatal dangers, apprehended for Northern society, may be and will be anticipated and provided against by measures already under consideration; and doubting if Slavery, while it prevents popular education, offers sufficient precaution against them, I think it is to be established convincingly, that Slavery alone is a sufficient cause, at this time, to account for any difference there may be between the value of property and all commercial and industrial prosperity, in Virginia and the neighboring free States.

COST AND VALUE OF LABOR.

Several thousand slaves were hired in Eastern Virginia, during the time of my visit there. The wages paid for able working-men, sound, healthy, in good condition, and with no especial vices, from twenty to thirty years old, were from $110 to $140; the average, as nearly as I could ascertain, from very extended inquiry, being $120 per year, with board and lodging, and certain other expenses. These wages must represent exactly the cost of slave-labor, because any considerations which would prevent the owner of a slave disposing of his labor for those wages, when the labor for his own purposes would not be worth as much, are so many hindrances upon the free disposal of his property, and thereby deduct from its actual value, as measured with money.

As the large majority of slaves are employed in agricultural labor, and many of those, hired at the prices I have mentioned, are taken directly from the labor of the farm, and are skilled in no other, these wages represent the cost of agricultural labor in Eastern Virginia.

In New York, the usual wages for similar men, if Americans, white or black, are exactly the same in the money part; for Irish or German laborers the most common wages are $10 per month, for summer, and $8 per month, for winter, or from $96 to $120 a year, the average being about $108.

The hirer has, in addition to paying wages for the slave, to feed and to clothe him; the free laborer requires also to be boarded, but not to be clothed by his employer. The opinion is universal in Virginia that the slaves are better fed than the Northern laborers. This is, however, a mistake, and we must consider that the board of the Northern laborer would cost at least as much more as the additional cost of clothing to the slave. Comparing man with man, with reference simply to equality of muscular power and endurance, I think, all these things considered, the wages for common laborers are *twenty-five per cent.* higher in Virginia than in New York. But let it be supposed they are equal.

LOSS OF PROFIT TO THE EMPLOYER, FROM THE ILLNESS OR DISABILITY, REAL OR COUNTERFEITED, OF THE LABORER TO WORK.

This, to the employer of free laborers, need be nothing. To the slave-master it is of varying consequence: sometimes small, often excessively embarrassing, and always a subject of anxiety

and suspicion. I have never made the inquiry on any plantation where as many as twenty negroes were employed together,
that I have not ascertained that one or more of the field-hands
was not at work on account of some illness, strain, bruise or
wound, of which he or she was complaining; and in such cases
I have hardly ever heard the proprietor or overseer fail to express his suspicion that the invalid was really as well able to
work as any one else on the plantation. It is said to be nearly
as difficult to form a satisfactory diagnosis of negroes' disorders,
as it is of infants', because their imagination of symptoms is so
vivid, and because not the smallest reliance is to be placed on
their accounts of what they have felt or done. If a man is
really ill, he fears lest he should be thought to be simulating,
and therefore exaggerates all his pains, and locates them
in whatever he supposes to be the most vital parts of his
system.

Frequently the invalid slaves will neglect or refuse to
use the remedies prescribed for their recovery. They will
conceal pills, for instance, under their tongue, and declare
they have swallowed them, when, from their producing
no effect, it will be afterwards evident that they have
not. This general custom I heard ascribed to habit, acquired when they were not very disagreeably ill, and were
loth to be made quite well enough to have to go to work
again.

Amusing incidents, illustrating this difficulty, I have heard
narrated, showing that the slave rather enjoys getting a severe
wound that lays him up:—he has his hand crushed by the fall
of a piece of timber, and after the pain is alleviated, is heard to
exclaim, "Bress der Lord—der haan b'long to masser—don't

reckon dis chile got no more corn to hoe dis yaar, no how."*

Mr. H., of North Carolina, observed to me, in relation to this difficulty, that a man who had had much experience with negroes could generally tell, with a good deal of certainty, by their tongue, and their pulse, and their general aspect, whether they were really ill or not.

" Last year," said he, " I hired out one of my negroes to a rail-road contractor. I suppose he found that he had to work harder than he would on the plantation, and became discontented, and one night he left the camp without asking leave. The next day he stopped at a public-house, and told the people he had fallen sick working on the rail-road, and was going home to his master. They suspected he had run away, and, as he had no pass, they arrested him and sent him to the jail. In the night the sheriff sent me word that there was a boy, who said he belonged to me, in the jail, and he was very sick indeed, and I had better come and take care of him. I immediately suspected how it was, and, as I was particularly engaged, I did not go near him till towards night, the next day. When I came to look at him, and heard his story, I felt quite sure in my own mind that he was not sick ; but, as he pretended to be suffering very much, I told the sheriff to give him plenty of salts and senna, and to be

* It is, perhaps, well I should say that this soliloquy was repeated to me by a Virginia planter, as if it had occurred within his own hearing. A similar illustration of the pleasure with which a slave finds himself exempted from labor, having been mentioned in the " Key to Uncle Tom's Cabin," the Reverend E. J. Stearns, of St. John's College, Maryland, in a rejoinder to that work, thinks it unnecessary to deny the truth of it, but, with the usual happy keenness of clerical controversialists, settles the matter without being personally disrespectful to Mrs. Stowe's authority, by quoting the *final* authority :—" ' No man ever hated his own flesh, but nourisheth it, and cherisheth it ;' *and again*, ' So ought men to love their wives as their own bodies.' "

careful that he did not get much of anything to eat. The next day I got a letter from the contractor, telling me that my nigger had run away, without any cause. So I rode over to the jail again, and told them to continue the same treatment until the boy got a good deal worse or a good deal better. Well, the rascal kept it up for a week, all the time groaning so you'd think he couldn't live many hours longer; but, after he had been in seven days, he all of a sudden said he'd got well, and he wanted something to eat. As soon as I heard of it, I sent them word to give him a good paddling,* and handcuff him, and send him back to the rail-road. I had to pay them for taking up a runaway, besides the sheriff's fees, and a week's board of the boy to the county."

But the same gentleman admitted that he had sometimes been mistaken, and had made men go to work when they afterwards proved to be really ill; therefore, when one of his people told him he was not able to work, he usually thought, "very likely he'll be all the better for a day's rest, whether he's really ill or not," and would let him off without being very particular in his examination. Lately he had been getting a new overseer, and when he was engaging him, he told him that this was his way. The overseer replied, "It's my way, too, now; it didn't use to be, but I had a lesson. There was a nigger one day at Mr. ——'s who was sulky, and complaining; he said he couldn't work. I looked at his tongue, and it was right clean, and I thought it was nothing but damned sulkiness so I paddled him, and made him go to work; but, two days after, he was under ground. He was a good eight hundred

* Not something to eat, but punishment with an instrument like a ferule.

dollar nigger, and it was a lesson to me about taming possums, that I ain't agoing to forget in a hurry."

The liability of women, especially, to disorders and irregularities which cannot be detected by exterior symptoms, but which may be easily aggravated into serious complaints, renders many of them nearly valueless for work, because of the ease with which they can impose upon their owners. "The women on a plantation," said one extensive Virginian slave-owner to me, "will hardly earn their salt, after they come to the breeding age : they don't come to the field, and you go to the quarters and ask the old nurse what's the matter, and she says, 'Oh, she's not well, master; she's not fit to work, sir ;' and what can you do ? You have to take her word for it that something or other is the matter with her, and you dare not set her to work ; and so she lay up till she feels like taking the air again, and plays the lady at your expense."

I was on one plantation where a woman had been excused from any sort of labor for more than two years, on the supposition that she was dying of phthisis. At last the overseer discovered that she was employed as a milliner and dress-maker by all the other colored ladies of the vicinity ; and upon taking her to the house, it was found that she had acquired a remarkable skill in these vocations. She was hired out the next year to a fashionable dress-maker in town, at handsome wages ; and as, after that, she did not again "raise blood," it was supposed that when she had done so before it had been by artificial means. Such tricks every army and navy surgeon is familiar with.

The interruption and disarrangement of operations of labor, occasioned by slaves "running away," frequently causes great inconvenience and loss to those who employ them. It is said to

often occur when no immediate motive can be guessed at for it—
when the slave has been well-treated, well-fed, and not overworked; and when he will be sure to suffer hardship from it, and
be subject to severe punishment on his return, or if he is caught.

This is often mentioned to illustrate the ingratitude and especial depravity of the African race. I should suspect it to be, if
it cannot be otherwise accounted for, the natural instinct of freedom in a man, working out capriciously, as the wild instincts of
domesticated beasts and birds sometimes do.

But the learned Dr. Cartwright, of the University of Louisiana, believes that slaves are subject to a peculiar form of mental
disease, termed by him *Drapetomania*, which, like a malady that
cats are liable to, manifests itself by an irrestrainable propensity
to *run away;* and in a work on the diseases of negroes, highly
esteemed at the South for its patriotism and erudition, he advises
planters of the proper preventive, and curative measures to be
taken for it.

He asserts that, "with the advantage of proper medical advice,
strictly followed, this troublesome practice of running away, that
many negroes have, can be almost entirely prevented." Its
symptoms and the usual empirical practice on the plantations
are described: "Before negroes run away, unless they are
frightened or panic-struck, they become sulky and dissatisfied.
The cause of this sulkiness and dissatisfaction should be inquired
into and removed, or they are apt to run away or fall into the
negro consumption." When sulky or dissatisfied without cause,
the experience of those having most practice with *drapetomania*,
the Doctor thinks, has been in favor of "whipping them *out of
it.*" It is vulgarly called, "whipping the devil *out of them*," he
afterwards informs us.

Another droll sort of "indisposition," thought to be peculiar to the slaves, and which must greatly affect their value, as compared with free laborers, is described by Dr. Cartwright, as follows:

"DYSÆSTHESIA ÆTHIOPICA, or Hebetude of Mind and Obtuse Sensibility of Body. * * * From the careless movements of the individuals affected with this complaint, they are apt to do much mischief, which appears as if intentional, but is mostly owing to the stupidness of mind and insensibility of the nerves induced· by the disease. Thus they break, waste, and destroy everything they handle—abuse horses and cattle—tear, burn, or rend their own clothing, and, paying no attention to the rights of property, steal others to replace what they have destroyed. They wander about at night, and keep in a half nodding state by day. They slight their work—cut up corn, cane, cotton, and tobacco, when hoeing it, as if for pure mischief. They raise disturbances with their overseers, and among their fellow-servants, without cause or motive, and seem to be insensible to pain when subjected to punishment. * * *

"When left to himself, the negro indulges in his natural disposition to idleness and sloth, and does not take exercise enough to expand his lungs and vitalize his blood, but dozes out a miserable existence in the midst of filth and uncleanliness, being too indolent, and having too little energy of mind, to provide for himself proper food and comfortable clothing and lodging. The consequence is, that the blood becomes so highly carbonized and deprived of oxygen that it not only becomes unfit to stimulate the brain to energy, but unfit to stimulate the nerves of sensation distributed to the body. * * *

"This is the disease called *Dysæsthesia* (a Greek term expressing the dull or obtuse sensation that always attends the complaint). When roused from sloth by the stimulus of hunger, he takes anything he can lay his hands on, and tramples on the rights as well as on the property of others, with perfect indifference. When driven to labor by the compulsive power of the white man, he performs the task assigned to him in a headlong, careless manner, treading down with his feet or cutting with his hoe the plants he is put to cultivate—breaking the tools he works with, and spoiling everything he touches that can be injured by careless handling. Hence the overseers call it 'rascality,' supposing that the mischief is intentionally done. * * *

"The term, 'rascality,' given to this disease by overseers, is founded on an erroneous hypothesis, and leads to an incorrect empirical treatment, which seldom or never cures it."

There are many complaints described in Dr. Cartwright's treatise, to which the negroes, in Slavery, seem to be peculiarly subject.

"More fatal than any other is congestion of the lungs, *peripneumonia notha*, often called cold plague, etc.   *   *   *

"The *Frambœsia*, Piam, or Yaws, is a *contagious* disease, communicable by contact among those who greatly neglect cleanliness.   It is supposed to be communicable, in a modified form, to the white race, among whom it resembles pseudo syphilis, or some disease of the nose, throat, or larynx.   *   *   *

"Negro-consumption, a disease almost unknown to medical men of the Northern States and of Europe, is also sometimes fearfully prevalent among the slaves.   'It is of importance,' says the Doctor, 'to know the pathognomic signs in its early stages, not only in regard to its treatment, but to detect impositions, as negroes, afflicted with this complaint are often for sale ; the acceleration of the pulse, on exercise, incapacitates them for labor, as they quickly give out, and have to leave their work.   This induces their owners to sell them, although they may not know the cause of their inability to labor.   Many of the negroes brought South, for sale, are in the incipient stages of this disease ; they are found to be inefficient laborers, and are sold in consequence thereof. The effect of superstition—a firm belief that he is poisoned or conjured —upon the patient's mind, already in a morbid state (dyæsthesia), and his health affected from hard usage, over-tasking or exposure, want of wholesome food, good clothing, warm, comfortable lodging, with the distressing idea (sometimes) that he is an object of hatred or dislike, both to his master or fellow-servants, and has no one to befriend him, tends directly to generate that erythism of mind which is the essential cause of negro-consumption.'   *   *   *   'Remedies should be assisted by removing the *original cause* of the dissatisfaction or trouble of mind, and by using every means to make the patient comfortable, satisfied and happy.' "

Longing for home generates a distinct malady, known to physicians as *Nostalgia*, and there is an analogy between the treatment commonly employed to cure it and that recommended in this last advice of Dr. Cartwright, which is very suggestive.

DISCIPLINE.

Under the slave system of labor, discipline must always be maintained by physical power. A lady of New York, spending a winter in a Southern city, had a hired slave-servant, who, one day, refused outright to perform some ordinary light domestic duty required of her. On the lady's gently remonstrating with her, she immediately replied: "You can't make me do it, and I won't do it: I aint afeard of you whippin' me." The servant was right; the lady could not whip her, and was too tender-hearted to call in a man, or to send her to the guard-house to be whipped, as is the custom with Southern ladies, when their patience is exhausted, under such circumstances. She endeavored, by kindness and by appeals to the girl's good sense, to obtain a moral control over her; but, after suffering continual annoyance and inconvenience, and after an intense trial of her feelings, for some time, she was at length obliged to go to her owner, and beg him to come and take her away from the house, on any terms. It was no better than having a lunatic or a mischievous and pilfering monomaniac quartered upon her.*

But often when courage and physical power, with the strength of the militia force and the army of the United States, if required, at the back of the master, are not wanting, there are a great variety of circumstances that make a resort to punishment inconvenient, if not impossible.

* The *Richmond American* has a letter from Raleigh, N. C., dated Sept. 18. which says: " On yesterday morning, a beautiful young lady, Miss Virginia Frost, daughter of Austin Frost, an engineer on the Petersburg and Weldon Rail-road, and residing in this city, was shot by a negro girl, and killed instantly. Cause—reproving her for insolent language."

Really well-trained, accomplished, and docile house-servants are seldom to be purchased or hired at the South, though they are found in old wealthy families rather oftener than first-rate English or French servants are at the North.   It is, doubtless, a convenience to have even moderately good servants who cannot, at any time of their improved value or your necessity, demand to have their pay increased, or who cannot be drawn away from you by prospect of smaller demands and kinder treatment at your neighbor's; but I believe few of those who are incessantly murmuring against this healthy operation of God's good law of supply and demand would be willing to purchase exemption from it, at the price with which the masters and mistresses of the South do.   They would pay, to get a certain amount of work done, three or four times as much, to the owner of the best sort of hired slaves, as they do to the commonest, stupidest Irish domestic drudges at the North, though the nominal wages by the week or year, in Virginia, are but little more than in New York.

The number of servants usually found in a Southern family, of any pretension, always amazes a Northern lady.   In one that I visited, there were exactly three negroes to each white, and this in a town, the negroes being employed solely in the house.

A Southern lady, of an old and wealthy family, who had been for some time visiting a friend of mine in New York, said to her, as she was preparing to return home: "I can not tell you how much, after being in your house so long, I dread to go home, and to have to take care of our servants again.   We have a much smaller family of whites than you, but we have twelve servants, and your two accomplish a great deal more, and do their work a great deal better than our twelve.   You think your girls are very stupid, and that they give you much trouble: but it is as

nothing.   There is hardly one of our servants that can be
trusted to do the simplest work without being stood over.   If I
order a room to be cleaned, or a fire to be made in a distant
chamber, I never can be sure I am obeyed unless I go there and
see for myself.   If I send a girl out to get anything I want for
preparing the dinner, she is as likely as not to forget what is
wanted, and not to come back till after the time at which dinner
should be ready.   A hand-organ in the street will draw all my
girls out of the house ; and while it remains near us I have no
more command over them than over so many monkeys.   The
parade of a military company has sometimes entirely prevented
me from having any dinner cooked ; and when the servants,
standing in the square looking at the soldiers, see my husband
coming after them, they only laugh, and run away to the other
side, like playful children.*   And, when I reprimand them, they
only say they don't mean to do anything wrong, or they wont
do it again, all the time laughing as though it was all a joke.
They don't mind it at all.   They are just as playful and careless
as any willful child ; and they never will do any work if you
don't compel them."

The slave employer, if he finds he has been so unfortunate as
to hire a sulky servant, that cannot be made to work to his
advantage, has no remedy but to solicit from his owner a deduction from the price he has agreed to pay for his labor, on the
same ground that one would from a livery-stable keeper, if he had
engaged a horse to go a journey, but found that he was not

---

* In the city of Columbia, S. C., the police are required to prevent the negroes
from running in this way after the military.   Any negro neglecting to leave
the vicinity of a parade, when ordered by a policeman or any military officer,
is required, by the ordinance, to be whipped at the guard-house.

strong or skillful enough to keep him upon the road.   But, if the slave is the property of his employer, and becomes "rascally," the usual remedy is that which the veterinary surgeon recommended when he was called upon for advice how to cure a balky horse: "*Sell* him, my lord." "Rascals" are "sent South" from Virginia, for the cure or alleviation of their complaint, in much greater numbers than consumptives are from the more Northern States.

"How do you manage, then, when a man misbehaves, or is sick?" I have been often asked by Southerners, in discussing this question.

If he is sick, I simply charge against him every half day of the time he is off work, and deduct it from his wages.   If he is careless, or refuses to do what in reason I demand of him, I discharge him, paying him wages to the time he leaves.   With new men in whom I have not confidence, I make a written agreement, before witnesses, on engaging them, that will permit me to do this.   As for "rascality," I never had but one case of anything approaching to what you call so.   A man insolently contradicted me in the field : I told him to leave his job and go to the house, took hold and finished it myself, then went to the house, made out a written statement of account, counted out the balance in money due him, gave him the statement and the money, and told him he must go.   He knew that he had failed of his duty, and that the law would sustain me, and we parted in a friendly manner, he expressing regret that his temper had driven him from a situation which had been agreeable and satisfactory to him.   The probability is, that this single experience educated him so far that his next employer would have no occasion to complain of his "rascality;" and I very much doubt if any amount of corporeal punishment would have improved his temper in the least.

That slaves have to be "humored" a great deal, and that they very frequently can not be made to do their master's will, I have seen much evidence.   Not that they often directly refuse to obey an order, but, when they are directed to do anything for which they have a disinclination, they undertake it in such a way that the desired result is sure not to be accomplished.   In small particulars for which a laborer's discretion must be trusted to in every-day work, but more especially when emergencies require some extraordinary duties to be performed, they are much less reliable than the ordinary run of laborers employed on our farms in New York.   They can not be driven by fear of punishment to do that which the laborers in free communities do cheerfully from their sense of duty, self-respect, or regard for their reputation and standing with their employer.   A gentleman who had some free men in his employment in Virginia, that he had procured in New York, told me that he had been astonished, when a dam that he had been building began to give way in a freshet, to see how much more readily than negroes they would obey his orders, and do their best without orders, running into the water waist deep, in mid-winter, without any hesitation or grumbling.

The manager of a large candle-factory in London, in which the laborers are treated with an unusual degree of confidence and generosity, writes thus in a report to his directors :

"The present year promises to be a very good one as regards profit, in consequence of the enormous increase in the demand for candles.   No mere driving of the men and boys, by ourselves and those in authority under us, would have produced the sudden and very great increase of manufacture, necessary for keeping pace with this demand.   It has been effected only by the hearty good-will with which the factory has worked, the men and boys making the great extra exertion, which they saw to be necessary to prevent our getting hopelessly in arrears with the orders, as heartily as if the question had been, how to avert some difficulty threatening themselves personally. One of the foremen remarked with truth, a few days back: "To look on them, one would think each was engaged in a little business of his own, so as to have only himself affected by the results of his work.' "

A farmer in Lincolnshire, England, told me that once, during an extraordinary harvest season, he had had a number of laborers at work without leaving the field or taking any repose for sixty hours—he himself working with them, and eating and drinking only with them during all the time. Such services men may give voluntarily, from their own regard to the value of property to be saved by it, or for the purpose of establishing their credit as worth good wages; but to require it of slaves would be intensely cruel, if not actually impossible. A man can work excessively on his own impulse as much easier than he can be driven to by another, as a horse travels easier in going towards his accustomed stable than in going from it. I mean—and every man who has ever served as a sailor or a soldier will know that it is no imaginary effect—that the actual fatigue, the waste of bodily energy, the expenditure of the physical capacity, is greater in one case than the other.

Sailors and soldiers both, are led by certain inducements to place themselves within certain limits, and for a certain time, both defined by contract, in a condition resembling, in many particulars, that of slaves; and, although they are bound by their voluntary contract and by legal and moral considerations to obey orders, the fact that force is also used to secure their obedience to their officers, scarcely ever fails to produce in them the identical vices which are complained of in slaves. They obey the letter, but defeat the intention of orders that do not please them, they are improvident, wasteful, reckless: they sham illness, and as Dr. Cartwright gives specific medical appellations to discontent, laziness, and rascality, so among sailors and soldiers, when men suddenly find themselves ill and unable to do their duty in times of peculiar danger, or when unusual labor is required, they are humorously said to be suffering under an attack of the powder-fever, the cape-fever, the ice-fever, the coast-fever, or the reefing-fever. The counteracting influences to these vices, which it is the first effort of every good officer to foster, are, first, regard to duty; second, patriotism; third, *esprit du corps*, or professional pride; fourth, self-respect, or personal pride; fifth, self-interest, hope of promotion, or of bounty, or of privileges in mitigation of their hard service, as reward for excellence. Things are never quickly done at sea, unless they are done with a will, or "cheerly," as the sailor's word is—that is, cheerfully. An army is never effective in the field when depressed in its *morale*.

None of these promptings to excellence can be operative, except in a very low degree, to counteract the indolent and vicious tendencies of the Slavery, much more pure than the slavery of the army or the ship, by which the exertions of the Virginia laborer are obtained for his employer.

It is very common, among the Virginians, to think that the relation of free-laborers to their employers is, by the effect of circumstances, rendered very little less slavish than that of their own slaves to them. It is true that in many respects the position of agricultural laborers, in some parts of England and other countries (where the land is owned and rented only in excessively large quantities, and the principle of competition has, therefore, very little influence to counteract the power of the capitalists to prevent a man's getting his living by labor, except on their conditions), approaches, in the degree of their moral subjection, to that of slaves.

But this is true only in a very few districts, nowhere in the United States, unless it be in the Slave States, where sometimes similar causes produce somewhat similar effects upon the poor whites. And, everywhere, the services rendered by the free-laborers are rendered not from fear of punishment, are claimed not by right of force, but are rendered in obedience to, and claimed by express right of, a contract voluntarily made : consequently, compared with that of the slave, their labor is actively, cheerfully, and discreetly given. Circumstances may have made it necessary for the laborer to accept the terms offered by the employer ; but those circumstances no more constitute slavery than do the circumstances, which induce merchants and manufacturers in towns to pay what they deem extravagant prices for flour, render them the slaves of the farmers, who say to them, "Pay these prices, or go without."

It is a very low mind that cannot appreciate the difference between services rendered from such motives and under such obligations, honorable, manly, and just obligations, voluntarily entered into, and the services of a slave, rendered from fear that he shall be whipped if he does not render them.

The employer of a free-laborer no more dare whip him than the laborer dare whip the employer. Their rights are equal, in all respects, before the law, and the claim of the laborer to his stipulated wages, his tacitly stipulated diet and lodging, is just as good, and renders him just as truly the owner of his employer, as the claim of the employer upon the free-laborer for his stipulated measure, by days or months, of muscular labor, and his tacitly stipulated exercise of skill and discretion, render him the owner of his employé. The man who would work cheerfully and to the best of his discretion, for the employer, in one case is a fool; the man who would not work cheerfully and to the best of his discretion, for his employer, in the other is dishonest and imprudent.

The following is from the organ of the New York city Know Nothings, of Feb. 21, 1855: "If to rise with the lark and labor the live-long day, saddled with care, loaded down with anxiety, until we sink under the burden, is freedom, then we are not slaves. If to do half this work, without any of its cares, or troubles, with the full quota of pleasure, is the want of it, then who would be free?"

Such a view of life is not only disgraceful to a man, but the prevalence of such ideas, however patriotic may be the foundation on which they have been cultivated, is most pernicious to the character of our own laboring-class, and to all industry into which competition can enter. There are some badly-educated American women who choose to die as seamstresses, rather than to live as cooks or chamber-maids, because they are taught by such writers that the position of a servant, or of those who sell their labor and skill by measure of time and not by measure of amount, is worse than that of slaves. Even prostitution is felt to be less a disgrace than this false parallel to Slavery, and so, unconsciously deluded by this false analogy, they answer this writer's question, actually preferring death to this imaginary degradation.

"It is with dogs," says the best authority on the subject, "as it is with horses; no work is so well done as that which is done cheerfully."* And it is with men, both black and white, as it is with horses and with dogs; it is even more so, because the strength and cunning of a man is less adapted to being "broken" to the will of another than that of either dogs or horses.

The writer, whose opinion, that Slavery is a better system for the laborer than the system of Northern States, I have just quoted, estimates that the labor of a slave is only half that, in a day, of a man actuated by anxiety for his own advantage at his work. If it were not that Slavery, present at the South and past in our own land and the lands where most of our laborers have been educated, had an influence still to make labor a less respected commodity than most others in our market, in consequence of which the mutual obligations of capitalist and laborer are sometimes less definitely felt than they should be, I think no one would be surprised to learn that this estimate of the difference in the amount of work accomplished in a day, by voluntary laborers and slave laborers, was not in the slightest degree extravagantly expressed. But upon this point I shall now give some exact information.

OF THE COMPARATIVE AMOUNT OF WORK ACCOMPLISHED IN A GIVEN TIME BY FREE AND SLAVE LABORERS.

Mr. T. R. Griscom, of Petersburg, Virginia, stated to me, that he once took accurate account of the labor expended in harvesting a large field of wheat; and the result was that one quarter of an acre a day was secured for each able hand engaged in cradling, raking, and binding. The crop was light, yielding not over six bushels to the acre. In New York a gang of fair

* Lieut. Col. W. N. HUTCHINSON, on Dog Breaking.

cradlers and binders would be expected, under ordinary circumstances, to secure a crop of wheat, yielding from twenty to thirty bushels to the acre, at the rate of about two acres a day for each man.

Mr. Griscom formerly resided in New Jersey; and since living in Virginia has had the superintendence of very large agricultural operations, conducted with slave-labor. After I had, in a letter, intended for publication, made use of this testimony, I called upon him to ask if he would object to my giving his name with it. He was so good as to permit me to do so, and said that I might add that the ordinary waste in harvesting wheat in Virginia, through the carelessness of the negroes, beyond that which occurs in the hands of ordinary Northern laborers, is equal in value to what a Northern farmer would often consider a satisfactory profit on his crop. He also wished me to say that it was his deliberate opinion, formed not without much and accurate observation, that four Virginia slaves do not, when engaged in ordinary agricultural operations, accomplish as much, on an average, as one ordinary free farm laborer in New Jersey.

Mr. Griscom is well known at Petersburg as a man remarkable for reliability, accuracy, and preciseness; and no man's judgment on this subject could be entitled to more respect.

Another man, who had superintended labor of the same character at the North and in Virginia, whom I questioned closely, agreed entirely with Mr. Griscom, believing that four negroes had to be supported on every farm in the State to accomplish the same work which was ordinarily done by one free laborer in New York.

A clergyman from Connecticut, who had resided for many years in Virginia, told me that what a slave expected to spend a day upon, a Northern laborer would, he was confident, usually accomplish by eleven o'clock in the morning.

In a letter on this subject, most of the facts given in which have been already narrated in this volume, written from Virginia to the *New York Daily Times*, I expressed the conviction that, at the most, not more than one-half as much labor was ordinarily accomplished in Virginia by a certain number of slaves, in a given time, as by an equal number of free laborers in New York. The publication of this letter induced a number of persons to make public the conclusions of their own experience or observations on this subject. So far as I know, these, in every case, sustained my conclusions, or, if any doubt was expressed, it was that I had under-estimated the superior economy of free-labor. As affording evidence more valuable than my own on this important point, from the better opportunities of forming sound judgment, which a residence at different times, in both Virginia and a free State had given the writers, I have reprinted, in an appendix, two of these letters, together with a quantity of other testimony from Southern witnesses on this subject, which I beg the reader, who has any doubt of the correctness of my information, not to neglect.

" DRIVING."

On mentioning to a gentleman in Virginia, who believed that slave-labor was better and cheaper than free-labor, Mr. Griscom's observation, he replied: that without doubting the correctness of the statement of that particular instance, he was sure that if four men did not harvest more than an acre of wheat a day, they could not have been well *driven*. He knew that, if properly driven, threatened with punishment, and punished if necessary, negroes would do as much work as it was possible for any white man to do. The same gentleman, however, at another time, told me that negroes were very seldom punished, not oftener, he presumed, than apprentices were, at the North; that the driving of them was generally left to overseers, who were the laziest and most worthless dogs in the world, frequently not demanding higher wages for their services than one of the negroes, they were given to manage, might be hired out for. Another gentleman told me that he would rather, if the law would permit it, have some of his negroes for overseers, than any white man he had ever been able to obtain in that capacity.

Another planter, whom I requested to examine a letter on the subject, that I had prepared for the *Daily Times*, that he might, if he could, refute my calculations, or give me any facts of an opposite character, after reading it said: "The truth is, that in general, a slave does not do half the work he easily might; and which, by being harsh enough with him, he can be made to do. When I came into possession of my plantation, I soon found the overseer then upon it was good for nothing, and told him I had no further occasion for his services: I then went to driving the negroes myself. In the morning, when I went out, one of them came up to me and asked what work he should go about. I told him to go into the swamp and cut some wood. 'Well, massa,' said he, 's'pose you wants me to do kordins we's been use to doin'; ebery niggar cut a cord a day.' 'A cord! that's what you have been used to doing, is it?' said I. 'Yes, massa, dat's wot dey always makes a niggar do roun' heah—a cord a day, dat's allers de task.'

'Well, now, old man,'* said I, 'you go and cut me two cords to-day.' 'Oh, massa! two cords! Nobody couldn do dat. Oh! massa, dat's too hard! Nebber heard o' nobody's cuttin' more 'n a cord o' wood in a day, roun' heah. No nigger couldn' do it.' 'Well, old man, you have two cords of wood cut to-night, or to-morrow morning you shall get two hundred lashes—that's all there is about it. So, look sharp!' And he did it, and ever since no negro has ever cut less than two cords a day for me, though my neighbors never get but one cord. It was just so with a great many other things—mauling rails —I always have two hundred rails mauled in a day; just twice what it is the custom of the country to expect of a negro, and just twice as many as my negroes had been made to do before I managed them myself.

This only makes it more probable that the amount of labor ordinarily and generally performed by slaves in Virginia is very small, compared with that done by the laborers of the free States, and confirms the correctness of the estimates that I have given.

These estimates, let it be recollected, in conclusion, are all deliberately and carefully made by gentlemen of liberal education, who have had unusual facilities of observing both at the North and at the South—gentlemen who own or employ slaves themselves, and who sustain Southern designs on the political questions connected with slavery. I have not given them because they were extreme, but because I could obtain no others equally exact. The conclusion to which they directly point is, that the

---

* "Old Man," is a common title of address to any middle-aged negro in Virginia, whose name is not known. "Boy" and "Old Man" may be applied to the same person. Of course, in this case, the slave is not to be supposed to be beyond his prime of strength.

cost of any certain amount of labor, by measure, of tasks and not of time, is *between three and four hundred per cent.* higher in Virginia than in the free States. To this is to be added the cost of clothing the slaves, of the time they lose in sickness, or otherwise, and of all they pilfer, damage, and destroy through carelessness, improvidence, recklessness, and "rascality."

Labor is the creator of wealth. There can be no honest wealth, no true prosperity without it; and in exact proportion to the economy of labor is the cost of production and the accumulation of profit upon the capital used in its employment.

Let any one allow as much as he can, in view of the testimony, for exaggeration in these estimates, and reduce them accordingly. It seems to me hardly possible that he should be able still to doubt, that in the additional cost of labor alone, a grand, if not all-sufficient cause may be found for the acknowledged slow progress and the poverty of Virginia, compared with the free States.

WHY FREE-LABOR COMPETITION DOES NOT DRIVE OUT SLAVERY IN VIRGINIA.

Considering that the wages of a week's labor would pay for the transportation of a laborer from the free States to a community where slave-labor predominates, it might, at the first thought upon the matter, appear impossible that there could be, for any length of time, any essential difference in the cost of labor between the two districts. The law of supply and demand is not, indeed, inoperative against slavery; it is a constant counteracting influence to its evils, and, if it were not for the internal slave-trade, which makes slaves valuable property, otherwise than for labor, it would probably, before this, unless the competition of free-labor had been excluded by know-nothing measures, have forced the adoption of *some* method of relieving the State of its heavy burden; but this great first law of Commerce acts very slowly.

The laborer who, in New York, gave a certain amount of labor for his wages in a day, soon finds, in Virginia, that the ordinary measure of labor is smaller than in New York: a "day's work" or a month's does not mean the same that it did in New York. He naturally adapts his wares to the market. Just as in New York a knavish custom having been sometime ago established, of selling a measure of three quarters of a bushel of certain articles under the name of a bushel, no man now finds it to his advantage to offer them by the full bushel, at a correspondingly higher price. Though every one cries out against the custom, and demands a bushel for a bushel, few are willing to pay proportionately for it; few are willing to sell it without being paid more than proportionately on account of their deviation from custom; and the custom must be reformed very slowly. So the laborer, finding that the capitalists of Virginia are accustomed to pay for a poor article at a high price, prefers to furnish them the poor article at their usual price, rather than a better article, unless at a more than correspondingly better price.

But there are other laws, also, that come in play in this case, to qualify the action of the laws of demand and supply.

"Man is a social animal." The largest part of the labor required in Virginia is, and long has been, performed by negroes. The negroes are a degraded people; degraded not merely by position, but actually immoral, low-lived; without healthy ambition; but little influenced by high moral considerations, and, in regard to labor, not all affected by regard for duty. This is universally recognized, and debasing fear, not cheering hope, is in general allowed to be their only stimulant to exertion. A capitalist was having a building erected in Petersburg, and his slaves were employed in carrying up the brick and mortar for the masons on their heads; a Northern man, standing near, remarked to him that they moved so indolently it seemed as if they were trying to see how long they could be in mounting the ladder without actually stopping. The builder started to reprove them, but after moving a step turned back and said: "It would only make them move more slowly still when I am not looking at them, if I should hurry them now. *And what motive have they to do better?* It's no concern of theirs how long the masons wait. I am sure, if I was in their place, I shouldn't move as fast as they do."

Now, let the white laborer come here from the North or from Europe—his nature demands a social life—shall he associate with the poor, slavish, degraded, low-lived, despised, unambitious negro, with whom labor and punishment are almost synonymous? or shall he be the friend and companion of the white man, in whose mind labor is habitually associated with no ideas of duty, responsibility, comfort, luxury, cultivation, or elevation and expansion either of mind or estate, as it is where the ordinary laborer is a free man—free to use his labor as a means of obtaining all these and all else that is to be respected, honored or envied in the world?

Associating with either or both, is it not inevitable that he will be rapidly demoralized—that he will soon learn to hate labor, give as little of it for his hire as he can, become base, cowardly, faithless—"worse than a nigger"?

Such, I am sure, is the fact, with regard to the majority of laborers who have come here, and I cannot doubt that such is the cause. And, when we reflect how little the great body of our working-men are consciously much affected by moral considerations, in their movements, one is tempted to suspect that the Almighty has endowed the great transatlantic migration with a new instinct, by which it is unconsciously repelled from the demoralizing and debilitating influence of slavery, as migrating birds have sometimes been thought to be from pestilential regions. I know not else how to account for the remarkable indisposition to be sent to Virginia, which I have seen manifested by poor Irishmen and Germans, who could have known, I think, no more of the evils of slavery to the whites, in the Slave States, than the slaves themselves know of the effect of conscription in France, and who certainly could have been governed by no considerations of self-respect. This experience I have had, in consequence of having been requested by several persons, in Virginia, to send them white laborers. I can understand better what induced two men of the same sort, who had previously lived a short time on farms in the Free State, to return north, after completing a short engagement to work upon a slave plantation, though they had obtained high wages, and were well treated by their employer, and could give no better reason to me, for their course, than that they "didn't like to work with them niggers."

That the native white population is thoroughly demoralized, in respect to those qualities essential to a good laborer, and that this demoralization is the direct result of slavery, I have given some evidence, which I received from a slave-holder, in one of my earlier letters (p. 82); but I will add the recorded testimony of others.

From the Patent Office Report, for 1847.

" As to the price of labor, our mechanics charge from one to two dollars a day. As to agricultural labor, we have none. Our poor are poor because *they will not work*, therefore are seldom employed.

" CHAS. YANCEY,
" Buckingham Co., Virginia."

The sentence, "as to agricultural labor, we have none," must mean no free-labor: the number of slaves in this county being, according to the census, 8,161, or nearly 3,000 more than the whole white population! There are, also, 250 free negroes in the county.

From a Correspondent of the American Agriculturist, Feb. 14, 1855.

" As to laborers, we work, chiefly, slaves, not because they are cheaper, but rather, because they are the only *reliable* labor we can get. The whites here engage to work *for less price than the blacks* can be got for ; yet, they will not work well, and *rarely work out the time specified.* If any of your friends come here, and wish to work whites, I would advise them, by all means, to bring them with them ; for, our white laborers are far inferior to our blacks, and our black labor is far inferior to what we read and hear of your laborers.

" C. G. G.,
" Albemarle Co., Virginia."

In Albemarle, there are over thirteen thousand slaves, to less than twelve thousand whites.

In the northwestern counties, Cabell, Mason, Brooke, and Tyler, in or adjoining which there are no large towns, but a free laboring population, with slaves in ratio to the freemen, as one to fifteen, only, the value of land is over seven dollars and three quarters an acre.

In Southampton, Surrey, James-Town, and New-Kent, in which the slave population is as 1 to 2·2, the value of land is but little more than half as much—$4 50 an acre .

In Surrey, Prince George, Charles City, and James, adjoining counties on James River, and originally having some of the most productive soil in the State, and now supplied with the public conveniences which have accrued in two hundred years of occupation, by a civilized and Christian community, the number of slaves being, at present, to that of whites, as 1 to 1·9, the value of land is but $6 an acre.

In Fairfax, another of the first-settled counties, and one in which, twenty years ago, land was even less in value than in the James River counties, it is now worth twice as much. The slave population, once greater than that of whites, has been reduced, by emigration and sale, till there are now less than half as many slaves as whites. In the place of slaves, has come another sort of people. The change which has taken place, and the cause of it, is thus simply described in the Agricultural Report of the County to the Commissioner of Patents. (*See Patent Office Report*, 1852.)

"In appearance, the county is so changed, in many parts, that a traveler, who passed over it ten years ago, would not now recognize it. Thousands and thousands of acres had been cultivated in tobacco, by the former proprietors, would not pay the cost, and were abandoned as worthless, and became covered with a wilderness of pines. These lands have been purchased by northern emigrants; the large tracts divided and subdivided, and cleared of pines; and neat farm-houses and barns, with smiling fields of grain and grass, in the season, salute the delighted gaze of the beholder. Ten years ago, it was a mooted question, whether Fairfax lands could be made productive; and, if so, would they pay the cost? This problem has been satisfactorily solved by many, and, in consequence of the above altered state of things, *school-houses and churches have doubled in number*."

There is much more evidence in my hands, but I think I may, as the lawyers say, rest on this. I see not how any one can still doubt that Slavery is the present cause of the comparative adversity or poverty of Virginia, or that Freedom would be found an immediate, certain, and, to all but the few slave-holders (they are not, I suppose, one to a hundred of the people), entirely satisfactory remedy.

But I cannot pass from Virginia without considering her condition from another and broader point of view.

It is very customary to speak of our Confederacy of States as The Great Experiment. The great experiment of what? Of the effect, I suppose is meant, of a form of government in which all men are declared to be equal; in which there are no privileged orders; no ruling class; in which the laboring class is dignified by being made, equally with the capitalist and the professional scholar, the recipient of governmental power.

Yet, the United States, in the aggregate, cannot rightly be considered as more than approximating such an experiment. It affords, however, thirty distinct experiments in governmental and social science, which might be studied and examined, one comparatively with another, most usefully. And I am convinced that the average progress in happiness and wealth, which has been made by the people of each State, is in almost exact ratio to the degree in which the democratic principle has been radically carried out in their constitution, laws, and customs.

In studying the question of the causes of the poverty of Virginia, I have been obliged to examine the past as well as the present character of her labor, and I have been astonished to see the important bearing which certain facts in her history have upon the great problem of statesmanship.

Men of literary taste or clerical habits are always apt to overlook the working-classes, and to confine the records they make of their own times, in a great degree, to the habits and fortunes of their own associates, or to those of people of superior rank to themselves, of whose sayings and doings their vanity, as well as their curiosity, leads them to most carefully inform themselves. The dumb masses have often been so lost in this shadow of egotism, that, in later days, it has been impossible to discern the very real influence their character and condition has had on the fortune and fate of nations.

Of the laborers in the colony of Virginia, although, after a self-sustaining community had been once firmly established, they undoubtedly formed a very large majority of all the people, very little notice is ever taken by any chronicler or historian, further than in simple memoranda of their arrival by the cargo or hundred. Information with regard to them is only to be obtained by a labored investigation of evidence incidentally recorded.

As very little of the knowledge thus attainable has been made readily accessible to the mass of the reading public, or to those who might most profit by it, I have thought it best to offer here a somewhat desultory review of the more significant facts relative to the industrial development of Virginia.

CHAPTER IV.

THE EXPERIENCE OF VIRGINIA.

SOME DATA AND PHENOMENA OF THE VIRGINIA EXPERIMENTS IN POLITICAL ECONOMY.

In the shipping-lists and other records of the first settlement of Virginia, a large proportion of the colonists are carefully designated "gentlemen." The circumstance, that the clergyman and surgeon-general have the honor to be mentioned in this company, but the untitled physician and surgeon are reckoned among the common people, will indicate pretty clearly the meaning of the distinction.

In the first ship, there are fifty "gentlemen," with one hairdresser, one tailor, one drummer, one mason, one blacksmith, four carpenters, and but eight professed laborers.

Speaking of the immigrants by the first three ships, Captain John Smith, in his autobiography, says there were not two dozen that had ever done a real day's work in their lives, before they left England. Of these, eight were Dutchmen and Poles. The rest of the nominal laborers had previously been gentlemen's lackeys and house-servants, or were bankrupt tradesmen and desperate loafers. "Ten good workmen would have done more substantial work than ten (of the best of them) in a week."

To keep them all from perishing, Smith was obliged to drive them to work almost at the sword's point; and when he had the whole responsibility of government to occupy his mind, and its various duties of superintendence to take up his time, he himself did more hard and irksome manual labor, with his own hands, than any other man in the colony.

Smith, of course, was unpopular, was conspired against, and denounced as a shrewd, ambitious, self-seeking demagogue. His enemies never dared try to tar and feather him; but they finally obtained his dismissal from the governorship. No sooner, however, did he leave the miserable rabble of snobs and flunkies to take care of themselves, than their absolute helplessness was made manifest. Presently they were reduced to such extremity as is described in the following passage from the "Observations of William Symmons, Doctor of Divinitie."

" —So great was our Famine, that a Saluage we slew, and buried, the poorer Sort tooke him up againe and eat him and so did diuers others one another, boyled and stewed with Roots and Herbs ! And one amongst the rest did kill his Wife, powdered her, and had eaten part of her before it was knowne, for which he was executed as he well deserued ; now whether she was better roasted, boyled or carbonado'd, I know not, but of such a Dish as powdered Wife I neuer heard of. This was that Time which still to this Day we call the staruing Time ; it were too vile to say and scarce to be belieued, what we endured : but the Occasion was our owne, for want of Prouidence, Industrie, and Gouernment, and not the barrennesse and defects of the Country, as is generally supposed."

At length, in a fit of desperation, the surviving adventurers packed what provisions their recklessness had not yet destroyed, in boats, abandoned their enterprise, and actually embarked with the intention of coasting to the northward until they should fall in with the honest laboring fishermen on the banks of Newfoundland, of whom they could ask charity. Before they got out of the river, however, they were met by Sir Thomas Dale, just arriving from England, with a Governor's commission. He obliged them to return, and, after a short experience of their laziness and imprudence, proclaimed martial law, ordered them all, gentle and simple, to work in gangs under overseers, and threatened to shoot the first man who refused to labor, or was disobedient.* Yet but six hours' work was all that it was deemed prudent or necessary to require. Smith says that one day's labor of each man was amply sufficient to provide him with food for a week; but most of the Colonists would actually starve rather than do this much.

William Box writes home an account of the dreadful amount of hard work that it is necessary to have done, but is careful to add—

"Neuertheleſs it must not be conceiued that this Buſineſs of planting a Colony excludes Gentlemen whose Breeding never knew what a Day's Labor was, for though they can not dig, use the Spade or practise the Ax, there is abundant Occasion for such to imploy the force of Knowledge, the Excuse of Counsel, the Operation and Power of their best Breeding and Qualities."

Smith, however, wrote to the Treasurer in London—

"When you send again I entreat you send rather but Thirty Carpenters, Husbandmen, Gardeners, Fishermen, Blacksmiths, Masons, and Diggers Up of Trees' Roots, well prouided, than a Thousand of such as we have, for except we be able to both lodge and feed them, the most will consume for want of Neceſsaries before they can be made good for any thing."

---

* One reads, not without admiration of the candor of the writer, the following observation of Mr. Howison: "If it be admitted that the Southern States of the American Union have acted wisely in enacting, for the slaves unhappily existing within their borders, laws different from those applied to the whites, then we presume that none who approve this distinction can object to the principle upon which the martial law of Sir Thomas Dale was introduced."—Dale found it necessary to apply to the Cavaliers the same motive to labor which their descendants now consider only requisite for the African race. Is it blood or education that is the essential evil?

He says elsewhere—

"They desired but to pack over so many as they could, saying Necefsity would make them get Victuals for themselves, as for good laborers they were more usefull here in England ; but they found it otherwayes, the Charge was all one to send a Workman as a Roarer, whose Clamors to appease we had much adoe to get Fish and Corne to maintaine them from one Supply till another came, with more Loyterers without Victuals still, to make us worse and worse : for the most of them would rather starve than worke."

The Colony still languishing, though things much improved under Sir Thomas Dale, in 1618 the company petitioned the Crown to make them a present of "vagabonds and condemned men," to be sent out as slaves ; and the King, thankful, probably, to get rid of the burden of taking care of these men, who had been too lazy heretofore to take care of themselves in any other way than by pilfering and knavery, was graciously pleased to grant their request.   The following year a hundred head of this valuable stock was driven out of Bridewell and other London knave-pens, on board ship, and exported to Virginia.

The next year, twenty head of black men, direct from Africa, were landed from a Dutch ship, in James River, and were immediately bought by the gentlemen of the Colony.

These were the first negro slaves in the country, at present included in the United States.   The same year the first cheerful labor by the voluntary immigrants to New England, by the May-Flower, was applied to the sterile soil of Massachusetts Bay.

Notwithstanding the gentlemen of Virginia were thus relieved from the necessity of personal labor, the Colony continued to demand from England such large supplies of provisions, and other stores, which it seemed well fitted to produce within itself, that the King ordered a commission to ascertain what was the secret of its remarkable adversity and continued helplessness and poverty.

An examination of the chartered Companies' books showed that more than one hundred and fifty thousand dollars had been then already sunk in the endeavor to establish and sustain the Colony.

Smith was examined at length.* Being asked what charge he thought, at the time he left, would have defrayed the necessary expenses of establishing the Colony on a safe footing, he answered, that twenty thousand pounds, if it could have been expended in *wages to good laborers and mechanics*, would have been amply sufficient, and added that one hundred *good hired hands* would have been worth more then a thousand of such as had been sent out, and that though Lord Delaware, Sir Thomas Dale, and Sir Thomas Gates, who had been Governors in Virginia since he was there, had been previously persuaded otherwise, they had now come to be of his mind about it.

In reply to the inquiry, what he thought were the defects of the government, he said it was generally complained that the supplies intended for the benefit of the Colony at large, were appropriated by a few individuals to their private advantage, and that even *the laborers sent out to work for the Company were sold to the highest bidders* among the private adventurers. God forbid, he continued, that those who transport these servants thither, and provide them with necessaries, should not be repaid, or that

* Smith had once been a slave himself, and had been driven to agricultural labor by his Tartar master, exactly as the African slaves now are in America. He knew very well, therefore, the different value of a slave, obliged to work for another's benefit, and a free man, working for himself. It is a curious thing, also, that finally he killed his owner, and fled to the North. See his Life, by himself.

masters should not there have the same privileges over their servants that they had in England; but it was an odious thing, and a source of corresponding evil, that when the cost of their shipment was not more than eight, or at the most, ten pounds each, they should be sold, as they were, to the planters, from the ships, at forty, fifty, and threescore pounds, and this *without any stipulation as to how they should be treated or maintained.* He would have these merchants made such merchandise of themselves, rather than suffer such a bad trade to continue longer, for it was enough to bring a well-settled commonwealth to misery, much more such a one as Virginia.

It was not discontinued until the revolution of 1776.

According to a letter of John Rolfe's, in 1619, there had been many complaints that the Governors, Captains and officers bought and sold men and boys, or set them over, from one to another, for a yearly rent; also that tenants and servants were frequently misused, and covenants were not kept with them, and the Council in England, in order to amend these abuses, ordered that a hundred men should be provided at the Company's charge, to serve and attend the Governor; fifty, the Deputy Governor; fifty, the Treasurer, and smaller numbers for the other officers, and likewise to each officer a competency sufficient to enable him to live well in his office, without resorting to those scandalous means. These servants they were required to deliver up in good order to their successors; but complaint is afterwards made that they generally failed to do so, and that many of them were sold to the planters, and the proceeds pocketed by the chivalrous cavaliers.

Being next asked how he would remedy the evils under which the Colony suffered, Smith recommended, first, that the officers should be held to a more strict accountability for the funds placed in their hands; second, that less should be expended from the common stock in maintaining the officers' and deputies' servants, and thirdly, that sufficient workmen, and means to maintain them, should be provided, and that the practice of sending out delinquents who could not be ruled by the laws of England should be stopped forthwith. To improve a commonwealth with debauched people, he maintained, was out of the question; no wise man would choose to seek his fortune in such company. There was more ado, he repeated, in conclusion, about the administration of their paltry government, than was necessary for that of the kingdoms of Ireland and Scotland; *the number of officers in Virginia, with their attendants, was greater than that of all the workers.*

The report of the investigating commission was never made public, but it resulted in an abrogation of the charter of the Company, and a bar upon their property, if not a formal confiscation of it, which has never been defended on any other grounds than such as are held to justify the forcible suppression of a public nuisance. The chief cause of the failure of the Colony had evidently been the indolence and imbecility of the people; nevertheless, the practice of sending out malefactors was not discontinued, nor were any pains taken to encourage the emigration of industrious poor men, eager to improve their circumstances.*

The king, however, had the sense to make the *gentlemen* of the Colony dependent neither on wages, nor partnership in profits,

---

* In 1614, shortly after Lord Delaware's return from Virginia, being in the House of Commons on the reception of a petition from Virginia, he made the capital observation: " All Virginia requires is but *a few honest laborers, burdened with children.*"

but wholly on their own individual good management. Patents of land, to any extent, were given to all applicants, except nonconformists, on the payment of a quit-rent to the crown, of two shillings an acre. This led to a large immigration of speculators, who immediately commenced planting tobacco, with all the laborers, of any sort, that they could command.

Four years later, Smith says, the Colony has increased wonderfully beyond expectation, and that tobacco is raised in such excessive quantities, that the market is already quite overstocked with it. He looks for a good effect to follow— that the small profit of raising tobacco "will cause the people to come together to work upon soap-ashes, iron, rape-oil, madder, pitch and tar, flax and hemp." We shall see that even he had not sufficiently appreciated the irreparable mischief which the degradation of labor must entail upon a community.

The more the people of the Colony increase in numbers, the more distinctly do they continue to be classed under the two grand divisions—gentlemen and laborers. Under the head of gentlemen are to be included the colonial officers, the clergy, and the large land-proprietors, sometimes still styled adventurers (a term equivalent to speculators,) but generally called planters. Lawyers and physicians are seldom mentioned. The laborers are sub-divided, under the three heads of heathen slaves, convict slaves or servants, and bond-servants: no doubt there were some freemen laboring for wages also, and a few mechanics and others, living by job-work, but there is never any mention of such.

CONVICT CHRISTIAN SLAVES.

Christian slaves, or servants, were criminals and state-prisoners, who were often given as property, by the English kings, to those they wished to reward among their courtiers and favorite officers, and by them sold to the colonists. The majority of them were not resolute ruffians, but idle and dissolute fellows, vagrants, and pickpockets. I have found no clear indication of their number, but, even before the confiscation of the Company's charter, it had been so great, and had occasioned Virginia so bad a reputation, that Smith wrote: "Some did choose to be hanged ere they would go thither, *and were*."

Shortly before the Revolution, the usual annual importation of felons into the adjoining smaller province of Maryland was three hundred and fifty in number; that to Virginia was probably larger.*

"The Fortunes and Misfortunes of the celebrated Moll Flanders, who was born in Newgate," a novel, by De Foe, written in 1683, first published in London, 1722, gives much evidence of the notorious character of the Virginia emigration, some of which I subjoin, in extracts.

" She often told me how the greateſt part of the Inhabitants of that Colony came thither in very indifferent Circumſtances from England; that, generally ſpeaking, they were of two Sorts ; either, firſt, ſuch as were brought over by Maſters of Ships, to be ſold as Servants; or, ſecond, ſuch as are tranſported, after having been found guilty of Crimes puniſhable with Death."

—" Depend upon it," ſays ſhe, " there are more Thieves and Rogues made by that one Priſon of Newgate, than by all the Clubs and Societies of Villains in the Nation. ' 'Tis that curſed Place,' ſays my Mother, ' that half peoples this Colony,' (Virginia).

" ' Hence, Child,' ſays ſhe, ' many a Newgate-Bird becomes a great Man, and we have,' continued ſhe, ' ſeveral Juſtices of the Peace, Officers of the trained Bands, and Magiſtrates of the Towns they live in, that have been burned in the Hand.' "

—" That he had ſome intimation, that if he would ſubmit to tranſport himſelf, he might be admitted to it without a Trial, but that he could not think of it with any Temper, and thought he could much eaſier ſubmit to be hanged."

* Grahame.

Transportation to Virginia was the choice, as appears by the context, and thus Smith's amusing assertion is confirmed.

"Some of them [convict paſsengers to Virginia] had neither Shirt nor Shift, Linen or Woolen, but what was on their Backs."

—"The Mortification of being brought on board, like a Priſoner, piqued him very much, ſince it was firſt told him that he ſhould tranſport himſelf, ſo that he might go as a Gentleman at Liberty. It is true he was not ordered to be ſold when he came there."

—"Ordered to be tranſported (to Virginia) in reſpite from the Gallows,

A VIRGINIA GENTLEMAN.—The Caſe was plain, he was born a Gentleman, and was not only unacquainted, but indolent, and when we did ſettle, would rather go into the Woods with his Gun—which they call, there, Hunting—than attend the natural Buſineſs of the Plantation."

The greater energy and industry of his wife, who had been a prostitute and a convict, only made him content to remain in Virginia.

—"An Engliſh Woman-ſervant and a Negro Man-ſervant, things abſolutely neceſsary for all People that pretended to ſettle in that Country."

It was not criminals alone that were sent into this bondage, but captives of war, of all nations, and State prisoners, victims of the Star Chamber and of the Ecclesiastical Courts; persons suspected of traitorous designs upon the monarchy, and infidels to the Court theology; all were herded together with petty pilferers, convicted murderers, and heathen blackamoors, and driven by overseers to work in the tobacco fields of their cavalier purchasers.

Charles II. ordered a shipment of Quakers to Virginia, where they were sold as slaves, for dissenting from *his* true church. Their non-resistance principles must have added much to their value. The common rascals, though always money's worth, were usually considered extra-hazardous. In 1720,

Beverly says: "as for malefactors condemned to transportation, *though the greedy planter will always buy them*, yet, it is to be feared they will be very injurious to the country, which has always suffered many murthers and robberies."

Medical science had not then been pushed to that profundity of analysis, which now distinguishes it, at the South; but, in the unprofessional records of the times, the distinguishing symptoms may be clearly recognized, of both *drapetomania* and *dysæsthesia*, and it is clear, I think, that these maladies prevailed among this class of laborers, to an exceedingly interesting extent. *Drapetomania* would, indeed, seem, though Professor Cartwright does not mention it, to have then been more prevalent among the whites than the negroes.   Dr. Little, in his History of Richmond, has not failed to notice this singular pathological fact.   He says that, in the earliest colonial newspapers, "Runaway servants are advertised; *generally white men*, convicts sold for their crimes; the nation, as well as the description of the person is given, and sometimes the manner of carrying himself, when in liquor.   *We find Englishmen, Irish, Welsh, and Scotch, all in print, as runaway convict slaves.*"

Owing, probably, to the neglect of sufficient quarantine precautions, *Dysæthesia Ethiopica* must have been introduced by the African traders, at an early period; and its contagion was not confined to the Ethiopian stock, but, perhaps, from their then more close association in the labors of the plantation, it too frequently, also, attacked the white slaves.   A case is mentioned by Beverly, where violent remedies were obliged to be used, to check it.

" The rigorous circumſcription of their Trade, the Perſecution of the Sectaries, and the little Demand for Tobacco, had like to have had very fatal Confequences. For the poor People (chiefly Servants who had ferved out their Bond, probably,) becoming thereby very uneafie, their Murmerings were watch'd and fed, by feveral mutinous and rebellious OLIVERIAN Soldiers, fent thither as Servants. Thefe depending upon the difcontented People of all Sorts, formed a villainous Plot to deftroy their Mafters, and afterwards to fet up for themfelves. This Plot was brought fo near to Perfection, that it was the very Night before the defigned Execution, e'er it was difcover'd; and then it came out by the relenting of one of their Accomplices, whofe name was BIRKENHEAD. This Man was Servant to Mr. SMITH of PURTON, in GLOUCESTER County, near which Place, viz., at POPLAR SPRING, the Mifcreants were to meet the Night following, and put in Execution their horrid Confpiracy." * * "Four of thefe Rogues were hanged; but BIRKENHEAD was gratified with his Freedom, and a Reward of Two Hundred Pounds Sterling. For the Discovery and happy Diffapointment of this Plot, an anniverfary Thankfgiving was appointed on the 13th of September, the Day it was to have been put in Execution. And it is great Pity fome other Days are not commemorated as well as that."

CHRISTIAN BOND-SERVANTS OR REDEMPTIONERS.

The term *servant* was, I believe, always applied, in the provincial days of Virginia, to white men and women, who were bound to service for a limited time, and the term slaves, to those held for life. Well-bred people now designate their slaves, both field hands and house servants, by that title. I presume the fashion of doing so arose after the Revolution, and was due to the same feeling which prevented the word slave from being permitted in the Constitution of the United States.

Poor people of all sorts, in England, were induced, by well-worked puffs of the delightful climate, and abundant, spontaneous productions of Virginia, to indenture themselves as servants for terms of years, for the sake of being transported thither. There was a profession of men, called *Spirits*, who made it their business to cajole weak young men and women, in this way, and then send them to the colony, and sell them to the planters, as servants or laborers. They were in such demand, that they were often disposed of on board ship, to the highest bidders, at profits of thirty or forty pounds to the spirited speculators.

The following advertisement is taken from the *Virginia Gazette*, March 3d, 1768:

JUST arrived, the Neptune, Captain Arbuckle, with one hundred and ten HEALTHY SERVANTS, Men, Women and Boys, among Whom are MANY VALUABLE TRADESMEN, viz.: Tailors, Weavers, Barbers, Blackſmiths, Carpenters and Joiners, Shoemakers, a Stay Maker, Cooper, Cabinet Maker, Bakers, Silverſmiths, a Gold and Silver Refiner, and many others.

The Sale will commence at Leedſtown, on the Rappahannoc, on Wedneſday, the 9th of this inſtant (March). A reaſonable Credit will be allowed on giving approved Security to

THOMAS HODGE.*

These servants stood in the relation of debtors to their masters, bound to discharge the cost of. their immigration "by the entire employment of their powers to the benefit of their creditors."† It was illegal for any man to deal with them, except their masters. Having no property of their own, by the penal laws, they were to be whipped at the rate of one stroke for each sixty cents of the fines imposed in like cases on freemen. Masters were forbidden to whip their servants naked, nor were they given permission to kill them, under any circumstances, but they were allowed by law to *dismember irreclaimable runaways*, if they thought best.‡ Any resistance or offer of violence, on the part of a servant to his master, subjected him to one year's additional servitude, and maid-servants, having illegitimate children, also

* Howison.   † Bancroft.   ‡ Hildreth.

forfeited to their masters one year's additional service; if, however, their master was the father, it was to be paid to the church-wardens. By a subsequent law, any unmarried white woman having a child, was to be fined fifteen pounds, or to be sold for five years; if she was already a servant, the time to commence at the end of the service for which she was bound: the child was to be bound out till thirty years of age.

The white servants, at an early period, were reported to be treated with great cruelty, and to be employed at unusual labors. Beverly denies that it was so in his time (1720). Probably, from the danger, which cruel treatment occasioned, of their revolt, as well as from the check which the reports of it produced upon the importation of servants, laws were passed to prevent cruelty, and to insure that wholesome diet and clothing should be provided for them.

"If a Mafter fhould be fo cruel as to ufe his Servant ill, who is faln fick, or lame in his Service and thereby rendered unfit for Labour, he muft be removed by the Church Wardens out of the Way of fuch Cruelty." "All Servants whatever, have their Complaints heard, without Fee or Reward; but if the Mafter be found faulty, the Charge of the Complaint is caft upon him, otherwife the bufinefs is done ex Officio." Mafters " are always to appear on the firft Complaint of their Servants, otherwife to forfeit the Service of them until they do appear." "All Servants' Complaints are to be received at any Time in Court without Procefs, and fhall not be delayed for want of Form; but the Merits of the fame fhall be immediately inquired into by the Juftices."*

None of these laws applied to negro slaves (or to any born out of Christendom); nor has there been any equally humane legislation in their behalf to this day. Whenever there shall be a sincere and earnest desire on the part of

* Beverly.

the controlling power of any slave State to legislate on Slavery *for the negro's sake*, the Virginia enactments of two centuries ago, with regard to the protection of white bond-servants, will serve as a model.

"An inexperienced examiner," says Mr. Howison, "of the present time, in reading the criminal code of Virginia as to slaves, would declare that it was stained with blood; and in truth it is appalling to note the number and the character of the offenses for which death is denounced against them. But it affords the purest consolation to reflect that these laws seldom operate in practice. The executive is clothed with the merciful power of selling slaves condemned to die, and transporting them beyond the limits of the State. The owner then receives value; but if the slave so transported returns, he is liable to execution, without reprieve, and the owner loses his value." Either these laws are barbarous or the transportation is unjust and unmerciful to those living out of the State. How would Virginia act, if Pennsylvania should pass a law, permitting the governor to set all criminals, deserving death, over the border, with a threat to kill them if they were ever seen within her limits again?

When the time for which these servants were covenanted to labor had expired, they, of course, were entitled to be at liberty. It was not customary to pay them anything as wages; but the law required that they should always be provided with two suits of clothes, ten bushels of corn, and a gun of twenty shillings value, when at length they became self-dependent. They could be made freemen of the province on application to the Governor, and after certain formalities. Chiefly recruited, originally, among the most miserable rabble of London, educated to agricultural labor as the yoke-mates of slaves and criminals, and then suddenly turned adrift with a Brumagem fire-lock and ten bushels of maize, to shift for themselves, their social elevation was not likely to be very rapid. Regard to family descent is a notoriously weak point among the wealthy people of Virginia, even at this day, "Poverty and the want of education on the part of the mass of the freedmen," says Hildreth, "kept them, too often, in a subservient position, and created in the Middle as well as the Southern.Colonies an inferior order of poor whites, a distinction of classes and an inequality almost unknown in republican New England."

HEATHEN OR INFIDEL SLAVES.

It was early enacted that all persons brought into the Colony, who had not been Christians in their own country, and even though they afterwards were converted, should be made and held slaves for life. One of the avowed objects of the Virginia speculation being to convert the native savages, a provision of the royal charter inculcated kindness to the Indians, and forbade their being made slaves. This was afterwards disregarded, and multitudes of them were brought into subjection, and held as slaves for life, on the ground that they were prisoners of war, and rightful subjects of oppression, in the name of Christ.

In 1662, forty-two years after the first importation of negroes, there being already many mulatto children, the paternity of which it would be disagreeable to inquire about, owing to the laws against libertinism, it was enacted, in direct contradiction to the supreme English law, that the children of slaves should follow the condition of the mother, and not ever of the father.

This law, which has been maintained to the present time, of course offers a direct encouragement to the most mischievous licentiousness. In the French, Dutch, Danish, German, Spanish, and Portuguese colonies, the white fathers of colored children have always been accustomed to educate and emancipate them, and endow them with property. In Virginia, and the English colonies generally, the white fathers of mulatto children have always been accustomed to use them in a way that most completely destroys the oft complacently-asserted claim, that the Anglo-Saxon race is possessed of deeper natural affection than the more demonstrative sort of mankind.

In 1669, that the cupidity of planters might not prevent them from permitting the christening of their slaves' children, from a doubt of their right to hold Christians in slavery, it was formally enacted that the Christian offspring of all slaves might be used as property, by the owners of the mothers of it.

Both these laws being, as is evident from repeated decisions of English Courts, "*unconstitutional*," or enacted in defiance of the common and fundamental law, at the time they were passed, no person can be legally defined a slave, in Virginia, except by his heathenism or infidelity, to this day. The law made no account of color, but only of creed, in distinguishing a man entitled to freedom from a man subject to be enslaved. The slavery of negroes, in Virginia, at this time, rests only on custom.*

Laws were afterwards passed, at various times, to discourage the emancipation of slaves by grateful or conscientious owners, and free negro-women were taxed in distinction from white.

---

* In England, Massachusetts, and Connecticut, Slavery ceased by decisions based on the Common Law, not by special legislative acts of abolition.

Slaves were, by special exception, denied trial by jury. When charged with a capital crime, a special commission was appointed to judge them, and, if they were condemned to death, their owners were remunerated for their loss from the public treasury.

In 1692, an act was passed for suppressing "outlying slaves." After setting forth that negroes, mulattoes, and other slaves, oft-times absent themselves from their masters, and lurk in obscure places, killing hogs, and committing other injuries to the planta-tions, it authorizes forces to be raised by the sheriffs, for hunting them, which, if they run away or resist being taken, may kill them with guns, or in "any other way whatsoever." For each slave so destroyed, the owner was entitled to obtain from the public treasury four thousand pounds of tobacco. In 1701, a proclamation was recorded, offering a reward of two thousand pounds of tobacco to whoever shall *kill* a certain runaway-slave Billy.

Planters, by special enactment, were not to be judged guilty of felony if they killed their own slaves.*

In 1687, when there was an insurrection of the slaves, the whole number of them in the colony fell little short of one third the whole number of inhabitants.† In 1724, the importation of Africans amounted to one thousand annually.‡ At the

---

* Cotemporaneously with these laws, it is not surprising to find that all persons who doubt the authority of the Bible, or who question the dogma of the Trinity, of whatever race or nation, are ineligible to office, and are subject to imprison-ment for three years if they express their opinions ; that Quakers are denied admission to the country, and, if they persist in coming, are ordered to be treated as felons; that strict measures are taken to prevent " the infection of Puritanism" from reaching the people, and to secure the formal observance of public worship; that fines, of from one to fifty pounds of tobacco, are laid on non-attendance at church on Sunday, Sunday traveling, profane swearing, "profanely getting drunk," etc.

† Burke.   ‡ Hildreth.

Revolution, Jefferson estimated the number of slaves in the State to be 270,000; that of whites, of all classes, 296,000. The number of the slaves in the Eastern counties was so great as to occasion continual uneasiness.

QUALITY AND EDUCATION OF THE LABORERS.

No one can fail to notice that, among all three of these varieties of laborers provided to the land-proprietors of Virginia, there could have been but very few accustomed to steady labor, before their arrival there. None of them, while they remained servants, had any direct interest in the result of their labors; there was nothing, in the nature of the relation between them and their masters, to make them interested in their master's wealth or welfare : between the large majority of them and their masters, there must have been the reverse of confidence and gratitude. They were worked, white and black slaves, criminal and bonded servants, all ganged together, under overseers whose own habits of labor had been formed in Virginia : whether they accomplished much or little, whether they labored skillfully or awkwardly, carefully or carelessly, it was all the same, so they but managed to escape chastisement.

THE PROPRIETORS.

The proprietary planters, who always were the commanding body in the province, received their character from certain emigrating offshoots of aristocratic English families. They endeavored to sustain, so far as it was possible in the wilderness, the manners, morals, politics, forms of religion, and other habits and fashions of the gentry and court of Charles the First. On this account, and because of their brave adherence to the king's party against the people's parliament, they are called Cavaliers. They did not leave their English homes from a desire of greater freedom, politically or morally, for they all belonged to the dominant party and the oppressing church.   Pure agriculture promised but little profit in the province, and the market was always glutted with its sole exporting staple : trade they held in contempt.   Their chief motive in coming to America seems to have been the hope to obtain the position, assume the airs, and enjoy the consequence in the New World which it was impossible for any but born noblemen and great land lords to possess in the old.   The anxiety of each to be master of his own people, upon his own estate, over which and over whom he could exercise the authority and support an imitation of the habits of a lord, induced them first to plant themselves at unsafe distances from each other, upon large properties of wild land, of no value except speculatively, and thus frequently to endanger the destruction of the colony by the Indians, and always to confine its industry to the bare support of its population and the profitless production of one poor herb.

Even before the seizure of the country by the king, and the general granting of patents to individuals, some of these gentlemen, ambitious to be lords of land, had obtained grants by special arrangement with the charter holders.   One of these, Captain Newport, who brought with him fifty servants and tenants, over whom he exercised a magistrate's authority, built a fortress for the defense of his settlement, and being a man of bravery, good judgment, and benevolent disposition, was an extremely valuable acquisition to the country.   But the others were of different character, and added to the disorder of the Colony.   " Among the rest," says Beverly, " one Captain Mar-tin, having made considerable preparations towards a settlement, obtained a suitable grant of land, and was made of the council there. But he, grasping still at more, *hanker'd after dominion*, as well as possession, and caused so many differences, that at last he put all things in distraction," etc.

In a letter of John Rolfe to the king, 1617, he says of the Virginia gentlemen : " All would be Keisars (kings), none inferior to the others."

Beverly again (writing about eighty years after the country was thrown open to private adventurers, and having still the advantage of personal intercourse with the gentry who were thus attracted to the country, himself a Virginian), speaks thus of the effect of the measure :

" This Liberty of taking up Land, and the ambition every Man had of being Lord of a vast, tho' unimprov'd Territory, * * * * has made the country fall into such an unhappy Settlement and Course of Trade, that to this Day, there is not one place of Cohabitation among them, that may reasonably bear the name of a Town."

THE EARLY TOBACCO CULTURE OF VIRGINIA.

The light, rich mould, resting on the sandy soils of Eastern Virginia, was exactly suited to the cultivation of tobacco, and no better climate for this plant was to be found on the globe. This had just been sufficiently proved, and a suitable method of culture learned experimentally, when the land was offered to individual proprietors by the king. Very little else was to be obtained from the soil which would be of value to send to Europe, without an application to it of a higher degree of art than the slaves, or stupid, careless servants of the proprietors could

readily be forced to use.   Although tobacco had then been introduced into England but a few years, an enormous number of
persons had initiated themselves in the appreciation of its myste-
rious value.   The king, having taken a violent prejudice against
it, though he saw no harm in the distillation of grain, had forbidden that it should be cultivated in England.   Virginia, therefore, had every advantage to supply the demand.

Merchants and the supercargoes of ships, arriving with slaves
from Africa, or manufactured goods, spirits, or other luxuries
from England, very gladly bartered them with the planters for
tobacco, but for nothing else.   Tobacco, therefore, stood for
money, and the passion for raising it, to the exclusion of everything else, became a mania, like the " California fever " of 1849.

The culture being once established, there were many reasons
growing out of the social structure of the colony which, for
more than a century, kept the industry of the Virginians confined to this one staple.   These reasons were chiefly the
difficulty of breaking the slaves, or training the bond-servants
to new methods of labor, the want of enterprise or ingenuity
in the proprietors to contrive other profitable occupations for
them, and the difficulty or expense of distributing the guard
or oversight, without which it was impossible to get any work
done at all, if the laborers were separated, or worked in any
other way than side by side, in gangs, as in the tobacco-fields.
Owing to these causes, the planters kept on raising tobacco
with hardly sufficient intermission to provide themselves with
the grossest animal sustenance, though often, by reason of
the excessive quantity raised, scarcely anything could be got
for it.

Tobacco is not now considered peculiarly and excessively

exhaustive : in a judicious rotation, especially as a preparation for wheat, it is an admirable fallow-crop, and, under a scientific system of agriculture, it is grown with no continued detriment to the soil. But in Virginia it was grown without interruption or alternation, and the fields rapidly deteriorated in fertility. As they did so, the crops grew smaller, in proportion to the labor expended upon them. Yet, from the continual importation of laborers, the total crops of the colony increased annually, and the market value fell proportionately to the better supply. With smaller return for labor, and lower prices, the planters soon found them-selves becoming bankrupts instead of nabobs.

How could they help themselves ? Only by forcing the merchants to pay them higher prices. But how to do that, when every planter had his crop pledged in advance, and was obliged to hurry it off at any price he could get for it, in order to pay for his food, and drink, and clothing, and to keep his head above water, at credit for the following year ?* The crop sup-plied more tobacco than was needed, but no one man would cease to plant it, or lessen his crop for the general good. Then, it was agreed, all men must be made to do so, and the colonial legislature was called upon to make them. Acts were accord-ingly passed, to prevent any planter from cultivating more than a certain number of plants to each hand he employed in labor, and prescribing the number of leaves which might be per-mitted to ripen upon each plant permitted to be grown. An inspection of all tobacco, after it had been prepared for

---

* " The merchants will trust them with tools and necessaries upon the credit of their crop, before it is grown. So they again plant every year a little more than the year before, and so buy everything they want, with the crop that is before them."—MOLL FLANDERS, 1683.

market, was decreed, and the inspectors were bound by oath, after having rejected all of inferior quality, to divide the good into two equal parts, and then to *burn and destroy* one of them. Thus, it was expected the quantity of tobacco offered for sale would be so small, that merchants would be glad to pay better prices for it, and the planters would be relieved of their embarrassment.

Simpler methods were sometimes employed, however. It was once ordered, that all creditors should be satisfied to take forty pounds for every hundred due them from the people of the province, at the time of the passage of the act, and that no man should be legally held to perform above one half of any covenants about freighting tobacco, into which he had previously had the good fortune to enter. It is quite probable that, at this time, higher-law opinions began to prevail among the creditors of the Virginia planters.

Attempts, even, were several times made, to stop the culture of tobacco altogether for a year, by legislative acts, with the intention of forcing the merchants to buy what was on hand, at higher prices, and with the hope that the people, if they were forbidden to spend their labor upon it, would direct it to some other industry. These schemes were always given up when it was found that the adjoining colonies were preparing to take advantage of them, by planting more extensively than usual.

Similar schemes have been proposed in good faith, and deliberately advocated before Southern Conventions, and in Southern newspapers, to remedy a similar evil, with which, in our own day, cotton-planters have afflicted themselves.

WHAT MIGHT HAVE BEEN.

If the fathers of Virginia had had the courage and manliness to enact for every person in their land, whose incompetency to exercise his natural rights should not have been specially, individually, and legally ascertained and declared, an equality of position before the law, and in the control of their government; if they had taken care that all children, of ordinary capacity, should be made by education intellectually competent to exercise their natural rights and perform their natural duties to society and to their posterity; if they had placed a reasonable limit upon the area of land which any one individual might control, to the exclusion of others from cultivating it; and if they had established that neither tobacco nor any other crop might be twice drawn in successive years, from the same soil, it may be thought that they would still have been exceeding the proper limits of governmental action —a point upon which it is natural their descendants should be nervously apprehensive; but, had they done so, there can be no doubt, I think, that the people, who would have occupied the territory of Virginia at this day, would have been in a far happier condition than those who now remain upon it; and I, myself, verily believe that Virginia would now have been even the richest, the best populated, and the happiest commonwealth in America.

But, for our benefit, they made an experiment of another sort of legislation, and, inconsistent as are the laws I have mentioned with our modern "democratic" notions, in one respect, the *laisser faire* principle reigned in their politics, as completely as it has since ever done in Virginia. No governmental interference was ever allowed to prevent the planters from defrauding their posterity of the natural wealth of the land. They were, therefore, able to live sumptuously, but ever discontentedly, as spendthrifts do, and always staggering with debt, though spending, with all their might, their capital stock, their land's fertility.

As their exhausted fields failed to meet the prodigal drafts of their luxury, they only made further clearings in the forest, and "threw out," to use their own phrase, so much of the land as they had ruined. Year after year the process continued; the richer districts were all, at length, gone over; the poorer soils of the slopes began to be attacked; the old-fields, recuperating in the prudent economy of nature, after many years, were again cleared, and, now with some aid of manure, again, for a short time, found capable of producing tobacco.

STYLE OF LIVING.

What this enormous, constant, and ruinous production of tobacco was needed to pay for, we are thus informed.

"The families being altogether in country-seats, they have their graziers, seedsmen, gardiners, brewers, bakers, butchers, and cooks, within themselves. They have plenty and variety of provision for their table; and, as for spicery, and other things that the country don't produce, they have constant supplies of them from *England*. The gentry pretend to have their victuals drest, and served up, as nicely as if they were in *London*. Their small drink is either wine and water, beer, milk and water, or water alone. Their richer sort generally brew their small beer with malt which they have from *England*, though barley grows there very well. Their strong drink is *Madeira* wine, cider, mobby punch, made either of rum from the *Caribbee* islands, or brandy distilled from their apples and peaches, besides *brandy*, wine, and strong beer, which they have constantly from *England*. They have their clothing of all sorts from *England*. The very furs that their hats are made of, perhaps, go first from thence; and most of their hides lie and rot, or are made use of only for covering dry goods in a leaky house. Indeed, some few hides, with much ado, are tanned and made into servants' shoes; but at so careless a rate, that the planters don't care to buy them if they can get others; and sometimes, perhaps, a better manager than ordinary will vouchsafe to make a pair of breeches of a deer-skin. Nay, they are such abominable ill-husbands, that though their country be over-run with wood, yet they have all their wooden ware from *England;* their cabinets, chairs, tables, stools, chests, boxes, cart-wheels, and all other things, even so much as their bowls and birchen brooms, to the eternal reproach of their laziness."—*Beverley,* 1620.

And "Moll Flanders" says, with a detail characteristic of the author of Robinson Crusoe:

"Here we had (by an arrival from England) a supply of all sorts of clothes, as well for my husband as myself; and I took especial care to buy for him all those things that I knew he delighted to have; as two good long wigs, two silver-hilted swords, three or four fine fowling-pieces, a fine saddle, with holsters and pistols, very handsome, with a scarlet cloak. . . . . And all this cargo arrived safe, and in good condition, with three women-servants, lusty wenches, suitable enough for the place and to the work we had for them to do, one of which happened to come double, having been got with child by one of the seamen."

They had also to support the little dignity of their little Court with perhaps—by favor of the King—as much rank as that of a real Knight, from England, at its head; and their little church, with its thorough-bred imported clergy, and its little imitation of the great Church of England's persecution of sectaries. A bishop could not be afforded them, and if a young Virginian wished to preach the Gospel of the Carpenter's Son, he crossed the ocean for a qualifying ceremony.[*]

---

[*] The province was divided into parishes, each of which was required to support a minister, at a salary of 16,000 pounds of tobacco, and handsome perquisites, such as two hundred pounds of tobacco for a marriage, and four hundred pounds for a funeral sermon. The church-wardens were required to collect the

THE WEALTH AND EXTRAVAGANCE OF THE ARISTOCRACY.

The masses of the people continued to gain in nothing, but that animal manliness and hatred of restraint which a life in a wild or thinly-inhabited country always has a strong tendency to encourage. But the planters, paying but a trifle for their labor and monopolizing its profits, and enjoying the advantage of any rise in the value of the land which might result from the constant immigration the country had to sustain, not-withstanding they were always embarrassed with debt, and always complaining of the low prices at which their creditors would have their tobacco, really grew richer and more lordly; and, had there not been so many, all jealous of each other's preforment, they probably would have become nobles indeed. They were, as a body, the nearest approach to the English aristocracy which America has ever possessed, not only in their follies and vices, but in their virtues and excellences. Of their habits, and the way these always continued, even until after the Revolution, to eat away the natural agricultural capital of the country, the following is given, by one of their descendants, in the pages of the *Southern Planter:*

minister's tobacco, and bring it to him in hogsheads, convenient for shipping, "that they might have more time for the Exercises of their Holy Office, and live in Decency becoming their Order." Beverley observes that "the labor of a dozen negroes does but answer this salary, and seldom yields a greater crop of sweet-scented tobacco than is allowed to each of the ministers." Besides their salary, a house and glebe was required to be provided the ministers; and it is mentioned that, sometimes, "stocks of cattle and negroes" were added by donation, for which they were only required to surrender an equal value on leaving the parish. All ministers were required to be ordained in England, and to be endorsed by the Governor, and there were laws to prevent dissenting preachers from entering the province. In 1720, a meeting of the Friends, in Nasemond County, was the only congregation of Dissenters; others had existed, Beverley mentions, but were now extinct; and, "it was observed, *by letting them alone, they decreased daily.*"

"The more wealthy proprietors, having no occupation of industry, spent their time mostly in seeking pleasure. Visits to each other were frequent and protracted. It was rare that any one of this class was without some company, either at home or abroad. Besides such exercise of reciprocal hospitality, every idle or homeless 'gentleman' of the whole country found in every mansion a comfortable sojourning-place, and, at least, the outward show, if not the reality of welcome, so long as he might choose to stay. Of course, visits from such persons were ordinary occurrences—and were sometimes protracted for weeks or months. That this particular neighborhood was not 'eaten out' by this class of genteel and honorable vagrants and spongers, was not because of their deficiency of numbers, or of active use of their facilities, but because they had like privileges in every part of the country. This race, fortunately, is now extinct; but many such individuals are still remembered, who, for many years of their adult life, and some for their whole life, pursued no other business, and had no other means of support, except visiting their friends; of course they counted their friends by hundreds.

"The wealthier proprietors were not only hospitable and kind hosts, but also refined and pleasing companions. Their fathers' wealth had served to give to them the education and manners of good society. With many excellent social and moral qualities, their habits of idleness and pleasure-seeking naturally led to the attendant and consequent vices. Social drinking was often carried to excess; and card-playing was sure to be introduced whenever as many neighbors dined together as served to make up a game of loo. Horse-racing was a favorite amusement of all classes; some of the farmers owned and ran race-horses, and nearly all reared horses of the high blood, and at the high cost required for the turf."

How like this is to the "true Irish gentleman," of ten or twenty years ago. But let it not be forgotten that, when the time of retribution came, the slaves suffered no physical want—the peasant starved.

No man of wealth, or with a moderate estate, thought of attending personally to his farming. Every detail of management was intrusted to the overseers, who were rarely stimulated by even the general superintendence and control of their employers. Overseers' wages were generally paid in a certain share or proportion of the crops they made. Thus, they had a direct interest in drawing from the land and labor as much as possible, during the current year of their engagement; and none whatever in preserving or increasing the productive power of the land for later times. It came to be recognized, as a maxim of agricultural morals, that "it was not *just* for a proprietor to interfere with, and change, his overseer's designed direction of the labors of the farm, inasmuch as any abstraction from immediate product, for the sake of future improvement, operated to lessen the overseer's profits for the present year." This doctrine accorded so well with the disposition of every indolent, careless, and wasteful proprietor, then it is no wonder that it came to be generally received, and conformed to in practice.

A carefully-drawn picture of the social condition and habits of the people of Virginia, at a period not long before the Revolution, is given by a writer for *Putnam's Monthly*, who, from the close topographical knowledge, of some parts of the State, he displays, and other internal evidence, is evidently also a Virginian. I quote what is most pertinent.

—"Newspapers, and literature at large, were a proscribed commodity, thanks to Sir William Berkeley and his successors.* He

---

* Sir William Berkeley had said, being then Governor of Virginia : " I thank God there are no free schools nor printing, and I hope we shall not have them these hundred years." At this time, when Boston contained five printing offices, and as many booksellers' shops, there was not one of either in all the rich and populous Southern colonies of Virginia, Maryland, and Carolina. Progress, since, in this particular, has closely corresponded with that of all other industrial progress in the slave countries. The publication of a book, at Richmond—an event occurring not oftener, on an average, than once a year—is as much a subject of universal congratulation, by all the public press of the South, as the birth of a royal heir is in England. No

[the Virginia gentleman] knew not what was going on in the next county, and the man who had made a journey to the little metropolis of Middle Plantation, or Williamsburg, was listened to, by his neighbors, as a miniature Herodotus. At intervals a vessel arrived from London or the West Indies, which brought, with a new Order in Council, or a fresh installment of negroes, some confused items of foreign news; or, perhaps, some young Virginian, fresh from Oxford or Cambridge, astonished the country gentlemen of his native county, with the last intelligence from the mother-country—the newest Parisian *mode*— or, better still, brought, in his traveling-trunk, the best productions of English or European writers, or the earlier numbers of the *Gentleman's Magazine*, or a file of London papers, which would afford pleasant reading, for the next month, to the neighbors for miles around."

" There were no cities in Virginia, even no towns, at the time of which we speak. The country gentleman had a peculiar and most genuine dislike to centralization in every form. He had an aversion, too, to much government, and gladly encountered the alternative of too little, if he was but left to lord it in peace and quiet over his ' large and well-conditioned household,' [a household, be it remembered, which might be numbered by hundreds]. Here he was supreme lord—a species of feudal baron, living in a sort of noble profusion and ease, which gave room for all his peculiarities and idiosyncrasies to spread themselves at will, and gratified at once his hobby of paramount rule, and his virtue of liberal and indiscriminate hospitality. In vain did Government, whether in London or Williamsburg, fulminate act after

---

book, I presume, ever paid for the cost of its publication, by its Southern circulation alone, unless it was a strongly sectional, or a religious book. There is a constant complaint that the circulation of Northern magazines at the South prevents Southern magazines from being supported; and frequent efforts are made to hinder people from taking them, by accusations of their hostility to Southern interests, or their indifference to Southern prejudices. It is a ridiculous mistake. The old *Southern Literary Messenger* probably sold more at the North, in proportion to its whole circulation, although it never flunkied to the North at all, than any Northern periodical sells at the South, in proportion to its Northern circulation. No Northern magazine would live a month, at least in its present excellence, on its Southern circulation alone; and none, I believe, not prepared expressly for the Southern market, has a tithe of its whole circulation in the Slave States. No Northen editor fears especially to offend the South, as is generally supposed; but many fear that, if they do offend the South, they will be calumniated and injured at the North.

act at this instinct; decreeing, even, that tobacco, the staple of Virginia, should not be shipped, except at certain spots upon the rivers; in vain were towns laid and incorporated. The cities did not appear, the towns were not built up; and these localities remain to this day, with their dilapidated wharves, and old crumbled warehouses —an eloquent memento of the vain attempt to force this stubborn race from what they clung to with the pertinacity of martyrs—their isolated country life.

"But this life was not in another sense isolated. At every court-day, the country was brought together; visits were courteously exchanged between neighbors; and the owner was proud of his fine-blooded horse, his trotting-mares, or his *six well-conditioned grays*, which thunder along with the old family chariot. This vehicle, which has come all the way from London, was, on all occasions of ceremony, of indispensable importance, and, in journeys of any length, it ever came prominently into play: that was no trifle to travel, in state, the twenty or thirty miles a day which it accomplished. The coachman must time his posts by the road-side taverns, or private residences competent to recruit the energies of himself, his animals, and the half-dozen persons, who temporarily existed in this moving mansion. The appearance of the coach was ever greeted, by the artisan or humble farmer, with great respect, but ill-concealed distaste. The pedestrian was covered with a cloud of dust, as it rolled grandly onward; and the humble carter must carefully keep from the middle of the road, otherwise a splintered wheel and a roll in the dirt would warn him to make way the next time for the 'gentry.' Honorable, hospitable, and, at the bottom of their hearts, kind and charitable, they yet nursed a high and overweening sense of their own importance and dignity. Long supremacy among their negroes and indented servants had taught them to expect implicit obedience from all inferiors; and, if any one, so unfortunate as to belong to the commons, and thus to be inferior to them in blood, refinement, or possessions, did not yield to their arrogance, every means was put in requisition to reduce him to his proper level. Such a man was always welcome to the best the 'gentleman Proprietor's' table afforded; he was treated kindly, assisted, if need be; but, with the profuse hospitality lavished on him, all connection between them ended. To do more would be to forget what, in the nature of things, he could never lose sight of—the fact that he was one of the gentry—his guest, a commoner."

That hospitality was ever so general a virtue among the *common people* in Old Virginia, as to entitle them to the reputation they have acquired for it, there is some reason to doubt. "There being no inns in the country, strangers were entertained at the houses of the inhabitants, and were *frequently involved in law-suits by the exorbitant claims of their hosts for indemnification of the expenses of their entertainment.*"* This refers to the latter days of the colony more especially.

INDUSTRIAL CONDITION OF VIRGINIA IN THE HALCYON PAST.

Beverley gives a detailed account of the industrial condition of the Province early in the eighteenth century.

"In extreme fruitfulnefs," he fays, "it is exceeded by no Other." "No Seed is fown there but it thrives, and moft of the Northern Plants are improved by being tranfplanted thither." "And yet there's very little Improvement made among them, feldom Anything us'd in Traffick but Tobacco." "Fruit trees are wonderfully quick of Growth. Yet they are very few that take any Care at all for an Orchard; nay, many that have good Orchards are fo negligent of them, as to let them go to Ruin, and expofe the Trees to be torn and bark'd by Cattle." "A Garden is nowhere fooner form'd than here, and yet they ha'nt many Gardens in the Country fit to bear the Name of Gardens." "All Sorts of Englifh Grain thrive yet, they don't make a Trade of any of them." "The Sheep increafe well, and bear good Fleeces; but they are generally fuffered to be torn off their Backs by Briars and Bufhes, or elfe are left rotting on the Dunghill with their Skins." "The Woods produce great variety of Incense and fweet Gums, Honey and Sugar. Yet there's no ufe made of any of them, either for Profit or Refrefhment." "All Sorts of Naval Stores may be produced there, as Pitch, Tar, Turpentine, Plank, Timber, and all Sorts of Mafts and Yards, befides Sails, Cordage and Iron; and all thefe may be tranfported by an easy Water-carriage."

"Thefe and a thoufand other Advantages that Country produces, which its Inhabitants make no manner of ufe of. They can fee their Naval Stores daily Benefit other People, who fend thither to build Ships. They receive no Benefit nor Refrefhment from the sweet

---

* Grahame's Hist. of N. A.

and precious Things they have growing amongſt them; but make uſe of the Induſtry of England for all ſuch Things.

" What Advantage do they ſee the neighboring Plantations make of their Grain and Proviſions, while they, who can produce them infinitely better, not only neglect the making a Trade thereof, but even a neceſsary Proviſion againſt an accidental Scarcity, contenting themſelves with a Supply of Food from Hand to Mouth; ſo, that if it ſhould pleaſe God to send them an unſeaſonable Year, there would not be found in the Country Proviſions ſufficient to ſupport the People for three Months extraordinary !

" They depend upon the Liberality of Nature, without endeavoring to improve its Gifts by Art or Induſtry. They ſponge upon the Bleſſings of a warm Sun and a fruitful Soil, and almoſt grutch the Pains of gathering in the Bounties of the Earth. I ſhould be aſhamed to publiſh this ſlothful Indolence of my Countrymen, but, that I hope it will ſome time or other rouſe them out of their Lethargy, and excite them to make the moſt of all theſe happy Advantages which Nature has given them; and if it does this, I am ſure they will have the Goodneſs to forgive me."—Beverley, p. 284.

We Americans have now a habit of congratulating each other on the material prosperity and independence of our country, and of glorifying our wise government and our "free institutions," as the cause of it. But we should not forget that we have lately, by the dignified and deliberate act of the Republic's servants, given free range, over millions of fertile acres, to essentially the same institutions of society which produced, and which still, ſpite of every advantageous surrounding, are still maintaining, in Virginia, that paralysis of enterprise and imbecility of industry, thus pathetically deplored a hundred and fifty years ago.

When Beverley speaks of the adjoining colonies, as taking the trade of Virginia, he can refer only to the more democratic and free-laboring Northern colonies. In the Carolinas, an exactly similar state of things existed to that in Virginia.

So early as 1676, it is recorded that "New England traders,

penetrating into the interior of the province of Albemarle, and bringing their goods to every man's door, had obtained a monopoly of the produce of the province. The proprietors in England endeavored, in vain, to substitute a direct intercourse with Britain, for this disadvantageous commerce."*

In 1677, the chief magistrate of this province was deposed and imprisoned by an insurrection of the people, consequent upon an attempt to interrupt the New England trade. The Assembly having once complained that the English proprietors did not give sufficient encouragement to immigration, and that the country consequently suffered from a deficiency of tradesmen and mechanics, they (the English proprietors) made answer that the inconvenience complained of was promoted by the complainants—

" By the lazy rapacity with which each desired to surround himself with a large expanse of property, over which he could exercise no other act of ownership than that of excluding the occupants by whom it might be most advantageously culti-vated."

The Assembly, however, followed its own counsel, and decreed that none should be sued for debt, within the limits of its juris-diction, for five years after his arrival; that no inhabitant should accept a power of attorney to collect debts contracted abroad, etc.   This had the desired effect of attracting immigration; but not of a very respectable or valuable character.   Virginia and Maryland both had laws of similar import.

That Beverley did not exaggerate the danger of famine, at a time when the annual export of tobacco, to pay for clothing, slaves, and other imported necessities and luxuries, was between

* Grahame's Hist. of North America, p. 120.

thirty and forty millions of pounds annually,* is evident from the legislative precautions taken to prevent it. The prices of every other product except corn were, at one time, fixed by law, with the avowed purpose of inducing farmers to plant it; three officers were appointed in every county, for the express purpose of obliging every settler to plant and tend sufficient corn-ground to insure an adequate supply to maintain his own family! Public granaries were established, to which every planter was ordered to contribute one bushel of corn, annually, to be disposed of as the Commonwealth should require. I am told, and the Southern agricultural journals confirm it, that such laws are needed now, in some parts of the cotton States, and would be advocated, but for the shame of publishing to the North the irreformable improvidence of the people.

Some of my readers may require yet to have it explained how it was that land monopoly, slavery, and servile or degraded and ignorant labor led to that state of things which Beverley bewailed, and which, indeed, to this day constitutes, strangely enough, both the glory and the shame, which is the basis alike of the weak vanity and the impotent anger of the sons of the Virginia cavaliers.

Manufactories and mechanic arts of all sorts thrive best in towns or dense communities, because different branches assist each other, not only morally, by stimulating mental activity, but materially. The carriage-maker calls upon the blacksmith, the currier, and the worker in leather; the blacksmith may, at any time, be glad of the services of the currier, the cobbler, or the wheel-wright, to mend his bellows. The spinners and weavers need to have near them, masons, machinists, and

* De Bow's Resources, iii., p. 347.

mill-wrights. All need farmers (not planters) to supply
their daily needs. In a country, therefore, where all men
"mind nothing but to be masters of a great estate, and to
plant themselves separately on their several plantations,"
trades and manufactures are not likely to thrive. But,
suppose one of these plantation lords to own a large number
of boys whose labor he desires to appropriate most advantageously to himself. The employment to which they must
be trained cannot be of such a character as to require the
use of much discretion; because there can be no sufficient
motive to induce them to exercise it, which does not involve
personal interest in the object of that employment, and
therefore, a partnership in its possession, or a receipt of
wages in some proportion to skill. In proportion, also,
to the amount of discretion required of a slave, the
reins of authority must be slackened. If he uses his own
skill, he must go his own way. If he goes his own way,
he will go negligently and with all possible indolence,
unless he has some advantage for himself to gain, by care
and dispatch. This he hardly can have, if the result of •his
labor is to inure wholly to the advantage of another. The
selfishness, therefore, of the owner of a slave-boy, will lead
him to undertake to make the boy labor at such simple work
and under such circumstances as will keep him most easily
and certainly under his control.

It is a fact that slave-mechanics, manufacturers' hands, stevedores, servants, and those engaged in almost all employments
superior to that of field-hands, in the Southern States, are,
nearly always, "gratified" with some sort of wages, or perquisites, or stimulants, to skill and industry, in some form; and

are more intelligent, more privileged, and more insubordinate than the general mass. This will be sufficiently apparent from observations I shall hereafter record.

THE REVOLUTION OF 1776.

"The struggle for equality in all the relations of life, for the liberty of man against the dominion of man, is necessarily founded on the consciousness of the importance of the individual.

"Their motto is, All by the People: their practice, Nothing for the People." —*Introduction to a History of the Nineteenth Century.*

GERVINUS.

Ignorance is weakness; and the ignorant man instinctively merges his ambition and his claims of justice with those of an aggregate—makes that aggregate an object of partiality and bigotry, and finds satisfaction for his enthusiasm in the success of those who guide and represent it, though that success in no wise affect his own interest.

The peculiar political aspiration of the people of Virginia, as a whole, was, on this account, less to maintain due consideration for individual rights, than to obtain and preserve communal independence and notoriety.

The wealthy and educated class, however, while they were entirely *en rapport* with the general communal spirit, were also remarkably characterized by personal assumption and dignity. And this, because the smallness of their number, proportionately to the whole people, and their widely-separated residences, gave to each a high local consideration and power, and led to inordinate self-respect.

The unusual and unexpected exactions of the exterior, royal government aroused, therefore, among the influential class of Virginians, a more passionate discontent than elsewhere; while the poor people were more ready, than those of other colonies, perhaps, to encourage a disposition in their leaders to communal independence.

Virginia, therefore, was early and determined, in the expression of her dissatisfaction with the royal impositions which led to the Revolution.

Yet great agitation, much, and rapid, and excited progress of thought, was necessary, before the aristocratic or the yeoman class could come to the point of actual treason, or bring to it the poor, and ignorant, and the superstitiously loyal.

If it was right for them to resist these demands of their king, the conscientious would ask, how should they define what demands it was not right to resist? If their royal master's authority was exercised by right divine, it was wrong for them to resist it at all—nay, even to feel discontent. If it was not by right divine, then by what right? On what right rests any governmental authority? Is there no alternative between despotism and anarchy? What is the basis of civil government?

There could be no hearty, united, and determined resistance, while these questions were left without some logically-satisfactory answer. The people at large could not be called upon, and stirred up to a spirited defense, without knowing, more clearly, what it was that was to be defended—what they were to gain. Stamp-acts and tea-taxes did not really trouble the great majority of Virginians, in the slightest degree, personally, only the people of some property—for the mass were still illiterate vagabonds; but, even among the better sort, no man could trust another, till each knew what all wanted, and to what limit all were prepared to stand out.

The best men in the Province—those in whose goodness,

wisdom, and bravery, their neighbors had most confidence—were, therefore, appointed to make a declaration of the principles and purposes by and for which the government of Virginia should thereafter be guided, and which should constitute a platform broad enough for all to stand upon, without jealousies and distrusts, and so just and reasonable as to command the respect and fealty of every individual, and of all classes.

The instrument of this declaration is still preserved, as a curious historical relic, in Virginia, and is interesting, if, for nothing else, as an evidence to what lengths men will go, when they have set their hearts upon an object and find it desperate business to accomplish it. For it announces principles which the intelligent classes in Virginia, always before and generally since, have held to be absurd, preposterous, and dangerous.

For instance, it asserts the equality of men, in freedom and independence—a "self-evident absurdity," as they now say; for a strong and wise man can, at any time, prevent or destroy the freedom and independence of a weak man, of which, proof is not wanting. That every man has certain "inherent rights" —one of which is named liberty; another absurdity, for the same reason. Another, the right of labor ("of obtaining property")—not only absurd, but very horrible : another, the right of enjoying the fruits of his labor, to the fullest degree compatible with security to all other men to equally enjoy the results of their labor—a dangerous and impracticable doctrine : another, the right of private judgment, in matters of religion and morality, so far as it can be exercised compatibly with the preservation to all of this and all other rights; of which, very little is now said.

On this original platform, reasonable or not reasonable—and

I do not want any one to doubt a moment that I consider it reasonable, and suppose that I see a meaning quite reconcilable with the facts considered to render it absurd, only I wish to be respectful to those who cannot—on this platform, they impliedly promised, if they should succeed in maintaining their independence of the power then deemed wickedly oppressive, to reorganize society; and they called upon all the people of Virginia, of all classes, of all degrees of muscular strength and intellectual capacity and acquirements, poor and rich, cavalier and base-blooded, to fraternize, and rise, and fight.

And they did it, fraternizing at the same time with others making similar professions, and having similar purposes; and they all fought together, and succeeded, all equally, in obtaining —not the security of these so-called natural rights, but—communal independence of their old king.

By the time they came to the work of forming the instruments of order for their to-be-reorganized society, there had evidently occurred a violent reaction from the fervency and highly stimulated judgment under which the Bill of Rights had been drawn up, among the influential people of Virginia—for the constitution of the new State was widely inconsistent with the principles of liberty, equality, and fraternity, previously distinctly proclaimed, and promised to be used as its supports and barriers.

The people, imposed upon and deprived of their acknowledged rights, be it observed, were, by chance, the weakest, most ignorant, and poorest—consequently, the least likely to regard the imposition, and the least able to resist it.

There were a few men, among those whose natural rights were respected, who did not like this, and who strongly protested against it.   Among them, Thomas Jefferson was foremost.

To the new Constitution of Virginia he strongly objected, in several particulars, not only on the score of consistency, but of justice and good judgment. For instance, that the majority of the tax-paying and fighting men of the State were unrepresented in its government; and, again, that things had been so managed that, even among those who were permitted to vote, there were nineteen thousand in the rich plantation-counties of the east, who could elect more members of the legislature than thirty thousand in the more free counties of the west; accordingly, the State would be virtually ruled, not by the people through their elected representatives, but by an oligarchy of slave-holders.*

A large majority of the people of the country were Dissenters from the Established Church of the English Colony ; yet, a proposal to realize the declared right of entire religious freedom was met by an opposition which occasioned, as Jefferson afterwards declared, the most severe political struggle in which he was ever engaged. The most that could be obtained at that time, after all, was an abrogation of the laws which denounced punishment for maintaining unorthodox opinions, and for not attending the Episcopal church; and acts exempting Dissenters from contributing to the support of the Episcopal clergy, and permitting them to build houses of worship of their own. It was not till several years later that any one else than the Episcopal clergymen were permitted to solemnize or legalize marriages, except by the purchase of a special license. The Episcopal church still continued to be the " Established Church," and other religious societies were merely " tolerated."†

* See Jefferson's Notes on Virginia, pages 172, 173.   † Howison, ii. 192.

THE ARISTOCRACY UNDERMINED.

Next to religious freedom, the most important change demanded by the avowed principles of the Revolution, was an alteration of the laws with regard to the descent of property. The laws of primogeniture and descent in tail, were felt to be unnatural, discouraging to industry, and, by their effect in aggravating the evils to society of the excessive possession and control of land, opposed to the declared right of all to the "means of obtaining wealth."

Mr. Howison thus clearly and truly describes these laws and their influence:

"Nothing can convey a more vivid idea of the strong aristocratic feeling pervading Virginia, than her course as to this scheme. In England, the courts had set their faces against entails, and permitted them to be *docked* by a fine and recovery; but the law-makers of the Old Dominion held all such innovations in high contempt, and, by a statute enacted in 1705, forbade their use. To complete their work in 1727, they enacted that slaves might be attached to lands, and might be entailed with them, subject to all the incidents proper to the system. Over the whole Eastern region, fine lands were held by families, who guarded their privileges with more than English jealousy.

"An aristocracy neither of talent, nor of learning, nor of moral worth, but of landed and slave interest, was (thus) fostered. The members of the Council of State were always chosen from this class; and in many respects they were regarded as the peerage of the land.

"Where lands could neither be sold nor mortgaged, debts must often have been contracted which were never paid; yet, the tenants in tail, lived in luxurious ease, to which others were strangers. The rich people of Virginia were then richer than at present, and the poor were poorer. There was no prospect for that equal distribution of property which is the legitimate reward of industry. Coaches, drawn by four horses, rolled from the doors of the aristocracy; and plate of gold and silver, in the utmost profusion, glittered on their boards, while the poor artisan and laborer worked for the necessaries of life, without any hope of ever gaining any portion of the property guarded by entail."

A bill, proposed by Jefferson, providing that thereafter all estates in tail should be converted into fee simple, so that the owner might sell, devise, mortgage, or otherwise dispose of them as he thought proper, was at length carried, after another very warm and protracted struggle.

Next, the law of primogeniture was attacked; a strong defense was made for it by the aristocratic party; and when they found it must be repealed, they urged, "in the spirit of compromise," that the Jewish rule of inheritance should be substituted: this gives the eldest son a double portion. Mr. Jefferson answered the proposal, with the remark, that unless the eldest son required a double portion of food, or would do double the work of any other, there was no justice in giving him double the property.

The law was repealed. Mr. Featherstonaugh, an English Tory who visited the United States in 1836, dates from this repeal all the adversity under which Virginia has since suffered. The seeds of much of the adversity which he witnessed were produced by the law: cutting it away did not destroy at once their vitality; but it removed a pernicious shade from labor, and, but for this timely relief, industry would not, I am convinced, be now known to have ever existed at all in Eastern Virginia, except by the evidence of the desert it had been forced to create.

The argument against all these changes was, not that they were not demanded by justice and sound principles of government, but, that it was not safe to move so rapidly. They were old institutions under which Virginia had existed for a century or more. They were unjust, it might, in some sense, be admitted, and their effects, it could not be denied, were sometimes rather unhappy; but destroy them, replace them with laws more abstractly just, and—who knew that there would not follow worse consequences? It was fanatical to push forward the experiment so rapidly. Besides, people had been born into the world under these laws, and had taken duties and responsibilities upon themselves, in the expectation that they would be sustained. They had a right to demand, it was urged, therefore, that they should be sustained: but now, when the right principles of law have been enunciated, leave it for posterity to enact them. It will then be every man's own fault, if he is not prepared for them.

Jefferson well understood the danger of this course. He urged that justice should be done, and right should be maintained then and there, and at all hazards. And with the prophetic mind of true statesmanship, such as we have had no approach to since, he uttered in 1787 this remarkable warning and prediction: men who pretend to be his disciples, should not pass it lightly—

" *The spirit of the times may alter—will alter.   Our rulers will become corrupt, our people careless.* It can never be too often repeated, that the time for fixing every essential right on a legal basis is while our rulers are honest, and ourselves united. From the conclusion of this war, we shall be going down hill. It will not then be necessary to resort every moment to the people for support. They will be forgotten, therefore, and their rights disregarded. *They will forget themselves, but in the sole faculty of making money,* and will never think of omitting to effect a due respect for their rights. The shackles, therefore, which shall not be knocked off at the conclusion of this war, will remain on us long— *will be made heavier and heavier, till our rights shall revive,* or expire in a convulsion."[*]

* Jefferson's Notes on Virginia, 239.

Impelled by these convictions, while the country was yet excited with all the turmoil and terror of invasion and war, while a price was yet set upon his head, as there last year was on the heads of men who were laboring to have his principles of government carried out in our young states, Mr. Jefferson, besides the radical improvements already noted, earnestly and confidently desired to have permanent enactments introduced into the laws for *the emancipation of the slaves*.*

EDUCATION AND EMANCIPATION OF THE SLAVE PEOPLE REFUSED.

The scheme of emancipation which Jefferson advocated would have provided that all negroes born after it had passed should be entitled to freedom; that they should remain with their parents until of a certain age, " then be brought up, at the public expense, to tillage, arts, or sciences, according to their geniuses, till the females should be eighteen, the males twenty-one years of age, when they should be colonized to such place as the circumstances of the time should render most proper, sending them out with implements of household and the handicraft arts, etc., etc.; that they should then be declared to be a free and independent people; that protection and assistance should be afforded them until they had acquired strength; and that, at the same time, an equal number of white people, *from other parts of the world, should be sent for, and induced, by proper encouragements, to migrate into Virginia*."† He apologizes at length for proposing to expatriate the negroes, on the ground of the impracticability of their amalgamation or comfortable association with the whites.

* Jefferson's Notes on Virginia, 203.   † Ib., 204.

To the great grief of its author, this project was not carried: he never afterwards ceased to bewail the neglect, or to deplore the consequences. But it is the grand characteristic of Jefferson, that he is not merely a philanthropist, a philosopher, and a patriot; he is also a strong practical statesman: he knows when to strike and when to hold. With the boldness, generosity, and clear moral vision, reached by the planters in the first struggle for their own liberty, the day for justice and liberality to those beneath them was past. Virginia, during his life-time, was in no condition to be asked to make sacrifices of property; and, after the seven years' exhausting war, to secure temporary peace and harmony, much was properly postponed; but he never ceased to hope that the spirit of the age, " the advancement of the human mind," as the country grew stronger and richer, would yet be able to grapple with the difficulty, and to solve it in accordance with republican principles. Alas! the human mind advances slowly when it has to drag slavery.

The following extracts are taken from the correspondence of Jefferson, published by Congress, 1854:

" TO M. WARVILLE.

" PARIS, February 12, 1788.

" SIR :—I am very sensible of the honor you propose to me of becoming a member of the society for the abolition of the Slave Trade. You know that nobody wishes more ardently to see an abolition, not only of the trade, but of the *condition* of Slavery."

———

" TO BENJAMIN BANNEKER.

" PHILADELPHIA, August 30, 1791.

" SIR :—I thank you sincerely for your letter of the 19th instant, and for the Almanac it contained. Nobody wishes more than I do to see such proofs as you exhibit, that nature has given to our black brethren talents equal to those of the other colors of men, and that appearance of a want of them is owing mainly to the degraded condition of their existence, both in Africa and America. I can add, with truth, that nobody wishes more ardently to see a good system commenced for raising the condition both of their body and mind to what it ought to be, as fast as the imbecility of their present existence and other circumstances, which cannot be neglected, will permit."

"TO ST. GEORGE TUCKER.

"MONTICELLO, August 28, 1797.

* * * "As to the mode of Emancipation, I am satisfied that must be a matter of compromise between the *passions and prejudices* and the *real* difficulties, which will each have their weight in that operation. But if something is not done, and soon done, we shall be the murderers of our own children. The sooner we put *some* plan under way, the greater hope there is that it *may* be permitted to proceed peaceably to its ultimate effect."

"TO MR. DARROW.

" MONTICELLO, May 1, 1815.

* * * " Some progress is sensibly made in it, yet not so much as I hoped and expected. But it will yield in time to temperate and steady pursuit, to the enlargement of the human mind, and its advancement in science. We are not in a world ungoverned by the laws and the power of a superior agent. Our efforts are in His hand, and directed by Him, and He will give them their effect in His own time. Where the disease is most deeply seated, there it will be slowest in eradication. In the Northern States, it was merely superficial and easily corrected ; in the Southern, it is incorporated with the whole system, and requires time, patience, and perseverance in the curative process. That it may finally be effected and its progress hastened, will be the last and fondest prayer of   THOMAS JEFFERSON."

I extract the following passages from a letter to Edward Coles, first published in the *National Intelligencer*, dated

"MONTICELLO, August 25, 1814.
" DEAR SIR :—Your favor of July 31 was duly received, and was read

with peculiar pleasure. The sentiments, breathed through the whole, do honor to both the head and heart of the writer. Mine on the subject of the Slavery of negroes have long since been in the possession of the public, and time has only served to give them stronger root.

" The love of justice and the love of country plead equally the cause of these people, and it is a mortal reproach to us that they should have pleaded it so long in vain, and should have produced not a single effort —nay, I fear, not much serious willingness—to relieve them and our-selves from our present condition of moral and political reprobation. From those of the former generation who were in the fullness of age when I came into public life—which was while our controversy with England was on paper only—I soon saw that nothing was to be hoped. Nursed and educated in the daily habit of seeing the degraded condition, both bodily and mental, of those unfortunate beings, not reflecting that that degradation was very much the work of themselves and their fathers, few minds had yet doubted but that they were as legitimate subjects of property as their horses or cattle. The quiet and mono-tonous course of colonial life had been disturbed by no alarm and little reflection on the value of liberty; and when alarm was taken at an enterprise on their own, it was not easy to carry them the whole length of the principles which they invoked for themselves. In the first or second session of the Legislature after I became a member, I drew to this subject the attention of Col. Bland, one of the oldest, ablest, and most respected members, and he undertook to move for certain moderate extensions of the protection of the laws to these people. I seconded his motion, and, as a younger member, was more spared in the debate; but he was denounced as an enemy to his country, and was treated with the greatest indecorum.

" From an early stage of our Revolution, other and more distant duties were assigned me, so that from that time till my return from Europe in 1789, and, I may say, till I returned to reside at home in 1809, I had little opportunity of knowing the progress of public sentiment here on this subject. I had always hoped that the younger generation, receiving their early impressions after the flame of liberty had been kindled in every breast, and had become, as it were, the vital spirit of every American, that the generous temperament of youth, analogous to the motion of their blood, and above the suggestions of avarice, would have sympathized with oppression wherever found, and proved their love of liberty beyond their own share of it. But my intercourse with them since my return has not been sufficient to ascertain that they had made toward this point the progress I had hoped. Your solitary but welcome voice is the first which has brought this sound to my ear, and I have considered the general silence which prevails on this subject as indicating an apathy unfavorable to our hopes. Yet the hour of emancipation is advancing in the march of time. It will come; and, whether brought on by the generous energy of our own minds, or by the bloody process of St. Domingo, excited and conducted by the power of our present enemy, if once stationed permanently within our country, offering asylum and arms to the oppressed, is a leaf of our own history, and not yet turned over."

Although the planters were not then willing to surrender the property they had in slaves, and desired to postpone emancipation until they could better afford to do so, it was universally known, felt, and acknowledged, that Slavery had been, and still continued to be, a great injury to the country, pernicious to morals, destructive to industry, and a dead weight upon enterprise. In the Convention of 1774, it was unanimously resolved, that:

"The abolition of domestic slavery is the greatest object of desire in those colonies where it was unhappily introduced in their infant state. But, previous to the enfranchisement of the slaves we have, it is necessary to exclude all further importations from Africa. Yet our repeated attempts to effect this by prohibitions, and by imposing duties which might amount to a prohibition, have been hitherto defeated by his Majesty's negative; thus preferring the immediate advantages of a few African corsairs to the lasting interests of the American States, and to the rights of human nature, deeply wounded by this infamous practice. Nay, the single interposition of an interested individual against a law, was scarcely ever known to fail of success, though in the opposite scale were placed the interests of a whole country. That this is so shameful an abuse of a power trusted with his Majesty for other purposes, as, if not reformed, would call for some legal restrictions."*

* American Archives, 4th series, i., 636.

At a general meeting of the freeholders of Prince George's county, in 1775, it was unanimously resolved: "That the African trade is injurious to this colony, obstructs the population of it by freemen, prevents manufacturers and other useful emigrants from settling among us, and occasions an increase of the balance of trade against this colony."[*]

In Princess Ann, Fairfax, (*Geo. Washington presiding*), Culpepper, Nansemond, Caroline, Hanover, and Surrey counties, resolutions of similar import were also passed at formal meetings of the freeholders, and generally by unanimous vote. Subsequently, in the discussion of the power of the general government with regard to Slavery, Mr. Mason said, in the Virginia Legislature:

"The present question concerns not the importing States alone, but the whole Union. The evil of having slaves was experienced during the late war. Had slaves been treated as they might have been by the enemy, they would have proved dangerous instruments in their hands. But their folly dealt by the slaves as it did by the Tories. Slavery discourages arts and manufactures. The poor despise labor when performed by slaves. They prevent the immigration of whites, who really enrich and strengthen a country. They produce the most pernicious effects on manners. Every master of slaves is born a petty tyrant. They bring the judgment of heaven on a country. By an inevitable chain of causes and effects Providence punishes national sins by national calamities. He lamented that some of our eastern brethren, from a lust of gain, have embarked in this nefarious traffic. As to the State being in the possession of the right to import, that was the case with many other rights now to be given up. He held it essential, in every point of view, that the General Government should have power to prevent the increase of slavery."

The importation of slaves from the West Indies and Africa was forbidden: the emancipation of those already living in the

[*] American Archives, 4th series, i., 494.

land was merely postponed, as it was distinctly understood, until a more convenient season.

EDUCATION AND ELEVATION ALSO REFUSED TO THE POOR WHITES.

Twenty-five acres of land, with such a cabin and other improvements upon it as "poor white people" are now generally content with in Virginia, could not have been, at the time of the Revolution, worth, on an average, more than one hundred dollars. The property of a majority of the able-bodied, tax paying men in the State, was then less than this.*

Mr. Jefferson says, the poorer class are accustomed to live almost entirely on animal food, " although a free use of vegetables is indispensable to their health and comfort." It is probable that but few of them were habituated to regular labor, and that a large part still lived by hunting, and were but slightly elevated, if any at all, above the savages they had displaced.

The father of American Democracy, believing in his heart that these men were unjustly denied the right of taking part in the election of their rulers, yet acknowledging the danger of intrusting power in the hands of men so grossly ignorant, was anxious that measures should be taken, simultaneously with those he advocated for the removal of the slave-laborers, to elevate their children, and, at all events, to draw out from them a fully educated class of free citizens—men who should understand and sympathize with their wants, yet be fully competent for the highest offices of State. He was too true to himself, however, to advocate any marked distinctions of classes in the laws, such as characterize the present school-laws of Virginia.

---

* Jefferson's Notes, comp. pp. 171, 172, 225.

He proposed that the whole State should, as soon as practicable, be divided into districts, each, at most, of six miles square, in every one of which a school-house, and competent teacher should be provided: that *all residents* in the district should be entitled to send their children to this school for three years, without payment, and by payment of a fixed moderate tuition fee, as much longer as they pleased: That out of the scholars whose parents were unable to give their children more complete education, the boy showing most genius, in each school district, should be chosen annually, to be advanced at the public expense, to a classical and mathematical, or High school: that from among the High school scholars, a certain number should be annually selected for promotion to a superior institution, where they should remain six years. This institution was intended to answer the purpose of a normal college, in supplying competent teachers for the common schools: but also from among its graduates, one-half of the most talented were to be offered three years' additional support by the State, while they pursued the study of arts and sciences at the University. This University—the present University of Virginia, at Charlottesville—is the only part of this scheme which has yet been realized. It is a school for the rich—for the sons of slave-holders almost exclusively.

"The general objects of this law," said Mr. Jefferson, "are to provide an education adapted to the years, to the capacity, and the condition of every one, and directed to their freedom and happiness." "Of the views of this law, none is more important, none more legitimate than that of rendering the people the safe, as they are the ultimate, guardians of their own liberty. The people themselves are the only safe depositories of government.

And to render them safe, their minds must be improved to a certain degree. This, indeed, is not all that is necessary, though it be essentially necessary."

The proposal met with no greater favor than that for the education and gradual emancipation of the slaves. However earnest Mr. Jefferson was, nothing can be more evident than that, even then, there was no sincere purpose on the part of the planters —that is, the rich and powerful—to constitute a truly Democratic government, or even to prepare the ground for it. Yet the results of what he was able to accomplish by the power of his eloquence, over their egotism and illiberality, are such as to encourage us never to fear, when we have an opportunity to legislate in advance of our age. The people of Virginia have not, to this day, as a body, approached to Jefferson's sound, practical and Christian views of governmental and social science. Yet, to his limited success in embodying those views in their Constitution and laws, they are indebted for most of their present limited prosperity.

THE SOCIAL RESULTS OF THE REVOLUTION.

Before the Revolution, there were, in Virginia, beside the temporary servile class, four distinct legal and social orders of the people: first, the aristocracy proper; second, the common free men; third, the poor whites, or non-freeholders, who had no vote on the matters of the Commonwealth; fourth, the slaves proper. The history of Virginia, since the Revolution, is a record of the industrial advantages resulting from the downfall of the old aristocracy and the formation of a younger—and, therefore, more vigorous,—broader—and, therefore, freer and less sharply defined—modern aristocracy. By comparing the industrial pro-

gress of the state with that of others, more democratically
organized and managed, and entirely or nearly free from Slavery
proper, an index is also given us of the injury the Commonwealth has experienced from Slavery, and from morbid pro-
slavery conservatism.

Neither the condition nor the character of the poor
people of the east was, on the whole, much improved by
the Revolution. The class of well-to-do planters, the wealthier
yeomen of the country, were chiefly elevated and benefited by
it.* Its effect on the old aristocracy was not directly ruinous;
it merely exposed its essential weakness, and revealed the heavy
expense to the Commonwealth by which it had hitherto been sustained. A generation passed away, before payment of the debt it
had been running up for nearly two centuries was demanded, and
its pride distinctly brought low.

The interval needs no particular account. The system of
husbandry—so to dignify the pernicious method of extract-
ing the wealth of the land, which prevailed—had necessarily, already, been somewhat modified. The great size
of the plantations was a principal hindrance to any extended improvement. The cultivated land was divided into
"in-fields" and "out-fields;" the former, being those nearest
the central establishment, received all the manure that was
made, and were planted with tobacco; the out-fields, were those
at such a distance that manure could not be afforded to be
carried to them. If not thought to be rich enough, without

* In the first Bill for organizing a militia, drawn up by Patrick Henry, the
people of the State were designated, as they would be in England, "gentlemen
and yeomen," the distinction of class being, even at such a time, and by such
a man, distinctly recognized.

the aid of manure, to produce a single crop of tobacco when first cleared up (after having been thrown out for many years), they were planted with maize, several years in succession, and, afterwards, cropped with maize and wheat alternately; or, if the wheat crop fell to less than three (3!) bushels an acre, with maize alone. Occasionally a "rest," of a year or two, would be permitted, during which the spontaneous growth of weeds was closely pastured. This process was continued as long as the land would produce five bushels of maize to the acre; when the crop fell below that, the land would be left alone twenty or thirty years (the length of time depending on the number of negroes the planter owned in proportion to the size of his plantation), when it would be again subjected to the same course.*

It was estimated that the crops of the whole State, just previous to the Revolution, were worth respectively—*per annum, communibus annis*—as follows:

Tobacco, - - - - - $1,650,000	Pork, - - - - - - $40,000
Wheat, - - - - - 666,666	Brandy and Whisky, - - 6,666
Maize, - - - - - - 200,000	Horses, - - - - - 6,666
All other agricultural productions, - - - - - - - 14,667

The tobacco-crop being still, if we except the small items of horses and distilled spirits, more than twice the value of all other agricultural productions, and ten times the value of all the shipping, lumber, naval stores, peltry, and other productions of the forest, fisheries, mines, and manufactures.

But its production was falling off, and Mr. Jefferson, commenting on the above statement, rejoices in the hope that it will soon be necessarily given up altogether. It is important to remember this; and I shall again refer to it—that the culture

---

* See Ruffin's Essay on Calcareous Manures.

of tobacco was *already* so little profitable that the amount grown was rapidly declining—and, that the philosophical statesman, who was the author of the bills for abrogating entails and primogeniture, saw, in the prospect of its entire discontinuance, subject for congratulation, rather than regret.

I can find no distinct statements or estimates, with regard to the material interests of Virginia, for a long time after the Revolution. It is certain that, owing to the causes I have mentioned, the culture of tobacco became necessarily less and less, on the Eastern Virginia plantations, and the labor owned upon them was necessarily devoted increasingly to the culture of wheat and maize. The income from the land and labor became constantly smaller; not because of the substitution of grain for tobacco, but because of the gradual but constant deterioration of the soil, which that substitution marked.

I use the awkward term, "income from property in land and labor," instead of the simple one, "profits of agriculture," because there never had yet been any legitimate profit of agriculture, in Virginia. From the beginning the planting aristocracy had merely been living on its capital; the whole labor of the country had been, and still, at the Revolution, continued to be engaged in nothing else but transmuting the soil of the country into tobacco—which was sent to England to purchase luxuries for its masters—and into bread for the bare support of its inhabitants, without making any return. Some manure, it is true, was occasionally deposited; but it was not, probably, one per cent. of the value of the capital of fertility which was washed into the sea between the periods at which it was applied. Entail, primogeniture, and Slavery, had been sufficient to hide the increasing poverty of the country under the ostentatious hospitality and pompous airs of the aristocracy. This extravagance, however, could not, under the most favorable circumstances, have lasted much longer. If the Revolution had not occurred, if these laws had not been changed, it is probable that a very much longer period would not have elapsed, before their repeal would have been desired by the aristocracy itself, as was the "Encumbered Estates Act" in Ireland, by its fine-blooded gentlemen, of Old Virginia habits, a few years since. Such pitiable calamity as Ireland suffered in the famine, is, perhaps, not possible in a country like Virginia; but, if the old system had been pursued on a short time longer, there would have been nothing left for the people but to emigrate in a body, or be reduced to a common level of extreme destitution.

But the revolutionary penance could only mitigate, not arrest, punitive justice, and, at length—at the close of the second war with England, which has occasioned a protracted dullness in the demand for tobacco—the hand of inevitable Nemesis is manifest. Many of the old Colonial proprietors are now dead, the plantations are generally divided according to the new laws. The young men, brought up among the negroes—"nursed, educated, and daily exercised in tyranny," as Mr. Jefferson described them to be—with luxurious and vicious propensities, and irrestrainable passions, are not able to meet the demands of their habits, much less to pay the interest of the long accumulating debts of their families. The law no longer protects them from the honest claims of the despised merchants. Lands and negroes have been mortgaged. The sale of negroes, from time to time, to traders, who are now beginning to ship them off in considerable number, to the cotton plantations of the Southern Slave States, satisfies the most pressing demands for a few years, but only makes the ultimate catastrophe more accumulative and overwhelming. The end of the rope is finally reached, and the worn out and used up old plantations are going a begging for purchasers, like foundered horses, at any price which shall give bare freedom to the poor young cavaliers. The iniquity of aristocracy is visited upon the children and upon the children's children, unto the third and fourth generations, and, in the world's open market, the exact value of grandfathers is at length ascertained.

The story is thus told by a Virginian in the *Southern Planter :*

" Every farm was greatly impoverished—almost every estate was seriously impaired—and some were involved in debt to nearly their value. Most of the proprietors had died, leaving families in reduced circumstances, and in some cases in great straits. No farm, whether of a rich or a poor proprietor, had escaped great exhaustion, and no property great dilapidation, unless because the proprietor had at first been too poor to join in the former expensive habits of his wealthier neighbors.

* * * "There was nothing left to waste, but time and labor ; and these continued to be wasted in the now fruitless efforts to cultivate to profit, or to replace the fertility of soil which had been destroyed. Luxury and expense had been greatly lessened. But on that account the universal prostration was even the more apparent. Many mansions were falling into decay. Few received any but trivial and indispensable repairs. No new mansion was erected, and rarely any other farm-building of value. There was still generally prevailing idleness among proprietors ; and also an abandonment of hope, which made every one desirous to sell his land and move to the fertile and far West, and a general emigration and dispersion was only prevented by the impossibility of finding purchasers for the lands, even at half the then low estimate of market prices."

And thus by Mr. Palfrey:

" By-and-by the father dies, and the land and the hundred negroes, more or less, are divided equally among the children.   The sons cannot live—at all events as they have been used to living—on a piece of exhausted tobacco-lands with a dozen or two of hands to till it.   The professions are full ; the trades too vulgar for them ; they have no way to get a subsistence.   They sell off the human-stock, and live off the proceeds, as long as they last ; and then become borrowing loafers about the Court-House tavern, or take their departure for parts unknown. Or they take to the Capitol, their only capital, long so well accredited there, of ' belonging to one of the first families in Virginia,' and get some small clerkship in one of the public offices, ——."

THE EFFECT OF DEMOCRACY.

The Democratic system, so far as it was established by the Revolution, was limited in its scope to what had been previously the middle white class, and the aristocracy.   Its first effect upon the latter I have shown to have been disastrous, but upon the great mass its operation must have been elevating and encouraging.   Even during this very same period of aristocratic dispersion, now known as the dark days of Virginia, because many flashing lights of her old gentry were then extinguished, I believe the condition of the major part of the people (leaving out of view, for the present, the slaves, and the politically debased whites), was steadily improving.   There were more rising than falling men.

Notwithstanding a constant emigration of the decayed families, and of the more enterprising of the poor, the population steadily augmented, though not so rapidly as in the adjoining more democratic States.*   If the apparent wealth of the country

* 1790 to 1810, population to sq. mile in Virginia increased from 10·68 to 13·92
        "   "   "   "   New York   "   7·56 to 21·31
        "   "   "   "   Pennsylvania   "   9·28 to 17·30

was not increasing, the foundation of a greater material prosperity was being laid, in the increase of the number of small,
but intelligent proprietors, and in the constantly growing necessity to abandon tobacco, and substitute grains, or varied
crops, as the staple productions of the country. The very circumstance that reduced the old pseudo-wealthy proprietors, was
favorable to this change, and to the application of intelligence to
a more profitable disposal of the remaining elements of wealth
in the land.

While multitudes abandoned their ancestral acres in despair,
or were driven from them by the recoil of their fathers' incon-
siderate expenditures, they were taken possession of by "new
men," endowed with more hopefulness and energy, if not more
intelligence than the old. Movement, though it be apparently
downward, is evidence of life, and is stimulating to the mind.
Every man who thought about it, saw that either tobacco must
be given up, or its method of culture essentially modified, or
that his land must continue to decrease in productive value.
With the new proprietors this was a matter of more consequence
than it had formerly been, because a larger proportion of their
capital was now absorbed in the land they owned, proportionately to that in slaves. In an address of Mr. Madison, afterwards President of the Confederacy, before an Agricultural
Society in Albemarle County, in 1819, the change then progressing in the economy of Virginia is thus alluded to :

" Whilst there was an abundance of fresh and fertile soil, it was the
interest of the cultivator to spread his labor over as great a surface as
possible. Land being cheap, and labor dear, and the land coöperating
powerfully with the labor, it was profitable to draw as much as possible
from the land. Labor is now comparatively cheaper, and land dearer.
It might be profitable, therefore, now, to contract the surface over which

labor is spread, even if the soil retained its freshness and fertility. But this is not the case. Much of the fertile soils are exhausted, and unfertile soils are brought into cultivation ; and both coöperating less with labor in producing the crop, it is necessary to consider how far labor can be profitably exerted on them : whether it ought not to be applied towards making them fertile, rather than in further impoverishing them ; or whether it might not be more profitably applied to mechanical operations, or domestic manufactures."

Among men of capital, intelligence, and social habits—for, without the stimulus of conversation or reading, improvements are accepted slowly—certain systematic methods of sustaining and improving landed estate began to prevail, immediately after the second war. Tobacco was given up, or cultivated only in its proper turn of a rotation ; artificial grasses were introduced, and, with the aid of gypsum, clover was made to grow upon the exhausted lands, and made use of as a green manure, to resuscitate them ; ambulatory pens, shifted yearly from field to field, came into use upon large farms, instead of the stationary central stockyards, thus saving the great labor of hauling fodder and manure between them and distant fields, and doing away with the "in and out-field" system. Cattle and horses were fed a much longer period of the year than formerly, and by some they were excluded from the tillage lands altogether, the growth of weeds and grasses having been found to be of more value to plow in as manure, than to be pastured.

Among American patriots of this period of our history, should always be classed John Taylor, of Caroline county, Virginia, the author of "Arator," and John S. Skinner, who, in 1819, commenced at Baltimore, in Maryland, the publication of the first special agricultural journal in America. Other men, many of whose names are enrolled among those of our national statesmen, were then united with them, in strenuous and concerted exertion, to give a better direction to the labor and agricultural capital of those States.

The convalescence of Virginia agriculture, however, if convalescent it may be considered ever to have been, should more especially be dated from the introduction of lime, as an application, in connection with better tillage, judicious rotations, and more frequent applications of dung and green crops, for the improvement of the land. And for this, Virginia is chiefly indebted to the study, experiments, preaching, and publications of Edmund Ruffin. Mr. Ruffin was, for many years, the editor of the *Virginia Farmers' Register*, but is best known as the author of "A Treatise on Calcareous Manures," than which no work on a similar subject has ever been published in Europe or America based on more scientifically careful investigation, and trusty, personal experience, or of equal practical value to those for whose benefit it was designed.

But, cotemporaneously with the invigoration of the planting class, the depression of the tobacco market, and the introduction of these improvements in agriculture which promised so much for the future of the State, there entered a still more potent element into the direction of her destiny. This was occasioned by the increasing profit and extending culture of cotton in the more Southern States, which gave rise to a demand for additional labor, increased the value of slaves, and, the African Slave Trade having been declared piracy, led to a great extension of the internal Slave Trade.

The value of the cotton exported from the United States was:

In 1794,	.	.	.	.	.	.	.	$500,000
1800,	.	.	.	.	.	.		5,000,000
1810,		.	.	.	.	.	.	15,000,000
1820,	.	.	.	.	.	.		22,000,000
1830,		.	.	.	.	.	.	30,000,000
1840,	.	.	.	.	.	.		64,000,000
1850,		.	.	.	.	.	.	72,000,000

Closely corresponding to the increase in the exportation of cotton, was the growth of the demand for labor; and as, in any slave-holding community, experience shows no other labor can be extensively made use of but that of slaves, the value of slaves *for sale* has steadily advanced in Virginia, with the extension of cotton fields over the lands conquered or purchased for that purpose of the Indians in Alabama and Florida; of France, in the valley of the Mississippi; and of Mexico, in Texas.*

The effect of this demand for slaves was directly contrary to those influences which I have described as being the foundation of renewed agricultural energy in Virginia. It concentrated the interest of the planter in his slaves, as in old times it had been concentrated in tobacco; the improvement, or even the sustentation of the value of his lands became a matter of minor importance; the taste for improving husbandry, except among the men of leisure, capital, and highly-cultivated minds, was fatally checked. Mr. Ruffin, a gentleman of ultra, and, it seems to a stranger, fanatical devotion to the perpetuation of slavery, yet otherwise a most sensible and reliable observer

---

* That the people of California should have decided not to permit slaves to be sold also in that great acquisition to our territory, has been an intense disappointment to Virginia slave-holders; and the influence of the State, for some time after this was determined, was very undecided with regard to further schemes of annexation.

and thinker, unintentionally gives his evidence against the Slave Trade, by describing the effect of the increased value it gave to negroes:

"A gang of slaves on a farm will increase to four times their original number in thirty or forty years. If a farmer is only able to feed and maintain his slaves, their increase in value may double the whole of his capital originally invested in farming before he closes the term of an ordinary life. But few farms are able to support this increasing expense, and also furnish the necessary supplies to the family of the owner; whence very many owners of large estates, in lands and negroes, are, throughout their lives, too poor to enjoy the comforts of life, or to incur the expenses necessary to improve their unprofitable farming. A man so situated may be said to be a slave to his own slaves. If the owner is industrious and frugal, he may be able to support the increasing numbers of his slaves, and to bequeath them undiminished to his children. But the income of few persons increases as fast as their slaves, and, if not, the consequence must be that some of them will be sold, that the others may be supported, and the sale of more is perhaps afterwards compelled to pay debts incurred in striving to put off that dreaded alternative. The slave at first almost starves his master, and at last is eaten by him—at least, he is exchanged for his value in food."

What a remarkable state of things is here pictured — the labor of a country almost exclusively applied to agriculture, and yet able to supply *itself*, but in few cases, with the coarsest food!

The interest of the slaves' owners being withdrawn, by their increasing value as transferable property, from their land, a gradual but rapid amelioration of their condition followed, as respects physical comfort. Since 1820, there has been a constant improvement in this respect. They are now worked no harder, in general, than is supposed to be desirable to bring them into high muscular and vital condition; they are better fed, clothed, and sheltered, and the pliant strap and scientific paddle have been substituted, as instruments of discipline, for the scoring lash and bruising cudgel.*

No similar progress, it is to be observed, has been made in the mental and moral economy of Slavery in Virginia; the laws and customs being a good deal less favorable, than formerly, to the education of the race, which is sufficiently explainable. The opinion being prevalent—and, I suppose, being well-founded —that negro property, as it increases in intelligence, decreases in security; as it becomes of greater value, and its security more important, more regard is naturally paid to the means of suppressing its ambition and dwarfing its intellect.

Of course, this increased care of the slaves' physical well-being adds to the current expenditure of their master, and makes all operations, involving labor, cost more than formerly; and, as its effect is to force more rapid breeding, and the number of slaves does not diminish, no corresponding encouragement is obtained from it for free-labor. Consequently, the internal slave-trade makes the cost of labor greater, and its quality worse, precisely in proportion to its activity. This, as I pointed out in the last chapter, is the grand reason of the exces-

---

* Hon. Humphrey Marshall, of Kentucky, in his defense of Mat. Ward, thus describes the strap:

"The strap, gentlemen, you are probably aware, is an instrument of refined modern torture, ordinarily used in whipping slaves. By the old system, the cow-hide—a severe punishment—cut and lacerated them so badly as to almost spoil their sale when brought to the lower markets. But this strap, I am told, is a vast improvement in the art of whipping negroes; and, it is said, that one of them may be punished by it within one inch of his life, and yet he will come out with no visible injury, and his skin will be as smooth and polished as a peeled onion!"

The paddle is a large, thin ferule of wood, in which many small holes are bored; when a blow is struck, these holes, from the rush and partial exhaustion of air in them, act like diminutive cups, and the continued application of the instrument has been described to me to produce precisely such a result as that attributed to the strap by Mr. M.

sively low market value of all real estate, and has occasioned the slow and stingy application of capital to mining and other industrial enterprises, in all other elements for the success of which Virginia is so exceedingly rich.

It was, for a long time, generally expected that the demand of the cotton-planters would gradually draw off all the slaves from Virginia, and that the State would thus be redeemed to freedom. The objection which had been chiefly urged against Jefferson's scheme of emancipation, certainly would have had less weight, during thirty years past, against a requirement that all slaves below mature age, remaining, after a certain future time, in the State, should be educated, freed, and transported; for the owners, who could not afford to lose the value of their property, could, at any time, have sold away their slaves, at very much more than their cost price, before the requirement went into effect.

It, therefore, became advisable to stigmatize such a proposition as tyrannical—to claim for a class the power of thus continuing to ruin the State, so long as they found in it their private profit, as a legal and vested right. On January 18, 1832, a member of the legislature, Mr. Gholson, proclaimed this, in the following cunning language. Be it observed that all existing nuisances, and those that are a part of them, are always called old-fashioned; which, oddly enough under such circumstances, is considered equivalent to respectable.

"It has always (perhaps erroneously) been considered, by steady and old-fashioned people, that the owner of land had a reasonable right to its annual profit, the owner of orchards to their annual fruits, * * and the owner of female slaves to their increase. * * It is on the justice and inviolability of this maxim that the master foregoes the service of the female slave, has her nursed and attended during the period of gestation, and raises the helpless infant offspring. The value of the property justifies the expense; and I do not hesitate to say, that in its increase consists much of our wealth."

That is to say, no law providing for the freedom of unborn generations is to be considered just; consequently, Mr. Jefferson's scheme was agrarian and preposterous.

The value of slaves for sale has, since then, pretty steadily advanced; the exportation has as steadily augmented; while the stock kept on hand is some three thousand more than it then was. The amiable letter-writer, whom the State of Jefferson now delights to honor, tells our simple New York Democrats, that if they had not been so foolish as to favor the admission of California as a Free State—if they had been able, as he desired, to force it to become a Slave State—it would have opened such a market for slaves as would have soon drained them all out of Virginia.

I do not believe, if prime field-hands should ever sell for ten thousand dollars a head, there would be one negro less kept in Virginia than there is now, when they are worth but one thousand.

How would this increasing demand be met, then?

Very easily: by the re-importation of breeding-slaves from the consuming States. Connecticut exports bullocks and barren cows by the thousand annually; and the drovers who take the working and fatted stock out, often drive back heifers from the districts in which the breeding of cattle is made less a matter of business, and is, therefore, less profitable than it is in that region of bleak pastures.

It is an assertion often made, and generally credited, that it is only since the rise of the abolition agitation that the people of the South have shown a determined disposition to perpetuate Slavery—that in Virginia, especially, the people would, ere this, have abolished, or greatly modified it, if they had not been exasperated to folly by the calumnious and impertinent meddling in the matter of those who had no business with it.

I have always, until recently, taken the truth of this assertion for granted; and have often, I am afraid, somewhat foolishly, repeated it. No doubt there is a certain basis of truth in it; no doubt the abolition agitation in the Free States has been, and is in many respects, injudicious; but I am induced to think this charge against it requires to be made with some reservation and explanation.

It certainly is a curious coincidence—and it can hardly be thought a mere coincidence, it seems to me—that the general indisposition to emancipate slaves has been very closely proportionate to the expense, or loss of cash property, which would attend it. If an accurate yearly price-current of slaves since the Revolution could be had, it would indicate the fluctuating probabilities of their general emancipation more exactly than the value of the English consolidated debt follows the varying prospects of peace or war.

From the day in which Jefferson inaugurated the agitation for the emancipation of the slaves, up to 1820, the Abolition party in Virginia, though it never succeeded in accomplishing the smallest of its legislative purposes, was strong in talent if not in number, and was in close fraternity and affiliation with the more successful party in the States now free.*   At this time the

* Benjamin Franklin was President, and George Washington and Thomas Jefferson correspondents, of the Ab-'ition Society of Pennsylvania, of which Passmore Williamson, lately lying in jail, in Philadelphia, is the present Secretary.

internal slave traffic was first recognized as a phenomena of pregnant importance; and Randolph and other Virginians lamented it, and deplored its probable consequences in Congress.

There were then (1820) in Virginia no men of education and influence who were not slave-owners—and as such, pecuniarily interested, more or less, in restraining legislation unfavorable to Slavery. During the next fifteen years, the Southern demand for slaves, and, consequently, their value as stock, constantly increasing, there would appear to have been a struggle between the consciences and the interests, or between the selfishness and the good judgment, of those who had constituted the anti-slavery influence of the State. Gradually the older and more powerful opponents of the perpetuation of the system passed off the field of action, and the younger were induced to accept what they found so increasingly profitable—at least, to be quiet, and leave its determined supporters to govern and represent the State.

In 1830, Daniel Webster said, in the Senate:

" I know full well, that it is, and has been, the settled policy of some persons in the South, *for years*, to represent the people of the North as disposed to interfere with them in their own exclusive and peculiar concerns. This is a delicate and sensitive point in Southern feeling; and of late years, it has always been touched, and generally with effect, whenever the object has been to unite the whole South against Northern men or Northern measures. This feeling, *always carefully kept alive*, and maintained at too intense a heat to admit discrimination or reflection, is a lever of great power in our political machine. It moves vast bodies, and gives to them one and the same direction. But it is without adequate cause, and the suspicion which exists is wholly groundless."

Remember that slave property still grew daily less productive, but more valuable.

Two years after the above declaration of Mr. Webster, an important debate occurred in the Virginia Legislature, with regard to Slavery. The Anti-Slavery party may be said to have then made its last demonstration, and final protest, against the policy which now, far more distinctly than formerly, was defended and maintained as an established permanent policy: whether most from a spirit of resistance to an abolition agitation at the North, or at home, or from the increasing value of slaves, the reader will judge.

On that occasion (in the Virginia Legislature, in the city of Richmond, fifty-six years after the Declaration of Independence), there were still not wanting some men who saw the evil of Slavery, and the rights of slaveholders in the same light that Jefferson, and Madison, and Mason, and Monroe, and Henry, and all the real statesmen of Virginia had done, and who were brave and magnanimous enough to utter their convictions. Thus, one Mr. Faulkner used the following language, especially significant in the italicised passage, of what he considered to be then the real obstacle in the way of measures for emancipation:

"Slavery, it is admitted, is an evil. It is an institution which presses heavily against the best interests of the State. It banishes free white labor—it exterminates the mechanic, the artisan, the manufacturer. It converts the energy of a community into indolence; its power into imbecility; its efficiency into weakness. Being thus injurious, have we not a right to demand its extermination? *Shall society suffer that the slaveholder may continue to gather his vigintial crop of human flesh?* What is his mere pecuniary claim, compared with the great interests of the common weal? Must the country languish and die, that the slaveholder may flourish? Shall all interests be subservient to one? Have not the middle classes their rights—rights incompatible with the existence of Slavery?

Mr. Brodnax: "That Slavery in Virginia is an evil, and a transcendent evil, it would be more than idle for any human being to doubt or deny.   It is a mildew, which has blighted every region it has touched, from the creation of the world.   Illustrations from the history of other countries and other times might be instructive; but we have evidence nearer at hand, in the short histories of the different States of this great confederacy, which are impressive in their admonitions, and conclusive in their character."

Mr. Summers: " Will gentlemen inform us when this subject will become less delicate—when it will be attended with fewer difficulties than at present—and at what period we shall be better enabled to meet them? Shall we be more adequate to the end proposed, after the resources of the State have been yet longer paralyzed by the withering, desolating influence of our present system? *Sir, every year's delay but augments the difficulties of this great business, and weakens our ability to compass it.*'*

PROGRESS OF THE EXPERIMENT, 1855—PRESENT POLICY, PLANS, AND PROSPECTS OF VIRGINIA.

Having suffered twenty-three years longer since this protest against her cherished policy was made in her Legislature, now at length has Virginia acquired the necessary strength and courage to undergo the painful operation necessary to free her from that chronic malady which, from the earliest period of her colonial infancy, has constantly debilitated and paralyzed her.

She is further from it than ever.   Like a poor man, rendered prematurely imbecile by his long endurance of pain, and who, conscious that every pretext against the application of the surgeon's relieving knife has been long since exhausted, finally, in unconquerable cowardice, discharges his faithful old family physician, feigns to despise his judgment, and throws

* Speeches delivered in the House of Delegates of Virginia, in relation to her colored population, January, 1832. Richmond, printed by Thomas W. White.

himself, in a flood of grateful tears, into the embrace of some
contemptible, bragging quack, who pretends that his disease
has hitherto been entirely misunderstood—who predicts that,
under his care, he will soon be the strongest man in town—
who diverts him with expensive nostrums, and amuses him
by humorous descriptions of his own debilitated form and
palsied movements; so Virginia now insultingly spurns
from her councils all who suggest that slavery is *ever* to
be eradicated, and not one man is allowed to enter her
Legislature who dares to declare and demand " the rights
of the middle class," nay, even to supplicate for them; and
if one should now petition for the passage of the amendment
proposed by Jefferson, he would actually be in danger of losing
his life. Such has been the influence of the extension of cotton
culture and the demand for slaves in Virginia—such is the
power of organized capital and educated wisdom, in a republic.

Virginia has this year passed through an exciting election—
the most so, probably, of any since the discussion of the Alien
and Sedition Acts. It was preceded by a prolonged and very
thorough canvass, with personal appeals to the conscience, the
patriotism, and especially to the pecuniary interests of the people,
by the rival candidates and their friends. The successful candidate is said to have made more than sixty addresses, in person,
to large assemblages of the electors convened to hear him
describe the policy he desired to pursue, and his reasons for it.

I have read with attention all the reports which I could
obtain of these expositions, in order to judge from them what
the people of Virginia now want or expect of their public
servants. Among the passages which are represented by the

reporters to have been received with great applause by the intelligent audience, on one occasion, are the following:

" Commerce has long ago spread her sails, and sailed away from you. You have not, as yet, dug more than coal enough to warm yourselves at your own hearths; you have set no tilt-hammer of Vulcan to strike blows worthy of gods in your own iron-foundries; you have not yet spun more than coarse cotton enough, in the way of manufacture, to clothe your own slaves.

" You have had no commerce, no mining, no manufactures.

" You have relied alone on the single power of agriculture—and such agriculture! Your sedge-patches outshine the sun. Your inattention to your only source of wealth has scared the very bosom of mother earth. Instead of having to feed cattle on a thousand hills, you have had to chase the stump-tailed steer through the sedge-patches to procure a tough beef-steak. (Laughter and applause.)

" The present condition of things has existed too long in Virginia. The landlord has skinned the tenant, and the tenant has skinned the land, until all have grown poor together. I have heard a story—I will not locate it here or there—about the condition of the prosperity of our agriculture. I was told by a gentleman in Washington, not long ago, that he was traveling in a county not a hundred miles from this place, and overtook one of our citizens on horseback, with, perhaps, a bag of hay for a saddle, without stirrups, and the leading line for a bridle, and he said: 'Stranger, whose house is that?' 'It is mine,' was the reply. They came to another. 'Whose house is that?' 'Mine, too, stranger.' To a third: 'And whose house is that?' 'That's mine, too, stranger; but don't suppose that I'm so darned poor as to own all the land about here.' (Laughter and applause.) We may own land, we may own slaves, we may own roadsteads and mines, we may have all the elements of wealth; but unless we apply intelligence, unless we adopt a thorough system of instruction, it is utterly impossible that we can develop, as we ought to develop, and as Virginia is prepared now to do, and to take the line of march towards the very eminence of prosperity." (Applause and continued merriment.)

And how does the fiddling Nero propose, it will be wondered, to remedy this so very amusing stupidity, poverty, and debility? Very simply and pleasantly. By building railroads and canals, ships and mills; by establishing manufactories, opening mines, and setting up smelting-works and foundries. And "Hurrah!" shout the tickled electors; "that's exactly what we want."

Indeed, it is what they want; but how are they going to get it? one is next anxious to ascertain. This question is neither asked nor answered. The confirmed paralytic and dyspeptic pauper is told: "All you want is a good digestion. Take plenty of exercise, walk twenty miles a day, swing dumb-bells, box, fence, row, and hunt; live generously; breakfast on cutlets *à la victime;* dine on salmon and venison with truffles; sup on canvas-backs, and don't spare pure old port." "Ah! that's it; I'm satisfied you understand my complaint," whispers the poor, bed-ridden wretch; "I put myself in your hands." "Good," returns the laughing charlatan; "you are now prepared to develop."

The same sagacious candidate, in a similar strain of eloquent mockery, depicts the intense ignorance which characterizes the people of Virginia; and affects to deplore it, though when a member of Congress he used publicly to boast of it, and congratulate himself upon it, as preventing disagreeable dissensions in his constituency. Now he laments it, and ridicules it, and promises, if they will make him governor, he will set about remedying it. How?

Actually, he has the impudence, as he stands there laughing at them, to pretend an admiration for the educational scheme of Jefferson, and to promise to recommend its adoption by the State.

And the poor mob appears to be imposed upon again; and, having a traditional confidence in the sincerity of Jefferson's democracy, they actually cheer him as if he was in earnest.

"He was in earnest," will the reader say, if about the time this book comes out, his first message will be reported in the newspapers, as containing a recommendation redeeming his promise?

Unless he also recommends—which I think would make an "activity" for a day or two in Wall street—Jefferson's sister scheme for the emancipation of the slaves, I should say, he was not in earnest, but was cruelly imposing again upon the ignorance of the poor, quack-ridden "Democracy;" for the Democratic scheme of education, proposed by Jefferson, is as impracticable and fallacious when disconnected from that sister scheme of his, as, when associated with it, it is admirable and necessary to a truly Democratic system of political economy.

Every Virginian possessing the average American development of brain, and not quite demented with avarice, or doctrinairism, must know this, if he has ever had any interest in the workings of the wretched attempts at public education employed in his State.

In the year ending Sept. 30, 1851, there were in ninety-eight counties, the School Commissioners of which made reports as required by law, 55,312 indigent children, between eight and eighteen years old, needing special State aid, to enable them to attend any school. Besides this number, there were those of forty counties, and the towns of Norfolk, Portsmouth, Williamsburg and Wheeling, of which report was neglected to be made. In 125 counties but 30,324, less than half the immense body of pauper-children living in them, were enabled or induced to attend school at all; and these (namely, the poor children mainly living nearest schools already established and supported by the wealthy for their own children), each on an average only eleven weeks and one day (less than one-quarter of the year). This pitiable result was obtained at a cost to the State of sixty-nine thousand dollars.

The Second Auditor's General Report on Education, from which I compile these facts, contains abstracts of sub-reports touching the working of the system then in operation, and which, I was assured by several worthy gentlemen in Richmond, was working most satisfactorily. These sub-reports were drawn up by the County School Commissioners and Superintendents, through whose hands what is called the Literary Fund is distributed. From them I shall make a few extracts, which will show how entirely impracticable—while the white population is so excessively distributed, as it needs must be, where there are many slaves—it will always be to contrive any *valuable* system of education for the families of those not able to pay for each scholar at a very high rate of tuition.

ALBEMARLE (White Population, 11,875 ; Slave do, 13,338).—"The Board of Commissioners state, that with the present appropriation to the county, they must be dependent upon the schools established by individual enterprise. They can, of course, proffer their assistance only where such schools exist."

"Your Superintendent would bring to your consideration the importance of recommending an increased per diem rate of tuition from four to five cents, as many of the best qualified teachers in the county object to take the indigent children into their schools on account of the reduced price per diem. He cannot furnish a synopsis of the proceedings of the Commissioners in the county, as very few reports have been furnished him."

AMELIA (Whites, 2,785 ; Slaves, 6.819 ; number of indigent children registered, 120 ; number of do., who attended school at any time within a year, 68).—No remarks.

BUCKINGHAM (White Population, 5,426 ; Slave, 8,161).—"The Board of School Commissioners report, that some of the Commissioners are unable, for the want of schools, to expend the money allotted to their districts.   They have no regular system of visiting the schools, nor do they, as a body, formally examine the teachers, leaving that to be done by those who patronize the schools.   Neither have they established schools where none existed.   The quota to this county is not sufficient to educate all the poor children.   The number of children and the time they are sent to school, is discretionary with the district commissioners."

CHARLOTTE (White Population, 4,615 ; Slave, 8,988).—" The Superintendent states that *in three or four of the districts, schools could not be obtained, and in others the children could not be induced to go ;* that it is utterly impossible to induce the district commissioners to have the accounts and reports made out according to form ; the consequence is, that there is a great difficulty in making the returns in due time."

CLARKE (Whites, 3,614 ; Slaves, 3,614).—" The Board has no regulations of a general character for the government of the district commissioners, as they have only acted in sessions of the Board.   The schools are not visited by them, nor can they judge of the qualifications of the teachers, because, from the insufficiency of their quota, they are obliged to send the indigent children to such established schools as are most convenient to the residence of the children."

FAUQUIER (Whites, 9,875 ; Slaves, 10,350).—" The Commissioners would call attention to the inadequacy of the school quota of this county, for the tuition of the indigent children within its limits.   They would further state, as the reason why they have not returned the number of poor children in their respective districts, that the duty is a very onerous one, and such as they are not able to perform without compensation, but that in the discharge of their duties they endeavor to aid the cause of education as much as they can, consistent with their own private interests, and are at all times ready to resign their trust to any who will perform the duties of the office more faithfully than themselves."

GLOUCESTER (Whites, 4,290 ; Slaves, 5,557).—" Some of the Commissioners have visited the schools in their districts, and are happy to state that there is a considerable improvement in the pupils, as well as in the management and the course of instruction on the part of the teachers.   The school quota of this county is entirely insufficient to educate the indigent children.   No preference is given to either sex."

GOOCHLAND (Whites, 3,863; Slaves, 5,845).—No remarks by board of school commissioners.

"The superintendent, as usual, has visited some of the schools, and has to say, that at some of them the scholars were progressing very well, whilst at others they were not doing so well as is desirable."

HALIFAX (Whites, 10,976; Slaves, 14,452; poor children, 803; attended school, 378).—"The individual commissioners have occasionally visited the schools to which they entered indigent children, and found that the poor children were improving in their studies as well as other children. The teachers are well qualified to teach spelling, reading, writing, and arithmetic, which is all that can be hoped for that class. The annual appropriation from the treasury, to the primary schools of this county, is not more than half enough to educate all the indigent children.

"They have no alterations to suggest in the present system. If any were made, it would not be to amend, but to make an entire alteration of the present system; but they do not believe that the county would adopt such a system as they would recommend."

HANOVER (Whites, 6,539; Slaves, 8,393).—"The school commissioners have paid some attention to visiting the schools in their districts. The teachers are generally persons of good moral character, and capable of conducting schools of respectable grades. Indigent children improve as well as others, and are generally making good progress.

"The commissioners have established several schools. They have aided in establishing others in neighborhoods where they could not otherwise have been established; and others might have been established to great advantage but for the want of funds. There appears to be an increasing desire among indigent persons to have their children educated, but the quota of the Literary fund for this county is not half sufficient to educate all of them. We have found but little difficulty in getting indigent children to attend school, except amongst the most ignorant or degraded class. No general rule has been adopted by them for the selection of children to be sent to school, except what the law requires."

RAPAHANNOCK (Whites, 5,642; Slaves, 3,844).—"The board of school commissioners state that the appropriation from the treasury is insufficient to educate all the poor of the county, yet as *there are many indigent children, whose parents cannot be prevailed upon to send them to school*, they generally enter all the indigent children who will attend school."

KING WILLIAM (Whites, 2,701 ; Slaves, 5,731).—" The commissioners report that such of the commissioners as have schools in their districts have visited them. They find the teachers well qualified to give instruction in the common branches of an English education, and that the indigent children, for the time they attend school, learn as well as other children. The appropriation from the treasury is fully sufficient for all who are entered, and the commissioners enter as many of that class as they or the teachers can get to attend school." (Number of poor children returned, 246 ; number sent to school within the year, 66.)

NANSEMOND (Whites, 5,424 ; Slaves, 4,715).—" A majority of the school commissioners find difficulty in getting indigent children to attend school regularly, *principally owing to the schools not being located near them;* they sometimes send children to another district. Some of the commissioners have visited the schools, and are well satisfied with the qualifications of the teachers. The children that attend make very fair improvement. Children from eight to eighteen have been admitted to school without regard to sex. The commissioners have not established any more schools, for want of funds ; they send to schools that have been established heretofore."

SUSSEX (Whites, 3,086; Slaves, 5,992).—" The commissioners state that they have no power in regulating the government of the schools. The qualifications of the teachers they believe to be as good as the small sum which they possess will command. They have no choice generally in the selection of teachers—the scholars entered are taken by the teachers as objects of charity, and not for the compensation they receive. The fund being insufficient to educate the poor of the county, the commissioners have made selections from among the children, giving the preference to those who would be most likely to attend the schools regularly."

SOUTHAMPTON (Whites, 5,940 ; Slaves, 5,755).—" The commissioners state, that the funds appropriated are very inadequate to the education of the poor children of the county ; that not one-half of them attend school at all, and of those the most of them were at school but a small portion of the year ; that the parents of many were willing and anxious for their children to attend, but the teachers would not receive them, because there was nothing to pay for their tuition. They further state, that *the irregular attendance of the poor children still continues to be one of the greatest difficulties they labor under in judiciously applying the funds allotted them ;* and, in consequence of this, the school commissioner is very much embarrassed in distributing his quota among the schools of his district, and consequently in determining the number of days he should enter to each teacher, as he can form no correct idea, from the number of children, how many days they are likely to make."

POWHATAN (Whites, 2,513; Slaves, 5,282).—No remarks. Number of poor children, 150; attended school, 60.

I do not mean to say that, if the people will submit to the necessary taxation, some enormously expensive system of education may not be adopted, which will be of great benefit to the State, and lead to a more rapid development of her resources, even though Slavery should still continue to separate, distract, and debilitate the associative energies of the indigent whites. I have not a doubt this can be done, and I sincerely trust it will be tried. But, except as an indirect step towards the abolition of Slavery, it will do hardly anything towards raising Virginia to an equality of intelligence with the Free States, or to that position of power and attractiveness which is indicated by her natural elements of wealth.

Nor can anything do this, but a free, self-dependent, self-supporting, and self-respecting, intelligent laboring people. Whether the negroes can be made a part of such a people, I need not here give an opinion; but I will say that I can see no evidence that they are advancing towards it, or that it is the general intention that they shall advance towards it. Whether, if the negroes were free, and remained as stupid, as helpless, as contented, as unhopeful and unambitious, and as indolent, as it is claimed they are at present, it would be possible to have any general population of white people of such a kind, I do not now care to answer. But I declare, with confidence, that it is evidently an absolute impossibility to have such a people, and such a development of the State, or such a degree of intelligence among the mass of free people as, under a republic, it is of vital importance to secure to them, while a peculiar, degraded, pitiable, or despicable class, capable of being used only as the instruments of labor in the hands of a more intelligent, is by law expressly provided for, and not merely left unfurnished with education by the State, but expressly prevented from being educated, expressly prevented from striving to improve its own capacity of usefulness through the impulse to improve its status in society. While such a class is carefully conserved for the purposes of labor, good, careful, high-spirited and high-purposed men, disposed to turn their own honest labor to good account, will avoid or go out from such a labor-market; and only bad, mean, low-minded, careless, and poor laboring people will come to it, or stay in it. So it always has been : so it is now.

So much for the remedies which the new governor imposes upon the people of Virginia, for the evils under which the State suffers.

What little he has time to say, directly of Slavery, he says only as the champion and advocate, before the electors at large, of the interests of the slaveholders, and in denunciation and defiance of those who may dare doubt the necessity of making that interest paramount to all others in the nation. But to the slaveholders themselves he especially commends himself, by the assertion, that if he could have had his way, California would have been a Slave State, and in that case slaves would have been worth five thousand dollars a-piece !

I know not much about Louis Blanc, except that he is very much detested by most people, and especially by the aristocracy and the stock-brokers of Europe, but I saw something which he said lately to the continental democratic refugees in England, which seems to me in itself true and good.

"The republican form of government is not the object : the object is, to restore to the dignity of human nature those whom the excess of poverty degrades, and to enlighten those whose intelligence, from want of education, is but a dim, vacillating lamp, in the midst of darkness ; the object is to make him that works enjoy all the fruits of his work ; the object is to enfranchise the people, by endeavoring gradually to abolish this double slavery—ignorance and misery.   A very difficult task, indeed, the accomplishment of which requires long study, deep meditation, and something more than discipline !   As to the republican form of government, it is a means, most valuable, certainly, and which we ought to strive to conquer, even at the cost of life, but which it is very imprudent to mistake for the aim, as the consequence might be to make us take the shadow for the substance, and run through a heap of ruins to fatal delusions."

I think this mistake has been made by the Virginia experimenters : the republican form of government has certainly failed to restore to much dignity of human nature that part of her population degraded by excess of poverty, or to very materially enlighten those whose intelligence, for want of education, was dim and vacillating.   I think, also, the people of Virginia have been running very fast through their "heap of ruins, towards fatal delusions"—fatal delusions, already warmly embraced, as will presently be seen.

The *Richmond Examiner* and the *Richmond Enquirer* are the chief organs of those who lead the long dominant party of Virginia.   They are conducted with more talent than any other journals of the State, and each receives a very much larger income from its subscribers than does any newspaper in the State which now ever distinctly admits Slavery to be an evil, desirable or possible to be remedied.

From the Richmond Enquirer, Sept. 6, 1855.

"We are happy to find that others of our Southern cotemporaries are wilting to discuss(?) the true and great question of the day—*The exist-ence of Slavery as a permanent institution in the South.*

"Every moment's additional reflection but convinces us of the abso-lute impregnability of the Southern position on this subject. Facts, which cannot be questioned, come thronging in support of the true doctrine—that Slavery is the best condition of the black race in this country, and that the true philanthropists should rather desire that race to remain in a state of servitude, than to become free, with the privileges of becoming worthless, * * * The Virginians need not be told that, as a class, there is not a more worthless or dissolute set of men than these free negroes. Our slaves, even, look upon most of them with contempt, and speak of them with a sneer. They deserve it. There are some few honorable exceptions—but, as a class, they are the most despicable characters our State contains. This is not peculiar to Virginia. In the Northern States as well as in the Southern—indeed, everywhere—this is the true state of facts; and we were not surprised, therefore, to see a *free* State refuse admission to the Randolph negroes. Without, then, going the length of declaring that Slavery *in the abstract*—Slavery everywhere — is a blessing to the laboring classes, may we not candidly and calmly, and upon the maturest and soberest reflection, say that to the black race of the Union it is a blessing, and perhaps the greatest blessing we can now confer upon them?"

From the Richmond Examiner, 1854.

"It is all a hallucination to suppose that we are ever going to get rid of African Slavery, or that it will ever be desirable to do so. It is a thing that we cannot do without, that is *righteous, profitable,* and permanent, and that belongs to Southern society as inherently, intri-cately, and durably as the white race itself. Yea, the white race will itself emigrate from the Southern States to Africa, California, or Poly-nesia, sooner than the African.

Let us make up our minds, therefore, to put up with and make the most of the institution. Let us not bother our brains about what *Providence* intends to do with our negroes in the distant future, but glory in and' profit to the utmost by what He has done for them in transplanting them here, and setting them to work on our plantations. Let the politicians and planters of the South, while encouraging the ' Baptists and Metho-dists,' (and other denominations having a less number of votes), in Chris-tianizing the negro, keep their slaves at hard work, under strict discipline, out of idleness and mischief, while they live; and, when they come to die, instead of sending them off to Africa, or manumitting them to a life of "freedom," licentiousness, and nuisance, will them over to their children, or direct them to be sold where they will be made to work hard, and be of service to their masters, and to the country. True philanthropy to the negro, begins, like charity, at home; and if Southern men would act as if the canopy of heaven were inscribed with a covenant, in letters of fire, that *the negro is here, and here forever; is our property, and ours forever; is never to be emancipated; is to be kept hard at work, and in rigid subjection all his days;* and is never to go to Africa, to Polynesia, or to Yankee Land (far worse than either), they would accomplish more good for the race in five years than they boast the institution itself to have accomplished in two centuries, and cut up by the roots a set of evils and fallacies that threaten to drive the white race a wandering in the western wilderness, sooner than Cuffee will go to preach the Gospel in Guinea."

I think these notions, if the policy of the State shall continue in accordance with them, will be proved to the satisfaction of all Northerners—all who do not trade with Virginia, at least—to be delusions, and fatal ones, before another seventy-nine years of the Republic is accomplished.

And that these papers do give a fair expression to the views and purposes of the present governing influence in Virginia, there is every reason to believe. Not of the majority of the people—they are not quite so demented yet—but of the majority of those whose monopoly of wealth and knowledge has a governing influence on a majority of the people: in a word, of those among the educated and wealthy slaveholders, whose combined patronage and talent, applied with an energy and facility for political labor, unknown to the more conscientious and liberal, is sufficient to make everybody else's interest dependent upon and subservient to their own.

There are certainly, in the State of Virginia, a very large

number of voters, strongly desirous, either from selfish or other motives, that the State should be freed from Slavery. I have conversed with enough myself almost to form a respectable party; and if a party, for that purpose, could once be thoroughly organized and equipped, and its aims well advertised, I have not the least doubt that a majority of the voters of the State would rejoice to enlist in it. But, suppose a man could have been found, with the necessary audacity to offer himself as a candidate to the people on this ground, in opposition alike to the Know Nothings and those who, with artful absurdity, assumed the name of Democrats, at the late election. There is not, probably, one newspaper in the State that could have afforded to support him. If there is, it is published at a manufacturing town, and within a stone's throw of a free State, and where, consequently, there are few, if any, resident slave-owners. If he had attempted to make the rural population acquainted with his plan, he would have had to do so, literally, by hunting them up, one by one. All the ordinary means of collecting assemblages would have been denied him, or he would have been able to make use of them only at very unusual expense. The poor traders and mechanics could not generally have afforded to listen to him, much less to vote for him, because, there being no vote by ballot in Virginia, it would be immediately known; they would be denounced as Abolitionists, and, at least, the slaveholders, who are their most valued customers, would decline employing men who so opposed their interests. Under these circumstances, with all the newspapers and bar-room orators, and many of the pulpits industriously coupling the audacious candidate's purposes with every ridiculous and detestable doctrine, scheme, and " ism," to which a name has ever been fixed, it would appear, to the most conscientious and earnest opponent of Slavery, who yet gives himself the vexation and loss of remaining in the State, a perfect waste of his vote to give it to a man so evidently unable to command a general vote of any significance; and he would determine, probably, to give it where it would tell against the least objectionable of the candidates who stood some chance of being successful. If I had been a Virginian, I should have voted myself for the gasconading mountebank who was elected governor, ambitious and expert for mischief as he certainly is, because I should have been conscientiously bound to prevent, as far as my vote would do it, the success of a party more directly opposed to Democratic principles than is that which disgraced itself by allowing him to be nominated as the exponent of its strength.

It can only be by affiliating itself with a party of great strength and success at the North, that a party opposed to the interest of the Slave stock-jobbers can get upon its legs in any Slave State. It must have a prestige of national success, to encourage the immense labor of sufficient organization for local success. Only by a resolute determination of the thinking men of the Democratic party in the free States, not to be driven from the Jeffersonian creed upon Slavery, can the Democratic party in Virginia be made responsive to the wants of the common people, or otherwise than obstructive in its action to their prosperity.

THE FUTURE PROSPECT.

Rail-roads and guano seem, just now, to give much life and improvement to Virginia.

Rail-roads, badly as they are managed, must encourage activity and punctuality in the people, besides increasing the value of exports of the country through which they pass, and diminishing the cost of imports by lessening the above-sea freightage expenses. Beside which, they cannot be prevented from disseminating intelligence and stirring thought, and in this way they will do more than any school-system at present possible.

Guano not only increases the immediate crops, to which it is applied, very profitably, but may be made the means of rapidly and permanently restoring the fertility of exhausted soils. Where judiciously employed, as it is by most men of wealth and education, it will do much good; where ignorantly or improvidently employed, with a thought only of immediate returns, it will probably lead to a still greater exhaustion of the soil, and lessen the real wealth of the poor farmer. Thus it would seem likely to better the wealthy and intelligent, and eventually injure the lower class. It must be added that there is now a very strong and most judiciously conducted State Agricultural Society, and one of the best agricultural journals in the United States (the *Southern Planter*) is published at Richmond.

The Constitution of the State has been democratized lately, so that poor people may vote, but no sufficient system of instruction has been instituted; and, though great promises are now made, it is probable, as I have shown, that, while Slavery lasts, there never can be. The majority of the people will, therefore, continue to be amused and used by greedy and ambitious speculators in politics; and, unless the West is more intelligent than it has thus far shown itself to be, the State will yet, for an indefinite time, be wholly ruled by the slaveholders, and everything else will continue, as heretofore, to be sacrificed to what they suppose to be their interests.

But, on the whole, the condition of the people has certainly improved, since the Revolution, both in comfort and in intelligence; less so, very much, than in the Free States, yet very distinctly.

The diffusion of intelligence, and, with it, of wealth, is likely to be even more rapid in future, and must be expected, eventually, to result in a revolution and reorganization of society, with Free Trade in Labor as its corner-stone. Whether this process shall be spasmodic and bloody, or gradual and peaceful, will depend on the manner in which it is resisted. It may come this century, it may come the next. The sooner the better, if broader and more important interests are not too greatly endangered. For, if soon, Virginia might yet be the most attractive field of enterprise and industry in America, and would rapidly be occupied by an ambitious and useful laboring population—the parent of an intelligent and respectable people.

As things are, citizens of the free States, especially needing good land on which to use their labor, with a mild climate, and other advantages available in Virginia, might, perhaps, colonize in the vicinity of rail-roads, or of the Ohio, and its navigable tributaries, with advantage, if they could settle together in sufficient numbers to give business to various kinds of industry. Under no other circumstances can I recommend any one in the free States to choose in Virginia a residence for a family, unless a move southward be deemed peculiarly desirable, as offering a chance to prolong life, imperiled in our harsher atmospheres.

CHAPTER V.

NORTH CAROLINA.

"MINE EASE IN MINE"—HOTEL.

THE largest and best hotel in Norfolk had been closed, shortly before I was there, from want of sufficient patronage to sustain it, and I was obliged to go to another house which, though quite pretending, was very shamefully kept. The land-lord paid scarcely the smallest attention to the wants of his guests, turned his back when inquiries were made of him, and replied insolently to complaints and requests. His slaves were far his superiors in manners and morals; but, not being one quarter in number what were needed, and consequently not being able to obey one quarter of the orders that were given them, their only study was to disregard, as far as they would be allowed to, all requisitions upon their time and labor. The smallest service could only be obtained by bully-ing or bribing. I had to make a bargain for every clean towel that I got during my stay.

I was first put in a very small room, in a corner of the house, next under the roof. The weather being stormy, and the roof leaky, water was frequently dripping from the ceiling upon the bed and driving in at the window, so as to stand in pools upon the floor. There was no fire-place in the room; the ladies' parlor was usually crowded by ladies and their friends, among whom I had no acquaintance, and, as it was freezing cold, I was obliged to spend most of my time in the stinking bar-room, where the landlord, all the time, sat with his boon companions, smoking and chewing and talking obscenely.

This crew of old reprobates frequently exercised their indignation upon Mrs. Stowe, and other "Infidel abolitionists;" and, on Sunday, having all attended church, afterwards mingled with their ordinary ribaldry laudations of the "evangelical" character of the sermons they had heard.

On the night I arrived, I was told that I would be provided, the next morning, with a room in which I could have a fire, and a similar promise was given me every twelve hours, for five days, before I obtained it; then, at last, I had to share it with two strangers.

When I left, the same petty sponging operation was practiced upon me as at Petersburg. The breakfast, for which half a dollar had been paid, was not ready until an hour after I had been called; and, when ready, consisted of cold salt fish; dried slices of bread and tainted butter; coffee, evidently made the day before and half re-warmed; no milk, the milkman not arriving so early in the morning, the servant said; and no sooner was I seated than the choice was presented to me, by the agitated book-keeper, of going without such as this, or of losing the train and so being obliged to stay in the house twenty-four hours longer.

Of course I dispensed with the breakfast, and hurried off with the porter, who was to take my baggage on a wheel-barrow to the station. The station was across the harbor, in Ports-

mouth.   Notwithstanding all the haste I could communicate
to him, we reached the ferry-landing just as the boat left,
too late by three seconds.   I looked at my watch; it lacked
but twenty minutes of the time at which the landlord and the
book-keeper and the breakfast-table waiter and the rail-road
company's advertisements had informed me that the train
left.   "Nebber mine, masser," said the porter, " dey wont go
widout 'ou—Baltimore boat haant ariv yet; dey doan go
till dat come in, such."

Somewhat relieved by this assurance, and by the arrival of
others at the landing, who evidently expected to reach the
train, I went into the market and bought a breakfast from
the cake and fruit stalls of the negro women.

In twenty minutes the ferry-boat returned, and after waiting some time at the landing, put out again; but when midway across the harbor, the wheels ceased to revolve, and for
fifteen minutes we drifted with the tide.   The fireman had
been asleep, the fires had got low, and the steam given out.
I observed that the crew, including the master or pilot, and
the engineer, were all negroes.

We reached the rail-road station about half an hour after the
time at which the train should have left.   There were several
persons, prepared for traveling, waiting about it, but there
was no sign of a departing train, and the ticket-office was
not open.   I paid the porter, sent him back, and was added
to the number of the waiters.

The delay was for the Baltimore boat, which arrived in
an hour after the time the train was advertised, uncondition-
ally, to start, and the first forward movement was more than
an hour and a half behind time.   A brakeman told me this

delay was not very unusual, and that an hour's waiting might be commonly calculated upon with safety.

The distançe from Portsmouth to Welden, N. C., eighty miles, was run in three hours and twenty minutes—twenty-five miles an hour. The road, which was formerly a very poor and unprofitable one, was bought up a few years ago, mainly, I believe, by Boston capital, and reconstructed in a substantial manner. The grades are light, and there are few curves. Fare $2\frac{3}{4}$ cents a mile.

At a way-station, a trader had ready a company of negroes, intended to be shipped South; but the "servants' car" being quite full already, they were obliged to be left for another train. As we departed from the station, I stood upon the platform of the rear car with two other men. One said to the other :—

" That's a good lot of niggers."

"Damn'd good ; I only wished they belonged to me."

I entered the car and took a seat, and presently they followed, and sat near me. Continuing their conversation thus commenced, they spoke of their bad luck in life. One appeared to have been a bar-keeper; the other an overseer. One said the highest wages he had ever been paid were two hundred dollars a year, and that year he hadn't laid up a cent. Soon after, the other, speaking with much energy and bitterness, said:

" I wish to God old Virginny was free of all the niggers."

" It would be a good thing if she was."

"Yes, sir ; and, I tell you, it would be a damn'd good thing for us poor fellows."

" I reckon it would, myself."

When we stopped at Weldon, a man was shouting from a

stage-coach, "passengers for Gaston! Hurry up! Stage is waiting!" As he repeated this the third time, I threw up to him my two valises, and proceeded to climb to the box, to take my seat.

"You are in a mighty hurry, aint ye!"

"Didn't you say the stage was waiting?"

"If ye'r goin' ter get any dinner to-day, you'd better get it here; won't have much other chance. Be right smart about it, too."

"Then you are not going yet?"

"You can get yer dinner, if ye want to."

"You'll call me, will you, when you are ready to go?"

"I shan't go without ye, ye needn't be afeard—go 'long in, and get yer dinner; this is the place, if anywar;—don't wan't to go without yer dinner, do ye?"

Before arriving at Weldon, a handbill, distributed by the proprietors of this inn, had been placed in my hands, from which I make the following extracts:

"We pledge our word of honor, as gentlemen, that if the fare at our table be inferior to that on the table of our enterprising competitor, we will not receive a cent from the traveler, but relinquish our claims to pay, as a merited forfeit, for what we would regard as a wanton imposition upon the rights and claims of the unsuspecting traveler.

"We have too much respect for the Ladies of our House, to make even a remote allusion to their domestic duties in a public circular. It will not, however, be regarded indelicate in us to say, that the duties performed by them have been, and are satisfactory to us, and, as far as we know, to the public. And we will only add, in this connection, that we take much pleasure in superintending both our "Cook-House" and Table in person, and in administering in person to the wants of our guests.

"We have made considerable improvements in our House of late, and those who wish to remain over at Weldon, will find, with us, **airy rooms,** clean beds, brisk fires, and attentive and orderly servants, with abundance of FRESH OYSTERS during the season, and every necessary and luxury that money can procure.

" It is not our wish to deceive strangers nor others ; and if, on visiting our House, they do not find things as here represented, they can publish us to the world as impostors, and the ignominy will be ours."

Going in to the house, I found most of the passengers by the train at dinner, and the few negro boys and girls in too much of a hurry to pay attention to any one in particular.   The only palatable viand within my reach was some cold sweet-potatoes ; of these I made a slight repast, paid the landlord, who stood like a sentry in the doorway, half a dollar, and in fifteen minutes, by my watch, from the time I had entered, went out, anxious to make sure of my seat on the box, for the coach was so small that but one passenger could be conveniently carried outside.   The coach was gone.

" O, yes, sir," said the landlord, hardly disguising his satisfaction ; " gone—yes, sir, some time ago ; you was in to dinner, was you, sir—pity ! you'll have to stay over till to-morrow now, won't you ?"

" I suppose so," said I, hardly willing to give up my intention to sleep in Raleigh that night, even to secure a clean bed and fresh oysters.   " Which road does the stage go upon ?"

" Along the county road."

" Which is that—this way through the woods ?"

" Yes, sir.—Carried off your baggage, did he?—Pity !   Suppose he forgot you.   Pity !"

" Thank you—yes, I suppose he did.   Is it a pretty good road ?"

" No, sir, 'taint first-rate—good many pretty bad slews.   You might go round by the Petersburg Rail-road, to-morrow. You'd overtake your baggage at Gaston."

"Thank you. It was not a very fast team, I know. I'm going to take a little run; and, if I shouldn't come back before night, you needn't keep a bed for me. Good day, sir."

I am pretty good on the legs for a short man, and it didn't take me long, by the *pas gymnastique*, to overtake the coach.

As I came up, the driver hailed me—

"Hallo! that you?"

"Why did not you wait for me, or call me when you wanted to go, as you promised?"

"Reckoned ye was inside—didn't look in, coz I asked if 'twas all right, and somebody—this 'ere gentleman, here"— (who had got my seat) "'Yes,' says he, 'all right;' so I reckoned 'twas, and driv along. Mustn't blame me. Ortn't to be so long swallerin' yer dinner—mind, next time!"

The road was as bad as anything, under the name of a road, can be conceived to be. Wherever the adjoining swamps, fallen trees, stumps, and plantation fences would admit of it, the coach was driven, with a great deal of dexterity, out of the road. When the wheels sunk in the mud, below the hubs, we were sometimes requested to get out and walk. An upset seemed every moment inevitable. At length, it came; and the driver, climbing on to the upper side, opened the door, and asked, with an irresistibly jolly drawl—

"Got mixed up some in here then, didn't ye? Ladies, hurt any? Well, come, get out here; don't wan't to stay here all night I reckon, do ye?—Aint nothing broke, as I see. We'll right her right up. Nary durn'd rail within a thousan' mile, I don't s'pose; better be lookin' roun'; got to get somethin' for a pry."

In four hours after I left the hotel at Weldon, the coach reached the bank of the Roanoke, a distance of fourteen miles, and stopped. "Here we are," said the driver, opening the door.

"Where are we—not in Gaston?"

"Durned nigh it. That ere's Gaston, over thar; and you just holler, and they'll come over arter you in the boat."

Gaston was a mile above us, and on the other side of the river. Nearly opposite to where we were was a house, and a scow drawn up on the beach; the distance across the river was, perhaps, a quarter of a mile. When the driver had got the luggage off, he gathered his reins, and said:

"Seems to me them gol-durned lazy niggers aint a goin' to come over arter you now; if they won't, you'd better go up to the rail-road bridge, some of ye, and get a boat, or else go down here to Free-town; some of them cussed free niggers 'll be glad of the job, I no doubt."

"But, confound it, driver! you are not going to leave us here, are you? we paid to be carried to Gaston."

"Can't help it; you are close to Gaston, any how, and if any man thinks he's goin' to hev me drive him up to the bridge to-night, he's damnably mistaken, he is, and I ain't a goin' to do it, not for no man, I ain't."

And away he drove, leaving us, all strangers, in a strange country, just at the edge of night, far from any house, to "holler."

The only way to stop him was to shoot him; and, as we were all good citizens, and traveled with faith in the protection of the law, and not like knights-errant, armed for adventure, we could not do that.

Good citizens? No, we were not; for we have all, to this

day, neglected to prosecute the fellow, or his employers. It would, to be sure, have cost us ten times any damages we should have been awarded; but, if we had been really good citizens, we should have been as willing to sacrifice the necessary loss, as knights-errant of old were to risk life to fight bloody giants. And, until many of us can have the nobleness to give ourselves the trouble and expense of killing off these impudent highwaymen of our time, at law, we have all got to suffer in their traps and stratagems.

We soon saw the "gol-durned lazy niggers" come to their scow, and after a scrutiny of our numbers, and a consultation among themselves, which evidently resulted in the conclusion that the job wouldn't pay, go back.

When it began to grow dark, leaving me as a baggage-guard. the rest of the coach's company walked up the bank of the river, and crossed by a rail-road bridge to Gaston. One of them afterwards returned with a gang of negroes, whom he had hired, and a large freight-boat, into which, across the snags which lined the shore, we passed all the baggage. Among the rest, there were some very large and heavy chests, belonging to two pretty women, who were moving, with their effects; and, although they remained in our company all the next day, they not only neglected to pay their share of the boat and negro-hire, but forgot to thank us, or even gratefully to smile upon us, for our long toil in the darkness for them.

Working up the swollen stream of the Roanoke, with setting-poles and oars, we at length reached Gaston. When I bought my tickets at the station in Portsmouth, I said: "I will take tickets to any place this side of Raleigh at which I can arrive before night. I wish to avoid traveling after dark." "You can go straight through to Raleigh, before dark," said the clerk. "You are sure of that?" "Yes, sir." On reaching Gaston, I inquired at what time the train for Raleigh had passed: "At three o'clock." According to the advertisement, it should have passed at two o'clock; and, under the most favorable circumstances, it could not have been possible for us, leaving Portsmouth at the time we did, to reach Gaston before four o'clock, or Raleigh in less than twenty-eight hours after the time promised. The next day, I asked one of the rail-road men how often the connection occurred, which is advertised in the Northern papers, as if it were a certain thing to take place at Gaston. "Not very often, sir; it hain't been once, in the last two weeks." Whenever the connection is not made, all passengers whom these rail-road freebooters have drawn into their ambush, are obliged to remain over a day, at Gaston; for, as is to be supposed, with such management, the business of the road will support but one train a day.

The route by sea, from Baltimore to Portsmouth, and thence by these lines, is advertised as the surest, cheapest, and most expeditious route to Raleigh. Among my stage companions, were some who lived beyond Raleigh. This was Friday. They would now not reach Raleigh till Saturday night, and such as could not conscientiously travel on Sunday, would be detained from home two days longer than if they had come the land route. One of them lived some eighty miles beyond Raleigh, and intended to proceed by a coach, which was to leave Saturday morning. He would probably be now detained till the following Wednesday, as the coach left Raleigh but twice a week.

The country from Portsmouth to Gaston, eighty miles, partly

in Virginia, and partly in North Carolina, is almost all pine forest, or cypress swamp; and on the little land that is cultivated, I saw no indication of any other crop than maize. The soil is light and poor. Between Weldon and Gaston there are heavier soils, and we passed several cotton fields, and substantial planters' mansions. On the low, flat lands bordering the banks of the Roanoke, the soil is of the character of that of James river, fine, fertile, mellow loam; and the maize crop seemed to have been heavy.

GASTON.

Gaston is a village of some twenty houses, shops and cabins, besides the rail-road store-houses, the hotel, and a nondescript building, which may be either a fancy barn, or a little church, getting high. From the manner in which passsengers are forced, by the management of the trains arriving here, to patronize it, the hotel, I presume, belongs to the rail-road companies. It is ill-kept, but affords some entertainment from its travesty of certain metropolitan vulgarities. I was chummed with a Southern gentleman, in a very small room. Finding the sheets on both our beds had been soiled by previous occupants, he made a row about it with the servants, and, after a long delay, had them changed; then, observing that it was probably the mistress's fault, and not the servants', he paid the negro whom he had been berating, for his trouble.

NEGROES ON PUBLIC CONVEYANCES.

Among our inside passengers, in the stage-coach, was a free colored woman; she was treated in no way differently from the white ladies. My room-mate said this was entirely customary at the South, and no Southerner would ever think of objecting to it. Notwithstanding which, I have known young Southerners to get very angry because negroes were not excluded from the public conveyances in which they had taken passage themselves, at the North; and I have always supposed that when they were so excluded, it was from fear of offending Southern travelers, more than anything else.

A South Carolina View of the Subject. (Correspondence of Willis's Musical World, New York).

" CHARLESTON, Dec. 31.

" I take advantage of the season of compliments (being a subscriber to your invaluable sheet), to tender you this scrap, as a reply to a piece in your paper of the 17th ult., with the caption : ' Intolerance of colored persons in New York.' The piece stated that up-town families (in New York) objected to hiring colored persons as servants, in consequence of ' conductors and drivers refusing to let them ride in city cars and omnibuses,' and colored boys, at most, may ride on the top. And after dwelling on this, you say, ' shame on such intolerant and outrageous prejudice and persecution of the colored race at the North !' You then say, ' even the slaveholder would cry shame upon us.' You never made a truer assertion in your life. For you first stated that they were even rejected when they had white children in their arms. My dear friend, if this was the only persecution that your colored people were compelled to yield submission to, then I might say nothing. Are they allowed (if they pay) to sit at the tables of your fashionable hotels ? Are they allowed a seat in the ' dress circle,' at your operas ? Are they not subject to all kinds of ill treatment from the whites ? Are they not pointed at, and hooted at by the whites (natives of the city), when dressed up a little extra, and if they offer a reply, are immediately overpowered by gangs of whites ? You appear to be a reasonable writer, which is the reason I put these queries, knowing they can only be answered in the affirmative.

" We at the South feel proud to allow them to occupy seats in our omnibuses (public conveyances), while they, with the affection of mothers, embrace our white children, and take them to ride. And in our most fashionable carriages, you will see the slave sitting alongside of *their owner.* You will see the slave clothed in the most comfortable of wearing apparel. And more. Touch that slave, if you dare, and you will see the owner's attachment. And thus, in a very few words, you have the contrast between the situation of the colored people at the North and South. Do teach the *detestable* Abolitionist of the North his duty, and open his eyes to the misery and starvation that surrounds his own home. *Teach him* to love his brethren of the South, and teach him to let Slavery alone in the South, while starvation and destitution surrounds him at the North; and oblige,

"BARON."

PHARMACEUTICAL SCIENCE.

Listening to a conversation among some men lounging on the river bank, and who were, probably, brakemen or engineers on the rail-roads, I took notes of the following interesting information:

"Nitrate of silver is a first-rater; you can get it at the 'pothecary shops in Richmond. But the best medicine there is, is this here Idee of Potasun. It's made out of two minerals; one on 'em they gets in the mountains of Scotland—that's the Idee; the other's steel-filings, and they mixes them cschemically until they works altogether into a solid stuff like saltpetre. Now, I tell you that's the stuff for medicine. It's the best thing a man can ever put into his self. It searches out every narve in his body."

GASTON TO RALEIGH—NIGHT TRAINS.

The train by which we were finally able to leave Gaston arrived the next day an hour and a half after its advertised time. The road was excellent and speed good, a heavy U rail having lately been substituted for a flat one. A new equipment of the road, throughout, is nearly complete. The cars of this train were very old, dirty, and with dilapidated and

moth-eaten furniture. They furnished me with a comfort, however, which I have never been able to try before—a full-length
lounge, on which, with my over-coat for a pillow, the car being
warmed, and, unintentionally well ventilated, I slept soundly
after dark. Why night-trains are not furnished with sleeping
apartments, has long been a wonder to me. We have now
smoking-rooms and water-closets on our trains; why not sleeping, dressing, and refreshment rooms? With these additions,
and good ventilation, we, could go from New York to New
Orleans by rail without stopping: as it is, a man of ordinary
constitution cannot go a quarter that distance without suffering
serious indisposition. Surely such improvements could not fail
to be remunerative, particularly on lines competing with water
communication.

The country passed through, so far as I observed, was almost
entirely covered with wood; and such of it as was cultivated,
very unproductive.

RALEIGH.

The city of Raleigh (old Sir Walter), the capital of North
Carolina, is a pleasing town—the streets wide and lined with
trees, and many white wooden mansions, all having little court-
yards of flowers and shrubbery around them. The State-House
is, in every way, a noble building, constructed of brownish-grey
granite, in Grecian style. It stands on an elevated position,
near the centre of the city, in a square field, which is shaded
by some tall old oaks, and could easily be made into an appropriate and beautiful little park; but which, with singular
negligence, or more singular economy (while $500,000 has
been spent upon the simple edifice), remains in a rude state

of undressed nature, and is used as a hog-pasture. A trifle of the expense, employed with doubtful advantage, to give a smooth exterior face to the blocks of stone, if laid out in grading, smoothing, and dressing its ground base, would have added indescribably to the beauty of the edifice. An architect should always begin his work upon the ground.

There are several other public buildings and institutions of charity and education, honorable to the State. A church, near the Capitol, not yet completed, is very beautiful; cruciform in ground plan, the walls of stone, and the interior wood-work of oiled native pine, and with, thus far, none of the irreligious falsities in stucco and paint that so generally disenchant all expression of worship in our city meeting-houses.

It is hard to admire what is common; and it is, perhaps, asking too much of the citizens of Raleigh, that they should plant for ornament, or even cause to be retained about such institutions as their Lunatic Asylum, the beautiful evergreens that crowd about the town; but can any man walk from the Capitol oaks to the pine grove, a little beyond the Deaf and Dumb Institution, and say that he would not far rather have the latter than the former to curtain in his habitation? If he can in summer, let him try it again, as I did, in a soft winter's day, when the evergreens fill the air with a balsamic odor, and the green light comes quivering through them, and the foot falls silently upon the elastic carpet they have spread, deluding one with all the feelings of spring.

The country, for miles about Raleigh, is nearly all pine forest, unfertile, and so little cultivated, that it is a mystery how a town of 2,500 inhabitants can obtain sufficient supplies from it to exist.

The public-house at which I stayed was, however, not only well supplied, but was excellently well kept, for a house of its class, in all other respects.   The landlord superintended his business personally, and was always attentive and obliging to his guests; and the servants were sufficiently numerous, intelligent, and well instructed.   Though I had no acquaintances in Raleigh, I remained, finding myself in such good quarters, several days.   I think the house was called " The Burlinghame."

A STAGE-COACH CAMPAIGN.

After this stay, rendered also partly necessary for the repair of damages to my clothing and baggage on the Weldon stage, I engaged a seat one day on the coach, advertised to leave at nine o'clock for Fayetteville.   At half-past nine, tired of waiting for its departure, I told the agent, as it was not ready to start, I would walk on a bit, and let them pick me up.   I found a rough road—for several miles a clayey surface and much water—and was obliged to pick my way a good deal through the woods on either side.   Stopping frequently, when I came to cultivated land, to examine the soil and the appearance of the stubble of the maize—the only crop—in three different fields I made five measurements at random, of fifty feet each, and found the stalks had stood, on an average, five feet by two feet one inch apart, and that, generally, they were not over an inch in diameter at the butt.   In one old-field, in process of clearing for new cultivation, I examined a most absurd little plow, with a share not more than six inches in depth, and eight in length on the sole, fastened by a socket to a stake, to which was fitted a short beam and stilts.   It was drawn by one mule, and its work among the stumps could only

be called scratching. A farmer told me that he considered
twenty-five bushels of corn a large crop, and that he generally
got as much as fifteen. He said that no money was to be got
by raising corn, and very few farmers here "made" any more than
they needed for their own force. It cost too much to get it to
market, and yet sometimes they had had to buy corn at a dollar
a bushel, and wagon it home from Raleigh, or further, enough
not having been raised in the country for home consumption.
Cotton was the only crop they got any money for. I, nevertheless, did not see a single cotton-field during the day. He
said that the largest crop of corn that he knew of, reckoned to
be fifty bushels to the acre, had been raised on some reclaimed
swamp, while it was still so wet that horses would mire on it
all the summer, and most of it had been tended entirely with
hoes.

A very fine oak tree, standing by itself on some elevated
ground, having attracted me to a considerable distance from
the road, I found that the spread of its branches covered a
circle of the diameter of forty-two paces.

After walking a few miles, the country became more flat, and
was covered with old forests of yellow pine, and, at nine miles
south of Raleigh, there were occasionally young long-leaved
pines : exceedingly beautiful they are while young, the color
being more agreeable than that of any other pine, and the
leaves, or *straw*, as its foliage is called here, long, graceful,
and lustrous. As the tree gets older, it becomes of a stiffer
character and darker color.

I do not think I passed, in ten miles, more than half a dozen
homesteads, and of these but one was above the character of a
hut or cabin.

A little after one o'clock I reached "Bank's," a plantation where the stage horses are changed, eleven miles from Raleigh; and the coach not having arrived, I asked for something to eat. A lunch was prepared for me in about fifteen minutes. There was nothing on the table, when I was invited to it, except some cold salt pork and pickled beets; but as long as I remained, at intervals of two or three minutes, additions would be made, till at last there had accumulated five different preparations of swine's flesh, and two or three of corn, most of them just cooked; the only vegetable, pickled beets.

Before I finished my repast, the coach arrived, and I took my seat.

"All right?" asked the driver.

"You haven't changed your horses."

"Goin' ter change the wheelers on top the hill; horses in the field there."

Having reached the hill top, the change was effected—a change, but no improvement. The fresh horses could do but little more than stand up; there was not one among them that would have sold for twenty-five dollars in New York. "There ain't a man in North Car'lina could drive them horses up the hills without a whip," said the driver. "You ought to get yesef a whip, massa," said one of the negroes. "*Durnation!* think I'm going to buy whips; the best whip in North Car'lina wouldn't last a week on this road." "Dat's a fac—dat ar is a fac; but look yeah, massa, ye let me hab yer stick, and I'll make a whip for ye; ye nebber can make Bawley go widout it, no now." The stick was a sapling rod, of which two or three lay on the coach top; the negro fastened a long leather thong to it. "Dah! ye can fetch old Bawley wi' dat." "Bawley" had been tackled in as the leader of the "spike team;" but, upon attempting to start, it was found that he couldn't be driven in that way at all, and the driver took him out and put him to the pole, within reach of the butt of his stick, and another horse was put on the lead.

One negro now took the leader by the head, and applied a stick lustily to his flanks; another, at the near wheeler, did the same; and the driver belabored Bawley from the box. But as soon as they began to move forward, and the negro let go the leader's head, he would face about. After this had been repeated many times, a new plan of operations was arranged that proved successful. Leaving the two wheelers to the care of the negroes, the driver was enabled to give all his attention to the leader. When the wheelers started, of course he was struck by the pole, upon which he would turn tail and start for the stable. The negroes kept the wheelers from following him, and the driver with his stick, and another negro with the bough of a tree, thrashed his face; he would then turn again, and, being hit by the pole, start ahead. So, after ten minutes of fearful outcry, we got off.

"How far is it to Mrs. Barclay's?" a passenger had asked. "Thirteen miles," answered a negro; "but I tell 'ou, massa, dais a heap to be said and talk 'bout 'fore 'ou see Missy Barclay's wid dem hosses." There was, indeed.

"Bawley—*you!* Bawley—Bawley! wha' 'bout?—ah!"

"*Rock!* wha' you doin'?—(durned sick horse—an't fit to be in a stage, nohow)."

"Bawley! you! g'up!"

"Oh! you dod-rotted Bob—*Bob!*—(he don't draw a pound, and he an't a goin' to)—*you*, Bob!—(well, he can't *stop, can he*, as long as the wheelers keep movin'?)   Bob!   I'll break yer legs, you don't git out the way."

"Oh, Bawley!—(no business to put such a lame hoss into the stage.)   Blamnation, Bawley!   Now, if you stop, I'll kill you."

"Wha' 'bout, Rock?   Dod burn that Rock!   You stop if you dare!   (I'll be durned to Hux if that ere hoss arn't all used up.)"

"You, *Bob!* get out de way, or I'll be ———."

"Oh! d'rot yer soul, Bawley—y're goin' to stop!   G'up! G'up!   *Rock!*   You all-fired ole villain!   Wha' 'bout?   (If they jus' git to stoppin', all hell couldn't git the mails through to-night.)"

After about three miles of this, they did stop.   The driver threw the reins down in despair.   After looking at the wheels, and seeing that we were on a good piece of road, nothing unusual to hinder progress, he put his hands in his pockets, and sat quietly a minute, and then began, in a business-like manner, to swear, no longer confining himself to the peculiar idiomatic profanity of the country, but using real, outright, old-fashioned, uncompromising English oaths, as loud as he could yell.   Then he stopped, and, after another pause, began to talk quietly to the horses:

"You, Bob, you won't draw?   Didn't you git enough last night?   (I jabbed my knife into his face twice when we got into that fix last night;" and the wounds on the horse's head showed that he spoke the truth.)   "I swar, Bob, if I have to come down thar, I'll *cut your throat.*"

He stopped again, and then sat down on the foot-board, and began to beat the wheelers as hard and as rapidly as possible with the butt of his stick.   They started, and, striking Bob with the pole, he jumped and turned round; but a happy stroke on "the raw" in his face brought him to his place; and the stick being applied just in time to the wheelers, he caught the pole and jumped ahead. We were off again.

"Turned over in that 'ere mire hole last night," said the driver. "Couldn't do anythin' with 'em—passengers camped out—thar's where they had their fire, under that tree; didn't get to Raleigh till nine o'clock this mornin'. That's the reason I wern't along arter you any sooner—hadn't got my breakfast; that's the reason the hosses don't draw no better to-day, too, I s'pose. *You*, Rock!—*Bawley!*—Bob!

After two miles more, the horses stopped once more. The driver now quietly took the leader off (he had never drawn at all), and tied him behind the coach. He then began beating the near-wheeler, a passenger did the same to Bawley—both standing on the ground—while I threw off my over-coat and walked on. For a time I could occasionally hear the cry, "Bawl—Rock!" and knew that the coach was moving again; gradually I outwalked the sound.

THE PINY WOOD.

I was now fairly in the Turpentine region of North Carolina. The road was a mere opening through a forest of the long-leafed pine; the trees from eight to eighteen inches in diameter, with straight trunks bare for nearly thirty feet, and their ever-green foliage forming a dense dark canopy at that hight, the surface of the ground undulating with long swells, occasionally low and wet. In the latter case, there was generally a mingling of deciduous trees and a water-course crossing the road, with a thicket of shrubs. The soil sandy, with occasionally veins of clay; the latter more commonly in the low ground, or in the descent to it. Very little grass, herbage, or under-wood; and the ground covered, except in the road, with the fallen pine-leaves. Every tree, on one, two, or three sides, was scarified for turpentine. In ten miles, I passed half a dozen cabins, one or two small clearings, in which corn had been planted, and one turpentine distillery, with a dozen sheds and cabins clustered about it.

In about an hour after I left the coach, the driver, mounted on Bob, overtook me: he was going on to get fresh horses.

After dark, I had some difficulty in keeping the road, there being frequent forks, and my only guide the telegraph wire. I had to cross three or four brooks, which were now high, and had sometimes floated off the logs which, in this country, are commonly placed, for the teamsters, along the side of the road, where it runs through water. I could generally jump from stump to stump; and, by wading a little at the edges in my staunch Scotch shooting boots, get across dry-shod. Where, however, the water was too deep, I always found, by going up or down stream, a short way, a fallen trunk across it, by which I got over.

I met the driver returning with two fresh horses; and at length, before eight o'clock, reached a long one-story cabin, which I found to be Mrs. Barclay's. It was right cheerful and comforting to open the door, from the dark, damp, chilly night, into a large room, filled with blazing light from a great fire of turpentine pine, by which two stalwart men were reading newspapers, a door opening into a back-ground of supper-table and kitchen, and a nice, stout, kindly-looking, Quaker-like old lady coming forward to welcome me.

As soon as I was warm, I was taken out to supper: seven

preparations of swine's flesh, two of maize, wheat cakes, broiled quails, cold roast turkey, coffee, and tea.

My bed-room was a house by itself, the only connection between it and the main building being a platform, or gallery, in front. A great fire burned here also in a broad fire-place; a stuffed easy-chair had been placed before it, and a tub of hot water, which I had not thought to ask for, to bathe my weary feet.

And this was a piny-woods stage-house! But genius will find its development, no matter where its lot is cast; and there is as much a genius for hospitality as for poetry. Mrs. Barclay is a Burns in her way, and with even more modesty; for, after twenty-four hours of the best entertainment that could be asked for, I was only charged one dollar. I paid two dollars for my stage-coach privileges—to wit, riding five miles and walking twenty-one.

At three o'clock in the morning, the three gentlemen' that I had left ten miles back at four o'clock the previous day, were dragged, shivering in the stage-coach, to the door. They had had no meal since breakfasting at Raleigh; and one of them was now so tired that he could not eat, but lay down on the floor before the fire and slept the half hour they were changing horses, or rather resting horses, for there was nothing left to change to.

I afterwards met one of the company in Fayetteville. Their night's adventure after I left them, and the continued cruelty to the horses, were really most distressing. The driver once got off the box, and struck the poor, miserable, sick "Rock" with a rail, and actually knocked him down in the road. At another time, after having got the fresh horses, when they, too, were "stalled," he took them out of the harness and turned them loose, and, refusing to give any answer to the inquiries of the passengers, looked about for a dry place, and laid down and went to sleep on the ground. One of the passengers had then walked on to Mrs. Barclay's, and obtained a pair of mules, with which the coach was finally brought to the house. The remainder kindled a fire, and tried to rest themselves by it. They were sixteen hours in coming thirty miles, suffering much from cold, and without food.

The next day I spent in visiting turpentine and rosin works, piny-wood farms, etc., under the obliging guidance of Mrs. Barclay's son-in-law, and in the evening again took the coach. The horses were better than on the previous stage: upon my remarking this to the driver, he said that the reason was, that they took care of this team themselves (the drivers); on the last stage the horses were left to negroes, who would not feed them regularly, nor take any decent care of them. "Why, what do you think?" said he, "when I got to Banks's, this morning, I found my team hadn't been fed all day; they hadn't been rubbed nor cleaned, nary durned thing done to 'em, and thar the cussed darkey was, fast asleep. Reckon I didn't gin him a wakin' up!"

"You don't mean the horses that you drove up?"

"Yes, I do, and they hadn't a cussed thing to eat till they got back to Barclay's!"

"How was it possible for you to drive them back?"

"Why, I don't suppose I could ha' done it if I'd had any passengers: (you *Suze!*) shall lose a mail again to-night, if this mare don't travel better, (durn ye, yer ugly, I believe). She's a good mare—a heap of go in her, but it takes right smart of work to get it out. *Suze!*"

So we toiled on, with incessant shouting, and many strange

piny-wood oaths, and horrid belaboring of the poor horses' backs, with the butt-end of a hickory whip-stalk, till I really thought their spinal-columns must break. The country, the same undulating pine forest, the track tortuous among the trees, which frequently stood so close that it required some care to work between them. Often we made detours from the original road to avoid a fallen tree, or a mire-hole, and all the time we were bouncing over protruding roots and small stumps. There was but little mud, the soil being sand, but now and then a deep slough. In one of these we found a wagon, heavily laden, stuck fast, and six mules and five negroes tugging at it. With our help it was got out of the way, and we passed on. Soon afterwards we met the return coach, apparently in a similar predicament; but one of the passengers, whom I questioned, replied: "No, not stalled, exactly, but somehow *the horses won't draw.* We have been more than three hours coming about four miles."

"How is it you have so many balky horses?" I asked the driver.

"The old man buys 'em up cheap, 'cause nobody else can do anything with 'em."

"I should not think you could do much with them, either—except to kill them."

"Well, that's what the old man says he buys 'em for. He was blowing me up for losing the mail t'other night; I told him, says I, 'you have to a'most kill them horses, 'fore you can make 'em draw a bit,' says I. 'Kill 'em, damn 'em, kill 'em, then; that's what I buy 'em for,' says he. 'I buy 'em a purpose to kill; that's all they are good for, ain't it?' says he. 'Don't s'pose they're going to last forever, do ye?' says he."

We stopped once, nearly half an hour, for some unexplained

reason, before a house on the road. The door of the house was open, an enormous fire was burning in it, and, at the suggestion of the driver, I went in to warm myself. It was a large log-cabin, of two rooms, with beds in each room, and with an apartment overhead, to which access was had by a ladder. Among the inmates were two women; one of them sat at the chimney-corner, smoking a pipe, and rocking a cradle; the other sat directly before the fire, and full ten feet distant. She was apparently young, but her face was as dry and impassive as a dead man's. She was doing nothing, and said but little; but, once in about a minute, would suddenly throw up her chin, and spit with perfect precision across the ten feet range, into the hottest embers of the fire. The furniture of the house was more scanty and rude than I ever saw before in any house, with women living in it, in the United States. Yet these people were not so poor but that they had a negro woman cutting and bringing wood for their fire.

It must be remembered that this is a long-settled country, having been occupied by Anglo-Saxons as early as any part of the Free States.

There is nothing that is more closely connected, both as cause and effect, with the prosperity and wealth of a country, than its means and modes of traveling, and of transportation of the necessities and luxuries of life. I saw this day, as I shall hereafter describe, three thousand barrels, of an article worth a dollar and a half a barrel in New York, thrown away, a mere heap of useless offal, because it would cost more to transport it than it would be worth. There was a single wagon, with a ton or two of sugar, and flour, and tea, and axes, and cotton cloths, unable to move, with six mules and five negroes at work upon it.

Raleigh is a large distributing post-office, getting a very heavy mail from the North; here was all that is sent by one of its main radii, traveling one day two miles an hour, the next four miles, and on each occasion failing to connect with the conveyances which we pay to scatter further the intelligence and wealth transmitted by it. Barbarous is too mild a term to apply to the manner in which even this was done. The improvidence, if not the cruelty, no sensible barbarian could have been guilty of.

Afterwards, merely to satisfy my mind (for there is a satisfaction in seeing even scoundrelism consistently carried out, if attempted at all in a business), I called on the agent of the line at Fayetteville, stated the case, and asked if any part of what I had paid for my passage would be returned me, on account of the disappointment and delay which I had suffered from the inability of the proprietor to carry out his contract with me. The impudence of the suggestion, of course, only created amusement; and I was smilingly informed that the business was not so "lucky" that the proprietor could afford to pay back money that he had once got into his hands.

A PRAYING BLACKSMITH.

At one of the stations for changing horses, an old colored man was taken into the coach. I ascertained from him that he was a blacksmith, and had been up the line to shoe the horses at the different stables. Probably he belonged (poor fellow,) to the man who bought horses to be killed in doing his work. After answering my inquiries, he lay down in the bottom of the coach, and slept until we reached Fayetteville. The next time we changed, the new driver inquired of the old one what passengers he had. "Only one gentleman, and old man Ned."

"Oh! is old man along—that's good—if we should turn over, or break down, or anything, reckon he could nigh about pray us up—he's right smart at prayin'."

"Well, I tell you, now, ole man can trot out as smart a prayer, when he's a mind to go in for't, as any man I ever heerd, durned if he can't."

The last ten miles we came over rapidly, smoothly, and quietly, by a plank-road, reaching Fayetteville about twelve, of a fine, clear, frosty night.

TALENT APPLIED TO INN-KEEPING.

Entering the office or bar-room of the stage-house, at which I had been advised to stay while in Fayetteville, I found it occupied by a group of old soakers, among whom was one of perhaps sixteen years of age. This lad, without removing the cigar which he had in his mouth, went to the bar, whither I followed him, and, without saying a word, placed an empty tumbler before me.

"I don't wish anything to drink," said I; "I am cold and tired, and I would like to go to a room. I intend to stay here some days, and I should be glad if you could give me a private room, and I should like to have a fire in it."

"Room with a fire in it?" he inquired, as he handed me the registry-book.

"Yes, and I will thank you to have it made immediately, and let my baggage be taken up."

He closed the book, after I had written my name, and returned to his seat at the stove, leaving me standing, and immediately engaged in conversation, without paying any attention to my request. I waited some time, during which a negro came into the room, and went out again. I then repeated my request, necessarily aloud, and in such a way as to be understood, not only by the boy, but by all the company. Immediately all conversation ceased, and every head was turned to look at me. Some faces showed evident signs of amusement. The lad paused a moment, spit upon the stove, and then—

" Want a room to yourself?"

" Yes, if convenient, and with a fire in it."

No answer and no movement, all the company staring at me as if I was a detected burglar.

" Perhaps you can't accommodate me?"

" Want a fire made in your room?"

" Why, yes, if convenient; but I should like to go to my room, at any rate; I am very tired."

After puffing and spitting for a moment, he rose and pulled a bell; then took his seat again. In about five minutes a negro came in, and during all this time there was silence.

" What'll you drink, Baker," said the lad, rising and going to the bar, and taking no notice of the negro's entrance. A boozy man followed him, and made some reply; the lad turned out two glasses of spirits, added water to one, and drank it in a gulp.*

" Can this boy show me to my room?" I asked.

" Anybody in number eleven, Peter?"

* The mother of this young man remonstrated with a friend of mine, for permitting his son to join a company of civil engineers, engaged, at the time, in surveying a route for a road—he would be subject to such fatiguing labor, and so much exposure to the elements; and congratulated herself that her own child was engaged in such an easy and gentleman-like employment as that of hotel-clerk and bar-keeper.

"Not as I knows on, sar."

"Take this man's baggage up there."

I followed the negro up to number eleven, which was a large back room, in the upper story, with four beds in it.

"Peter," said I, "I want a fire made here."

"Want a fire, sar?"

"Yes, I want you to make a fire."

"Wan't a fire, master, this time o' night?"

"Why, yes! I want a fire! Where are you going with the lamp?"

"Want a lamp, massa?"

"Want a lamp? Certainly, I do."

After about ten minutes, I heard a man splitting wood in the yard, and, in ten more, Peter brought in three sticks of green wood, and some chips; then, the little bed-lamp having burned out, he went into an adjoining room, where I heard him talking to some one, evidently awakened by his entrance to get a match; that failing, he went for another. By one o'clock, my fire was made.

"Peter," said I, "are you going to wait on me, while I stay here?"

"Yes, sar; I 'tends to dis room."

"Very well; take this, and, when I leave, I'll give you another, if you take good care of me. Now, I wan't you to get me some water."

"I'll get you some water in de morning, sar."

"I want some to-night—some water and some towels; don't you think you can get them for me?"

"I reckon so, massa, if you wants 'em. Want 'em 'fore you go to bed?"

"Yes; and get another lamp."

"Want a lamp?"

"Yes, of course."

"Won't the fire do you?"

"No; bring a lamp. That one won't burn without filling; you need not try it."

The water and the lamp came, after a long time.

In the morning, early, I was awakened by a knock at the door.

"Who's there?"

"Me, massa; I wants your boots to black."

I got up, opened the door, and returned to bed. Falling asleep, I was soon again awakened by Peter throwing down an armful of wood upon the floor. Slept again, and was again awakened, by Peter's throwing up the window, to empty out the contents of the wash-bowl, etc. The room was filled with smoke of the fat light-wood: Peter had already made a fire for me to dress by; but I again fell asleep, and, when I next awoke, the breakfast-bell was ringing. Peter had gone off, and left both the window and the door open. The smoke had been blown out, and the fire had burned out. My boots had been taken away, and not returned; and the bell-wire was broken. I dressed, and walked to the bar-room in my stockings, and asked the bar-keeper—a polite, full-grown man—for my boots. He did not know where they were, and rang the bell for Peter. Peter came, was reprimanded for his forgetfulness, and departed. Ten minutes elapsed, and he did not return. I again requested that he should be called; and, this time, he came with my boots. He had had to stop to black them; having, he said, been too busy to do it before breakfast.

The following evening, as it grew too cold to write in my room, I went down, and found Peter, and told him I wanted a fire again, and that he might get me a couple of candles. When he came up, he brought one of the little bed-lamps, with a capacity of oil for fifteen minutes' use. I sent him down again to the office, with a request to the proprietor that I might be furnished with candles. He returned, and reported that there were no candles in the house.

"Then, get me a larger lamp."

"Aint no larger lamps, nuther, sar;—none to spare."

"Then go out, and see if you can't buy me some candles, somewhere."

"Aint no stores open, Sunday, massa, and I don't know where I can buy 'em."

"Then go down, and tell the bar-keeper, with my compliments, that I wish to write in my room, and I would be obliged to him if he would send me a light, of some sort; something that will last longer, and give more light, than these little lamps."

"He won't give you none, massa—not if you hab a fire. Can't you see by da light of da fire? When a gentleman hab a fire in his room, dey don't count he wants no more light 'n dat."

"Well, make the fire, and I'll go down and see about it."

As I reached the foot of the stairs, the bell rung, and I went in to tea. The tea-table was moderately well lighted with candles. I waited till the company had generally left it, and then said to one of the waiters:

"Here are two dimes: I want you to bring me, as soon as you can, two of these candles to number eleven; do you understand?"

"Yes, sar; I'll fotch 'em, sar."

And he did.

"FIRE!   TURN OUT!"

About eight o'clock, there was an alarm of fire.   Going into
the street, I was surprised to observe how leisurely the people
were walking towards the house in flames, standing very prominently, as it did, upon a hill, at one end of the town.   As I
passed a church, the congregation was coming out; but very
few quickened their step above a strolling pace.   Arrived near
the house, I was still more astonished to see how few, of the
crowd assembled, were occupied in restraining the progress
of the fire, or in saving the furniture, and at the prevailing
stupidity, confusion, and want of system and concert of action,
in the labor for this purpose.   A large majority of those who
were thus engaged were negroes.   As I returned towards the
hotel, a gentleman, walking, with a lady, before me, on the
side-walk, accosted a negro whom he met:

"What! Moses!   That you?   Why were you not here
sooner?"

"Why, Mass Richard, I was a singing, an' I didn' her de
bells and——I see twant in our ward, sar, and so I didn' see
as dar was zactly 'casion for me to hurry mysef to def.   Ef eed
a been in our ward, Mass Richard, I'd a rallied, you knows
I would.   Mose would ha rallied, ef eed a been in our ward—
ha! ha! ha!—you knows it, Mass Richard!"

And he passed on, laughing comically, without further re-

Turpentine is the crude sap of pine-trees. It varies somewhat, in character and in freedom of flow, with the different
varieties; the long-leafed pine (*Pinus Palustris*) yielding it more
freely than any other.

There are very large forests of this tree in North and South
Carolina, Georgia, and Alabama; and the turpentine business is
carried on, to some extent, in all these States.   In North Carolina, however, much more largely than in the others; because,
in it, cotton is rather less productive than in the others, in an
average of years.   Negroes are, therefore, in rather less demand;
and their owners oftener see their profit in employing them in
turpentine orchards than in the cotton-fields.

In the region in which the true turpentine-trees grow, indeed,
there is no soil suitable for growing cotton; and it is only in the
swampy parts, or on the borders of streams flowing through it,
that there is any attempt at agriculture.   The farmer, in the
forest, makes nothing for sale but turpentine, and, when he
cultivates the land, his only crop is maize; and of this, I was
often told, not more than five bushels from an acre is usually
obtained.   Of course, no one would continue long to raise
such crops, if he had wages to pay for the labor; but,
having inherited or reared the laborers, the farmer does not
often regard them as costing him anything more than what
he has to pay for their clothes and food—which is very little.

Few turpentine-farmers raise as much maize as they need for
their own family; and those who carry on the business most
largely and systematically, frequently purchase all the food of
their hands.   Maize and bacon are, therefore, very largely
imported into North Carolina, chiefly from Ohio, by the Balti-

more and Wheeling rail-road, and from Baltimore to Wilmington or Newbern, by sea.

The turpentine forest is from thirty to eighty miles wide, and extends from near the north-line of North Carolina to the Gulf of Mexico. Until lately, even in North Carolina, the business of collecting turpentine has been confined to such parts of the forest as were situated most conveniently to market—the value of the commodity not warranting long inland transportation. Recently, the demand has increased, owing, probably, to the enlarged consumption of spirits of turpentine in "burning fluids;" and the business has been extended into the depths of the forest. It is yet thought a hazardous venture to start the business where more than thirty miles of wagoning is required to bring the spirits of turpentine to a rail-road, or navigable water.*

If we enter, in the winter, a part of a forest that is about to be converted into a "turpentine orchard," we come upon negroes engaged in making boxes, in which the sap is to be collected the following spring. They continue at this work from November to March, or until, as the warm weather approaches, the sap flows freely, and they are needed to remove it from the boxes into barrels. These "boxes" are not made of boards, nailed to-gether in a cubical form, as might be supposed; nor are they log-troughs, such as, at the North, maple-sap is collected in. They are cavities dug in the trunk of the tree itself. A long, narrow ax, made in Connecticut, especially for this purpose, is used for this wood-pecking operation; and some skill is required to use it properly. We may see the green hands doing 'prentice

* Since this was written, a great decline of prices has occurred.

work upon any stray oaks, or other *non*-turpentine trees they can find in the low grounds.

The boxes are made at from six inches to a foot above the roots, and are shaped like a distended waistcoat-pocket. The lower lip is horizontal—the upper, arched; the bottom of the box is about four inches below the lower lip, and eight or ten below the upper. On a tree of medium size, a box should be made to hold a quart. The less the ax approaches towards the centre of the tree, to obtain the proper capacity in the box, the better, as the vitality of the tree is less endangered; but this is little thought about.

An expert hand will make a box in less than ten minutes; and seventy-five to a hundred—according to the size and proximity of the trees—is considered a day's work.

The boxes being made, the bark, and a few of the outer rings of the wood of the tree, are cut off ("hacked") along the edge of the upper lip. From this excoriation, the sap begins to flow about the fifteenth of March, and gradually fills the boxes, from which it is taken by a spoon or ladle, of a peculiar form, and collected into barrels.

The turpentine barrels are made by negro coopers; the staves split from pine-logs, shaved and trimmed. They are hooped with split oak-saplings. Coopers' wages, when hired out, are from $1 50 to $2 a day. A good cooper is expected to make six or seven barrels a day. They are of the rudest construction possible—the staves being straight, and forming a simple cylinder—thirty inches long and eighteen inches diameter, headed up at both ends, with a square hole in one end, where the turpentine is poured in.

In from seven to ten days after the first hacking, the trees are again scarified. This is done with a hatchet, or with an instrument made for the purpose. A very slight chip, or shave, above the former, is all that is needed to be removed; the object being merely to expose a new surface of the cellular tissue—the flow from the former being clogged by congelations of the sap.

These hackings being made three or four times a month, the excoriation is constantly advancing higher up the trunk. The slighter the cut, the less the tree is injured, and the slower the advance, and the longer and the more conveniently may the process be carried on: nevertheless, in ninety-nine "orchards" out of a hundred, you will see that the chip has always been much broader and deeper than, with the slightest care to restrict it, it needed to have been. If the "dipping" has commenced when you visit the orchard, you will notice that the turpentine collected has much rubbish—chips and leaves—in it, considerably injuring its value. The greater part of this might have been avoided, by having the negroes clean out the boxes in which it had fallen, in the winter; but they seldom take this trouble.

In some orchards, you will see that many trees have been killed by fire. The wire-grass, which grew among the trees the previous year, is frequently set on fire, either accidentally or purposely, when dead and dry, in the spring. It burns slowly, and with little flame, and the living trees, the bark of which is not very inflammable, are seldom injured. But where a tree has been boxed, and the chips lie about it, these take fire, and burn with more flame; so that frequently the turpentine in the box, and on the scarified wood above it, also takes fire, and burns with such intensity as to kill the tree. The danger might be avoided by raking away the chips and leaves, for a foot or two about the roots; but I nowhere saw this precaution taken. I mention these things, by the way, as further illustration of the general inefficient direction of slave-labor; or as indicating, as might be rather claimed by the owners, that the high cost of the labor prevents its direction to these minor points of economy.

By the middle of March, the turpentine is flowing abundantly, and the negroes must be employed in hacking, as each tree requires to be freshly scarified once in a week, or ten days. Soon afterwards, it is necessary to commence dipping, or the removal of the turpentine from the boxes to barrels. There are two ways of arranging the labor for this purpose used by the larger proprietors. In one, all the negroes employed are divided into two classes—"hackers" and "dippers." The hackers are wholly employed in scarifying the trees. A task, of a certain number of trees, is given to each, which he is required to go over, hacking each tree, once in seven or eight days. The dippers are constantly employed in emptying the boxes, as they fill with turpentine. The other way—and this is more common—is to give each hand a task of trees, each of which he is required to both hack and dip statedly. Twenty-five hundred trees give a man five days' employment hacking, and one day dipping, in a week.

From one to four boxes are made in each tree, according to its size; a few inches of bark being left between them. The greater number of trees, from which turpentine is now obtained, are from a foot to eighteen inches in diameter, and have three boxes each. The hacking is carried on year after year, until, in the oldest orchards, it is extended twelve or fifteen feet, and ladders have to be used to carry it further up the trunks of the trees. The turpentine flows from the most recent hack, down over the previously scarified wood of the tree, towards the box, a considerable proportion of it congealing by the way, and remaining attached to the wood. From this adhering portion, a part of the spirits or oil has evaporated in the process of drying; it is, therefore, of less value than that which is taken, in a more liquid condition, from the box. It is occasionally—perhaps but once a year—scraped off, and barreled by itself. It is, therefore, known in market as "scrape;" while that which is dipped from the box, and which is of considerably higher value, is termed "dip." The flow of the first year, having but a small surface of wood to traverse, and being, therefore, less exposed to evaporation than the flow of later years, is of higher value than the ordinary dip. It is called "virgin dip." In many of the orchards, at a distance from market, and where, of course, all classes of turpentine are of less value, I observed that the trees had never been scraped—the proprietor having boxed and hacked more trees than he could apply force enough to both dip and scrape. The dip is lessened, however, by allowing the scrape to accumulate; for much of the flow is thus often made to drop outside of the box. The price of turpentine being now much higher than usual, many of the small proprietors are this year scraping their trees, that have not scraped before. This old "scrape" will be of inferior quality.

DISTILLATION OF TURPENTINE.

A considerable amount of turpentine is shipped in barrels to Northern ports, where it is distilled; a larger amount is distilled in the State. The proprietors of the large turpentine orchards, themselves, have stills; and those collecting but a small quantity sell to them, or to custom distilleries, owned by those who make distilling alone their business.

The stills used for making spirits or oil of turpentine from the crude gum, are of copper, not materially different in form from common ardent-spirit stills, and have a capacity of from five to twenty barrels; an average size being, perhaps, ten barrels.

The forest distilleries are usually placed in a ravine or valley, where water can be brought to them in troughs, so as to flow, at an elevation of fifteen feet from the ground, into the condensing tank. At a point at which the ground will decline from it in one direction, the still is set in a brick furnace. A floor or scaffold is erected on a level with the bottom of the still-head, and a roof covers all. The still-head is taken off, and barrels of turpentine, full of rubbish as it is collected by the negroes, are emptied in. When the still is full, or nearly so, the still-head is put on, and the joint made tight with clay; fire is made, and soon a small, transparent stream of spirits begins to flow from the mouth of the worm, and is caught directly in the barrel in which it finally comes to market. When all the spirits, which can be profitably extracted, are thus drawn off, the fire is raked out of the furnace, a spigot is drawn from a spout at the bottom of the still, and the residuum flows out—a dark, thick fluid, appearing, as it runs, like molasses.

ROSIN.

This residuum is resin, or the rosin of commerce. There is not a sufficient demand for rosin, except of the first qualities, to make it worth transporting from the inland distilleries; it is ordinarily, therefore, conducted off to a little distance, in a wooden trough, and allowed to flow from it to waste upon the ground. At the first distillery I visited, which had been in operation but one year, there lay a congealed pool of rosin, estimated to contain over three thousand barrels. Its appearance was very beautiful; firm and glair; varying in color, and glistening like polished porphyry. The rosin from "virgin dip" turpentine, only, was saved here. At the distilleries on the river-banks, a second quality is also saved, while a poorer description is still let run to waste. When it is intended to save the rosin, it is drawn off into a vat of water, which separates the chips and other rubbish, that were contained in the gum, and it is then barreled for market.

To prevent the spirits soaking through the wood and evaporating, the barrels are all washed on the inside with glue. They are made as carefully as possible, and are often brought from the North, and sold at three or four dollars a-piece. Notwithstanding all precaution, the waste from

leakage and evaporation is often great, owing to the exceedingly subtile nature of the fluid.

The turpentine lands that I saw were valued at from $5
to $20 an acre. They have sometimes been sold at $2 an
acre; and those of Georgia and Alabama can be purchased,
to any extent, at that price. From 500 to 1,000 trees (or
2,000 boxes), I judged, stand usually upon an acre. The
quantity of turpentine that would flow from these, in a year,
I cannot state reliably. According to some statements given
me, it would be about fourteen barrels of dip, and two
barrels of scrape. Fourteen barrels of dip would give, in
distillation, two barrels of spirits, and eight of resin.

At a fifteen barrel still, I found one white man and one negro
employed under the oversight of the owner. It kept employed
twenty-five men hacking and dipping; running twice, that is,
using thirty barrels crude turpentine, a day. Besides these
hands, were two coopers, and several wagoners. The wages
of ordinary practiced turpentine hands (slaves) are about $120
a year, with board, clothing, etc., as usual.

A North Carolina turpentine orchard, with the ordinary
treatment, lasts fifty years. The trees are subject to the
attack of an insect which rapidly kills them. Those most
severely hacked are chiefly liable to this danger.

The turpentine business is considered to be extremely favorable to health and long life. It is sometimes engaged in by
persons afflicted with pulmonary complaints, with the belief that
it has a remedial effect.

When the original long-leafed pine has been destroyed, and
the ground cultivated a few years, and then "turned out," a
bastard variety springs up, which grows with rapidity, but is

of no value for turpentine, and of but little for timber. The true variety, rich in turpentine, is of very slow growth. On one trunk, seven inches in diameter, I counted eighty-five rings. Whether there will be a renewed spontaneous growth of the true long-leafed pine, where they are allowed to gradually decay on the ground, I am unable to say.

TAR.

Tar is an extract from the pine-wood obtained by charring it. It is made wholly from the heart or "light wood" of the long-leafed pine, which is split into billets of a size convenient for handling and arranging in the tar-kiln. Trees which have been used up in the turpentine business, are the best to use for making tar. The billets are piled in a conical heap, which is covered with turf, much as coal-pits are made at the North. The kiln is usually made upon a hillock, and trenches are made under it, having a mouth a little below it on the hill-side. The proper burning of the kiln to produce the most tar, is an art to be learned by practice. It is made to burn very slowly, to gradually roast out the juices of the pine, so that they will run down, collect in the trench, and flow out at its mouth, where, in the commingled condition known as tar, they are ladled into barrels.

This is an exceedingly slovenly process, the tar being mixed with sand, and collecting other impurities as it flows through the kiln, and searches a way out on and through the ground. It is for the reason that it is prepared with more care, so as to be free from the admixture of sand, that the tar of Northern Europe always stands at a higher value, and competes with the Carolina tar, even in our own ports.

A new patent process of roasting the pine in iron ovens, the fire not being in contact with it, has lately been introduced, and gives good promise of removing this reproach. The tar is said to be of much superior quality and to be obtained more expeditiously and economically than by the old method.

PITCH.

Pitch is a concentration of tar obtained by boiling it. I was unable to obtain any particulars of the process of manufacturing it.

SLAVES AND OTHER PEOPLE IN THE TURPENTINE FORESTS.

The negroes employed in this branch of industry, seemed to me to be unusually intelligent and cheerful. Decidedly they are superior in every moral and intellectual respect to the great mass of the white people inhabiting the turpentine forest. Among the latter there is a large number, I should think a majority, of entirely uneducated, poverty-stricken vagabonds. I mean by vagabonds, simply, people without habitual, definite occupation or reliable means of livelihood. They are poor, having almost no property but their own bodies; and the use of these, that is, their labor, they are not accustomed to hire out statedly and regularly, so as to obtain capital by wages, but only occasionally by the day or job, when driven to it by necessity. A family of these people will commonly hire, or "squat" and build, a little log cabin, so made that it is only a shelter from rain, the sides not being chinked, and having no more furniture or pretension to comfort than is commonly provided a criminal in the cell of a prison. They will cultivate a little corn, and possibly a few roods of potatoes,

cow-peas and coleworts. They will own a few swine, that find
their living in the forest; and pretty certainly, also, a rifle and
dogs; and the men, ostensibly, occupy most of their time in
hunting.

A gentleman of Fayetteville told me that he had, several
times, appraised, under oath, the whole household property of
families of this class at less than $20. If they have need of
money to purchase clothing, etc., they obtain it by selling
their game or meal. If they have none of this to spare, or an
insufficiency, they will work for a neighboring farmer for a few
days, and they usually get for their labor fifty cents a day,
finding themselves. The farmers say, that they do not like to
employ them, because they cannot be relied upon to finish
what they undertake, or to work according to directions; and

because, being white men, they cannot "drive" them. That is to say, their labor is even more inefficient and unmanageable than that of slaves.

That I have not formed an exaggerated estimate of the proportion of such a class, will appear to the reader more probable from the testimony of a pious colporteur, given before a public meeting in Charleston, in February, 1855. I quote from a Charleston paper's report. The colporteur had been stationed at —— county, N. C.:—"*The larger portion* of the inhabitants seemed to be totally given up to a species of mental hallucination, which carried them captive at its will. They nearly all believed implicitly in witchcraft, and attributed everything that happened, good or bad, to the agency of persons whom they supposed possessed of evil spirits."

The majority of what I have termed turpentine-farmers—meaning the small proprietors of the long-leafed pine forest land, are people but a grade superior, in character or condition, to these vagabonds. They have habitations more like houses—log-cabins, commonly, sometimes chinked, oftener not—without windows of glass, but with a few pieces of substantial old-fashioned heir-loom furniture ; a vegetable garden, in which, however, you will find no vegetable but what they call "collards" (colewort) for "greens"; fewer dogs ; more swine, and larger clearings for maize, but no better crops than the poorer class. Their property is, nevertheless, often of considerable money value, consisting mainly of negroes, who, associating intimately with their masters, are of superior intelligence to the slaves of the wealthier classes.

The larger proprietors, who are also often cotton planters, cultivating the richer low lands, are, sometimes, gentlemen of

good estate—intelligent, cultivated, and hospitable.   The num-
of these, however, is extremely small.

NORTH CAROLINA FISHERIES.—SLAVE FISHERMEN.

The shad and herring fisheries upon the sounds and inlets of
the North Carolina coast are an important branch of industry,
and a source of considerable wealth.   The men employed in
them are mainly negroes, slave and free; and the manner in
which they are conducted is interesting, and in some respects
novel.

The largest sweep seines in the world are used.   The gentleman to whom I am indebted for the most of my information,
was the proprietor of a seine over two miles in length.   It was
manned by a force of forty negroes, most of whom were hired at
a dollar a day, for the fishing season, which usually commences
between the tenth and fifteenth of March, and lasts fifty days.
In favorable years the profits are very great.   In extremely unfavorable years, many of the proprietors are made bankrupt.

Cleaning, curing and packing-houses are erected on the shore,
as near as they conveniently may be to a point on the beach
suitable for drawing the seine.   Six or eight windlasses, worked
by horses, are fixed along the shore, on each side of this point.
There are two large seine-boats, in each of which there is one
captain, two seine-tenders, and eight or ten oarsmen.   In making
a cast of the net, one-half of it is arranged on the stern of each
of the boats, which, having previously been placed in a suitable
position—perhaps a mile off shore, in front of the buildings—
are rowed from each other, the captains steering, and the seine-
tenders throwing off, until the seine is all cast between them.
This is usually done in such a way that it describes the arc of a

circle, the chord of which is diagonal with the shore. The hawsers attached to the ends of the seine are brought first to the outer windlasses, and are wound in by the horses. As the operation of gathering in the seine occupies several hours, the boat-hands, as soon as they have brought the hawsers to the shore, draw their boats up, and go to sleep.

As the wings approach the shore, the hawsers are from time to time carried to the other windlasses, to contract the sweep of the seine. After the gaff of the net reaches the shore, lines attached toward the bunt are carried to the windlasses, and the boats' crews are awakened, and arrange the wing of the seine, as fast as it comes in, upon the boat again. Of course, as the cast was made diagonally with the shore, one wing is beached before the other. By the time the fish in the bunt have been secured, both boats are ready for another cast, and the boatmen proceed to make it, while the shore-gang is engaged in sorting and gutting the "take."

My informant, who had $50,000 invested in his fishing establishment, among other items of expenditure, mentioned that he had used seventy kegs of gunpowder the previous year, and amused himself for a few moments with letting me try to conjecture in what way villainous saltpetre could be put to use in taking fish.

There is evidence of a subsidence of this coast, in many places, at a comparatively recent period; many stumps of trees, evidently standing where they grew, being found some way below the present surface, in the swamps and salt marshes. Where the formation of the shore and the surface, or the strength of the currents of water, which have flowed over the sunken land, has been such as to prevent a later deposit, the

stumps of great cypress trees, not in the least decayed, yet protrude from the bottom of the sounds.   These would obstruct the
passage of a net, and must be removed from a fishing-ground.

The operation of removing them is carried on during the summer, after the close of the fishing season.   The position of a
stump having been ascertained by divers, two large seine-boats
are moored over it, alongside each other, and a log is laid across
them, to which is attached, perpendicularly, between the boats, a
spar, fifteen feet long.   The end of a chain is hooked to the log,
between the boats, the other end of which is fastened by divers
to the stump which it is wished to raise.   A double-purchase
tackle leads from the end of the spar to a ring-bolt in the bows
of one of the boats, with the fall leading aft, to be bowsed upon
by the crews.   The mechanical advantages of the windlass, the
lever, and the pulley being thus combined, the chain is wound on
to the log, until either the stump yields, and is brought to the
surface, or the boats' gunwales are brought to the water's edge.

When the latter is the case, and the stump still remains firm,
a new power must be applied.   A spile, pointed with iron, six
inches in diameter, and twenty feet long, is set upon the stump
by a diver, who goes down with it, and gives it that direction
which, in his judgment, is best, and driven into it by mauls and
sledges, a scaffold being erected between the boats for men to
stand on while driving it.   In very large stumps, the spile is
often driven till its top reaches the water; so that when it is drawn
out, a cavity is left in the stump, ten feet in depth.   A tube is
now used, which is made by welding together three musket-
barrels, with a breech at one end, in which is the tube of a per-
cussion breech, with the ordinary position of the nipple reversed,
so that when it is screwed on with a detonating cap, the latter

will protrude within the barrel. This breech is then inserted within a cylindrical tin box, six inches in diameter, and varying in length, according to the supposed strength of the stump; and soap or tallow is smeared about the place of insertion, to make it water-tight. The box contains several pounds of gunpowder.

The long iron tube is elevated, and the diver goes down again, and guides it into the hole in the stump, with the canister in his arms. It has reached the bottom—the diver has come up, and is drawn into one of the boats—an iron rod is inserted in the mouth of the tube—all hands crouch low, and hold hard—the rod is let go—crack!—whoo—oosch! The sea swells, boils, and breaks upward. If the boats do not rise with it, they must sink; if they rise, and the chain does not break, the stump must rise with them. At the same moment the heart of cypress is riven; its furthest rootlets quiver; the very earth trembles, and loses courage to hold it; "up comes the stump, or down go the niggers!"

If I owned a yacht, I think I would make a trip to Currituck next summer, to witness this Titanic dentistry. Who could have invented it? Not a Carolinian; it is too ingenious: not a Yankee; it is too reckless: not a sailor; it is too hard upon the boats.

The success of the operation evidently depends mainly on the discretion and skill of the diver. My informant, who thought that he removed last summer over a thousand stumps, using for the purpose seventy kegs of gunpowder, employed several divers, all of them negroes. Some of them could remain under water, and work there to better advantage than others; but all were admirably skillful, and this, much in proportion to the practice and experience they had had. They wear, when diving, three or four pairs of flannel drawers and shirts. Nothing is required of them when they are not wanted to go to the bottom, and, while the other hands are at work, they may lounge, or go to sleep in the boat, which they do, in their wet garments. Whenever a diver displays unusual hardihood, skill, or perseverance, he is rewarded with whisky; or, as they are commonly allowed, while diving, as much whisky as they want, with money. Each of them would generally get every day from quarter to half a-dollar in this way, above the wages paid for them, according to the skill and industry with which they had worked. On this account, said my informant, " the harder the work you give them to do, the better they like it." His divers very frequently had intermittent fevers, but would very rarely let this keep them out of their boats. Even in the midst of a severe "shake," they would generally insist that they were "well enough to dive."

What! slaves eager to work, and working cheerfully, earnestly and skillfully? Even so. Being for the time managed as freemen, their ambition stimulated by wages, suddenly they, too, reveal sterling manhood, and honor their Creator.

SCOTCH HIGHLANDERS.—IMMIGRATION.

In the vicinity of Fayetteville, there are many Scotch Highlanders. The emigration of these people to North Carolina commenced in the early Colony days, and has been continued, at intervals, to the present time. They come direct, in a small class of vessels, to Wilmington.*

Very few Highlanders come to New York, or to other parts of the United States; the largest proportion of those emi-

---

* There is a credible tradition that Flora Macdonald once lived in North Carolina.

grating, arrive at Quebec, and remain in Canada. In this they are led simply by their clannishness; like sheep, they follow one another without looking right or left for an easier leap; the stream once started, there is no diverting it. I remember to have found the Highlanders at home familiar with the names of districts and towns in Canada, though they had no knowledge whatever of the United States, and used the names Canada and America synonymously. Probably, in some districts of the Highlands, no one knows of any other port in America than Wilmington. You frequently fiud people who can speak Gaelic, in North Carolina; and, sometimes, a small settlement where it is the common tongue: there are even one or two churches in the State, in which the services are performed in Gaelic.

The immigrants of the present generation have, nearly all, come to Fayetteville. Most of them are very poor, and obtain employment as laborers, as soon as they can get it, after their arrival. In a year or two, they will have saved money enough from their wages to purchase a few acres of piny-wood land, upon which they raise a cabin, make a clearing, and go to raising corn and a family. They are distinguished for frugality and industry; and, unless they are very intemperate—as too many of them are—are certain in a few years to acquire money enough to buy a negro, which they are said to be invariably ambitious to possess. Before they die, they will have got a family or two of young negroes about them, to be divided as a patrimony among their children. With a moderate competence they are content, and seldom become wealthy. Their children do not appear, generally, to retain their thrifty habits. I saw a number of girls, of Highland blood, employed in a cotton factory near Fayetteville. In modesty, cleanliness, and neatness of apparel, though evidently poor, they certainly compared favorably with the girls employed in a cotton mill that I visited near Glasgow, a few years ago; but the proprietor told me that they very seldom laid up anything, and spent the greater part of their earnings very foolishly, as fast as they received them.

A young man, employed in this factory, to whom the proprietor, having told me he was more intelligent and trustworthy than most of his class, had introduced me, finding that I was from the North, voluntarily told me that Slavery was a great weight upon poor people here, and he wished that he lived in a Free State.

WAGONERS.

Having observed, from my room in the hotel at Fayetteville, a number of remarkable, bright lights, I walked out, about eleven o'clock, in the direction in which they had appeared, and found, upon the edge of an old-field, near the town, a camp of wagoners, with half-a-dozen fires, around some of which were clustered groups of white men and women and negroes cooking and eating their suppers (black and white from the same kettle, in many cases), some singing Methodist songs, and some listening to a banjo or fiddle-player. A still larger number appeared to be asleep, generally lying under low tents, about as large as those used by the French soldier. There were thirty or forty great wagons, with mules, cattle, or horses, feeding from troughs set upon their poles. The grouping of all among some old sycamore trees, with the fantastic shadows and wavering lights, the free flames and black brooding smoke of the pitch-pine fires, produced a most interesting and attractive spectacle, and detained me long in admiration. I could easily imagine myself to be on the Oregon or California trail, a thousand miles from the realm of civilization—not readily realize that I was within the limits of one of the oldest towns on the American continent.

These were the farmers of the distant highland districts, and their slaves, come to market with their produce. Next morning I counted sixty of their great wagons in the main street of the little town. They would generally hold, in the body, as much as seventy-five bushels of grain, were very strongly built, and drawn by from two to six horses; the near wheeler always having a large Spanish saddle on his back, for their driver. The merchants stood in the doors of their stores, or walked out into the street to observe their contents—generally of corn, meal, flour or cotton—and to traffic for them. I observed that the negroes often took part in the bargaining, and was told by a merchant, that both the selling of the produce, and the selection and purchase of goods for the farmer's family, was often left entirely to them.

Several of the wagons had come, I found, from a hundred miles distant; and one of them from beyond the Blue Ridge, nearly two hundred miles. In this tedious way, until lately, nearly all the commerce between the back country and the river towns and sea-ports of Virginia and North Carolina has been carried on, strong teams of horses toiling on, less than a score of miles a day, with the lumbering wagons, the roads running through a sparsely settled district of clay soil, and much worse, even, than those of the sandy lands I have described. Every night, foul or fair, the driver and attendants, often including the farmer himself, and part of his family, camp out on the road-side.

BOAT-TRANSPORTATION.

At Gaston I had seen a number of long, narrow, canoe-like boats, of light draft, in which the produce of the country along the head waters of the Roanoke was brought to market. They were generally manned by three men each, who were sheltered at night under a hood of canvas, stretched upon poles, in the stern of the boat. The mouth of this hood opened upon a bed of clay, laid upon the boat's bottom, on which a fire was made, that would keep them warm, and cook their food. An equally picturesque scene with that of the wagon camp was a collection of these boats, moored at night under the steep river bank, the

negroes reclining under the dusky hoods, or sitting on the gunwales, cooking and eating their hoe-cake, smoking, singing, or
telling of their adventures on the passage. The cargoes of these
boats were chiefly composed of meal, hides, and tobacco, and at
Gaston they were transhipped, by rail, to some of the Virginia
ports.

TOBACCO ROLLERS.

Until within a recent period, much tobacco has been brought
to market, from the more remote districts of North Carolina and
Virginia, by a very rude method, called "rolling," which was
performed in this wise. Felloes, like those of cart-wheels, were
hewn with an ax, and fitted to a cask of tobacco, at a little distance each side the bilge; holes were bored with an auger,
and long wooden pins driven in, fastening them to the cask; a
large hole was then bored in the middle of each head, and a spar
driven through, which formed an axle-tree. To this, long poles,
used as shafts, were attached, holes being bored through the ends
of them, which slipped over the axle-tree, and they were secured
by linch-pins. One horse was tackled in between the poles, and
another attached tandem, before him. On the leader's back, a
kettle and a bag of meal were hung; and on the shaft-horse was
strapped a blanket, or bear-skin, which served as a saddle for the
driver by day, and a bed-cover by night. Small farmers themselves often brought in their tobacco in this way; but there were
also a set of men who made it their principal occupation, and
whose calling was that of "tobacco-rollers." They contracted
with the large planters to take their whole crop to the market-
town at a certain price, furnishing horses, felloes, etc., themselves. It was their custom to so arrange their starting, that

many would come together on the road, and so proceed, making a considerable camp, wherever they stopped for the night; and many such companies, by a previous agreement, would arrive in the towns together. A hard set they must have been—for the citizens now tell how, when they were young, all quiet housekeepers were kept in a state of excited alarm during the seasons when the tobacco-rollers were in town; and they well remember with what respect and consideration they were treated by all discreet people; for the quarrel of one, was made that of the whole body.

IMPROVED MEANS OF TRANSPORT.

Rail-roads and canals, running westward from the navigable water at Baltimore, Richmond, Petersburg, and Charleston, now shorten the distance to which it is necessary for the horse transportation of the products of much of the upper country to be carried. A large district of Central and Western North Carolina, however, is still unpierced by either rail-road or serviceable canal; and much of this finds its readiest communication with the sea, and by that to the rest of the world, by the Cape Fear river. Fayetteville is the point of transfer from wagon to boat, being at the head of navigation.

In 1820, a company was chartered, to make the river above Fayetteville navigable for boats, with a capital of $100,000. About $80,000 were raised and spent, probably without good judgment; certainly without accomplishing anything; and this failure operated for a long time to discourage the further employment of capital (which is much less concentrated in this than in the adjoining States), in public works. The Cape Fear river improvements have been persevered in with fluctuating energy at different periods, and are now directed by the State. The main object in view at present, is to obtain a boat-transportation from certain coal-beds to the ocean. The coal is bituminous—some of it of a very desirable quality, would be readily and cheaply mined, and the beds are of exhaustless extent. If it could be brought from the mines to the ocean with but one transhipment, and untaxed with heavy tolls, it could, without doubt, be sold with a good profit in New York and New England. It is calculated, also, that it would bear rail-road freight to Fayetteville, and thence two handlings to get it to sea; and for this purpose a rail-road had been projected, and a charter obtained, shortly before my visit. Gentlemen interested told me then, that they had scarcely any hopes of getting a sufficient amount of stock taken to proceed, but they should try to get a loan from the corporations of Fayetteville and Wilmington. When I returned through Western North Carolina, some months afterwards, I was informed that when about one-sixth of the amount of stock required to be taken by a certain date, before any use could be made of the charter, had been subscribed for, and when it was thought no more subscriptions could be obtained, a stranger had suddenly subscribed, in behalf of certain New Yorkers, for all the remainder. It was reported to be the design of these capitalists, if it should be found practicable upon careful survey, to carry the road to a point on the coast where they had discovered a neglected harbor, with great natural advantages for commerce, the charter having, by accident, been so loosely worded as to admit of this change in the terminus of the road. The New Yorkers were supposed to have made large purchases of land in the vicinity of this new harbor, and probably at other points, where the value of land would be favorably influenced by the work. How much truth there was in this report, I do not know, but my informant, having just come from Fayetteville, told me that the people there believed it, and were in transports of delight with the prospect it afforded them. Not one word was said about the "impudent intermeddling of Northerners," not the slightest indignation expressed, that the "profits of their own legitimate business should thus be stolen from them by the mercenary New Yorkers."

Paragraphs like the following may often be seen in juxtaposition, in the Southern papers :

"The Farmersville coal field, on Deep river, Chatham county, N. C. which was purchased some four years ago for $0,000, was sold last week to a Northern Company, for $91,000, cash. There are 900 acres of land in the tract."

———

* * * * "It is plain that a new and glorious destiny awaits the South, and beckons us onward to a career of independence. Shall we train and discipline our energies for the coming crisis, or *shall we continue the tributary and dependent vassals of Northern brokers and money-changers?* Now is the time for the South to begin in earnest the work of self-development! Now is the time to break asunder the fetters of commercial subjection, and to prepare for that more complete independence that awaits us !"—*Richmond Enquirer.*

A rail-road from Charlotte to Raleigh, from which the line to navigable waters is already complete, is now building, and will much shorten the necessary wagoning of produce to market from the central district of the State, and will, doubtless, stimulate a greatly increased production.

The advantages offered by rail-roads, to the farmers of inland districts, are strikingly shown by the following fact: A gentleman, near Raleigh, who had a quantity of wheat to dispose of, seeing it quoted at high prices, in a paper of Petersburg, Va., and seeing, at the same time, the advertisement of a commission-house there, wrote to the latter, making an offer of it. The next day he received a reply, by mail, and by the train a bundle of sacks, in which he immediately forwarded the wheat, and, by the following return mail, received his pay, at the rate of $1 20 a bushel, the top price of the winter. At the same time, only forty miles from where he lived, off the line of the rail-road, wheat was selling at 60 cents a bushel. There was one county, during the time I was in North Carolina, to and through which the roads were absolutely impassable, and out of which, I was told, no intelligence had been received, at the capitol, for more than a month. It is not, therefore, incredible that it should cost 60 cents to move a bushel of wheat forty miles.

WAGON COMPETITION WITH RAIL-ROADS.

Rail-roads do not, however, so readily and entirely change the channels in which farmers have been accustomed for a long time to float their trade, especially in thinly settled districts, as might be expected. I was told of a farmer who persisted in wagoning his produce one hundred miles, making several trips during the winter to do so, for several years after he had the opportunity of using a cheap and direct communication, with a better market, by rail-road. The farmer, unaccustomed to the usual mercantile forms, shrinks from them, and is afraid to deal in a large way. He does not like to trust agents, particularly strangers at a distance, and many in North Carolina are unable to deal at all by correspondence. He enjoys much more, after the Fall plowing is done, and the horses are no longer required for field-work, to hitch them to the big wagon, load it with a little of everything he has made, and bring it to town, under his own guard and guidance, camping o'nights, on the road; and then, to talk over the news of the year, and trade with his old town cronies, as his father used to when he was a boy, and he began to go down with him. Then, with some new store goods for his family and his "people;" molasses, sugar, and coffee, and a new coffee-mill, or other Down-east notion, to return leisurely as he went, so that, when he reaches home, two or three weeks' absence shall make his arrival something of an event.

PLANK-ROADS.

Plank-roads, it will be obvious, from these considerations, are admirably adapted to all the circumstances of this country. They suit the habits of the people, and the value of land being small, and the country heavily timbered, they may be built at a low cost. On them the farmer may drive his wagon, as he has been accustomed in the Winter, but carrying double his usual load, and in less time, and with much less liability to accidents.

The first plank-road in the State of New York was laid, I believe, in 1844, and in 1846 there were several in operation; and the public, generally, began to be informed of their mode of construction and their advantages.

It is creditable to the citizens of North Carolina, that they so soon appreciated the peculiar advantages offered them in the invention, and took measures to avail themselves of it. In 1847 an engineer was procured from New York, and, under his direction, a plank-road commenced, running westwardly from Fayetteville, into the middle of the productive region I have referred to.

The road so commencing, now forms a great trunk road, running northwest more than a hundred miles. From this trunk there are many laterals, drawing from districts which in the winter season are almost inaccessible by the old earth roads. The plank-roads are as good in winter, when the farmer has leisure to drive to market, as they are in summer; and he can take upon them a much heavier load, thirty-five miles a day, than he formerly wore out his horses and exhausted his patience to drag seventeen. So well are the advantages appreciated in the State, that over forty new companies, for building plank-roads, have been incorporated by one legislature.

NORTH CAROLINA CHARACTER.

North Carolina has a proverbial reputation for the ignorance and torpidity of her people; being, in this respect, at the head of the Slave States. I do not find the reason of this in any innate quality of the popular mind; but, rather, in the circumstances under which it finds its development. Owing to the general poverty of the soil in the Eastern part of the State, and to the almost exclusive employment of slave-labor on the soils productive of cotton; owing, also, to the difficulty and expense of reaching market with bulky produce from the interior and western districts, population and wealth is more divided than in the other Atlantic States; industry is almost entirely rural, and there is but little communication or concert of action among the small and scattered proprietors of capital. For the same reason, the advantages of education are more difficult to be enjoyed, the distance at which families reside apart preventing children from coming

together in such numbers as to give remunerative employment
to a teacher. The teachers are, generally, totally unfitted for
their business; young men, as a clergyman informed me, themselves not only unadvanced beyond the lowest knowledge of the
elements of primary school learning, but often coarse, vulgar,
and profane in their language and behavior, who take up teaching as a temporary business, to supply the demand of a neighborhood of people as ignorant and uncultivated as themselves.

The native white population of North Carolina is,	550,267
The whole white population under 20 years, is,	301,106
Leaving white adults over 20,	249,161
Of these there are natives who cannot read and write,	73,226*

Being more than one fourth of the native white adults.

SLAVERY IN NORTH CAROLINA.

But the aspect of North Carolina with regard to slavery,
is, in some respects, less lamentable than that of Virginia. There is not only less bigotry upon the subject,
and more freedom of conversation, but I saw here, in
the institution, more of patriarchal character than in any
other State. The slave more frequently appears as a family
servant—a member of his master's family, interested with
him in his fortune, good or bad. This is a result of the
less concentration of wealth in families or individuals, occasioned
by the circumstances I have described. Slavery thus loses much
of its inhumanity. It is still questionable, however, if, as the
subject race approaches civilization, the dominant race is not
proportionately detained in its onward progress. One is forced
often to question, too, in viewing slavery in this aspect, whether
humanity and the accumulation of wealth, the prosperity of

* Official Census Report, pp. 369, 299, 317.

the master, and the happiness and improvement of the subject, are not in some degree incompatible.

———

CAPE FEAR RIVER.

I left Fayetteville in a steam-boat (advertised for 8 o'clock,
left at 8.45) bound down Cape Fear river to Wilmington. A
description of the river, with incidents of the passage, will serve
to show the character of most of the navigable streams of the
cotton States, flowing into the Atlantic and the Gulf, and of
the manner of their navigation.

The water was eighteen feet above its lowest summer stages;
the banks steep, thirty feet high from the present water surface—
from fifty to one hundred feet apart—and covered with large
trees and luxuriant vegetation; the course crooked; the current
very rapid; the trees overhanging the banks, and frequently
falling into the channel—making the navigation hazardous.
The river is subject to very rapid rising. The master told me
that he had sometimes left his boat aground at night, and, on
returning in the morning, found it floating in twenty-five feet
water, over the same spot. The difference between the extremes
of low stages and floods is as much as seventy feet. In summer, there are sometimes but eighteen inches of water on the
bars: the boat I was in drew but fourteen inches, light. She
was a stern-wheel craft—the boiler and engine (high pressure)
being placed at opposite ends, to balance weights. Her burden
was three hundred barrels, or sixty tons measurement. This is
the character of most of the boats navigating the river—of
which there are now twelve. Larger boats are almost useless
in summer, from their liability to ground; and even the smaller

ones, at low stages of water, carry no freight, but are employed to tow up "flats," or shallow barges. At this season of the year, however, the steamboats are loaded close to the water's edge.

The bulk of our freight was turpentine; and the close proximity of this to the furnaces suggested a danger fully equal to that from snags or grounding. On calling the attention of a fellow-passenger to it, he told me that a friend of his was once awakened from sleep, while lying in a berth on one of these boats, by a sudden, confused sound. Thinking the boiler had burst, he drew the bed-clothing over his head, and laid quiet, to avoid breathing the steam; until, feeling the boat ground, he ran out, and discovered that she was on fire near the furnace. Having some valuable freight near by, which he was desirous to save, and seeing no immediate danger, though left alone on the boat, he snatched a bucket, and, drawing water from alongside, applied it with such skill and rapidity as soon to quench the flames, and eventually to entirely extinguish the fire. Upon the return of the crew, a few repairs were made, steam was got up again, and the boat proceeded to her destination in safety. He afterwards ascertained that three hundred kegs of gunpowder were stowed beneath the deck that had been on fire—a circumstance which sufficiently accounted for the panic-flight of the crew.

WOODING-UP.

Soon after leaving, we passed the ZEPHYR, wooding-up: an hour later, our own boat was run to the bank, men jumped from her fore and aft, and fastened head and stern lines to the trees, and we also commenced wooding.

The trees had been cut away so as to leave a clear space to the top of the bank, which was some fifty feet from the boat, and moderately steep. Wood, cut, split, and piled in ranks, stood at the top of it, and a shoot of plank, two feet wide and thirty long, conveyed it nearly to the water. The crew rushed to the wood-piles—master, passengers, and all, but the engineer and chambermaid, deserting the boat—and the wood was first passed down, as many as could, throwing into the shoot, and others forming a line, and tossing it, from one to another, down the bank. From the water's edge it was passed, in the same way, to its place on board, with great rapidity—the crew exciting themselves with yells. They were all blacks, but one.

On a tree, near the top of the bank, a little box was nailed, on which a piece of paper was tacked, with this inscription:

" *Notic*
" *to all persons takin' wood from this landin' pleas*
" *to leav a ticket payable to the subscriber, at*
" *$1,75 a cord as heretofore.*
                        " *Amos Sikes.*"

and the master—just before the wood was all on board—hastily filled a blank order (torn from a book, like a check-book, leaving a memorandum of the amount, etc.) on the owner of the boat for payment, to Mr. SIKES, for two cords of pine-wood, at $1 75, and two cords of light-wood, at $2—and left it in the box. The wood used had been measured in the ranks with a rod, carried for the purpose, by the master, at the moment he reached the bank.

Before, with all possible haste, we had finished wooding, the ZEPHYR passed us; and, during the rest of the day, she kept out of our sight. As often as we met a steam-boat, or passed any flats or rafts, our men were calling out to know how far ahead of us she was; and when the answer came back each time, in an increasing number of miles, they told us that our boat was more than usually sluggish, owing to an uncommonly heavy freight; but, still, for some time, they were ready to make bets that we should get first to Wilmington.

Several times we were hailed from the shore, to take on a passenger, or some light freight; and these requests, as long as it was possible, were promptly complied with—the boat being run up, so as to rest her bow upon the bank, and then shouldered off by the men, as if she had been a skiff.

SLAVE AND FREE-LABOR IN THE GLUE TRADE.

There were but three through-passengers, besides myself. Among them, was a glue-manufacturer, of Baltimore—getting orders from the turpentine-distillers—and a turpentine-farmer and distiller. The glue-manufacturer said that, in his factory, they had formerly employed slaves; had since used Irishmen, and now employed Germans altogether. Their operations were carried on night and day, and one gang of the men had to relieve another. The slaves they had employed never would be *on hand*, when the hour for relieving came. It was also necessary to be careful that certain operations should be performed at a certain time, and some judgment and watchfulness was necessary, to fix this time: the slaves never could be made to care enough for the matter, to be depended upon for discretion, in this respect; and great injury was frequently done in consequence. Some of the operations were disagreeable, and they would put one another up to thinking and saying that they ought not to be required to do such dirty work—and try to have their owners get them away from it.

Irishmen, he said, worked very well and, to a certain extent, faithfully, and, for a time, they liked them very much; but they found that, in about a fortnight, an Irishman always thought he knew more than his master, and would exercise his discretion a little too much, as well as often directly disregard his orders. Irishmen were, he said, "*too* faithful"—that is, self-confident and officious.

At length, at a hurried time, they had employed one or two Germans. The Irishmen, of course, soon quarreled with them, and threatened to leave, if they were kept. Whereupon, they were, themselves, all discharged, and a full crew of Germans, at much less wages, taken; and they proved excellent hands—steady, plodding, reliable, though they never pretended to know anything, and said nothing about what they could do. They were easily instructed, obeyed orders faithfully, and worked fairly for their wages, without boasting or grumbling.

The turpentine-distiller gave a good account of some of his men; but said he was sure they never performed half so much work as he himself could; and they sometimes would, of their own accord, do twice as much, in a day, as could usually be got out of them. He employed a Scotchman at the "still;" but he never would have white people at ordinary work, because he couldn't drive them. He added, with the utmost simplicity—and I do not think any one present saw, at the time, how much the remark expressed more than it was intended to—" I never can drive a white man, for I know I could never bear to be driven myself, by anybody."

The other passenger was "a North of England man," as I suspected from the first words I heard from him—though he had been in this country for about twenty years. He was a mechanic, and employed several slaves; but testified strongly of the expensive character of their labor; and declared, without any reserve, that the system was ruinous in its effects upon the character of all classes of working-men.

The country on the river-bank was nearly all wooded, with, occasionally, a field of corn, which, even in the low alluvial meadows, sometimes overflowed by the river, and enriched by its deposit, had evidently yielded but a very meagre crop— the stalks standing singly, at great distances, and very small. The greater part, even of these once rich low lands, that had been in cultivation, were now "turned out," and covered, either with pines, or broom-sedge and brushwood.

At some seventy or eighty miles, I should think, below Fay-etteville, the banks became lower, and there was much swamp land, in which the ground was often covered with a confusion of logs and sawn lumber, mingled with other rubbish, left by floods of the river. The standing timber was very large, and many of the trees were hung with the long, waving drapery of the tyllin-dria, or Spanish moss, which, as well as the mistletoe, I here first saw in profusion. There was also a thick network among the trees, of beautiful climbing plants. I observed some very large grape-vines, and many trees of greater size than I ever saw of their species before. I infer that this soil, properly reclaimed, and protected from floods of the river, might be most profitably used in the culture of the various half-tropical trees and shrubs, of whose fruits we now import so large and costly an amount. The fig, I have been informed, grows and bears luxuriantly at Wilmington, seldom or never suffering in its wood, though a crop of fruit may be occasionally injured by a severe late spring frost. The almond, doubtless, would succeed equally well, so also the olive; but of none of these is there the slightest commercial value produced in North Carolina, or in all our country.

In the evening we passed many boats and rafts, blazing with great fires, made upon a thick bed of clay, and their crews singing at their sweeps. Twenty miles above Wilmington, the shores became marshy, the river wide, and the woody screen that had hitherto, in a great degree, hid the nakedness of the land, was withdrawn, leaving open to view only broad, reedy savannahs, on either side.

We reached Wilmington, the port at the mouth of the river, at half-past nine. Taking a carriage, I was driven first to one hotel, and afterwards to another. They were both so crowded with guests, and excessive business duties so prevented the clerks from being tolerably civil to me, that I feared if I remained in either of them, I should have another Norfolk experience. While I was endeavoring to ascertain if there was a third public-house, in which I might, perhaps, obtain a private room, my eye fell upon an advertisement of a new rail-road line of passage to Charleston. A boat, to take passengers to the rail-road, was to start every night from Wilmington, at ten o'clock. It was already something past ten, but being pretty sure that she would not get off punctually, and having a strong resisting impulse to being packed away in a close room, with any chance stranger the clerk of the house might choose to couple me with, I shouldered my baggage, and ran for the wharves. At half-past ten I was looking at Wilmington over the stern of another little wheelbarrow-steamboat, pushing back up the river. When or how I was to be taken to Charleston, I had not yet been able to ascertain. The captain assured me it was all right, and demanded twenty dollars. Being in his power, I gave it to him, and received in return a pocketful of tickets, guaranteeing the bearer passage from place to place; not one of which places had I ever heard of before, except Charleston.

The cabin was small, dirty, crowded, close and smoky. Finding a warm spot in the deck, over the furnace, and to leeward of the chimney, I pillowed myself on my luggage, and went to sleep.

The ringing of the boat's bell awoke me, after no great lapse of time, and I found we were in a small creek, heading southward. Presently we reached a wharf, near which stood a locomotive and train. A long, narrow plank having been run out, half a dozen white men, including myself, went on shore. Then followed as many negroes, who appeared to be a recent purchase of their owner. Owing, probably, to an unusually low tide, there was a steep ascent from the boat to the wharf, and I was amused to see the anxiety of this gentleman for the safe landing of his property, and especially to hear him curse them for their carelessness, as if their lives were of much greater value to him than to themselves. One of them was a woman. All carried over their shoulders some little baggage, probably all their personal effects, slung in a blanket; and one had a dog, whose safe landing caused him nearly as much anxiety as his own did *his* owner.

"Gib me da dog, now," said the dog's owner, standing half way up the plank.

"Damn the dog," said the negro's owner; "give me your hand up here. Let go of the dog; d'ye hear! Let him take care of himself."

But the negro hugged the dog, and brought him safely on shore.

After a short delay, the train started: the single passenger car was a very fine one (made at Wilmington, Delaware), and just sufficiently warmed. I should have slept again if it had not been that two of the six inmates were drunk—one of them uproariously, and the other blandly. The latter had got possessed with the idea that I was the conductor—probably because I wore a cap—and in whatever part of the car I seated myself, would, as often as once in five minutes, come to make some inquiry of me, usually first apologizing with, "Hope I don't intrude, sir, as the immortal says."

CHAPTER VI.

SOUTH CAROLINA AND GEORGIA.

PASSING through long stretches of cypress swamps, with occasional intervals of either pine-barrens, or clear water ponds, in about two hours we came, in the midst of the woods, to the end of the rails. In the vicinity could be seen a small tent, a shanty of loose boards, and a large, subdued fire, around which, upon the ground, there were a considerable number of men, stretched out asleep. This was the camp of the hands engaged in laying the rails, and who were thus daily extending the distance which the locomotive could run.

The conductor told me that there was here a break of about eighty miles in the rail, over which I should be transferred by a stage coach, which would come as soon as possible after the driver knew that the train had arrived. To inform him of this, the locomotive screamed loud and long.

The negro property, which had been brought up in a freight car, was immediately let out on the stoppage of the train. As it stepped on to the platform, its owner asked, "Are you all here?"

"Yes, massa, we is all heah," answered one; "Do dysef no harm, for we's all heah," added another, quoting Saint Peter, in an under tone.

The negroes immediately gathered some wood, and, taking a

brand from the rail-road hands, made a fire for themselves; then, all but the woman, opening their bundles, wrapped themselves in their blankets and went to sleep. The woman, bare-headed, and very inadequately clothed as she was, stood for a long time alone, perfectly still, erect and statue-like, with her head bowed, gazing in the fire. She had taken no part in the light chat of the others, and had given them no assistance in making the fire. Her dress, too, was not the usual plantation apparel. It was all sadly suggestive.

The principal other freight of the train was one hundred and twenty bales of northern hay. It belonged, as the conductor told me, to a planter who lived some twenty miles beyond here, and who had bought it in Wilmington at a dollar and a half a hundred weight, to feed to his mules. Including the steam-boat and rail-road freight, and all the labor of getting it to his stables, its entire cost to him would not be much less than two dollars a hundred. This would be at least four times as much as it would have cost to raise and make it in the interior of New York or New England. Now, there are not only several forage crops which can be raised in South Carolina, that cannot be grown on account of the severity of the winter in the free States, but, on a farm near Fayetteville, a few days before, I had seen a crop of natural grass growing in half-cultivated land, dead upon the ground; which, I think, would have made, if it had been cut and well treated in the summer, three tons of hay to the acre. The owner of the land said that there was no better hay than it would have made, but he hadn't had time to attend to it. He had as much as his hands could do of other work at the period of the year when it should have been made.

Probably the case was similar with the planter who had bought this northern hay at a price four times that which it would have cost a northern farmer to make it.   He had preferred to employ his slaves at other business.

The inference must be either that there was most improbably-foolish, bad management, or that the slaves were more profitably employed in cultivating cotton, than they could have been in cultivating maize, or other forage crops.

I put the case, some days afterwards, to an English merchant, who had had good opportunities, and made it a part of his business, to study such matters.

"I have no doubt," said he, "that, if hay cannot be obtained here, other valuable forage can, with less labor than anywhere at the North; and all the Southern agricultural journals sustain this opinion, and declare it to be purely bad management that neglects these crops, and devotes labor to cotton, so exclusively.   Probably, it is so   at the present cost of forage. Nevertheless, the fact is also true, as the planters assert, that they cannot afford to apply their labor to anything else but cotton.   And yet, they complain that the price of cotton is so low, that there is no profit in growing it; which is evidently false.   You see that they prefer buying hay, to raising it, at, to say the least, three times what it costs your Northern farmers to raise it.   Of course, if cotton could be grown in New York and Ohio, it could be afforded at one-third the cost it is here— say at three cents per pound.   And that is my solution of the Slavery question.   Bring cotton down to three cents a pound, and there would be more abolitionists in South Carolina than in Massachusetts.   If that can be brought about, in any way—and it is not impossible that we may live to see it, as our railways are extended in India, and the French enlarge their free-labor plantations in Algiers—there will be an end of Slavery."

It was just one o'clock when the stage-coach came for us. There was but one passenger beside myself—a Philadelphia gentleman, going to Columbia. We proceeded very slowly for about three miles, across a swamp, upon a "corduroy road;" then more rapidly, over rough ground, being tossed about in the coach most severely, for six or eight miles further. Besides the driver, there was on the box the agent or superintendent of the coach line, who now opened the doors, and we found ourselves before a log stable, in the midst of a forest of large pines. The driver took out a horse, and, mounting him, rode off, and we collected wood, splitting it with a hatchet that was carried on the coach, and, lighting it from the coach lamp, made a fire. It was very cold, ice half an inch thick, and a heavy hoar frost. We complained to the agent that there was no straw in the coach bottom, while there were large holes bored in it, that kept our feet excessively cold. He said that there was no straw to be had in the country. They were obliged to bed their horses with pine leaves, which were damp, and would be of no service to us. The necessity for the holes he did not immediately explain, and we, in the exercise of our Yankee privilege, resolved that they were made with reference to the habit of expectoration, which we had observed in the car to be very general and excessive.

In about half an hour the driver of the new stage came to us on the horse that the first had ridden away. A new set of horses was brought out, and attached to the coach, and we were driven on again. An hour later, the sun rose; we were still in pine-barrens, once in several miles passing through a clearing, with a log farm-house, and a few negro huts about it; often through cypress swamps, and long pools of water. At the end of ten miles we breakfasted, and changed horses and drivers at a steam saw-mill. A few miles further on, we were asked to get on the top of the coach, while it was driven through a swamp, in which the water was over the road, for a quarter of a mile, to such a depth that it covered the foot-board. The horses really groaned, as they pushed the thin ice away with their necks, and were very near swimming. The holes in the coach bottom, the agent now told us, were to allow the water that would here enter the body to flow out. At the end of these ten miles we changed again, at a cotton planter's house—a very neat, well-built house, having pine trees about it, but very poor, old, negro quarters.

Since the long ford we had kept the top, the inside of the coach being wet, and I had been greatly pleased with the driving —the coachman, a steady, reliable sort of fellow, saying but little to his horses, and doing what swearing he thought necessary in English; driving, too, with great judgment and skill. The coach was a fine, roomy, old-fashioned, fragrant, leathery affair, and the horses the best I had seen this side of Virginia. I could not resist expressing my pleasure with the whole establishment. The new team was admirable; four sleek, well-governed, eager, sorrel cobs, and the driver, a staid, bronzed-faced man, keeping them tight in hand, drove quietly and neatly, his whip in the socket. After about fifteen minutes, during which he had been engaged in hushing down their too great impetuosity, he took out a large silver hunting-watch, and asked what time it was.

"Quarter past eleven," said the agent.

"Twelve minutes past," said the Philadelphian.

"Well, fourteen, only, I am," said the agent.

"Thirteen," said I.

"Just thirteen, I am," said the driver, slipping back his watch to its place, and then, to the agent, "ha'an't touched a hand of her since I left old Lancaster."

Suddenly guessing the meaning of what had been for some time astonishing me—"You are from the North?" I asked.

"Yes, sir."

"And you, too, Mr. Agent?"

"Yes, sir."

"And the coach, and the cattle, and all?"

"All from Pennsylvania."

"How long have you been here?"

"We have been here about a fortnight, stocking the road. We commenced regular trips yesterday. You are the first passenger through, sir."

It was, in fact, merely a transfer from one of the old National Road lines, complete. After a little further conversation, I asked, "How do you like the country, here?"

"Very nice country," said the agent.

"Rather poor soil, I should say."

"It's the cussedest poor country God ever created," snapped out the driver.

"You have to keep your horses on ——"

"*Shucks!* damn it."

NATURE IN EASTERN SOUTH CAROLINA.

The character of the scenery was novel to me, the surface very flat, the soil a fine-grained, silvery white sand, shaded by a continuous forest of large pines, which had shed their lower branches, so that we could see from the coach-top, to the distance of a quarter of a mile, everything upon the ground. In the swamps, which were frequent and extensive, and on their borders, the pines gave place to cypresses, with great pedestal trunks, and protuberant roots, throwing up an awkward dwarf progeny of shrub cypress, and curious bulbous-like stumps, called " cypress-knees." Mingled with these were a few of our common deciduous trees, the white-shafted sycamore, the gray beech, and the shrubby black-jack oak, with broad leaves, brown and dead, yet glossy, and reflecting the sun-beams. Somewhat rarely, the red cedar, and, more frequently than any other except the cypress, the beautiful holly. Added to these, there was often a thick undergrowth of evergreen shrubs. Vines and creepers of various kinds grew to the tops of the tallest trees, and dangled beneath and between their branches, in intricate net-work. The tylandria hung in festoons, sometimes several feet in length, and often completely clothed the trunks, and every branch of the trees in the low ground. It is like a fringe of tangled hair, of a light gray pearly color, and sometimes produces exquisite effects when slightly veiling the dark green, purple and scarlet of the cedar, and the holly with their berries. The mistletoe also grew in large, vivid, green tufts, on the ends of the branches of the oldest and largest trees. A small, fine and wiry, dead grass, hardly perceptible, even in the most open ground, from the coach tops, was the only sign of herbage. Large black buzzards were constantly in sight, sailing slowly, high above the tree-tops. Flocks of larks, quails, and robins were common, as were also doves, swiftly flying in small companies. The red-headed woodpecker could at any time be heard hammering the old tree-trunks, and would sometimes show himself, after his rat-tat, cocking his head archly, and listening to hear if the worm moved under the bark. The drivers told me that they had, on previous days, as they went over the road, seen deer, turkeys, and wild hogs.

THE PEOPLE.

At every tenth mile, or thereabout, we changed horses; and, generally, were allowed half an hour, to stroll in the neighborhood of the stable—the agent observing that we could reach the end of the staging some hours before the cars should leave to take us further; and, as there were no good accommodations for sleeping there, we would pass the time quite as pleasantly on the road. We dined at "Marion County House," a pleasant little village (and the only village we saw during the day), with a fine pine-grove, a broad street, a court-house, a church or two, a school-house, and a dozen or twenty dwellings. Towards night, we crossed the Great Pedee of the maps, the *Big* Pedee of the natives, in a flat-boat. A large quantity of cotton, in bales, was upon the bank, ready for loading into a steam-boat—when one should arrive—for Charleston.

The country was very thinly peopled; lone houses often being several miles apart. The large majority of the dwellings were of logs, and even those of the white people were often without glass windows. In the better class of cabins, the roof is usually built with a curve, so as to project eight or ten feet beyond the log-wall; and a part of this space, exterior to the logs, is inclosed with boards, making an additional small room—the remainder forms an open porch. The whole cabin is often elevated on four corner-posts, two or three feet from the ground, so that the air may circulate under it. The fire-place is built at the end of the house, of sticks and clay, and the chimney is carried up outside, and often detached from the log-walls; but the roof is extended at the gable, until in a line with its outer side. The porch has a railing in front,

and a wide shelf at the end, on which a bucket of water, a gourd, and hand-basin, are usually placed. There are chairs, or benches, in the porch, and you often see women sitting at work in it, as in Germany.

The logs are usually hewn but little; and, of course, as they are laid up, there will be wide interstices between them—which are increased by subsequent shrinking. These, very commonly, are not "chinked," or filled up in any way; nor is the wall lined on the inside. Through the chinks, as you pass along the road,

you may often see all that is going on in the house; and, at
night, the light of the fire shines brightly out on all sides.

Cabins, of this class, would almost always be flanked by two
or three negro-huts.   The cabins of the poorest class of whites
were of a meaner sort—being mere square pens of logs, roofed
over, provided with a chimney, and usually with a shed of
boards, supported by rough posts, before the door.

Occasionally, where the silvery sand was darkened by a
considerable intermixture of mould, there would be a large
plantation, with negro-quarters, and a cotton-press and gin-
house. We passed half a dozen of these, perhaps, during the
day. Where the owners resided in them, they would have
comfortable-looking residences, not unlike the better class of
New England farm-houses.   On the largest one, however,
there was no residence for the owner, at all, only a small cot-
tage, or whitewashed cabin, for the overseer.   It was a very
large plantation, and all the buildings were substantial and
commodious, except the negro-cabins, which were the smallest
I had seen—I thought not more than twelve feet square, in-
teriorly. They stood in two rows, with a wide street between
them. They were built of logs, with no windows—no opening
at all, except the doorway, with a chimney of sticks and mud;
with no trees about them, no porches, or shades, of any kind.
Except for the chimney—the purpose of which I should not
readily have guessed—if I had seen one of them in New England,
I should have conjectured that it had been built for a powder-
house, or perhaps an ice-house—never for an animal to sleep in.

We stopped, for some time, on this plantation, near where
some thirty men and women were at work, repairing the road.
The women were in majority, and were engaged at exactly the

same labor as the men; driving the carts, loading them with dirt, and dumping them upon the road; cutting down trees, and drawing wood by hand, to lay across the miry places; hoeing, and shoveling.

They were dressed in coarse gray gowns, generally very much burned, and very dirty; which, for greater convenience of working in the mud, were reefed up with a cord drawn tightly around the body, a little above the hips—the spare amount of skirt bagging out between this and the waist-proper. On their legs were loose leggins, or pieces of blanket or bagging wrapped about, and lashed with thongs; and they wore very heavy shoes. Most of them had handkerchiefs, only, tied around their heads, some wore men's caps, or old slouched hats, and several were bare-headed.

The overseer rode about among them, on a horse, carrying in his hand a raw-hide whip, constantly directing and encouraging them; but, as my companion and I, both, several times noticed, as often as he visited one end of the line of operations, the hands at the other end would discontinue their labor, until he turned to ride towards them again.   Clumsy, awkward, gross, elephantine in all their movements; pouting, grinning, and leering at us; sly, sensual, and shameless, in all their expressions and demeanor; I never before had witnessed, I thought, anything more revolting than the whole scene.

At length, the overseer dismounted from his horse, and, giving him to a boy to take to the stables, got upon the coach, and rode with us several miles.   From the conversation I had with him, as well as from what I saw of his conduct in the field, I judged that he was an uncommonly fit man for his duties; at least ordinarily amiable in disposition, and not passionate; but deliberate, watchful, and efficient.   I thought he would be not only a good economist, but a firm and considerate officer or master.

If these women, and their children after them, were always naturally and necessarily to remain of the character and capacity stamped on their faces—as is probably the opinion of their owner, in common with most wealthy South Carolina planters— I don't know that they could be much less miserably situated, or guided more for their own good and that of the world, than they were.   They were fat enough, and didn't look as if they were at all overworked, or harassed by cares, or oppressed by a consciousness of their degradation.   If that is all—as some think.

Afterwards, while we were changing at a house near a crossing of roads, strolling off in the woods for a short distance, I came upon two small white-topped wagons, each with a pair of horses feeding at its pole; near them was a dull camp fire, with a bake-kettle and coffee-pot, some blankets and a chest upon the ground; and an old negro, sitting with his head bowed down over a meal sack, while a negro boy was combing his wool with a common horse-card. "Good evening, uncle," said I, approaching them. "Good evening, sar," he answered, without looking up.

"Where are you going?"

"Well, we ain't goin' nower, master; we's peddlin' tobacco roun."

"Oh! peddling tobacco. Where did you come from?"

"From Rockingham County, Norf Car'lina, master."

"How long have you been coming from there?"

"'Twill be seven weeks, to-morrow, sar, since we left home."

"Have you most sold out?"

"We had a hundred and seventy-five boxes in both wagons, and we's sold all but sixty. Want to buy some tobacco, master?" (Looking up.)

"No, thank you; I am only waiting here, while the coach changes. How much tobacco is there in a box?"

"Seventy-five pound."

"Are these the boxes?"

"No, them is our provision boxes, master. Show de gemman some of der tobacco, dah." (To the boy.)

A couple of negroes here passed along near us: the old man hailed them:

"Ho dah, boys! Doan you want to buy some backey?"

"No." (Decidedly.)

"Well, I'm sorry for it." (Reproachfully.)

"Are you bound homeward, now?" I asked.

"No, massa; wish me was; got to sell all our tobackey fuss; you don't want none, master, does you? Doan you tink it pretty fair tobacco, sar, just try it: its right sweet, reckon you'll find."

"I don't wish any, thank you; I never use it. Is your master with you?"

"No, sar; he's gone across to Marion, to-day."

"Do you like to be traveling about, in this way?"

"Yes, master; I likes it very well."

"Better than staying at home, eh?"

"Well, I likes my country better dan dis; must say dat, master, likes my country better dan dis. I'se a free nigger in my country, master."

"Oh, you are a free man, are you! North Carolina is a better country than this, for free men, I suppose."

"Yes, master, I likes my country de best; I gets five dollar a month for dat boy." (Hastily, to change the subject.)

"He is your son, is he?"

"Yes, sar; he drives dat wagon, I drives dis; and I haant seen him fore, master, for six weeks, till dis mornin'."

"How were you separated?"

"We separated six weeks ago, sar, and we agreed to meet here, last night. We didn', dough, till dis mornin'."

The old man's tone softened, and he regarded his son with earnestness.

"'Pears dough, we was bofe heah, last night; but I couldn't find dem till dis mornin'. Dis mornin' some niggars tole me dar war a niggar camped off yander in de wood; and I knew 'twas him, and I went an' found him right off."

"And what wages do you get for yourself?"

"Ten dollars a month, máster."

"That's pretty good wages."

"Yes, master, any niggar can get good wages if he's a mind to be industrious, no matter wedder he's slave or free."

"So you don't like this country as well as North Carolina?"

"No, master. Fac is, master, 'pears like wite folks doan ginerally like niggars in dis country; day doan' ginerally talk so to niggars like as do in my country,; de niggars ain't so happy heah; 'pears like de wite folks was kind o' different, somehow. I doan' like dis country so well; my country suits me very well."

"Well, I've been thinking, myself, the niggers did not look so well here as they did in North Carolina and Virginia; they are not so well clothed, and they don't appear so bright as they do there."

"Well, massa, Sundays dey is mighty well clothed, dis country; 'pears like dere an't nobody looks better Sundays dan dey do. But Lord! workin' days, seems like dey haden no close dey could keep on 'um at all, master. Dey is a'mos' naked, wen deys at work, some on 'em. Why, master, up in our country, de wite folks, why, some on 'em has ten or twelve niggars; dey doan' hev no real big plantation, like dey has heah, but some on 'em has ten or twelve niggars, may be, and dey juss lives and talks along wid 'em; and dey treats 'um most as if dem was dar own chile. Dey doan' keep no niggars dey can't treat so; dey wont keep 'em, wont be bodered wid 'em. If dey gets a niggar and he doan behave himself, day wont keep him;

dey juss tell him, sar, he must look up anudder master, and
if he doan' find hisself one, I tell 'ou, when de trader cum along,
dey sell him, and he totes him away.   Dey allers sell off all de
bad niggers out of our country; dat's de way all de bad nigga:
and all dem no-account niggar keep a cumin' down heah; dat's
de way on't, master."

"Yes, that's the way of it, I suppose; these big plantations
are not just the best thing for niggers, I see that plainly."

"Master, you want raise in dis country, was 'ou?"

"No; I came from the North."

"I tort so, sar, I knew 'ou wan't one of dis country people,
'peared like 'ou was one o' my country people, way 'ou
talks; and I loves dem kine of people.   Won't you take
some whisky, sar?"   Heah, you boy! bring dat jug of
whisky dah, out o' my wagon; in dah, in dat box under dem
foddar."

"No, don't trouble yourself, I am very much obliged to you;
but I don't like to drink whisky."

"Like to have you drink some, massa, if you'd like it.   You's
right welcome to it. 'Pears like I know you was one of my
country people.   Ever been in Greensboro' massa? dat's in
Guilford."

"No, I never was there.   I came from New York, further
North than your country."

"New York, did 'ou, massa? I heerd New York was what
dey calls a Free State; all de niggars free dah."

"Yes, that is so."

"Not no slaves at all; well, I expec dat's a good ting, for all
de niggars to be free.   Greensboro' is a right comely town;
tain't like dese heah Souf Car'lina towns."

"I have heard it spoken of as a very beautiful town, and there are some very nice people there."

"Yes, dere's Mr. —— ——, I knows him, he's a mighty good man."

"Do you know Mr. ——?"

"O, yes sar, he's a mighty fine man, he is, massa; ain't no better kind of man dan him."

"Well, I must go, or the coach will be kept waiting for me. Good-by to you."

"Far'well, master, far'well, 'pears like it's done me good to see a man dat's cum out of my country again. Far'well, master."

We took supper at an exquisitely neat log-cabin, standing a short distance off the road, with a beautiful ever-green oak, the first I had observed, in front of it. There was no glass in the windows, but drapery of white muslin restrained the currents of air, and during the day would let in sufficient light, while a great blazing wood-fire both warmed and lighted the room by night. A rifle and powder-horn hung near the fire-place, and the master of the house, a fine, hearty, companionable fellow, said that he had lately shot three deer, and that there were plenty of cats, and foxes, as well as turkeys, hares, squirrels and other small game in the vicinity. It was a perfectly charming little backwoods farm-house, good wife, supper, and all; but one disagreeable blot darkened the otherwise most agreeable picture of rustic civilization—we were waited upon at table by two excessively dirty, slovenly-dressed, negro girls. In the rear of the cabin were two hovels, each lighted by large fires, and apparently crowded with other slaves belonging to the family.

Between nine and ten at night, we reached the end of the completed rail-road, coming up in search for that we had left the previous night. There was another camp and fire of the workmen, and in a little white frame-house we found a company of engineers. There were two trains and locomotives on the track, and a gang of negroes was loading cotton into one of them.

NEGRO *JODLING.* "THE CAROLINA YELL."

I strolled off until I reached an opening in the woods, in which was a cotton-field and some negro-cabins, and beyond it large girdled trees, among which were two negroes with dogs, barking, yelping, hacking, shouting, and whistling, after 'coons and 'possums. Returning to the rail-road, I found a comfortable, warm passenger-car, and, wrapped in my blanket, went to sleep. At midnight I was awakened by loud laughter, and, looking out, saw that the loading gang of negroes had made a fire, and were enjoying a right merry repast. Suddenly, one raised such a sound as I never heard before ; a long, loud, musical shout, rising, and falling, and breaking into falsetto, his voice ringing through the woods in the clear, frosty night air, like a bugle-call. As he finished, the melody was caught up by another, and then, another, and then, by several in chorus. When there was silence again, one of them cried out, as if bursting with amusement : " Did yer see de dog ?—when I began eeohing, he turn roun' an' look me straight into der face ; ha! ha! ha!" and the whole party broke into the loudest peals of laughter, as if it was the very best joke they had ever heard.

After a few minutes I could hear one urging the rest to come to work again, and soon he stepped towards the cotton bales, saying, "Come, brederen, come ; let's go at it ; come now, eoho ! roll away ! eeoho-eeoho-weeioho-i !"—and the rest taking it up as before, in a few moments they all had their shoulders to a bale of cotton, and were rolling it up the embankment.

About half-past three, I was awakened again by the whistle of the locomotive, answering, I suppose, the horn of a stage-coach, which in a few minutes drove up, bringing a mail. A negro man and woman, sleeping near me, replenished the fire; two other passengers came in and we started.

In the woods I saw a negro by a fire, while it was still night, shaving shingles very industriously. He did not even stop to look at the train. No doubt he was a slave, working by task, and of his own accord at night, that he might have the more daylight for his own purposes.

The negroes greatly enjoy fine blazing fires in the open air, and make them at every opportunity. The train on this road was provided with a man and maid-servant to attend to the fire and wait on the passengers—a very good arrangement, by the way, yet to be adopted on our own long passenger trains. When we arrived at a junction where we were to change cars, as soon as all the passengers had left the train, they also left; but instead of going into the station-house with us, they immediately collected some pine branches and chips, and getting a brand from the locomotive, made a fire upon the ground, and seated themselves by it. Other negroes soon began to join them, and as they approached were called to, "Doan' yer cum widout som' wood? Doan' yer cum widout som' wood!" and every one had to make his contribution. At another place, near a cotton plantation, I found a woman collecting pine straw into heaps, to be carted to the cattle-pens. She, too, had a fire **near** her. "What are you doing with a fire, aunty?" "Oh, jus' to warm my hans wen dey gits cold, massa." The weather was then almost uncomfortably warm to a Northern man.

We were running during the forenoon, for a hundred miles or more, in a southerly direction, on nearly a straight course, through about the middle of the State of South Carolina. The greater part of this distance, the flat, sandy pine barrens continued, scarcely a foot of grading, for many miles at a time, having been required in the construction of the rail-road. As the swamps, which were still frequent, were crossed on piles and tressel-work, the roads must have been built very cheaply— the land damages being nothing. We passed from the track of one company to that of another, several times during the day —the speed was from fifteen to twenty miles an hour, with usually very long stoppages at the stations. A conductor said they could easily run forty miles, and had done it, including stoppages; but they were forbidden now to make fast time, from the injury it did the road—the superstructure being much more shaken and liable to displacement in these light sands than on our Northern roads. The locomotives that I saw were all made in Philadelphia; the cars were all from the Hartford, Conn., and Worcester, Mass., manufactories, and, invariably, elegant and comfortable. The roads seemed to be doing a heavy freighting business with cotton. We passed at the turn-outs half a dozen trains, with nearly a thousand bales on each, but the number of passengers was always small. A slave country can never, it is evident, furnish a passenger traffic of much value. I should suppose a majority of the trains, which I saw used in the South, were not paying for the fuel and wages expended in running them.

For an hour or two we got above the sandy zone, and into the second, middle, or "wave" region of the State. The surface here was extremely undulating, gracefully swelling and dipping in bluffs and dells—the soil a mellow, brown loam, with some indications of fertility, especially in the valleys. Yet most of the ground was occupied by pine woods (probably old-field pines, on exhausted cotton-fields.) For a few miles, on a gently sloping surface of the same sort of soil, there were some enormously large cotton-fields.

I saw women working again, in large gangs, with men. In one case they were distributing manure—ditch scrapings it appeared to be—and the mode of operation was this: the manure had been already carted into heaps upon the ground; a number of the women were carrying it from the heap in baskets, on their heads, and one in her apron, and spreading it with their hands between the ridges on which the cotton grew last year; the rest followed with great, long-handled, heavy, clumsy hoes, and pulled down the ridges over the manure, and so made new ridges for the next planting. I asked a young planter who continued with me a good part of the day, why they did not use plows. He said this was rather rough land, and a plow wouldn't work in it very well. It was light soil, and smooth enough for a parade ground. The fact is, in certain parts of South Carolina, a plow is yet an almost unknown instrument of tillage.

About noon we turned east, on a track running direct to Charleston. Pine barrens continued alternating with swamp, with some cotton and corn-fields on the edges of the latter. A few of the pines were "boxed" for turpentine; and I understood

that one or two companies from North Carolina had been ope-
rating here for several years.   Plantations were not very often
seen along the road through the sand, but stations, at which
cotton was stored and loading, were comparatively frequent.

At one of the stations an empty car had been attached to the
train; I had gone into it, and was standing at one end of it,
when an elderly countryman with a young woman and three little
children entered and took seats at the other.   The old man
took out a roll of deerskin, in which were bank-bills, and some
small change.

" How much did he say 'twould be ?" he inquired.

" Seventy cents."

" For both on us?'

" For each on us."

" Both on us, I reckon."

" Reckon it's each."

" I've got jess seventy-five cents in hard money."

"Give it to him, and tell him it's all yer got; reckon he'll let
us go."

At this I moved, to attract their attention ; the old man
started, and looked towards me for a moment, and said no more.
I soon afterwards walked out on the platform, passing him, and
the conductor came in, and collected their fare; I then returned,
and stood near them, looking out the window of the door.   The
old man had a good-humored, thin, withered, very brown face,
and there was a speaking twinkle in his eye.   He was dressed
in clothes much of the Quaker cut—a broad-brimmed, low hat;
white cotton shirt, open in front, and without cravat, showing
his hairy breast; a long-skirted, snuff-colored coat, of very coarse
homespun, short trowsers, of brown drilling, red woolen stock-

ings, and heavy cow-hide shoes. He presently asked the time of day; I gave it to him, and we continued in conversation, as follows:

"Right cold weather."

"Yes."

"G'wine to Branchville?"

"I am going beyond there—to Charleston."

"Ah—come from Hamburg this mornin'?"

"No—from beyond there."

"Did ye?—where'd you come from?"

"From Wilmington."

"How long yer ben comin'?"

"I left Wilmington night before last, about ten o'clock. I have been ever since on the road."

"Reckon yer a night-bird."

"What?"

"Reckon you are a night-bird—what we calls a night-hawk, keeps a goin' at night, you know."

"Yes—I've been going most of two nights."

"Reckon so, kinder red your eyes is. Live in Charleston, do ye?"

"No, I live in New York."

"New York—that's a good ways, yet, aint it?"

"Yes."

"Reckon yer arter a chicken, up here."

"No."

"Ah, ha—reckon ye are."

The young woman laughed, lifted her shoulder, and looked out the window.

"Reckon ye'll get somebody's chicken."

"I'm afraid not."

The young woman laughed again, and tossed her head.

"Oh, reckon ye will—ah, ha! But yer mustn't mind my fun."

"Not at all, not at all. Where did *you* come from?"

"Up here to ——; g'wine hum; g'wine to stop down here, next deeper. How do you go, w'en you get to Charleston?"

"I am going on to New Orleans."

"Is New York beyond New Orleans?"

"Beyond New Orleans? Oh, no."

"*In* New Orleans, is't?"

"What?"

"*New York is somewhere in New Orleans, ain't it?*"

"No; it's the other way—beyond Wilmington."

"Oh! Been pretty cold thar?"

"Yes; there was a foot and a half of snow there, last week, I hear."

"Lord o'massy! why! have to feed all the cattle!—whew!—ha!—whew!—don't wonner ye com' away."

"You are a farmer."

"Yes."

"Well, I am a farmer, too."

"Be ye—to New York?"

"Yes; how much land have you got?"

"A hundred and twenty-five acres; how much have you?"

"Just about the same. What's your land worth, here?"

"Some on't—what we call swamp-land—kinder low and wet like, you know—that's worth five dollars an acre; and mainly it's worth a dollar and a half or two dollars—that's takin' a common trac' of upland. What's yours worth?"

" A hundred and fifty to two hundred dollars."

" What !"

" A hundred and fifty to two hundred."

" Dollars ?"

" Yes."

" Not an acre ?"

" Yes."

" Good Lord ! yer might as well buy niggers to onst. Do you work any niggers ?"

" No."

" May be they don't have niggers—that is, slaves—to New York."

" No, we do not. It's against the law."

" Yes, I heerd 'twas, some place. How do yer get yer work done ?"

" I hire white men—Irishmen, generally."

" Do they work good ?"

" Yes, better than negroes, I think, and don't cost nearly as much."

" What do yer have to give 'em ?"

" Eight or nine dollars a month, and board, for common hands, by the year."

" Hi, Lordy ! and they work up right smart, do they ? Why, yer can't get any kind of a good nigger less'n twelve dollars a month."

" And board ?"

" And board 'em ? yes ; and clothe, and blank, and shoe 'em, too."

He owned no negroes himself, and did not hire any. " They," his family, " made their own crap." They raised maize, and sweet potatoes, and cow-peas. He reckoned, in general, they made about three barrels of maize to the acre; sometimes, as much as five. He described to me, as a novelty, a plow, with "a sort of a wing, like, on one side," that pushed off, and turned over a slice of the ground; from which it appeared that he had, until recently, never seen a mould-board; the common plows of this country being constructed on the same principles as those of the Chinese, and only rooting the ground, like a hog or a mole —not cleaving and turning. He had never heard of working a plow with more than one horse. He was frank and good-natured; embarrassed his daughter by coarse jokes about herself and her babies, and asked me if I would not go home with him, and, when I declined, pressed me to come and see them when I returned. That I might do so, he gave me directions how to get to his farm; observing, that I must start pretty early in the day—because it would not be safe for a stranger to try to cross the swamp after dark. The moment the train began to check its speed, before stopping at the place at which he was to leave, he said to his daughter, " Come, gal! quick now; gather up yer young ones!" and stepped out, pulling her after him, on to the platform. As they walked off, I noticed that he strode ahead, like an Indian or a gipsy-man, and she carried in her arms two of the children and a bundle, while the third child held to her skirts.

A party of fashionably-dressed people took the train for Charleston. Two families, apparently, returning from a visit to their plantations. They came to the station in handsome coaches. Some minutes before the rest, there entered the car, in which I was then again alone, and reclining on a bench in the corner, an old nurse, with a baby, and two young negro women, having care of half a dozen children, mostly girls, from three to fifteen years of age. As they closed the door, the negro girls seemed to resume a conversation, or quarrel. Their language was loud and obscene, such as I never heard before from any but the most depraved and beastly women of the streets. Upon observing me, they dropped their voices, but not with any appearance of shame, and continued their altercation, until their mistresses entered. The white children, in the mean time, had listened, without any appearance of wonder or annoyance. The moment the ladies opened the door, they became silent.

From the Southern Cultivator, June, 1855.

" Children are fond of the company of negroes, not only because the deference shown them makes them feel perfectly at ease, but the subjects of conversation are on a level with their capacity ; while the simple tales, and the witch and ghost stories, so common among negroes, excite the young imagination and enlist the feelings. If, in this association, the child becomes familiar with indelicate, vulgar, and lascivious manners and conversation, an impression is made upon the mind and heart, which lasts for years—perhaps for life. Could we, in all cases, trace effects to their real causes, I doubt not but many young men and women, of respectable parentage and bright prospects, who have made shipwreck of all their earthly hopes, have been led to the fatal step by the seeds of corruption which, in the days of childhood and youth, were sown in their hearts by the indelicate and lascivious manners and conversation of their fathers' negroes."

From an Address of Chancellor Harper, prepared for and read before the Society for the Advancement of Learning, of South Carolina.

" I have said the tendency of our institution is to elevate the female character, as well as that of the other sex, for similar reasons.

"And, permit me to say, that this elevation of the female character is no less important and essential to us, than the moral and intellectual cultivation of the other sex. It would, indeed, be intolerable, if, when one class of society is necessarily degraded in this respect, no compensation were made by the superior elevation and purity of the other. Not only essential purity of conduct, but the utmost purity of manners. And, I will add, though it may incur the formidable charge of affectation or prudery, *a greater severity of decorum than is required elsewhere, is necessary among us.* Always should be strenuously resisted the attempts, which have sometimes been made, to introduce among us the freedom of foreign European, and, especially, of continental manners: Let us say: we will not have *the manners* of South Carolina changed."

CHARLESTON.

Before night, the train arrived at Charleston, where I remained several days.

Charleston, more than any town at the North, has the character of an old town, where careful government and the influence of social organization has been long in operation. It is much more metropolitan and convenient than any other Southern town; and yet, it seems to have adopted the requirements of modern luxury with an ill grace, and to be yielding to the demands of commerce and the increasing mobility of civilized men slowly and reluctantly.

I saw as much close packing, filth, and squalor, in certain blocks, inhabited by laboring whites, in Charleston, as I have witnessed in any Northern town of its size; and greater evidences of brutality and ruffianly character, than I have ever happened to see, among an equal population of this class, before.

The frequent drumming which is heard, the State military school, the cannon in position on the parade-ground, the citadel, the guard-house, with its martial ceremonies, the frequent parades of militia (the ranks mainly filled by foreign-born citizens), and, especially, the numerous armed-police, which is under military discipline, might lead one to imagine that the town was in a state of siege or revolution.

SAVANNAH.

Savannah, which is but half a day's sail from Charleston, has, on the other hand, a curiously rural and modest aspect, for a place of its population and commerce. A very large proportion of the buildings stand detached from each other, and are surrounded by gardens, or courts, shaded by trees, or occupied by shrubbery. There are a great number of small public squares, and some of the streets are double, with rows of trees in the centre.

Charleston and Savannah are so easily accessible from the North, and are, in consequence, so much visited, and so much written about, that there is no occasion for me to particularly describe them, or their vicinity. Both towns are chiefly interesting from that in them which is indescribable, and which strangers cannot be expected to fully appreciate.

SLAVE FUNERALS AND BURYING-GROUNDS.

I described a negro-funeral that I witnessed in Richmond, Va. In Charleston, I saw one of a very different character. Those in attendance were mainly women, and they all proceeded on foot to the grave, following the corpse, carried in a hearse. The exercises were simple and decorous, after the form used in the Presbyterian church, and were conducted by a well-dressed and dignified elderly negro. The women were generally dressed in white, and wore bonnets, which were temporarily covered with a kind of hood, made of dark cambric. There was no show whatever of feeling, emotion, or excitement. The grave was filled by the negroes, before the crowd, which was quite large, dispersed. Besides myself, only one white man,

probably a policeman, was in attendance.   The burying-ground
was a rough "vacant lot" in the midst of the town.   The only
monuments were a few wooden posts, and one small marble
tablet.

While riding, aimlessly, in the suburbs of Savannah, on returning from a visit to the beautiful rural cemetery of the wealthy
whites, which Willis has, with his usual facility and grace, a little
over-pictured, I came upon a square field, in the midst of an open
pine-wood, partially inclosed with a dilapidated wooden paling.
It proved to be a grave-yard for the negroes of the town.   Dis-
mounting, and fastening my horse to a gate-post, I walked in,
and found much, in the monuments, to interest me.   Some of
these were mere billets of wood, others were of brick and marble, and some were pieces of plank, cut in the ordinary form of
tomb-stones.   Many family-lots were inclosed with railings, and
a few flowers or evergreen shrubs had sometimes been planted
on the graves; but these were generally broken down and withered, and the ground was overgrown with weeds and briars.   I
spent some time in examining the inscriptions, the greater number of which were evidently painted by self-taught negroes, and
were curiously illustrative both of their condition and character.
I transcribed a few of them, as literally as possible, as follow:

"SACRED

TO THE MEMORY

OF HENRY. Gleve, ho

Dide JANUARY 19 1849

Age 44."

"BALDWING
In men of CHARLES
who died NOV
20. THE 1846
aged 62 years Blessed are the
dead who dieth
in the LORD
Even so said
the SPerit.   For
the Rest From
Thair"

[The remainder rotted off.]

"DEAR
WIFE OF
JAMES DELBUG
BORN 1814   DIED 1852."

To Momu
y, of,
M a
gare
-t . Born
August
29 and
died oc
tober 29 1852

[The following on marble.]

To record the worth fidelity and virtue of Reynolda Watts, (who died on the 2d day of May 1829 at the age of 24 years, in giving birth to her 3d child).

Reared from infancy by an affectionate mistress and trained by her in the paths of virtue, She was strictly moral in her deportment, faithful and devoted in her duty and heart and soul a

[Sand drifted over the remainder.]

There were a few others, of similar character to the above, erected by whites to the memory of favorite servants. The following was on a large brick tomb :

"This tablet is erected to record the demise of Rev. HENRY CUNNINGHAM, Founder and subsequent pastor of the 2d African Church for 39 years, who yielded his spirit to its master the 29 of March 1842, aged 83 years."

[Followed by an inscription to the memory of Mrs. Cunningham.]

"This vault is erected by the 2d African Church, as a token of respect."

The following is upon a large stone table. The reader will observe its date ; but I must add that, while in North Carolina, I heard of two recent occasions, in which public religious services had been interrupted, and the preachers—very estimable colored men—publicly whipped.

"Sacred to the memory of Andrew Brian pastor of 1st colored Baptist church in Savannah. God was Pleased to lay his honour near his heart and impress the worth and weight of souls upon his mind that he was constrained to Preach the Gospel to dieng world, particularly to the sable sons of africa. though he labored under many disadvantage yet thought in the school of Christ, he was able to bring out new and old out of the treasury And he has done more good among the poor slaves than all the learned Doctors·in America. He was im prisoned for the Gospel without any ceremony was severely whipped. But while under the lash he told his prosecutor he rejoiced not only to be whipped but he was willing for to suffer death for the cause of CHRIST.

"He continued preaching the Gospel until Oct. 6 1812. He was supposed to be 96 years of age, his remains were interd with peculiar respect an address was delivered by the Rev. Mr Johnston Dr. Kolluck Thomas Williams & Henry Cunningham He was an honour to human nature an ornament to religion and a friend to mankind. His memory is still precious in the (hearts) of the living.

"Afflicted long he bore the rod
With calm submission to his maker God.

His mind was tranquil and serene
No terrors in his looks was seen
A SAVIOURS smile dispelled the gloom
And smoothed the passage to the tomb.

"I heard a voice from Heaven saying unto me, Write, Blessed are the dead which die in the Lord from henceforth! Yea saith the Spirit that they may rest from the labours.

"This stone is erected by the First Colored Church as a token of love for their most faithful pastor.   A. D. 1821."

THE RICE COAST.

——————— PLANTATION, February —.

I left town yesterday morning, on horseback, with a letter in my pocket to Mr. X., a rice-planter, under whose roof I am now writing. The weather was fine, and, indeed, since I left Virginia, the weather, for out-of-door purposes, has been as fine as can be imagined. The exercise of walking or of riding, warms one, at any time between sunrise and sunset, sufficiently to allow an overcoat to be dispensed with, while the air is yet brisk and stimulating. The public-houses are overcrowded with Northerners, who congratulate themselves on having escaped from the severe cold, of which they hear from home.

All, however, who know the country, out of the large towns, say that they have suffered more from cold here, than ever at the North; because, except at a few first class hotels, and in the better sort of mansions and plantation residences, any provision for keeping houses warm is so entirely neglected. It is, indeed, too cool to sit quietly, even at midday, out of sunshine, and at night it is often frosty. As a general rule, with such exceptions as I have indicated, it will be full two hours after one has asked for a fire in his room, before the servants can be got to make it.

The idea of closing a door or window to exclude cold air, seems really never to have reached any of the negroes. From the time I left Richmond, until I arrived at Charleston, I never but once knew a servant to close a door on leaving a room, unless he was requested at the moment to do so.

The public houses of the smaller towns, and the country houses generally, are so loosely built, and so rarely have unbroken glass windows, that to sit by a fire, and to avoid remaining in a draught at the same time, is never to be expected.

As the number of Northerners, and especially of invalids, who come hither in winter, is every year increasing, more comfortable accommodations along the line of travel must soon be provided ; if not by native, then by Northern enterprise. Some of the hotels in Florida, indeed, are already, I understand, under the management of Northerners; and this winter cooks and waiters have been procured for them from the North. I observe, also, that one of them advertises that meats and vegetables are received by every steamer from New York.

As soon as comfortable quarters, and means of conveyance are extensively provided, at not immoderately great expense, there must be a great migration here every winter. The climate and the scenery, as well as the society of the more wealthy planters' families, are attractive, not to invalids alone, but even more to men and women who are able to enjoy invigorating recreations. Nowhere in the world could a man, with a sound body and a quiet conscience, live more pleasantly, at least, as a guest, it seems to me, than here where I am. I was awakened this morning by a servant making a fire for me to dress by. Opening the window, I found a clear, brisk air, but without frost—the mercury standing at 35° F. There was not a sign of winter, except that a few cypress trees, hung with seed, attached to pretty pendulous tassels, were leafless. A grove which surrounded the house was all in dark verdure; there were green oranges on trees nearer the window; the buds were swelling on a jessamine-vine, and a number of camelia-japonicas were in full bloom; one of them, at least seven feet high, and a large, compact shrub, must have had several hundred blossoms on it. Sparrows were chirping, doves cooing, and a mocking-bird whistling loudly. I walked to the stable, and saw the clean and neatly-dressed negroes grooming thorough-bred horses. They pawed the ground, and tossed their heads, and drew deep inspirations, and danced as they were led out, in exuberance of animal spirits, and I felt as they did. We drove ten miles to church, in the forenoon, with the carriage-top thrown back, and with our overcoats laid aside; nevertheless, when we returned, and came into the house, we found a crackling wood fire, in the old-fashioned fire-place, as comfortable as it was cheerful. Two lads, the sons of my host, had returned the night before from a "marooning party," with a boat-load of venison, wild fowl and fish, and at dinner this evening there were delicacies which are not to be had in perfection, it is said, anywhere else than on a rice-plantation. The woods and waters around us abound, not only with game, but with most interesting subjects of observation to the naturalist and the artist. Everything encourages cheerfulness, and invites to healthful life.

Now to think how people are baking in their oven-houses at home, or waddling out in the deep snow or mud, or across the frozen ruts, wrapped up to a Falstaffian rotundity in flannels and furs, one can but wonder that those who have means stay there, any more than these stay here in summer; and that my host would no more think of doing than the wild-goose.

But I must tell how I got here, and what I saw by the way.

A narrow belt of cleared land—"vacant lots"—only separated the town from the pine-forest—that great broad forest which extends uninterruptedly, and merely dotted with a few small corn and cotton-fields, from Delaware to Louisiana.

Having some doubt about the road, I asked a direction of a man on horseback, who overtook and was passing me. In reply, he said it was a very straight road, and we should go in company, for a mile or two. He inquired if I was a stranger; and, when he heard that I was from the North, and now first visiting the South, he remarked that there was "no better place for me to go to than that for which I was bound. Mr. X. was a very fine man—rich, got a splendid plantation, lived well, had plenty of company always, and there were a number of other show plantations near his. He reckoned I would visit some of them."

I asked what he called "show plantations." "Plantations belonging to rich people," he said, "where they had everything fixed up nice. There were several places that had that name; their owners always went out and lived on them part of the year, and then they kept a kind of open house, and were always ready to receive company. He reckoned I might go and stay a month round on them kind of places on ———— river, and it would not cost me a cent. They always had a great many Northerners going to see them, those gentlemen had. Almost every Northerner, that came here, was invited right out, to visit some of them, and, in summer, a good many of them went to the North themselves."

During the forenoon, my road continued broad and straight, and I was told that it was the chief outlet and thoroughfare of a very extensive agricultural district. There was very little land in cultivation within sight of the road, however; not a mile of it fenced, in twenty, and the only houses were log-cabins. The soil varied from a coarse, clean, yellow sand, to a dark, brown, sandy loam. There were indications that most of the land had, at some time, been under cultivation—had been worn out, and deserted.

Long teams of mules, driven by negroes, toiled slowly towards the town, with loads of rice, or cotton. A stage-coach, with six horses to hasten it through the heavy road, covered me, as it passed, with dust; and, once or twice, I met a stylish carriage (not the old Virginia "family chariot, with its six well-conditioned grays," but its descendant in fashion), with fashionably-clad gentlemen and ladies, and primly-liveried negro-servants; but much the greatest traffic of the road was done by small one-horse carts, driven by white men, or women.

"THE CRACKERS."

These carts, all but their wheels, which come from the North, look as if they were made by their owners, in the woods, with no better tools than axes and jack-knives. Very little iron is used in their construction; the different parts being held together by wooden pins, and lashings of hide. The harness is made chiefly of ropes and undressed hide; but there is always a high-peaked riding-saddle, in which the driver prefers to sit, rather than on his cart. Once, I met a woman riding in this way, with a load of children in the cart behind her. From the axle-tree, often hung a gourd, or an iron kettle. One man carried a rifle on his pommel. Sometimes, these carts would contain a single bale of cotton, more commonly, an assorted cargo of maize, sweet potatoes, poultry, game, hides, and peltry, with, always, some bundles of corn-leaves, to be fed to the horse. Women and children were often passengers, or traveled on foot, in company with the carts, which were usually furnished with a low tilt. Many of them, I found, had been two or three days on the road, bringing down a little crop to market; whole families coming with it, to get reclothed with the proceeds.

The men with the carts were generally slight, with high cheek-bones and sunken eyes, and were of less than the usual stature of the Anglo-Saxon race. They were dressed in long-skirted homespun coats, wore slouched hats, and heavy boots, outside their trowsers. As they met me, they usually bowed, and often offered a remark upon the weather, or the roads, in a bold, but not uncourteous manner—showing themselves to be, at least, in one respect, better off than the majority of European peasants, whose educated servility of character rarely fails to manifest itself, when they meet a well-dressed stranger.

The household markets of most of the Southern towns seem to be mainly supplied by the poor country people, who, driving in in this style, bring all sorts of produce to exchange for such small stores and articles of apparel as they must needs obtain from the shops. Sometimes, owing to the great extent of the back country from which the supplies are gathered, they are offered in great abundance and variety; at other times, from the want of regular market-men, there will be a scarcity, and prices will be very high.

A stranger cannot but express surprise and amusement at the appearance and manners of these country traffickers in the mar-

ket-place.   The "wild Irish" hardly differ more from the English gentry, than these rustics from the better class of planters
and towns-people, with whom the traveler more commonly
comes in contact.   Their language, even, is almost incompre-
hensible, and seems exceedingly droll, to a Northern man.   I
have found it quite impossible to report it.

I shall not soon forget the figure of a little old white woman,
wearing a man's hat, smoking a pipe, driving a little black bull
with reins; sitting, herself, bolt upright, upon the axle-tree of
a little truck, on which she was returning from market.   I was
riding with a gentleman of the town at the time, and, as she
bowed to him with an expression of ineffable self-satisfaction, I
asked if he knew her.   He had known her for twenty years, he
said, and until lately she had always come into town about once

a week, on foot, bringing fowls, eggs, potatoes, or herbs, for sale, in a basket. The bull she had probably picked up astray, when a calf, and reared and broken it herself; and the cart and harness she had made herself; but he did not think anybody in the land felt richer than she did now, or prouder of her establishment.

In the afternoon, I left the main road, and, towards night, reached a much more cultivated district. The forest of pines still extended uninterruptedly on one side of the way, but on the other was a continued succession of very large fields, of rich dark soil—evidently reclaimed swamp-land—which had been cultivated the previous year, in Sea Island cotton, or maize. Beyond them, a flat surface of still lower land, with a silver thread of water curling through it, extended, Holland-like, to the horizon. Usually at as great a distance as a quarter of a mile from the road, and from a half mile to a mile apart, were the residences of the planters—large white houses, with groves of evergreen trees about them; and between these and the road were little villages of slave-cabins.

My directions not having been sufficiently explicit, I rode in, by a private lane, to one of these. It consisted of some thirty neatly-whitewashed cottages, with a broad avenue, planted with Pride-of-China trees between them.

The cottages were framed buildings, boarded on the outside, with shingle roofs and brick chimneys; they stood fifty feet apart, with gardens and pig-yards, enclosed by palings, between them. At one, which was evidently the "sick house," or hospital, there were several negroes, of both sexes, wrapped in blankets, and reclining on the door steps or on the ground, basking in the sunshine. Some of them looked ill, but all were chatting and laughing as I rode up to make an inquiry. I learned that it was not the plantation I was intending to visit, and received a direction, as usual, so indistinct and incorrect that it led me wrong.

At another plantation which I soon afterwards reached, I found the "settlement" arranged in the same way, the cabins only being of a slightly different form. In the middle of one row was a well-house, and opposite it, on the other row, was a mill-house, with stones, at which the negroes grind their corn. It is a kind of pestle and mortar; and I was informed afterwards that the negroes prefer to take their allowance of corn and crack it for themselves, rather than to receive meal, because they think the mill-ground meal does not make as sweet bread.

At the head of the settlement, in a garden looking down the street, was an overseer's house, and here the road divided, running each way at right angles; on one side to barns and a landing on the river, on the other toward the mansion of the proprietor. A negro boy opened the gate of the latter, and I entered.

On either side, at fifty feet distant, were rows of old live oak trees, their branches and twigs slightly hung with a delicate fringe of gray moss, and their dark, shining, green foliage, meeting and intermingling naturally but densely overhead. The sunlight streamed through and played aslant the lustrous leaves, and fluttering, pendulous moss; the arch was low and broad; the trunks were huge and gnarled, and there was a heavy groining of strong, rough, knotty branches. I stopped my horse and held my breath; for I have hardly in all my life seen anything so impressively grand and beautiful. I thought of old Kit North's rhapsody on trees; and it was no rhapsody—it was all here and real: "Light, shade, shelter, coolness, freshness, music, dew, and dreams dropping through their umbrageous twilight— dropping direct, soft, sweet, soothing, and restorative from heaven."

Alas! no angels; only little black babies, toddling about with an older child or two to watch them, occupied the aisle. At the upper end was the owner's mansion, with a circular court-yard around it, and an irregular plantation of great trees; one of the oaks, as I afterwards learned, seven feet in diameter of trunk, and covering with its branches a circle of one hundred and twenty feet in diameter. As I approached it, a smart servant came out to take my horse. I obtained from him a direction to the residence of the gentleman I was searching for, and rode away, glad that I had stumbled into so charming a place.

After riding a few miles further I reached my destination.

A RICE PLANTATION.

Mr. X. has two plantations on the river, besides a large tract of poor pine forest land, extending some miles back upon the upland, and reaching above the malarious region. In the upper part of this pine land is a house, occupied by his overseer during the malarious season, when it is dangerous for any but negroes to remain during the night in the vicinity of the swamps or rice-fields. Even those few who have been born in the region, and have grown up subject to the malaria, are generally weakly and short-lived. The negroes do not enjoy as good health on rice plantations as elsewhere; and the greater difficulty with which their lives are preserved, through infancy especially, shows that the subtle poison of the miasma is not innocuous to them; but Mr. X. boasts a steady increase of his negro stock of five per

cent. per annum, which is better than is averaged on the plantations of the interior.

As to the degree of danger to others, " I would as soon stand
fifty feet from the best Kentucky rifleman and be shot at by
the hour, as to spend a night on my plantation in summer,"
a Charleston gentleman said to me.   And the following two
instances of the deadly work it sometimes does were mentioned
to me by another : A party of six ladies and gentlemen went
out of town to spend a day at the mansion of a rice-planter, on
an island.   By an accident to their boat, their return before night
was prevented, and they went back and shut themselves within
the house, had fires made, around which they sat all night, and
took every other precaution to guard against the miasma.   Nevertheless, four of them died from its effects, within a week ; and
the other two suffered severely.   Two brothers owned a plantation
on which they had spent the winter ; one of them, as summer
approached, was careful to go to another residence every night ;
the other delayed to do so until it was too late.   One morning
he was found to be ill ; a physician could not be procured until
late in the afternoon, by which time his recovery was hopeless.
The sick man besought his brother not to hazard his own life
by remaining with him ; and he was obliged, before the sun set,
to take the last farewell, and leave him with the servants, in
whose care, in the course of the night, he died.

The plantation which contains Mr. X.'s winter residence, has
but a small extent of rice land, the greater part of it being
reclaimed upland swamp soil, suitable for the culture of Sea
Island cotton, which, at the present market, might be grown
upon it with profit.   But, as his force of slaves has ordinarily
been more profitably engaged in the rice-fields, all this has been

for many years " turned out," and is now overgrown with pines. The other plantation contains over five hundred acres of rice-land, fitted for irrigation; the remainder is unusually fertile, reclaimed upland swamp, and some hundred acres of it are culti-vated for maize and Sea Island cotton.

There is a "negro settlement" on each; but both plantations, although a mile or two apart, are worked together as one, under one overseer—the hands being drafted from one to another as their labor is required.   Somewhat over seven hundred acres are at the present time under the plow in the two plantations: the whole number of negroes is two hundred, and they are reckoned to be equal to about one hundred prime hands—an unusual strength for that number of all classes.   The overseer lives, in winter, near the settlement of the larger plantation, Mr. X. near that of the smaller.

It is an old family estate, inherited by Mr. X.'s wife, who, with her children, were born and brought up upon it in close intimacy with the negroes, a large proportion of whom were also included in her inheritance, or have been since born upon the estate.   Mr. X. himself is a New England farmer's son, and has been a successful merchant and manufacturer.   He is also a religious man, without the dementifying bigotry or self-important humility, so frequently implied by that appellation to a New Englander, but generous, composed and cheerful in disposition, as well as conscientious.

The patriarchal institution should be seen here under its most favorable aspects; not only from the ties of long family associa-tion, common traditions, common memories, and, if ever, com-mon interests, between the slaves and their rulers, but, also, from the practical talent for organization and administration, gained among the rugged fields, the complicated looms, and the exact and comprehensive counting-houses of New England, which directs the labor.

The house-servants are more intelligent, understand and perform their duties better, and are more appropriately dressed, than any I have seen before. The labor required of them is light, and they are treated with much more consideration for their health and comfort than is usually given to that of free domestics. They live in brick cabins, adjoining the house and stables, and one of these, into which I have looked, is neatly and comfortably furnished. Several of the house-servants, as is usual, are mulattoes, and good-looking. The mulattoes are generally preferred for in-door occupations. Slaves brought up to house-work dread to be employed at field-labor; and those accustomed to the comparatively unconstrained life of the negro-settlement, detest the close control and careful movements required of the house-servants. It is a punishment for a lazy field-hand, to employ him in menial duties at the house, as it is to set a sneaking sailor to do the work of a cabin-servant; and it is equally a punishment to a neglectful house-servant, to banish him to the field-gangs. All the household economy is, of course, carried on in a style appropriate to a wealthy gentleman's residence—not more so, nor less so, that I observe, than in an establishment of similar grade at the North.

It is a custom with Mr. X., when on the estate, to look each day at all the work going on, inspect the buildings, boats, embankments and sluice-ways, and examine the sick. Yesterday I accompanied him in one of these daily rounds.

After a ride of several miles through the woods, in the rear of the plantations, we came to his largest negro-settlement. There was a street, or common, two hundred feet wide, on which the cabins of the negroes fronted. Each cabin was a framed building, the walls boarded and whitewashed on the outside, lathed and plastered within, the roof shingled; forty-two feet long, twenty-one feet wide, divided into two family tenements, each twenty-one by twenty-one; each tenement divided into three rooms—one, the common household apartment, twenty-one by ten; each of the others (bed-rooms), ten by ten. There was a brick fire-place in the middle of the long side of each living room, the chimneys rising in one, in the middle of the roof. Besides these rooms, each tenement had a cock-loft, entered by steps from the household room. Each tenement is occupied, on an average, by five persons. There were in them closets, with locks and keys, and a varying quantity of rude furniture. Each cabin stood two hundred feet from the next, and the street in front of them being two hundred feet wide, they were just that distance apart each way. The people were nearly all absent at work, and had locked their outer doors, taking the keys with them. Each cabin has a front and back door, and each room a window, closed by a wooden shutter, swinging outward, on hinges. Between each tenement and the next house, is a small piece of ground, inclosed with palings, in which are coops of fowl with chickens, hovels for nests, and for sows with pig. There were a great many fowls in the street. The negroes' swine are allowed to run in the woods, each owner having his own distinguished by a peculiar mark. In the rear of the yards were gardens—a half-acre to each family. Internally the cabins appeared dirty and disordered, which was rather a pleasant indication that their home-life was not much interfered with, though I found certain police regulations were enforced.

The cabin nearest the overseer's house was used as a nursery. Having driven up to this, Mr. X. inquired first of an old nurse

how the children were; whether there had been any births since his last visit; spoke to two convalescent young mothers, that were lounging on the floor of the portico, with the children, and then asked if there were any sick people.

"Nobody, oney dat boy, Sam, sar."

"What Sam is that?"

"Dat little Sam, sar; Tom's Sue's Sam, sar."

"What's the matter with him?"

"Don' 'spec dere's noting much de matter wid him now,

sar. He came in Sa'dy, complainin' he had de stomach-ache, an' I gin him some ile, sar; 'spec he mus' be well, dis time, but he din go out dis mornin'."

" Well, I'll see to him."

Mr. X. went to Tom's Sue's cabin, looked at the boy, and, concluding that he was well, though he lay abed, and pretended to cry with pain, ordered him to go out to work. Then, meeting the overseer, who was just riding away, on some business off the plantation, he remained some time in conversation with him, while I occupied myself in making a sketch of the nursery and the street of the settlement in my note-book. On the verandah and the steps of the nursery, there were twenty-seven children, most of them infants, that had been left there by their mothers, while they were working their tasks in the fields. They probably make a visit to them once or twice during the day, to nurse them, and receive them to take to their cabins, or where they like, when they have finished their tasks—generally in the middle of the afternoon. The older children were fed with porridge, by the general nurse. A number of girls, eight or ten years old, were occupied in holding and tending the youngest infants. Those a little older—the crawlers—were in the pen, and those big enough to toddle were playing on the steps, or before the house. Some of these, with two or three bigger ones, were singing and dancing about a fire that they had made on the ground. They were not at all disturbed or interrupted in their amusement by the presence of their owner and myself. At twelve years of age, the children are first put to regular field-work; until then no labor is required of them, except, perhaps, occasionally, they are charged with some light kind of duty, such as frightening birds from corn. When first sent to the field, one-quarter of an able-bodied hand's day's work is ordinarily allotted to them, as their task.

But very few of the babies were in arms; such as were not, generally lay on the floor, rolling about, or sat still, sucking their thumbs. The nurse was a kind-looking old negro woman, with, no doubt, philoprogenitiveness well developed; but she paid very little attention to them, only sometimes chiding the older ones for laughing or singing too loud. I watched for half an hour, and in all that time not a baby of them began to cry; nor have I ever heard one, at two or three other plantation-nurseries which I have visited. I remember, in Amsterdam, to have seen two or three similar collections of children, voluntarily deposited by their mothers, who went out from home to work. These seemed to be looked out for by two or three poor women, who probably received a small fee for their trouble, from the parent thus relieved. Not being able to converse in Dutch, I could get no particular information about it; but I especially noticed, in each case, that there was no crying or fretting. On the contrary, they appeared to be peculiarly well-disposed and jolly, as if they were already on the straight road to the right place, and were fully satisfied with the vehicles they had got to drive through the world. They had, in short, thus early learned that it did not do any good to cry—for the nurse couldn't, if she would, feed, or cuddle, or play with one every time she was wanted to. I make a note of it, as indicating how young the little twig is bent, how early the formation of habits commences, and that, even in babyhood, the "product of happiness is to be found, not so much in increasing your numerator, as in lessening your denominator."

From the settlement, we drove to the "mill"—not a flouring

mill, though I believe there is a run of stones in it—but a monster barn, with more extensive and better machinery for threshing and storing rice, driven by a steam-engine, than I have ever seen used for grain on any farm in Europe or America before. Adjoining the mill-house were shops and sheds, in which blacksmiths, carpenters, and other mechanics—all slaves, belonging to Mr. X.—were at work. He called my attention to the excellence of their workmanship, and said that they exercised as much ingenuity and skill as the ordinary mechanics that he was used to employ in New England. He pointed out to me some carpenter's work, a part of which had been executed by a New England mechanic, and a part by one of his own hands, which indicated that the latter was much the better workman.

I was gratified by this, for I had been so often told, in Virginia, by gentlemen, anxious to convince me that the negro was incapable of being educated or improved to a condition in which it would be safe to trust him with himself—that no negro-mechanic could ever be taught, or induced to work carefully or nicely—that I had begun to believe it might be so.

We were attended through the mill-house by a respectable-looking, orderly, and gentlemanly-mannered mulatto, who was called, by his master, "the watchman." His duties, however, as they were described to me, were those of a steward, or intendant. He carried, by a strap at his waist, a very large number of keys, and had charge of all the stores of provisions, tools, and materials of the plantations, as well as of all their produce, before it was shipped to market. He weighed and measured out all the rations of the slaves and the cattle; superintended the mechanics, and himself made and repaired, as was necessary, all the machinery, including the steam-engine.

In all these departments, his authority was superior to that of the overseer. The overseer received his private allowance of family provisions from him, as did also the head-servant at the mansion, who was his brother. His responsibility was much greater than that of the overseer; and Mr. X. said, he would trust him with much more than he would any overseer he had ever known.

Anxious to learn how this trustworthiness and intelligence, so unusual in a slave, had been developed or ascertained, I inquired of his history, which was, briefly, as follows.

Being the son of a favorite house-servant, he had been, as a child, associated with the white family, and received by chance something of the early education of the white children. When old enough, he had been employed, for some years, as a waiter; but, at his own request, was eventually allowed to learn the blacksmith's trade, in the plantation-shop. Showing ingenuity and talent, he was afterwards employed to make and repair the plantation cotton-gins. Finally, his owner took him to a steam-engine builder, and paid $500 to have him instructed as a machinist. After he had become a skillful workman, he obtained employment, as an engineer; and for some years continued in this occupation, and was allowed to spend his wages for himself. Finding, however, that he was acquiring dissipated habits, and wasting all his earnings, Mr. X. eventually brought him, much against his inclinations, back to the plantations. Being allowed peculiar privileges, and given duties wholly flattering to his self-respect, he soon became contented; and, of course, was able to be extremely valuable to his owner.

I have seen another slave-engineer. The gentleman who employed him told me that he was a man of talent, and of great

worth of character.   He had desired to make him free, but his
owner, who was a member of the Board of Brokers, and of Dr.
————'s Church, in New York, believed that Providence designed the negro race for slavery, and refused to sell him for
that purpose.   He thought it better that he (his owner) should
continue to receive two hundred dollars a year for his services,
while he continued able to work, and then he should feel
responsible that he did not starve, or come upon the public for
a support, in his old age.   The man himself, having light and
agreeable duties, well provided for, furnished with plenty of
spending money in gratuities by his employer, patronized and
flattered by the white people, honored and looked up to by those
of his own color, was rather indifferent in the matter; or even,
perhaps, preferred to remain a slave, to being transported for
life, to Africa.

The watchman was a fine-looking fellow: as we were returning from church, on Sunday, he had passed us, well-dressed and
well-mounted, and as he raised his hat, to salute us, there was
nothing in his manner or appearance, except his color, to distinguish him from a gentleman of good-breeding and fortune.

When we were leaving the house, to go to church, on Sunday,
after all the white family had entered their carriages, or mounted
their horses, the head house-servant also mounted a horse—as
he did so, slipping a coin into the hands of the boy who had
been holding him.   Afterwards, we passed a family of negroes,
in a light wagon—the oldest among them driving the horse.   On
my inquiring if the slaves were allowed to take horses to drive
to church, I was informed that, in each of these three cases, the
horses belonged to the negroes who were driving or riding them.
The old man was infirm, and Mr. X. had given him a horse, to

enable him to move about. He was probably employed to look after the cattle at pasture, or at something in which it was necessary, for his usefulness, that he should have a horse : I say this, because I afterwards found, in similar cases on other plantations, that it was so.

But the watchman and the house-servant had bought their horses with money. The watchman was believed to own three horses ; and, to account for his wealth, Mr. X.'s son told me that his father considered him a very valuable servant, and frequently encouraged him in his good behavior, with handsome gratuities. He receives, probably, considerably higher wages, in fact (in the form of presents), than the white overseer. He knew his father gave him two hundred dollars at once, a short time ago. The watchman has a private house, and, no doubt, lives in considerable luxury.

Will it be said, " therefore, Slavery is neither necessarily degrading nor inhumane ?" On the other hand, so far as it is not, there is no apology for it. It may be that this fine fellow, if he had been born a freeman, would be no better employed than he is here ; but, in that case, where is the advantage ? Certainly not in the economy of the arrangement. And if he was self-dependent, and if, especially, he had to provide for the present and future of those he loved, and was able to do so, would he not necessarily live a happier, stronger, better, and more respectable man ?

But, to arrive at this conclusion, we have had to suppose such a state of society for the free laborer as to make it a matter of certainty that by the development of industry, talent, and providence, he is able to provide for himself and for those whose happiness is linked with his own.

As a general rule, this is the case in all free-labor countries. Nowhere, I suspect, are the exceptions to it so frequent as are the exceptions to humane and generous treatment of slaves by their masters.   Nevertheless, it is the first duty of those who think Slavery wrong to remove to the utmost all such excuse for it as is to be found in the occasional hardships and frequent debasement and ignorance of the laboring class in free communities.

After passing through tool-rooms, corn-rooms, mule-stables, store-rooms, and a large garden, in which vegetables to be distributed among the negroes, as well as for the family, are grown, we walked to the rice-land.   It is divided by embankments into fields of about twenty acres each, but varying somewhat in size, according to the course of the river.   The arrangements are such that each field may be flooded independently of the rest, and they are subdivided by open ditches into rectangular plats of a quarter acre each.   We first proceeded to where twenty or thirty women and girls were engaged in raking together, in heaps and winrows, the stubble and rubbish left on the field after the last crop, and burning it.   The main object of this operation is to kill all the seeds of weeds, or of rice, on the ground.   Ordinarily it is done by tasks—a certain number of the small divisions of the field being given to each hand to burn in a day ; but owing to a more than usual amount of rain having fallen lately, and some other causes, making the work harder in some places than others, the women were now working by the day, under the direction of a "driver," a negro man, who walked about among them, taking care that they left nothing unburned. Mr. X. inspected the ground they had gone over, to see whether the driver had done his duty.   It had been sufficiently well burned, but, not more than quarter as much ground had been gone over, he said, as was usually burned in task-work,—and he thought they had been very lazy, and reprimanded them for it. The driver made some little apology, but the women offered no reply, keeping steadily, and it seemed sullenly, on at their work.

In the next field, twenty men, or boys, for none of them looked as if they were full-grown, were plowing, each with a single mule, and a light, New-York-made plow. The soil was very friable, the plowing easy, and the mules proceeded at a smart pace; the furrows were straight, regular, and well turned. Their task was nominally an acre and a quarter a day; somewhat less actually, as the measure includes the space occupied by the ditches, which are two to three feet wide, running around each quarter of an acre. The plowing gang was superintended by a driver who was provided with a watch; and while we were looking at them he called out that it was twelve o'clock. The mules were immediately taken from the plows, and the plow-boys mounting them, leapt the ditches, and cantered off to the stables, to feed them. One or two were ordered to take their plows to the blacksmith, for repairs.

FOOD.

The plowmen got their dinner at this time: those not using horses do not usually dine till they have finished their tasks; but this, I believe, is optional with them. They commence work at sunrise, and at about eight o'clock have breakfast brought to them in the field, each hand having left a bucket with the cook for that purpose. All who are working in connection leave their work together, and gather in a social company about a fire, where they generally spend about half an hour, at breakfast time.   The provisions furnished them consist mainly of meal, rice and vegetables, with salt and molasses, and occasionally bacon, fish, and coffee.   The allowance is a peck of meal, or an equivalent quantity of rice per week, to each working hand, old or young, besides small stores.   Mr. X. says that he has lately given a less amount of meat than is now usual on plantations, having observed that the general health of the negroes is not as good as formerly, when no meat at all was customarily given them.   The general impression among planters is, that the negroes work much better for being supplied with three or four pounds of bacon a week.

Leaving the rice-land, we went next to some of the upland fields, where we found several other gangs of negroes at work; one entirely of men engaged in ditching; another of women, and another of boys and girls, "listing" an old corn-field with hoes. All of them were working by tasks, and were overlooked by negro drivers.   They all labored with greater rapidity and cheerfulness than any slaves I have before seen; and the women struck their hoes as if they were strong, and well able to engage in muscular labor.   The expression of their faces was generally repulsive, and their *tout ensemble* anything but agreeable to the eye.   The dress of most of them was uncouth and cumbrous, dirty and ragged; reefed up, as I have once before described, at the hips, so as to show their heavy legs, wrapped round with a piece of old blanket, in lieu of leggings or stockings.   Most of them worked with bare arms, but wore strong shoes on their feet, and handkerchiefs on their heads; some of them were smoking, and each gang had a fire burning on the ground, near where they were at work, to light their pipes and warm their breakfast by.   Mr. X. said this was always their custom, even in summer. To each gang a boy or girl was also attached, whose business it was to bring water for them to drink, and to go for anything required by the driver. The drivers would frequently call back a hand to go over again some piece of his or her task that had not been worked to his satisfaction, and were constantly calling to one or another, with a harsh and peremptory voice, to strike harder or hoe deeper, and otherwise taking care that the work was well done. Mr. X. asked if Little Sam ("Tom's Sue's Sam") worked yet with the "three-quarter" hands, and learning that he did, ordered him to be put with the full hands, observing that though rather short, he was strong and stout, and, being twenty years old, well able to do a man's work.

The field-hands are all divided into four classes, according to their physical capacities. The children beginning as "quarter-hands," advancing to "half-hands," and then to "three-quarter hands;" and, finally, when mature, and able-bodied, healthy and strong, to "full hands." As they decline in strength, from age, sickness, or other cause, they retrograde in the scale, and proportionately less labor is required of them. Many, of naturally weak frame, never are put among the full hands. Finally, the aged are left out at the annual classification, and no more regular field-work is required of them, although they are generally provided with some light, sedentary occupation. I saw one old woman picking "tailings" of rice out of a heap of chaff, an occupation at which she was literally not earning her salt. Mr. X. told me she was a native African, having been brought when a girl from the Guinea coast. She spoke almost unintelligibly; but after some other conversation, in which I had not

been able to understand a word she said, he jokingly proposed to send her back to Africa. She expressed her preference to remain where she was, very emphatically. " Why?"
She did not answer readily, but being pressed, threw up her
palsied hands, and said furiously, " I lubs 'ou mas'r, oh, I
lubs 'ou. I don't want go 'way from 'ou."

The field hands, are nearly always worked in gangs, the
strength of a gang varying according to the work that en-
gages it; usually it numbers twenty or more, and is directed
by a driver. As on most large plantations, whether of rice
or cotton, in Eastern Georgia and South Carolina, nearly
all ordinary and regular work is performed *by tasks:* that
is to say, each hand has his labor for the day marked out
before him, and can take his own time to do it in. For
instance, in making drains in light, clean meadow land, each
man or woman of the full hands is required to dig one thousand
cubic feet; in swamp-land that is being prepared for rice
culture, where there are not many stumps, the task for a
ditcher is five hundred feet; while in a very strong cypress
swamp, only two hundred feet is required; in hoeing rice, a
certain number of rows, equal to one-half or two-thirds of
an acre, according to the condition of the land; in sowing
rice (strewing in drills), two acres; in reaping rice (if it
stands well), three-quarters of an acre ; or, sometimes a gang
will be required to reap, tie in sheaves, and carry to the
stack-yard the produce of a certain area, commonly equal to
one fourth the number of acres that there are hands working
together. Hoeing cotton, corn, or potatoes; one half to one
acre. Threshing; five to six hundred sheaves. In plowing
rice-land (light, clean, mellow soil) with a yoke of oxen, one

acre a day, including the ground lost in and near the drains—
the oxen being changed at noon. A cooper, also, for instance,
is required to make barrels at the rate of eighteen a week.
Drawing staves; 500 a day. Hoop poles; 120. Squaring
timber; 100 ft. Laying worm-fence; 50 panels per hand.
Post and rail do., posts set $2\frac{1}{2}$ to 3 ft. deep, 9 ft. apart, nine
or ten panels per hand. In getting fuel from the woods,
(pine, to be cut and split,) one cord is the task for a day.
In "mauling rails," the taskman selecting the trees (pine)
that he judges will split easiest, one hundred a day, ends not
sharpened.

These are the tasks for first class able-bodied men, they
are lessened by one quarter for three quarter hands, and proportionately for the lighter classes.   In allotting the tasks,
the drivers are expected to put the weaker hands, where (if
there is any choice in the appearance of the ground, as where
certain rows in hoeing corn would be less weedy than others,)
they will be favored.

These tasks certainly would not be considered excessively
hard, by a Northern laborer; and, in point of fact, the more
industrious and active hands finish them often by two o'clock.
I saw one or two leaving the field soon after one o'clock,
several about two; and between three and four, I met a dozen
women and several men coming home to their cabins, having
finished their day's work.

Under this "Organization of Labor," most of the slaves work
rapidly and well.   In nearly all ordinary work, custom has settled the extent of the task, and it is difficult to increase it.   The
driver who marks it out, has to remain on the ground until
it is finished, and has no interest in over-measuring it; and

if it should be systematically increased very much, there is danger of a general stampede to the "swamp"—a danger the slave can always hold before his master's cupidity. In fact, it is looked upon in this region as a proscriptive right of the negroes to have this incitement to diligence offered them; and the man who denied it, or who attempted to lessen it, would, it is said, suffer in his reputation, as well as experience much annoyance from the obstinate "rascality" of his negroes. Notwithstanding this, I have heard a man assert, boastingly, that he made his negroes habitually perform double the customary tasks. Thus we get a glimpse again of the black side. If he is allowed the power to do this, what may not a man do?

SLAVE DRIVERS.

It is the driver's duty to make the tasked hands do their work well. If, in their haste to finish it, they neglect to do it properly, he "sets them back," so that carelessness will hinder more than it will hasten the completion of their tasks.

In the selection of drivers, regard seems to be had to size and strength—at least, nearly all the drivers I have seen are tall and strong men—but a great deal of judgment, requiring greater capacity of mind than the ordinary slave is often supposed to be possessed of, is certainly needed in them. A good driver is very valuable and usually holds office for life. His authority is not limited to the direction of labor in the field, but extends to the general deportment of the negroes. He is made to do the duties of policeman, and even of police magistrate. It is his duty, for instance, on Mr. X.'s estate, to keep order in the settlement; and, if two

persons, men or women, are fighting, it is his duty to immediately separate them, and then to "whip them both."

Before any field of work is entered upon by a gang, the
driver who is to superintend them has to measure and stake
off the tasks. To do this at all accurately, in irregular-
shaped fields, must require considerable powers of calculation.
A driver, with a boy to set the stakes, I was told, would
accurately lay out forty acres a day, in half-acre tasks. The
only instrument used is a five-foot measuring rod. When
the gang comes to the field, he points out to each person his
or her duty for the day, and then walks about among them,
looking out that each proceeds properly. If, after a hard
day's labor, he sees that the gang has been overtasked, owing
to a miscalculation of the difficulty of the work, he may excuse the completion of the tasks; but he is not allowed to
extend them. In the case of uncompleted tasks, the body
of the gang begin new tasks the next day, and only a sufficient number are detailed from it to complete, during the
day, the unfinished tasks of the day before. The relation
of the driver to the working hands seems to be similar to
that of the boatswain to the seamen in the navy, or of the
sergeant to the privates in the army.

Having generally had long experience on the plantation,
the advice of the drivers is commonly taken in nearly all the
administration, and frequently they are, *de facto*, the mana-
gers. Orders on important points of the plantation economy,
I have heard given by the proprietor directly to them, without the overseer's being consulted or informed of them; and
it is often left with them to decide when and how long to
flow the rice-grounds—the proprietor and overseer deferring

to their more experienced judgment. Where the drivers are discreet, experienced and trusty, the overseer is frequently employed merely as a matter of form, to comply with the laws requiring the superintendence or presence of a white man among every body of slaves; and his duty is rather to inspect and report, than to govern. Mr. X. considers his overseer an uncommonly efficient and faithful one, but he would not employ him, even during the summer, when he is absent for several months, if the law did not require it. He has sometimes left his plantation in care of one of the drivers for a considerable length of time, after having discharged an overseer; and he thinks it has then been quite as well conducted as ever. His overseer consults the drivers on all important points, and is governed by their advice.

PUNISHMENT.

Mr. X. said, that though overseers sometimes punished the negroes severely, and otherwise ill-treated them, it is their more common fault to indulge them foolishly in their disposition to idleness, or in other ways to curry favor with them, so they may not inform the proprietor of their own misconduct or neglect. He has his overseer bound to certain rules, by written contract; and it is stipulated that he can discharge him at any moment, without remuneration for his loss of time and inconvenience, if he should at any time be dissatisfied with him. One of the rules is, that he shall never punish a negro with his own hands, and that corporeal punishment, when necessary, shall be inflicted by the drivers. The advantage of this is, that it secures time for deliberation, and prevents punishment being made in sudden passion. His drivers are not allowed to carry their whips with them in the field; so that if the overseer wishes a hand punished, it is necessary to call a driver; and the driver has then to go to his cabin, which is, perhaps, a mile or two distant, to get his whip, before it can be applied.

I asked how often the necessity of punishment occurred?

"Sometimes, perhaps, not once for two or three weeks; then it will seem as if the devil had got into them all, and there is a good deal of it."

SLAVES TAKING CARE OF THEMSELVES.

As the negroes finish the labor, required of them by Mr. X., at three or four o'clock in the afternoon, they can employ the remainder of the day in laboring for themselves, if they choose. Each family has a half-acre of land allotted to it, for a garden; besides which, there is a large vegetable garden, cultivated by a gardener for the plantation, from which they are supplied, to a greater or less extent. They are at liberty to sell whatever they choose from the products of their own garden, and to make what they can by keeping swine and fowls. Mr. X.'s family have no other supply of poultry and eggs than what is obtained by purchase from his own negroes; they frequently, also, purchase game from them. The only restriction upon their traffic is a "liquor law." They are not allowed to buy or sell ardent spirits. This prohibition, like liquor laws elsewhere, unfortunately, cannot be enforced; and, of late years, grog shops, at which stolen goods are bought from the slaves, and poisonous liquors—chiefly the worst whisky, much watered and made stupefying by an infusion of tobacco—are clandestinely sold to them, have become an established evil, and the planters find themselves almost powerless to cope with it. They have, here, lately organized an association for this purpose, and have brought several offenders to trial; but, as it is a penitentiary offense, the culprit spares no pains or expense to avoid conviction—and it is almost impossible, in a community of which so large a proportion is poor and degraded, to have a jury sufficiently honest and intelligent to permit the law to be executed.

A remarkable illustration of this evil has lately occurred. A planter, discovering that a considerable quantity of cotton had been stolen from him, informed the patrol of the neighboring planters of it. A strategem was made use of, to detect the thief, and, what was of much more importance—there being no question but that this was a slave—to discover for whom the thief worked. A lot of cotton was prepared, by mixing hair with it, and put in a tempting place. A negro was seen to take it, and was followed by scouts, to a grog-shop, several miles distant, where he sold it—its real value being nearly ten dollars—for ten cents, taking his pay in liquor. The man was arrested, and, the theft being made to appear, by the hair, before a justice, obtained bail in $2,000, to answer at the higher Court. Some of the best legal counsel of the State has been engaged, to obtain, if possible, his conviction.

This difficulty in the management of slaves is a great and very rapidly increasing one. Everywhere that I have been, I have found the planters provoked and angry about it. A swarm of Jews, within the last ten years, has settled in nearly every Southern town, many of them men of no character, opening cheap clothing and trinket shops; ruining, or driving out of business, many of the old retailers, and engaging in an unlawful trade with the simple negroes, which is found very profitable.

From the Charleston Standard, Nov. 23d, 1854.

"This abominable practice of trading with slaves, is not only taking our produce from us, but injuring our slave property. It is true the ᴖwner of slaves may lock, watch, and whip, as much as he pleases—the negroes will steal and trade, as long as white persons hold out to them temptations to steal and bring to them. Three-fourths of the persons who are guilty, you can get no fine from ; and, if they have some property, all they have to do is to confess a judgment to a friend, go to jail, and swear out. It is no uncommon thing for a man to be convicted of offenses against the State, and against the persons and property of individuals, and pay the fines, costs, and damages, by swearing out of jail, and then go and commit similar offenses. The State, or the party injured, has the cost of all these prosecutions and suits to pay, besides the trouble of attending Court : the guilty is convicted, the injured prosecutor punished."

The law which prevents the reception of the evidence of a negro in courts, here strikes back, with a most annoying force, upon the dominant power itself. In the mischief thus arising, we see a striking illustration of the danger which stands before the South, whenever its prosperity shall invite extensive immigration, and lead what would otherwise be a healthy competition to flow through its channels of industry.

This injury to slave property, from grog-shops, furnishes the grand argument for the Maine Law at the South.

From an Address to the people of Georgia, by a Committee of the State Temperance Society, prior to the election of 1855.

"We propose to turn the 2,200 *foreign* grog-shop keepers, in Georgia, out of office, and ask them to help us. They (the Know-Nothings) reply, 'We have no time for that now—we are trying to turn *foreigners* out of office ;' and when we call upon the Democratic party for aid, they excuse themselves, upon the ground that they have work enough to do in keeping these foreigners in office."

From the Penfield (Ga.) Temperance Banner, Sept. 29th, 1855.

"OUR SLAVE POPULATION.

"We take the following from the *Savannah Journal and Courier,* and would ask every candid reader if the evils referred to ought not to be corrected.   How shall it be done?

" ' By reference to the recent homicide of a negro, in another column, some facts will be seen suggestive of a state of things, in this part of our population, which should not exist, and which cannot endure without danger, both to them and to us.   The collision, which terminated thus fatally, occurred at an hour past midnight—at a time when none but the evil-disposed are stirring, unless driven by necessity ; and yet, at that hour, those negroes and others, as many as chose, were passing about the country, with ample opportunity to commit any act which might happen to enter their heads.   In fact, they did engage, in the public highway, in a broil terminating in homicide.   It is not difficult to imagine that their evil passions might have taken a very different direction, with as little danger of meeting control or obstacle.

" ' But it is shown, too, that to the impunity thus given them by the darkness of midnight, was added the incitement to crime drawn from the abuse of liquor.   They had just left one of those resorts where the negro is supplied with the most villainously-poisonous compounds, fit only to excite him to deeds of blood and violence.   The part that this had in the slaughter of Saturday night, we are enabled only to imagine ; but experience would teach us that its share was by no means small.   Indeed, we have the declaration of the slayer, that the blow, by which he was exasperated so as to return it by the fatal stab, was inflicted by a bottle of brandy !   In this fact, we fear, is a clue to the whole history of the transaction.'

" Here, evidently, are considerations deserving the grave notice of, not only those who own negroes, but of all others who live in a society where they are held."

LAWS OF TRADE ON THE PLANTATION.

Mr. X. remarks that his arrangements allow his servants no excuse for dealing with these fellows.   He has a rule to purchase everything they desire to sell, and to give them a high price for it, himself.   Eggs constitute a circulating medium on the plantation.   Their par value is considered to be twelve for a dime, at which they may always be exchanged for cash, or left on deposit, without interest, at his kitchen.

Whatever he takes of them that he cannot use in his own family, or has not occasion to give to others of his servants, is sent to town, to be resold. The negroes do not commonly take money for the articles he has of them, but the value of them is put to their credit, and a regular account kept with them. He has a store, usually well supplied with articles that they most want, which are purchased in large quantities, and sold to them at wholesale prices; thus giving them a great advantage in dealing with him rather than with the grog-shops. His slaves are sometimes his creditors to large amounts; at the present time he says he owes them about five hundred dollars. A woman has charge of the store, and when there is anything called for that she cannot supply, it is usually ordered by the next conveyance, of his factors in town.

SUGGESTIVE.

The ascertained practicability of thus dealing with slaves, together with the obvious advantages of the method of working them by tasks, which I have described, seem to me to indicate that it is not so impracticable as is generally supposed, if only it was desired by those having the power, to rapidly extinguish Slavery, and while doing so, to educate the negro for taking care of himself, in freedom. Let, for instance, any slave be provided with all things he will demand, as far as practicable, and charge him for them at certain prices—honest, market prices for his necessities, higher prices for harmless luxuries, and excessive, but not absolutely prohibitory, prices for everything likely to do him harm. Credit him, at a fixed price, for every day's work he does, and for all above a certain easily accomplished task in a day, at an increased price, so that his reward will be in an increasing ratio to his perseverance. Let the prices of provisions be so proportioned to the price of task-work, that it will be about as easy as it is now for him to obtain a bare subsistence. When he has no food and shelter due him, let him be confined in solitude, or otherwise punished, until he asks for opportunity to earn exemption from punishment, by labor.

When he desires to marry, and can persuade any woman to marry him, let the two be dealt with as in partnership. Thus, a young man or young woman will be attractive, somewhat in proportion to his or her reputation for industry and providence. Thus, industry and providence will become fashionable. Oblige them to purchase food for their children, and let them have the benefit of their children's labor, and they will be careful to teach their children to avoid waste, and to honor labor. Let those who have not gained credit while hale and young, sufficient to support themselves in comfort when prevented by age or infirmity from further labor, be supported by a tax upon all the negroes of the plantation, or of a community. Improvidence, and pretense of inability to labor, will then be disgraceful.

When any man has a balance to his credit equal to his value as a slave, let that constitute him a free man. It will be optional with him and his employer, whether he shall continue longer in the relation of servant. If desirable for both that he should, it is probable that he will ; for unless he is honest, prudent, industrious and discreet, he will not have acquired the means of purchasing his freedom.

If he is so, he will remain where he is, unless he is more wanted elsewhere ; a fact that will be established by his being called away by higher wages, or the prospect of greater ease and comfort elsewhere. If he is so drawn off, it is better for all parties concerned that he should go. Better for his old master; for he would not refuse him sufficient wages to induce him to stay, unless he could get the work, he wanted him to do, done cheaper than he would justly do it. Poor wages would certainly, in the long run, buy but poor work; fair wages, fair work.

Of course there will be exceptional cases, but they will always operate as cautions for the future, not only to the parties suffering, but to all who observe them. And be sure they will not be suffered, among ignorant people, to be lost. This is the beneficent function of gossip, with which wise and broad-working minds have nothing to do, such not being benefited by the iteration of the lessons of life.

Married persons, of course, can only become free together. In the appraisement of their value, let that of their young children be included, so that they cannot be parted from them; but with regard to children old enough to earn something more than their living, let it be optional what they do for them.

Such a system would simply combine the commendable elements of the emancipation law of Cuba,* and those of the reformatory punishment system, now in successful operation in some of the British penal colonies, with a few practical modifications. Further modifications would, doubtless, be needed, which

---

* In Cuba every slave has the privilege of emancipating himself, by paying a price which does not depend upon the selfish exactions of the masters; but it is either a fixed price, or else is fixed, in each case, by disinterested appraisers. The consequence is, that emancipations are constantly going on, and the free people of color are becoming enlightened, cultivated, and wealthy. In no part of the United States do they occupy the high social position which they enjoy in Cuba.

any man who has had much practical experience in dealing with slaves might readily suggest. Much might be learned from the experience of the system pursued in the penal colonies, some account of which may be seen in the report of the Prisoners' Aid Society of New York, for 1854, or in a previous little work of my own. I have here only desired to suggest, apropos to my friend's experience, the practicability of providing the negroes an education in essential social morality, while they are drawing towards personal freedom; a desideratum with those who do not consider Slavery a purely and eternally desirable thing for both slave and slave-master, which the present system, I think, is calculated, as far as possible, in every direction to oppose. My reasons for thus thinking, I may hereafter give, in some detail.

Education in theology and letters could be easily combined with such a plan as I have hinted at; or, if a State should wish to encourage the improvement of its negro constituent—as, in the progress of enlightenment and Christianity, may be hoped to eventually occur—a simple provision of the law, making a certain standard of proficiency the condition of political freedom, would probably create a natural demand for education, which commerce, under its inexorable higher-laws, would be obliged to satisfy.

SPECIAL NATURAL DEPRAVITY OF NEGROES.

I do not think, after all I have heard to favor it, that there is any good reason to consider the negro, naturally and essentially, the moral inferior of the white; or, that if he is so, it is in those elements of character which should forever prevent us from trusting him with equal social munities with ourselves.

So far as I have observed, slaves show themselves worthy of trust most, where their masters are most considerate and liberal towards them. Far more so, for instance, on the small farms of North Carolina than on the plantations of Virginia and South Carolina. Mr. X.'s slaves are permitted to purchase fire-arms and ammunition, and to keep them in their cabins; and his wife and daughters reside with him, among them, the doors of the house never locked, or windows closed, perfectly defenseless, and miles distant from any other white family.

Another evidence that negroes, even in slavery, when trusted, may prove wonderfully reliable, I will subjoin, in a letter written by Mr. Alexander Smets, of Savannah, to a friend in New York, in 1853. It is hardly necessary to say, that the "servants" spoken of were negroes, and the "suspicious characters," providentially removed, were whites. The letter was not written for publication:

"The epidemic which spread destruction and desolation through our city, and many other places in most of the Southern States, was, with the exception of that of 1820, the most deadly that was ever known here. Its appearance being sudden, the inhabitants were seized with a panic, which caused an immediate *sauve qui peut* seldom witnessed before. I left, or rather fled, for the sake of my daughters, to Sparta, Hancock county. They were dreadfully frightened.

"Of a population of fifteen thousand, six thousand, who could not get away, remained, nearly all of whom were more or less seized with the prevailing disease. The negroes, with very few exceptions, escaped.

"Amidst the desolation and gloom pervading the deserted streets, there was a feature that showed our slaves in a favorable light. There were entire blocks of houses, which were either entirely deserted, the owners in many instances having, in their flight, forgotten to lock them up, or left in charge of the servants. A finer opportunity for plunder could not be desired by thieves; and yet the city was remarkable, during the time, for order and quietness. There were scarcely any robberies committed, and as regards fires, so common in the winter, none!

Every householder, whose premises had escaped the fury of the late terrific storm, found them in the same condition he had left them. Had not the yellow fever scared away or killed those suspicious characters, whose existence is a problem, and who prowl about every city, I fear that our city might have been laid waste. Of the whole board of directors of five banks, three or four remained, and these at one time were sick. Several of the clerks were left, each in the possession of a single one. For several weeks it was difficult to get anything to eat; the bakers were either sick or dead. The markets closed, no country-man dared venture himself into the city with the usual supplies for the table, and the packets had discontinued their trips. I shall stop, other-wise I could fill a volume with the occurrences and incidents of the dismal period of the epidemic."

SLAVE "MARRIAGES" AND FUNERALS.

While watching the negroes in the field, Mr. X. addressed a girl, who was vigorously plying a hoe near us.

"Is that Lucy?——Ah, Lucy, what's this I hear about you?"

The girl simpered; but did not answer nor discontinue her work.

"What is this I hear about you and Sam, eh?"

The girl grinned; and, still hoeing away with all her might, whispered "Yes, sir."

"Sam came to see me this morning."

"If master pleases."

"Very well; you may come up to the house Saturday night, and your mistress will have something for you."

Mr. X. does not absolutely refuse to allow his negroes to "marry off the place," as most large slave-owners do, but he discourages intercourse, as much as possible, between his negroes and those of other plantations; and they are usually satisfied to choose from among themselves.

When a man and woman wish to live with each other, they

are required to *ask leave* of their master; and, unless there are
some very obvious objections, this is always granted: a cabin is
allotted to them, and presents are made of dresses and house-
keeping articles. A marriage ceremony, in the same form as
that used by free people, is conducted by the negro preacher,
and they are encouraged to make the occasion memorable and
gratifying to all, by general festivity. The master and mistress,
when on the plantation, usually honor the wedding by their
attendance; and, if they are favorite servants, it is held in the
house, and the ceremony performed by a white minister.

A beautiful, dense, evergreen grove is used as the burial-
ground of the negroes. The funerals are always at night, and
are described as being very quaint and picturesque—all the
negroes of the neighborhood marching in procession from the
cabin of the deceased person to the grave, carrying light-wood
torches, and singing hymns, in their sad, wailing, chanting manner. At the head of each recent grave stands a wooden post.

SLAVE CHAPELS AND SLAVE WORSHIP.

On most of the large rice plantations which I have seen in
this vicinity, there is a small chapel, which the negroes call their
prayer-house. The owner of one of these told me that, having
furnished the prayer-house with seats having a back-rail, his
negroes petitioned him to remove it, because it did not leave
them *room enough to pray*. It was explained to me that it is
their custom, in social worship, to work themselves up to a great
pitch of excitement, in which they yell and cry aloud, and,
finally, shriek and leap up, clapping their hands and dancing,
as it is done at heathen festivals. The back-rail they found
to seriously impede this exercise.

Mr. X. told me that he had endeavored, with but little success, to prevent this shouting and jumping of the negroes at their meetings on his plantation, from a conviction that there was not the slightest element of religious sentiment in it. He considered it to be engaged in more as an exciting amusement than from any really religious impulse.   In the town churches, except, perhaps, those managed and conducted almost exclusively by negroes, the slaves are said to commonly engage in religious exercises in a sober and decorous manner; yet, a member of a Presbyterian church in a Southern city told me, that he had seen the negroes, in his own house of worship, during " a season of revival," leap from their seats, throw their arms wildly in the air, shout vehemently and unintelligibly, cry, groan, rend their clothes, and fall into cataleptic trances.

SLAVE CLERGY.

On almost every large plantation, and in every neighborhood of small ones, there is one man who has come to be considered the head or pastor of the local church.   The office among the negroes, as among all other people, confers a certain importance and power.   A part of the reverence attaching to the duties is given to the person; vanity and self-confidence are cultivated, and a higher ambition aroused than can usually enter the mind of a slave.   The self-respect of the preacher is also often increased by the consideration in which he is held by his master, as well as his fellows ; thus, the preachers generally have an air of superiority to other negroes ; they acquire a remarkable memory of words, phrases, and forms ; a curious sort of poetic talent is developed, and a habit is obtained of rhapsodizing and exciting furious emotions, to a great degree spurious and temporary, in

themselves and others, through the imagination. I was introduced, the other day, to a preacher, who was represented to be
quite distinguished among them. I took his hand, respectfully,
and said I was happy to meet him. He seemed to take this for
a joke, and laughed heartily. He was a "driver," and my friend
said:

"He drives the negroes at the cotton all the week, and Sundays he drives them at the Gospel—don't you, Ned?"

He commenced to reply in some scriptural phrase, soberly;
but, before he could say three words, began to laugh again, and
reeled off like a drunken man—entirely overcome with merriment. He recovered himself in a moment, and returned to us.

"They say he preaches very powerfully, too."

"Yes, Massa! 'kordin' to der grace—*yah! yah!*"

And he staggered off again, with the peculiar hearty negro
guffaw. My friend's tone was, I suppose, slightly humorous,
but I was grave, and really meant to treat him respectfully,
wishing to draw him into conversation; but he had got the
impression that it was intended to make fun of him, and,
generously assuming a merry humor, I found it impossible to
get a serious reply.

A RELIGIOUS SERVICE AMONG THE CRACKERS.

A majority of the public houses of worship at the South
are small, rude structures of logs, or rough boards, built by
the united labor or contributions of the people of a large
neighborhood or district of country, and are used as places
of assembly for all public purposes. Few of them have
any regular clergymen, but preachers of different denominations go from one to another, sometimes in a defined rotation,

or "circuit," so that they may be expected at each of their stations at regular intervals. A late report of the Southern Aid Society states that hardly one-fifth of the preachers are regularly educated for their business, and that "you would starve a host of them if you debarred them from seeking additional support for their families by worldly occupation." In one presbytery of the Presbyterian Church, which is, perhaps, the richest, and includes the most educated body of people of all the Southern Churches, there are twenty-one ministers whose wages are not over two hundred and fifty dollars each. The proportion of ministers, of all sorts, to people, is estimated at one to thirteen hundred. (In the Free States it is estimated at one to nine hundred.) The report of this Society also states, that "within the limits of the United States religious destitution lies comparatively at the South and Southwest; and that from the first settlement of the country the North has preserved a decided religious superiority over the South, especially in three important particulars: in ample supply of Christian institutions; extensive supply of Christian truth; and thorough Christian regimen, both in the Church and in the community." It is added that, "while the Southwestern States have always needed a stronger arm of the Christian ministry to raise them up toward a Christian equality with their Northern brethren, their supply in this respect has always been decidedly inferior." The reason of this is the same with that which explains the general ignorance of the people of the South: The effect of Slavery in preventing social association of the whites, and in encouraging vagabond and improvident habits of life among the poor.

The two largest denominations of Christians at the South are the Methodists and Baptists—the last having a numerical superiority. There are some subdivisions of each, and of the Baptists especially, the nature of which I do not understand. Two grand divisions of the Baptists are known as the Hard Shells and the Soft Shells. There is an intense rivalry and jealousy among these various sects and sub-sects, and the controversy between them is carried on with a bitterness and persistence exceeding anything which I have known at the North, and in a manner which curiously indicates how the terms Christianity, piety, etc., are misapplied to partisanship, and conditions of the imagination.

A general want of deep reverence of character is evidenced in the frequent familiar and public use of expressions of rare reverence, and in high-colored descriptions of personal feelings and sentiments, which, if actual, can only be among a man's dearest, most interior, secret, stillest, and most uncommunicable experiences. Men talk in public places, in the churches, and in barrooms, in the stage-coach, and at the fireside, of their personal and peculiar relationship with the Deity, and of the mutations of their harmony with His Spirit, just as they do about their family and business matters. Of the familiar use of Scripture expressions by the negroes, I have already spoken. This is not confined to them, but is general among all the lower and middle classes. (When I speak of classes, I usually refer, as in this case, more especially to degree in education and information.) The following advertisement of a "reforming" dram-seller is an illustration:

" 'FAITH WITHOUT WORKS IS DEAD,'

IN order to engage in a more 'honorable' business, I offer for sale, cheap for cash, my stock of

LIQUORS, BAR-FIXTURES, BILLIARD TABLE,

etc., etc. If not sold privately, by the 20th day of May, I will sell the same at public auction. 'Shew me thy faith without thy works, and I will shew thee my faith by my works.'   E. KEYSER."

The religious service which I am about to describe, was held in a less than usually rude meeting-house, the boards by which it was inclosed being planed, the windows glazed, and the seats for the white people provided with backs. It stood in a small clearing of the woods, and there was no habitation within two miles of it. When I reached it with my friends, the services had already commenced. Fastened to trees, in a circle about the house, there were many saddled horses and mules, and a few attached to carts or wagons. There were two smouldering camp-fires, around which sat circles of negroes and white boys, roasting potatoes in the ashes.

In the house were some fifty white people, generally dressed in homespun, and of the class called "crackers," though I was told that some of them owned a good many negroes, and were by no means so poor as their appearance indicated. About one-third of the house, at the end opposite the desk, was covered by a gallery or cock-loft, under and in which, distinctly separated from the whites, was a dense body of negroes; the men on one side, the women on another. The whites were seated promiscuously in the body of the house. The negroes present outnumbered the whites, but the exercises at this time seemed to have no reference to them; there were many more waiting about the doors outside, and they were expecting to enjoy a meeting to themselves, after the whites had left the house. They were generally neatly dressed, more so than the majority of the whites present, but in a distinctly plantation or slave style. A few of them wore somewhat expensive articles, evidently of their own selection and purchase, but I observed, with some surprise, that not one of the women had a bonnet upon her head, all wearing handkerchiefs, generally of gay patterns, and becomingly arranged. I inquired if this was entirely a matter of taste, and was told that it, no doubt, was generally so, though the masters would not probably allow them to wear bonnets, if they should be disposed to, and should purchase them themselves, as it would be thought presuming. In the towns, the colored women often, but not generally, wear bonnets.

During all the exercises, people of both classes were frequently going out and coming in; the women had brought their babies with them, and these made much disturbance. A negro girl would sometimes come forward to take a child out; perhaps the child would prefer not to be taken out and would make loud and angry objections; it would then be fed. Several were allowed to crawl about the floor, carrying handfuls of corn-bread and roast potatoes about with them; one had a fancy to enter the pulpit; which it succeeded in climbing into three times, and was as often taken away, in spite of loud and tearful expostulations, by its father. Dogs were not excluded; and outside, the doors and windows all being open, there was much neighing and braying, unused as were the mules and horses to see so many of their kind assembled.

The preliminary devotional exercises—a Scripture reading, singing, and painfully irreverential and meaningless harangues nominally addressed to the Deity, but really to the audience —being concluded, the sermon was commenced by reading a text, with which, however, it had, so far as I could discover, no further association. Without often being violent in his manner, the speaker nearly all the time cried aloud at the utmost stretch of his voice, as if calling to some one a long distance off; as his discourse was extemporaneous, however, he sometimes returned with curious effect to his natural conversational tone; and as he was gifted with a strong imagination, and possessed of a good deal of dramatic power, he kept the attention of the people very well. There was no argument upon any point that the congregation were likely to have much difference of opinion upon, nor any special connection between one sentence and another; yet there was a constant, sly, sectarian skirmishing, and a frequently recurring cannonade upon French infidelity and socialism, and several crushing charges upon Fourier, the Pope of Rome, Tom Paine, Voltaire, "Roosu," and Jo Smith. The audience were frequently reminded that the preacher did not want their attention, for any purpose of his own; but that he demanded a respectful hearing as "the Ambassador of Christ." He had the habit of frequently repeating a phrase, or of bringing forward the same idea in a slightly different form, a great many times. The following passage, of which I took notes, presents an example of this, followed by one of the best instances of his dramatic talent that occurred. He was leaning far over the desk, with his arm stretched forward, gesticulating violently, yelling at the highest key, and catching breath with an effort:

"A—ah! why don't you come to Christ? ah! what's the reason? ah! Is it because he was of *lowly birth?* ah! Is that it? *Is it* because he was born in a manger? ah! Is it because he was of a humble origin? ah! Is it because he was lowly born? a-ha! Is it because, ah!—is it because, ah!—because he was called a Nazarene? Is it because he was born in a stable?—or is it because—because he was of humble origin?

Or is it—is it because"—He drew back, and after a moment's silence put his hand to his chin, and began walking up and down the platform of the pulpit, soliloquizing. "It can't be —it can't be—?"—then lifting his eyes and gradually turning towards the audience, while he continued to speak in a low, thoughtful tone: "perhaps you don't like the messenger —is that the reason? I'm the Ambassador of the great and glorious King; it's his invitation, 'taint mine. You musn't mind me. I ain't no account. Suppose a ragged, insignificant little boy should come running in here and tell you, 'Mister, your house's a-fire!' would you mind the ragged, insignificant little boy, and refuse to listen to him, because he didn't look respectable?"

At the end of the sermon he stepped down from the pulpit, and, crossing the house towards the negroes, said, quietly, as he walked, "I take great interest in the poor blacks; and this evening I am going to hold a meeting specially for you." With this, he turned back, and without reëntering the pulpit, but strolling up and down before it, read a hymn, at the conclusion of which, he laid his book down, and, speaking for a moment, with natural emphasis, said:

"I don't want to create a tumultuous scene, now;— that isn't my intention. I don't want to make an excitement,—that aint what I want,—but I feel that there's some here that I may never see again, ah! and, as I may never have another opportunity, I feel it my duty as an Ambassador of Jesus Christ, ah! before I go ——" By this time he had returned to the high key and whining yell. Exactly what he felt it his duty to do, I did not understand; but evidently to employ some more powerful agency of awakening, than arguments and appeals to the understanding; and, before I could conjecture, in the least, of what sort this was to be, while he was yet speaking calmly, deprecating excitement, my attention was attracted to several men, who had previously appeared sleepy and indifferent, but who now suddenly began to sigh, raise their heads, and *shed tears*—some standing up, so that they might be observed in doing this by the whole congregation—the tears running down their noses without any interruption. The speaker, presently, was crying aloud, with a mournful, distressed, beseeching shriek, as if he was himself suffering torture: "Oh, any of you fond parents, who know that any of your dear, sweet, little ones may be, oh! at any moment snatched right away from your bosom, and cast into hell fire, oh! there to suffer torment forever and ever, and ever and ever—Oh! come out here and help us pray for·them! Oh, any of you wives that has got an unconverted husband, that won't go along with you to eternal glory, but is set upon being separated from you, oh! and taking up his bed in hell—Oh! I call upon you, if you love him, now to come out here and jine us in praying for him. Oh, if there's a husband here, whose wife is still in the bond of iniquity," etc., through a long category.

It was immediately evident that a large part of the audience understood his wish to be the reverse of what he had declared, and considered themselves called upon to assist him; and it was astonishing to see with what readiness the faces of those who, up to the moment he gave the signal, had appeared drowsy and stupid, were made to express agonizing excitement, sighing, groaning, and weeping. Rising in their seats, and walking up to the pulpit, they grasped each other's hands agonizingly, and remained, some kneeling, others standing, with their faces towards the remainder of the assembly. There was great confusion and tumult, and the poor children, evidently impressed by the terrified tone of the howling preacher, with the expectation of some immediately impending calamity, shrieked, and ran hither and thither, till negro girls came forward, laughing at the imposition, and carried them out.

At length, when some twenty had gathered around the preacher, and it became evident that no more could be drawn out, he stopped a moment for breath, and then repeated a verse of a hymn, which being sung, he again commenced to cry aloud, calling now upon all the unconverted, who were *willing* to be saved, to kneel. A few did so, and another verse was sung, followed by another more fervent exhortation. So it went on ; at each verse his entreaties, warnings, and threats, and the responsive groans, sobs, and ejaculations of his coterie grew louder and stronger. Those who refused to kneel, were addressed as standing on the brink of the infernal pit, into which a diabolical divinity was momentarily on the point of satisfying the necessities of his character by hurling them off.

All this time about a dozen of the audience remained standing, many were kneeling, and the larger part had taken their seats—all having risen at the commencement of the singing. Those who continued standing were mainly wild-looking young fellows, who glanced with smiles at one another, as if they needed encouragement to brazen it out. A few young women were evidently fearfully excited, and perceptibly trembled, but for some reason dared not kneel, or compromise, by sitting. One of these, a good-looking and gayly-dressed girl, stood near, and directly before the preacher, her lips compressed, and her eyes fixed fiercely and defiantly upon him.   He for some time concentrated his force upon her; but she was too strong for him, he could not bring her down.   At length, shaking his finger toward her, with a terrible expression, as if he had the power, and did not lack the inclination to damn her for her resistance to his will, he said: "I tell you this is *the last call !*"   She bit her lips, and turned paler, but still stood erect, and defiant of the immense magnetism concentrated upon her, and he gave it up himself, quite exhausted with the effort.

The last verse of the hymn was sung.   A comparatively quiet and sober repetition of Scripture phrases, strung together heterogeneously and without meaning, in the form of prayer, followed, a benediction was pronouced, and in five minutes all the people were out of the door, with no trace of the previous excitement left, but most of the men talking eagerly of the price of cotton, and negroes, and other news.

The negroes kept their place during all of the tumult; there may have been a sympathetic groan or exclamation uttered by one or two of them, but generally they expressed only the interest of curiosity in the proceedings, such as Europeans might at a performance of the dancing dervishes, an Indian pow-wow, or an exhibition of "psychological" or "spiritual" phenomena, making it very evident that the emotion of the performers was optionally engaged in, as an appropriate part of divine service. There was generally a self-satisfied smile upon their faces; and I have no doubt they felt that they could do it with a good deal more energy and abandon, if they were called upon.   I did not wish to detain my companion to witness how they succeeded, when their turn came; and I can only judge from the fact, that those I saw the next morning were so hoarse that they could scarcely speak, that the religious exercises they most enjoy are rather hard upon the lungs, whatever their effect may be upon the soul.

CHAPTER VII.

RICE AND ITS CULTURE.

ALTHOUGH nineteen-twentieths of all the rice raised in the United States is grown within a district of narrow limits, on the sea-coast of the Carolinas and Georgia, the crop forms a not unimportant item among the total productions of the country.* The crop of 1849 was supposed to be more than two hundred and fifteen million pounds, and the amount exported was equal, in value, to one-third of all the wheat and flour, and to one-sixth of all the vegetable food, of every kind, sent abroad. The exportation of 1851 was exceeded in value, according to the Patent Office Report, only by that of cotton, flour, and tobacco.

Rice is raised in limited quantity in all of the Southern States, and probably might be in some of the North. Rice has been grown on the Thames in England, and is extensively cultivated in Westphalia, Lombardy, and Hungary, in a climate not differing, materially, from that of Southern Ohio or Pennsylvania. Travelers have found a variety of rice extensively cultivated among the Himalayan mountains, at an

---

* The number of Rice Plantations is as follows, viz. :

S. Carolina—Plantations raising 20,000 lbs. and over,					-	446
Georgia,	"	"	"	"	-	88
N. Carolina,	"	"	"	"	-	25
Total,	-	-	-	-	-	559

elevation but little below the line of constant snow. It is true that a hot climate is necessary for a large production ; but these facts contradict the common assertion, that rice can only be grown under such circumstances of climate as must be fatal to any but negro labor.*

In Louisiana and the Mississippi valley, where the rice culture is, at present, very limited, there are millions of acres of now unproductive wilderness, admirably adapted to its requirements, and here, "it is a well known fact," says a writer in De Bow's *Review*, "that *the rice plantations, both as regards whites and blacks, are more healthy than the sugar and cotton.*" The only restriction, therefore, upon the production of rice to a thousand fold greater extent than at present, is the cost of labor in the Southern States.

From the New Orleans Delta, Feb'y 20, 1853.

"It is shown in a petition to the legislature of Louisiana, asking for a grant of State land to the petitioners, as an encouragement to them to undertake extensive rice culture, in the State, that the cultivation of rice, in Louisiana, is not attended with the unusual sickness that it is in the Atlantic States. This is an important fact, and reference is made to the Parish of Plaquemines, where there is a rice-growing district, of some thirty or forty miles, on each side of the river, making forty thousand or more barrels of rough rice, yearly ; and where the health of the inhabitants, both white and black, is about the same that it is in other parts of the State, where no rice is grown. The reason assigned is, the Mississippi water, owing to its peculiar character, is not near so liable to stagnate or decompose, and produce miasms, as the fresh, clear waters of the Eastern rivers. It has been the impression of most of the residents of Plaquemines, that that Parish has always been, except when the cholera prevailed, one of the healthiest in the State."

---

* The rice commonly reported to grow wild, abundantly, in Wisconsin, and lately reproduced from seed in Connecticut, is not, I believe, properly called rice, but is of the family of oats.

" Another specimen of Creole rice may now be seen at the Reading Room of the Exchange, side by side with the " Gold Seed" we noticed a short time since. It came from the Parish of Plaquemines, and is of the sort very generally cultivated there. J. Blodget Britton, Esq., the founder of the Louisiana Rice Mill Company, selected it as a fair sample of what is now produced in that district. He informs us that it resembles the white husk upland variety of South Carolina, though having, where care is used in its culture, a larger kernel, but is not so highly esteemed in commerce as the " Gold Seed ; it is, however, greatly preferred by the Creoles, on account of its flavor.

Mr. Britton has been traveling much through the Atlantic States, from Georgia to Massachusetts, in quest of information upon the subject of rice culture and milling, and recently has visited the principal rice districts of this State, collecting and imparting all the information in his power. He says there are few, very few persons in Louisiana who are at all aware of the great capability of our batture lands for the production of rice, and of a quality, too, he thinks, that will equal any in the world. All that is wanted is, good seed and proper culture. Some of the grain he has found is even larger than the large Ward rice of the Georgetown District, S. C., and some equally tough and hard, indeed, tougher and harder, he thinks, and possessing all the requisites for fine milling. But a fact, by no means the least important, he has ascertained. He is thoroughly satisfied, after hundreds of inquiries, that the cultivation of rice on the Mississippi bottoms does not cause unusual sickness, as is the case to the eastward. This he attributes to the purifying qualities of the sediment of the river water. Dr. Wilkinson, of the Parish of Plaquemines, whom we regard as high authority, has also given his assurance of this."

Rice continues to be cultivated extensively on the coast of Georgia and the Carolinas, notwithstanding the high price of labor which Slavery and the demand for cotton has occasioned, only because there are unusual facilities there for forming plantations, in which, while the soil is exceedingly rich and easily tilled, and the climate favorable, the ground may be covered at will with water until nearly all other plants are killed, so as to save much of the labor which would otherwise be necessary in the cultivation of the crop; and may as readily be drained, when the requirements of the rice itself make it desirable.

Some of the economical advantages thus obtained, might certainly be made available, under other circumstances, for other crops. Luxuriant crops of grain and leguminous plants are sometimes grown upon the rice fields, and I have little doubt that there are many swamps, bordering upon our Northern rivers, which might be converted into fields of irrigation, with great profit. On this account, I shall describe the rice plantation somewhat elaborately.

THE ATLANTIC RICE DISTRICT.

A large part of all the country next the coast, fifty miles or more in width, in North and South Carolina and Georgia, is occupied by flat cypress swamps and reedy marshes. That which is not so is sandy, sterile, and overgrown with pines, and only of any value for agriculture where, at depressions of the surface, vegetable mould has been collected by the flow of rain water. The nearer we approach the sea, the more does water predominate, till at length land appears only in islands or capes; this is the so-called Sea Island region. Below all, however, there stretches along the whole coast a low and narrow sand bar—a kind of defensive outwork of the land, seldom inhabited except by lost Indians and runaway negroes, who subsist by hunting and fishing. There are, upon it, several government relief stations and light-houses, far less frequent, alas! than skeleton hulks of old ships, which, half buried—like victims of war—in the sand, give sad evidence of the fury of the sea, and of the firmness with which its onsets are received.

At distant intervals there are shallow breaches, through which the quiet tide twice a day steals in, swelling the neutral lagoons, and damming the outlet of the fresh water streams, till their current is destroyed or turned back, and their flood dispersed far and wide over the debatable land of the cypress swamps.

Then when heavy rains in the interior have swollen the rivers, their eddying currents deposit, all along the edges of the sandy islands and capes of the swamp, the rich freight they have brought from the calcareous or granitic mountains in which they rise, with the organic waste of the great forests through which they flow. With all is mingled the silicious wash of the nearest shore and the rich silt of the salt lagoons, aroused from their bottoms in extraordinary assaults of the ocean.

This is the soil of the rice plantations, which are always formed in such parts of the tidal swamps, adjoining the mainland or the sandy islands, as are left nearly dry at the ebb of the water. The surface must be level, or with only slight inclinations towards the natural drains in which the retiring tide withdraws; and it must be at such a distance from the sea, that there is no taste of salt in the water by which it is flooded, at the rise of tide.

MAKING A RICE FIELD.

In such a situation, the rice fields are first constructed as follows: Their outline being determined upon, the trees are cut upon it for a space of fifty feet in width; a ditch is then dug at the ebb of the water, the earth thrown out from which soon suffices to prevent the return of ordinary tides, and the laborers are thus permitted to work uninterruptedly. An embankment is then formed, upon the site of the first made ditch, sufficiently thick and high to resist the heaviest floods which can be anticipated. It is usually five feet in hight, and fifteen in breadth at the base, and all stumps and roots are removed from the earth of which it is formed, as, in digging the first ditch, they have been from its base. The earth for it is obtained' by digging a great ditch fifteen or twenty feet inside of it; and if more is afterwards needed, it is brought from a distance, rather than lessen its security by loosening the ground near its base.

While this embanking has been going on, the trees may have been felled over all the ground within, and, with the underbrush, drawn into piles or rows. At a dry time in the spring, fire is set to the windward side of these, and they are more or less successfully consumed. Often the logs remain, as do always the stumps, encumbering the rice field for many years. Usually, too, the larger trees are only girdled, and their charred or rotting trunks stand for years, rueful corpses of the old forests.

The cleared land is next divided into fields of convenient size, by embankments similar to, but not as large as, the main river embankment, the object of them being only to keep the water that is to be let into one field out of the next, which may not be prepared for it; commonly they are seven or eight feet wide at base and three feet high, with ditches of proportionate size adjoining them; a margin of eight or ten feet being left between the ditches and the embankments. Each field must be provided with a separate trunk and gate, to let in or exclude the water of the river; and if it is a back field, a canal, embanked on either side, is sometimes necessary to be made for this purpose. Such a canal is generally made wide enough to admit of the passage of a scow for the transportation of the crop.

These operations being concluded, the cultivation of the land is commenced; but, owing to the withdrawal of shade, the decay of roots and recent vegetable deposit, and the drainage of the water with which the earth has hitherto been saturated, there continues for several years to be a gradual subsidence of the surface, making it necessary to provide more ditches to remove the water, after a flooding of the field, with sufficient rapidity and completeness. These ditches, which are, perhaps, but two feet wide and deep, are dug between the crops, from time to time, until all the fields are divided into rectangular beds of a half or a quarter-acre each. Now, when the gates are open, at the fall of tide, any water that is on the beds flows rapidly into these minor drains (or "quarter ditches"), from these into the outside ditches of each field, and from these through the field trunks into the canal, or the main embankment ditch, and from this through the main trunk into the river. The gates in the trunk are made with valves, that are closed by the rise of water in the river, so as not to again admit it. Another set of gates, provided with valves opening the other way, are shut down, and the former are drawn up, when it is wished to admit the water, and to prevent its outflow.

The fields can each be flooded to any hight, and the water retained upon them to any length of time desired. The only exceptions to this sometimes occur on those plantations nearest the sea, and those furthest removed from it. On the lower plantations, the tide does not always fall low enough, for a few days at a time, to draw off the water completely; and on the upper ones, it may not always rise high enough to sufficiently flood the fields. The planter must then wait for spring-tides, or for a wind from seaward, that shall "set up" the water in the river.

"FRESHES" AND "SALTS."

In times of freshet of the river, too, it will be impossible to drain a greater or less number of the plantations upon it. These circumstances occurring at critical periods of the growth of the rice-plant, always have a great effect upon the crop, and are referred to in factors' and brokers' reports, and are often noticed in the commercial newspapers.

There is another circumstance, however, connected with the character of the season for rain, that still more essentially concerns the interests of the rice-planters, especially those nearest the ocean. In a very dry season, the rivers being low, the ocean water, impregnated with salt, is carried further up than usual. Salt is poisonous to the rice-plant; while, on the other hand, unless it is flooded from the river, no crop can be made. The longer the drought continues, the greater this difficulty becomes, and the higher up it extends.

An expanse of old rice ground, a nearly perfect plain surface, with its waving, clean, bright verdure, stretching unbroken, except by the straight and parallel lines of ditch and wall, to the horizon's edge before you, bounded on one side by the silver thread of the river, on the other by the dark curtain of the pine forest, is said to be a very beautiful sight. But the new plantation, as I saw it in February, the ground covered thickly with small stumps, and strown with brands and cinders, and half-burnt logs, with here and there an old trunk still standing, seared and burned, and denuded of foliage, with a company of clumsy and uncouth black women, armed with axes, shovels and hoes, and directed by a stalwart black man, armed with a whip, all slopping about in the black, unctuous mire at the bottom of the ditches, is a very dreary scene.

CHOPPING, MASHING, TRENCHING, AND SOWING.

In preparing the ground for the crop, it is first thoroughly "chopped," as the operation with the thick, clumsy, heavy hoe is appropriately termed. This rudely turns, mixes, and levels the surface, two or three inches in depth. It is repeated as near as possible to the planting time, the soil being made as fine and friable, by crushing the clods, as possible—whence this second hoeing is termed the "mash." From the middle of March to the first of April planting commences, the first operation in which is opening drills, or, as it is termed on the plantation, "trenching." This is done with narrow hoes, the drills or trenches being chopped out about four inches wide, two inches deep, and thirteen inches apart. To guide the trenchers, a few drills are first opened by expert hands, four feet four inches apart, stakes being set to direct them; the common hands then open two between each of these guide rows, measuring the distance only by the eye. The accuracy with which the lines are made straight is said to be astonishing; and this, as well as the plowing, and many other operations performed by negroes, as I have had occasion to notice with colored laborers at the North, no less than among the slaves, indicates that the race generally has a good "mathematical eye," much more so at least than the Irish.

As fast as the trenches are made, light hands follow, strewing

the seed in them.   It is sowed very thickly through the breadth
of the trenches, so that from two to three bushels of rice are
used upon an acre.   The seed is lightly covered with hoes as
rapidly as possible after it is sowed.

FLOWING, AND CULTIVATION OF THE CROP.

The force employed must always be large enough to complete
the sowing of each field on the day it is begun.   The outer gate
in the trunk is opened as soon as the sowing is finished; and on
the next rise of tide the water flows in, fills the ditches, and
gradually rises until the whole ground is covered.

This is termed the " sprout flow," and the water is left on the
field until the seed sprouts—from a week to a fortnight, according to the warmth of the season.   It is then drawn off, and
the field is left until the points of the shoots of the young
plants appear above ground, when the second flooding is given
it, called the "point flow."   At this time, the water remains
on till all the grass and weeds that have come up with the rice
are killed, and until the rice itself is three or four inches in
hight, and so strong that the birds cannot pull it up.   As soon
as the ground is sufficiently dry, after the "point flow," the rice
is hoed, and a fortnight or three weeks later it is hoed again,
remaining dry in the mean time.   As soon, after the second
hoeing, as the weeds are killed by the sun (or, if rainy weather,
immediately, so as to float them off), the field is again flooded,
the water being allowed to rise at first well above all the plants,
that the weeds and rubbish which will float may drift to the
sides of the field, where they are raked out, dried and burned:
the water is then lowered, so that the points of the rice may be
seen above it.   The rice will be from six inches to one foot in

hight at this time, and the water remains on at the same hight for two or three weeks. The exact time for drawing it off is determined by the appearance of the rice, and is a point requiring an experienced and discreet judgment to decide. This is called the "long flow."

The field is again left to dry, after which it receives a third and a fourth hoeing, and, when it is judged to need it, the water is again let on to a depth that will not quite cover the rice, and now remains on till harvest.

The negroes are employed, until the rice is headed, in wading through it, and collecting and bringing out in baskets any aquatic grasses or volunteer rice that have grown in the trenches. "Volunteer rice" is such as is produced by seed that has remained on the ground during the winter, and is of such inferior quality that, if it is left to be threshed with the crop, it injures its salable value much more than the addition it makes to its quantity is worth.

When the rice has headed, the water is raised still higher, for the purpose of supporting the heavy crop, and to prevent the straw from being tangled or "laid" by the wind, until it is ripe for the sickle.

The system of culture and irrigation which I have described is that most extensively practiced; but there are several modifications of it, used to a greater or less extent. One of these is called "planting in the open trench;" in which the seed is prepared by washing it with muddy water, and drying it, so that a slight coating of clay remains upon it, which, after it is sown, is sufficient to prevent its rising out of the trench when the field is flooded. This saves the labor of covering it, and the water being let on at once after the sowing, it is protected from birds.

The water remains until the plant has attained a certain size and color (commonly from two to three weeks), when it is withdrawn, and the subsequent culture is the same as I have described, after the second or "point" flow, in the first plan. The "long flow" and the "lay-by flow" are sometimes united, the water being gradually raised, as the plant increases in hight, and only drawn off temporarily and partially, to supply its place with fresh, to prevent stagnation, or to admit the negroes to go over the field to collect weeds, etc. When this follows the open trench planting, the rice is flooded during all but perhaps two weeks of its growth, and receives but two instead of four hoeings. Some keep the water on as much as possible, only drawing off for barely the time required for the negroes to hoe it, when necessary to free the crop from weeds. Good planters use these and other modifications of the usual plan, according to the season, each having occasional advantages.

It will be obvious that in each method, the irrigation, by protecting the seed and plants, destroying weeds and vermin, and mechanically sustaining the crop, allows a great deal of labor to be dispensed with, which, with an unirrigated crop, would be desirable. This economy of labor is probably of greater consequence than the excessive moisture afforded the plant. Crops of rice have been grown on ordinarily dry upland, in the interior of the State, quite as large as the average of those of the tidalswamps, but, of course, with an immensely greater expense in tillage.

I should remark, also, that as moisture can be commanded at pleasure, it is of much less consequence to be particular as to the time of seeding, than it would otherwise be. One field is sowed after another, during a period of two months. The flowings, tillage and harvest of one may follow that of another, in almost equally prolonged succession. A large plantation of rice may therefore be taken proper care of with a much smaller force of hands than would otherwise be necessary. Many of these advantages, the Northern farmer should not neglect to consider, would be possessed by grass meadows, similarly subject to irrigation.

HARVEST.

The rice-harvest commences early in September. The water having been all drawn off the field the previous ebb tide, the negroes reap the rice with sickles, taking three or four rows of it at a cut. The stubble is left about a foot in hight, and the rice is laid across the top of it, so that it will dry rapidly. One or two days afterwards it is tied in small sheaves, and then immediately carried to the barn or stack-yard. This is often some miles distant; yet the whole crop of many plantations is transported to it on the heads of the laborers. This work, at the hottest season of the year, in the midst of the recently-exposed mire of the rice-fields, is acknowledged to be exceedingly severe, and must be very hazardous to the health, even of negroes. Overseers, who consider themselves acclimated, and who, perhaps, only spend the day on the plantation, often at this time contract intermittent fever, which, though not in itself immediately dangerous, shatters the constitution, and renders them peculiarly liable to pneumonia, or other complaints which are fatal. When there is a canal running in the rear of the plantation, a part of the transportation of the crop is made by scows; and very recently, a low, broad-wheeled cart or truck, which can be drawn by negroes on the embankments, has been introduced, first at the suggestion of a Northerner, to relieve the labor.

The rice is neatly stacked, much as wheat is in Scotland, in round, thatched stacks. Threshing commences immediately after harvest, and on many plantations proceeds very tediously, in the old way of threshing wheat, with flails, by hand, occupying the best of the plantation force for the most of the winter. It is done on an earthen floor, in the open air, and the rice is cleaned by carrying it on the heads of the negroes, by a ladder, up on to a platform, twenty feet from the ground, and pouring it slowly down, so that the wind will drive off the chaff, and leave the grain in a heap, under the platform. But on most large plantations, threshing-machines, much the same as are used with us, driven either by horse-power or by steam-power, have been lately adopted, of course, with great economy. Where horse-power is used for threshing, the wind is still often relied upon for removing the chaff, as of old; but where steam-engines are employed, there are often connected with the threshing-mill, very complete separators and fanners, together with elevators and other labor-saving machinery, some of it the best for such purposes that I have ever seen.

HULLING.

After the ordinary threshing and cleaning from chaff, the rice still remains covered with a close, rough husk, which can only be removed by a peculiar machine, that lightly pounds it, so as to crack the husk without breaking the rice. Many of the largest plantations are provided with these mills, but it is now found more profitable (where the expense of procuring them has not been already incurred), to sell the rice "in the rough," as it

is termed, before the husk is removed.   There are very extensive rice-hulling mills in most large towns in Europe and
America.   In most of the European States a discriminating
duty in favor of rough rice is laid on its importation, to protect
these establishments.   The real economy of the system is
probably to be found in the fact, that rice in the rough bears
transportation better than that which is cleaned on the plantation; also, that when fresh cleaned it is brighter and more
salable.   Rice in the rough is also termed "paddy," an East
Indian word, having originally this signification.

The usual crop of rice is from thirty to sixty bushels from an
acre, but even as high as one hundred bushels is sometimes
obtained.   Its weight (in the rough) is from forty-one to forty-
nine pounds per bushel.   The usual price paid for it (in the
rough), in Charleston and Savannah, is from eighty cents to one
dollar a bushel.

Planters usually employ their factors—merchants residing in
Charleston, Savannah, or Wilmington, the three rice ports—to
sell their crop by sample.   The purchasers are merchants, or
mill-owners, or the agents of foreign rice-mills.   These factors
are also employed by the planters as their general business
agents, making the necessary purchase of stores and stock for
their plantation and family supply.   Their commission is 2½ per
cent.

Rice is used in the rice-district as a constant article of food,
never being absent from the breakfast and dinner-table of many
families.   On the rice-plantations, particularly those furnished
with a hulling-mill, it is given a good deal to the negroes, more
especially during the seasons of their harvest labor, and at the
holidays.   From this circumstance, I judge that it is thought

better food than maize, although the cracked and inferior rice, that would be unmerchantable, is alone given them. Some planters, however, say that the cracked rice (broken in the process of removing the hull) is better than the prime, and they prefer it for their own table. Rice is screened after the hull is removed, so as to produce several different classes, the difference in which is mainly in size, the lower denominations including only chips and powder of the grain. The classes are indicated as follows, at the mills of Mr. Bilby, of New York, where one thousand bushels of paddy, or rough rice, produced:

.16,078 lbs. of " best head" rice.	3,243 lbs. of " broken" rice.
596 " of " best prime" rice.	570 " of " chits" or " small."
9,190 " of " good to fair."	5,210 " of " flour" or " douse."

In the Carolina mills the product is divided into "prime," "middling" (broken), "small" or "chits," and "flour" or "douse."

Prime rice, at the best mills, is not only separated from all of inferior quality, and from all sand and impurities, but each grain is actually polished ; the last operation at the mill being, to force it through a rapidly revolving cylinder, of woven wire, between which and a sheep-skin flap it is obliged to rub its way to the shoot, which lets it out into the sack or barrel in which it is transferred to the grocer.

Having thus described its progress, from the dark mire of its amphibious birth till it has become, at length, the clean, lustrous, translucent, pearly, and most beautiful of grains, I will add directions for preparing it for the table, according to the most esteemed plantation method.

Rice is increased in bulk, by boiling, 150 per cent., and in weight, 100 per cent. Wash it thoroughly in cold water; have your pot of water (two quarts for every half-pint of rice) boiling—add salt at discretion; put the rice in, and stir it while boiling; let it boil four minutes (some say ten, and some say fifteen); then pour off the water as close as you can without stirring the rice; set the pot on some coals, and cover it; let it remain twenty minutes, and then dish up. Each grain, by this method, will be swollen and soft, without having lost its individuality, and the dish will be light, palatable, and nutritious. Those who prefer a sodden, starchy, porridge-like mess, may boil it longer, and neglect to steam it. A very delicate breakfast-roll is made in Georgia, by mixing hominy or rice, boiled soft, with rice-flour, and milk, in a stiff batter, to which an egg and salt may be added. It is kept over night in a cool place, and baked, so as to brought hot to the breakfast-table.

SLAVE LABOR AS APPLIED ON THE RICE PLANTATIONS.

The system of working slaves by tasks, common on the large cotton plantations of the Atlantic States, as well as the rice plantations, has certainly great advantages. The slave works more rapidly, energetically, and, within narrow limits, with much greater use of discretion, or skill, than he is often found to do elsewhere. Could the hope of reward for faithfulness be added to the fear of punishment for negligence, and some encouragement be offered to the laborer, to apply his mind to a more distant and elevated result than release from his day's toil— as, it seems to me, there easily might be—it would, inevitably, have not only an improving effect upon his character, but would make way for a vastly more economical application of his labor.

On the contrary, however, the tasked laborer is always watched as closely as possible—a driver standing by, often with a whip in his hand, that he may be afraid to do his work slightingly. Under the most favorable circumstances, by the most liberal and intelligent proprietors, he is trusted as little as possible to use his own discretion, and it is taken for granted that he will never do anything desired of him that he dares avoid.

Take men of any original character of mind, and use them as mere animal machines, to be operated only by the motive-power of fear; provide for the necessities of their animal life in such a way that the cravings of their body shall afford no stimulus to contrivance, labor, and providence; work them mechanically, under a task-master, so that they shall have no occasion to use discretion, except to avoid the imposition of additional labor, or other punishment; deny them, as much as possible, the means of enlarged information, and high mental culture—and what can be expected of them, but continued, if not continually increasing stupidity, indolence, wastefulness, and treachery?

Put the best race of men under heaven into a land where all industry is obliged to bear the weight of such a system, and inevitably their ingenuity, enterprise, and skill will be paralyzed, the land will be impoverished, its resources of wealth will remain undeveloped, or will be wasted; and only by the favor of some extraordinary advantage can it compare, in prosperity, with countries adjoining, in which a more simple, natural, and healthy system of labor prevails.

Such *is* the case with the Slave States. On what does their wealth and prosperity, such as it is, depend? On certain circumstances of topography, climate, and soil, that give them almost a monopoly of supplying to the world the most important article of its commerce.

Conventions of planters, met to consider preposterous propo-

sitions for "regulating the Cotton Market," annually confess that if the price of this staple should be very greatly
reduced, by its extended culture in other parts of the world, or
by any cause greatly diminishing its consumption, every proprietor at the South would be ruined. If this humiliating state of
things, extending over so large a region, and yet so distinctly
defined by the identical lines that separate the Slave from the
Free States, is not caused by the peculiar system of labor which
distinguishes the former, there is, at least, an appearance of
reason in the fanaticism that votes, on that supposition, not to
extend the area devoted to the experiment.

On the rice plantation which I have particularly described, the
slaves were, I judge, treated with at least as much discretion
and judicious consideration of economy, consistently with humane regard to their health, comfort, and morals, as on any
other in all the Slave States; yet I could not avoid observing—and I certainly took no pains to do so, nor were any special
facilities offered me for it—repeated instances of that waste and
misapplication of labor which it can never be possible to guard
against, when the agents of industry are slaves. Many such
evidences of waste it would not be easy to specify; and others,
which remain in my memory after some weeks, do not adequately account for the general impression that all I saw gave me; but
there were, for instance, under my observation, gates left open and
bars left down, against standing orders; rails removed from fences
by the negroes, as was conjectured, to kindle their fires with;
mules lamed, and implements broken, by careless usage; a flat-
boat, carelessly secured, going adrift on the river; men ordered
to cart rails for a new fence, depositing them so that a double
expense of labor would be required to lay them, more than

would have been needed if they had been placed, as they might almost as easily have been, by a slight exercise of forethought; men, ordered to fill up holes made by alligators or craw-fish in an important embankment, discovered to have merely patched over the outside, having taken pains only to make it *appear* that they had executed their task—not having been overlooked while doing it, by a driver; men, not having performed duties that were entrusted to them, making statements which their owner was obliged to receive as sufficient excuse, though, he told me, he felt assured they were false—all going to show habitual carelessness, indolence, and mere eye-service.

The constant misapplication and waste of labor on many of the rice plantations, is inconceivably great. Owing to the proverbial stupidity and dogged prejudice of the negro (but peculiar to him only as he is more carefully poisoned with ignorance than the laborer of other countries), it is exceedingly difficult to introduce new and improved methods of applying his labor. He always strongly objects to all new-fashioned implements; and, if they are forced into his hands, will do his best to break them, or to make them only do such work as shall compare unfavorably with what he has been accustomed to do without them. It is a common thing, I am told, to see a large gang of negroes, each carrying about four shovelsful of earth upon a board balanced on his head, walking slowly along on the embankment, so as to travel around two sides of a large field, perhaps for a mile, to fill a breach—a job which an equal number of Irishmen would accomplish, by laying planks across the field and running wheelbarrows upon them, in a tenth of the time. The clumsy iron hoe is, almost everywhere, made to do the work of pick, spade, shovel, and plow. I have seen it used to dig a grave. On many plantations, a plow has never been used; the land being entirely prepared for the crop by *chopping* with the hoe, as I have described. There is reason, perhaps, for this, on the newly-cleared rice-ground, encumbered, as it is, with the close-standing stumps and strong roots and protuberances of the late cypress swamp; though, I should suppose, it would be more economical to grub these by hand, sufficiently to admit of the use of a strong plow. On old plantations, where the stumps have been removed, the surface is like a garden-bed—the soil a dark, rich, mellow, and exceedingly fine loam, the proportion of sand varying very much in different districts; but always considerable, and sufficient, I must think, to prevent an injurious glazing from the plow, unless the land is very poorly drained. Yet, even on these, the plow is not in general use.

Trials have been made on some of the South Carolina plantations of English horse-drills, I understood, without satisfactory success; but I can hardly doubt that with as good laborers as the common English clod-hoppers, some modification of them might be substituted advantageously for the very laborious hoe and hand-process of planting. I should think, too, the horse-hoe, now much used in England for cleaning wheat (which is drilled nearly one-half closer than rice usually is), might be adapted to rice-culture, with much saving of labor over the present method of hand-hoeing. Half an acre a day is the usual task of a negro at this operation. Garrett's horse-hoe, on light land, will easily go over ten acres, employing one horse, and one man and a boy. The Judges of the Royal Agricultural Society, at a trial in 1851, reported that the work done by it was far superior to any hand-hoeing. It requires to be guided, of course, with great carefulness, and, perhaps, could not be entrusted to ordinary slave field-hands.

I am not aware that any application of the reaping-machines, now in use on every large grain farm at the North, has been made in the rice harvest. By the use of a portable tram-way for them to run upon, I should think they might be substituted for the present exceedingly slow and toilsome method of reaping with the sickle, with economy and great relief to the laborers. Such portable tram-ways are in use in England for removing the turnip crop from miry fields in winter; and men earn sixty cents a day by contracting to remove heavy crops at the rate of $1 50 an acre, shifting the trams themselves. It is probable, therefore, that the rice crop might be taken out of the wet ground, and carried much more rapidly, and at less expense, to the stack-yard, in this way, than by the slow and cruel method now employed.

Could these, and other labor-saving appliances, in general use elsewhere, be introduced, and competition of labor be obtained, the cost of raising rice might probably be reduced one-half.

That free labor, even of whites, can be used in rice culture, if not in Carolina, certainly in Louisiana, the poor Creoles of that State have proved. But even for Carolina, free laborers might be procured by thousands, within a year, from the rice-region of China, if good treatment and moderate wages, dependent on hard work and good behavior, could be sufficiently assured to them. That they would suffer no more from malaria than do the negroes, there can be little doubt. And why, except for the sake of consistency, or for the purpose of bullying the moral sense of the rest of mankind, South Carolina should propose to reëstablish the African slave-trade, while this resource is left, I cannot see. If the British and Spanish treat the Chinese laborers, which they have imported to the West Indies, worse than if they were negroes, as is said, no evidence is offered that such cruelty is necessary. The Chinese have heathen vices enough, certainly; but the want of docility and pains-taking industry are not among them. And, looking from the purely economical point of view, if orderly industry can be bought of them cheaply, nothing more is required. And as regards the other main consideration on which the re-opening of the slave-trade is advocated—the saving of sinners—the souls of the Chinese are probably as precious in the eyes of weeping angels, as those of the questionably-human races of Africa.

TREATMENT OF NEGROES ON THE RICE PLANTATIONS.

That the slaves on Mr. X.'s plantation were treated with all the kindness which a reasonable desire to make their labor profitable, and a loyal regard for the laws of the State for the preservation of Slavery would allow, was evident. A little more than that in fact, for privileges were sometimes openly allowed them, contrary to the laws. I was also satisfied, by the representations made to me, that many of the published reports as to the suffering of the slaves on the rice-plantations—like that in "Porter's Tropical Agriculture," for instance—are greatly exaggerated, or, at least, have but very limited application. That the slaves are sometimes liable, however, to be treated with excessive cruelty, and that often their situation must be very unpleasant, will be apparent from a very few considerations.

In the first place, if the humane Mr. X. could, with impunity, disregard the laws, for the purpose of increasing the comforts of his negroes, in so important a particular as by allowing them to possess, and keep in their cabins, guns and ammunition, for their own sport, as he did, what should prevent a heartless and unprincipled man, if such a one could be rich enough to own a rice-plantation, from equally disregarding the laws, in the exercise of his ill humor? Mr. X. told me that he had sold but three slaves off his plantation in twenty years—and these either went willingly, or were banished for exceedingly and persistingly bad conduct. But during the very week that I was on his plantation, one of his neighbors sold an excellent man to a trader, without any previous intimation to him that he intended to do so, without having any fault to find with him, and without the slightest regard, apparently, to the strong ties of kindred which were ruptured in the transaction.

This gentleman, too, though spoken of as eccentric, was evidently under no social taboo, and was, I believed, considered a "pious" man.*

Again, Mr. X. had established regulations, to prevent his negroes from being punished by his subordinates, in the heat of sudden anger. Still another of his neighbors at the time of my visit, while in a drunken frolic, not only flogged a number of his negroes, without cause, but attempted to shoot and stab them; and if he did not succeed in killing any of them outright, was only prevented from doing so by what the law would have considered—and often has considered—an act of insubordination to be justifiably punished with death.

During the summer, for from four to six months, at least, not one rice-planter in a hundred resides on his plantation, but leaves it, with all his slaves, in charge of an overseer. The

---

* Within fifty miles of this plantation, I heard a Presbyterian clergyman urge a man, whom he had never before seen, to purchase some slaves of him, which he had inherited, and had in his possession for many years.

overseers for rice-plantations have to be chosen from among a population of whites comparatively very limited in number: from among those, namely, that have been born and reared in the miasmatic district of the coast; or, if they are taken from elsewhere, they must be very reckless and mercenary men who engage in so dangerous an occupation.

Mr. X.'s overseer was considered an uncommonly valuable one. He had been in his employment for eight years, a longer time than Mr. X. had ever known any other overseer to remain on one plantation; yet I have shown that Mr. X. thought it necessary to restrain his authority within the narrowest possible limits which the law would permit.

He spoke of the character of overseers in general, as planters universally have, whenever I have asked information on the point, as exceedingly bad. It was rare that an overseer remained more than two years in succession on the same plantation; and often they were changed every year. They were almost universally drunken and dissolute, and constantly liable to neglect their duties. Their families, when they had them, were generally unhappy. They were excessively extravagant; and but a few ever saved anything year by year from their wages.

The *Southern Agriculturist*, published at Charleston, South Carolina, says:—

" Overseers are changed every year : a few remain four or five years ; but the average length of time they remain on the same plantation will not exceed two years.

—" What are the general characters of overseers? They are taken from the lowest grade of society, and seldom have had the privilege of a religious education, and have no fear of offending God, and consequently no check on their natural propensities ; they give way to passion, intemperance, and every sin, and become savages in their conduct."— *Southern Agriculturist*, Vol. IV., page 351.

A writer in the "*South Carolinian*," published at the capital of the State, says :—

—"Somehow, many persons improperly consider overseeing as a degrading occupation. I do not see why. Probably the notion arises from the impression that everything is done on a plantation by dint of lashing. When this is the case, it is the fault of the overseer. My opinion is, that of all punishments it is the least efficacious, and that fifteen or twenty lashes, lightly inflicted, are as much as should ever be given. For serious offenses, other punishments, such as solitary confinement, should be resorted to. I am happy to think this idea is rapidly gaining ground among planters ; and could they entirely control their overseers, or obtain overseers of better education, a most important change in this particular would soon be accomplished."

The writer is speaking of the cotton planters of the interior, who reside on their plantations, and are under no necessity of leaving them during the summer, as are rice-planters.

These extracts, in connection with the well known facts to which I have referred, prove, beyond a question, that the slaves of the most humane rice-planters are exceedingly likely to be subject to the uncontrolled tyranny of men of the most heartless and reckless disposition.

The precariousness of the much-vaunted happiness of the slaves can need but one further reflection to be appreciated. No white man can be condemned for any cruelty or neglect, no matter how fiendish, on slave testimony. The rice-plantations generally are in a region very sparsely occupied by whites : the plantations are nearly all very large—often miles across : many a one of them occupying the whole of an island—and rarely is there more than one white man upon a plantation at a time, during the summer. Upon this one man each slave is dependent, even for the necessities of life.

What laboring man in the free States can truly be told that

the slaves are better off than he is? Nay, in Europe, who desires to change his circumstances for these? Does not Mr. Geo. Sanders rather overdo his part, when he tells the French Democrats that the working-men of France are in far worse circumstances than the American slaves? What Frenchman, about starving to death, is desirous that his wife and children shall be "provided for" during life, in the Carolina method? Disgraceful to mankind as is the Napoleonic usurpation, this is more so. It is not our business to interfere with it, I may admit; but I must expose the sophistry by which we are coaxed to aid and comfort it.

CHAPTER VIII.

EXPERIMENTAL POLITICAL ECONOMY OF SOUTH CAROLINA AND GEORGIA.

"Ill fares the land, to hastening ills a prey,
Where wealth accumulates and men decay."
The Deserted Village.

" Laws grind the poor, and rich men guide the law."— *The Traveler.*

" Laws, to be just, must give a reciprocation of right; without this, they are mere arbitrary rules."—*Jefferson.*

" It is plain that a party so confided in as even a common plowman must be, ought not to have his sense of responsibility blunted."—*Blackwood.*

" But, gentlemen, there are two kinds of labor; intelligent and unintelligent labor : the former is that which gives character to a nation, and in giving character gives wealth and power. Hence, I say, encourage the education of all the people, for by so doing you will promote the elevation of character, and give that dignity to the founders of wealth, which is justly their due."—*Abbott Lawrence.*

ARISTOCRACY, or an established superior class, necessitates inferiority, or a subject class, at whose expense, in some way, the aristocracy is supported. In a rude society, aristocracy may be an economical institution, inasmuch as by the same means that it has power to rule the people, it is able also to defend their commonwealth. The ruder, the more barbarous, and the more villainous the state of society, the more easily will aristocratic government be supported by the people, as being less expensive than a constant liability to more improvident and unsystematized plundering of the results of labor. As society approaches civilization, and the people of a state grow more and more gentle, discreet, and individually proud, self-disciplined, and self-maintaining, the use of an aristocracy becomes less, and the burden of supporting it is less contentedly borne. Finally, mankind arrives at the Democratic republic, in which the clerks and guards of the common business of a common wealth, instead of being made the rulers are simply members of the partnership of a community, appointed by their fellow-partners to transact, agreeably to their instructions, such business as they shall have agreed to have done in common.

Every real movement of societies towards this system will be favorable to their moral, mental, and material prosperity. A man will, as a general rule, always work harder, more skillfully, and with more exercise of discretion, for himself than for any one else; especially so if his work for another is not wholly voluntary, and his task self-imposed. So of bodies of men: all the faculties and talents, art-conception, inventive-genius, investigating-enterprise, order and precision, as well as muscular power, will be developed and exerted by any man, and by any body of men, in proportion to the individual freedom with which they are directed, in proportion to the voluntariness—the good will with which they are exercised.

And where a man has these ease, delight, and comfort-producing faculties exercised for him by another, whether superior or inferior to him, the less will he be likely to exercise them for himself—the less perfectly, the less productively.

Whatever is to the real advantage of any man, must be, in some degree, to the advantage of others, to all others in the world, but especially all others in his community.

Thus slavery, or aristocracy, a ruling or a subject class in a community, is in itself a very great hindrance to its industrial progress; that is, to its acquisition of wealth—moral, æsthetic, and mental, as well as material wealth.

This is the way Democrats reason.

SOUTH CAROLINA POLITICAL AND SOCIAL ECONOMY.

I do not wish to attribute to the South Carolinians any principles or motives which they would generally be disposed, themselves, to doubt or deny. I believe they will generally, at once, concede the statement to be correct, that it has always been the opinion of the rulers of their community, that it is impossible to educate the laboring mass to a sufficiently good judgment to enable them to take part in directing affairs of state, and that the proper capacity and fitness for these duties is only to be obtained among those whom wealth has relieved from the necessity of labor, and therefore special encouragement should be given to this class to extend its education to the uttermost. The most intelligent government, it is believed, will be the best; and as it is impracticable to make the average intelligence of all sorts of people equal to the highest intelligence of some, the policy of South Carolina community has been to develop the highest possible culture in a few, and to manage, in one way or another, to give political control to these few. To develop, not the highest average intelligence practicable among the people, and to trust government to this high average, but to develop the highest attainable intelligence in some originally fortunate ones, and to give government into the hands of this higher intelligence.

The Democratic theory of the social organization is everywhere ridiculed and rejected, in public as well as in private, in the forum as well as the newspapers.

The late Governor Hammond declared:—

"I endorse, without reserve, the sentiment of Gov. McDuffie, that 'Slavery is the very corner-stone of our republican edifice,' while I repudiate, as ridiculously absurd, that much lauded, but nowhere accredited, motto of Mr. Jefferson, that 'all men are born free and equal.' "*

And a late Chancellor of the State, in an address to its Society of Learning, asked—in a connection which indicated that he entertained no doubt that the opinions of his audience coincided with his own:—

"Would you do a benefit to the horse or the ox, by giving him a cultivated understanding, or fine feelings? So far as the *mere laborer* has the pride, the knowledge, or the aspirations of a free man, he is unfitted for his situation, and must doubly feel its infelicity. If there are sordid, servile, and laborious offices to be performed, is it not better that there should be sordid, servile, and laborious beings to perform them?"†

So far as the polity of South Carolina has differed from that of the other American States, it has been by its being more strongly, steadily, and consistently pervaded by these ideas, than theirs; and it is as the exponent of this polity, that its history and present condition most challenges examination.

ORIGIN AND EARLY CHARACTER.

In South Carolina, as in Virginia, the influential settlers were "gentlemen." "Many of them," says Hewitt, the first historian

---

* Letter to Thomas Clarkson, by Gov. Hammond, of South Carolina.—DE BOW's *Review.*

† The *Charleston Standard,* of Nov. —, 1855, contains a report of the annual address to the graduating class of the State Military Asylum, of another address to the literary societies of the institution, and an editorial article on education; in all which, the Democratic educational system of the North, and of Prussia, is ridiculed and condemned; and, by the two orators, the proposition is advocated, that the State should educate only its capitalists and the officers or overseers, who, under orders of the capitalists, shall command and direct the laborers.

of the Colony, "pampered citizens, whose wants luxury had increased, and rendered them impatient of fatigue, and the restraint of legal authority."*

In the first fundamental constitution of the Colony, provision was made for a race of hereditary tenants to have farms of ten acres each; one-eighth of the produce of which was to be paid over, as rent, to the gentlemen—lords of the manor. Two classes of hereditary nobility were provided for. Decisions of the lords of the manor, or of any of the nobility, in matters concerning their tenantry, were without judicial appeal. No man was eligible to any office, except he was the possessor of a certain definite extent of landed estate—larger or smaller, according to the dignity of his office. Negro slavery was provided for, and every freeman was declared to have absolute power, extending to life and death, over his slaves.

This constitution is supposed to have been drafted by John Locke; but Locke's opinion of negro slavery was certainly very inconsistent with any design to provide for its permanent establishment in the Colony. He describes it, elsewhere, to be "the state of war continued between a lawful conqueror and his captive;" * * * "so opposite to the generous temper and courage of our nation, that 'tis hardly to be conceived that an Englishman, much less a gentleman, should plead for it."

Having the least democratic government, South Carolina was, almost from the first, distinguished as the worst governed, most insubordinate, and most licentious and immoral of all the English settlements in America. Negroes, from Africa, were not only eagerly purchased, but wars were made upon the Indians of the

* Hewitt's History of South Carolina and Georgia. London, 1779; vol. i., page 75.

country, for the purpose of capturing them, and using them as slaves. The different tribes of Indians were encouraged to war with one another, and the prisoners of each and all tribes and parties, were bought for slaves. So successfully was this cat-and-monkey trick performed, that multitudes of Carolina Indians were exported, as slaves, to the West Indies, where they were exchanged for rum, which thereby became very cheap in the Colony, and made drunkenness very common. Sea-rovers and filibusters were openly and joyfully received, and sup-plied with every necessity—even with arms and ammunition—in exchange for treasure that had been taken from ships, or plundered towns, on the Spanish main. Several of these free-booters purchased land, and became resident planters of the Colony.* Party spirit and party tyranny were stronger than they have often been, anywhere in the world; and the cavalier party in the legislature, although the constitution guaranteed religious freedom, and two-thirds of the people were Dissenters, did not hesitate, when they had a majority of one, to use the opportunity to disfranchise all who refused to accept the dog-mas of their church, and so rid themselves, if possible, of their opposition forever.

Costly churches were erected, and clergymen were supported in luxury, at the expense of the Colony. "The Dissenters," says Hewitt, "were not only obliged to erect and uphold their own churches, and maintain their clergy by private contributions, but also to contribute their share, in the way of taxes, towards the maintainance of the establishment. This, indeed, many of them considered a grievance; but, having but few friends in the

---

* Hewitt, i., 116.

provincial assembly, no redress could be obtained for them. Besides, the establishment gave its adherents many advantageous privileges, in point of power and authority, over persons of other denominations." The English-born of the Colony were, nearly all, gradually drawn into the establishment, by the worldly advantages it offered. The Scotch and Irish, only, steadfastly adhered to their conviction, and maintained the Presbyterian organization and worship.*

THE ORIGIN OF "AMERICANISM."

The proprietors, having permitted a band of French refugees to settle in the Colony, and, for their encouragement, ordered that they should have equal rights with the Anglo-Saxons, the latter immediately began to persecute and oppress them by every means in their power. "Their haughty spirit could not brook the thoughts of sitting in assembly with the rivals of the English nation, for power and dominion." They maintained that the proprietors had no right to make low foreigners partakers of the privileges of natural-born Englishmen; that their marriages, having been performed by a clergyman who had not been ordained by an English bishop, were unlawful, and their children were bastards; they insisted that they should be allowed no vote; that they should not be returned on any jury, nor sworn for the trial of issues between subject and subject.†

---

* Cotemporaneously with the infernal negro-laws of the Province, the enslavement of Indians, and the public entertainment of pirates, laws were also maintained to regulate the deportment of the people, on Sundays, for punishing those who used profane language, etc., and the legislature refused to enforce payment of debts due to creditors living out of the Province.

† Hewitt, i., 111.

THE EARLY BLACK CODE.

The laws to protect the masters against the slaves, were of a severity that no necessity could justify; while there was scarcely a semblance of law to guard the slaves against the inhumanity of the whites. Slaves, endeavoring to flee from the cruelties to which they were generally subjected,[*] were permitted to be shot, and were required, when recaptured alive, on pain of heavy penalties upon their owners, to be mutilated in a manner too bad to mention. If they died in consequence, their owners were entitled to compensation for their loss, from the colonial treasury. Slaves, committing burglary, were punished by being slowly burned to death.[†]

EARLY LAND MONOPOLISTS—ORIGIN OF THE "SAND-HILLERS."

About 1730, Hewitt says:—

" The old planters now acquiring, every year, greater strength of hands by the large importation of negroes, and extensive credit in England, began to turn their attention, *more closely than ever*, to the lands of the Province (that is, to the engrossment of landed estate). A spirit of emulation broke out among them, for securing tracts of the richest lands of the Province ; but especially such as were most conveniently situated for navigation."

Complaints were made to the legislature that

" All the valuable lands on navigable rivers and creeks, adjacent to Port Royal, had been run out in exorbitant tracts, under color of patents granted, by proprietors, to Cassiques and Landgraves, by which the complainants, who had, at the hazard of their lives, defended the country, were hindered of obtaining such lands as could be useful and beneficial, at the established quit rents, although the Attorney and Solicitor-General of England had declared such patents void."

[*] Hewitt, i., 120; ii., 96.   [†] Hildreth.

The state of the Colony, at the end of the year 1773, is thus described:

"Each planter, *eager in pursuit of large possessions of land*, * * strenuously vied with his neighbor for a superiority of fortune, and seemed impatient of every restraint that hindered or cramped him in his favorite pursuit."

EARLY LABOR MONOPOLISTS.

The profits of rice culture, in which no poor man could engage, increased the ability, without at all diminishing the eagerness of the richer class to possess slaves. No regard to the general welfare could restrain the importation.

In an address to the King, about 1750, it is stated: "The only commodity of consequence produced, is rice." The "negroes are ready to revolt on the first opportunity, and are *eight times as many in number as there are white men able to bear arms.*" "At the lowest computation," the export of rice is declared to be two hundred and twenty thousand pounds sterling in value, and to require the use of one hundred and sixty ships. This crop was almost wholly the produce of slave-labor. Little or no result of the labor of white men was exported, and the free laboring men were constantly engaged in trying to preserve something of their few legal rights, from the rapacity and ambition of the rich, slave-owning aristocracy.

PROGRESS.

The tendency which, during the last century, has been perceptible in every Christian land, and among all people intimately associated with the civilized world, towards pure democracy, has, from time to time, been revealed in South Carolina, in the gradual modification of the aristocratic system; but, even now, no man can be admitted to a seat in the legislature of the State, unless he is the owner of real estate to the value of, at least, one hundred and fifty pounds sterling; and, to be eligible to the upper house, he must possess a freehold estate of, at least, three hundred pounds value. The number of representatives, from any particular part of the State, is proportionate, not to the number of citizens residing in it, but to the value of property owned in it.

Five-sixths of the whole white population of the State, residing in those counties where there are the fewest slaves, have but seventy-eight out of one hundred and twenty-two representatives. The Pendleton district, with over 26,000 white inhabitants, is represented by seven members; the two parishes of St. Philip and St. Michael, with less than 19,000 white inhabitants, send eighteen. Nowhere else, in the United States, and, probably, not even in England, are elections so entirely contests of money and of personal influence, and less expressions of judgment, upon subjects of difference in politics, as in South Carolina. In many parts, if I was rightly informed, no effective opposition can ever be offered to the will of some few of the "old families, who usually have a good understanding among themselves, who shall be chosen to fill any offices at all desirable.*

As far as the slaves are concerned, there has been no essential political progress at all. The laws have been only slightly modified in conformity with more humane, but not more

* "There's Beaufort, for instance," I was told; "if you had asked any well-informed Carolinian the name of its representatives, at any time in the last forty years, he would have replied; 'It is ——, or ——, or ——, or ——.' It is always a question only of succession, among the young gentlemen of those four families."

philosophical views of the modern legislators.   And even as late as 1808, two slaves were publicly and judicially burned alive, over a slow fire, in the city of Charleston.   In 1816 a grand jury declared in their official presentment, that instances of negro homicide were common, and that the murderers were allowed to continue in the full exercise of their powers as masters and mistresses.   In the annual message of Governor Adams to the legislature, this year (1855), he observes :

" The administration of our laws, in relation to our colored population, by our courts of magistrates and freeholders, as these courts are at present constituted, calls loudly for reform.   *Their decisions are rarely in conformity with justice or humanity.*   I have felt constrained, in a majority of the cases brought to my notice, either to modify the sentence, or set it aside altogether.   I recommend, in all cases involving life, that the trial of slaves and free persons of color be held at the court-house of the district in which the offense is committed ; that the clerk, ordinary, and sheriff of the district, constitute a court to try such cases."

To this time, whether with justice, I know not, South Carolinians have a reputation generally, at the South, not only of being the most bigoted and fanatical conservators of Slavery, but also of being hard masters to their slaves.   I have, several times, been cautioned by other Southerners, not to draw general conclusions with regard to the condition of slaves in the South at large, from what I saw and heard of those belonging to persons born in South Carolina. If this report is unjust to the South Carolinians, I think it probably is not without foundation in some truth ; and probably this : that the South Carolina planters have more faith in the Divine right of masters over subjects than those of other origin and education, and consequently are more determined and thorough in the exercise of despotic power.   None will deny,

at any rate, that there is a difference of this kind between South
Carolina planters and all others, nor doubt that it has had
considerable influence on the economy, public and private, of
the State.

The ruling intellect of the State has now, as it originally
had, more than that of any other American community, a
profound conviction, that God created men to live in distinct
classes or castes, one beneath another, one subject to another. As far as possible, this ruling intellect tries to make
practicably reconciliable the social system of the State with
the Constitution of the Confederacy, from which it finds it
inconvenient to make itself, alone, independent. The whole
legislation of the State is a succession of miserable compromises for this purpose. One year, a little is yielded to the
common people within the State; the next, an effort is made
to bully the General Government or the democratic States
into some retreat from the Confederate principles; the next,
circulars are sent to the other Slave States, to coax or shame
them into joining South Carolina in seceding from the hateful
connection with States which, purely because they are disposed to be consistently democratic, are hated and despised
by her rulers.

RESULTS.

It is not, I suppose, to be questioned, that in those qualities for
which a man is honored in society—for refinement of manners, and
the power of being agreeable to social equals—the wealth which
has been accumulated in a few hands, from the long unrequited
labor and suffering of the slaves (I speak of the past, when no one
will doubt their suffering), has given some few South Carolinians

a superiority over most of the citizens of the more democratic States.   One could beat up recruits for a dinner-party, or a ball room, in Charleston, as well, at least, as anywhere else in America—better than anywhere at the North.   And the qualifications for this purpose are certainly most desirable ones, and, where generally possessed, add more than profundity of judgment in metaphysics, or skill in bargaining, to the wealth of a community.   It may be a question, nevertheless, if they are not sometimes acquired at too great an expense—a question of social economy.

I am disposed, from the pleasure I have myself received from the little intercourse I by chance have had with educated Carolinians, to do them all justice on this point—a point on which they habitually make such great claims.   But I must observe, also, that I have been astonished by the profound ignorance and unmitigated stupidity I have found in some planters of the State, of considerable wealth, and owning large numbers of slaves.   There are notorious anecdotes of wealthy Carolinians, also, which show them to be sometimes not only ignorant and stupid, but quite as vulgar as the most ridiculous palace-builders in New York.   Nevertheless, let us believe that there is less vulgar display, and more intrinsic elegance, and habitual mental refinement in the best society of South Carolina, than in any distinct class anywhere among us.   This is to be expected from their social system.

Leisure, and bountiful provision for the future being secured, it is also almost a matter of course, that men will amuse themselves with literature, arts and science.   South Carolina has, therefore, always boasted several men of learning (men learned in the classics, and abstract science), and many belle-lettre

scholars.   Yet scarce anything has been accomplished by them
for the advancement of learning and science, and there have been
fewer valuable inventions and discoveries, or designs in art, or
literary compositions of a high rank, or anything else, contrived
or executed for the good of the whole community, or the world
at large (cotton and rice-growing excepted), in South Carolina,
than in any community of equal numbers and wealth, probably
in the world.   What Hewitt said of the wealthy class, previous
to the Revolution, is still remarkably true of it:

" In the progress of society, they have not advanced beyond that period
in which men are distinguished more by their external than internal
accomplishments.   Hence it happens, that beauty, figure, agility, and
strength form the principal distinctions among them.   Among English
people, they are chiefly known by the number of their slaves, the value
of their annual produce, or the extent of their landed estate.   They discover no bad taste for the polite arts, such as music, drawing, fencing,
and dancing.   And it is acknowledged by all, but especially by strangers,
that the ladies considerably outshine the men.   Several natives, who
have had their education in Britain, have distinguished themselves by
their knowledge in the laws and constitution of their country ; but those
who have been bred in the province, having their ideas confined in a
narrower sphere, have, as yet, made little figure as men of genius or
learning."*

Such were and are the few rich.   What of the many poor?

THE FREE LABORING CLASS AT THE REVOLUTION.

In an account of an interview, given by a South Carolina
gentleman, between General Marion, himself, and the Baron de
Kalb, during the Revolutionary war, the following conversation
is reported :

" He received us politely, observing that we were the first Carolinians

---

* Calhoun was educated in Connecticut, and he was the son of a poor Irishman.

that he had seen, which had not a little surprised him. * * * 'I thought,' said he, 'that British tyranny would have sent great numbers of the South Carolinians to join our arms; but so far from it, they are all, as we are told, running to take British protections; surely, they are not tired already of fighting for liberty.'

"We told him the reason was very plain to us, who were inhabitants of that country, and knew very well the state of things there.

"'Aye?' said he; 'well, what can the reason be?'

"'Why, sir,' said Marion, 'the people of Carolina form two classes, the rich and the poor. The poor are generally very poor, because, not being necessary to the rich, who have slaves to do all their work, they get no employment of them. Being thus unsupported by the rich, they continue poor and *low spirited*. They seldom get money; and, indeed, what little they do get, is laid out in brandy, to raise their spirits, and not on books and newspapers, to get information. Hence, they know nothing of the comparative blessings of our country, or of the dangers which threaten it, and therefore care nothing about it.* As to the other class (continued Marion), the rich, they are generally very rich, and, consequently, afraid to stir unless a fair chance offer, lest the British should burn their houses and furniture, and carry off their negroes and stock.'"†

And on another occasion, near the close of his life, Marion is reported to have discoursed as follows:

"What, sir! keep a nation in ignorance, rather than vote a little of

* It is a fact, I believe, that the British recruited more men, during the war, in South Carolina, than were ever induced to take up arms against them. The Tories of the North were generally men of wealth, and the patriots were the common people. In Carolina, it was the reverse. The great mass of the people were perfectly indifferent, and took sides with the party that offered them the best pay. Even the patriotism of the planters could, in many cases, be ascribed to the fact that the Revolution relieved them of their liabilities to their creditors, most of them being excessively in debt to their English factors. It was not until an express exception from the non-exportation clause of the "American Association," of the article of rice, had been made for her special benefit, that the Colony was induced to join the others in the agreement of commercial non-intercourse with Great Britain, which preceded the outbreak of the Revolution.

† The Life of General Francis Marion, by Brig. Gen. P. Horrey, of Marion's Brigade, and M. L. Weems.

their own money for education? Only let such politicians remember what poor Carolina has already lost through her *ignorance*. What was it brought the British, last war, to Carolina, but her lack of knowledge? Had the people been enlightened, they would have been united; and had they been united, they would never have been attacked a second time by the British. For, after the drubbing they got from us at Fort Moultrie, in 1776, they would have as soon attacked the devil as have attacked Carolina again, had they not heard that they were '*a house divided against itself*'—or, in other words, had amongst us a great number of Tories, men who through mere ignorance were disaffected to the cause of liberty, and ready to join the British, against their own countrymen. Thus, ignorance begat toryism, and toryism begat losses in Carolina, of which few have any idea."

He then goes on to show that, owing to the foothold the British gained in Carolina, the war was protracted two years; and makes a curious estimate of the loss to Carolina in those two years, at $15,100,000. "As a proof," he continues, "that such hellish tragedies would never have been acted, had our State been enlightened, only let us look at the people of New England: Religion had taught them that God created men to be happy; that, to be happy, they must have virtue; that virtue is not to be attained without knowledge; nor knowledge without instruction; nor public instruction without free schools; nor free schools without legislative order."

PRESENT CONDITION OF THE FREE LABORING CLASS.

Since the Revolution, the effects of the republican general government, and the influence of the democratic societies of the North, have certainly forced some improvement upon the State; but how slowly these counteract the results of its ruling, interior, social and political polity, may be judged from the following extract from a recent message of Governor Seabrook, to the Legislature:

" Education has been provided by the Legislature, but for one class of the citizens of the State, which is the wealthy class. For the middle and poorer classes of society it has done nothing, since no organized system has been adopted for that purpose. You have appropriated seventy-five thousand dollars annually to free schools ; but, under the present mode of applying it, that liberality is really the profusion of the prodigal, rather than the judicious generosity which confers real benefit. The few who are educated at public expense in those excellent and truly useful institutions, the Arsenal and Citadel Academies [military schools], form almost the only exception to the truth of this remark. Ten years ago, twenty thousand adults, besides children, were unable to read or write, in South Carolina. Has our free-school system dispelled any of this ignorance ? Are there not any reasonable fears to be entertained that the number has increased since that period ?"

And in the message of Gov. Adams, December, 1855, urging the appointment of a State Superintendent of Education, he says :

" Make, at least, this effort, and if it results in nothing—if, in consequence of insurmountable difficulties in our condition, no improvement can be made on the present system, and the poor of the land are hopelessly doomed to ignorance, poverty, and crime—you will, at least, feel conscious of having done your duty, and the public anxiety on the subject will be quieted."

A Southern-born gentleman, who had resided in South Carolina during many years, and who has lately been a traveler in Spanish America, in expressing to me his doubts of the utter degeneracy, as commonly understood, of the Spanish and Hispano-Indian races, and his conviction of their many good qualities and capabilities, said, that he had seen, among the worst of them, and those who had been most unfavorably circumstanced, none so entirely debased, so wanting in all energy, industry, purpose of life, and in everything to be respected and valued, as among extensive communities on the banks of the Congaree, in South Carolina. The latter, he said, in answer to

my inquiries, "are the descendants of the former proprietors of
nearly all the land of the region; but, for generations, their
fathers have been gradually selling off to the richer planters
moving in among them, and living on the purchase money of
their lands, and their children have been brought up in listless,
aimless, and idle independence, more destructive to them, as a
race, than even forced and servile industry might have been.
They are more ignorant, their superstitions are more degrading,
they are much less enduring and industrious, far less cheerful
and animated, and very much more incapable of being improved
and elevated, than the most degraded peons of Mexico. Their
chief sustenance is a porridge of cow-peas, and the greatest
luxury with which they are acquainted is a stew of bacon and
peas, with red pepper, which they call 'Hopping John.' "

Let the reader recall to mind Hewitt's description of the
knavery exercised by the early gentlemen of the Colony, in the
mad passion to acquire large landed estates, and consider that
these are their children, and he will see the repetition of the
Virginia lesson, and the words again verified—"visiting the
sins of the fathers upon the children, unto the third and fourth
generation."

THE SAND-HILLERS.

Not very essentially different is the condition of a class
of people living in the pine-barrens nearest the coast, as
described to me by a rice-planter. They seldom have any meat,
he said, except they steal hogs, which belong to the planters,
or their negroes, and their chief diet is rice and milk. "They
are small, gaunt, and cadaverous, and their skin is just the
color of the sand-hills they live on. They are quite incapable

of applying themselves steadily to any labor, and their habits are very much like those of the old Indians."

A Northern gentleman, who had been spending a year in South Carolina, said to me, after speaking respectfully of the character of some of the wealthier class, " but the poor whites, out in the country, are the meanest people I ever saw : half of them would be considered objects of charity in New York. When I was at —— Springs, in the summer, I took too long a walk one day, and stopped at a miserable shanty to rest myself. There were four grown-up girls in the shanty : one of them was weaving, and the rest did not seem to have anything to do. I found their father was a blacksmith, who had been working at his trade in the neighborhood for forty years : all that time he had lived in that hovel, and was evidently still in abject poverty. I asked the girl at the loom how much she could make a day by her work. She did not know, but I ascertained that the stuff she wove was bought at a factory in the vicinity, to be used for bagging yarn ; and she was paid in yarn—so many pounds of yarn for a piece of the bagging. She traded off the yarn at a store for what she had to buy, at the rate of a dollar and ten cents for this number of pounds of it. If she worked steadily from daylight to dark she could make not more than a seventh part of a piece in a day. Her wages, therefore, were less than sixteen cents a day, boarding herself."

" These people," he continued, " are regarded by the better class with as little respect as the slaves; and, in fact, they have hardly more self-respect. One day, when I was riding out with a gentleman, we passed a house, at the door of which an old man and four rather good-looking girls made their appearance. The gentleman told me that two of the girls were notorious harlots, and that their father was understood not to object to their bearing that character."

He added further evidence of a similar character, indicating that a very slight value is placed upon female virtue among this class. A Southern physician expressed the opinion to me that if an accurate record could be had of the births of illegitimate children, as in Sweden and France, it would be found to be as great, among the poor people in the part of the country in which he practiced, as of those born in wedlock. A planter told me that any white girl who could be hired to work for wages would certainly be a girl of easy virtue; and he would not believe that such was not the case with all our female domestics at the north. The northern gentleman who related to me the facts repeated on the last page, told me he was convinced that real chastity among the young women of the non-slaveholding class in South Carolina was as rare as the want of it among farmers' daughters at the north. I can only say, in the absence of reliable data upon the subject, that the difference in the manners and conversation and general demeanor of the two is not unfavorable to this conclusion.

I am not unaware that it is often asserted, as an advantage of slavery (in the elaborate defense of the institution by Chancellor Harper, for instance), that the ease with which the passions of men of the superior caste are gratified by the loose morality, or inability to resist, of female slaves, is a security of the chastity of the white women. I can only explain this, consistently with my impression of the actual state of things, by supposing that these writers ignore entirely, as it is a constant custom for Southern writers to do, the condition of the poorer class of the white population. (Witness, for instance, Mrs. Tyler's letter to the Duchess of Sutherland.)   Chancellor Harper says: "It is related rather as a matter of tradition, not unmingled with wonder, that a Carolinian woman of education and family proved false to her conjugal faith."   And it is, I presume, to women of education and "family" alone that he referred, in claiming an especial glory to the South in this particular.   In any case, the claim is unfounded of a higher character, in this respect, than belongs to women favorably situated in the free states, though those of the south are unexcelled in the world for every quality which commands respect, admiration and love.

In speaking of the severity of the laws with regard to free negroes at the south, a Southerner remarked : "It is impossible that we should not always have a class of free colored people, because of the fundamental law, *partus sequiter ventrem.*   There must always be women among the lower class of whites, so poor that their favors can be purchased by the slaves, and the off-spring must be constitutionally entitled to freedom ; and although it may be kidnapped, or illegally sold into slavery by the mother, it cannot be enacted that all persons of color shall be, considered *ipse facto,* slaves."

The *Richmond Enquirer,* of the 12th June, 1855, gives an account of a case decided in the Botecourt Circuit Court, as follows :

"ELIZA CRAWFORD, AND FIVE CHILDREN, COLORED, SUING FOR THEIR FREEDOM.—The case was decided in favor of the plaintiffs, the evidence being full and complete that the chief plaintiff, Eliza, was born of a white woman, of Georgia.   She is now about thirty-five years of age, and has been in slavery between fifteen and twenty years."

The reports of the agents employed by religious associations to travel among the poor of South Carolina, indicate, strongly, a state of ignorance and superstition in the population of large districts, hardly exceeded in Mexico, and unparalleled, so far as I know, in civilized Europe. The log-book of a colporteur yields, for instance, the following statistical results of a few days' observations in his cruising-ground :

"Visited sixty families, numbering two hundred and twenty-one souls over ten years of age; only twenty-three could read, and seventeen write. Forty-one families destitute of the Bible. Average of their going to church, once in seven years. Several, between thirty and forty-five years old, had heard but one or two sermons in their lives. Some grown-up youths had never heard a sermon or prayer, until my visit, and did not know of such a being as the Saviour; and boys and girls, from ten to fifteen years old, did not know who made them. All of one family rushed away, when I knelt to pray, to a neighbor's, begging them to tell what I meant by it. Other families fell on their faces, instead of kneeling."*

The slave-labor of the State is almost exclusively devoted to the culture of cotton and rice. Live stock, meat, corn, breadstuffs, and forage—though the soil and climate of a large part are entirely favorable to their production—are very largely imported; and, for nearly all sorts of skillfully manufactured goods, the people are quite dependent on the Free States. Trade, and skilled labor of all sorts, is mainly in the hands of persons from the Free States, or foreign countries, and the population of this class is rapidly increasing. Previous to an election for a sheriff, in Charleston, in 1855, two hundred and fifty-two foreigners were naturalized in five days. The pecu-

---

* Any amount of similar testimony may be obtained at the offices of those noble institutions, the Southern Aid Society and the American Tract Society, in New York. It is curious how little complaint is made of the impertinence of these Northern societies : why are not their agents sent back, in tar and feathers, to "take care of their own vicious and wretched poor?"

niary inducements to emigration may be judged from the following facts:

"Lands, with heavy timber upon them, are selling, within twenty miles of Charleston, for prices varying from one to five 'dollars an acre. Wood is selling at six dollars and a half a cord, by the boat-load, delivered at the wharf; and at seven dollars and a half by the wood-factors, in the city. Masts and spars are brought from Boston. Brick, made from clay, which costs nothing, is worth twelve dollars a thousand."*

I lately saw it stated in a Charleston paper, that the most prosperous community in the State was one composed exclusively of Germans, in the hill country of the West. The observation was apropos to the foundation among them of an educational institution, of a high order; and it appeared that they had considerable manufactories in successful operation, and were succeeding so well, in farming and other industry—undoubtedly free laboring—as to have capital to spare to aid a rail-road enterprise.

The estimation in which the foreign-born working-people are held by the enlightened natives, may be judged from the following extract from a South Carolina newspaper,† which also gives a hint of the predominant feeling among the capitalists towards that class of the poor natives who bring their own industry in competition with that of the slaves.

"A large proportion of the mechanical force that migrate to the South, are a curse instead of a blessing; they are generally a worthless, unprincipled class—enemies to our peculiar institutions, and formidable

---

* *Charleston Standard*, 1855, in advocacy of reopening the African Slave-trade.

† The *Carolinian*, I think; but, in cutting it out, I omitted to note the authority and date.

barriers to the success of our native mechanics. Not so, however, with another class who migrate southward—we mean that class known as merchants ; they are generally intelligent and trustworthy, and they seldom fail to discover their true interests. They become slaveholders and landed proprietors ; and, in ninety-nine cases out of a hundred, they are better qualified to become constituents of our institution, than even a certain class of our native-born—who, from want of capacity, are perfect drones in society, continually carping about slave competition and their inability to acquire respectable position and employment, when, in fact, their natural acquirements and ambition do not excel the wisdom of the mole—they never look beyond the point of their nose, or aspire to anything beyond the capacity of a drudge in society. * *

"The intelligent mercantile class, who come among us from the North, and settle, are generally valuable acquisitions to society, and every way qualified to sustain 'our institution ;' but the mechanics, most of them, are pests to society, dangerous among the slave population, and ever ready to form combinations against the interest of the slaveholder, against the laws of the country, and against the peace of the Commonwealth."

This must refer to some movements, which have lately been made, for enlarging the basis of suffrage, and for permitting the people to vote directly for Presidential electors. South Carolina stands alone among all the States in this, that the Presidential electors are chosen by the legislature. No native even can exceed, in idolatry to Slavery, the mass of the ignorant foreign-born laborers. Their hatred of the negro is proportionate to the equality of their intellect and character to his : and their regard for Slavery, to their disinclination to compete with him, in a fair field.

The Census Report, which should be the best authority in the matter, is evidently more than ordinarily unreliable, as an index to the average material wealth of the people of this State. There is every reason to suppose that the condition of the poorest of the people was often left unascertained, generally, in the Slave

States—the vagabond habits of many of them keeping them out of the reach of the marshals; also, I am sure, from what I have heard, that the marshals were generally excessively lazy, and neglectful of their duty, among that class which was most ignorant, or indifferent on the subject.*

By the returns of the South Carolina marshals, the cash value of land, in the State, appears to be $5·08 an acre; by the legislative documents of the State, for the same year, the cash value of real estate, exclusive of town lots, appears to be but sixty cents an acre. (The value of land is given in the several counties, and foots up, in the one case, $10,082,427, and $82,431,684 in the other; so it can be no typographical error.) The marshals were directed to make out their returns from the assessment rolls, and, where the assessments were made on sums less than the intrinsic value of the land, to add the necessary per centage. The average addition made, under this provision, by the South Carolina marshals, is over 800 per cent.; while, at page 46 of the official Abstract of the Census, the difference between the real and assessed value of real and personal estate, in South Carolina, is shown to be but one-seventieth of one per cent.

Attention was called to these discrepancies, immediately after the publication of the document, by a writer in the *National Era*, at Washington—but no explanation has ever been made; and, until one is offered, either the honesty or the competency of the South Carolina marshals must be so doubtful, that

---

* I have seen an advertisement of a deputy Census marshal, in Alabama or Georgia, announcing that he would be at a certain tavern in his district, on a certain day, for the purpose of receiving from the people of the vicinity—who were requested to call upon him—the information it was his duty to obtain from them.

it is hardly worth while to particularly study their other returns.

In looking for other reliable data for an estimate of happiness
which South Carolina statesmanship had secured at home, for
the mass of that part of its people not systematically and
with avowed intention held in subjection and degradation,
I find, in an address of another chief magistrate of the State
(Governor Hammond) before the South Carolina Institute, the
following exposition :

"According to the best calculations which, in the absence of statistic
facts, can be made, it is believed that, of the 300,000 *white* inhabitants
of South Carolina, there are not less than 50,000, whose industry, such
as it is, and compensated as it is, is not, in the present condition of
things, and does not promise, hereafter, to be, adequate to procure them,
honestly, such a support as every white person in this country is and
feels himself entitled to."

"Some cannot be said to work at all. They obtain a precarious
subsistence by occasional jobs, by hunting, by fishing, sometimes by
plundering fields or folds, and, too often, by what is, in its effects, far
worse—trading with slaves, and seducing them to plunder for their
benefit."

In another part of the same address, Gov. Hammond says,
that "$18 or, at the most, $19 will cover the whole necessary
annual cost of a full supply of wholesome and palatable food,
purchased in the market;" meaning, generally, in South Carolina.
From a comparison of these two extracts, it will be evident that
$19 per annum is high wages for the labor of one-sixth of all
the white population of South Carolina—and that one-sixth
exclusive of the classes not obliged to labor for their living.

Mr. Bancroft says, in his Essay on the Decline of the Roman
People :

"When Tiberius Sempronius Gracchus, on his way to Spain,

to serve in the army before Numantia, traveled through Italy, he was led to observe the impoverishment of the great body of citizens in the rural districts.   Instead of little farms, studding the country with their pleasant aspect, and nursing an independent race, he beheld nearly all the lands of Italy engrossed by large proprietors ; and the plow was in the hands of the slave.   In the early periods of the State, Cincinnatus, at work in his field, was the model of patriotism ; agriculture and war had been the labor and office of freemen ; but of these the greater number had now been excluded from employment by the increase of slavery, and its tendency to confer the exclusive possession of the soil on the few.   The palaces of the wealthy towered in the landscape in solitary grandeur ; the plebeians hid themselves in miserable hovels.   Deprived of the dignity of freeholders, they could not even hope for occupation ; for the opulent land-owner preferred rather to make use of his slaves, whom he could not but maintain, and who constituted his family.   Excepting the small number of the immeasurably rich, and a feeble, but constantly decreasing class of independent husbandmen, poverty was extreme."

No observant traveler can pass through South Carolina, and extend his observation beyond the illumined ground of hospitality, and not perceive a state of things similar to that here described.   The slaveholders have, as far as possible with their capital, secured the best circumstances for the employment of that slave-labor which is the most valuable part of their capital. They need no assistance from the poor white man : his presence near them is disagreeable and unprofitable.   Condemned to the poorest land, and restricted to the labor of merely providing for themselves the simple necessities of life, they are equally indifferent and incompetent to materially improve their minds or their wealth.

Few will wish to ask whether the condition of the non-slaveholders is compensated by the progress of knowledge and the abundance of happiness among the slaveholders.   This is impossible, considering the relative numbers of each.   But it will be interesting to see how this distinct separation of classes, into the ignorant and the cultivated, is opposed to an economical direction of the forced labor of the slaves, leads, everywhere, to improvidence and waste in the use of the natural resources of the country, and prevents a rapid increase of wealth, even among the opulent and educated.

A man finding himself chiefly distinguished from a class despised of his comrades, by his superior intellectual cultivation, naturally cultivates his intellect further in those directions which wealth gives him a monopoly of pursuing, in preference to those in which he must advance on equal terms with the poor. The greater the class distinctions, the more general will be the habit of lazy contemplation and reflection—of dilettanteism—and the less that of practical industry and the capacity for laborious personal observation and invention. The South Carolina gentleman is ambitious to generalize, either in war, or in politics, or in society; but to closely superintend and carry out his own plans, is excessively irksome and difficult for him. Consequently he is obliged to depend upon uncultivated, ignorant, and immoral poor men. What is the result on his plantations?

"No improvements can be effected—no ameliorations, either of negroes or land, can be expected, if overseers are invested with the chief authority, and changed every two years. Each one has his peculiarities in managing affairs; plants differently, works differently, establishes different rules for the government of negroes, wants other implements, and has different views about feeding working-animals and rearing stock—while none of them feel, or can be expected to feel, any *permanent interest* in their employers' concerns. Unless, therefore, the latter establishes a system of his own, rigidly adheres to it, and compels all his overseers to conform to it, it is obvious that everything must be, and continue, at sixes and sevens, with a total or partial revolution every one, two, or four years. It is not enough, that he should exercise a sort of general superintendence. That may save him from speedy ruin, and, perhaps, even enable him to get along tolerably well; but, if he desires *really to improve*, he must descend to particulars, and infuse into every plantation operation the spirit of an intelligent guardian of a permanent interest.

"How much better, then, would everything be conducted, if the planter himself took upon him the steady, uniform, and entire direction of all his affairs, and pursued a system of his own, even in the smallest matters, for a series of years. Unfortunately, too, it happens that few overseers can be long retained on the same place. They are fond of change. If not, they become careless, or, if they think you have a high opinion of them, demand such an increase of wages as you cannot give; and, in case you refuse, will leave you, and even take less from another, rather than you. Such is the disposition of many of them.

"These difficulties, like almost all others, would be overcome, by the planter assuming the chief management himself. The overseer would see that you were in no way dependent on him—could not become careless, without speedy detection—and would be more contented to remain.

"Every planter will assent at once, I am sure, to the proposition. The difficulty is, that so few will carry it out—and one or two cannot do it. Overseers who can choose employers—which most overseers worth having can do—will not submit to it, if they can avoid it. It is necessary, therefore, that most, if not all planters, should unite in carrying out the system; and what I have written has been in the hope that it might possibly have some influence in bringing about so desirable a consummation."*

Another member of the favored class elucidates the working of the system as follows. [By "the man of literature" it will be evident that the orator means the man whose main motive of life is recreation.]

"Literature will enable one to take a comprehensive view of agriculture; to compare systems of different countries, and choose what is best for his own purposes; to trace effects to causes; to analyze his lands, perceive their defects, and apply the remedies. On the other hand, * * * we know that success in agriculture depends on

---

* Southern Agriculturist, Charleston, vol. iv., p. 323.

minute attention to objects, separately, trifling, but, aggregately, of the greatest importance—indeed, absolutely essential to success. The man of literature, who is habituated to generalize his thoughts, cannot devote his atention to minutiæ, even though he may be conscious of their importance. Further, it is in vain to possess a knowledge of planting, without possessing a knowledge of the proper management of slaves. They are an impelling power; and, if not properly directed, will lead to failure. Now, the very means of acquiring literature, if not the acquisition itself, incapacitates us from being able to compete with men in their knowledge of trickery. Nothing but an early knowledge of their powers of evasion will allow us to detect their duplicity, and prevent us from becoming the dupes of their superior cunning, or sagacity in roguery, if you please, in our relative situations. It is their business to deceive us, and ours to detect the deceit. The man of literary knowledge enters the field at disadvantage, and must be imposed upon. Perhaps the strongest argument is, that the acquisition of knowledge makes his taste fastidious, so that he compounds to be imposed upon.*

In De Bow's *Review*, a monthly periodical, especially devoted to the advocacy of the theories, interests, and measures of the South Carolina school of politicians, for November, 1855, is an article on the agriculture of South Carolina, by a South Carolinian; written for "*The Carolinian*" newspaper, and endorsed by the Editor of the *Review*—who is Superintendent of the U. S. Census, and also himself a Carolinian-born—as "an able and valuable essay." It is so. By carefully weighing and connecting a variety of statistical information, many most interesting conclusions are reached—all of which, but for their length, I would copy. One section of them will, however, suffice for my purpose.

"The average value of the productive industry of the State does not exceed, as shown in the table, $62 per head of the entire population,

---

* Address, before the St. Andrew's, Ashley, and Stone River Agricultural Association, by their President, J. S. Brisbane, Esq., 1844.

omitting the two cities, Charleston and Columbia. Full one-half, or more, of this amount is consumed on the plantation or farm, as necessary means of subsistence ; leaving about $31 as the value of cotton and other marketable produce, per head. Of this $31, about one-third, upon an average, is required to meet the necessary expenses of clothing, overseers' wages, or superintendence, taxes, physicians' and blacksmiths' bills, to say nothing of the expense of renewing the loss of mule and horse-power, and other necessary charges occasionally incurred, leaving a net profit of only $20.66 per head of the entire population. We have seen that the entire capital of the State, in land and labor, is, at a moderate estimate, $269,000,000, or full $400 *per capita*, not including, in this estimate of value, that portion of the population which is a charge upon the active capital. If the natural increase is computed in the account, that of course will, in most cases, more than cover this part of the expense. This, however, is foreign to the matter in hand. But to this capital of $400 per head must be added a capital of not less than $176 more, to cover the regular losses from death and decline in the labor actually employed ; which reduces the net profit on the capital to three and six-tenths per cent. per annum. All the capital in labor is sunk in the average period of about twenty-two years; and $271, the laboring part of capital, being $12.34 per annum, which is the interest of $176, at seven per cent. per annum.

" Let us now suppose the production per head one hundred dollars (and it is over this amount in half of the Eastern States), after making the same deductions as above, for subsistence and other expenses, there would still be left a net profit of $59.66 per head. If, under the influence of such a profit from the cultivation of fertile lands, the population were doubled (as soon it would be), such lands might, and probably would, be enhanced to five times the present value of the lands of this State ; while such a profit would pay more than eight per cent. on the capital thus enhanced, and the lands then be worth more than the same' lands now, with all the slaves upon them. The large amount of lands now necessarily cultivated to produce a given amount of cotton, corn, or other produce, being three or four times the quantity necessary, if they were of first quality, and the consequent increased amount of labor expended in cultivation, show conclusively the low condition of our agriculture.

" It is too obvious to require extended illustration, that the slow advance of our population mainly arises from the impoverished condition of our lands. As lands become exhausted, the returns are not only small and unremunerating, but crops become uncertain, from casualties and vicissitudes of season, subsistence more precarious, and obtained at greater cost The striking fact that those districts possessing naturally the best soils are almost stationary in population, while districts of inferior soils naturally are filling up, show not only the exhausted state of the soil in the former, but prove that the character of slave-labor, and the system of cultivation adopted, are unfriendly to density of population.

"The exhaustion of our lands, above alluded to, is further evinced by the fact that, in the last thirty years, they have remained generally stationary in price ; and, in many instances, have actually declined. Another fact, very significant of this truth, is the regularly increased amount of lands cultivated in different crops per hand, particularly in cotton, while the amount produced is proportionably less."

The business committee of the South Carolina State Agricultural Society reported, Aug. 9, 1855 :—

"Our old-fields are enlarging, our homesteads have been decreasing fearfully in number. * * * We are not only losing some of our most energetic and useful citizens to supply the bone and sinew of other States, but we are losing our slave population, which is the true wealth of the State, our stocks of hogs, horses, mules, and cattle are diminishing in size and decreasing in number, and our purses are strained for the last cent to supply their places from the Northwestern States."

The absurd state and sectional pride of the South Carolinians, their simple and profound contempt for everything foreign except despotism ; their scornful hatred especially of all honestly democratic States, and of everything that proceeds from them; the ridiculous cockerel-like manner in which they swell, strut, bluster, and bully in their confederate relations, is so trite a subject of amusement at the North, that I can only allude to it as affording another evidence of a decayed and stultified people.   In this particular they are hardly surpassed by the most bigoted old Turks, or the most interior mandarins of the Yellow Dragon.

The following extract from the letter of a gentleman who manifests every disposition to take things quietly, but who is a straightforward, honest man, presents, in a clear and forcible manner, the present predicament of the State, and the urgent need for more statesmanlike policy in her legislation. It is published in the *Charleston Standard*, the editor of which calls attention to it, as worthy of especial consideration by every enlightened mind, North or South. Two grand juries of South Carolina (it is not, I believe, generally known at the North) have lately, in the most solemn manner, recommended a renewed importation of slaves from Africa, as the only remedy which the pride of the people of the State will permit them to make use of, for their half-acknowledged debility. The proposal is favored by the most influential newspapers of the State; and a committee of the Legislature, to whom the subject was referred, has given its approval of the measure, on theological, moral and economical grounds, though recommending, from considerations of temporary policy, that no action should at present be taken in the matter:

"For my own part, I do not think that happiness necessarily consists in crowded communities, though I confess that in crowded communities we find more to satisfy the taste, and more of the comforts of social life. Nor do I believe that the stability of the institution of domestic Slavery depends upon its covering the same precise extent of superficial area, or upon its possessing the same precise amount of political power as that which is possessed by the Free States of this confederacy. I believe that there is the possibility of happiness everywhere, and that Slavery is destined to an existence perpetual as the hills on which it has been planted, and is destined to survive the forms of social constitution which oppose it, no matter what may be the present action of our people. But still, if we must have towns and cities like the North, if we must have manufacturing establishments, if our country must be cut up into small parcels, and must bloom like a garden, if our rail-roads are to find the business which is to make them profitable, and our rivers are to be rendered navigable, and our forests planted, and the whole country become resonant with the sounds of active industry, and if, besides all this, we must have Kansas and Nebraska slave territory—and I confess it would seem to be more in accordance with the schemes of an overruling Providence—*we must have the population.* If we have these results, we must have men to work them. But it has been my unfortunate experience to find in the men who mourn the most over the prostrate condition of the State, and who browbeat me when I say a word in its favor, the very men who shrink from every desirable measure of escape.

"If we propose to bring over among us the artisans and farmers from Central Europe, who have made their roads, their canals, their farms, their gardens, and by their wants have given value to every vacant spot of land in New York and the New England States, they raise a finger of warning at us. These men, when they come, they tell us, will exclude our slaves from their legitimate employments, and will create a sentiment, even in the Slave States themselves, against the institution.

"This, to a great extent, is true. There can be no question but that when slaves are cheap, free labor will come to union with them. Free enterprise will take the slave, as the cheapest labor it can get; but when slaves are dear, as they are now, it is equally certain that free enterprise, instead of using Slavery, will combine against it; and the truth is, therefore, that while near ten thousand foreigners have come to Charleston within the last thirty years, near ten thousand negroes have left it in the same time. But when, to obviate it, we propose to re-open the slave-trade, and present enough of slaves to counteract the tendency of free-labor, they raise up both hands in pious horror.

"The man who will buy the negro that has been torn from his home in North Carolina or Virginia—the negro who has been elevated to a sense of natural and social relations by the influence of enlightened institutions, and the blessed precepts of the Gospel, and who may come with his heart-strings bleeding from the recent rupture, will stand aghast at the enormity of buying from the merchant of Massachusetts or New York the savage African, who knows no ties of relationship, and whose condition at home was one of hopeless slavery to a master not less a savage than himself. *If men are to make a fuss upon this subject, they must begin with the domestic slave trade.*"

The amount of it, then, is this: Improvement and progress in South Carolina is forbidden by its present system. There are two ways, in one of which the difficulty must be met: by offering encouragement to the emigration of men from regions in which Slavery has not destroyed the capacity to labor in the people, or by the importation of savages.   In the first case, Slavery will have to be given up; in the latter, free or skilled labor must be dispensed with, and the great majority of whites must be still further degraded and pauperized.

South Carolina must meet her destiny: either be democratized or barbarianized.

I have no doubt hundreds of her planters will say, when they read this—and they may read it, though the poor people may not—"Let it be so: barbarism rather than voluntarily yield a hair's breadth to this base-born agrarianism.   The penalty will not come in our time—at least not on us."

One hundred years hence, the men whose wealth and talent will rule South Carolina, will be, in large part, the descendants of those now living in poverty, ignorance, and the vices of stupid and imbecile minds.   Will they still be taking counsel of their pride, cramming their children with the ancient sophistries of tyranny, and harden their hearts to resist the demands of vulgar Humanity?

Later than in Virginia the spirit of manliness and of personal aspiration will permeate the people of South Carolina; and they will demand freedom, equality and fraternity in the social organization. Later, yet it will come, and will prevail. But how much will, in the meanwhile, have been lost.

GEORGIA.
" Non sibi sed aliis;"

The settlement of Georgia did not originate in mercenary and

ambitious motives. The design of the founders of the Colony
was to provide for the poor and unfortunate—more especially
for discharged prisoners—an asylum in which they might be
hoped, when free from the social submergement and weight of
disgrace which disabled them in England, to support themselves
by honest industry. A corporation for this purpose having
been framed, a seal was adopted on which the cap of Liberty
was a prominent emblem, with the motto, " *Non sibi sed aliis*,"
"signifying," says Hewitt, " that neither the first Trustees, nor
their successors could have any views of interest, it being entirely designed for the benefit and happiness of others."

Conscious that the class for whom they were to provide were
most liable, under the best of circumstances, to continue to
suffer from their own weak character, the Trustees set about the
formation of a constitution, or code of laws, which should, as far
as possible, guard their beneficiaries from temptation to trust to
anything but honest and persevering industry for success, and
which should educate them to sobriety, self-confidence, and perseverance in labor.

In the first place, therefore, they obtained from the king a
guarantee to all of whatever birth, or previous condition or persuasion of mind, who should settle in the Colony, equality of
rights with each other, and with all the free-born subjects of the
king, native of Great Britain ; and to all, except Papists, perfect
religious freedom. Negro slavery was expressly prohibited to
exist in the Colony. Trade with the West Indies was forbidden,
to prevent the importation of rum. Restrictions were placed
upon the trade with the Indians—always a fruitful source of
danger in the frontier settlements in America, and no less a
school of knavery, and of all vicious habits, than the jails of

London. To prevent large tracts from falling, in process of time, under one possessor, land was to be granted to the settlers only in tail male, subject, on the failure of a male heir, to return to the government of the Colony, by which it should be granted anew to such other persons, as should be judged for the best interest of the commonwealth, provision being made for widows and female children. Land, in any case, was to be granted only on condition that it should be made productive ; and if it should fail to have been fenced, cleared, and cultivated in eighteen years after it was granted, in order to remove the temptation to hold it longer, in idleness, for speculation, it was stipulated that it should revert to the government. Under no consideration was any one person or family, however large or wealthy, to be granted more than five hundred acres of land within the Colony.

A secondary purpose of the corporation, by which their project was recommended to the favor of the king, was to form outposts, to guard the Carolinas from invasion by the Spaniards, then strongly fortified in Florida. For this purpose, all grants of land were made on condition that the grantees should be prepared to take arms, whenever called upon by proper authority.

"The first embarkations of poor people from England (I quote from Hewitt), being collected from towns and cities, were found equally idle and useless members of society abroad, as they had been at home. A hardy and bold race of men, inured to rural labor and fatigue, they (the Trustees) were persuaded would be much better adapted, both to cultivation and defense." A hundred and thirty frugal and industrious laboring men were therefore procured from Scotland, and one hundred and seventy more of the same sort from Germany. The liberal and democratic character of the Colony rapidly added to it additional forces of these honest and self-reliant people. They were settled at posts of danger and barrenness, on the extreme frontier, while the moral strength of the English invalids was attempted to be nursed on the banks of the Savannah, in the nearest part of the Colony to the South Carolina plantations.*   A sad error, this.

Like children, weak in good resolution, unaccustomed to labor, habitually despondent, and ready to despair at the first occurrence of unexpected difficulty, the English settlers needed to be constantly cheered and animated.   That the laws designed to remove temptation to vice, and to restrain unhealthy specula- tion, operated, in some degree, also, to check enterprise, and restrict competition among traders and men of capital, there can be no question.   But, if it be remembered how largely the Colony was composed of people whose first and best business it should have been to produce food, and build shelter for themselves, and not to transfer goods, I can see no grounds for esteeming, according to a common assumption, that the first constitution and laws of Georgia were the worst which could have been de- vised for their purpose.   Considering that they were drawn in an age when, by many, feudalism was still deemed the highest pos- sible attainment of political and social science, they seem to me to have been an extraordinarily sagacious production.

These people, of course, were indolent, dejected, and soon dis- contented.   Like all such unfortunates, they labored to find, in the errors of others, or in circumstances over which they had no control, the grounds of that unhappiness which resulted from their own misconduct or indolence.

The merchants, who thought their interests would be served

* Hewitt, ii., 45.

by a liquor and a slave-traffic, and by a free trade with drunken Indians, found nothing but hardship and danger in the restrictions of the law. The South Carolinians, over the river, had slaves to do their work for them, made themselves jolly with cheap rum, and entertained Indians and pirates with great profit. The ignorant, poor people were very ready to believe themselves oppressed; that it was impossible for white people to work in that climate, especially without cheap liquor, to sustain their strength, and were easily persuaded to raise an outcry for free trade and Slavery. Ungrateful, "they could," says Hewitt, "view the design of the Trustees in no other light than that of having decoyed them into misery," and "they frankly told them that nothing could prevent the Colony from being totally deserted, but the same encouragement with their more fortunate neighbors in Carolina."*

"But the Highlanders," says the same chronicler, strangely enough, "instead of joining in this application, to a man remonstrated against the introduction of slaves." "They considered perpetual Slavery as shocking to human nature, and deemed the *permission of it a grievance*, and which, in some future day, might also prove a scourge, and make many feel the smart of that oppression they [the poor Englishmen,] so earnestly desired to introduce." So it was also with the industrious Germans.

And for twenty years, the people were thus divided in two parties: those who had been coaxed to come out because of their bravery, hardihood and industry, forming the bulk of one— conservative and democratic; the speculators, traders, office-

* Hewitt, ii., 149

holders, and the ignorant rabble of loafers at Savannah, who
had been sent out for charity's sake, the other—disorganizing
and pro-slavery.

Many of the arguments of the latter were identical with those
we now hear. "They judged that the British [read *American*]
Constitution, zealous for the rights and liberties of mankind,
could not permit subjects [read *citizens*] to be deprived of the
common privileges of all Colonists" [read *white men*]. "That
the chief cause of all their calamities was, the strict adherence to
a chimerical and impracticable scheme" [read *infidel and fanatical isms*]. "The leading men at New Inverness and Ebenezer
—the Scotch and German settlements—[read *Lawrence*] who opposed the introduction of slaves, were traduced and persecuted."
"The standing toast at Savannah was, 'THE ONE THING NEEDFUL',"
meaning Slavery. The churches were induced to represent it
as desirable that Africans should be imported, that they might
be converted to Christianity. The clergy were flattered to
to preach and pray for it as an institution sanctioned by the
Bible. The South Carolinians constantly said all they could,
to increase the discouragement of the Georgians, and to assist
them to obtain an abrogation of the proviso against slaves.*

At length, after slaves had been for some time imported and
held in defiance of the law, or an evasion had been practiced, by obtaining them from South Carolina on a life-
lease, the benevolent Trustees, "weary of the complaints of the
people," were persuaded to resign their charter. The king at
once accepted it, appointed a royal governor, and removed
all restraint to Slavery.

* Hewitt and Hildreth.

One can, I think, with considerable confidence anticipate, that though Kansas should be forced, in this second year of its settlement, to submit to the permission of Slavery, the strong sentiment of a large part of the settlers against it, and the free-labor character sustained up to the present time, by so many of them, will, in a degree, restrict the evil of Slavery, and insure a better character to its future population, than would be the case if, from the outset, Slavery had been welcomed, and inconsiderately submitted to by all the people.

It is but reasonable to suppose, that during the much larger protection from, and resistance to Slavery, enjoyed by the first settlers of Georgia, habits of hopeful labor, and genuine, honest industry, had been established among much of its rural English, as well as retained, and more than ever cherished by the Scotch and German portion of its population. Such men would naturally disdain, for a long time, to avail themselves of the unrequited labor of slaves; or, if using it, would be less demoralized by its use than others, and would educate their families, not only in their own habits, but to some degree in their own sentiments of respect for labor.

Being the most vigorous in body as well as in mind, the number of their descendants would be large in proportion to those of the more effeminate class. Thus, unless the after immigration, or other circumstances, should be very much against it, the customs, the opinions, the popular legislation, and whole character of the general body politic of the State might have been expected to be greatly and favorably influenced by these early laws and these early habits and sentiments of a part of its people.

This element has, of course, been greatly smothered; yet in our own day, it is obvious to the traveler, and notorious in the stock market, that there is more life, enterprise, skill, and industry in Georgia than in any other of the old Slave Commonwealths.

In a letter from a native Alabamian to a New York paper (the *Times*), it is thus testified:

"Georgia has the reputation of being the *Yankee land of the South*, and it is well deserved. She has the idea of doing—the will and the hand to undertake and accomplish—and you have only to be abroad among her people to see that she intends to lead the way in the race of Southern empire. Already over eight hundred miles of rail-road have been finished; but this is only one item of her rapid advance. Factories, improved means of agriculture, diversified labor, endowed institutions, are all contributing to her progress. I have known many Georgians who are settled over the Southwest in the different States, and have always found them a very industrious, moral, elevated people."

And the present laws of Georgia show the effects of the early democratic education of the Colony, as do those of South Carolina the reverse influences attending her settlement; being still much less undemocratic, with regard to the whites, much less inhumane with regard to the blacks, than those of the other pre-revolutionary Slave States. Although advantage continues to be taken of that provision of the Constitution, which permits slave property to be represented in our national councils, Georgia repudiates, in her internal politics, the absurd and unjust principle of it. The vote of every freeman counts one, and but one, though he owns a hundred slaves.* The wickedness and danger

---

* A friend of mine once said to a Georgian: "I confess, H., whenever I am reminded that your power in our Congress, by the reason of the hundred slaves you own, counts as sixty-one to my one, because I happen to live at the North, and choose to invest the results of my labor in rail-roads, instead of niggers, I have a very strong indisposition to submit to it."

"I declare," answered the Georgian, "I should think you would; I never

of the internal slave trade is distinctly recognized, by a provision of her laws forbidding the importation of slaves from other States. A provision which, unfortunately, however, like nearly all laws against the evils of Slavery, is so easily evaded as to be entirely useless, except as an act of conscience. The restrictive laws of the State, upon negroes—as those forbidding their instruction, and those with regard to free colored seamen—are less frequently enforced, and are more unpopular, and more violently, because less honestly, defended, than in any other State. More stringent and outrageous means have also been taken to prevent the "infection of abolitionism" reaching the people in Georgia, than in any other State, evidently because the apprehension of it by the ruling class has been greater than elsewhere. There still stands unrepealed an act of the legislature, offering a large reward for the head of a citizen of New York, who has committed no crime recognized by the constitution of the confederacy.

But, let us consider, what was the effect of abrogating the law of freedom?

It was several years before slaves began to be much used—showing that, during the greatest clamor for them, there were very few persons who personally wanted them. Ultimately, however, large speculations began to be made with their labor; and, at the same time, the richer class—as in Virginia and Caro-

thought of it in that light before; it's wrong, and you ought not to submit to it —and, if I were you, I would not."

Howison, the Virginia historian, said, in 1848: "It would be hard to find an equitable objection to this compromise (the slave representation). The instrument containing it was adopted by the Northern States, and they have ever since acquiesced without resistance; and if it was right for the Union, it seems, *a fortiori*, right for Virginia."

As the people of Virginia has since decided that it is not right for Virginia, as have those of Georgia for their State, it would seem, " *a fortiori*," not right for the Union. [See Appendix A.]

lina—commenced to secure for themselves, and to withdraw from the labor of the free poor, the most available land of the country. Many planters were attracted from South Carolina, the general immigration continued, and more capitalists were numbered in it. Were the poor people, or the people in general, out of those engaged in commerce, benefited thereby? Not at all. Instead of giving them profitable employment, these capitalists bought slaves in large numbers, and monopolized for them, in a great degree, the valuable opportunities and encouragements to labor, which the Colony afforded. These slaves they obliged to obtain whatever of value the country would produce, returning them only the small share of these productions necessary to sustain their lives. Whatever else they wanted, they obtained direct, or through the merchants, from England; paying for it from the remainder of the productions of the labor of their slaves.

The poor white people remained as before, except that the results of the labor of the industrious had to be sold in competition with that of the labor of the slaves.

In short, the abrogation of the law was equivalent, in its effects on the people for whose benefit the Colony was founded, to what, upon honest tradesmen, would be a general granting of licenses, to those who could afford to pay enough for them, to sell stolen goods.

Of course, the wealth of the land was more rapidly worked out, and there was a rapid increase of exports and imports, which Southern politicians and historians cite as evidence of the benevolence of Slavery, and which Hewitt especially points to, as proof that Slavery had been "the one thing needful" for the prosperity of the Colony.

The following picture, by a native Georgian, of what was the richest part of Georgia, when Hewitt wrote, will show at what expense this rapid increase of wealth—that is, of wealthy people and of trade, in the Colony—was obtained:

"The classic hut occupied a lovely spot, overshadowed by majestic hickories, towering poplars, and strong-armed oaks. The little plain on which it stood, was terminated, at the distance of about fifty feet from the door, by the brow of a hill, which descended rather abruptly to a noble spring, that gushed joyously forth from among the roots of a stately beech, at its foot. The stream from this fountain scarcely burst into view, before it hid itself in the dark shade of a field of cane, which overspread the dale through which it flowed, and marked its windings, until it turned from sight, among vine-covered hills, at a distance far beyond that to which the eye could have traced it, without the help of its evergreen belt. A remark of the Captain's, as we viewed this lovely country, will give the reader my apology for the minuteness of the fore-going description : 'These lands,' said he, 'will never wear out. Where they lie level, they will be just as good, fifty years hence, as they are now.' Forty-two years afterwards, I visited the spot on which he stood when he made the remark. The sun poured his whole strength upon the bald hill which once supported the sequestered school-house ; many a deep-washed gully met at a sickly bog, where had gushed the limpid fountain ; a dying willow rose from the soil which had nourished the venerable beech ; flocks wandered among the dwarf pines, and cropped a scanty meal from the vale where the rich cane had bowed and rustled to every breeze, and all around was barren, dreary, and cheerless."*

I will quote from graver authority : De Bow's Resources of the South, from Fenner's Southern Medical Reports :

"The native soil of Middle Georgia is a rich, argillaceous loam, resting on a firm, clay foundation. In some of the richer counties, nearly all the lands have been cut down, and appropriated to tillage ; a large maximum of which have been worn out, leaving a desolate picture for the traveler to behold. Decaying tenements, red, old hills, stripped of

---

* Georgia Scenes, by the Rev. and Hon. Judge Longstreet, now President of the University of Mississippi. Harper's edition, p. 76.

their native growth and virgin soil, and washed into deep gullies, with here and there patches of Bermuda grass and stunted pine shrubs, struggling for subsistence on what was once one of the richest soils in America."

In 1854, the Hon. Mr. Stephens, M. C., from Georgia, in a speech in the House of Representatives, attempted to show that the agricultural productions of his State were more valuable than those of Ohio, and thereby to obtain an economical argument for Slavery. In order to do so, he left hay—the most valuable crop of Ohio, and large quantities of which are exported to the Slave States, but of which none of consequence is raised in Georgia—entirely out of the calculation; giving as a reason that corn-fodder was not returned from Georgia. Corn-fodder is a crop of comparatively small value, but that of Ohio, which was also omitted, would, if returned, have far exceeded that of Georgia. He then placed absurdly low prices upon the great staples of Ohio, and unusually high ones upon those of Georgia, and even put higher prices upon the same articles in his Georgia than in his Ohio table. The truth is, though Georgia has every advantage in climate, and enjoys, in common with other Slave States, a natural protection in the culture of the great staple of cotton, her average agricultural productions, by the ordinary commercial method of calculation—taking the prices for all crops from those ruling at a common market—are probably less than half in value those of Ohio. In mechanical and manufactured articles, the production of which requires intelligence and trained skill in the laborer, Ohio has a still greater superiority. This disgraceful argument for Slavery has probably been placed in the hands of nearly every man who can read, in the State of Georgia. A refutation of it, proving Slavery to be a restraint upon their prosperity, would be denied a general distribution through the post-offices.

In De Bow's *Review*, for August, 1855, may be found a table, based on the census, in which the value of the productive industry, in the year 1850, in Georgia, is said to be $63,797,659. The same in Ohio, *without counting the value of live stock of any kind*, $149,577,898. The year 1850 was an especially unfavorable one for the most valuable crops of Ohio.

It is impossible to obtain statistics which will show definitely the distribution of wealth in any of the Slave States. From a study of pages 94 and 95 of the official compendium of the census, it appears probable that only twenty-seven in a hundred of the white families in Georgia are possessed of slaves, and that one fifth of these own over one-half of all the slaves in the State. That is, less than one-fiftieth of the white people own one-half of the property in slaves. The small number of the very wealthy, without doubt, own more than that proportion of the wealth of the State in land, in houses, in furniture, and in all the material comforts of life. In Carolina the distribution is much more unequal.

And how general is that intelligence which has made Georgia " the Banner State of the South ?"

Of the *free native* population of Georgia, according to the census returns, one in nine and a half, on an average, are without the smallest rudiments of school-education (cannot read or write). In Maine, which among the old Free States compares most closely with Georgia in density of population (that of one being 16, the other 15 to square mile), the proportion is one in two hundred and forty-one. With other Free States, a comparison would be still more unfavorable to the Georgia experiment, and more accurate returns would, doubtless, increase the contrast.*

In Georgia, the mail expenses are equal to twenty-five cents a head of the population. The postage receipts are only sixteen cents a head, on an average. In Maine, the cost of transporting the United States mails would be paid by a tax of nine cents upon each inhabitant. The people, however, voluntarily pay twenty-one and a half cents a head, on an average, for the intelligence conveyed in them. The people of Maine, with but one more inhabitant to a square mile, pay to the United States government considerably more than twice the cost of their mail-service; those of Georgia, less than two-thirds the cost of theirs.

The truth is—I judge from observation—it is a distinct "better class" that gives Georgia its reputation for great prosperity; and that class, though intelligence, and consequently wealth, is more diffused than in South or North Carolina, is not a large one, compared with the whole population. It must be also admitted that it is very largely composed and directed in enterprise by persons born in the Free States. The number of these, propor-

---

* The following table shows the *native white* population, and the number of *native white adults* ignorant of letters, in a few States :

	Population.	Ignorant Adults.
Maine, - - - - - - -	549,674	1,999
North Carolina, - - - - -	550,267	73,226
Massachusetts, - - - - -	819,044	1,055
Tennessee, - - - - - -	749,661	77,017
Ohio, - - - - - - -	1,732,698	51,968
Virginia, - - - - -	871,393	75,868
Connecticut, - - - - - -	324,095	726
Maryland, - - - - - -	366,650	17,364
Rhode Island, - - - - - -	119,975	981
Louisiana, - - - - - -	187,558	14,950
New York, - - - - - -	2,388,830	23,241
Missouri, - - - - - -	514,527	34,448

tionately to all the white population, is much greater than in any other Slave State.

Until one has closely observed the operation of Slavery upon the poor free people of a slave community, it is but natural to attribute their condition only to causes which, in free communities, would be considered unfavorable to the rapid accumulation of wealth. The poor people of Georgia are mostly seen dwelling upon soils naturally unfertile, or made barren by the wasteful necessity of previous slave-holding occupants; and it is customary with travelers, and with their more fortunate neighbors, to attribute their poverty to this circumstance.

If this were the case, Slavery would still be primarily responsible for their condition ; because, by concentrating in one man's hands the profits of the labor of many hands, it gives him power to purchase for that labor the most profitable field to be obtained for its application, and thus drives to the least profitable the man who can use merely the results of his own personal labor.*

But it is a mistake to suppose that the poverty of the soil necessitates the poverty of its occupants. It may account for a sparse settlement, but does not for such general idleness or ill-paid industry as is evident among the poor whites of Georgia.

There is no part of Georgia which equals, in poverty of natural agricultural resources, Cape Cod, in Massachusetts. But

* About forty years ago, Governor Woolcot, of Connecticut, addressed to the Legislature of that State the following observation, in connection with a circular letter on the subject of State Rights, sent to him by the Legislature of Virginia :

"Where agricultural labor is wholly or chiefly performed by slaves, it must constitute the principal revenue of the community. The owners of the slaves must be the chief owners of the soil, and those laborers who are too poor to own slaves, though nominally free, must be dependent on an aristocratic order, and remain without power or political influence."

there is hardly a poor woman's cow on the Cape that is not better housed and more comfortably provided for than a majority of the white people of Georgia. A majority of the people of the Cape have far better houses, better furniture, better food, and altogether live, I have no doubt, in more comfort than the majority of even the slave-holders of Georgia.* The people of the Cape have manners and customs, and a character peculiar to themselves, as have the "Crackers" and "Sand-hillers," of Georgia. In both there is frankness, boldness, and simplicity; but in the one it is associated with intelligence, discretion, and an expansion of mind, resulting from considerable education; in the other with ignorance, improvidence, laziness, and the prejudices of narrow minds.

It may be thought that the people of the Cape, though they have less agricultural elements of wealth than the Sand-hillers of Georgia, have other advantages, exceeding theirs, for the profitable application of their industry. An examination of the facts will show the contrary to be the case, very markedly, especially so, as regards mining and manufacturing. The inducements to a sea-faring life and to fishing alone, of the Cape Cod people, perhaps exceed those of the Georgians; but do the Georgians make anything like a corresponding use of their facilities of the same kind? On the contrary, I found a gang of New Englanders, and probably in part Cape Cod men, fishing in Georgia

---

* The following description is given of the residence of "Thomas Gibson, Esq., one of the magistrates of the county," in Georgia Scenes: "The Squire's dwelling [he has a large family], consisted of but one room, which answered the three-fold purpose of dining-room, bed-room, and kitchen. The house was constructed of logs, and the floor was of puncheons [a term which means split-logs, with their faces a little smoothed with the axe]."

See also, Lyell's Second Tour in the United States, and Parson's Tour among the Planters.

waters, salting their fish with salt made on the Cape by evaporating the waters of the same ocean that washes the coast of
Georgia, and selling them to Georgia planters, to be fed to
Georgia slaves. Ships are built on the Cape, from lumber procured by the Cape men from the Georgia forests; and then,
being manned by Cape seamen, are profitably employed in exporting the Georgia slave staples. Is there one Georgia built
ship, manned by one native Georgia seaman?* Is there one
Georgia fishing-smack? Has there ever been a Georgia whaler?
or a Georgia sealer? Never. Yet Georgia is nearer the great
sealing and whaling ground, and is nearer the chief market for
fish than the Cape. Why have not the poor Sand-hillers turned
their attention to something besides raising corn and bacon, eating clay, drinking whisky, and disputing on the meaning of the
Greek $\beta\alpha\pi\tau\omega$, for which alone they are distinguished, seeing the
small profit of these occupations?† Because, as Marion said,
they have no spirit to labor—they have no care for the future
this side of heaven, to gain which they must think it was especially provided for them that no works should be necessary—
only faith and $\beta\alpha\pi\tau\iota\sigma\mu\alpha$—whichever that shall turn out to be.

It is evident that a large part of the people of Georgia still
have the vagrant and hopeless habits and character of Oglethorpe's first colonists, somewhat favorably modified, it is true,
by the physical circumstances which have made them superior to
absolute charity or legal crime, and also, perhaps, by the influ-

---

* In the year 1854, there were built in Maine 168,632 tons of shipping, in craft,
averaging over 500 tons each. In Georgia, where the natural advantages for
the business are at least equally great, there were built 667 tons, all in small
craft.

† See "Letters of a Pedagogue in Georgia," in *Putnam's Magazine*, and
Lyell's Second Tour.

ence of a freely preached, though exceedingly degraded, form of Christianity. They are still coarse and irrestrainable in appetite and temper; with perverted, eccentric and intemperate spiritual impulses; faithless in the value of their own labor, and almost imbecile for personal elevation. Had Oglethorpe's democratic designs been sustained, who believes that no better result to them would have been arrived at?

This year an appeal is made to the *patriotism and honor* of the slave-holders of Georgia, to contribute each one dollar, for every slave he owns, to the fund of a Society, the declared object of which is to assist in extending Slavery, and establishing it in a great region, hitherto protected from its influence. This Society should have for its motto the words of Cæsar:

"With men we will get money, and with money we will get men."

NOTE ON SHIP BUILDING.

Kentucky and Missouri, as compared with—Maine being excepted—each of the Southern States, have facilities and advantages for ship building, superior, if it were not for Slavery, to those of *any* Northern State. In two or three of them (Free Trade States), there is a bounty paid from the State treasury to the owners of all ships built in them, to draw Northern mechanics or increase the enterprise of the natives.

More than seven-eighths part of the tonnage, nevertheless, is from the Free States, and of the rest, the largest part is built at Baltimore and in the District of Columbia, under free labor influences, as appears by the following table which exhibits the number of vessels built, and their gross tonnage in each State last year (1854):

States, etc.	Ships and Barques.	Brigs.	Schooners.	Sloops.	Steamers.	Total.	Tons.
Maine - - - -	56	78	90	12	3	348	168,632
New Hampshire - -	19	—	—	—	2	11	11,980
Massachusetts - - -	82	4	87	4	3	180	91,570
Rhode Island - - -	5	—	3	1	2	11	5,726
Connecticut - - -	10	1	30	8	2	51	10,691
Vermont - - - -	—	—	1	3	—	4	227
New York - - - -	46	10	89	85	70	300	117,107
New Jersey - - -	—	—	33	27	9	69	8,554
Pennsylvania - - - -	7	4	27	124	75	237	36,768
Delaware - - -	—	—	29	1	4	34	3,021
Maryland - - -	13	3	101	1	4	122	20,252
District of Columbia -	—	—	—	42	2	44	2,814
Virginia - - - -	1	—	9	3	6	9	3,228
North Carolina - -	—	—	32	3	3	38	2,532
South Carolina - - -	—	—	13	10	—	23	1,162
Georgia - - - -	—	—	1	—	2	3	667
Florida - - - -	—	—	7	—	—	7	562
Alabama - - - -	1	—	4	2	2	9	2,000
Mississippi - - - -	—	—	3	—	—	3	77
Louisiana - - -	1	—	6	5	2	14	1,509
Tennessee - - - -	—	—	—	—	—	2	209
Missouri - - - -	—	—	—	2	7	9	3,071
Kentucky - - - -	—	—	—	—	—	22	6,824
Illinois - - - -	1	3	8	4	1	17	3,304
Wisconsin - - - -	—	—	26	—	—	26	2,947
Ohio - - - -	—	4	20	27	41	92	17,046
Indiana - - - -	—	—	—	—	—	4	2,400
Michigan - - -	1	5	22	12	8	48	7,788
Texas - - - -	1	—	—	—	—	1	125
California - - -	—	—	11	10	5	26	1,023
Total - - - -	334	112	661	386	281	1774	535,936

" In the European market, Georgia pine enjoys an undisputed preëminence over all other American pines, etc., etc."—*Report of W. B. Bullock, Collector at Savannah, to Sec'y Treas'y. Con. Doc. No. 6, p. 644, 1846.*

" Ship building was once followed to a great extent, in North Carolina; but at present, there is not enough tonnage to do the coasting trade, [it] having to rely on canal boats of Norfolk and the New England vessels."—*Report to Sec'y Treas'y, Doc. No. 6, p. 368, 1846.*

The *New Orleans Delta* says:

"We possess the finest ship timber in the world, in inexhaustible quantities, which is easy of access, and can be cheaply transported to any given point. Almost every day this timber is cut down, split, hewed and sawed into proper lengths and shapes, and sent to Northern ship-yards thousands of miles off, where it is used in the construction of vessels, many of which come back here to engage in the transportation of Southern produce. Now, wouldn't it be cheaper to build the ships where the timber is, than to send that same timber off some thousands of miles, and there build the ships? Of course it would. This proposition is clear. There would be a vast saving in expense, to say nothing of local advantages added, to which the bonus offered by the State ought to give a stimulus to the business, such as would make it grow and prosper, until it become one of the most important pursuits of the State."

NOTE ON MANUFACTURES AND INDUSTRY OTHER THAN AGRICULTURAL AND NAVAL.

The greater part of Georgia is abundantly provided with running water, frequently affording excellent milling power. The mineral wealth of the State is said, by geologists, to be very great, but is, at present, almost entirely undeveloped, except in gold, which is somewhat extensively mined, without much profit. More attention has been given to manufacturing —thus far, with but indifferent success; but I cannot doubt that, if the same judgment, skill, and close scrutiny of details, were given to cotton manufacturing, that is now evidently applied to the management of rail-roads in Georgia, it would be well rewarded. The cost of the raw material must be from ten to twenty per cent. less than in Massachusetts, yet I saw Lowell cottons, both fine and coarse, for sale, almost under the roof of Georgia factories. Cotton goods manufactured in Georgia are sent to New York for sale, and are there sold by

New York jobbers to Georgia retailers, who re-transport them to the vicinity in which the cotton was grown, spun, and wove, to be sold, by the yard or piece, to the planter. I saw the goods, with the mill marks, and was informed that this was the case, by a Georgia merchant.

Land-rent, water-power, timber, fuel, and raw material for cotton manufacturing, are all much cheaper in Georgia than in New England. The only other item of importance, in esti-mating the cost of manufacturing, must be the cost of labor, which includes, of course, the efficiency of the laborers. By the census, it appears that the average wages of the female operatives in the Georgia cotton factories was, in 1850, $7·39 a month; in Massachusetts, $14·57 a month.

Negroes were worth $180 a year, and found in clothes, food, and medical attendance, by the hirer, to work on rail-roads, when I was in Georgia. The same year, a Georgia planter, being hard pressed, sent to New York, for Irish laborers to work on his plantation—hiring them, probably, at $10 a month, and found in food only, losing their own time when ill—a very significant fact. New England factory-girls have been induced to go to Georgia to work in newly-established cotton factories, by the offer of high wages, but have found their position so unpleasant—owing to the general degradation of the laboring class—as very soon to be forced to return.

A correspondent of the *Charleston News*, writing from Sparta, Georgia, July, 1855, says:

" A large cotton factory has been in operation here about three years, but is now about being closed, and to-day will probably terminate its existence. It unpleasantly reminded us of a fate of a similar enter-prise which so signally failed, after a brief career, in our own city.

Why is it so ?   It would seem to be reasonable, at least that, surrounded with the raw material, unencumbered with the cost of transportation to Northern cities, Southern manufactories should not only compete, but successfully maintain a higher position than those so far removed from the cotton-growing region.   But so it is, with few exceptions, our own Graniteville being among them."

In the "Southern Commercial Convention," which met at New Orleans, this year (1855), one of the orators distinguished himself by his splendid delivery of the following sublime passage, adapted for the occasion from the speech in the British Parliament, on taxes, which we have all seen in the "Child's First Speaker:"

"It is time that we should look about us, and see in what relation we stand to the North.   From the rattle with which the nurse tickles the ear of the child born in the South, to the shroud that covers the cold form of the dead, everything comes to us from the North.   We rise from between sheets made in Northern looms, and pillows of Northern feathers, to wash in basins made in the North, dry our beards on Northern towels, and dress ourselves in garments woven in Northern looms ; we eat from Northern plates and dishes ; our rooms are swept with Northern brooms, our gardens dug with Northern spades, and our bread kneaded in trays or dishes of Northern wood, or tin ; and the very wood which feeds our fires is cut with Northern axes, helved with hickory brought from Connecticut and New York."

This state of things another gentleman—who, also, thought Slavery the most economical labor-system in the world—proposed to remedy as follows :

" *Resolved*, That this Convention recommend to each of the Southern States to encourage the establishment of a direct trade with Europe. either by an exemption from taxation, for a limited time, on the goods imported ; or by allowing the importers an equivalent drawback or bounty ; or by such other mode as, to the legislators of the respective States, may seem best.

" *Resolved*, That to further this great object, Congress be recommended to make such appropriations for deepening the inlets to harbors, and other purposes, as may be deemed necessary."

Fifty other, at least, equally puerile propositions were gravely listened to ; but not one man dared to insinuate that Slavery had ever done any harm to the South, or to suggest that anything should be done about it, except to maintain and extend it.

And to this school of statesmanship the "Democratic" party, year after year, is obliged to surrender its power.

" With men we will get money, and with money we will get men."

CHAPTER IX.

ALABAMA.

SAVANNAH TO NEW ORLEANS.

I LEFT Savannah for the West, by the Macon road; the train started punctually to a second, at its advertised time; the speed was not great, but regular, and less time was lost unnecessarily, at way-stations, than usually on our Northern roads.

I have traveled more than five hundred miles on the Georgia roads, and I am glad to say that all of them seemed to be exceedingly well managed. The speed upon them is not generally more than from fifteen to twenty miles an hour; but it is made, as advertised, with considerable punctuality. The roads are admirably engineered and constructed, and their equipment will compare favorably with that of any other roads on the continent. There are now very nearly, if not quite, one thousand miles of rail-road in the State, and more building. The Savannah and Macon line—the first built—was commenced in 1834. The increased commerce of the city of Savannah, which followed its completion, stimulated many other rail-road enterprises, not only within the State, but elsewhere at the South, particularly in South Carolina. Many of these were rashly pushed forward by men of no experience, and but little commercial judgment; the roads were injudiciously laid out, and have been badly managed, and, of course, have occasioned disastrous losses. The Savannah and Macon road has, however, been very successful. The receipts are now over $1,000,000 annually; the road is well stocked, is out of debt, and its business is constantly increasing; the stock is above par, and the stockholders are receiving eight per cent. dividends, with a handsome surplus on hand. It has been always, in a great degree, under the management of Northern men—was engineered, and is still worked chiefly by Northern men, and a large amount of its stock is owned at the North. I am told that most of the mechanics, and of the successful merchants and tradesmen of Savannah came originally from the North, or are the sons of Northern men.

Partly by rail and partly by rapid stage-coaching (the coaches, horses and drivers again from the North), I crossed the State in about twenty-four hours. The rail-road is since entirely completed from Savannah to Montgomery, in Alabama, and is being extended slowly towards the Mississippi; of course with the expectation that it will eventually reach the Pacific, and thus make Savannah "the gate to the commerce of the world." Ship-masters will hope that, when either it or its rival in South Carolina has secured that honor, they will succeed, better than they yet have done, in removing the bars, physical and legal, by which commerce is now annoyed in its endeavors to serve them.

At Columbus, I spent several days. It is the largest manufacturing town, south of Richmond, in the Slave States. It is situated at the falls, and the head of steamboat navigation of the Chatahooche, the western boundary of Georgia. The water-power is sufficient to drive two hundred thousand spindles, with a proportionate number of looms. There are, probably, at present from fifteen to twenty thousand spindles running. The operatives in the cotton-mills are said to be mainly "Cracker girls" (poor whites from the country), who earn, in good times, by piece-work, from $8 to $12 a month. There are, besides the cotton-mills, one woolen-mill, one paper-mill, a foundry, a cotton-gin factory, a machine-shop, etc. The laborers in all these are mainly whites, and they are in such a condition that, if temporarily thrown out of employment, great numbers of them are at once reduced to a state of destitution, and are dependent upon credit or charity for their daily food. Public entertainments were being held at the time of my visit, the profits to be applied to the relief of operatives in mills which had been stopped by the effects of a late flood of the river. Yet Slavery is constantly boasted to be a perfect safeguard against such distress.

I had seen in no place, since I left Washington, so much gambling, intoxication, and cruel treatment of servants in public, as in Columbus. This, possibly, was accidental; but I must caution persons, traveling for health or pleasure, to avoid stopping in the town. The hotel in which I lodged was disgustingly dirty; the table revolting; the waiters stupid, inattentive, and annoying. It was the stage-house; but I was informed that the other public-house was no better. There are very good inns at Macon, and at Montgomery, Alabama; and it will be best for an invalid proceeding from Savannah westward, if possible, not to spend a night between these towns.

I should add that I met with much courtesy from strangers, and saw as much real hospitality of disposition among the people near Columbus, as anywhere else in the South. I was much gratified by a visit to the garden of Mr. Peabody, a horticulturist, who has succeeded wonderfully in cultivating strawberries upon a poor, sandy soil, in a climate of great heat and dryness, by a thin mulching of leaves.

A day's journey took me from Columbus, through a hilly wilderness, with a few dreary villages, and many isolated cotton farms, with comfortless habitations for black and white upon them, to Montgomery, the capital of Alabama.

Montgomery is a prosperous town, with very pleasant suburbs, and a remarkably enterprising population, among which there is a considerable proportion of Northern and foreign-born business-men and mechanics.

I spent a week here very pleasantly, and then left for Mobile, on the steamboat Fashion, a clean and well-ordered boat, with polite and obliging officers. We were two days and a half making the passage, the boat stopping at almost every bluff and landing to take on cotton, until she had a freight of nineteen hundred bales, which was built up on the guards, seven or eight tiers in hight, and until it reached the hurricane deck. The boat was thus brought so deep that her guards were in the water, and the ripple of the river constantly washed over them. There are two hundred landings on the Alabama river, and three hundred on the Bigby (Tombeckbee of the geographers), at which the boats advertise to call, if required, for passengers or freight. This, of course, makes the passage exceedingly tedious.

The principal town at which we landed was Selma, a thriving and pleasant place, situated upon the most perfectly level natural plain I ever saw. In one corner of the town, while rambling on shore, I came upon a tall, ill-proportioned, broken-windowed brick barrack ; it had no grounds about it, was close upon the highway, was in every way dirty, neglected, and forlorn in expression. I inquired what it was, and was informed, the

"Young Ladies' College." There were a number of pretty private gardens in the town, in which I noticed several evergreen oaks, the first I had seen since leaving Savannah.

At Claiborne, another considerable village upon the river, we landed, at nine o'clock on a Sunday night. It is situated upon a bluff, a hundred and fifty feet high, with a nearly perpendicular bank, upon the river. The boat came to the shore at the foot of a plank slide-way, down which cotton was sent to it, from a warehouse at the top.

There was something truly Western in the direct, reckless way in which the boat was loaded. A strong gang-plank being placed at right angles to the slide-way, a bale of cotton was let slide from the top, and, coming down with fearful velocity, on striking the gang-plank, it would rebound up and out on to the boat, against a barricade of bales previously arranged to receive it. The moment it struck this barricade, it would be dashed at by two or three men, and jerked out of the way, and others would roll it to its place for the voyage, on the tiers aft. The mate, standing near the bottom of the slide, as soon as the men had removed one bale to what he thought a safe distance, would shout to those aloft, and down would come another. Not unfrequently, a bale would not strike fairly on its end, and would rebound off, diagonally, overboard; or would be thrown up with such force as to go over the barricade, breaking stanchions and railings, and scattering the passengers on the berth deck. Negro hands were sent to the top of the bank, to roll the bales to the side, and Irishmen were kept below to remove them, and stow them. On asking the mate (with some surmisings) the reason of this arrangement, he said :

"The niggers are worth too much to be risked here; if the Paddies are knocked overboard, or get their backs broke, nobody loses anything!"

The boat being detained the greater part of the night, and the bounding bales making too much noise to allow me to sleep, I ascended the bank by a flight of two hundred steps, placed by the side of the slide-way, and took a walk in the village. In the principal street, I came upon a group of seven negroes, talking in lively, pleasant tones: presently, one of them commenced to sing, and in a few moments all the others joined in, taking different parts, singing with great skill and taste— better than I ever heard a group of young men in a Northern village, without previous arrangement, but much as I have heard a strolling party of young soldiers, or a company of students, or apprentices, in the streets of a German town, at night. After concluding the song, which was of a sentimental character, and probably had been learned at a concert or theatre, in the village, they continued in conversation, till one of them began to whistle: in a few moments all joined in, taking several different parts, as before, and making a peculiarly plaintive music. Soon after this, they walked all together, singing, and talking soberly, by turns, slowly away. I allowed them to pass me, but kept near them, until they reached a cabin, in the outskirts of the village. Stopping near this a few minutes, two of them danced the "juba," while the rest whistled and applauded. After some further chat, one said to the rest: "Come, gentlemen, let's go in and see the ladies," opening the door of the cabin. They entered, and were received by three negro girls, with great heartiness; then all found seats on beds, and stools, and chests, around a great wood fire, and

when I passed again, in a few minutes, they were again
singing.

THE MUSICAL TALENT OF NEGROES.

The love of music which characterizes the negro, the readiness
with which he acquires skill in the art, his power of memorizing
and improvising music is most marked and constant. I think,
also, that sweet musical voices are more common with the
negro than with the white race—certainly than with the white
race in America. I have frequently been startled by clear, bell-
like tones, from a negro woman in conversation, while walking
the streets of a Southern town, and have listened to them with
a thrill of pleasure. A gentleman in Savannah told me that,
in the morning after the performance of an opera in that city,
he had heard more than one negro, who could in no way have
heard it before, whistling the most difficult airs, with perfect accuracy. I have heard ladies say that, whenever they have obtained
any new and choice music, almost as soon as they had learned
it themselves, their servants would have caught the air, and
they were likely to hear it whistled in the streets, the first night
they were out. In all of the Southern cities, there are music
bands, composed of negroes, often of great excellence. The military parades are usually accompanied by a negro brass band.

Dr. Cartwright, arguing that the negro is a race of inferior
capabilities, says that the negro does not understand harmony;
his songs are mere sounds, without sense or meaning. My
observations are of but little value upon such a point, as I have
had no musical education; but they would lead me to the contrary opinion. The common plantation-negroes, or deck-hands
of the steamboats—whose minds are so little cultivated that

they cannot count twenty—will often, in rolling cotton-bales, or carrying wood on board the boat, fall to singing, each taking a different part, and carrying it on with great spirit and independence, and in perfect harmony, as I never heard singers, who had not been considerably educated, at the North.

MATHEMATICAL CAPACITY.

Touching the intellectual capacity of negroes: I was dining with a gentleman, when he asked the waiter—a lad of eighteen—to tell him what the time was. The boy, after studying the clock, replied incorrectly; and the gentleman said it was impossible for him to make the simple calculation necessary. He had promised to give him a dollar, a year ago, whenever he could tell the time by the clock; had taken a good deal of trouble to teach him, but he did not seem to make any progress. I have since met with another negro boy, having the same remarkable inability—both the lads being intelligent, and learning easily in other respects: the first could read. I doubt if it is a general deficiency of the race; both these boys had marked depressions where phrenologists locate the organ of calculation.

A gentleman, whom I visited, in Montgomery, had a carpenter, who was remarkable for his mathematical capacities. Without having had any instruction, he was able to give very close and accurate estimates for the quantity of all descriptions of lumber, to be used in building a large and handsome dwelling, of the time to be employed upon it, and of its cost. He was an excellent workman; and, when not occupied with work directly for his master, obtained employment of others—making engagements, and taking contracts for jobs, without being required to consult his master. He had been purchased for two thousand dollars, and his ordinary wages were two dollars a day.   He earned considerable money besides, for himself, by overwork at his trade, and still more in another way.

SLAVE HIGH LIFE.

He was a good violinist and dancer, and, two nights a week, taught a negro dancing-school, from which he received two dollars a night, which, of course, he spent for his own pleasure. During the winter, the negroes, in Montgomery, have their "assemblies," or dress balls, which are got up "regardless of expense," in very grand style.   Tickets are advertised to these balls, "admitting one gentleman and two ladies, $1;" and "Ladies are assured that they may rely on the strictest order and propriety being observed."   Cards of invitation, finely engraved with handsome vignettes, are sent, not only to the fashionable slaves, but to some of the more esteemed white people, who, however, take no part, except as lookers-on.   All the fashionable dances are executed; no one is admitted, except in full dress: there are the regular masters of ceremonies, floor committees, etc.; and a grand supper always forms a part of the entertainment.

While in a book-store, in Montgomery, I saw a negro looking at some very showy London valentines.   After examining the embossed envelopes, and the colored engravings of hearts and darts, and cupids and doves, he would ask the clerk to read the poetry, and listen while he did so, with the air of a profound critic.   I heard ten dollars mentioned as the price of one of them; and I presume he was ready to pay that price, if he could find an adequate expression of his sentiment.

My friend had so much confidence in the discretion and

faithfulness of his carpenter, that he seldom gave him any orders or directions. To enable him to execute some business with greater celerity, he, one day, in my observation, took a horse that his master was intending to use himself. When asked why he did so, he mentioned the object he had in view, and said : "I thought I needed him more than you did"—and was not reproved.

On visiting a piece of ground that his master owned, out of town, we found him engaged, with two black men and one white—a native, country fellow—in putting up a fence. The latter was acting under his orders; and, upon inquiry, I found that, seeing that the work was needed to be done immediately, he had hired him, as well as the two blacks, without consulting his master. It was the first case I had seen of a white man acting under the orders of a negro, though I have several times since seen Irishmen doing so.

This gay carpenter's wife was a woman of serious sentiments, and preferred prayer-meetings to balls; so they did not agree very well. She belonged to another gentleman, who did not live in the town, and was at service in another family than that with which her husband was connected. She had informed her owner that, if he would like to take her into the country with him, she had no particular objections to being separated from her husband. She did not like him very much—he was "so gay."

NATURAL AFFECTION OF NEGROES.

It is frequently remarked by Southerners, in palliation of the cruelty of separating relatives, that the affections of negroes for one another are very slight. I have been told by more than one lady that she was sure her nurse did not have half the affection for her own children that she did for her mistress's. But it is evident that this loyalty is not peculiar to the black race. Probably there are many white people in Europe, even in this day, who would let their children's lives be sacrificed to save the life of the son of their sovereign. They teach this as a duty, and use the Bible to make it appear so, in Prussia, if not in England.

A very excellent lady, to show me how little cruelty there was in the separation of husband and wife, told me that when she lived at home, on her father's plantation, in South Carolina, he had given her a girl for a dressing-maid. This girl, after a time, married a man on the plantation. The marriage ceremony was performed by an Episcopal clergyman, according to the prayer-book form—the parties, of course, promising to cleave together until death should part them. A year later, the lady herself was to be married, and was to remove with her husband to his residence in Alabama. She told the girl she could do as she pleased—go with her and leave her husband, or remain with her husband and be separated from her. She preferred to cleave to her mistress. She accordingly parted from her husband, with some expressions of regret for the necessity, but with no appearance of grief or sadness. Neither did the husband complain. A month after she reached her new residence in Alabama, she found a new husband; and it was supposed that her former husband had suited himself with a new woman. She had now been living ten years in Alabama, and had several children; she was expecting soon to be taken with her mistress on a visit to the old plantation in South Carolina, and laughed as she spoke of probably meeting her old husband again.

A slave, who was hired (not owned) by a friend of mine in

Savannah, called upon him one morning while I was there, to say that he wished to marry a woman in the evening, and wanted a ticket from him to authorize the ceremony.

"I thought you were married," said my friend.

"Yes, master, but that woman hab leáve me, and go 'long wid 'nodder man."

"Indeed! Why, you had several children by her, did not you?"

"Yes, master, we hab thirteen, but now she gone 'long wid 'nodder man."

"But will your church permit you to marry another woman so soon?"

"Yes, master; I tell 'em de woman I had leave me, and go 'long wid 'nodder man, and she say she don't mean to come back, and I can't be 'spected to lib widout any woman at all, so dey say dey grant me de divorce."

A pleasant example of the child-like confidence which a slave frequently has in his sovereign, when he is a good-hearted and trustworthy man, occurred to me at a hotel, where I had been waited upon for several days by an unusually good servant. One morning, while making a fire for me, he said—

"Dey say Congress is going to be bruck up in tree weeks— I'se glad enough o' dat."

"Glad of it—why so?"

"I'se got a master dah; I'll be a heap glad when he's come back."

"You want to see him again, eh?"

"Yes, sar. I won't stay long in dis place wen he com, nudder. I'll hab im get noder place for me. I don' like dis place, no how; dis place don' suit me; never saw sich a place. Dey kceps me up most all night; I haan been used to sich treatem. Dey haan got but one servant for all dis hall; dey ought to hab two at de least.   I'm de olest servant in de house; all de odder ole servant is gone."

"And they have got Irishmen in their places."

"Yes! and what kine of servant is dey?   Ha! all de Irishmen dat ever I see haden so much sense in dar heds as I could carry in de palm of my han.   I was de head waiter allers in my master's house till my brudder grew up, and I learned him; he's de head waiter now.   And dis heah ant no kine of place for my sort; I don' stay here no longer wen my master come back."

A few mornings after this, he did not come into my room, as usual; I was out during the forenoon; when I returned, he came to me, and said:

"You must excuse me dat I din't be heah to brush your clothes dis mornin', sar; dey had me in de guard-house, last night."

"Had you in the guard-house—what for?"

"Because I was out widout a pass.   You see I don' sleep heah, sar, and I was jes gwine down to de boat, 'bout two o'clock, and dey took me, and put me in de guard-house."

"And what kind of accommodations do they give you at the guard-house?"

"Why, dey makes me pay a dollar for 'em.   I offered dem two dollars las' night, if dey let me go.   I tort dat's de way dey do; make you pay two dollar, or else dey gives you a right smart whippin'; but dey didn'—I don' know why.   I tell you, sar, I nebber felt so mortify in all my life, as wen dey lets me out de guard-house dis mornin', right before all de people in dat ar market-place."

"Well, I suppose it was your own fault."

"*No, sar!* not my own fault 'tall, sar; dey ought to gib me a pass; why not? dey knows I's a married man. Do dey tink I is gwine to sleep heah wid dese nasty niggers? No, sar! I lie out dah on de floor in de passage, and catch my deff of cold first. I aint been use to sich treatem. *I's got a master.* My master's member Congress. Wen dat broks up, he mus fine me nodder place mighty quick. I don' stay heah. I's always been a family servant. You see, sar, I aint use to such treatem. Nebber was sole yet in all my life. My missis' fader was worf four hundred tousand dollar, and we had two plantation. Nebber was in a field in my life—allers was in de house ebber since I was a little chile. I was a kine of pet boy, you see, master. I allers wait on my masser myself till my little brudder got big enough; den I want to go 'way. Oh, I'se a wild chile, you see, sar, and I want to clear out and hab some fun to myself. I's a kine of favorite allers to my mistress. She 'ould do anything for me. She wanted to learn me to read, but I'se too wild. She would gib me a first-rate education, I 'spose, only I's so wild I wouldn'."

"Can't you read at all!"

"Well, I ken read some, but not very well. Dat is, you see, master, dere's *some* of de letters I can't read, not all on 'em I can't; no sar; but I ken read some."

THE CITIZENS.

There were about one hundred passengers on the Fashion, besides a number of poor people and negroes on the lower deck. They were, generally, cotton-planters, going to Mobile on business, or emigrants bound to Texas or Arkansas. They were usually well dressed, but were a rough, coarse style of people, drinking a great deal, and most of the time under a little alcoholic excitement.   Not sociable, except when the topics of cotton, land, and negroes, were started ; interested, however, in talk about theatres and the turf ; very profane ; often showing the handles of concealed weapons about their persons, but not quarrelsome, avoiding disputes and altercations, and respectful to one another in forms of words ; very ill-informed, except on plantation business ; their language very ungrammatical, idiomatic, and extravagant. Their grand characteristics—simplicity of motive, vague, shallow, and purely objective habits of thought ; spontaneity and truthfulness of utterance, and bold, self-reliant movement.

With all their individual independence, I soon could perceive a very great homogeneousness of character, by which they were distinguishable from any other people with whom I had before been thrown in contact ; and I began to study it with interest, as the Anglo-Saxon development of the Southwest.

I found that, more than any people I had ever seen, they were unrateable by dress, taste, forms, and expenditures.   I was perplexed by finding, apparently united in the same individual, the self-possession and confidence of the well equipped gentleman, and the coarseness and low tastes of the uncivilized boor—frankness and reserve, recklessness and self restraint, extravagance, and penuriousness.

There was one man, who " lived, when he was to home," as he told me, " in the Red River Country," in the northeastern part of Texas, having emigrated thither from Alabama, some years before. He was a tall, thin, awkward person, and wore a suit of clothes (probably bought " ready-made") which would have better suited a short, fat figure. Under his waistcoat he carried a large knife, with the hilt generally protruding at the breast.   He had been with his family to his former home, to do a little business, and visit his relatives, and was now returning to his plantation.   His wife was a pale and harassed looking woman; and he scarce ever paid her the smallest attention, not even sitting near her at the public table.   Of his children, however, he seemed very fond; and they had a negro servant in attendance upon them, whom he was constantly scolding and threatening.   Having been from home for six weeks, his impatience to return was very great, and was constantly aggravated by the frequent and long continued stoppages of the boat.   "Time's money, time's money!" he would be constantly saying, while we were taking on cotton, "time's worth more 'n money to me now; a hundred per cent. more, 'cause I left my niggers all alone, not a dam white man within four mile on 'em."

I asked how many negroes he had.

" I've got twenty on 'em to home, and thar they ar! and thar they ar! and thar aint a dam soul of a white fellow within four mile on 'em."

" They are picking cotton, I suppose?"

"No, I got through pickin' fore I left."

" What work have they to do, then, now?"

" I set em to clairin', but they aint doin' a dam thing—not a dam thing, they aint; that's wat they are doin', that is—not a dam thing.   I know that, as well as you do.   That's the reason time's an object.   I told the capting so wen I came a board: 'says I, capting, says I, time is in the objective case with me.' No, sir, they aint doin' a dam solitary thing; that's what they are up to.   I know that as well as anybody; I do.   But I'll make it up, I'll make it up, when I get thar, now you'd better believe."

Once, when a lot of cotton, baled with unusual neatness, was coming on board, and some doubt had been expressed as to the economy of the method of baling, he said very loudly :

"Well, now, I'd be willin' to bet my salvation, that them thar's the heaviest bales that's come on to this boat."

"I'll bet you a hundred dollars of it," answered one.

"Well, if I was in the habit of bettin', I'd do it. I aint a bettin' man. But I am a cotton man, I am, and I don't car who knows it. I know cotton, I do. I'm dam if I know anythin' but cotton. I ought to know cotton, I had. I've been at it ever sin' I was a chile."

"Stranger," he asked me once, "did you ever come up on the Leweezay? She's a right smart, pretty boat, she is, the Leweezay; the best I ever see on the Alabamy river. They wanted me to wait and come down on her, but I told 'em time was in the objective case to me. She is a right pretty boat, and her capting's a high-tone gentleman ; haint no objections to find with him—he's a high-tone gentleman, that's what he is. But the pilot—well, damn him ! He run her right out of the river, up into the woods—didn't run her in the river, at all. When I go aboard a steam-boat, I like to keep in the river, somewar ; but that pilot, he took her right up into the woods. It was just clairin' land. Clairin' land, and playin' hell ginerally, all night ; not follering the river at all. I believe he was drunk. He must have been drunk, for I could keep a boat in the river myself. I'll never go in a boat where the pilot's drunk all the time. I take a glass too much myself, sometimes ; but I don't hold two hundred lives in the holler of my hand. I was in my berth, and he run her straight out of the river, slap up into the furest. It threw me clean out of my berth, out onter the floor; I didn't sleep any more while I was aboard. The Leweezay's a right smart, pretty little boat, and her capting's a high-tone gentleman. They hev good livin' aboard of her, too. Haan't no objections on that score; weddin' fixins all the time; but I won't go in a boat war the pilot's drunk. I set some vally on the life of two hundred souls. They wanted to hev me come down on her, but I told 'em time was in the objective case."

There were three young negroes, carried by another Texan, on the deck, outside the cabin. I don't know why they were not allowed to be with the other emigrant slaves, on the lower deck, unless the owner was afraid of their trying to get away, and had no handcuffs small enough for them. They were boys; the oldest twelve or fourteen years old, the youngest not more than seven. They had evidently been bought lately by their present owner, and probably had just been taken from their parents. They lay on the deck and slept, with no bed but the passengers' luggage, and no cover but a single blanket for each. Early one morning, after a very stormy night, when they must have suffered much from the driving rain and cold, I saw their owner with a glass of spirits, giving each a few swallows from it. The older ones smacked their lips, and said, "Tank 'ou, massa;" but the little one couldn't drink it, and cried aloud, when he was forced to. The older ones were very playful and quarrelsome, and continually teasing the younger, who seemed very sad, or homesick and sulky. He would get very angry at their mischievous fun, and sometimes strike them. He would then be driven into a corner, where he would lie on his back, and kick at them in a perfect frenzy of anger and grief. The two boys would continue to laugh at him, and frequently the passengers would stand about, and be amused by it. Once, when they had plagued him in this way for some time, he jumped up on to the cotton-bales, and made as if he would have plunged overboard. One of the older boys caught him by the ankle, and held him till his master came and hauled him in, and gave him a severe flogging with a rope's end. A number of passengers collected about them, and I heard several say, " That's what he wants." Red River said to me, " I've been a watchin' that ar boy, and I see what's the matter with him; he's got the devil in him right bad, and he'll hev to take a right many of them warmins before it'll be got out."

The crew of the boat, as I have intimated, was composed partly of Irishmen, and partly of negroes; the latter were slaves, and were hired of their owners at $40 a month—the same wages paid to the Irishmen. A dollar of their wages was given to the negroes themselves, for each Sunday they were on the passage. So far as convenient, they were kept at work separately from the white hands; they were also messed separately. On Sunday I observed them dining in a group, on the cotton-bales. The food, which was given to them in tubs, from the kitchen, was various and abundant, consisting of bean-porridge, bacon, corn bread, ship's biscuit, potatoes, duff (pudding), and gravy. There was one knife used only, among ten of them; the bacon was cut and torn into shares; splinters of the bone and of fire-wood were used for forks; the porridge was passed from one to another, and drank out of the tub; but though excessively dirty and beast-like in their appearance and manners, they were good-natured and jocose as usual.

"Heah! you Bill," said one to another, who was on a higher

tier of cotton, " pass down de dessart. You! up dar on de hill;
de dessart! Augh! don't you know what de dessart be? De
duff, you fool."

" Does any of de gemmen want some o' dese potatum?" asked
another ; and no answer being given, he turned the tub full of
potatoes overboard, without any hesitation. It was evident he
had never had to think on one day how he should be able to
live the next.

Whenever we landed at night or on Sunday, for wood or cotton, there would be many negroes come on board from the
neighboring plantations, to sell eggs to the steward.

Sunday was observed by the discontinuance of public gambling
in the cabin, and in no other way. At midnight gambling was
resumed, and during the whole passage was never at any other
time discontinued, night or day, so far as I saw. There were
three men that seemed to be professional sharpers, and who
probably played into each other's hands. One young man lost
all the money he had with him—several hundred dollars.

MOBILE.

Mobile, in its central, business part, is very compactly built,
dirty, and noisy, with little elegance, or evidence of taste or
public spirit, in its people. A small, central, open square—the
only public ground that I saw—was used as a horse and hog
pasture, and clothes drying-yard. Out of the busier quarter,
there is a good deal of the appearance of a thriving New England village—almost all the dwelling-houses having plots of
ground enclosed around them, planted with trees and shrubs.
The finest trees are the magnolia and live oak; and the most
valuable shrub is the Cherokee rose, which is much used for

hedges and screens. It is evergreen, and its leaves are glossy and beautiful at all seasons, and in March it blooms profusely. There is an abundance, also, of the Cape jessamine. It is as beautiful as a camelia; and, when in blossom, scents the whole air with a most delicate and delicious fragrance. At a market-garden, near the town which I visited, I found most of the best Northern and Belgian pears fruiting well, and apparently healthy, and well-suited in climate, on quince-stocks. Figs are abundant, and bananas and oranges are said to be grown with some care, and slight winter protection.

The Battle House, kept by Boston men, with Irish servants, I found an excellent hotel; but with higher charges than I had ever paid before. Prices, generally, in Mobile, range very high. There are large numbers of foreign merchants in the population; but a great deficiency of tradesmen and mechanics.

While I was at Montgomery, my hat was one day taken from the dining-room, at dinner-time, by some one who left, in its place, for me, a very battered and greasy substitute, which I could not wear, if I had chosen to. I asked the landlord what I should do to effect a reëxchange: "Be before him, to-morrow." Following this cool advice, and, in the mean time, wearing a cap, I obtained my hat the next day; but so ill used, that I should not have known it, but for Mr. Beebe's name, stamped within it. Not succeeding in fitting myself with a new hat, I desired to have my old one pressed, when in Mobile; but I could not find a working hatter in the place, though it boasts a population of thirty thousand souls. Finally, a hat-dealer, a German Jew, I think he was, with whom I had left it while looking further, returned it to me, with a charge of one dollar, for brushing it—the benefit of which brushing I was unable, in the least, to perceive. A friend informed me that he found it cheaper to have all his furniture and clothing made for him, in New York, to order, when he needed any, and sent on by express, than to get it in Mobile.

The great abundance of the best timber for the purpose, in the United States, growing in the vicinity of the town, has lately induced some persons to attempt ship-building at Mobile. The mechanics employed are mainly from the North.

The great business of the town is the transfer of cotton, from the producer to the manufacturer, from the wagon and the steam-boat to the sea-going ship. Like all the other cotton-ports, Mobile labors under the disadvantage of a shallow harbor. At the wharves, there were only a few small craft and steam-boats. All large sea-going vessels lie some thirty miles below, and their freights are transhipped in lighters.

There appears to be a good deal of wealth and luxury, as well as senseless extravagance, in the town. English merchants affect the character of the society, considerably; some very favorably—some, very much otherwise. Many of them own slaves, and, probably, all employ them; but Slavery seems to be of more value to them from the amusement it affords, than in any other way. " So-and-so advertises 'a valuable drayman, and a good blacksmith and horse-shoer, for sale, on reasonable terms;' an acclimated double-entry book-keeper, kind in harness, is what I want," said one; " those Virginia patriarchs haven't any enterprise, or they'd send on a stock of such goods every spring, to be kept over through the fever, so they could warrant them."

" I don't know where you'll find one," replied another; " but if you are wanting a private chaplain, there's one I have heard, in ——— street, several times, that could probably be bought for a fair price; and I will warrant him sound enough in wind, if not in doctrine."

" I wouldn't care for his doctrine, if I bought him; I don't care how black he is, feed him right, and, in a month, he will be as orthodox as an archbishop."

MOBILE TO NEW ORLEANS.

The steam-boat by which I made the passage along the north shore of the Mexican Gulf to New Orleans, was New York built, and owned by a New-Yorker; and the Northern usage of selling passage tickets, to be returned on leaving the boat, was retained upon it. I was sitting near a group of Texans and emigrating planters, when a waiter passed along, crying the usual request, that passengers who had not obtained tickets, would call at the captain's office for that purpose. " What's that? What's that?" they shouted; " What did he mean? What is it?" " Why, it's a dun," said one. " Damned if 'taint," continued one and another; "he is dunnin' on us, sure," and some started from the seats, as if they thought it insulting. " Well, it's the first time I ever was dunned by a nigger, I'll swar," said one. This seemed to place it in a humorous aspect; and, after a hearty laugh, they resumed their discussion of the advantages offered to emigrants in different parts of Texas, and elsewhere.

A party of very fashionably-dressed and gay, vulgar people, were placed near me at the dinner-table; opposite, a stout, strong, rough and grim-looking Texan, and his quiet, amiable wife. There was an unusual number of passengers, and consequently a great deficiency of waiters, and the only one in our vicinity had been entirely engaged with the fashionable party;

their plates had all been changed, and he had opened two or three bottles of wine for them, without paying any regard to the rest of us. At length the Texan, who had been holding a plate ready to hand to the waiter, and following his motions for a long time, with an eye full of hunger and disgust, as he was again dashing off to execute an order, shouted, with a voice loud enough to be heard the length of the boat, while he looked defiantly at the small, moustached person opposite, who had given the order, " *Boy!*" "Sir," said the negro, turning at once. "Give us something to eat here! damned if I—" "Hush," said his wife, clapping her hand on his mouth. "Well, if—" "Hush, my dear, hush," said his wife, again putting her hand across his mouth, but joining in the universal smile. The fashionable people did not call upon the waiter again till we all had got "something to eat."

There was a young man on the boat who had been a passenger with me in coming down the river. He was bound for Texas; and while on board the Fashion I had heard him saying that he had met with "a right smart bad streak of luck" on his way, having lost a valuable negro. "I thought you were going on with those men to Texas, the other day," said I.

"No," he replied, "I left my sister in Mobile, when I went back after my nigger, and when I came down again, I found that she had found an old acquaintance there, and they had concluded to get married; so I staid to see the wedding."

"Rather quick work."

"Well, I reckon they'd both thought about it when they knew each other before; but I didn't know it, and it kind o' took me by surprise. So my other sister, she concluded Ann had done so well stopping in Mobile, she'd stop and keep com-

pany with her a spell; and so I've got to go 'long alone. Makes
me feel kind o' lonesome—losing that nigger too."

"Did you say that you went back after the nigger? I
thought he died?"

"Well, you see I had brought him along as far as Mobile, and
he got away from me there, and slipped aboard a steam-boat
going back, and hid himself. I found out that he was aboard of
her pretty soon after she got off, and I sent telegraphic dis-
patches to several places along up the river, to the captain, to
put him in a jail, ashore, for me. I know he got one of them at
Cahawba, but he didn't mind it till he got to Montgomery.
Well, the nigger didn't have any attention paid to him. They
just put him in irons; likely enough he didn't get much to eat,
or have anything to cover himself, and he took cold, and got
sick—got pneumonia—and when they got to Montgomery, they
made him walk up to the jail, and there wan't no fire, and
nothin' to lie on, nor nothin' for him in the jail, and it made
quick work with him. Before I could get up there he was dead.
I see an attorney here to Mobile, and he offered to take the case,
and prosecute the captain; and he says if he don't recover every
red cent the man's worth, he wont ask me for a fee. It comes
kinder hard on me. I bought the nigger up, counting I should
make a speculation on him; reckoned I'd take him to Texas if
I couldn't turn him to good advantage at Mobile. As niggers
is goin' here now, I expect 'twas a dead loss of eight hundred
dollars, right out of pocket."

There were a large number of steerage passengers occupying
the main deck, forward of the shaft. Many of them were Irish,
late immigrants, but the large majority were slaves, going on to
New Orleans to be sold, or moving with their masters to Texas.

There was a fiddle or two among them, and they were very merry, dancing and singing. A few, however, refused to join in the amusement, and looked very disconsolate. A large proportion of them were boys and girls, under twenty years of age.

On the forecastle-deck there was a party of emigrants, moving with wagons. There were three men, a father and his two sons, or sons-in-law, with their families, including a dozen or more women and children. They had two wagons, covered with calico and bed-ticks, supported by hoops, in which they carried their furniture and stores, and in which they also slept at night, the women in one, and the men in the other. They had six horses, two mules, and two pair of cattle with them. I asked the old man why he had taken his cattle along with him, when he was going so far by sea, and found that he had informed himself accurately of what it would cost him to hire or buy cattle at Galveston; and that taking into account the probable delay he would experience in looking for them there, he had calculated that he could afford to pay the freight on them, to have them with him, to go on at once into the country on his arrival, rather than to sell them at Mobile.

"But," said he, "there was one thing I didn't cakulate on, and I don't understand it; the capting chorged me two dollars and a half for 'wherfage.' I don't know what that means, do you? I want to know, because I don't car' to be imposed upon by nobody. I paid it without sayin' a word, 'cause I never traveled on the water before; next time I do, I shall be more sassy." I asked where he was going. "Didn't know much about it," he said, "but reckoned he could find a place where there was a good range, and plenty of game. If 'twas as good a range (pasture) as 'twas to Alabama when he first came there, he'd be satisfied." After he'd got his family safe through acclimating this time, he reckoned he shouldn't move again. He had moved about a good deal in his life. There was his littlest boy, he said, looking kindly at a poor, thin, blue-faced little child—he reckoned they'd be apt to *leave* him; he had got *tropsical*, and was of mighty weak constitution, nat'rally; 'twouldn't take much to carry him off, and, of course, a family must be exposed a good deal, moving so this time of year. They should try to find some heavy timbered land—good land, and go to clearing; didn't calculate to make any crops the first year—didn't calculate on it, though perhaps they might if they had good luck. They had come from an eastern county of Alabama. Had sold out his farm for two dollars an acre; best land in the district was worth four; land was naturally kind of thin, and now 'twas pretty much all worn out there. He had moved first from North Carolina, with his father. They never made anything to sell but cotton; made corn for their own use. Never had any negroes; reckoned he'd done about as well as if he had had them; reckoned a little better on the whole. No, he should not work negroes in Texas. "Niggers is so kerless, and want so much lookin' arter; they is so monstrous lazy; they won't do no work, you know, less you are clus to 'em all the time, and I don't feel like it. I couldn't, at my time of life, begin a-using the lash; and you know they do have to take that, all on 'em—and a heap on't, sometimes."

"I don't know much about it; they don't have slaves where I live."

"Then you come from a Free State; well, they've talked some of makin' Alabamy a Free State."

"I didn't know that."

"O, yes, there was a good deal of talk one time, as if they was goin' to do it right off. O, yes; there was two or three of the States this way, one time, come pretty nigh freein' the niggers—lettin' 'em all go free."

"And what do you think of it?"

"Well, I'll tell you what I think on it; I'd like it if we could get rid on 'em to yonst. I wouldn't like to hev 'em freed, if they was gwine to hang 'round. They ought to get some country, and put 'em war they could be by themselves. It wouldn't do no good to free 'em, and let 'em hang round, because they is so monstrous lazy; if they hadn't got nobody to take keer on 'em, you see they wouldn't do nothin' but juss nat'rally laze round, and steal, and pilfer, and no man couldn't live, you see, war they was—if they was free, no man couldn't live. And then, I've two objections; that's one on 'em—no man couldn't live—and this ere's the other: Now suppose they was free, you see they'd all think themselves just as good as we; of course they would, if they was free. Now, just suppose you had a family of children, how would you like to hev a niggar feelin' just as good as a white man? how'd you like to hev a niggar steppin' up to your darter? Of course you wouldn't; and that's the reason I wouldn't like to hev 'em free; but I tell you, I don't think its right to hev 'em slaves so; that's the fac—taant right to keep 'em as they is."

CHAPTER X.

EXPERIENCE OF ALABAMA.

"And if these sorts of men surprise less by their wandering, as for the most part, without wandering, the business of their life was impossible; of those again who dedicate their life to the soil, we should certainly expect that they at least were fixed. By no means! Even without possession, occupation is conceivable; and we behold the eager farmer forsaking the ground which for years had yielded him profit and enjoyment. Impatiently he searches after similar, or greater profit, be it far or near. Nay, the owner himself will abandon his new grubbed clearage so soon as, by his cultivation, he has rendered it commodious for a less enterprising husbandman; once more he presses into the wilderness; again makes space for himself in the forests; in recompense of that first toiling a double and treble space; on which also, it may be, he thinks not to continue." —*Meister's Travels. Gœthe.*

ECONOMICAL EXPERIENCE.

The territorial Government of Alabama was established in 1816, and in 1818 she was admitted as a State into the Union. In 1820, her population was 128,000; in 1850, it had increased to 772,000; the increase of the previous ten years having been 30 per cent. (that of South Carolina was 5 per cent.; of Georgia, 31; Mississippi, 60; Michigan, 87; Wisconsin, 890). A large part of Alabama has yet a strikingly frontier character. Even from the State-house, in the fine and promising town of Montgomery, the eye falls in every direction upon a dense forest, boundless as the sea, and producing in the mind the same solemn sensation. Towns frequently referred to as important points in the stages of your journey, when you reach them, you are surprised to find consist of not more than three or four cabins, a tavern or grocery, a blacksmith's shop, and a stable.

A stranger once meeting a coach, in which I was riding, asked the driver whether it would be prudent for him to pass through one of these places, that we had just come from; he had heard that there were more than fifty cases of small-pox in the town. "There ain't fifty people in the town, nor within ten mile on't," answered the driver, who was a northerner. The best of the country roads are but little better than open passages for strong vehicles through the woods, made by cutting away the trees.

The greater number of planters own from ten to twenty slaves only, though plantations on which from fifty to a hundred are employed are not uncommon, especially on the rich alluvial soils of the southern part of the State. Many of the largest and most productive plantations are extremely unhealthy in summer, and their owners seldom reside upon them, except temporarily. Several of the larger towns, like Montgomery, remarkable in the midst of the wilderness which surrounds them, for the neatness and tasteful character of the houses and gardens which they contain, are in a considerable degree, made up of the residences of gentlemen who own large plantations in the hotter and less healthful parts of the State. Many of these have been educated in the older States, and with minds enlarged and liberalized by travel, they form, with their families, cultivated and attractive society.

Much the larger proportion of the planters of the State live in log-houses, some of them very neat and comfortable, but frequently rude in construction, not *chinked*, with windows unglazed, and wanting in many of the commonest conveniences possessed by the poorest class of Northern farmers and laborers of the older States. Many of those who live in this way, possess considerable numbers of slaves, and are every year buying more. Their early frontier life seems to have destroyed all capacity to enjoy many of the usual luxuries of civilized life.

Notwithstanding the youth of the State, there is a constant and extensive emigration from it, as well as immigration to it. Large planters, as their stock increases, are always anxious to enlarge the area of their land, and will often pay a high price for that of any poor neighbor, who, embarrassed by debt, can be tempted to move on. There is a rapid tendency in Alabama, as in the older Slave States, to the enlargement of plantations. The poorer class are steadily driven to occupy poor land, or move forward on to the frontier.

In an Address before the Chunnenuggee Horticultural Society, by Hon. C. C. Clay, Jr., reported by the author in De Bow's Review, December, 1855, I find the following passage. I need add not a word to it to show how the political experiment of old Virginia, the Carolinas, and Georgia, is being repeated to the same cursed result in young Alabama. The author, it is fair to say, is devoted to the sustentation of Slavery, and would not, for the world, be suspected of favoring any scheme for arresting this havoc of wealth, further than by chemical science :

"I can show you, with sorrow, in the older portions of Alabama, and in my native county of Madison, the sad memorials of the artless and exhausting culture of cotton. Our small planters, after taking the cream off their lands, unable to restore them by rest, manures, or otherwise, are going further west and south, in search of other virgin lands, which they may and will despoil and impoverish in like manner. *Our wealthier planters, with greater means and no more skill, are buying out their poorer neighbors, extending their plantations, and adding to their slave force. The wealthy few, who are able to live on smaller profits, and to give their blasted fields some rest, are thus pushing off the many, who are merely independent.*

"Of the twenty millions of dollars annually realized from the sales of the cotton crop of Alabama, nearly all not expended in supporting the producers is reinvested in land and negroes. Thus the white population has decreased, and the slave increased, almost *pari passu* in several counties of our State. In 1825, Madison county cast about 3,000 votes; now she cannot cast exceeding 2,300. *In traversing that county one will discover numerous farm-houses, once the abode of industrious and intelligent freemen, now occupied by slaves, or tenantless, deserted, and dilapidated ; he will observe fields, once fertile, now unfenced, abandoned, and covered with those evil harbingers—fox-tail and broom-sedge; he will see the moss growing on the mouldering walls of once thrifty villages ; and will find ' one only master grasps the whole domain' that once furnished happy homes for a dozen white families. Indeed, a country in its infancy, where, fifty years ago, scarce a forest tree had been felled by the axe of the pioneer, is already exhibiting the painful signs of senility and decay, apparent in Virginia and the Carolinas; the freshness of its agricultural glory is gone; the vigor of its youth is extinct, and the spirit of desolation seems brooding over it.*"

CHAPTER XI.

LOUISIANA.

NEW ORLEANS.

I was awakened, in the morning, by the loud ringing of a hand-bell; and, turning out of my berth, dressed by dim lamp-light. The waiters were serving coffee and collecting baggage; and, upon stepping out of the cabin, I found that the boat was made fast to a long wooden jetty, and the passengers were going ashore. A passage-ticket for New Orleans was handed me, as I crossed the gang-plank. There was a rail-track and a train of cars upon the wharf, but no locomotive; and I got my baggage checked, and walked on toward the shore.

It was early day-light—a fog rested on the water, and only the nearest point could be discerned. There were many small buildings near the jetty, erected on piles over the water—bathing-houses, bowling-alleys, and billiard-rooms, with other indications of a place of holiday resort—and, on reaching the shore, I found a slumbering village. The first house from the wharf had a garden about it, with complex alleys, and tables, and arbors, and rustic seats, and cut shrubs, and shells, and statues, and vases, and a lamp was feebly burning in a large lantern over the entrance-gate. I was thinking how like it was to a rural restaurant in France or Germany, when a locomotive backed, scream-ing hoarsely, down the jetty; and I returned to get my seat.

Off we puffed, past the restaurant, into the village—the name of which I did not inquire, everybody near me seemed so cold and cross, and I have not learned it since—through the little village of white houses—whatever it was—and away into a dense, gray cypress forest. For three or four rods, each side of the track, the trees had all been felled and removed, leaving a dreary strip of swamp, covered with stumps. This was bounded and intersected by broad ditches, or narrow and shallow canals, with a great number of very small punts in them—which, I suppose, are used for shrimp catching. So it continued, for two or three miles; then the ground became dryer, there was an abrupt termination of the grey wood. The fog was lifting and drifting off, in ragged, rosy clouds, and liberty of the eye was given over a flat country, skirted still, and finally bounded, in the back-ground, with the swamp-forest. There were scattered, irregularly over it, a few low houses, one story high, all having verandahs before them.

At length, a broad road struck in by the side of the track; the houses became frequent; soon it was a village street, with smoke ascending from breakfast fires; windows and doors opening, girls sweeping steps, bakers' wagons passing, and broad streets, little built upon, breaking off at right angles.

At the corners of these streets, were high poles, connected at the top by a rope, and furnished with blocks and halyards, by which great square lanterns were slung over the middle of the carriage-way. I thought again of France, and of the dread cry, "*a la lanterne!*" and turning to one of my cold and cross companions—a man wrapped in a loose coat, with a cowl over his head—I asked the name of the village, for my geography was at fault. I had expected to be landed at New Orleans by the boat, and had not been informed of the rail-road arrangement, and had no idea in what part of Louisiana we might be.

"Note Anglische, sare," was the gruff reply.

There was a sign, " *Café du Faubourg*," and, putting my head out of the window, I saw that we were thundering into New Orleans.   We reached the terminus, which was surrounded with *fiacres*, in the style of Paris.   "To the hotel St. Charles," I said to a driver, confused with the loud French and quiet English of the crowd about me.   " *Oui*, yer 'onor," was the reply of my Irish-born fellow-citizen: another passenger was got, and away we rattled through narrow dirty streets, among grimy old stuccoed walls; high, arched windows and doors, balconies and entresols, and French noises and French smells (nothing so strong, in associations, as old smells); French signs, ten to one of English, but with funny polygomatic arrangements, sometimes, from which less influential families were not excluded; thus:

"APARTEMENTS TO LET.

A LA FEE AUX ROSES.

WEIN BIER EN DETAIL.

CHAMBRES A LOUER.

UPHOLSTERS IN ALL ITS BRANCHES.

KOSSUTH COFFEE HOUSE.

DEPOT DES GRAINES POUR LES OISEAUX.

To Loyaute Intelligence Office, only for the girls and women answerung ho!   On demande, 50 hommes pour la chemin-de-fer.   Wanted to work in the Rail-road some men now.

Defense d'afficher!"

The other fare, whom I had not ventured to speak to, was set down at a *salle pour la vente des* somethings, and soon after the *fiacre* turned out upon a broad place, covered with bales of cotton, and casks of sugar, and weighing scales, and disclosing an astonishing number of steam-boats, lying all close together in a line, the ends of which were lost in the mist, which still hung upon the river.

Now the signs became English, and the new brick buildings American. We turned into a broad street, in which shutters were being taken from great glass store-fronts, and clerks were exercising their ingenuity in the display of muslin, and silks, and shawls. In the middle of the broad street there was an open space of waste ground, looking as if the corporation had not been able to pave the whole of it at once, and had left this interval to be attended to when the treasury was better filled. Crossing through a gap in this waste, we entered a narrow street of high buildings, French, Spanish, and English signs, the latter predominating; and at the second block, I was landed before the great Grecian portico of the stupendous, tasteless, ill-contrived and inconvenient St. Charles Hotel.

After a bath and breakfast, I returned, with great interest, to wander in the old French town, the characteristics of which I have sufficiently indicated. Among the houses, one occasionally sees a relic of ancient Spanish builders, while all the newer edifices have the characteristics of the unartistic and dollar pursuing Yankees.

I was delighted when I reached the old Place d'Armes, now a public garden, bright with the orange and lemon trees, and roses, and myrtles, and laurels, and jessamines of the south of France. Fronting upon it is the old Hotel de Ville, still the city court-house, a quaint old French structure, with scaly and vermiculated surface, and deep-worn door-sills, and smooth-rubbed corners; the most picturesque and historic-looking public building, except the highly-preserved, little old court-house at Newport, that I can now think of in the United States.

Adjoining it is an old Spanish cathedral, damaged by paint, and late alterations and repairs, but still a fine thing in our desert of the reverend in architecture. Enough, that while it is not new, it is not shabby, and is not tricked out with much frippery,* gingerbread and confectionery work. The door is open; coaches and crippled beggars are near it. A priest, with a face in which the expression of an owl and an ape are combined, is coming out. If he were not otherwise to be heartily welcomed to fresh air and sunlight, he should be so for the sake of the Sister of Charity who is following him, probably to some death-bed, with a corpse-like face herself, haggard but composed, pensive and absorbed, and with the eyes of a broken heart. I may yet meet them looking down compassionately and soothingly, in some far distant pestilent or war-hospital. In lieu of holy-water then, here is money for the poor-box, though the devil share it unfairly with good angels.

Dark shadows, and dusky light, and deep subdued, low organ strains pervade the interior; and, on the bare floor, here are the kneeling women—"good" and "bad" women—and, ah! yes, white and black women, bowed in equality before their common Father. "Ridiculously absurd idea," say democratic Governors McDuffie and Hammond; "Self-evident," said our ancestors, and so must say the voice of conscience, in all free, humble hearts.

* Contemptible; from the root Fripper, to wear out.—WEBSTER.

In the crowded market-place, there were not only the pure old Indian Americans, and the Spanish, French, English, Celtic, and African, but nearly all possible mixed varieties of these, and no doubt of some other breeds of mankind.

GRADATIONS OF COLOR.

The various grades of the colored people are designated by the French as follows, according to the greater or less predominance of negro blood:

Sacatra, - - - - -	griffe and negress.
Griffe, - - - - -	negro and mulatto.
Marabon, - - - - -	mulatto and griffe.
Mulatto, - - - - -	white and negro.
Quarteron, - - - - -	white and mulatto.
Metif, - - - - -	white and quarteron.
Meamelouc, - - - - -	white and metif.
Quarteron, - - -	white and meamelouc.
Sang-mele, - - - - -	white and quarteron.

And all these, with the sub-varieties of them, French, Spanish, English, and Indian, and the sub-sub-varieties, such as Anglo-Indian-mulatto, I believe experts pretend to be able to distinguish. Whether distinguishable or not, it is certain they all exist in New Orleans.

They say that the cross of the French and Spanish with the African produces a finer and a healthier result than that of the more Northern European races. Certainly, the French Quadroons are very handsome and healthy in appearance; and I should not be surprised if really thorough and sufficient scientific observation should show them to be more vigorous than either of the parent races.

Some of the colored women spoke French, Spanish, and English, as their customers demanded.*

Three taverns, bearing the sign of "The Pig and Whistle," indicated the recent English, a cabaret to the Universal Republic, with a red flag, the French, and the Gasthaus zum Rhein platz, the Teutonic contributions to the strength of our nation. A policeman, with the richest Irish brogue, directed me back to the St. Charles.

FINE STOCK.

In front of a large New York clothing store, twenty-two negroes were standing in a row. They each wore a suit of blue cloth clothing, and a black hat, and each held a bundle of additional clothing, and a pair of shoes, in his hands. They were all, but one, who was probably a driver having charge of them, young men, not over twenty-five, and the majority, I should think, were between eighteen and twenty-two years of age. Their owner was probably in the clothing store, settling for the outfit he had purchased for them, and they were waiting to be led to the steam-boat, which should convey them to his plantation. They were silent and sober, like a file of soldiers "standing at ease;" and, perhaps, were gratified by the admiration their fine manly figures and uniform dress obtained from the passers by.

*[From the New Orleans Picayune.]
"FIFTY DOLLARS REWARD.—Ran away from the subscriber, about two months ago, a bright mulatto girl, named Mary, about twenty-five years of age, almost white, and reddish hair, front teeth out, a cut on her upper lip; about five feet five inches high; has a scar on her forehead; she passes for free; talks *French, Italian, Dutch, English, and Spanish.*
                                                              "ANDRE GRASSO.
  "Upper side of St. Mary's Market."

"Well, now, that ar's the likeliest lot of niggers I ever see," said one, to me. "Some feller's bin roun', and just made his pick out o' all the jails* in Orleens. Must ha' cost him a heap o' rocks. I don't reckon thar's a nigger in that crowd that wouldn't fetch twelve hundred dollars, at a vandue. Twenty thousand dollars wouldn' be no banter for 'em. Dam'd if they aint just the best gang o' cotton-hands ever I see. Give me half on 'em, and I'd sign off—wouldn' ask nothing more."

Louisiana or Texas, thought I, pays Virginia twenty-odd thousand dollars for that lot of bone and muscle. Virginia's interest in continuing the business may be imagined, especially if, in their place, could come free laborers, to help her people at the work she needs to have done; but where is the advantage of it to Louisiana, and especially to Texas? Yonder is a steam-boat load of the same material—bone and muscle—which, at the same sort of valuation, is worth two hundred and odd thousand dollars; and off it goes, past Texas, through Louisiana —far away yet, up the river, and Wisconsin or Iowa will get it, two hundred thousand dollars' worth, to say nothing of the thalers and silver groschen, in those strong chests—all for nothing.

In ten years' time, how many mills, and bridges, and school-houses, and miles of rail-road, will the Germans have built? And how much cloth and fish will they want from Massachusetts, iron from Pennsylvania, and tin from Banca, hemp from Russia, tea from China, and coffee from Brazil, fruit from Spain, wine from Ohio, and oil and gold from the Pacific, silk from France, sugar from Louisiana, cotton from Texas, and rags from Italy,

* The private establishments, in which stocks of slaves are kept for sale in New Orleans, are called jails.

lead from Illinois, and antimony from Hungary, notions from Connecticut, and machines from New Jersey, and intelligence from everywhere?

And how much of all these things will the best two hundred Virginians that Louisiana can buy, at any price, demand of commerce, in ten years?

The world's prejudice against Slavery is not inconsistent with natural depravity. Every man's selfishness, everywhere, unless he is a slave-owner, or means to be one, should war with it.

But would the Germans be willing to live in the warm climate —and, if Virginia did not furnish negroes—could Texas furnish us cotton?

Hundreds of them have told me they would prefer to live in the South, were it not for Slavery, and its influences. As to whether they could, listen to Mr. Darby, the surveyor and geographer of Louisiana:

" Between the 9th of July, 1805, to the 7th of May, 1815, incredible as it may appear to many persons, I actually traveled [in Southern Alabama, Mississippi, Louisiana and, what is now, Texas] twenty thousand miles, mostly on foot. During the whole of this period, I was not confined one month, put all my indispositions together, and not one moment, by any malady attributable to climate. I have slept in the open air for weeks together, in the hottest summer nights, and endured this mode of life in the most matted woods, perhaps, in the world. During my survey of the Sabine river, myself, and the men that attended me, existed, for several weeks, on flesh and fish, without bread or salt, and without sickness, of any kind. That nine-tenths of the distempers of warm climates may be guarded against, I do not harbor a single doubt.

" If climate operates extensively upon the actions of human beings, it is principally their amusements that are regulated by proximity to the tropics. Dancing might be called the principal amusement of both sexes, in Louisiana. Beholding the airy sweep of a Creole dance, the length of time that an assembly will persevere in the sport, at any season of the year, cold or warm, indolence would be the last charge that candor could lodge against such a people."

" Copying from Montesquieu," elsewhere says Mr. Darby, himself a slaveholder, " climate has been called upon to account for stains on the human character, imprinted by the hand of political mistake. No country where Negro Slavery is established but must have part in the wounds committed on nature and justice."

A writer in *Household Words*, speaking of the "popular fallacy, that a man cannot do a hard day's work in the climate of India," says :

" I have seen as hard work, real bone and muscle work, done by citizens of the United Kingdom in the East, as was ever achieved in the cold West, and all upon rice and curry—not curry and rice—in which the rice has formed the real meal, and the curry has merely helped to give it a relish, as a sort of substantial Kitchener's zest, or Harvey's sauce. I have seen, likewise, Moormen, Malabars, and others of the Indian laboring classes, perform a day's work that would terrify a London porter, or coal-whipper, or a country navvy, or ploughman ; and under the direct rays of a sun, that has made a wooden platform too hot to stand on, in thin shoes, without literally dancing with pain, as I have done many a day, within six degrees of the line."

MECHANICS AND LABORERS.

A mechanic, English by birth, who had lived in New Orleans for several years, always going up the river in the summer, to escape the danger of fever in the city, told me that he could lay up money much more rapidly there than in New York. The expenses of living were not necessarily greater than in New York. If a man kept house, and provided for himself, he could live much cheaper than at boarding-houses. Many unmarried mechanics, therefore, lived with colored mistresses, who were commonly vile and dishonest. He was at a boarding-house, where he paid four dollars a week. In New York he had paid three dollars, but the board was not as good as in New Orleans. "The reason," said he, "that people say it costs so much more to live here than in New York is, that what they think treats in New York, they consider necessaries here. Everybody lives freer, and spends their money more willingly here." When he first came to New Orleans, a New England mechanic came with him. He supposed him to have been previously a man of sober habits; but almost immediately after he got to New Orleans, he got into bad ways, and in a few months he was so often drunk, and brought so much scandal on their boarding-house, that he was turned out of it. Soon after this, he called on him, and borrowed two dollars. He said he could not live in New Orleans, it was too expensive, and he was going to Texas. This was several years before, and he had not heard from him since. He had left a family in New England; and this he said was a very common course with New England boys, who had been "too carefully brought up at home," when they came to New Orleans. The master mechanics, who bought up slaves, and took contracts for work, he said, made more money than any others. They did so because they did very poor work—poorer than white mechanics could generally be got to do. But nearly all work was done in New Orleans more hastily and carelessly than in New York, though he thought it was bad enough there. The slave-holding bosses could get no white men to work with their slaves, except Irishmen or Germans—no man who had any regard for his position among his fellow-craftsmen would ever let himself be seen working with a negro. He said I could see any day in Canal street, "a most revolting sight"—Irishmen waiting on negro masons. He had seen, one morning as he was going to his work, a negro carrying some mortar, when another negro hailed him with a loud laugh: "Hallo! you is turned Irishman, is 'ou?" White working men were rapidly displacing the slaves in all sorts of work, and he hoped and believed it would not be many years before every negro would be driven out of the town. He thought acclimated white men could do more hard work than negroes, even in the hottest weather, if they were temperate, and avoided too stimulating food. That, he said, was the general opinion among those of them who staid over summer. Those who drank much whisky and cordials, and kept up old habits of eating, just as if they were in England, were the ones who complained most of the climate, and who thought white men were not made to work in it. He had staid as late as July, and returned in September, and he never saw the day in which he could not do as much work as he did in London.

A New-Yorker, that I questioned about this, said: "I have worked through the very hottest weather, steadily, day after day, and done more work than any three niggers in the State, and been no worse for it. A man has only got to take some care of himself."

Going to Lafayette, on the top of an omnibus, I heard an Irishman, somewhat over-stimulated, as Irishmen are apt to be, loudly declare himself an abolitionist; a companion endeavored in vain to stop him, or make him recant, and finally declared he would not ride any further with him if he would not be more discreet.

The *Morehouse* (Louisiana) *Advocate*, in an article abusive of foreigners, thus describes what, if foreign born working men were not generally so ignorant and easily imposed upon as they are, would undoubtedly be (although they certainly have not yet generally been) their sentiments with regard to Slavery:

"The great mass of foreigners who come to our shores are laborers, and consequently come in competition with slave labor. It is to their interest to abolish Slavery; and we know full well the disposition of man to promote all things which advance his own interests. These men come from nations where Slavery is not allowed, and they drink in abolition sentiments from their mothers' breasts; they (all the white race), entertain an utter abhorrence of being put on a level with blacks, whether in the field or in the work-shop. Could Slavery be abolished, there would be a greater demand for laborers, and the prices of labor must be greatly enhanced. These may be termed the internal evidences of the abolitionism of foreigners.

"But we may find near home facts to corroborate these 'internal' evidences: It is well known that there exists a great antipathy among draymen and rivermen of New Orleans (who are almost to a man foreigners) to the participation of slaves in these branches of industry."

It is obvious that free men have very much gained the field of labor in New Orleans to themselves. The majority of the cartmen, hackney-coach men, porters, rail-road hands, public waiters, and common laborers, as well as of skilled mechanics, appear to be white men; and of the negroes employed in those avocations, a considerable proportion are free.

This is the case here more than in any other town in Slavery, although the climate is torrid, and inconvenient or dangerous to strangers; because New Orleans is more extensively engaged in commerce, and because there is, by the passing and sojourning immigration from Europe, constantly in the city a sufficient number of free laborers, to sustain, by competition and association with each other, the habits of free-labor communities. It is plainly perceptible that the white working men in New Orleans have more business-like manners, and more assured self-respect, than those of smaller towns. They are even not without *esprit du corps*.

As Commerce, or any high form of industry requires intelligence in its laborers, slaves can never be brought together in dense communities, but their intelligence will increase to a degree dangerous to those who enjoy the benefit of their labor. The slave must be kept dependent, day by day, upon his master for his daily bread, or he will find, and will declare his independence, in all respects, of him. This condition disqualifies the slave for any but the simplest and rudest forms of labor; and every attempt to bring his labor into competition with free labor can only be successful at the hazard of insurrection. Hundreds of slaves in New Orleans must be constantly reflecting and saying to one another, "I am as capable of taking care of myself as this Irish hod-carrier, or this German market-gardener; why can't I have the enjoyment of my labor as well as they? I am as capable of taking care of my own family as much as they of theirs; why should I be subject to have them taken from me by those other men who call themselves our owners? Our children have as much brains as the children of these white neighbors of ours, who not long ago were cooks and waiters at the hotels, why should they be spurned from the school-rooms? I helped to build the school-house, and have not been paid for it. One thing I know, if I can't have my rights, I can have my pleasures; and if they won't give me wages I can take them."

That this influence of association in labor with free-men cannot fail to be appreciated by intelligent observers, will be evident from the following paragraph from the *New Orleans Crescent*, although it was probably written to show only the amusing and picturesque aspect of the slave community:

" GUINEA-LIKE.—Passing along Baronne street, between Perdido and Poydras streets, any Sunday afternoon, the white passer-by might easily suppose himself in Guinea, Caffraria, or any other thickly-peopled region in the land of Ham. Where the darkies all come from, what they do there, or where they go to, constitute a problem somewhat beyond our algebra. It seems to be a sort of nigger exchange. We know there are in that vicinity a colored church, colored ice-cream saloon, colored restaurant, colored coffee-houses, and a colored barbershop, which, we have heard say, has a back communication with one of the groggeries, for the benefit of slaves; but as the police haven't found it out yet, we suppose it ain't so. However, if the ebony dandies who attend Sunday evening 'change, would keep within their various retreats, or leave a path about three feet wide on the side-walk, for the free passage of people who are so unlucky as to be white, we wouldn't complain; but to have to elbow one's way through a crowd of woolly-heads on such a day as yesterday, their natural muskiness made more villainous by the fumes of whisky, is too much for delicate olfactories like ours. A fight, last evening, between two white men at one of the doggeries, afforded much edification to the darkies standing around, and seemed to confirm them in their opinion, that white folks, after all, ain't much."

Similar complaints to the following, which I take from the *New Orleans Crescent*, I have heard, or seen in the journals, at Richmond, Savannah, Louisville, and most other large manufacturing, or commercial towns of the South.

" PASSES TO NEGROES.—Something must be done to regulate and prescribe the manner in which passes shall be given to slaves. This is a matter that should no longer be shirked or avoided. The Common Council should act promptly. The slave population of this city is already demoralized to a deplorable extent, all owing to the indiscriminate license and indulgence extended them by masters, mistresses, and guardians, and to the practice of *forging passes*, which has now become a regular business in New Orleans. The greater portion of the evil flows from forged passes. As things now stand, any negro can obtain a pass for four bits or a dollar, from miserable wretches who obtain a living by such infamous practices. The consequence is that hundreds spend their nights drinking, carousing, gambling, and contracting the worst of habits, which not only make them *useless to their owners*, but dangerous pests to society. We know of many negroes, completely ruined, morally and physically, by such causes. The inherent vice in the negro character always comes out when unrestrained, and there is no degradation too low for him to descend.

"Well, for the remedy to cure this crying evil. Prosecuting the forgers is out of the question; for where one conviction could be obtained, thousands of fraudulent passes would be written. *Slave evidence weighs nothing against white forgers and scoundrels.* Hence the necessity of adopting some other mode of prevention. It has been suggested to us, that if the Council would adopt a form for passes, different each month, to be obtained by masters from the Chief of Police, exclusively, that a great deal of good would be at once accomplished. We have no doubt of it. Further, we believe that all owners and guardians would cheerfully submit to the inconvenience in order to obtain so desirable an end. We trust the Common Council will pay some little attention to these suggestions."

How many men, accustomed to the close calculations necessary to successful enterprises, can listen to these suggestions, without asking themselves whether a system, that requires to be sustained by such inconvenient defenses, had not better be thrown up altogether?

First and last, I spent some weeks in New Orleans and its vicinity. I doubt if there is a city in the world, where the resident population has been so divided in its origin, or where there is such a variety in the tastes, habits, manners, and moral codes of the citizens. Although this injures civic enterprise—which the peculiar situation of the city greatly demands to be directed to means of cleanliness, convenience, comfort, and health—it also gives a greater scope to the working of individual enterprise, taste, genius, and conscience; so that nowhere are the higher qualities of man—as displayed in generosity, hospitality, benevolence, and courage—better developed, or the lower qualities, likening him to a beast, less interfered with, by law or the action of public opinion.

There is one, among the multitudinous classifications of society in New Orleans, which is a very peculiar and characteristic result of the prejudices, vices, and customs of the various elements of color, class, and nation, which have been there brought together.

I refer to a class composed of the illegitimate offspring of white men and colored women (mulattoes or quadroons), who, from habits of early life, the advantages of education, and the use of wealth, are too much superior to the negroes, in general, to associate with them, and are not allowed by law, or the popular prejudice, to marry white people. The girls are frequently sent to Paris to be educated, and are very accomplished. They are generally pretty, and often handsome. I have rarely, if ever, met more beautiful women, than one or two of them, that I saw by chance, in the streets. They are much better formed, and have a much more graceful and elegant carriage than Americans in general, while they seem to have commonly inherited or acquired much of the taste and skill, in the selection and arrangement, and the way of wearing dresses and ornaments, that is the especial distinction of the women of Paris. Their beauty and attractiveness being their fortune, they cultivate and cherish with diligence every charm or accomplishment they are possessed of.

Of course, men are attracted by them, associate with them, are captivated, and become attached to them, and, not being able to marry them legally, and with the usual forms and securities for constancy, make such arrangements "as can be agreed upon." When a man makes a declaration of love to a girl of this class, she will admit or deny, as the case may be, her happiness in receiving it; but, supposing she is favorably disposed, she will usually refer the applicant to her mother. The mother inquires, like a Countess of Kew, into the circumstances of the suitor; ascertains whether he is able to maintain a family, and, if satisfied with him, in these and other respects, requires from him security that he will support her daughter in a style suitable to the habits she has been bred to, and that, if he should ever leave her, he will give her a certain sum for her future support, and a certain additional sum for each of the children she shall then have.

The wealth, thus secured, will, of course, vary—as in society with higher assumptions of morality—with the value of the lady in the market; that is, with her attractiveness, and the number and value of other suitors she may have, or may reasonably expect. Of course, I do not mean that love has nothing at all to do with it; but love is sedulously restrained, and held firmly in hand, until the road of competency is seen to be clear, with less humbug than our English custom requires about it. Everything being satisfactorily arranged, a tenement in a certain quarter of the town is usually hired, and the couple move into it and go to housekeeping—living as if they were married. The woman is not, of course, to be wholly deprived of the society of others—her former acquaintances are continued, and she sustains her relations as daughter, sister, and friend. Of course, too, her husband (she calls him so—why shouldn't she?) will be likely to continue, also, more or less in, and form a part of, this kind of society. There are parties and balls —*bals masqués*—and all the movements and customs of other fashionable society, which they can enjoy in it, if they

wish.* The women of this sort are represented to be exceedingly affectionate in disposition, and constant beyond reproach.

During all the time a man sustains this relation, he will
commonly be moving, also, in reputable society on the other
side of the town; not improbably, eventually he marries, and
and has a family establishment elsewhere. Before doing this, he
may separate from his *placée* (so she is termed). If so, he pays
her according to agreement, and as much more, perhaps, as his
affection for her, or his sense of the cruelty of the proceeding,
may lead him to ; and she has the world before her again, in
the position of a widow. Many men continue, for a long time,
to support both establishments—particularly, if their legal marriage is one *de convenance*. But many others form so strong
attachments, that the relation is never discontinued, but becomes,
indeed, that of marriage, except that it is not legalized or sol-
emnized. These men leave their estate, at death, to their
children, to whom they may have previously given every advantage of education they could command. What becomes of the

* "THE GLOBE BALL ROOM,
Corner of St. Claude and St. Peter streets, abreast of the Old Basin,
WILL OPEN THIS EVENING, October 16, when a Society Ball will
   be given.
No ladies admitted without masks.
Gentlemen, fifty cents—Ladies, gratis.
Doors open at 9½ o'clock. Ball to commence at 10 o'clock.
No person admitted with weapons, by order of the Council.
A superior orchestra has been engaged for the season.
The public may be assured of the most strict order, as there will be at all
times, an efficient police in attendance.
Attached to the establishment is a superior Bar, well stocked with wines
and liquors ; also, a Restaurant, where may be had all such delicacies as the
market affords.
All ladies are requested to procure free tickets in the Mask Room, as no lady
will be admitted into the ball room without one.
                                        A. WHITLOCK, Manager."

boys, I am not informed; the girls, sometimes, are removed to other countries, where their color does not prevent their living reputable lives; but, of course, mainly continue in the same society, and are fated to a life similar to that of their mothers.

I have described this custom as it was described to me; I need hardly say in only its best aspects. The crime and heart-breaking sorrow that must frequently result from it, must be evident to every reflective reader.

A gentleman, of New England education, gave me the following account of his acquaintance with the quadroon society. On first coming to New Orleans, he was drawn into the social circles usually frequented by New England people, and some time afterwards was introduced by a friend to a quadroon family, in which there were three pretty and accomplished young women. They were intelligent and well informed; their musical taste was especially well cultivated; they were interested in the literature of the day, and their conversation upon it was characterized by good sense and refined discrimination. He never saw any indication of a want of purity of character or delicacy of feeling in them. He was much attracted by them, and for some time visited them very frequently. Having then discontinued his intimacy, at length one of the girls asked him why he did not come to see them as often as he had formerly done. He frankly replied that he had found their society so fascinating, that he had thought it best to restrict himself in the enjoyment of it, lest it should become necessary to his happiness; and out of regard to his general plans of life, and the feelings of his friends, he could not permit himself to indulge the purpose to be united to one of them, according to the usual custom with their class. The young woman was evidently much pained, but

not at all offended, and immediately acknowledged and com-
mended the propriety and good sense of his resolution.

One reason which leads this way of living to be frequently
adopted by unmarried men, who come to New Orleans to carry
on business, is, that it is much cheaper than living at hotels and
boarding-houses. As no young man ordinarily dare think of
marrying, until he has made a fortune to support the extravagant
style of house-keeping, and gratify the expensive tastes of young
women, as fashion is now educating them, many are obliged to
make up their minds never to marry. Such a one undertook to
show me that it was cheaper for him to *placer* than to live in
any other way that he could be expected to in New Orleans.
He hired, at a low rent, two apartments in the older part of the
town ; his placée did not, except occasionally, require a servant ;
she did the marketing, and performed all the ordinary duties of
house-keeping herself ; she took care of his clothes, and in every
way was economical and saving in her habits—it being her
interest, if her affection for him were not sufficient, to make him
as much comfort and as little expense as possible, that he might
be the more strongly attached to her, and have the less occasion
to leave her. He concluded by assuring me that whatever might
be said against it, it certainly was better than the way in which
most young men lived who depended on salaries in New York.

While we have so little real social democracy that we manifest
our respect less to character and mental and æsthetic attainments than to offices and positions, we must dress extravagantly,
must be housed extravagantly, must spend an extravagant portion of time in senseless employments, must neglect the essential
means of comfort and health, and must forget taste for the necessary means of display ; because these are badges and signs of

positions superior, at least, to those of our servants and proletaires.

A woman may have spent a year in learning how a loaf of bread and a dish of soup can be made, a steak broiled, and a potatoe boiled, in a perfectly wholesome and yet palatable manner; things which it is certain that not one American man or woman among a thousand has ever seen, or has any correct idea about. She may have spent ten years in the study of beauty, of taste and domestic fine-art, and thus possess an unfailing power of self-cheering and of elevating the lives of all in her house, and it will command for her, if her husband is a book-keeper, or an editor, or an actor, on a small salary, less respect and less influence—for her children, less exterior social advantages—than the woman with no solid acquirements will possess, if her husband is able to pay a thousand dollars rent for a stone-veneered dwelling, and furnish a stylish carriage for her to send cards from.

Perhaps I am wrong in saying that this is so. I believe in New York it is not so. But such is the general opinion, and by this unfortunate opinion the mass of young minds are ruled.

But, regardless of social position and reputation with the world, how rarely are we educated to be happy, without excessive expenditure. The taste of our young men and of our young women is so little or so badly cultivated that they have hardly any conception of comfort without splendor, or of beauty beyond fashion. There are, therefore, so few houses built in our towns with prime regard to health and simple convenience, and there are so few of us sufficiently educated as purveyors and cooks, to provide a palatable variety of good food, except at a wasteful expense, that a large income is really made necessary for a merely wholesome and comfortable family life.

Our young men, therefore, shrink from marriage until they can command business positions, from which they can safely undertake to pay rent for stone veneering, and suites of parlors, to buy theatrical furniture, and to support idle, if not sickly families, "in a style of barbaric splendor." Those less conscientious and more bold—how often are they detected in peculations and reckless gambling speculations.

And when there is generally so little comprehension of the more noble sources of pleasure which may be commanded with moderate wealth, are their passions dormant while a pure domestic life is held to be so far in the future?

The Irish are faithless of the future, improvident, passionate, and marry young. The Scotch are cool, ambitious, and penurious, and, much less often than the Irish, marry without seeing their way clear to household comfort. Is there no philosophical connection between these differences of character and the fact that licentiousness is exceedingly prevalent in Scotland, while Ireland is more free from it than any other country in the world?

It is asserted by Southerners who have lived at the North, and Northerners who have lived at the South, that although the facilities for licentiousness are much greater at the South, the evil of licentiousness is much greater at the North. Not because the average standard of "respectable position" requires a less expenditure at the South, for the contrary is the case.* But it is said licentiousness at the North is far more capti-

* A gentleman in an inland Southern town said to me, "I have now but one servant; if I should marry, I should be obliged to buy three more, and that alone would withdraw from my capital at least three thousand dollars."

vating, irresistible, and ruinous than at the South. Its very intrigues, cloaks, hazards, and expenses, instead of repressing the passions of young men, exasperate them, and increase its degrading effect upon their character, producing hypocrisy, interfering with high ambitions, destroying self-respect, causing the worst possible results to their health, and giving them habits which are inimical to future domestic contentment and virtue.

With regard to young men in towns, I think this may be true, though in rural life the advantage of the North, I believe, is incomparable.

Mrs. Douglass, a Virginia woman, who was tried, convicted and punished, a year or two since, for teaching a number of slaves to read, contrary to law, says, in a letter from her jail :

" This subject demands the attention, not only of the religious population, but of statesmen and law-makers. It is one great evil hanging over the Southern Slave States, destroying domestic happiness, and the peace of thousands. It is summed up in the single word—*amalgamation.* This, and this only, causes the vast extent of ignorance, degradation and crime, that lies like a black cloud over the whole South. And the practice is more general than even the Southerners are willing to allow.

" Neither is it to be found only in the lower order of the white population. It pervades the entire society. Its followers are to be found among all ranks, occupations and professions. The white mothers and daughters of the South have suffered under it for years—have seen their dearest affections trampled upon—their hopes of domestic happiness destroyed, and their future lives embittered, even to agony, by those who should be all in all to them, as husbands, sons, and brothers. I cannot use too strong language in reference to this subject, for I know that it will meet with a heart-felt response from every Southern woman."

A negress was hung this year in Alabama, for the murder of her child. At her trial, she confessed her guilt. She said her owner was the father of the child, and that her mistress knew it, and treated it so cruelly in consequence, that she had killed it to save it from further suffering, and also to remove a provocation to her own ill-treatment.

A large planter told me the reason he sent his boys to the North to be educated was, that there was no possibility of their being brought up in decency at home. Another planter told me that he was intending to move to a free country on this account. He said that the practice was not occasional or general, it was universal. "There is not," he said, "a likely-looking black girl in this State, that is not the paramour of a white man. There is not an old plantation in which the grandchildren of the owner are not whipped in the field by his overseer. I cannot bear that the blood of the —— should run in the veins of slaves." He was of an old Scotch family.

There is but one step between the way of living which I have described to be so common with young men in New Orleans, and a natural, virtuous, and commendable way of living. It is, to be sure, a step most important and needful to a good state of society. But let any one visit the hospitals of New York, and inquire into the causes of disease, and it will be seen that there is a way of living, fearfully prevalent among us, which is but a step, and that often a short one, above the life of beasts.

Whether there is less licentiousness in New Orleans than in New York, it is impossible to more than guess; but it is certain that there is less obvious licentiousness, and that the physical penalties of it, however it may be with the moral, are less horrible and general.

The late lamented Dr. Kelly, a most sensible and religious man, for several years superintending physician at the Blackwell's Island S. hospital, has more than once expressed his conviction to me, that at least one in five of the whole population of New York city is tainted with the incurable disease which is born only in the lowest form of licentiousness. Another physician tells me that he has often been called upon by old men, of the most respectable position, and officers of the churches, who were suffering the most acute distress from the sins of their youth. When we reflect that this suffering is not only incurable, but, under some circumstances, contagious, and endlessly transmissible to offspring, we shall see the sins of society punished in it, as well as of individuals.

May it not be that the effect of our present laws, which are intended to be prohibitory of licentiousness, is only to change the form and outward appearance of the vice, and rather to increase than to diminish its essential evil? Such has been the conclusion, as is well known, of the legislative power of Prussia and Denmark.

RED RIVER EMIGRANT CRAFT.

On Saturday morning I found that two boats, the Swamp Fox and the St. Charles, were advertised to leave in the evening, for Shreveport, on the Red River. I went to the levee, and, finding the St. Charles to be the best of the two, I asked her clerk if I could engage a state-room. There was just one state-room berth left unengaged; I was requested to place my name against its number on the passenger-book—and did so, understanding that it was thus secured for me.

Having taken leave of my friends, I had my baggage brought down, and went on board at half-past three—the boat being advertised to sail at four. Four o'clock passed, and freight was still being taken on—a fire had been made in the furnace, and the boat's big bell was rung. I noticed that the Swamp Fox was also firing up, and that her bell rang whenever ours did—though she was not advertised to sail till five. At length, when five o'clock came, the clerk told me he thought, perhaps, they would not be able to get off at all that night—there was so much freight still to come on board. Six o'clock arrived, and he felt certain that, if they did get off that night, it would not be till very late. At half-past six, he said the captain had not come on board yet, and he was quite sure they would not be able to get off that night. I prepared to return to the hotel, and asked if they would leave in the morning. He thought not. He was confident they would not. He was positive they could not leave now, before Monday, at twelve o'clock—I might rely upon it.

Monday morning, *The Picayune* stated, editorially, that the floating palace, the St. Charles, would leave for Shreveport, at five o'clock, and, if anybody wanted to make a quick and luxurious trip up Red River, with a jolly soul, Captain Lickup was in command. It also stated, in another paragraph, that, if any of its friends had business up Red River, Captain Pitchup was a whole-souled veteran in that trade, and was going up with that remarkably low-draft favorite, the Swamp Fox, to leave at four o'clock that evening. Both boats were also announced, in the advertising columns, to leave at four o'clock.

As the clerk had told me the St. Charles would leave at noon, however, I thought there might have been a misprint in the newspaper announcements, and so went on board again before twelve. The clerk informed me that the newspaper was right —they had finally concluded not to sail till four o'clock. Before four, I returned again, and the boat again fired up, and rang her bell. So did the Swamp Fox. Neither, however, was quite ready to leave at four o'clock. Not quite ready at five. Even at six—not yet quite ready. At seven, the fires having burned out in the furnace, and the stevedores having gone away, leaving a quantity of freight yet on the dock, without advising this time with the clerk, I had my baggage re-transferred to the hotel.

A similar performance was repeated on Tuesday.

On Wednesday, I found the berth I had engaged occupied by a very strong man, who was not very polite, when I informed him that I believed there was some mistake—that the berth he was using had been engaged to me. I went to the clerk, who said that he was sorry, but that, as I had not staid on board at night, and had not paid for the berth, he had not been sure that I should go, and he had, therefore, given it to the gentleman who now had it in possession, and whom, he thought, it would not be best to try to reason out of it. He was very busy, he observed, because the boat was going to start at four o'clock; if I would now pay him the price of passage, he would do the best he could for me. When he had time to examine, he could probably put me in some state-room, if not quite as good a one as that I had lost. I could, at any rate, put my baggage in his private state-room, until the boat got off, and then he would make some satisfactory arrangements for me. I inquired if it was quite certain that the boat would get off at four; for I had been asked to dine with a friend, at three o'clock. There was not the smallest doubt that she would leave at four. They were all ready, at that moment, and only waited till four, because the agent had advertised that they would—merely a technical point of honor.

But, by some error of calculation, I suppose, she didn't go at four. Nor at five. Nor at six.

At seven o'clock, the Swamp Fox and the St. Charles were both discharging dense smoke from their chimneys, blowing steam, and ringing bells. It was apparent that each was making every exertion to get off before the other. The captains of both boats stood at the break of the hurricane deck, as if they were waiting impatiently for mails to come on board.

The St. Charles was crowded with passengers, and her decks were piled high with freight. Bumboatmen, about the bows, were offering shells, and oranges, and bananas; and newsboys, and peddlers, and tract distributers, were squeezing about with their wares among the passengers. I had confidence in their instinct; there had been no such numbers of them the previous evenings, and I made up my mind, although past seven o'clock, that the St. Charles would not let her fires go down again.

Among the peddlers there were two of "cheap literature," and among their yellow covers, each had two or three copies of the cheap edition (pamphlet) of Uncle Tom's Cabin. They did not cry it out as they did the other books they had, but held it forth among others, so its title could be seen. One of them told me he carried it because gentlemen often inquired for it, and he sold a good many : at least three copies were sold to passengers on the boat. Another young man, who looked like a beneficiary of the Education Society, endeavoring to pass a college vacation in a useful and profitable manner, was peddling a Bible Defense of Slavery, which he made eloquent appeals, in the manner of a pastoral visit, to us, each personally, to purchase. He said it was prepared by a clergyman of Kentucky, and every slave-holder ought to possess it. When he came to me, I told him that I

owned no slaves, and therefore had no occasion for it. He answered that the world was before me, and I perhaps yet might
own many of them. I replied so decidedly that I should not,
that he appeared to be satisfied that my conscience would not
need the book, and turned back again to a man sitting beside
me, who had before refused to look at it. He now urged again
that he should do so, and forced it into his hands, open at the
title-page on which was a vignette, representing a circle of
colored gentlemen and ladies, sitting around a fire-place, with a
white person standing behind them, like a servant, reading from
a book. "Here we see the African race as it is in America,
under the blessed—"

"Now you go to hell! I've told you three times, as civilly
as I could, I didn't want your book. If you bring it here again
I'll throw it overboard. I own niggers; and I calculate to own
more of 'em, if I can get 'em, but I don't want any damned
preachin' about it."

That was the last I saw of the book-peddler.

It was twenty minutes after seven when the captain observed,
scanning the levee in every direction, to see if there was another
cart or carriage coming towards us, "No use waiting any longer,
I reckon: throw off, Mr. Heady." (The Swamp Fox did not
leave, I afterwards heard, till Saturday.)

We backed out, winded round head up, and as we began to
breast the current, a dozen of the negro boat-hands, standing on
the freight, piled up on the low forecastle, began to sing, waving
hats and handkerchiefs, and shirts lashed to poles, towards the
people who stood on the sterns of the steam-boats at the
levee. After losing a few lines, I copied literally into my
note-book:

" Ye see dem boat way dah ahead.
> CHORUS.—Oahoiohieu.

De San Charles is arter 'em, dey mus go behine.
> CHO.—Oahoiohieu.

So stir up dah, my livelies, stir her up ; (pointing to the furnaces).
> CHO.—Oahoiohieu.

Dey's burnin' not'n but fat and rosum.
> CHO.—Oahoiohieu.

Oh, we is gwine up de Red River, oh !
> CHO.—Oahoiohieu.

Oh, we mus part from you dah asho'.
> CHO.—Oahoiohieu.

Give my lub to Dinah, oh !
> CHO.—Oahoiohieu.

For we is gwine up de Red River.
> CHO.—Oahoiohieu.

Yes, we is gwine up de Red River.
> CHO.—Oahoiohieu.

Oh we must part from you dah oh.
> CHO.—Oahoiohieu."

[The wit introduced into these songs has, I suspect, been rather over-estimated. On another occasion I took down the following :

" John come down in de holler,
> Oh, work and talk and holler,
> Oh, John, come down in de holler,
Ime gwine away to-morrow.
> Oh, John, &c.

Ime gwine away to marry,
> Oh, John, &c.

Get my cloves in order,
> Oh, John, &c.

I'se gwine away to-morrow,
        Oh, John, &c.

Oh, work and talk and holler,
        Oh, John, &c.

Massa guv me dollar,
        Oh, John, &c.

Don't cry yer eyes out, honey,
        Oh, John, &c.

I'm gwine to get some money,
        Oh, John, &c.

But I'll come back to-morrow,
        Oh, John, &c.

So work and talk and holler,
        Oh, John, &c.

Work all day and Sunday,
        Oh, John, &c.

Massa get de money,
        Oh, John, &c.

After the conclusion of this song, and after the negroes had left the bows, and were coming aft along the guards, we passed two or three colored nurses, walking with children on the river bank; as we did so the singers jumped on some cotton bales, bowed very low to them, took off their hats, and swung and waved them, and renewed their song:

God bless you all, dah! ladies!
        Oh, John come down in de holler,

Farwell, de Lord be wid you, honey,
        Oh, John, come down, &c.

Done cry yerself to def,
        Oh, John, &c.

I'm gwine down to New Orleans,
        Oh, John, &c.

I'll come back, dough, bime-by,
    Oh, John, &c,

So far-you-well, my honey,
    Oh, John, &c.

Far-you-well, all you dah, shore,
    Oh, John, &c.

And save your cotton for de Dalmo!
    Oh, John, &c.]

As soon as the song was ended, I went into the cabin to remind the clerk to obtain a berth for me. I found two brilliant supper tables reaching the whole length of the long cabin, and a file of men standing on each side of both of them, ready to take seats as soon as the signal was given.

The clerk was in his room, with two other men, and appeared to be more occupied than ever. His manner was, I thought, now rather cool, not to say rude; and he very distinctly informed me that every berth was occupied, and he didn't know where I was to sleep. He judged I was able to take care of myself; and if I was not, he was quite sure that he had too much to do to give all his time to my surveillance. I then went to the captain, and told him that I thought myself entitled to a berth. I had paid for one, and should not have taken passage in the boat, if it had not been promised me. I was not disposed to fight for it, particularly as the gentleman occupying the berth engaged to me was a good deal bigger fellow than I, and also carried a bigger knife; but I thought the clerk was accountable to me for a berth, and I begged that he would inform him so. He replied that the clerk probably knew his business; he had nothing to do with it; and walked away from me. I then addressed myself to a second clerk, or sub-officer of some denomination, who more good-naturedly informed me that half the company were in the same condition as myself, and I needn't be alarmed, cots would be provided for us.

As I saw that the supper-table was likely to be crowded, I asked if there would be a second table. "Yes, they'll keep on eatin' till they all get through." I walked the deck till I saw those who had been first seated at the table coming out; then going in, I found the table still crowded, while many stood waiting to take seats as fast as any were vacated. I obtained one for myself at length, and had no sooner occupied it than two half-intoxicated and garrulous men took the adjoining stools.

It was near nine o'clock before the tables were cleared away, and immediately afterwards the waiters began to rig a framework for sleeping-cots in their place. These cots were simply canvas shelves, five feet and a half long, two wide, and less than two feet apart, perpendicularly. A waiter, whose good will I had purchased at the supper-table, gave me a hint to secure one of them for myself, as soon as they were erected, by putting my hat in it. I did so, and saw that others did the same. I chose a cot as near as possible to the midship doors of the cabin, perceiving that there was not likely to be the best possible air, after all the passengers were laid up for the night, in this compact manner.

Nearly as fast as the cots were ready they were occupied. To make sure that mine was not stolen from me, I also, without much undressing, laid myself away. A single blanket was the only bed-clothing provided. I had not lain long, before I was driven, by an exceedingly offensive smell, to search for a cleaner neighborhood; but I found all the cots fore and aft, were either occupied or engaged. I immediately returned, and that I might have a dernier resort, left my shawl in that I had first obtained.

In the forward part of the cabin there was a bar, a stove, a table, and a placard of rules, forbidding smoking, gambling, and swearing in the cabin, and a close company of drinkers, smokers, card-players, and constant swearers. I went out, and stepped down to the boiler-deck. The boat had been provided with very poor wood, and the firemen were crowding it into the furnaces whenever they could find room for it, driving smaller sticks between the larger ones at the top, by a battering-ram method.

Most of the firemen were Irish born; one with whom I conversed was English. He said they were divided into three watches, each working four hours at a time, and all hands liable to be called, when wooding, or landing, or taking on freight, to assist the deck-hands. They were paid now but thirty dollars a month—ordinarily forty, and sometimes sixty—and board. He was a sailor bred. This boat-life was harder than sea-faring, but the pay was better, and trips were short. The regular thing was to make two trips, and then lay up for a spree. It would be too hard upon a man, he thought, to pursue it regularly; two trips " on end" was as much as a man could stand. He must then take a "refreshment." Working this way for three weeks, and then refreshing for about one, he did not think it was unhealthy, no more so than ordinary sea-faring. He concluded, by informing me that the most striking peculiarity of the business was, that it kept a man, notwithstanding wholesale periodical refreshment, very dry. He was of opinion that after the information I had obtained, if I gave him at least the price of a single drink, and some tobacco, it would be characteristic of a gentleman.

Going round behind the furnace, I found a large quantity of freight: hogsheads, barrels, cases, bales, boxes, nail-rods, rolls of leather, plows, cotton bale-rope, and fire-wood, all thrown together in the most confused manner, with hot steam-pipes, and parts of the engine crossing through it. As I explored further aft, I found negroes lying asleep in all postures, upon the freight. A single group only, of five or six, appeared to be awake, and as I drew near to them they commenced to sing a Methodist hymn, not loudly, as negroes generally do, but, as it seemed to me, with a good deal of tenderness and feeling; a few white people— men, women and children—were lying here and there, among the negroes. Altogether, I heard we had two hundred of these deck passengers, black and white. A stove, by which they could fry bacon, was the only furniture provided for them by the boat. They carried with them their provisions for the voyage, and had their choice of the freight for beds.

As I came to the bows again, and was about to ascend to the cabin, two men came down, one of whom I recognized to have been my cot neighbor. "Where's a bucket?" said he; "by thunder! this fellow was so strong I could not sleep by him, so I stumped him to come down and wash his feet." "I am much obliged to you," said I, and I was, very much; the man had been lying in the cot beneath mine, which I now returned to, and soon fell asleep.

I awoke about midnight. There was an unusual jar in the boat, and an evident excitement among people talking on deck. I rolled out of my cot, and stepped out on to the gallery. The steamboat "Kimball" was running head-and-head with us, and so close that one might have jumped easily from our paddle-box on to her guards. A few other passengers had turned out beside myself, and most of the waiters were leaning on the rail of the gallery. Occasionally a few words of banter passed between them and the waiters of the Kimball; below, the firemen were shouting as they crowded the furnaces, and some one could be heard cheering them: "Shove her up, boys! Shove her up! Give her hell!" "She's got to hold a conversation with us before she gets by, anyhow," said one of the negroes. "Ye har' that ar' whistlin'," said a white man; "tell ye thar an't any too much water in her bilers when ye har that." I laughed silently, but was not without a slight expectant sensation, which Mr. Burke would have called sublime. At length the Kimball slowly drew ahead, crossed our bow, and the contest was given up. "De ole lady too heavy," said a waiter; "if I could pitch a few ton of dat freight off her bow, I'd bet de Kimball would be askin' her to show de way, mighty quick."

At half-past four o'clock a hand-bell was rung in the cabin, and soon afterwards I was informed that I must get up, that the servants might remove the cot arrangement, and clear the cabin for the breakfast-table.

Breakfast was not ready till half-past seven. In the mean time, having washed in the barber's shop, I walked on the hurricane deck, where I got very damp and faint. The passengers, one set after another, and then the pilots, clerks, mates, and engineers, and then the free-colored people, and then the waiters, chambermaids, and passengers' body servants, having breakfasted, the tables were cleared, and the cabin was swept. The tables were then again laid for dinner. Thus the greater part of the cabin was constantly occupied, and the passengers who had not state-rooms to retreat to were driven to herd in the vicinity of the card-tables and the bar, the lobby (Social Hall, I believe

it's called), in which most of the passengers' baggage was deposited, or to go outside. Every part of the boat, except the bleak
hurricane deck, was crowded; and so large a number of equally
uncomfortable and disagreeable people I think I never saw elsewhere together. We made very slow progress, landing, it seems
to me, after we entered Red River, at every " bend," " bottom,"
" bayou," " point," and " plantation" that came in sight; often
for no other object than to roll out a barrel of flour, or a keg of
nails; sometimes merely to furnish newspapers to a wealthy
planter, who had much cotton to send to market, and whom
it was therefore desirable to please.

I was sitting one day on the forward gallery, watching a pair
of ducks, that were alternately floating on the river, and flying
further ahead as the steamer approached them. A man standing
near me drew a long barreled and very finely-finished pistol
from his coat pocket, and, resting it against a stanchion, took
aim at them. They were, I judged, full the boat's own length
—not less than two hundred feet—from us and were just raising
their wings to fly, when he fired. One of them only rose; the
other flapped round and round, and when within ten yards of the
boat, dived. The bullet had broken its wing. So remarkable a
shot excited, of course, not a little admiration and conversation.
Half a dozen other men drew pistols, or revolvers, which they
appeared to carry habitually, and several were fired at floating
chips, or objects on the shore. I saw no more remarkable
shooting, however; and that the duck should have been hit at
such a distance, was generally considered a piece of luck. A
man who had been " in the Rangers" said that all his company
could put a ball into a tree, the size of a man's body, at sixty
paces, at every shot, with Colt's army revolver, not taking

steady aim, but firing at the jerk of the arm. He did not be-lieve that any dueling-pistol could be fired with more accuracy.

This pistol episode was almost the only entertainment in which the passengers engaged themselves, except eating, drink-ing, smoking, conversation, and card-playing. Gambling was constantly going on, day and night. I don't think there was an interruption to it of fifteen minutes in three days. The conversa-tion was almost exclusively confined to the topics of steam-boats, liquors, cards, black-land, red-land, bottom-land, timber-land, warrants and locations, sugar, cotton, corn, and negroes.

After the first night, I preferred to sleep on the trunks in the social hall, rather than among the cots, in the crowded cabin, and several others did the same. There were, in fact, not cots enough for all the passengers excluded from the state-rooms. I found that some, and I presume most of the passengers, by making the clerk believe that they would otherwise take the Swamp Fox, had obtained their passage at considerably less price than I had paid.

On the third day, just after the dinner-bell had rung, and most of the passengers had gone into the cabin, I was sitting alone on the gallery, reading a pamphlet, when a well-dressed, middle-aged man accosted me.

"Is that the book they call Uncle Tom's Cabin, you are read-ing, sir?"

"No, sir."

"I did not know but it was; I see that there are two or three gentlemen on board that have got it. I suppose I might have got it in New Orleans: I wish I had. Have you ever seen it, sir?"

"Yes, sir."

"I'm told it shows up Slavery in very high colors."

"Yes, sir, it shows the evils of Slavery very strongly."

He took a chair near me, and said that, if it represented extreme cases as if they were general, it was not fair.

Perceiving that he was disposed to discuss the matter, I said that I was a Northern man, and perhaps not very well able to judge; but that I thought that a certain degree of cruelty was necessary to make slave-labor profitable, and that not many were disposed to be more severe than they thought necessary. I believed there was very little wanton cruelty.

He answered, that northern men were much mistaken in supposing that slaves were generally ill-treated. He was a merchant, and owned a plantation, and he just wished I could see his negroes.

"Why, sir," said he, "my niggers' children all go regularly to a Sunday-school, just the same as my own, and learn verses, and catechism, and hymns. Every one of my grown-up niggers are pious, every one of them, and members of the church. I've got an old man that can pray——well, sir, I only wish I had as good a gift at praying! I wish you could just hear him pray. There are cases in which niggers are badly used; but they are not common. There are brutes everywhere. You have men, at the North, who whip their wives—and they kill them, sometimes."

"Certainly, we have, sir; there are plenty of brutes at the North; but our law, you must remember, does not compel women to submit themselves to their power, nor refuse to receive their testimony against them. A wife, cruelly treated, can escape from her husband, and can compel him to give her subsistence, and to cease from doing her harm. A woman could defend herself against her husband's cruelty, and the law would sustain her."

"It would not be safe to receive negroes' testimony against white people; they would be always plotting against their masters, if you did."

"Wives are not always plotting against their husbands."

"Husband and wife is a very different thing from master and slave."

"Your remark, that a bad man might whip his wife, suggested an analogy, sir."

"If the law was to forbid whipping altogether, the authority of the master would be at an end."

"And if you allow bad men to own slaves, and allow them to whip them, and deny the slave the privilege of resisting cruelty, and refuse testimony, except from those most unlikely to witness cruelty from a master, on his own plantation, to his own slave, do you not show that you think it is necessary to permit cruelty, in order to sustain the authority of masters, in general, over their slaves? That is, you establish cruelty as a necessity of Slavery —do you not?"

"No more than it is of marriage, because men may whip their wives cruelly."

"Excuse me, sir; the law does all it can, to prevent cruelty between husband and wife; between master and slave it does not, because it cannot, without weakening the necessary authority of the master—that is, without destroying Slavery. It is, therefore, a fair argument against Slavery, to show how cruelly this necessity, of sustaining the authority of cruel and passionate men over their slaves, sometimes operates. Some people have thought that a similar argument lay against some of our Northern laws, with regard to marriage. No one objected to the case being argued, and scores of books, some of them novels, have been written about it; and, in consequence, these laws have been repealed, and marriage has become a simple civil contract, with every relic of involuntary servitude abolished, as far as the civil law is concerned."

He asked what it was *Uncle Tom* "tried to make out."

I narrated the Red River episode, and asked if such things could not possibly occur.

"Yes," replied he; "but very rarely. I don't know a man, in my parish, that could do such a thing. There are two men, though, in ———, bad enough to do it, I believe; but it isn't a likely story, at all. In the first place, no colored woman would be likely to offer any resistance, if a white man should want to seduce her."

After further conversation, he said, that a planter had been tried for injuring one of his negroes, at the Court in his parish, the preceding summer. He had had, among his girls, a *favorite*, and suspecting that she was unduly kind to one of his men, under an impulse of jealousy, he mutilated him. There was not sufficient testimony to convict him; "but," he said "everybody believes he was guilty, and ought to have been punished. Nobody thinks there was any good reason for his being jealous of the boy."

I said this story corroborated the truthfulness of Uncle Tom's Cabin; it showed that it was all possible.

"Yes," he answered, "perhaps it may; but, then, nobody would have any respect for a man that would treat his niggers cruelly."

I wondered, as I went into dinner, and glanced at the long

rows of surly faces, how many men there were there, whose passions would be much restrained by the fear of losing the respect of their neighbors.*

I think very few of them would be very much controlled by such an influence, but I should do them injustice if I neglected to add my conviction, that as a general rule the slaves of this rough, strait-forward pioneer class, enjoy privileges and are less liable to severe labor or excessive punishment than the majority of those belonging to wealthy proprietors, who work on large plantations under overseers. They are less well provided for and are more neglected in every way; but I am inclined to think that the greatest kindness that can be done to a slave, is to neglect him and so encourage, if not force him, to exercise some care over himself.

My original purpose had been to go high up Red River at this time, but the long delay in the boat's leaving New Orleans, and her slow passage, obliged me to change my plans, and I went no further than Grand Ecore. It was not till the following autumn that I was able to proceed beyond there.

ANOTHER SORT OF CRAFT.

When I returned to New Orleans I did so by the steam-boat Dalmau—a very pleasant and orderly boat, with very polite and obliging officers. The company of passengers was also an agreeable one, a large number of them being wealthy planters with their families, generally intelligent and somewhat cultivated peo-

---

* John Randolph, of Roanoke, once said, on the floor of Congress (touching the internal slave-trade): "What are the trophies of this infernal traffic? The handcuff, the manacles, the blood-stained cowhide. What man is worse received in society for being a hard master? Who denies the hand of sister or daughter to such monsters?"

ple.   Many were of French descent, and a few could not speak
English.

A gentleman, northern born, who had been liberally educated
in New England, and had traveled abroad, but had been some
years living in Texas, observed to me, that he thought Carlyle
had said the best thing for Slavery, and acknowledged himself a
disciple to his views of it.   He thought labor of mind and body,
directed to the development of the material of man's comfort
(and so to his mental and moral progress), was what was most
needed of all men.   The negroes in Africa were doing nothing
for the world. If Slavery should be abolished, those here would,
he assumed, do nothing. As they are, they are doing much.
It was best for the world that Slavery should continue, and therefore, we must rest content with a rather low standard of mental attainments and moral character, which he admitted prevailed
in the Slave States. It was Utopian to ask for the same manifes-
tation of civilization at the South, that might be aimed at in a
free country ; but if it were not for the South and its Slavery,
the aims of the Free States would be also Utopian.   Moral and
intellectual improvement, at the North and in Europe, was based,
in a degree, on cheap cotton and so on Slavery. Men gave more
time to study and thought, because they gave less to providing
themselves with shirts.

He thought there was certainly progress and improvement at
the South, and it would continue ; but it was much more limited,
and less calculated upon and provided for, than at the North.
And while the chief labor was done by slaves, and they remained
a large proportion of the people, there could be no *atmosphere* of
progress and improvement, as where all men were desirous and
able to improve, and the interests of each were favored by the

improvement in every way of all.   At the North there was a constant electric current of progress, which no màn could resist being moved by.   At the South, every second man was a nonconductor and broke the chain.   Individuals at the South were enterprising, but they could move only themselves.

He had little respect for the religion which the negroes acquired in Slavery.   They learned to copy the manifestations of religion of the whites in a parrot-like way, and connected these manifestations with excitements of mind and body, which were no way essentially different, or of higher nature than those which all savage tribes were accustomed to connect with their heathen worship.

But materially they were vastly better off than savages. They were, generally well provided for, and seldom suffered from hunger and cold, as savages constantly did.   He thought the wild, hard Texas men made the best of masters; and the slaves were, in general, better treated in Texas than in any other part of the South.

There were occasional exceptions, certainly.   One had occurred lately near Nacogdoches.   A man had tied up a slave in a fit of anger, and had drawn a live cat down his back, so she would strike her claws into his skin and tear it.   The slave was seriously injured; and it having become notorious how he was injured, his master was brought to a regular trial.   He had not been convicted, for want of sufficient legal evidence; but there was so great popular indignation, that he would have to move out of that region of country, to save himself from a lynching. I think he said this man's anger was also founded on jealousy.

He sneered at any other defense of Slavery, than the utilitarian one.   Every man in the world ought to work for the benefit of mankind at large, as well as himself—the negroes would not do so, unless they were forced to, and Slavery was justified by its results, not to the South but to the world. It was nonsense to say that Slavery was sustained for the benefit of the negro. It was unsafe and would be uneconomical, and, therefore, bad for the world at large, to give the negro knowledge and to improve his intelligence. If he should be systematically instructed in matters, safe in themselves for him to be informed upon, as the Bible, for instance, he would instruct himself in other matters, and would soon get beyond the control of the whites, who retained authority over him only by their superior intelligence and knowledge.

There was no need to pretend that the negro was incapable of being greatly improved. No men improved faster under favorable circumstances. The difference between town-bred and plantation-bred slaves, in point of general intelligence, was always very striking. He had been in business intercourse for many years with a gentleman whose book-keeping and correspondence had been almost altogether carried on by a slave, and it was admirably done; his manner of expression was terse, pointed, and appropriate, and his business abilities every way admirable. His owner could not possibly have obtained more valuable services from a white clerk.

He owned but one slave himself, and that was an old woman, whom he had bought purely from motives of compassion. He had supported her for several years, and had never received the smallest return from her labor.

"If you are right in your justification of Slavery," said I, "why not knock her in the head? She's no longer of any use to the world, only an incumbrance, using a certain amount of corn and cotton, which would otherwise go to make study cheaper, and so advance the general improvement of the world."

"Yes," he replied, laughing, "but then we can't afford to throw charity overboard."

"You throw your theory overboard in saying so, I think. To obtain cheap cotton, you would throw overboard all political morality. I think it a dear bargain."

Would throw overboard all compromises and compacts, I might have added, when they stood in the way of greater profit from Slavery.

But he said it was fanaticism, not morality, that would be thrown overboard. Prudence would retain Slavery, and sensible morality with it. And on this point we agreed, with great friendliness, to differ.

RIGOLET DU BON DIEU AND CANE RIVER.

At Grand Ecore, the Red River divides into two streams, which reunite some forty miles below; one of these, called Cane River, which was formerly the principal channel, is now only navigable when Red River is running above its ordinary level; and the other, called Rigolet du Bon Dieu (streamlet of the good God), takes, at low stages, sometimes even the whole stream.

At Nachitoches, a few miles below Grand Ecore, on Cane River, I found a very good hotel, kept by a Mr. Brown, and remained several days. As is very frequently the case in Southern towns, the hotel had no bar-room in it; but the guests went to a large public bar-room, in the immediate vicinity, for lunch and drink. This bar-room had a billiard-room connected with it, and was kept by a Frenchman, and French wines seemed to be more consumed in it than whisky, or fiercer liquids. At the hotel, bottles of claret and sauterne were placed upon the table at dinner, for the free use of the guests, and the same custom prevails on most of the Louisiana steam-boats. Even on the St. Charles, claret was every day placed upon the table, and I noticed that the coarse Texans, who most patronized the bar, and whose stomachs were most seared with whisky, availed themselves very little of it. Light wines are much more extensively consumed in Louisiana than anywhere else in the United States. In summer, among the Creoles and the wealthier Americans, claret is the usual drink at breakfast. The cheapness with which it can be imported, removes the temptation to deleterious adulterations, and I have no doubt that it is far more wholesome than water, or any of the ordinary beverages; while its habitual use, like that of light malt liquors, seems to generally satisfy that universal demand for stimulants which in America, more than anywhere else in the world, leads mankind so strongly to gluttony, by which it is deadened, or to intemperance in the use of strong drinks, or to habitual excessive nervous or mental excitements—more or less akin to insanity. I question much, if tea, or coffee, or tobacco, as ordinarily used, or excessive labor, mental or bodily, is not worse in its effects than claret and beer, as ordinarily used in countries where these are cheap, and in general use. Insanity, fanaticisms, dyspepsia, and the disease of drunkenness are not unknown in those countries, but are much less common than in the United States, and claret and beer drinkers are less liable to them, I think, than others. Different climates and different constitutions, however, evidently demand difference of stimuli, as of food.

Wholesome water and wholesome fresh fruits are not to be obtained by the traveler, in the largest part of the United States. Bacon, fat and salt, is the stock article of diet. He must satisfy his appetite with this, or with coarse or most indigestible forms of bread. In either case he will have an unnatural thirst, and the only means ordinarily offered him at country houses, for satisfying this, will be an exceedingly dirty and unpalatable decoction of coffee, of which the people usually consume an excessive quantity, or alcoholic liquors, of the most fiery and pernicious description.

There is no reason, I believe, why every farmer in the United States should not now make a wine for his own family use, which, with most persons, would be most advantageously and economically substituted for coffee and tea, and which use would soon make more palatable than any other beverage, for ordinary purposes. I do not suppose that the general use of light wines would entirely prevent drunkenness. The drunkard is a diseased person, and drunkenness prevails more in the United States than elsewhere, from those peculiarities, whatever they are, of climate and circumstances, which produce habits of greater rapidity and intensity of action in the people, from the want of satisfactory social recreations—the church and the bar-room being, in many communities, the only general friendly meeting-ground—and from ignorance of, and inability to procure simple and delicate food and stimulants, and, at the South especially, from an entire absence of education, among the whites, to self-control. Immigrants, who have no advantage over us, as the poor generally have not, in this last particular, are even more subject to the disease of drunkenness, after they have been here a few years, than natives.

The intelligent foreigner, unless he has unusual opportunities of observing the fearful prevalence and virulence, and uncontrollability of the drunkard's disease in our climate, generally deems the Maine Law wholly unjustifiable, and is astonished that it can be favored at all, by intelligent citizens; but he, invariably, soon deduces, from his personal experience, a necessity for changing the character of his stimulants, or of considerably lessening the quantity he shall use of those to which he is accustomed. Otherwise, he also soon becomes a fanatic, a dyspeptic, or a drunkard.

The Maine Law, while it will—in those communities where it can be enforced—restore many drunkards, may, perhaps, in the long run, lead to the prevalence of other excitements, not less immoral or unhealthy than drunkenness, though less obviously and notoriously so. What our people want, is less the removal of certain temptations, than the ability and the knowledge to satisfy the demands of their nature in a healthy way. Certain elements of civilization are more diffused, in some parts of our country, than they are anywhere in Europe; but others are wanting, more than anywhere else in the world. Our civilization is one-sided, irregular, and awkward. We must grow accustomed to exhaust our judgment and self-control less in matters of pure business, and to apply it more to religion and politics and the good government of our individual bodies and minds, with their various appetites, impulses, functions, and longings. Our needed temperance reformation is not to stand on one leg. Amputation of a vicious habit does not remove vice from the system. Little good will be done by an attempt to remove the sustenance of disease, if the food of health is not provided.

THE LOWER RED RIVER COUNTRY.

The Red River bottoms are nearly the best cotton lands in the world; but the crops suffer upon them, in a wet season, and sometimes are totally destroyed by "the rot," or "the worm." The production, on the old plantations, already falls far below what it was formerly—but deep plowing will at once restore their fertility; the soil being of unknown depth. Earth, from the bottom of a well, forty-three feet deep, is found to produce an excessively rank growth of the cotton-plant, though the production of cotton wool upon it is very small. Land, on the river, is now worth from $15 to $40 an acre. Improved plantations average, perhaps, $20 in value.

At a distance of a mile or two from the river-bottoms, in the vicinity of Nachitoches, the land rises into low, sandy hills, bearing pine, and some oak. Only superior tracts of this are cultivated; the cotton produced is of shorter staple, and the crop is smaller, but more uniform, being much less injured by heavy rains, and other contingencies. This land is worth from $2 to $6 an acre, and is comparatively healthy. Much the larger part of it belongs to the State, and is of use only for grazing, and for this is of but littlevalue. Considerable herds of poor cattle are, however, kept upon it, by men who make it their business, and who, if they have any farms, raise nothing but maize upon them. They seldom own slaves, or more than a single family of them for house-servants, but hire Spaniards, to assist them in herding cattle.

The "range" is said to be very much worse than formerly, and the quality of the cattle to have greatly deteriorated within twenty years; yet they looked to me superior to any I had seen previously in the South.

Walking out, on Sunday, in the country, I came by chance upon the negro quarters of a large plantation, which were built right upon what appeared to be a public road. They were apparently intended for the accommodation of about one hundred slaves. The residents were mending clothes, washing, and cooking, and looked well-fed and contented. They were generally creoles, and spoke English, French, and Spanish, among themselves. The cabins were small, built mostly of hewn plank, set

upright, and chinked with rags and mud, roofed with split clapboards, and provided with stick and mud chimney. There was but one room, and no loft, to each cabin; or, where there were two rooms, they were occupied by two families. Several of them, into which, without intrusion, I was able to see, were very destitute of furniture—nothing being perceptible but two very dirty beds, and a few rude stools, standing upon a bare earth floor.   There was no window, of any kind—all light and ventilation being by the door or chimney.   In one, a curtain or screen, of gunny-bagging, was hung across the doorway.   In another, I saw a shelf of crockery.   On another large plantation, I observed exceedingly comfortable, though cheap and rude, quarters for the negroes—each cabin being of good size, with brick chimney, and a broad shed or gallery before the door.

While returning to town, I met six negroes—one of them a woman—riding on horseback.   Soon afterwards I saw them stop, and two rode back some distance, and then raced their horses, the others cheering, as they passed them.   Nearer town, I met a group of boys and children—among them English, Spanish, and mulattoes—carrying several game cocks under their arms, and evidently being about to set them to fighting.   Two negroes that I met, carried guns.   During the day many negroes were in town, peddling eggs, nuts, brooms, and fowls.   I looked into the cathedral, and found a respectable, and—viewed from behind their backs—very New England-like congregation, listening attentively to a sermon from an animated Frenchman.   The negroes and all colored persons occupied distinct seats from the whites. There is, besides this Romish cathedral, a little Episcopal chapel, twenty feet by forty in size, but I believe no other church in the town.

SECRET AGENTS.

I was told that there was more morality, and more immorality in Nachitoches than in almost any other place of its size in the United States; and that in Alexandria, a town some distance below it, on Red River, there was about as much immorality without any morality at all.

Two drovers were sitting by the fire, waiting for breakfast, at the hotel; one, who looked and spoke more like a New-Englander than a Southerner, said to the other:

"I had a high old dream, last night."

"What was it?"

"Dreamt I was in hell."

"Rough country?"

"Boggy—sulphur bogs. By-and-by I came to a great pair of doors. Something kinder drew me right to 'em, and I had to open 'em, and go in. As soon as I got in, the doors slammed to, behind me, and there I see old boss Devil lying asleep, on a red hot sofy. He woke up, and rubbed his eyes, and when he see me, he says, 'Halloo! that you?' 'Yes, *sir*,' says I. 'Where'd you come from?' says he. 'From Alexandria, sir,' says I. 'I thought so,' says he, and he took down a big book, and wrote something in it with a red hot spike. 'Well, sir, what's going on now in Alexandria?' says he. 'Having a protracted meeting there, sir,' says I. 'Look here, my friend,' says he, 'you may stop lying, now you've got here.' 'I aint lying, sir,' says I. 'Oh!' says he, 'I beg your pardon; I thought it was Alexandria on Red River, you meant.' 'So it was,' says I, 'and they are having a protracted meeting there, as sure as you're alive.' 'Hell they are!' says he, jumpin' right up; 'boy, bring my boots!' A little black devil fetched him a pair of hot brass boots, and he began to draw 'em on. 'Whose doin' is that?' says he. 'Elder Slocum's, sir,' says I. 'Elder Slocum's! Why in hell couldn't you have said so, before?' says he; 'no use in my goin' if he's round; here, boy, take away these boots;' and he kicked 'em off, and laid down again."

SPANISH CREOLES.

French blood rather predominates in the population in the vicinity of Nachitoches, but there is also a considerable amount of the Spanish and Indian mongrel breed. These are often handsome people, but vagabonds, almost to a man. Scarcely any of them have any regular occupation, unless it be that of herding cattle; but they raise a little maize, and fish a little, and hunt a little, and smoke and lounge a great deal, and are very regular in their attendance on divine worship, at the cathedral.

In the public bar-room I heard a person, who I suppose would claim the appellation of a gentleman, narrating how he had over-reached a political opponent, in securing the "Spanish vote" at an election, and it appeared from the conversation that it was considered entirely, and as a matter of course, purchasable by the highest bidder. A man who would purchase votes at the North, would be very careful not to mention it publicly.

The children in the streets speak Spanish, and French, and English, with the negro dialect, indifferently; and a school-house exposes a sign, "ECOLE PRIMAIRE ANGLAIS ET FRANÇAIS."

There are also a considerable number of Italians in this neighborhood. Some of them are refugee revolutionists. The men are chiefly mechanics, and are represented to be well-behaved and valuable citizens. I have met one who, coming from Trieste, could speak Italian, German, French, Russian, and English. Yankees, of course, there are, and Anglo-Saxon Americans from every quarter. The slaves are, some French and Spanish Creole negroes, and many from "Old Virginny."

GALLIC AND HISPANO-AFRIC CREOLES.

There are also, in the vicinity, a large number of free-colored planters. In going down Cane River, the Dalmau called at several of their plantations, to take on cotton, and the captain told me that in fifteen miles of a well-settled and cultivated country, on the bank of the river, beginning ten miles below Nachitoches, he did not know but one pure-blooded white man. The plantations appeared no way different from the generality of those of the white Creoles; and on some of them were large, handsome, and comfortable houses. These free-colored people are all descended from the progeny of old French or Spanish planters, and their negro slaves. Such a progeny, born before Louisiana was annexed to the United States, and the descendants of it, are entitled to freedom.

The first person of whom I made inquiries about them, at Nachitoches, told me that they were a lazy, beastly set—slaves and all on an equality, socially—no order or discipline on their plantations, but everything going to ruin. Also that they had sore eyes, and lost their teeth early, and had few children, and showed other scrofulous symptoms, and evidences of weak constitution, as Professor Cartwright says they must. I think this gentleman must have read De Bow's *Review*, and taken these facts for granted, without personal knowledge; for neither my own observation, nor any information that I could obtain from others, at all confirmed his statement. Two merchants, to whom I had letters of introduction, and to whom I repeated them, assured me that they were entirely imaginary. They had extensive dealings with the colored planters, and were confident that they enjoyed better health than the whites living in their vicinity. They could not recollect a single instance of those indications of weak constitution which had been mentioned to me. The colored planters, within their knowledge, had large and healthy families; they were honest, and industrious, and paid their debts quite as punctually as the white planters, and were, so far as they could judge, without an intimate acquaintance, good citizens, in all respects. One of them had lately spent $40,000 in a law suit, and it was believed that they were increasing in wealth. If you have occasion to call at their houses, I was told, you will be received in a gentlemanly manner, and find they live in the same style with white people of the same wealth. They speak French among themselves, but all are able to converse in English also, and many of them are well educated.

The driver of the stage from Nachitoches towards Alexandria, described them as being rather distant and reserved towards white people with whom they were not well acquainted; but said, that he had often staid over night at their houses, and knew them intimately, and he was nowhere else so well treated, and he never saw more gentleman-like people. He appeared to have been especially impressed by the domestic and social happiness he had witnessed in their houses.

The Captain of the Dalmau, Mr. Brown of the Hotel, and two intelligent planters, who had had frequent opportunities of inter course with them, as far as their knowledge extended, confirmed these accounts.

The barber of the Dalmau was a handsome light coloured young man. While he was once dressing my hair he said to me:

"You are an Eastern man, I think, sir."

"Yes: how did you know?"

"There's something in the appearance of an Eastern man that I generally know him by."

"Couldn't you tell me what it is?"

"Well, sir, there's more refinement in an Eastern man, both in his look and his manner, than in a Southerner, in general— Are you from Massachusetts or New York, sir?"

"New York."

"I lived in New York myself, one year: at West Troy."

"Ah—what were you doing there?"

"I was at school, sir."

Perceiving from this that he was a free-man, I asked if he preferred living at the South to the North. He said he didn't like the Northern winter, and he was born and bred in Louisiana, and felt more at home there. Finally he said his best reason was, that a colored man could make more money in Louisiana than at the North. There were no white barbers there, and a barber was paid nearly four times as much for his work as he was at the North.

"I presume you have no family?"

"No, sir."

"If you should marry, would you not find it more agreeable to live at the North?"

"I'd never marry in Louisiana, sir."

"Why not?"

"Because I'd never be married to any but a virtuous woman, and there are no virtuous women among the colored people here!"

"What do you mean?"

"There are very few, sir."

"What, among the free?"

"Very few, sir. There are some very rich colored people, planters, some of them are worth four or five hundred thousand dollars. Among them I suppose there are virtuous women; but they are very few. You see, sir, it's no disgrace to a colored girl to *placer*. It's considered hardly anything different from marrying."

I asked if he knew any of the colored planters on Cane River. He did and had relatives among them. He thought there were virtuous girls there. They were rich, too, some of them. He said they rather avoided white people, because they could not associate pleasantly with them. They were uncertain of their position with them, and were afraid, if they were not reserved, they would be thought to be taking liberties, and would be subject to insults, which they could not very well resent. Yet there were some white people that they knew well, with whom they associated a good deal, and pleasantly. White men, sometimes, married a rich colored girl; but he never knew a colored man to marry a white girl. (I subsequently heard of one such case.) He said that colored people could associate with whites much more easily and comfortably at the South than the North; this was one reason he preferred to live at the South. He was kept at a greater distance from white people, and more insulted, on account of his color, at the North than in Louisiana. He thought the colored people at Cane River were thriving and happy, and there was no truth in what I had heard about their health or their thriftlessness. He was sure they were quite as forehanded as their white creole neighbors.

He asked if I knew what the colored people at the North had concluded about emigration. He did not incline to go to Africa himself; but he would like to live in a community where he was on an equality with the rest, and he preferred it should be in a warm climate. He didn't want to go out of the United States. He was an American, and he didn't want to be anything else.

He did not think the slaves were fit to be freed all at once. They ought to be somewhat educated, and gradually emancipated, and sent to Africa. They would never come to anything here, because the white people would never give them a chance.

The New Orleans correspondent of the New York *Times*, writes, under date of April 3, 1853, as follows :

" Last year an act was passed, providing for the emancipation of slaves in this State by their owners, with the proviso, that no emancipated negro should have the privilege of remaining in the State, who was not liberated three months after the passage of the act. A number of slaves who had purchased themselves, and others who had been voluntarily emancipated by their masters, refused to take out their papers, as the three months had expired, and they would be forced to leave the State. In preference to leaving Louisiana for a Free State, they had rather remain here under a nominal Slavery; and they give as a reason, that they are better treated and respected in the South, and can make more money, than in the North ! There are also a number of cases now in our Courts, where negroes are suing for their freedom, they having been once emancipated, and afterwards run off by parties and sold. In all these cases the liveliest interest is felt, more so than by your Abolitionists, for the rights of the claimants. And there is no State in the Union where the rights of persons of every description are more respected and protected than in Louisiana ; but we want no insolent interference of fanatics and hypocritical philanthropists."

It is true, that the rights of colored people to freedom, under the laws, are generally maintained with great energy in Louisiana. Suits to recover freedom are nowhere else so common, and nowhere else so successful. The crime of kidnapping and selling, as slaves, persons legally free, is evidently a very frequent one. The bar of Louisiana is more talented and respectable than that of any other Southern State, perhaps than that of any State ; and is most honorably conservative of the rights of the weak.

The excessive use of metaphors and figures of speech, and of rhodomontade, which characterizes Southern legal oratory in general, will as surely subject a lawyer to ridicule among his brethren in New Orleans as in New York. In many of the courts, pleadings are oftener in the French than the English language; and it is indispensable for a lawyer to have a free command of both languages.

I afterwards spent a night at the house of a white planter, who told me that, when he was a boy, he had lived at Alexandria. It was then under the Spanish rule; and, "the people they was all sorts. They was French and Spanish, and Egyptian and Indian, and Mulattoes and Niggers."

"Egyptians?"

"Yes, there was some of the real old Egyptians there then."

"Where did they come from?"

"From some of the Northern Islands."

"What language did they speak?"

"Well they had a language of their own that some of 'em used among themselves; Egyptian, I suppose it was, but they could talk in French and Spanish, too."

"What color were they?"

"They was black; but not very black. Oh! they was citizens, as good as any; they passed for white folks."

"Did they keep close by themselves, or did they intermarry with white folks?"

"They married mulattoes, mostly, I believe. There was heaps of mulattoes in Alexandria then—free niggers—their fathers was French and Spanish men, and their mothers right black niggers. Good many of them had Egyptian blood in 'em, too."

He believed the Egyptians had disappeared since then. He had lately made a visit to Alexandria, and had seen none of them. The free mulattoes were always healthy, so far as he knew. He thought they were rather more healthy than white people. Upon close questioning, he thought those of them that were nearest to white were rather weakly. A good many that he remembered were rich, and their fathers had them educated and brought up just as they did their white children.

The Egyptians were probably Spanish Gipsies; though I have never heard of any of them being in America in any other way.

Some time subsequently to my Red River trip, I made a short visit to Washington and Opelousas. Washington was formerly called Niggerville, from the number of free negroes living in the village. A German merchant, living in Washington, told me there were few now living in the place; but in the parish of Opelousas (parish, in Louisiana, is equivalent to county) there were many. Often, he said, they were wealthy and thriving, and they owned some of the best of the cotton and sugar plantations. Some of them were educated; he did not know how or where. One planter that he did business with, kept his books and wrote business-letters in a better manner than most white planters.

Between Washington and Opelousas, a distance of about six miles, if I recollect rightly, three handsome houses, attached to first-rate plantations, were pointed out to me as belonging to free colored men.

On the steam-boat Alice Glaze, running to Washington, I noticed among some Creole ladies a very plainly-dressed young woman, not as dark as the rest, but of a warmer brown, and a more nectarine-like texture of skin, remarkably well formed, with very fine, wavy black hair.   Although she was plainly dressed, it was not until I saw her dining between two perfectly black women, that I thought of her being a slave.   She was lighter in color than most English women, and had a soft and downcast eye, and a modest and sensitive expression.

I have seen, I suppose, a hundred advertisements of runaway slaves, who were described as being so white that they might be mistaken for white persons.   I append some specimens :—

From the *Republican Banner and Nashville Whig*, July 14, 1849.

"Two Hundred Dollars Reward.—Ran away from the subscriber, on the 23d of June last, a bright mulatto woman, named Julia, about twenty-five years of age.   She is of common size, nearly white, and very likely.   She is a good seamstress, and can read a little.   She may attempt to *pass for white;* dresses fine.   She took with her Anna, her child, eight or nine years old, and considerably darker than her mother.   * * *   She once belonged to a Mr. Helm, of Columbia, Tennessee.

"I will give a reward, &c.

"A. W. Johnson."

From the *Savannah Republican*, Oct. 8, 1855.

"Fifty Dollars Reward.—Ran away from the subscriber, on the 22d ulto., my negro man, Albert, who is 27 years old, *very white, so much so that he would not be suspected of being a negro.*   Has blue eyes, and very light hair.   Wore, when he left, a long thin beard, and rode a chestnut sorrel horse, with about $70 belonging to himself.

"He is about five feet eight inches high, and weighs about 140 pounds.   Has a very humble and meek appearance ; can neither read nor write, and is a very kind and amiable fellow ; speaks much like a low country negro.   He has, no doubt, been led off by some miserable wretch, during my absence in New York.

"The above reward will be paid for his delivery to me, or to Tinson & Mackey, Savannah, or for his apprehension and confinement in any jail where I can get him.

"I. M. Tison.

"Bethel, Glynn Co., Ga."

From the *New Orleans Picayune.*

"Two Hundred Dollars Reward.—Ran away from the subscriber, last November, *a white negro man*, about thirty-five years old, hight about five feet eight or ten inches, blue eyes, has a yellow woolly head, very fair skin (particularly under his clothes). * * * Said negro man was raised in Columbia, S. C., and is well known by the name of Dick Frazier. * * * He was lately known to be working on the rail-road in Alabama, near Moore's Turnout, and *passed as a white man*, by the name of Jesse Teams. I will give the above reward, &c.

"Barnwell Court House, S. C.   J. D. Allen.

"P. S.—Said man has a good-shaped foot and leg ; and his foot is very small and hollow."

From the *Richmond* (Virginia) *Whig.*

"One Hundred Dollars Reward will be given for the apprehension of my negro, Edmund Kenney. He has straight hair, and complexion so nearly white that it is believed a stranger would suppose there was no African blood in him. He was with my boy Dick, a short time since, in Norfolk, and offered him for sale, and was apprehended, but escaped under pretense of being a white man.

"Anderson Bowles."

An intelligent man, whom I met at Washington, who had been traveling most of the time for two years, in the planting districts of the Louisiana, having business with planters, told me that the free negroes of the State in general, so far as he had observed, were just equal, in all respects, to the white Creoles. Much the largest part of them, he said, are poor, thriftless, unambitious, and live wretchedly ; but there are many, opulent, intelligent, and educated. The best house and most tasteful grounds that he had visited in the State, belong to a nearly full-blooded negro—a very dark man. He and his family are well educated, and though French is their habitual tongue, they speak English with freedom ; and one of them with much more elegance than most liberally educated whites in the South. They had a private tutor in their family.   They owned, he presumed, a hundred slaves.

Court was in session at Opelousas during my visit, and among the crowd of people in attendance, there were a number of well-dressed, and self-respecting-looking colored men ; but they kept together, in groups by themselves, not mingling or conversing at all with the whites.

OPELOUSAS AND WASHINGTON.

Opelousas is a pleasant village, with shaded streets, and many substantial mansions, and pretty cottages.   The soil in the vicinity is very rich, and there are many large plantations.

Washington is a mean, scattering village, on a narrow bayou, and is the shipping port of Opelousas, and of a large planting and grazing district.   The inhabitants seemed to be mostly Germans.   In the inn yard were five German peddlers' wagons. These peddlers, I ascertained, usually purchased their outfit of their countrymen in Washington, and were present in unusual numbers at the time of my visit, to give evidence in the court sitting at Opelousas.   They testified that they each had been in the habit of purchasing from one house, goods to the value of from one to two hundred dollars a month.   There were also several other Germans, travelers and clerks, in the village, boarding at the hotel.

GERMAN FOOLS.

The educated German, who has grafted upon the thorough-ness, the conscientiousness, and the pleasant, social traits of his countrymen, the rapidity, directness, and self-reliance of the American, is the most agreeable, and if not yet the most useful,

certainly the most promising man in our country. But I don't
know any people so disagreeable, or so despicable as those young
Germans, who have learned to copy all that is vulgar and vicious
in the American character, and who are ashamed of their own
natural characteristics. They speak, even to each other, all the
while, a bastard English; and their chief accomplishment is to
decorate it with a profusion of cant, and profane and obscene
phrases and words. These at Washington carried knives in
their bosoms, and were constantly offering familiar observations
to me, and the other New-Yorker at the hotel, nearly always
commencing with the exclamation, "Oh! Christ! gents." One
of them told me, aside, with great contempt, that the rest were
Jews, but that they pretended to be infidels.

The house was well filled with guests, and my friend and myself were told that we must sleep together. In the room containing our bed, there were three other beds; and although the
outside of the house was pierced with windows, nowhere more
than four feet apart, not one of them opened out of our room.
A door opened into the hall, another into the dining-room, and
at the side of our bed was a window into the dining-room,
through which, betimes in the morning, we could, with our heads
on our pillows, see the girls setting the breakfast-tables. Both
the doors were provided with glass windows, without curtains.
Hither, about eleven o'clock, we *retired*. Soon afterwards, hearing something moving under the bed, I asked, "Who's there?"
and was answered by a girl, who was burrowing for eggs; part of
the stores of the establishment being kept in boxes, in this convenient locality. Later, I was awakened by a stranger attempting to enter my bed. I expostulated, and he replied that it was
his bed, and nobody else had a right to his place in it. Who

was I, he asked, angrily, and where was his partner. " Here I am," answered a voice from another bed; and without another word, he left us. I slept but little, and woke feverish, and with a headache, caused by the want of ventilation.

FIGHTS.

While at the dinner-table, a man asked, as one might at the North, if the steamer had arrived, if there had been " any fights to-day ?" After dinner, while we were sitting on the gallery, loud cursing, and threatening voices were heard in the direction of the bar-room, which, as at Nachitoches, was detached, and at a little distance from the hotel. The company, except myself and the other New-Yorker, immediately ran towards it. After ten minutes, one returned, and said :

" I don't believe there'll be any fight; they are both cowards."

" Are they preparing for a fight?"

" O, yes ; they are loading pistols in the coffee-room, and there's a man outside, in the street, who has a revolver and a knife, and who is challenging another to come out. He swears he'll wait there till he does come out; but in my opinion he'll think better of it, when he finds that the other feller's got pistols, too."

" What's the occasion of the quarrel ?"

" Why, the man in the street says the other one insulted him this morning, and that he had his hand on his knife, at the very moment he did so, so he couldn't reply. And now he says he's ready to talk with him, and he wants to have him come out, and as many of his friends as are a mind to may come with him ; he's got enough for all of 'em, he says. He's got two revolvers, I believe."

We did not hear how it it ended; but, about an hour afterwards, I saw three men, with pistols in their hands, coming from the bar-room.

The next day, I saw, in the streets of the same town, two boys running from another, who was pursuing them with a large, open dirk-knife in his hand, and every appearance of ungovernable rage in his face.

The boat, for which I was waiting, not arriving, I asked the landlady—who appeared to be a German Jewess—if I could not have a better sleeping-room. She showed me one, which she said I might use for a single night; but, if I remained another, I must not refuse to give it up. It had been occupied by another gentleman, and she thought he might return the next day, and would want it again; and, if I remained in it, he would be very angry that they had not reserved it for him, although they were under no obligation to. "He is a dangerous man," she observed, "and my husband, he's a quick-tempered man, and, if they get to quarreling about it, there'll be knives about, sure. It always frightens me to see knives drawn."

A TEXAS DROVER'S RELIGION.

A Texas drover, who staid over night at the hotel, being asked, as he was about to leave in the morning, if he was not going to have his horse shod, replied:

"No sir! it'll be a damned long spell 'fore I pay for having a horse shod. I reckon if God Almighty had thought it right hosses should have iron on thar feet, he'd a put it thar himself. I don't pretend to be a pious man myself; but I a'nt a-goin' to run agin the will of God Almighty, though thar's some, that calls themselves ministers of Christ, that does it."

CREOLE BALL.

I attended a Creole ball, while at Washington. The ladies were, on an average, more beautiful, better formed, and more becomingly dressed, as well as much better dancers, than they would ever be found in a country ball room at the North; but, what was chiefly remarkable, was the exquisite skill and taste displayed in the dressing of their hair. The ball was conducted with the greatest propriety; and broke up earlier than public balls usually do at the North.

COURT AT OPELOUSAS.

Nearly all of the large number of people, in attendance on the Court, who came in from the country, rode on horseback. The majority of them were of French blood; but the leading and richest men seemed to be all English. Pleadings were made by each counsel—first in the English, and afterwards in the French language. A juryman mentioned, at dinner, that the man who sat beside him, on the jury, was a Spaniard, and understood very little French, and scarcely a word of English; and was constantly asking him what it was that was being said. There were also a good many Germans, and, as I before mentioned, several free colored persons: I saw not one Irishman. The Court-room was strewed, to the depth of an inch or two, with saw-dust, to absorb the tobacco juice; and the spitting was incessant, by men of every race.

TRANSACTIONS IN THE NIGGER TRADE.

On the gallery of the hotel, after dinner, a fine-looking man —who was on the best of terms with every one—familiar with the judge—and who had been particularly polite to me, at the dinner-table, said to another :

"I hear you were very unlucky with that girl you bought of me, last year?"

"Yes, I was; very unlucky. She died with her first child, and the child died, too."

"Well, that was right hard for you. She was a fine girl. I don't reckon you lost less than five thousand dollars, when she died."

"No, sir; not a dollar less."

"Well, it came right hard upon you—just beginning so."

"Yes, I was foolish, I suppose, to risk so much on the life of a single woman; but I've got a good start again now, for all that. I've got two right likely girls; one of them's got a fine boy, four months old, and the other's with child—and old Pine Knot's as hearty as ever."

"Is he? Hasn't been sick at all, eh?"

"Yes; he was sick very soon after I bought him of you; but he got well soon."

"That's right. I'd rather a nigger would be sick early, after he comes into this country; for he's bound to be acclimated, sooner or later, and the longer it's put off, the harder it goes with him."

The man was a regular negro trader. He told me that he had a partner in Kentucky, and that they owned a farm there, and another one here. His partner bought negroes, as opportunity offered to get them advantageously, and kept them on their Kentucky farm; and he went on occasionally, and brought the surplus to their Louisiana plantation—where he held them for sale.

"So-and-so is very hard upon you," said another man, to him as he still sat, smoking his cigar, on the gallery, after dinner.

"Why so ? He's no business to complain; I told him just exactly what the nigger was, before I sold him (laughing, as if there was a concealed joke). It was all right—all right. I heard that he sold him again for a thousand dollars; and the people that bought him, gave him two hundred dollars to let them off from the bargain. I'm sure he can't complain of me. It was a fair transaction. He knew just what he was buying."

FRENCH AND SPANISH BLOODED LOUISIANIANS.

Of the Creoles, in general, the commercial traveler said, that the greater part live very poorly. He had sometimes found it difficult to get food, even when he was in urgent need of it, at their houses. The lowest class live much from hand to mouth; and are often in extreme destitution. This was more particularly the case with those who lived on the rivers; those who resided on the prairies were seldom so much reduced. The former now live only on those parts of the river to which the back-swamp approaches nearest; that is, where there is but little valuable land, that can be appropriated for plantation-purposes. They almost all reside in communities, very closely housed in poor cabins. If there is any considerable number of them, there is to be always found, among the cluster of their cabins, a church, and a billiard and a gambling-room—and the latter is always occupied, and play going on.

They almost all appear excessively apathetic, sleepy, and stupid, if you see them at home; and they are always longing and waiting for some excitement. They live for excitement, and will not labor, unless it is violently, for a short time, to gratify some passion.

This was as much the case with the women as the men. The women were often handsome, stately, and graceful, and, ordinarily, exceedingly kind; but languid, and incredibly indolent, unless there was a ball, or some other excitement, to engage them. Under excitement, they were splendidly animated, impetuous, and eccentric. One moment they seemed possessed by a devil, and the next by an angel.

The Creoles are inveterate gamblers—rich and poor alike. The majority of wealthy Creoles, he said, do nothing to improve their estate; and are very apt to live beyond their income. They borrow and play, and keep borrowing to play, as long as they can; but they will not part with their land, and especially with their home, as long as they can help it, by any sacrifice.

The men are generally dissolute. They have large families, and a great deal of family affection. He did not know that they had more than Anglo-Saxons; but they certainly manifested a great deal more, and, he thought, had more domestic happiness. If a Creole farmer's child marries, he will build a house for the new couple, adjoining his own; and, when another marries, he builds another house—so, often his whole front on the river is at length occupied. Then he begins to build others, back of the first—and so, there gradually forms a little village, wherever there is a large Creole family, owning any considerable piece of land. The children are poorly educated, and are not brought up to industry, at all.

The planters living near them, as their needs increase, lend them money, and get mortgages on their land, or, in some way or other, if it is of any value, force them to part with it. Thus they are every year reduced, more and more, to the poorest lands; and the majority now are able to get but a very poor living, and would not be able to live at all, in a Northern climate. They are, nevertheless—even the poorest of them— habitually gay and careless, as well as kind-hearted, hospitable, and dissolute—working little, and spending much of their time at church, or at balls, or at the gaming-table.

There are very many wealthy Creole planters, who are as cultivated and intelligent as the better class of American planters, and usually more refined. The Creoles, he said, did not work their slaves as hard as the Americans; but, on the other hand, they did not feed or clothe them nearly as well, and he had noticed universally, on the Creole plantations, a large number of "used-up hands"—slaves, sore and crippled, or invalided for some cause. On all sugar plantations, he said, they work the negroes excessively, in the grinding season; often cruelly. Under the usual system, to keep the fires burning, and the works constantly supplied, eighteen hours' work was required of every negro, in twenty-four—leaving but six for rest. The work of most of them, too, was very hard. They were gene-rally, during the grinding season, liberally supplied with food and coffee, and were induced, as much as possible, to make a kind of frolic of it; yet, on the Creole plantations, he thought they did not, even in the grinding season, often get meat.

I remarked that the law, in Louisiana, required that meat should be regularly served to the negroes.

" O, those laws are very little regarded."

" Indeed ?"

" Certainly. Suppose you are my neighbor; if you maltreat your negroes, and tell me of it, or I see it, am I going to prefer charges against you to the magistrates? I might possibly get you punished, according to law; but, if I did, or did not, I should have you, and your family and friends, far and near, for my mortal enemies. There is a law of the State that negroes shall not be worked on Sundays; but I have seen negroes at work almost every Sunday, when I have been in the country, since I have lived in Louisiana.* I spent a Sunday once with a gentleman, who did not work his hands at all on Sunday, even in the grinding season; and he had got some of his neighbors to help him build a school-house—which was used as a church, on Sunday. He said, there was not a plantation on either side of him, as far as he could see, where the slaves were not generally worked on Sunday; but that, after the church was started, several of them quit the practice, and made their negroes go to the meeting. This made others discontented; and, after a year or two, the planters voted new trustees to the school, and these forbid the house to be used for any other than school purposes. This was done, he had no doubt, for the purpose of breaking up the meetings, and to lessen the discontent of the slaves which were worked on Sunday."

It was said that the custom of working the negroes on Sunday was much less common than formerly; if so, he thought that it must have formerly been universal.

He had lived, when a boy, for several years on a farm in Western New York, and afterwards, for some time, at Rochester, and was well acquainted with the people generally, in the valley of the Genesee.

---

* I also saw slaves at work every Sunday that I was in Louisiana. The law permits slaves to be worked, I believe, on Sunday; but requires that some compensation shall be made to them when they are—such as a subsequent holiday.

I asked him if he thought, among the intelligent class of farmers and planters, people of equal property lived more happily
in New York or Louisiana. He replied immediately, as if he
had carefully considered the topic, that, with some rare exceptions,
farmers worth forty thousand dollars lived in far greater comfort,
and enjoyed more refined and elegant leisure, than planters worth
three hundred thousand, and that farmers of the ordinary class,
who labored with their own hands, and were worth some six
thousand dollars, in the Genesee valley, lived in far greater comfort, and in all respects more enviably, than planters worth forty
thousand dollars in Louisiana. The contrast was especially
favorable to the New York farmer, in respect to books and newspapers. He might travel several days, and call on a hundred
planters, and hardly see in their houses more than a single newspaper a-piece, in most cases; perhaps none at all: nor any books
except a Bible, and some Government publications, that had been
franked to them through the post-office, and perhaps a few religious tracts or school-books.

The most striking difference that he observed between the
Anglo-Americans of Louisiana and New York, was the impul-
sive and unreflective habit of the former, in doing business. He
mentioned, as illustrative of this, the almost universal passion
among the planters for increasing their negro-stock. It appeared
evident to him, that the market price of negroes was much higher than the prices of cotton and sugar warranted; but it seemed
as if no planter ever made any calculation of that kind. The
majority of planters, he thought, would always run in debt to the
extent of their credit for negroes, whatever was asked for them,
without making any calculation of the reasonable prospects
of their been able to pay their debts. When any one made a

good crop, he would always expect that his next one would be better, and make purchases in advance upon such expectation. When they were dunned, they would attribute their inability to pay, to accidental short crops, and always were going ahead risking everything, in confidence that another year luck would favor them, and a big crop make all right.

If they had a full crop, probably there would be good crops everywhere else, and prices would fall, and then they would whine and complain, as if the merchants were to blame for it, and would insinuate that no one could be expected to pay his debts when prices were so low, and that it would be dangerous to press such an unjust claim. And, if the crops met with any misfortune, from floods, or rot, or vermin, they would cry about it like children when rain fell upon a holiday, as if they had never thought of the possibility of such a thing, and were very hard used.

The following resolutions were proposed (and perhaps passed) in the Southern Commercial Convention, at New Orleans, this year (1855).

" *Resolved,* That this Convention strongly recommends the Chambers of Commerce and Commission Merchants of our Southern and Southwestern cities to adopt such a system of laws and regulations as will put a stop to the dangerous practice, heretofore existing, of making advances to planters, in anticipation of their crops—a practice entirely at variance with everything like safety in business-transactions, and tending directly to establish the relations of master and slave between the merchant and planter, by bringing the latter into the most abject and servile bondage.

" *Resolved,* That this Convention recommend, in the most urgent manner, that the planters of the Southern and Southwestern States patronize exclusively our home merchants, and that our Chambers of Commerce, and merchants generally, exert all their influence to exclude foreign agents from the purchase and sale of produce in any of our Southern and Southwestern cities.

" *Resolved, further,* That this Convention recommend to the Legislatures of the Southern and South-Western States to pass laws, making it a penitentiary offense for the planters to ask of the merchants to make such pecuniary advances."

He had talked with many sugar-planters who were very strong Cuba war and annexation men, and had rarely found that any of these had given the first thought to the probable effect the annexation of Cuba would have on their home interests. It was mainly a romantic excitement and enthusiasm, inflamed by senseless appeals to their patriotism and their combativeness. They had got the idea, that patriotism was necessarily associated with hatred and contempt of any other country but their own, and the only foreigners to be regarded with favor were those who desired to surrender themselves to us.

They never reflected that the annexation of Cuba would necessarily be attended by the removal of the duty on sugar, and would bring them into competition with the sugar-planters of that island, where the advantages for growing cane were so much greater than in Louisiana.

To some of the very wealthy planters who favored the movement, and who were understood to have taken some of the Junta stock, he gave credit for greater sagacity. He thought it was the purpose of these men, if Cuba could be annexed, to get possession of large estates there : then, with the advantages of their greater skill in sugar-making, and better machinery than that which yet was in use in Cuba, and with much cheaper land and labor, and a far better climate for cane growing than that of Louisiana, it would be easy for them to accumulate large fortunes in a few years ; but he thought the sugar-planters who remained in Louisiana would be ruined by it.

The principal subscribers to the Junta stock at the South, he thought, were land speculators; persons who expected that, by now favoring the movement, they would be able to obtain from the revolutionary government large grants of land in the island, as gratuities in reward of their services or at nominal prices, which after annexation would rise very rapidly in value; or persons who now owned wild land in the States, and who thought that if Cuba were annexed the African slave-trade would be reëstablished, either openly or clandestinely, with the States, and their lands be increased in value, by the greater cheapness with which they could then be stocked with laborers.

I find these views confirmed in a published letter from a Louisiana planter, to one of the members of Congress, from that State; and I insert an extract of that letter, as it is evidently from a sensible and far-thinking man, to show on how insecure a basis rests the prosperity of the slave-holding interest in Louisiana. The fact would seem to be, that, if it were not for the tariff on foreign sugars, sugar could not be produced at all by slave labor; and that a discontinuance of sugar culture would almost desolate the State.

" The question now naturally comes up to you and to me, do we Louisianians desire the possession of Cuba? It is not what the provision dealers of the West, or the ship-owners of the North may wish for, but what the State of Louisiania, as a State, may deem consistent with her best interests. My own opinion on the subject is not a new one. It was long ago expressed to high officers of our Government, neither of whom ever hesitated to acknowledge that it was, in the main, correct. That opinion was and is, *that the acquisition of Cuba would prove the ruin of our State.* I found this opinion on the following reasons : Cuba has already land enough in cultivation to produce, when directed by American skill, energy, and capital, twenty millions of tons of sugar. In addition to this she has virgin soil, only needing roads to bring it, with a people of the least pretension to enterprise, into active working, sufficient nearly to double this ; all of which would be soon brought into productiveness were it our own, with the whole American market free to it. If any man supposes that the culture of sugar in our State can be sustained in the face of this, I have only to say that he can suppose anything. We have very nearly, if not quite, eighty millions invested in the sugar culture. My idea is that *three-fourths of this would, so far as the State is concerned, be annihilated at a blow.* The planter who is in debt, would find his negroes and machinery sold and dispatched to Cuba for him, and he who is independent would go there in self-defense. What will become of the other portion of the capital ? It consists of land, on which I maintain there can be produced no other crop but sugar, under present auspices, that will bear the contest with cocoa,* and the expense and risk of levees, as it regards the larger part of it, and the difficulty of transportation for the remainder. But supposing that it will be taken up by some other cultivation, that in any case must be a work of time, and in this case a very long time for unacclimated men. It is not unreasonable, then, to suppose that this whole capital will, for purposes of taxation, be withdrawn from Louisiana. From whence, then, is to come the revenue for the support of our State Government, for the payment of the interest on our debt, and the eventual redemption of the principal ? Perhaps repudiation may be recommended ; but you and I, my dear sir, are too old-fashioned to rob in that manner, or in any other. The only resort, then, is double taxation on the cotton planter, which will drive him, without much difficulty, to Texas, to Arkansas, and Mississippi."

VISIT TO A SUGAR PLANTATION.

I came to Mr. R.'s plantation by a steam-boat, late at night. As the boat approached the shore, near his house, her big bell having been rung some ten minutes previously, a negro came out with a lantern to meet her. The boat's bow was run boldly against the bank ; I leaped ashore, the clerk threw out a newspaper and a package, saying to the negro, " That's for your

---

* Cocoa is a grass much more pernicious, and more difficult of extirpation when it once gets a footing upon a sugar plantation, than the Canada thistle, or any other weed known at the North. Several plantations have been ruined by it, and given up as worthless by their owners.

master, and that's for so and so, tell your master, and ask him to give it to him." The boat bounded off by her own elasticity, the starboard wheel was backed for a turn or two, and the next minute the great edifice was driving up the stream again—not a rope having been lifted, nor any other movement having been made on board, except by the pilot and engineer.

"Do you belong to Mr. R.?" I asked the negro. "Yes, sir; is you going to our house, master?" "Yes." "I'll show you the way, then, sir;" and he conducted me in, leaving the parcels the clerk had thrown out, where they had fallen, on the bank.

A negro woman prepared a bed for me, waited at the door till I had put out my light, and then returned to tuck in the musquito-bar tightly about the bed. This was merely from custom, as there were no musquitoes at that season. In the morning the same woman awakened me, opened the curtains, and asked me to take the money which she had found in the pockets of my clothing, while she took it out to be brushed.

Mr. R. is a Southerner by birth, but was educated at the North, where, also, and in foreign countries, he has spent a large part of his life. He is a man of more than usual precision of mind, energetic and humane; and while his negroes seemed to be better disciplined than any others I had seen, they evidently regarded him with affection, respect, and pride.

He had been ill for some weeks previous to my visit, and when he walked out with me, on the second day, it was the first time since the commencement of his illness that his field-hands had seen him.

The first negroes we met were half a dozen women, who were going up to the nursery to suckle their children—the overseer's bell having been just rung (at eleven o'clock), to call them in from work for that purpose.. Mr. R. said that he allowed them two hours to be with their children while nursing at noon, and to leave work an hour earlier at night than the other field-hands. The women all stopped as we met them, and asked, with much animation:

"Oh, master! how is ou?"

"Well, I'm getting up. How are you, girls?"

"Oh, we's well, sir."

"The children all well?"

"Yes, master, all but Sukey's, sir."

"Sukey's? What, isn't that well yet?"

"No, master."

"But it's getting well, is it not?"

"Yes, master."

Soon after we met a boy, driving a cart. He pulled up as he came against us, and, taking off his hat, asked, "How is 'ou, master?"

"I'm getting well, you see. If I don't get about, and look after you, I'm afraid we shan't have much of a crop. I don't know what you niggers will do for Christmas money."

"Ha!—look heah, massa!—you jus' go right straight on de ways you's goin'; see suthin' make you laugh, ha! ha! (meaning the work that had been done while he was ill, and the good promise of a crop).

The plantation contained about nine hundred acres of tillage land, and a large tract of "swamp," or woodland, was attached to it. The tillage land was inclosed all in one field by a strong cypress post and rail fence, and was drained by two canals, five feet deep, running about twenty feet apart, and parallel—the earth from both being thrown together, so as to make a high, dry road between them, straight through the middle of the plantation.

Fronting upon the river, and but six or eight rods from the public road, which everywhere runs close along the shore inside the levee, was the mansion of the proprietor : an old Creole house, the lower story of brick and the second of wood, with a broad gallery, shaded by the extended roof, running all around it ; the roof steep, and shedding water on four sides, with ornaments of turned wood where lines met, and broken by several small dormer windows. The gallery was supported by round brick columns, and arches. The parlors, library and sleeping rooms of the white family were all on the second floor. Between the house and the street was a yard, planted formally with orange-trees and other evergreens. A little on one side of the house stood a large two-story, square dove-cot, which is a universal appendage of a sugar-planter's house. In the rear of the house was another large yard, in which, irregularly placed, were houses for the family servants, a kitchen, stable, carriage-house, smoke-house, etc. Behind this rear-yard there was a vegetable garden, of an acre or more, in the charge of a negro gardener ; a line of fig-trees were planted along the fence, but all the ground inclosed was intended to be cropped with vegetables for the family, and for the supply of " the people." I was pleased to notice, however, that the negro-gardener had, of his own accord, planted some violets and other flowering plants. From a corner of the court a road ran to the sugar-works and the negro settlement, which were five or six hundred yards from the house.

The negro houses were exactly like those I described on the Georgia Rice Plantation, except that they were provided with broad galleries in front. They were as neat and well-made externally as the cottages usually provided by large manufacturing companies in New-England, to be rented to their workmen. The clothing furnished the negroes, and the rations of bacon and meal, were the same as on other good plantations. During the grinding season extra rations of flour were served, and hot coffee was kept constantly in the sugar-house, and the hands on duty were allowed to drink it almost *ad libitum*. They were also allowed to drink freely of the hot *sirop*, of which they were extremely fond. A generous allowance of *sirop*, or molasses, was also given out to them, with their other rations, every week during the winter and early summer. In extremely hot weather it was thought to be unfavorable to health, and was discontinued. Rations of tobacco were also served. At Christmas, a sum of money, equal to one dollar for each hogshead of sugar made on the plantation, was divided among the negroes. The last year this had amounted to over two dollars a head. It was usually given to the heads of families. If any had been particularly careless or lazy, it was remembered at this Christmas dole. Of course, the effect of this arrangement, small as was the amount received by each person, was to give the laborers a direct interest in the economical direction of their labor: the advantage of it was said to be very evident.

Mr. R. had purchased the plantation but three years before of a Creole, and afterwards had somewhat increased its area by buying out several poor people, who had owned small farms adjoining. He had greatly extended and improved the drainage, and had nearly doubled the force of negroes employed upon it, adding to the number that he purchased with the land, nearly as many more whom he had inherited, and whom he transferred to it from an old cotton plantation that he had formerly lived upon.

He had considerably more than doubled the stock of mules and oxen; had built entirely new cabins for all the negroes, and new sugar-works and stables. His whole capital, he said, when he first bought the plantation, would not have paid half the price of it and of the cost of stocking it as he had done. Most men when they buy a plantation, he informed me, go very heavily in debt; frequently the purchase is made three quarters on credit.

"Buying a plantation," were his words, "whether a sugar or cotton plantation, in this country, is usually essentially a gambling operation. The capital invested in a sugar plantation of the size of mine ought not to be less than $150,000. The purchaser pays down what he can, and usually gives security for the payment of the balance in six annual installments, with interest (10 per cent. per annum) from the date of the purchase. Success in sugar as well as cotton planting, is dependent on so many circumstances, that it is as much trusting to luck as betting on a throw of dice. If his first crop proves a bad one, he must borrow money of the Jews in New Orleans to pay his first note; they will sell him this on the best terms they can, and often at not less than 25 per cent. per annum. If three or four bad crops follow one another, he is ruined. But this is seldom the case, and he lives on, one year gaining a little on his debts, but almost as often enlarging them. Three or four years ago there was hardly a planter in Louisiana or Mississippi that was not in very embarrassed circumstances, nearly every one having his crops pledged to his creditors long before they were secured. The good prices and good crops of the last few years have set them all on their legs again; and this year all the jewelers' shops, and stores of rich furniture and dry-goods, in New Orleans, were cleared out by the middle of the season, and everybody feels strong and cheerful. I have myself been particularly fortunate; I have made three good crops in succession. Last year I made six hundred and fifty hogsheads of sugar, and twelve hundred barrels of molasses. The molasses alone brought me a sum sufficient to pay all my plantation expenses; and the sugar yields me a clear profit of twenty-five per cent. on my whole investment. If I make another crop this year as good as that, I shall be able to discount my outstanding notes, and shall be clear of debt at the end of four years, instead of six, which was the best I had hoped for."

On another plantation that I visited, where the working force was considered equal to one hundred field-hands, the sugar works cost $40,000, and seven hundred barrels of sugar had been made. On this plantation there was a steam-pump, which drained the rear of the plantation over a levee, when the back-water from the swamp would have prevented perfect drainage.

Mr. R. modestly credited his extraordinary success to "luck;" but I was satisfied, upon examining his improvements, and considering the reasons, which he readily gave me, for every operation which he showed, or described to me, that intelligence, study, and enterprise had seldom better claims to reward. Adjoining his plantation there was another of nearly twice the size, on which an equal number of negroes and only half the number of cattle were employed; and the proprietor, I was told, had had rather bad luck: he had, in fact, made but little more than half the quantity of sugar which Mr. R. had done. I inquired of the latter if there was any advantage in his soil over that of his neighbor's. "I think not," he replied; "my best cane was made on a piece of land adjoining his, which, before I bought it, was thought unfit for cultivation. The great advantage I had over him last year, mainly arose from my having secured a more complete drainage of all my land."

The soil of the greater part of the plantation was a fine, dark, sandy loam ; some of it, at the greatest distance from the river, was lighter in color, and more clayey ; and in one part, where there was a very slight depression of the surface over about fifty acres, there was a dark, stiffish soil. It was this to which Mr. R. alluded as having produced his best cane. It had been considered too low, wet, tenacious, and unfertile to be worthy of cultivation by the former owner, and was covered with bushes and weeds when he took it. The improvement had been effected entirely by draining and fall-plowing. In fall-plowing, as a remedy for tenacity of soil, this gentleman's experience had given him great faith. At various points on my tour, I found most conflicting opinions upon this point, many (among them the President of a State Agricultural Society) having invariably observed pernicious effects result from it.

SUGAR CANE IN LOUISIANA.

The Sugar-cane is a perennial-rooted plant, and the stalk does not attain its full size, under favorable circumstances, in less growing time than twelve months ; and seed does not usually form upon it until the thirteenth or fourteenth month. This function (termed *arrowing*) it only performs in a very hot and steadily hot climate, somewhat rarely even in the West Indies. The plant is, at all stages, extremely susceptible to cold, a moderate frost not only suspending its growth, but disorganizing it so that the chemical qualities of its sap are changed, and it is rendered valueless for sugar-making.

As frosts of considerable severity are common in all parts of Louisiana, during three months of the year, of course the sugar-cane is there never permitted to attain its full growth.   To so much greater perfection does it arrive in the West Indies, that the cane produced on one acre will yield from 3,000 to 6,000 lbs. of sugar, while in Louisiana 1,000 is considered the average obtained.   "I could make sugar in the climate of Cuba," said a Louisiana planter to me, "for half the price that, under the most favorable circumstances, it must cost here."   In addition to the natural uncongeniality of the climate, the ground on which it grows in Louisiana, being lower than the surface of the river, is much of the time made cold by the infiltration of moisture.   It is, therefore, only by reason of the extreme fertility of this alluvial deposit, assisted by a careful method of cultivation, that the cane is forced to a state of maturity which enables it to yield an amount of sugar which, with the assistance of a governmental protection against foreign competition, will be remunerative to the planter.

THE ECONOMY OF LOUISIANA.

I must confess that there seems to me room for grave doubt if the capital, labor, and especially the human life, which have been and which continue to be spent in converting the swamps of Louisiana into sugar plantations, and in defending them against the annual assaults of the river, and the fever and the cholera, could not have been better employed somewhere else. It is claimed as a great advantage of Slavery, as well as of Protection, that what has been done for this purpose never would have been done without it.   If it would not, the obvious reason is, that the wages, or prospect of profit would not have been sufficient to induce free men to undergo the inconveniences and the danger incident to the enterprise. There is now great wealth in Louisiana; but I question if greater wealth would not have been obtained by the same expenditure of human labor, and happiness, and life, in other directions.

CANE CULTURE.

Planting commences immediately after the sugar-manufacturing season is concluded—usually in January. New or fallow land is prepared by plowing the whole surface: on this plantation the plow used was made in Kentucky, and was of a very good model, plowing seven to nine inches deep, with a single pair of mules. The ground being then harrowed, drills are opened with a double mould-board plow, seven feet apart. Cuttings of cane for seed are to be planted in them. These are reserved from the crop in the autumn, when some of the best cane on the plantation is selected for this purpose, while still standing.* This is cut off at the roots, and laid up in heaps or stacks, in such a manner that the leaves and tops protect the stalks from frost. The heaps are called mattresses; they are two or three feet high, and as many yards across. At the plant ing season they are opened, and the cane comes out moist and green, and sweet, with the buds or eyes, which protrude at the joints, swelling. The immature top parts of the stalk are cut off, and they are loaded into carts, and carried to the ground prepared for planting. The carts used are large, with high side-

---

* It is only on the best plantations that the seed-cane is selected with this care. On another plantation that I visited during the planting season, I noticed that the best part of the stalk had been cut off for grinding, and only the less valuable part saved for seed; and this, I apprehend, is the general practice. The best cuttings probably produce the most vigorous plants.

boards, and are drawn by three mules—one large one being in the shafts, and two lighter ones abreast, before her. The drivers are boys, who use the whip a great deal, and drive rapidly.

In the field I found the laborers working in three divisions—the first, consisting of light hands, brought the cane by arms-full from the cart, and laid it by the side of the furrows; the second planted it, and the third covered it. Planting is done by laying the cuttings at the bottom of the furrow, in such a way that there shall be three always together, with the eyes of each a little removed from those of the others—that is, all "breaking joints." They are thinly covered with earth, drawn over them with hoes. The other tools were so well selected on this planta-tion, that I expressed surprise at the clumsiness of the hoes, particularly as the soil was light, and entirely free from stones. "Such hoes as you use at the North would not last a negro a day," said the planter.

Cane will grow for several years from the roots of the old plants, and, when it is allowed to do so, a very considerable part of the expense is avoided; but the vigor of the plant is less when growing from this source than when starting from cuttings, and the crop, when thus obtained, is annually less and less pro-ductive, until, after a number of years, depending upon the rigor of the seasons, fresh shoots cease to spring from the stubble. This sprouting of cane from the stools of the last crop is termed "ratooning." In the West India plantations the cane is frequently allowed to ratoon for eight successive crops. In Louisiana it is usual to plant once in three years, trusting to the ratooning for two crops only, and this was the practice on Mr. R.'s plantation. The cost of sugar growing would be very greatly increased if the crop needed planting every year; for all the cane grown upon an acre will not furnish seed for more than four acres—consequently one-twelfth of the whole of each crop has to be reserved for the planting of the following crop, even when two-thirds of this is to be of ratoon cane.

Planting is finished in a favorable season—early in March. Tillage is commenced immediately afterwards, by plowing *from* the rows of young cane, and subsequently continued very much after the usual plan of tillage for potatoes, when planted in drills, with us. By or before the first of July, the crop is all well earthed up, the rows of cane growing from the crest of a rounded bed, seven feet wide, with deep water-furrows between each. The cane is at this time five or six feet high; and that growing from each bed forms arches with that of the next, so as to completely shade the ground. The furrows between the beds are carefully cleaned out; so that in the most drenching torrents of rain, the water is rapidly carried off into the drains, and thence to the swamp; and the crop then requires no further labor upon it until frost is apprehended, or the season for grinding arrives.

The nearly three months' interval, commencing at the intensest heat of summer, corresponds in the allotment of labor to the period of winter in Northern agriculture, because the winter itself, on the sugar-plantations, is the planting-season. The negroes are employed in cutting and carting wood for boiling the cane-juice, in making necessary repairs or additions to the sugar-house, and otherwise preparing for the grinding-season.

THE GRINDING SEASON.

The grinding-season is the harvest of the sugar-planter; it commences in October, and continues for two or three months,

during which time, the greatest possible activity and the utmost
labor of which the hands are capable, are required to secure the
product of the previous labor of the year. Mr. R. assured me
that during the last grinding-season nearly every man, woman,
and child on his plantation, including his overseer and himself,
were at work fully eighteen hours a day. From the moment
grinding first commences, until the end of the season, it is never
discontinued; the fires under the boiler never go out, and the
negroes rest only for six hours in the twenty-four, by relays—
three-quarters of them being constantly at work.

HARD WORK.

Notwithstanding the severity of the labor required of them at
this time, Mr. R. said that his negroes were as glad as he was
himself to have the time for grinding arrive, and they worked
with greater cheerfulness than at any other season.   How can
those persons who are always so ready to maintain that the
slaves work less than free laborers in free countries, and that for
that reason they are to be envied by them, account for this?
That at Mr. R.'s plantation it was the case that the slaves enjoyed most that season of the year when the hardest labor was
required of them, I have, in addition to Mr. R.'s own evidence,
good reason to believe, which I shall presently report.   And the
reason of it evidently is, that they are then better paid; they
have better and more varied food and stimulants than usual, but
especially they have a degree of freedom, and of social pleasure,
and a variety of occupation which brings a recreation of the
mind, and to a certain degree gives them strength for, and pleasure in, their labor.   Men of sense have discovered that when
they desire to get extraordinary exertions from their slaves, it is

better to offer them rewards than to whip them; to encourage them, rather than to drive them.

If the season has been favorable, so that the cane is strong, and well matured, it will endure a smart early frost without injury, particularly if the ground is well drained; but as rapidly as possible, after the season has arrived at which frosts are to be expected, the whole crop is cut, and put in mattresses, from which it is taken to the grinding-mill as fast as it can be made to use it.

The business of manufacturing sugar is everywhere carried on in connection with the planting of the cane. The shortness of the season during which the cane can be used is the reason assigned for this : the proprietors would not be willing to trust to custom-mills to manufacture their produce with the necessary rapidity. If cane should be cultivated in connection with other crops—that is, on small farms, instead of great " sugar only" plantations— neighborhood custom-mills would probably be employed. The profit of a sugar-plantation is now large, much in proportion to its size (if it be proportionately stocked); because only a very large supply of cane will warrant the proprietor in providing the most economical manufacturing apparatus. In 1849 there were 1,474 sugar estates in Louisiana, producing 236,547 hhds. of sugar; but it is thought that half of this quantity was produced on less than 200 estates—that is, that one-eighth of the planta-tions produced one-half the sugar. The sugar-works on some of the large estates cost over $100,000, and many of them manu-facture over 1,000,000 lbs. per annum. The profits of these, in a favorable season, are immense.

The apparatus used upon the better class of plantations is very admirable, and improvements are yearly being made, which

indicate high scientific acquirements, and much mechanical ingenuity on the part of the inventors. The whole process of sugar
manufacturing, although chemical analysis proves that a large
amount of saccharine is still wasted, has been within a few years
greatly improved, principally by reason of the experiments and
discoveries of the French chemists, whose labors have been
directed by the purpose to lessen the cost of beet-sugar. Apparatus for various processes in the manufacture, which they have
invented or recommended, has been improved, and brought into
practical operation on a large scale on some of the Louisiana
plantations, the owners of which are among the most intelligent,
enterprising, and wealthy men of business in the United States.
Forty-three plantations in the State are now furnished with apparatus constructed in accordance with the best scientific knowledge on the subject; and 914 are driven by steam-engines—
leaving but 560 to be worked by horse-power. Mr. R.'s sugar-
house, for making brown sugar, was furnished with the best kind
of apparatus, at a cost of $20,000. Preparations were making
for the addition of works for the manufacture of white loaf
sugar, which would cost $20,000 more. I visited one planta-
tion on which the sugar works were said to have cost over
$100,000.

SUGAR MANUFACTURING.

The first operation in the manufacture of sugar from cane is,
to express the saccharine juice it contains; this is done by passing it twice between rollers, on the same plan that apples are
crushed in our best cider-mills. A great deal of ingenuity has
been applied to the construction of the mills for this purpose,
and they have been, from time to time, improved, but are yet far

from satisfactory in their operation, as it is known that the crushed cane still retains nearly one-third of its original moisture, with a large share of the saccharine principle which belonged to it before it was passed between the rollers. No plan has yet been devised by which this can be economically secured.

The expressed juice is strained into a vessel, in which it is heated to a temperature of about 140° F., when it is clarified by the application of lime, the chemical action of which is not, I believe, perfectly understood; the effect is, to cause a precipitate of impurities, and to give a yellow color to the juice. In addition to this, the juice is sometimes further clarified by filtration. The next operation is the reduction of the cane-juice—by the evaporation of the greater part of its constituent water—to syrup. This is effected by the action of heat, which is applied in different ways, according to the apparatus used. There are seven different forms of this, in general use in Louisiana. In the simplest and rudest, the juice is boiled in open kettles; in the most improved, it is boiled in vacuo, on the principle that liquids boil at lower temperature, as the pressure of the atmosphere is removed. The sugar made by the latter process is much superior to that made by the former, which is always much burnt, and less pure, and it is also obtained at a much less expenditure for fuel.

The syrup having reached the proper degree of concentration, is next drawn off into vessels, in which it remains until granulation takes place. To separate the uncrystallizable syrup from the granulated sugar, in the more usual method, the mass of saccharine matter is placed in hogsheads, in the bottoms of which are holes, in which are inserted pieces of cane, which reach above the contents. As the granulation proceeds, a contraction takes place, which leaves an opening about the canes, by which the remaining liquid drains to the bottom, and, the canes being loosely inserted, it flows through the holes, out of the hogshead, leaving the comparatively dry sugar now completely granulated. The hogsheads are set upon a staging, or loose floor, over a large vat, in which the drainage is collected. This drainage is molasses. It is afterwards pumped out of the tanks into barrels, for market; commonly the purchaser buys it in the tank and provides barrels for its removal. Seventy gallons of molasses for each hogshead of sugar is considered a large estimate. The sugar is now in the condition known as "Muscovado," or raw brown sugar. Its color and quality depend on the caution and skill that have been used in the manufacture, and the excellence of the apparatus employed. The best Louisiana sugar is not inferior to any other plantation sugar of the world.

The raw sugar is further improved by filtering it (in the state of syrup), through animal black, or charcoal, made from bones, in the same way that liquors are "fined." This is done on several plantations. But the business of refining sugars is mainly carried on in well-known establishments, in all our large cities, and I need not describe it. In New York, alone, one thousand hogsheads a day are refined, and one house alone supplies to commerce as much as the whole manufacture of France. The difference between raw or brown sugar, and refined or white sugar, is simply one of cleanliness and purity.

Modern improvements have so greatly reduced the cost of refining sugar, that the consumption of the pure article, proportionately to that of the raw, has very rapidly increased; and it is probable that in a few years the use of the latter will be almost entirely discontinued for general purposes. Refined, or cleaned sugar is, doubtless, more wholesome, and can only be thought less palatable from habit or association. Pure sugar is now generally considered, by the best authorities, to be a very digestible and nutritious article of diet to most persons—even to infants—and the old idea that it injures the teeth, except mechanically, is considered a fallacy. But this is true only, I believe, of sugar in a pure crystallized or grained state; when cooked in the form of confectionery, or in combination with fatty substances, it seems to be very unwholesome.

"ACADIENS."

At one corner of Mr. R.'s plantation, there was a hamlet of Acadians (descendants of the refugees of Acadia), about a dozen small houses or huts, built of wood or clay, in the old French peasant style. The residents owned small farms, on which they raised a little corn and rice; but Mr. R. described them as lazy vagabonds, doing but little work, and spending much time in shooting, fishing, and play. He wanted very much to buy all their land, and get them to move away. He had already bought out some of them, and had made arrangements to get hold of the land of some of the rest. He was willing to pay them two or three times as much as their property was actually worth, to get them to move off. As fast as he got possession, he destroyed their houses and gardens, removed their fences and trees, and brought all their land into his cane-plantation.

Some of them were mechanics. One was a very good mason, and he employed him in building his sugar-works and refinery; but he would be glad to get rid of them all, and should then depend entirely on slave mechanics—of these he had several already, and he could buy more when he needed them.

Why did he so dislike to have these poor people living near him? Because, he said, they demoralized his negroes. The slaves seeing them living in apparent comfort, without much property and without steady labor, could not help thinking that it was not necessary for men to work so hard as they themselves were obliged to; that if they were free they would not need to work. Besides, the intercourse of these people with the negroes was not favorable to good discipline. They would get the negroes to do them little services, and would pay them with luxuries which he did not wish them to have. It was better that negroes never saw anybody off their own plantation; that they had no intercourse with other white men than their owner or overseer; especially, it was best that they should not see white men who did not command their respect, and whom they did not always feel to be superior to themselves, and able to command them.

" CHICKEN THIEVES."

The nuisance of petty traders dealing with the negroes, and encouraging them to pilfer, which I found everywhere a great annoyance to planters, seems to be greater on the Mississippi "Coast" than anywhere else. The traders generally come on boats, which they moor at night on the shore, adjoining the negro-quarters, and float away whenever they have obtained any booty, with very small chance of detection. One day, during my visit at Mr. R.'s, a neighbor called to apprise him that one of these tra-ding-boats was in the vicinity, that he might take precautions to prevent his negroes dealing with it. " The law," he observed, with much feeling, " is entirely inadequate to protect us against these rascals; it rather protects them than us. They easily evade detection in breaking it; and we can never get them punished, except we go beyond or against the law ourselves." To show me how vexatious the evil was, he mentioned that a large brass cock and some pipe had been lately stolen from his sugar-works, and that he had ascertained that one of his negroes had taken it and sold it on board one of these boats for seventy-five cents, and had immediately spent the money, chiefly for whisky, on the same boat. It had cost him thirty dollars to replace it. Mr. R. said that he had lately caught one of his own negroes going towards one of the "chicken thieves," (so the traders' boats are called) with a piece of machinery, that he had unscrewed from his sugar-works, which was worth eighty dollars, and which might very likely have been sold for a drink. If the negro had succeeded in reaching the boat, as he would if he had not been on the watch, he could never have recovered it. There would have been no witnesses to the sale; the stolen goods would have been hid on board until the boat reached New Orleans; or, if an officer came to search the boat, they would have been dropped into the river, before he got on board.

This neighbor of Mr. R.'s was a Creole, and had been educated in France. Conversing on the inconveniences of Slavery, he acknowledged that it was not only an uneconomical system, but a morally wrong one; "but," he said, "it was not instituted by us—we are not responsible for it. It is unfortunately fixed upon us; we could not do away with it if we wished; our duty is only to make the best of a bad thing; to lessen its evils as much as we can, so far as we have to do with it individually."

Mr. R. himself also acknowleged Slavery to be a very great evil, morally and economically. It was a curse upon the South; he had no doubt at all about it: nothing would be more desirable than its removal, if it were possible to be accomplished. But he did not think it could be abolished without instituting greater evils than those sought to be remedied. Its influence on the character of the whites was what was most deplorable. He was sorry to think that his children would have to be subject to it. He thought that eventually, if he were able to afford it, he would free his slaves and send them to Africa.

A SLAVE ABOLITIONIST.

When I left Mr. R.'s, I was driven about twenty miles in a buggy, by one of his house servants. He was inclined to be talkative and communicative; and as he expressed great affection and respect for his owner, I felt at liberty to question him on some points upon which I had always previously avoided conversing with slaves. He spoke rapidly, garrulously; and it was only necessary for me to give a direction to his thoughts, by my inquiries. I was careful to avoid leading questions, and not to show such an interest as would lead him to reply guardedly. I charged my memory as much as possible with his very words, when this was of consequence, and made the following record of the conversation, within half an hour after I left him.

He first said that he supposed that I would see that he was not a " Creole nigger;" he came from Virginia. He reckoned the Virginia negroes were better looking than those who were raised here; there were no black people anywhere in the world who were so " well made" as those who were born in Virginia. He asked if I lived in New Orleans; and where? I told him that I lived at the North; he asked:

" Da's a great many brack folks dah, massa?"

" No; very few."

"Da's a great many in Virginia ; more'n da is heah?"

"But I came from beyond Virginia—from New York."

He had heard there were a great many black folk in New York. I said there were a good many in the city; but few in the country. Did I live in the country? What people did I have for servants? Thought, if I hired all my labor, it must be very dear. He inquired further about negroes there. I told him they were all free, and described their general condition; told him what led them to congregate in cities, and what the effect was. He said the negroes, both slave and free, who lived in New Orleans, were better off than those who lived in the country. Why? Because they make more money, and it is "gayer" there, and there is more "society." He then drew a contrast between Virginia—as he recollected it—and Louisiana. There is but one road in this country. In Virginia, there are roads running in every direction, and often crossing each other. You could see so much more "society," and there was so much more "variety" than here. He would not like now to go back to Virginia to live, because he had got used to this country, and had all his acquaintances here, and knew the ways of the people. He could speak French. He would like to go to New Orleans, though; would rather live in New Orleans than any other place in the world.

After a silence of some minutes, he said, abruptly;

"If I was free, I would go to Virginia, and see my old mudder." He had left her when he was thirteen years old. He reckoned he was now thirty-three. "I don't well know, dough, exactly, how old I is; but, I rec'lect, de day I was taken away, my ole mudder she tell me I was tirteen year old." He did not like to come away at all; he "felt dreadful bad;" but, now he was used to it, he liked living here. He came across the Blue Ridge, and he recollected that, when he first saw it, he thought it was a dark piece of sky, and he wondered what it would be like when they came close to it. He was brought, with a great many other negroes, in wagons, to Louisville; and then they were put on board a steam-boat, and brought down here. He was sold to a Creole, and was put on this plantation, and had been on it ever since. He had been twice sold, along with it. Folks didn't very often sell their servants here, as they did in Virginia. They were selling their servants, in Virginia, all the time; but, here, they did not very often sell them, except they run away. When a man would run away, and they could not do anything with him, they always sold him off. The people were almost all French. "Were there any French in New York?" he asked. I told him there were; but not as many as in Louisiana. "I s'pose dah is more of French people in Lusiana, dan dah is any-whar else in all de world—a'nt dah, massa?'

"Except in France."

"Wa's dat, sar?"

"France is the country where all the Frenchmen came from, in the first place."

"Wa's dat France, massa?"

"France is a country across the ocean, the big water, beyond Virginia, where all the Frenchmen first came from; just as the black people all came first from Africa, you know."

"I've heered, massa, dat dey sell one anoder dah, in de fus place. Does you know, sar, was dat so?" This was said very gravely, and with some expression of emotion.

I explained the savage custom of making slaves of prisoners of war, and described the constant wars of the native Africans. I told him that they were better off here than they would be to be the slaves of cruel savages, in Africa. He turned, and looked me anxiously in the face, like a child, and asked:

"*Is* de brack folks better off to be here, massa?"

I answered that I thought so; and described the heathenish barbarism of the people of Africa. I made exception of Liberia, knowing that his master thought of some time sending him there, and described it as a place that was settled by negroes, who went back there from this country. He said he had heard of it, and that they had sent a great many free negroes from New Orleans there.

After a moment's pause, he inquired, very gravely, again:

"Why is it, massa, when de brack people is free, dey wants to send 'em away out of dis country?"

The question took me aback. After bungling a little—for I did not like to tell him the white people were afraid to have them stay here—I said that it was thought to be a better place for them there. But, he should think, that, when they had got used to this country, they would be better off here. He would not like to go out of this country. He wouldn't like even to go to Virginia, though Virginia was such a pleasant country; he had been here so long, seemed like this was the best place for him to live. To avoid discussion of the point, I asked what he would do, if he was free?

"If I was free, massa; if I was free (with great animation), I would —— well, sar, de fus thing I would do, if I was free, I would go to work for a year, and get some money for myself, —den—den—den, massa, dis is what I do—I buy me, fus place, a little house, and little lot land, and den—no; den—den—I would go to old Virginny, and see my old mudder. Yes, sar,

I would like to do dat fus thing; den, when I com back, de fus thing I'd do, I'd get me a wife; den, I'd take her to my house, and I would live with her dar; and I would raise things in my garden, and take 'em to New Orleans, and sell 'em dar, in de market. Dat's de way I would live, if I was free."

He said, in answer to further inquiries, that there were many free negroes all about this region. Some of them were very rich. He pointed out to me three plantations, within twenty miles, which were owned by colored men. These bought black folks, he said, and had servants of their own. They were very bad masters, very hard and cruel—hadn't any feeling. "You might think master, dat dey would be good to dar own nation; but dey is not. I will tell you de truth, massa; I know I'se got to answer; and it's a fact, dey is very bad masters, sar. I'd rather be a servant to any man in de world, dan to a brack man. If I was sold to a brack man, I'd drown myself. I would dat—I'd drown myself!—dough I shouldn't like to do dat nudder; but I wouldn't be sold to a colored master for anyting."

If he had got to be sold, he would like best to have an American master buy him. The French people did not clothe their servants well; though they now did much better than when he first came to Louisiana. The French masters were very severe, and "dey whip dar niggers most to deff—dey whip de flesh off of 'em."

Nor did they feed them as well as the Americans did. "Why, sometimes, massa, dey only gives 'em dry corn—don't give out no meat at all." I told him this could not be so, for the law required that every master should serve out meat to his negroes. "Oh, but some on 'em don't mind Law, if he does say so, massa. Law never here; don't know anything about him. *Very often,* dey only gives 'em dry corn—I knows dat; I sees de niggers. Didn't you see de niggers on our plantation, sar? Well, you nebber see such a good-looking lot of niggers as ours on any of de French plantations, did you, massa? Why, dey all looks fat, and dey's all got good clothes, and dey look as if dey all had plenty to eat, and hadn't got no work to do, ha! ha! ha! Don't dey? But dey does work, dough. Dey does a heap of work. But dey don't work so hard as dey does on some ob de French plantations. Oh, dey does work *too* hard on dem, sometimes."

" You work hard, in the grinding season, don't you?"

" Oh, yes; den we works hard; we has to work hard den: harder dan any oder time of year. But, I tell 'ou, massa, I likes to hab de grinding season come; yes, I does—rader dan any oder time of year, dough we works so hard den. I wish it was grinding season all de year roun'—only Sundays."

"Why?"

"Because—oh, because it's merry and lively. All de brack people like it when we begin to grind."

" You have to keep grinding Sundays?"

" Yes, can't stop, when we begin to grind, till we get tru."

" You don't often work Sundays, except then?"

"No, massa; nebber works Sundays, except when der crap's weedy, and we want to get tru 'fore rain comes; den, wen we work a Sunday, massa gives us some oder day for holiday— Monday, if we get tru."

He said that, on the French plantations, they oftener work Sundays than on the American. They used to work almost always on Sundays, on the French plantations, when he was first brought to Louisiana; but they did not so much now.

We were passing a hamlet of cottages, occupied by Acadians, or what the planters call *habitans*, poor white, French Creoles. The negroes had always been represented to me to despise the habitans, and to look upon them as their own inferiors; but William spoke of them respectfully; and, when I tempted him to sneer at their indolence and vagabond habits, refused to do so, but insisted very strenuously that they were " very good people," orderly and industrious. He assured me that I was mistaken in supposing that the Creoles, who did not own slaves, did not live comfortably, or that they did not work as hard as they ought to for their living. There were no better sort of people than they were, he thought.

Some of the cottagers were engaged in threshing rice, which they performed by the ancient process of treading with horses walking in a circle. There were five horses, and three men driving them. He explained this operation to me, and told me that the negroes beat out the rice with sticks. He asked if wheat was not threshed by engines. In answer to inquiries, he said that the negroes raised rice in considerable quantity in wet places on the edge of the swamp, in the rear of the plantation. They also raised corn, potatoes, and pumpkins. His master allowed them land for this, and they sold their crop, or consumed it themselves; generally they sold it. They worked at night, and on Sundays on their patches, and after the sugar and corn-crops of the plantation were " laid by," his master allowed them to have Saturday afternoons to work their own crops in.

He again recurred to the fortunate condition of the negroes on his master's plantation. He thought it was the best plantation in the State, and he did not believe there was a better lot of negroes in the State; some few of them, whom his master had brought from his plantation, were old ; but altogether, they were "as right good a lot of niggers" as could be found anywhere. They could do all the work that was necessary to be done on the plantation. On some old plantations they had not nearly so many negroes as they needed to make the crop, and they " drove 'em awful hard ;" but it wasn't so on his master's : they could do all the work, and do it well, and it was the best worked plantation, and made the most sugar to the hand, of any plantation he knew of. All the niggers had enough to eat, and were well clothed ; their quarters were good, and they got a good many presents.

" Well, now, wouldn't you rather live on such a plantation than to be free, William ?"

"Oh! no, sir, I'd rather be free! Oh, yes, sir, I'd like it better to be free ; I would dat, master."

" Why would you ?"

" Why, you see, master, if I was free—if I was *free*, I'd have *all* my time to myself. I'd rather work for myself. I'd like dat better."

" But then, you know, you'd have to take care of yourself, and you'd get poor."

"No, sir, I would not get poor, I would get rich ; for you see, master, then I'd work *all de time* for myself."

" Suppose all the black people on your plantation, or all the black people in the country were made free at once, what do you think would become of them ?—what would they do, do you think ?   You don't suppose there would be much sugar raised, do you ?"

" Why, yes, master, I do. Why not, sir ? What *would* de brack people do ? Wouldn't dey hab to work for dar libben ?

and de wite people own all de land—war dey goin' to work? Dey hire demself right out again, and work all de same as before. And den, wen dey work for demself, dey work *harder* dan dey do now to get more wages—a heap harder. I tink so, sir. *I* would do so, sir. I would work for hire. I don't own any land; I hab to work right away again for massa, to get some money."

Perceiving from the readiness of these answers that the subject had been a familiar one with him, I immediately asked : "The black people talk among themselves about this, do they; and they think so, generally?"

"Oh! yes, sir; dey talk so; dat's wat dey tink."

"Then they talk about being free a good deal, do they?"

"Yes, sir. Dey—dat is, dey say dey wish it was so; dat's all dey talk, master—dat's all, sir."

His caution was evidently excited, and I inquired no further. We were passing a large old plantation, the cabins of the negroes upon which were mere hovels—small, without windows, and dilapidated. A large gang of negroes were at work by the road-side, planting cane. Two white men were sitting on horse-back, looking at them, and a negro-driver was walking among them, with a whip in his hand.

William said that this was an old Creole plantation, and the negroes on it were worked very hard. There was three times as much land in it as in his master's, and only about the same number of negroes to work it. I observed, however, that a good deal of land had been left uncultivated the previous year. The slaves appeared to be working hard; they were shabbily clothed, and had a cowed expression, looking on the ground, not even glancing at us, as we passed, and were perfectly silent.

"Dem's all Creole niggers," said William: "ain't no Virgin-

ny niggers dah. I reckon you didn't see no such looking niggers as dem on our plantation, did you, master?"

After answering some inquiries about the levee, close inside
of which the road continually ran, he asked me about the levee
at New York; and when informed that we had not any levee,
asked me with a good deal of surprise, how we kept the water
out? I explained to him that the land was higher than the
the water, and was not liable, as it was in Louisiana, to be
overflowed. I had much difficulty in making him understand
this. He seemed never to have considered that it was not the
natural order of things that land should be lower than water, or
that men should be able to live on land, except by excluding
water artificially. At length, when he got the idea, he made a
curious observation.

"I suppose dis State is de lowest State dar is in de world.
Dar ain't no odder State dat is so low as dis is. I s'pose it is
five thousand five hundred feet lower dan any odder State."

"What?"

"I s'pose, master, dat dis heah State is *five thousand five hundred feet* lower down dan any odder, ain't it, sir?"

"I don't understand you."

"I say dis heah is de lowest ob de States, master. I s'pose
its *five thousand five hundred feet* lower dan any odder; lower
down, ain't it, master?"

"Yes, it's very low."

This is a very good illustration of the child-like manner
and habits of the negroes, and which in him were particularly
observable, notwithstanding the shrewdness of some of his observations. Such a mingling of simplicity and shrewdness, in-
genuousness and slyness, detracted much from the weight of his

opinions and purposes in regard to freedom. I could not but
have a strong doubt if he would keep to his word, if the opportunity were allowed him to try his ability to take care of himself.

EXPENSES OF SUGAR PLANTATIONS.

In the year 1846, the Secretary of the Treasury of the United
States addressed a circular of inquiries to persons engaged in
various business throughout the country, to obtain information
of the national resources. In reply to this circular, forty-eight
sugar planters, of St. Mary's Parish, Louisiana, having compared
notes, made the following statement of the usual expenses of a
plantation, which might be expected to produce, one year with
another, one hundred hogsheads of sugar:

Statement.

Household and family expenses, - - - - -	$1,000
Overseer's salary, - - - - - - -	400
Food and clothing for 15 working hands, at $30, - -	450
Food and clothing for 15 old negroes and children, at $15,	225
1½ per cent. on capital invested (which is about $40,000), to keep it in repair, - - - - - -	600
	2,675

50 hogsheads sugar, at 4 cents per pound (net proceeds), - - - - - -	$2,000	
25 hogsheads sugar, at 3 cents per pound (net proceeds), - - - - - -	750	
25 hogsheads sugar, at 2 cents per pound (net proceeds) - - - - - -	500	
4,000 gallons of molasses, at 10 cents, - -	400	
		3,650

Leaving a profit of - - - - - - -	$975

Another gentleman furnished the following estimate of the

expenses of one of the larger class of plantations, working one hundred slaves, and producing, per annum, four to five hundred hogsheads of sugar.

Overseer,	$1,500
Physician's attendance (by contract, $3 a head, of all ages,)	300
Yearly repairs to engine, copper work, resetting of sugar kettles, etc., at least	900
Engineer, during grinding season,	200
Pork, 50 pounds per day—say, per annum, 90 hogsheads, at $12,	1,080
Hoops,	80
Clothing, two full suits per annum, shoes, caps, hats, and 100 blankets, at least $15 per slave,	1,500
Mules or horses, and cattle to replace, at least	500
Implements of husbandry, iron, nails, lime, etc., at least	1,000
Factor's commission, 2½ per cent.,	500
	$7,560

It may be noticed that in this estimate the working force is considered as being equal, in first class hands, to but one-third of the whole number of slaves.

In the report of an Agricultural Society, the gross product of one hand, on a well-regulated sugar estate, is put down at the cultivation of five acres—producing 5000 pounds of sugar, and 125 gallons of molasses; the former valued on the spot at 5½ cents per pound, and the latter at 18 cents per gallon—together, $297·50. The annual expenses, per hand, including wages paid, horses, mules, and oxen, physician's bills, etc., $105. An estate of eighty negroes annually costs $8,330. The items are as follows: Salt meat, and spirits, $830; clothing, $1,200; medical attendance and medicines, $400; Indian corn, $1,090;*

---

* Total for food and drink of negroes, and other live stock, $24 per head of the negroes, per annum. For clothing, $15.

overseer and sugar-maker's salary, $1,000; taxes, $300.   The capital invested in 1,200 acres of land, with its stock of slaves, horses, mules, and working-oxen, is estimated at $147,200.   One-third, or 400 acres, being cultivated annually in cane, it is estimated, will yield 400,000 pounds, at $5\frac{1}{2}$ cents, and 10,000 gallons molasses at 18 cents—together, $23,800.   Deduct annual expense, as before, $8,330, an apparent profit remains of $15,470, or 10 3-7 per cent. interest on the investment.   The crop upon which these estimates were based, has been considered an uncommonly fine one.

BOARD AND CLOTHING.

These estimates are all made by persons anxious to maintain the necessity of protection to the continued production of sugar in the United States, and who are, therefore, under temptation, from this desire, if nothing else, to over-estimate expenditures.

I want those who believe that the free competative system of labor is less humane to the laborer than the slave system, to observe the estimates, which are undoubtedly generous ones, at least, made by these most respectable planters, of the cost of maintaining their slaves.   In the first statement, the cost of clothing and boarding a first-rate, hard-working man is stated to be $30 a year.   A suit of winter clothing and a pair of thin pantaloons for summer, a blanket for bedding, a pair of shoes and a hat, must at least be included under the head of clothing, we must suppose; and these, however poor, could not certainly cost, altogether, less than ten dollars.   For food, then, we must infer that $20 a year is a fair estimate, which is $5\frac{1}{2}$ cents a day. This is for the best hands; light hands are estimated at half this cost.   Does the food of a first-rate laborer, anywhere in the free world, cost less? The lowest price paid by agricultural laborers in the Free States of America, for board, is 21 cents a day, that is, $1·50 a week; in manufacturing towns they oftener pay at least twice that.

On most plantations, I suppose, but by no means on all, the slaves cultivate "patches," and raise poultry for themselves. The produce is nearly always sold to get money to buy tobacco and Sunday finery. But these additions to the usual allowance cannot be said to be provided for them by their masters. The labor expended in this way for themselves does not average half a day a week per slave; and many planters will not allow their slaves to cultivate patches, because it tempts them to reserve for and to expend in the night-work the strength they want employed in their service during the day, and also because the produce thus obtained is made to cover much plundering of their master's crops, and of his live stock. The free laborer also, in addition to his board, nearly always spends something for luxuries—tobacco, fruit and confectionery, to say nothing of dress and intellectual luxuries and recreations.*

The fact is that ninety-nine in a hundred of our free laborers, from choice and not from necessity—for the same provisions cost

---

* "Most persons allow their negroes to cultivate a small crop of their own. For a number of reasons the practice is a bad one. It is next to impossible to keep them from working the crop on the Sabbath. They labor at night when they should be at rest. There is no saving more than to give them the same amount; for, like all other animals, the negro is only capable of doing a certain amount of work without injury. To this point he may be worked at his regular task, and any labor beyond this is an injury to both master and slave. They will pilfer to add to what cotton or corn they have made. If they sell the crop and trade for themselves, they are apt to be cheated out of a good portion of their labor. They will have many things in their possession, under color of purchases, which we know not whether they have obtained honestly."—*Southern Cultivator*.

more in Louisiana than they do anywhere in the northern States—
live, in respect to food, at least four times as well as the average of
the hardest worked slaves on the Louisiana sugar plantations.
And for two or three months in the year, it is known that these
are worked with much greater severity than free laborers at the
North ever are. For on no farm, and in no factory or mine,
even when double wages are paid for night-work, did I ever hear
of men or women working regularly eighteen hours a day. If
ever done, it is only when some accident makes it especially
desirable during a very few days.

I have not compared the comfort of the light hands, in which,
besides the aged and children, are evidently included most of
the females of the plantation, with that of factory girls and apprentices; but who of those at the North was ever expected to
find board at four cents a day, and obliged to save money
enough out of such an allowance to provide him or herself with
clothing? but that, manifestly and beyond the smallest doubt of
error (except in favor of free labor), expresses the condition of
the Louisiana slave. Forty-eight of the most worthy planters
of the State attest it in an official document, published by order
of Congress.

There is no reason for supposing that the slaves are much, if
any, better fed elsewhere than in Louisiana. I was expressly
told in Virginia that I should find them better fed in Louisiana,
because the laws of this State made it necessary for owners to
give them a certain allowance of meat and corn. In the same
Report of Mr. Secretary Walker, a gentleman in South Carolina
testifies that he considers that the "furnishing" (food and clothing) of "full-tasked hands" costs fifteen dollars a year.*

* P. W. Fraser, p. 574, Pub. Doc. VI., 1846.

The United States army is generally recruited from our laboring class, and a well-conditioned and respectable laborer is
seldom induced to join it.   The following, taken from an advertisement, for recruits, in the *Richmond Enquirer*, shows the
food provided :

"DAILY RATIONS.—One and a quarter pounds of beef, one
and three-sixteenths pounds of bread; and at the rate of eight
quarts of beans, eight pounds of sugar, four pounds of coffee,
two quarts of salt, four pounds of candles, and four pounds of
soap, to every hundred rations."

From an advertisement for slaves to be hired by the year, to
work on a canal, in the *Daily Georgian :*

"WEEKLY ALLOWANCE.—They will be provided with three
and a half pounds of pork or bacon, and ten quarts of gourd
seed corn per week, lodged in comfortable shanties, and attended
by a skillful physician."

The expense of boarding, clothes, taxes, and so forth, of a
male slave, is estimated by Robt. C. Hall, a Maryland planter,
at $45 per annum ; this in a climate but little milder than that of
New York, and in a breeding state.   By J. D. Messenger, Jeru-
salem, Virginia : " the usual estimate for an able-bodied laborer—
three barrels of corn, and 250 pounds of well-cured bacon,
seldom using beef or pork ; peas and potatoes substitute about
one-third the allowance of bread," (maize).   By R. G. Morris,
Amherst County, Va. : "not much beef is used on our estates ;
bacon, however, is used much more freely, three pounds a week
being the usual allowance.   The quantity of milk used by slaves
is frequently considerable."—*Pat. Office Report*, 1848.

The following "Essay on the Management of Slaves, by
Robert Collins, of Macon, Georgia," has been printed in many

of the Southern papers, and will show the ideal of slave life, under the most intelligent and humane owners, and in the most favorable circumstances.

" In attempting an essay upon this subject, we can gather but little aid from the long historical record which we have of the institution : for, although we learn that slaves were nearly always employed in labor, we yet see no account of how they were clothed or fed ; nor find any data of comparative results of different modes of treatment, or labor, whereby we can be guided in our search after a system, comprising the greatest benefits.   We must, therefore, rely upon the observation, experience, and practice of the present time, as the only sources of useful and correct information upon the subject.

" The writer has been accustomed to Slavery, from his earliest days, and, for thirty years, has been much interested in their management, both on plantations and public works ; and has, therefore, been prompt-ed, by his own interests, as well as inclination, to try every reasonable mode of management, treatment, living, and labor ; and the results of a long experience have fully satisfied him, and proven beyond doubt, that the best interests of all parties are most promoted by a kind and liberal treatment on the part of the owner, and the requirement of proper dis-cipline and strict obedience on the part of the slave.   Indeed, the Crea-tor seems to have planted in the negro an innate principle of protection against the abuse of arbitrary power ; and it is this law of nature which imperatively associates the true interest of the owner with the good treatment and comfort of the slave.   Hence, abuses and harsh treatment carry their own antidote, as all such cases recoil upon the head of the owner.   Every attempt to force the slave beyond the limits of reasonable service, by cruelty or hard treatment, so far from extorting more work, only tends to make him unprofitable, unmanageable—a vexation and a curse.

" It being, therefore, so manifestly against the interest of all parties, as well as opposed to the natural feelings of humanity, and refinement, and the civilization of the age, a case of cruelty, or abuse of a slave by his owner, is seldom known, and universally condemned.

" NEGRO HOUSES.

*   *   *   *   *   *   *

" The houses should be placed, if possible, under the shades of the native forests; but, where that cannot be done, the china, or mulberry, or some quick growth should be immediately transplanted, so as to cover the buildings, in some degree, from the rays of the summer's sun. The buildings should be placed about two feet above the ground, so that the air can pass freely under them, and also be well ventilated with doors and windows. They should be sufficiently large—say about sixteen by twenty feet—and but one family should be put in a house; there is nothing more injurious to health, or demoralizing in feeling, than crowding them together. They had much better sleep in the open air, than in crowded, tight houses. Each house, or family, should be furnished with suitable bedding and blankets; for while a proper outfit costs a few dollars in the beginning, they save twice as much in the end—they add greatly to the comfort and health of the slave, and enable him much better to perform the labor required.

"FEEDING OF SLAVES.

"In former years, the writer tried many ways and expedients to economize in the provision of slaves, by using more of the vegetable and cheap articles of diet, and less of the more costly and substantial. But time and experience have fully proven the error of a stinted policy; and, for many years, the following uniform mode has been adopted, with much success and satisfaction both to the owner and to the slave.

"The allowance now given per week to each hand—men, women, boys, and girls, that are old enough to go in the field to work—is five pounds of good, clean bacon, and one quart of molasses, with as much good bread as they require; and in the fall, or sickly season of the year, or on sickly places, the addition of one pint of strong coffee, sweetened with sugar, every morning, before going to work. These provisions are given out on some designated night of each week; and, for families, it is put together; but, to single hands, it is given to each separately, and they then unite in squads, or messes, and have their meat cooked for them, by a woman who is detailed for that purpose, or keep it to themselves, as they please. Their bread is baked daily, in loaves, by a woman who is kept for that duty. Each house, or family, should have a garden attached, for raising their own vegetables.

"This mode of allowancing relieves their owner from much trouble, in daily supervising their provisions, and is much more satisfactory to the slave. Under this system of treatment, a word of complaint, in relation to their living, is seldom heard. Some planters, however, differ on this subject, and prefer the plan of cooking and eating at one common table ; and, it is possible, with a small number of hands, and where the owner is willing to devote a good deal of attention to that matter, that he may save a small amount ; but it will not be as satisfactory, and it will, probably, not gain enough to pay for the trouble. Children, of course, must be fed and attended to, as their wants require ; they are not likely to be neglected, as they pay a good interest upon the amount of care and expense bestowed upon them.

"NEGRO CLOTHING.

"The proper and usual quantity of clothes, for plantation hands, is two suits of cotton, for spring and summer, and two suits of woolen, for winter ; four pair of shoes, and three hats, which, with such articles of dress as the negro merits, and the owner chooses to give, make up the year's allowance. Neatness in dress is important to the health, comfort, and pride of a negro—all of which should be encouraged by the owner. They should be induced to think well of themselves ; and the more pride and self-respect you can instill into them, the better they will behave, and the more serviceable they will be ; so they should always be aided and encouraged in dressing, and their own peculiar fancies indulged to a reasonable extent.

"HOURS OF WORK.

"In the winter time, and in the sickly season of the year, all hands should take breakfast before leaving their houses. This they can do, and get to work by sunrise, and stop no more until twelve o'clock ; then rest one hour for dinner ; then work until night. In the spring and summer, they should go to work at light, and stop at eight o'clock, for breakfast ; then work until twelve o'clock, and stop two hours for dinner ; and work from two till night. All hands stop on Saturday, at twelve o'clock, and take the afternoon for cleaning up their houses and clothes, so as to make a neat appearance on Sunday morning.

"TASK WORK.

"The usual custom of planters is, to work without tasks, during the cultivation of their crops ; but, in gathering cotton, tasks are common, and experience has proven that, whenever work is of that kind of character, it is much better to do so. If the overseer has judgment, he will get more work, and the negroes will be better satisfied ; he will generally make an effort, and gain time, to devote to his own jobs or pleasures.

" NEGRO CROPS.

" It was, at one period, much the custom of planters, to give each hand a small piece of land, to cultivate on their own account, if they chose to do so ; but this system has not been found to result well. It gives an excuse for trading, and encourages a traffic on their own account, and presents a temptation and opportunity, during the process of gathering, for an unscrupulous fellow to mix a little of his master's produce with his own. It is much better to give each hand, whose conduct has been such as to merit it, an equivalent in money at the end of the year : it is much less trouble, and more advantageous to both parties.

" DISCIPLINE.

" In regard to the general management or discipline on plantations or public works, it is of great consequence to have perfect system and regularity, and a strict adherence to the rules that may be adopted for the government of the place. Each hand should know his duty, and be required to perform it ; but, as before intimated, the owner has nothing to gain by oppression or over-driving, but something to lose : for he cannot, by such means, extort more work. But still, if it becomes necessary to punish the negro for not doing his duty, or the violation of rules, it does not make' him revengeful, as it would an Indian or white man, but it rather tends to win his attachment, and promote his happiness and well-being. Slaves have no respect or affection for a master who indulges them over-much, or who, from fear, or false humanity, fails to assume that degree of authority necessary to promote industry, and enforce good order. At the same time, proper and suitable indulgences and privileges should be granted for the gratification and amusement of the negro ; but they should always be exercised by special permission—for they are a people ever ready to practice upon the old maxim of ' give an inch, and take an ell.'

" Negroes are by nature tyrannical in their dispositions ; and, if allowed, the stronger will abuse the weaker ; husbands will often abuse their wives and mothers their children—so that it becomes a prominent duty of owners and overseers to keep peace, and prevent quarreling and disputes among them ; and summary punishment should follow any violation of this rule.

" Slaves are also a people that enjoy religious privileges. Many of them place much value upon it ; and, to every reasonable extent, that advantage should be allowed them. They are never injured by preaching, but thousands become wiser and better people, and more trustworthy servants, by their attendance at church. Religious services should be provided and encouraged on every plantation. A zealous and vehement style, both in doctrine and manner, is best adapted to their temperament; they are good believers in mysteries and miracles, ready converts, and adhere with much pertinacity to their opinions, when formed.

"No card-playing, nor gambling of any description should be allowed, under severe penalties. And the Maine liquor law should be rigidly enforced on every estate.

"MARRYING AMONG SLAVES.

"Taking wives and husbands among their fellow-servants, at home, should be as much encouraged as possible; and although inter-marrying with those belonging to other estates should not be absolutely prohibited, yet is always likely to lead to difficulties and troubles, and should be avoided as much as possible. They cannot live together as they ought, and are constantly liable to separation, in the changing of property. It is true they usually have but little ceremony in forming these connections, and many of them look upon their obligation to each other very lightly; but in others, again, is found a degree of faithfulness, fidelity, and affection, which owners admire; and hence they always dislike to separate those manifesting such traits of character.

"SICKNESS.

"Proper and prompt attention, in cases of sickness, is a vastly important matter among slaves. Many plantations are inconvenient to medical aid; therefore owners and overseers should always understand the treatment of such common cases as usually occur on places under their charge. This is easily done; and many times a single dose of some mild and well understood medicine, given at the beginning of a complaint, removes the cause, and effects a cure at once, when delay or neglect might render it a serious one. A few common medicines, with plain and proper directions pasted on each bottle, should be kept on all plantations.

"A bountiful supply of red pepper should be cultivated, and kept on hand, and used freely, in damp sections, where sore throats are apt to prevail, and also in all fall complaints. It acts by creating a glow over the whole body, without any narcotic effect; it produces general arterial excitement, and prevents, in a considerable degree, that languor and apathy of the system which renders it susceptible to chills and fevers;

it may be given in any way or form which their taste or fancy may dictate."

Mr. M. W. Phillips, an ardent and constant writer on agricultural economy, in connection with Slavery, and a most philanthropic man, writing to the New York *Tribune*, for the very purpose of proving that the condition of the slaves is better than that of free-laborers, says, of his own model plantation:

" We now have in this estate 1,168 acres of land ; on the place 66 negroes, twenty work horses and mules, five yoke of choice oxen.

" We plant 270 or 280 acres in cotton, and 125 in corn.

" We send to the field thirty-four negroes, old and young, rating them at thirty hands ; have one carpenter ; a woman who cooks for the above, with all children in charge.

" There are five women, one boy of 14, a girl of 7, and two small boys of 3 and 4 (which have been rather puny to endure ordinary treatment), about the house.   Another woman cooks and washes for overseer (belonging to him).   Thus ten are deducted from the sixty-six, leaving fifty-six, who get, weighed out daily, twenty-two to twenty-four pounds of fat bacon.   Of these, three are children from 2 months to 6 years old (seven and a half ounces of bacon a day each; three pounds a week). In addition, they have unlimited access to vegetables and meal.   No cooking permitted in negro houses—all cooked by the cook at her house, thirty-two by sixteen, with large brick chimney and brick oven. I do not know what meat each one gets, only that all are satisfied.   I prefer that children should have at dinner the pot liquor and bread, with not much meat, finding our children are healthier.   We churn for butter every day, negroes getting all sour milk, but excluding from children.

" We have an overseer at $600 ; we furnish meat and bread for himself, wife and three children, a house with two rooms and a passage, a kitchen, store-room and horse bed.   Our rule is, to eat breakfast before going to work from middle of October to March, then an hour for dinner ; in the summer they take breakfast out with them, and eat from six to seven ; come to dinner at twelve.   About 1st of May, all hands stop from twelve till three o'clock, at which time nothing is done, unless to wash babes by mothers ; this is nooning.

" We give two summer suits, and a straw hat, two winter suits, a wool hat and two pair of shoes ; a blanket worth two dollars, every two years.

" All wood is hauled for fires in winter, and for cooking ; washing done every Saturday afternoon by all the females ; all clothing made by house women.   Cistern water used entirely.

" We lost one of our best fellows a year ago.   His death was caused by a mule, though he lived for months after the injury, not having his mind, or able to go about.   Also, three children, born at a birth, not living an hour.   This comprises all deaths for some five to ten years. Our children are as hearty and as saucy boys and girls as can be shown anywhere.

" We require all negroes to attend family worship every Sabbath morn and eve—at the latter time an hour is spent in instruction by myself, or frequently by some visiting preacher.   They all are required to attend preaching one Sabbath in each month, two and a half miles off, and can go further another Sabbath if they desire it.   We permit no wives or husbands off the place, require marriages with a proper ceremony, *always providing partners.*

" Our women with young children come to the cook-house to nurse their children at breakfast, at nine and a half, twelve, and in the afternoon (nooning, of course, excepted, as they are then in, but always three times a day, besides the noon).   Each family has a house 16 x 18, brick chimney, and house two to three feet above earth.

" Many negroes here have as comfortable quarters as any man would need, even to sleeping between sheets.   My carpenter is employed at home.   We make corn and meat usually.   For twenty-three years I have sold more of each than I have bought by a fair margin.

" Negroes have no need of furniture ; they have bedsteads, bedding and seats, with chests or trunks for clothes—about as much as laborers have anywhere. This is unimportant, yet I like to be square up before all people.

" We might make more money by a different treatment, and we might spend more money on our negroes, if we would listen to questionable friends, of neither negroes nor ourselves.   We act from principle, and never cared to shape our course to please man.   I have examined much into the treatment of slaves, having, some twenty years ago, practiced medicine, with an opportunity to see how different diet and treatment affected health.   Half pound of sound bacon, with vegetables and bread in plenty, and cistern-water, is, in my opinion, a certain preventive of disease ; but the cook must be watched, and water carriers noticed. Negroes fed on three-quarters of a pound of bacon and bread are more prone to disease than if with less meat, but with vegetables.

" We do not permit negroes to stir out before day, nor to get wet if possible, nor do any night work, save feeding horses and shelling corn. We allow no swearing, calling harsh names, wrangling, nor any encroachment on each other's rights. We give a day, or a half-day's holiday occasionally during the summer, two to four days at Christmas, and a dance when the young ones desire it. No work done yesterday or to day, having had to work very hard to get out of the grass, and, working so faithfully without trouble, we gave two days' holiday. Although very hard work this year, owing to so much rain, no grown negro has required more than calling his name, and telling him to hurry. Our present manager has been here three years, and in the vicinity another year.

" I have written thus freely to let many of your readers see that all negroes are not treated here as many would make out. I believe I could show families treated much better than my own is ; but my own know all the circumstances, and are as well content as any laborers are on this broad earth.

" I write not to please, having nothing to gain by it, nor with any expectation of adding one mite to the happiness of many of your readers who make themselves miserable by trying to attend to other people's affairs. I belong to the Southern wing of the Democracy, and have nothing to ask for. Yet I would desire that all my fellow-citizens of this Republic would work for the common good, so that we may fulfill the great object of our mission—serve God with fidelity.

" I saw more destitution in Philadelphia, in the winter of 1828, than I have seen in the South in forty years. I have seen a negro in Philadelphia buy one cent's worth of wood. I never saw negroes beg for food *but those belonging to one man.* These are facts. We have hard masters here, but they are more talked against than hard masters are there. I have seen an able-bodied negro woman in Philadelphia—a good cook, washer and ironer—work for months for her food only, while here, even if free, she would have been paid $10 to $20 per month.

" *The poor white folks of the South fare worse than slaves.* Laziness fares not well anywhere.

" Yours, with respect, etc.,

" M. W. PHILLIPS.
" LOG HALL, EDWARDS, MISS., July 9, 1854."

What advantage have the slaves, under this most enlightened and humane management, over the occupants of our poor-houses? In all the items of food, oversight, clothing, bedding, furniture, religious instruction, medical attendance, defense from quarreling—in everything except the amount of labor, and the provision of partners, our poor-houses provide (so far as I know, and I have visited not a few), at least equally well. But our laboring people are not generally anxious to be admitted to the poor-house. Far from it. They universally consider it a deplorable misfortune which obliges them to go to it. Our poor-houses are seldom crowded. They seldom, in the rural districts, contain any but a few imbeciles and cripples.

Louisiana is the only State in which meat is required, by law, to be furnished the slaves. I believe it is four pounds a week, with a barrel of corn (flour barrel of ears of maize) per month, and salt. In North Carolina the prescribed allowance is "a quart of corn per day." In no other States does the law define the quantity, but it is required, in general terms, to be sufficient for the health of the slave; and I have no doubt that suffering from want of food is exceedingly rare. The food is everywhere, however, coarse, crude, and wanting in variety; much more so than that of our prison convicts. In fact, under favorable circumstances, on the large plantations the slave's allowance does not equal either in quantity or quality that which we furnish the rogues in our penitentiaries. In the New Hampshire, Vermont, Massachusetts, Connecticut, and Pennsylvania state-prisons, the weekly allowance of meat (which is in variety—not merely bacon) is always from one to three pounds more than that recommended by Mr. Collins, and which his slaves received with "much satisfaction," after "a stinted policy" had been given up, and three to five pounds more than that provided by Mr. Phillips. A greater variety of vegetables and condiments is also provided;

and in New Hampshire, Vermont, and Pennsylvania, the quantity of potatoes or porridge furnished is officially reported to be " unlimited." Our laborers certainly do not generally look with envying eyes upon the comforts of a prison.

Does argument, that the condition of free-laborers is, on the whole, better than that of slaves, or that simply they are generally better fed, and more comfortably provided, seem to any one to be unnecessary? Many of our newspapers, of the largest circulation, and certainly of great influence among people— probably not very reflective, but certainly not fools—take the contrary for granted, whenever its suits their purpose. The Southern newspapers, so far as I know, do so, without exception. And very few Southern writers, on any subject whatever, can get through a book, or even a business or friendly letter, to be sent North, without, in some form or other, asserting that Northern laborers might well envy the condition of the slaves. A great many Southern gentlemen—gentlemen whom I respect much for their moral character, if not for their faculties of observation— have asserted it so strongly and confidently, as to shut my mouth, and by assuring me that they had personally observed the condition of Northern laborers themselves, and really knew that I was wrong, have for a time half convinced me against my own long experience. (And perhaps I should say that my experience has been gained, not only as an employer, in different parts of the North, but as a laborer; for I have been a farm laborer, associating and faring equally with the generality of Northern laborers, myself.) I have, since my return, received letters to the same effect: I have heard the assertion repeated by several travelers, and even by Northerners, who had resided long in the South: I have heard it publicly repeated in Tamma-

ny Hall, and elsewhere, by Northern Democrats : I have seen it
in European books and journals : I have, in times past, taken its
truth for granted, and repeated it myself.   Such is the effect of
the continued iteration of falsehood.

Since my return I have made it a subject of careful and
extended inquiry.   I have received reliable and unprejudiced
information in the matter, or have examined personally the food,
the wages, and the habits of the laborers in more than one hundred
different farmers' families, in every free State (except California),
and in Canada.   I have made personal observations and inquiries
of the same sort in Great Britain, Germany, France, and Belgium.
In Europe, where there are large landed estates, which are rented
by lordly proprietors to the peasant farmers, or where land is divided into such small portions that its owners are unable to make
use of the best modern labor-saving implements, the condition of
the laborer, as respects food, often is as bad as that of the slave
often is—never worse than that sometimes is.   But, in general,
even in France, I do not believe it is generally or frequently
worse ; I believe it is, in the large majority of cases, much better
than that of the majority of slaves.   And as respects higher
things than the necessities of life—in their intellectual, moral and
social condition, with some exceptions on large farms and large
estates in England, bad as is that of the mass of European laborers, the man is a brute or a devil who, with my information, would
prefer that of the American slave.   As to our own laborers, in the
Free States, I have already said enough for my present purpose.

But it is time to speak of the extreme cases, of which so
much use has been made, in the process of destroying the confidence of the people of the United States in the freedom of trade,
as applied to labor.

In the year 1855, the severest winter ever known occurred at New York, in conjunction with unprecedentedly high prices of food and fuel, extraordinary business depression, unparalleled marine disasters, and the failure of establishments employing large numbers of men and women. At the same time, there continued to arrive, daily, from five hundred to one thousand of the poorer class of European peasantry. Many of these came, expecting to find the usual demand and the usual reward for labor, and were quite unprepared to support themselves for any length of time, unless they could obtain work and wages. There was consequently great distress.

We all did what we thought we could, or ought, to relieve it; and with such success, that not one single case of actual starvation is known to have occurred in a close compacted population of over a million, of which it was generally reported, fifty thousand were out of employment. Those who needed charitable assistance were, in nearly every case, recent foreign immigrants, sickly people, cripples, drunkards, or knaves taking advantage of the public benevolence, to neglect to provide for themselves. Most of those who received assistance would have thrown a slave's ordinary allowance in the face of the giver, as an insult; and this often occurred with more palatable and suitable provisions. Hundreds and hundreds, to my personal knowledge, during the worst of this dreadful season, refused to work for money-wages that would have purchased them ten times the slave's allowance of the slave's food. In repeated instances, men who represented themselves to be suffering for food, refused to work for a dollar a day. A laborer, employed by a neighbor of mine, on wages and board, refused to work unless he was better fed. "What's the matter," said my neighbor; "don't you have

enough ?"   " Enough; yes, such as it is."   " You have good
meat, good bread, and a variety of vegetables ; what do you
want else ?"   " Why, I want pies and puddings, too, to be sure."
Another laborer left another neighbor of mine, because he never
had any meat offered him, except beef and pork ; he " didn't see
why he shouldn't have chickens."

And these men went to New York, and joined themselves to
that army on which our Southern friends exercise their pity—
of laborers out of work—of men who are supposed to envy the
condition of the slave, because " the slave never dies for want of
food."*

In the depth of winter, a reliable man wrote us from Indiana :

" Here, at Rensselaer, a good mechanic, a joiner or shoemaker, for
instance—and numbers are needed here—may obtain for his labor in one
week :

2 bushels of corn,	25 pounds of pork,
1 bushel of wheat,	1 good turkey,
5 pounds of sugar,	3 pounds of butter,
½ pound of tea,	1 pound of coffee,
10 pounds of beef,	1 bushel of potatoes,

and have a couple of dollars left in his pocket, to start with the next
Monday morning."

The moment the ice thawed in the spring, the demand for

---

* Among the thousands of applicants for soup, and bread, and fuel, as charity,
I never saw, during " the famine" in New York, one negro. The noble Five
Points Pease said to me, " The negro seems to be more provident than the Celt.
The poor blacks always manage to keep themselves more decent and comfortable than the poor whites. They very rarely complain, or ask for charity ;
and I have often found them sharing their food with white people, who were too
poor to provide for themselves." A great deal of falsehood is circulated and
accredited about the sufferings of the free-negroes at the North. Their condition is bad enough, but no worse than that of any men educated and treated as
they are, must be ; and it is, I think, on an average, far better than that of the
slave.

mechanics exceeded the supply, and the workmen had the
master-hand of the capitalists. In June, the following rates
were willingly paid to the different classes of workmen—some
of the trades being on strike for higher:

	Per Week.			Per Week.
Boiler-maker, - -	$12 to $20		Harness-maker, - -	$10
Blacksmith, - - -	12 to 20		Mason, - - - - - 10 to	15
Baker, - - - -	9 to 14		Omnibus-driver, - -	10
Barber, - - - - -	7 to 10		Printer, - - - - - 10 to	25
Bricklayer, - - - - 14 to	15		Plumber, - - - -	15
Boat-builder, - - -	15		Painter (house), - -	15
Cooper, - - - - - 8 to	12		Piano-forte maker, - 10 to	14
Carpenter (house), -	15		Shipwright, - - - -	18
Confectioner, - - - 8 to	12		Ship-caulker, - - -	18
Cigar-maker, - - - 9 to	25		Ship-fastener, - - -	18
Car-driver (city cars),	10		Shoemaker, - - -	16
Car-conductor, "	10½		Sign painter, - - - 25 to	30
Engineer, common, - 12 to	15		Sail-maker, - - - -	15
Engineer, locomotive,	15		Tailor, - - - - - 8 to	17

At this time I hired a gardener, who had been boarding for a
month or two in the city, and paying for his board and lodging
$3 a week. I saw him at the dinner-table of his boarding-house,
and I knew that the table was better supplied with a variety of
wholesome food, and was more attractive, than that of the majority of slave-owners with whom I have dined.

Amasa Walker, formerly Secretary of State in Massachusetts,
is the authority for the following table, showing the average
wages of a common (field-hand) laborer in Boston (where immigrants are constantly arriving, and where, consequently, there is
often a necessity, from their ignorance and accidents, of charity,
to provide for able-bodied persons), and the prices of ten different articles of sustenance, at three different periods:

WAGES OF LABOR AND FOOD AT BOSTON.

	1836. Wages. $1·25 per day.	1840. Wages. $1 per day.	1843. Wages. $1 per day.
1 barrel flour, - -	$9·50	$5·50	$4·75
25 lbs. sugar, at 9c. -	2·25	2·00	1·62
10 gals. molasses, 42½c.	4·25	2·70	1·80
100 lbs. pork, - - - -	4·50	8·50	5·00
14 lbs. coffee, 12½c. -	1·75	1·50	5·00
28 lbs. rice, - - - -	1·25	1·00	75
1 bushel corn meal, -	96	65	62
1 do. rye meal, -	1·08	83	73
30 lbs. butter, 22c. -	6·60	4.80	4·20
20 lbs. cheese, 10c. -	2.00	1·60	1·40
	$44·00	$28·98	$22·00

This shows that in 1836 it required the labor of thirty-four
and a half days to pay for the commodities mentioned; while in
1840 it required only the labor of twenty-nine days, and in 1843
that of only twenty-three and a half days to pay for the same.
If we compare the ordinary allowance of food given to slaves
per month—as, for instance, sixteen pounds pork, one bushel
corn meal, and, say one quart of molasses, on an average, and
a half pint of salt—with that which it is shown by this table
the free laborer is usually able to obtain by a month's labor,
we can estimate the comparative general comfort of each.

I am not all disposed to neglect the allegation that there
is sometimes great suffering among our free laborers. Our
system is by no means perfect; no one thinks it so: no one
objects to its imperfections being pointed out.   There was no
subject so much discussed in New York that winter as the
causes, political and social, which rendered us liable to have
laborers, under the worst possible combination of circumstances,
liable to difficulty in procuring satisfactory food.

But this difficulty, as a serious thing, is a very rare and exceptional one (I speak of the whole of the Free States): that it is so, and that our laborers are ordinarily better fed and clothed than the slaves, is evident from their demands and expectations, when they are deemed to be suffering. When any real suffering does occur, it is mainly a consequence and a punishment of their own carelessness and improvidence, and is in the nature of a remedy.

And in every respect, for the laborer the competitive system, in its present lawless and uncertain state, is far preferable to the slave system; and any laborer, even if he were a mere sensualist and materialist, would be a fool to wish himself a slave.

One New York newspaper, having a very large circulation at the South, but a still larger at the North, in discussing this matter, last winter, fearlessly and distinctly declared—as if its readers were expected to accept the truth of the assertion at once, and without argument—that the only sufficient prevention of destitution among a laboring class was to be found in Slavery; that there was always an abundance of food in the Slave States, and hinted that it might yet be necessary, as a security against famine, to extend Slavery over the present Free States. This article is still being copied by the Southern papers, as testimony of an unwilling witness to the benevolence and necessity of eternal Slavery.

The extracts following, from Southern papers, will show what has occurred in the Slave country, in the mean while:

"For several weeks past, we have noticed accounts of distress among the poor in some sections of the South, for the want of bread, particularly in Western Georgia, East and Middle Alabama. Over in Coosa, corn-cribs are lifted nightly; and one poor fellow (corn thief) lately got caught between the logs, and killed! It is said there are many grain-hoarders in the destitute regions, awaiting higher prices! The L—d pity the poor, for his brother man will not have any mercy upon his brother."—*Pickens Republican, Carrolton, Ala., June 5,* 1855.

"We regret that we are unable to publish the letter of Governor Winston, accompanied by a memorial to him from the citizens of a portion of Randolph county, showing a great destitution of breadstuffs in that section, and calling loudly for relief.

"The Claiborne *Southerner* says, also, that great destitution in regard to provisions of all kinds, especially corn, prevails in some portions of Perry county."—*Sunny South, Jacksonville, Ala., May* 26, 1855.

"As for wheat, the yield in Talladega, Tallapoosa, Chambers, and Macon, is better even than was anticipated. Flour is still high, but a fortnight will lower the price very materially. We think that wheat is bound to go down to $1·25 to $1·50 per bushel, though a fine article commands now $2·25.

"Having escaped famine—as we hope we have—we trust the planting community of Alabama will never again suffer themselves to be brought so closely in view of it. Their want of thrift and foresight has come remarkably near placing the whole country in an awful condition. It is only to a kind Providence that we owe a deliverance from a great calamity, which would have been clearly the result of man's short-sightedness."—*Montgomery Mail, copied in Savannah Georgian, June* 25, 1855.

"Wheat crops, however, are coming in good, above an average ; but oats are entirely cut off. I am issuing commissary, this week, for the County, to distribute some corn, bought by the Commissioner's Court, for the destitute of our County ; and could you have witnessed the applicants, and heard their stories, for the last few days, I am satisfied you could draw a picture that would excite the sympathy of the most selfish heart. I am free to confess that I had no idea of the destitution that prevails in this County. Why, sir, what do you think of a widow and her children living, for three days and nights, on boiled weeds, called pepper grass ?—yet such, I am credibly informed, has been the case in Chambers County."—*From a letter to the editor of the Montgomery (Ala.) Journal, from Hon. Samuel Pearson, Judge of Probate, for Chambers County, Alabama.*

"FAMINE IN UPPER GEORGIA.—We have sad news from the north part of Georgia. The *Dalton Times* says that many people are without corn, or means to procure any. And, besides, there is none for sale. In some neighborhoods, a bushel could not be obtained for love or money. Poor men are offering to work for a peck of corn a day. If they plead " our children will starve," they are answered, " so will mine, if I part with the little I have." Horses and mules are turned out into the woods, to wait for grass, or starve, The consequence is, that those who have land can only plant what they can with the hoe—they cannot plough. It is seriously argued that, unless assisted soon, many of the poor class of that section will perish."— *California Paper.**

No approach to anything like such a state of things as these extracts portray (which extended over parts of three agricultural States) ever occurred, I am sure, in any rural district of the Free States. Even in our most thickly-peopled manufacturing districts, to which the staple articles of food are brought from far-distant regions, assistance from abroad, to sustain the poor, has never been asked ; nor do I believe the poor have ever been reduced, for weeks together, to a diet of corn. But this famine at the South occurred in a region where most productive land can be purchased for from three to seven dollars an acre; where maize and wheat grow kindly ; where cattle, sheep, and hogs, may be pastured over thousands of acres, at no rent; where fuel has no value, and at a season of the year when clothing or shelter is hardly necessary to comfort.

It is a remarkable fact that this frightful famine, unprecedented in North America, was scarcely noticed, in the smallest way, by

* In the obscure country papers, of Northern Alabama and Georgia, and Western South Carolina, I have seen many more descriptions, similar to these, of this famine; but I cannot now lay my hand on them. These I have by accident, not having taken pains to collect them for this purpose. In a district of the Slave States, where it is boasted that more than a hundred bushels of maize to the acre has been raised, and where not one out of five hundred of the people is engaged in any other than agricultural industry, I have myself bought maize, which had been raised by free labor, in Ohio, at two dollars a bushel.

any of those Southern papers which, in the ordinary course of things, ever reach the North.   In the Charleston, Savannah, and Mobile papers, received at our commercial reading-rooms, I have not been able to find any mention of it at all—a single, short, second-hand paragraph in a market report, excepted.   But these journals had columns of reports from our papers, and from their private correspondents, as well as pages of comment, on the distress of the laborers in New York City the preceding winter.

In 1837, the year of repudiation in Mississippi, a New Orleans editor describes the effects of the money-pressure upon the planters, as follows:

"They are now left without provisions, and the means of living and using their industry for the present year.   In this dilemma, planters, whose crops have been from 100 to 700 bales, find themselves forced to sacrifice many of their slaves, in order to get the common necessaries of life, for the support of themselves and the rest of their negroes.   In many places, heavy planters compel their slaves to fish for the means of subsistence, rather than sell them at such ruinous rates.   There are, at this moment, thousands of slaves in Mississippi, that know not where the next morsel is to come from.   The master must be ruined, to save the wretches from being starved."

Absolute starvation is as rare, probably, in Slavery, as in freedom; but I do not believe it is more so.   An instance is just recorded in the *New Orleans Delta*.   Other papers omit to notice it—as they usually do facts which it may be feared will do discredit to Slavery—and even the *Delta*, as will be seen, is anxious that the responsibility of the publication should be, at least, shared by the Coroner:

"INQUEST—DEATH FROM NEGLECT AND STARVATION.—The body of an old negro, named Bob, belonging to Mr. S. B. Davis, was found lying dead in the woods, near Marigny Canal, on the Gentilly Road, yesterday.

The Coroner held an inquest ; and, after hearing the evidence, the Jury returned a verdict of 'Death from starvation and exposure, through neglect of his master.' It appeared from the evidence, that the negro was too old to work any more, being near seventy ; and so they drove him forth into the woods to die. He had been without food for forty-eight hours, when found by Mr. Wilbank, who lives near the place, and who brought him into his premises on a wheelbarrow, gave him something to eat, and endeavored to revive his failing energies, which had been exhausted from exposure and want of food. Every effort to save his life, however, was unavailing, and he died shortly after being brought to Mr. Wilbank's. The above statement we publish, as it was furnished us by the Coroner."—*Sept.* 18, 1855.

This is the truth, then—is it not?—The slaves are generally sufficiently well fed to be in good physical working condition; but not as well as our free laborers generally are : Slavery, in practice, affords no safety against occasional suffering for want of food among laborers, or even against their starvation, any more than the democratic, or free system ; while it withholds all encouragement from the laborer to improve his faculties and his skill; destroys his self-respect; misdirects and debases his ambition, and withholds all the natural motives, which lead men to endeavor to increase their capacity of usefulness to their country and the world. To all this, the *occasional suffering* of the free laborer is favorable, on the whole. The occasional suffering of the slave has no such advantage. To deceit, indolence, malevolence, and thievery, it may lead, as may the suffering—though it is much less likely to—of the free laborer ; but to industry, cultivation of skill, perseverance, economy, and virtuous habits, neither the suffering, nor the dread of it as a possibility, ever can lead the slave, as it generally does the free laborer, unless it is by inducing him to run away.

I cannot leave this subject, without expressing my conviction of the great evil which the necessity felt by so many, to apologize for Slavery at every convenient opportunity, is working in our own society. It is to be attributed, very much, to this source, I think—the growing disposition to look upon the laborer, the artisan, the handicraftsman—the man who is employed at any of those callings in which it is commonly thought safe and proper to educate slaves—as a less fortunate and respectable man than the tradesman, the clerk, the "professional" man. To make Slavery less hateful, the condition and prospects of free laboring people are habitually disparaged. Our children are familiarized with comparisons unfavorable to the happiness and respectability of our own working class, and are led to believe that men who work for a living are seldom successful; that they are peculiarly dependent on others; that others have to be careful of them, and often provide for them out of charity and pity. And many of our working men are themselves influenced by this idea, and look upon their customers as in some way their superiors; and in consequence of this feeling they get a habit of thinking themselves ill-used, and unfortunate, poorly compensated for their labor; therefore, also, they work—the majority of our native mechanics—less soundly, and thoroughly, artistically, conscientiously, and with love and pride in their craft; more slightingly, carelessly, mechanically, and like to slaves than they formerly did. Our most conscientious and reliable work-men are no longer natives; they are from Germany, where yet the ancient guilds, with their honors to WORKMANSHIP, and conferring FREEDOM on passed and accepted workmen, are not quite lost.

This mischievous influence of Slavery upon ourselves, is rarely appreciated as it should be. Clarence Cook, in his admirable lecture—"The Head and the Hand"—is almost the only one of our public instructors by whom I have heard it at all adequately recognized.

This book is already so much too large, that I cannot dwell upon the subject; but I must declare my conviction, that the common notions, not only in the comparison of our free work-men with slaves, but of free work-men with free men of sedentary and effeminate callings, are fallacies, and have no other foundation than the political degradation of work-men in our own Slave communities, and the undemocratic communities of Europe. Certain I am, that in my experience, the young men of good sense, sobriety and industry, who have been educated as artisans, have been more successful, in every view, than the young men of similar quality, who have been educated as clerks. Where, too, so much capital as is necessary to prepare a man for the learned professions has been used to prepare workers in the industrial fields of science, it has been better, sooner, and with more honor, repaid in results. There is infinitely more room and need for the genius of Michael Angelo in a garden, or a ship-yard, or a blacksmith's or carpenter's shop, than in the sales-room, the counting-house, the pulpit, or the court-house. Nor need the cobbler's stall, if a man have by nature great endowments for statesmenship, be the smallest restriction upon their development. I believe, in fact, it yet is not; and that it is still easier for a great mind to direct itself to great things, and to gain a position to work great things, in hammering leather, than in engrossing pleas and filing declarations.

And I consider the skilled work-man to be always more independent of charity—to be in a more reliable and respectable position, actually, in society, than the skilled clerk, or the skilled professional man; so far, that is to say, as the mere callings of each are concerned. A larger proportion of the clergymen, lawyers, doctors, salesmen, tradesmen, merchants, speculators in land, and planters, of the United States, are involved in debt, and will never pay their debts, than of the laborers, yeomen farmers, mechanics, and artisans. The former class are more likely to become hopelessly bankrupt from personal accidents than the latter. The mechanic may lose his right hand, and his acquired skill being no longer available, he will be comparatively helpless; but the physician, the lawyer, may lose their eyes, or their hearing; the clergyman may suffer in his throat; the tradesman in his lungs; the planter and speculator, by fire, or rot, or worm, or war, and thus become equally incapable of self-support with the crippled mechanic.

As to success of the farm-laborer in gaining wealth, I cannot now speak with equal confidence as of the mechanic; but that sensible and industrious farmers, who have started in life with no capital but a good common-school education, and a good farm-boy's skill and strength for labor, more often spend a happy and grateful old age among children and children's children, of whom they are proud, than men of any other calling in our country, I have not a doubt.

In every way, I repeat it, the idea that a muscular or handicraft occupation, if directed with the genius and thought it always may and should be, is lower or less fortunate, and less likely to be attended with honor in a free country, than the occupations of transfer, scheming, copying and adapting of forms and precedents, is a most false and pernicious one. It is true, only, that a man without any education may be a bad workman, while he cannot well be even a bad clerk, lawyer, or physician. But genius, taste, energy, and dexterity, as well as capital in general knowledge, and culture of the mind, are even more valuable, and are at this time more wanted in our market, and are better paid for in the artisan and mechanic, than they are in the tradesman, or the professional man. The only basis for the contrary notion that I know of, is that slaves are excluded from trade and "the professions," and that therefore, wherever the influence of Slavery extends, those occupations to which slaves are condemned are considered to belong to a lower *caste* of the community, and so to degrade those who engage in them.

APPENDIX.

From a native Virginian, who has resided in New York:

"*To the Editor of the N. Y. Daily Times.*

"Sir :—You will not object, I think, to receive an endorsement from a Southern man of the statements contained in number seven of 'Letters on the productions, industry, and resources of the Southern States,' published in your issue on Thursday last.   *   *   *

"Where you would see one white laborer on a Northern farm, scores of blacks should appear on the Virginia plantation, *the best of them only performing each day one-fourth a white man's daily task, and all requiring an incessant watch to get even this small modicum of labor.* Yet they eat as much again as a white man, must have their two suits of clothes and shoes yearly, and although the heartiest, healthiest looking men and women anywhere on earth, actually lose for their owners or employers one-sixth their time on account of real or pretended sickness. Be assured, our model Virginia farmer has his hands full, and is not to be envied as a jolly fox-hunting idler, lording it over 'ranks of slaves in chains.' No, sir ; he must be up by 'the dawn's early light,' and head the column, direct in person the commencing operations, urging, and coaxing ; must praise and punish—but too glad to reward the meritorious, granting liberty (*i. e.* leave of absence,) often to his own servant, that he dare not take himself, because he must not leave home for fear something will go wrong ere his return.   Hence but too many give up, to overseers or other irresponsible persons, the care and management of their estates, rather than undergo such constant annoyance and confinement.   Poor culture, scanty crops, and worn-out land, is the inevitable result ; and yet, harassed and trammeled as they are, no one but a Southerner regards them with the slightest degree of compassion or even forbearance, and our good friends, the Abolitionists, would have ' all the rest of mankind' rank them with pirates and cut-throats. But my object in this communication is not to sympathize with nor ask sympathy on behalf of slave-holders. For, however sinning or sinned against, they seem quite able to take their own part, if molested ; and are remarkably indifferent, withal, as to the opinions expressed by ignorant ranters concerning them.

" If I have the ability, my desire is to draw a parallel between the state and condition of Northern and Southern farmers and farming. The Northern farmer does undoubtedly experience a full share of those troubles and cares attendant even upon the most easy and favorable system of farming ; but, sir, can he have any such responsibility as that resting upon the owner of from 50 to 300 ignorant, lazy negroes?

*   *   *   *   *   *   *   *   *   *   *

" You must plow deep, follow up quickly, and sow with powerful fertilizers, attend closely to the growing crop, gather in rapidly before blight or mildew can come and destroy, says our Northern farmer. On a farm of three hundred acres, thus managed with five hands, two extra during harvest, I can raise thirty bushels of wheat to the acre. Now picture the condition of him South, and hear his answer. With from three to fifteen hundred acres of land, and a host of negroes great and small, his cares and troubles are without end. ' The hands,' able men and women, to say nothing of children, and old ones laid by from age or other infirmity, have wants innumerable. Some are sick, others pretend to be so, many obstinate, indolent, or fractious—each class requires different treatment ; so that without mentioning the actual daily wants, as provisions, clothing, etc., etc., the poor man's time, and thoughts—indeed, every faculty of mind—must be exercised on behalf of those who have no minds of their own.

" His answer, then, to the Northern farmer is : ' I have not one hand on my place capable and willing to do the work you name.' They tell me that ' five of them could not perform the task required of one.' They have never been used to do it, and no amount of force or persuasion will induce them to try ; their task is so much per day, all over that I agree to pay them for, at the same rate I allow free laborers—but 'tis seldom they make extra time, except to get money enough to buy tobacco, rum, or sometimes fine clothes. Can it be wondered at that systematic farming, such as we see North and East, is unknown or not practiced to any great degree South? The two systems will not harmonize.

" R. J. W."

From a native New Yorker, who has resided in Virginia:

"*To the Editor of the New York Daily Times.*

" I have read with deep interest the series of letters from the South, published in your columns. Circumstances have made me quite familiar with the field of your correspondent's investigation, much more familiar than he is at present, and yet I am happy to say, that his letters are more satisfactory than any I have ever seen relating to the South. It is now about ten years since, going from this State, I first became familiar with those facts in regard to the results of slave-labor, etc., that your correspondent and his readers are so much surprised at. I have talked those subjects over as he is doing, with the planters along the shores of the Chesapeake, and on both sides of the James River, through the Tidewater, the middle and the mountainous districts east of the Blue Ridge, and in many of those rich counties in the Valley of Virginia. I may add that subsequently, spending my winters at the South for my health, I have become well nigh as familiar with the States of North and South Carolina, and Georgia, as I am with Virginia. I have, therefore, almost of necessity, given not a little thought to the questions your correspondent is discussing.

" His statement, in regard to the comparative value of slave and free-labor, will surprise those who have given little or no attention to the subject. I wish to confirm his statements on this subject. In Eastern Virginia I have repeatedly been told that the task of one cord of wood a day, or five cords a week, rain or shine, is the general task, and one of the most profitable day's work that the slave does for his master. And this, it should be remembered, is generally pine wood, cut from trees as straight and beautiful as ever grew. The reason of this ' profitableness' is the fact that the labor requires so little mental effort. The grand secret of the difference between free and slave-labor is, that the latter is without intelligence, and without motive. If the former, in Western New York, has a piece of work to perform, the first thought is, how it can be done with the least labor, and the most expeditiously. He thinks, he plans, before he commences, and while about his labor. His mind labors as much as his body, and this mental labor saves a vast deal of physical labor. Besides this, he is urged on by the strongest motives. He enjoys the products of his labor. The more intelligent and earnest his labors, the richer are his rewards. Slave-labor is exactly the opposite of this. It is unintelligent labor—labor without thought

—without plan—without motive. It is little more than brute force. To one who has not witnessed it, it is utterly inconceivable how little labor a slave, or a company of slaves, will accomplish in a given time. Their awkwardness, their slowness, the utter absence of all skill and ingenuity in accomplishing the work before them, are absolutely painful to one who has been accustomed to seeing work done with any sort of spirit and life. Often they spend hours in doing what, with a little thought, might be dispatched in a few moments, or perhaps avoided altogether. This is a necessary result of employing labor which is without intelligence and without motive. I have often thought of a remark made to me by a planter, in New Kent County, Virginia. We were riding past a field where some of his hands were making a sort of wicker-work fence, peculiar to Eastern Virginia. 'There,' said he, in a decidedly fretted tone, 'those "boys" have been — days in making that piece of fence.' I expressed my astonishment that they could have spent so much time, and yet have accomplished so very little. He assured me it was so—and after a slight pause, the tones of his voice entirely changed, said : 'Well, I believe they have done as well as I would in their circumstances !' And so it is. The slave is without motive, without inducement to exertion. His food, his clothing, and all his wants are supplied as they are, without care on his part, and when these are supplied he has nothing more to hope for. He can make no provision for old age, he can lay up nothing for his children, he has no voice at all in the disposal of the results of his earnings. What cares he whether his labor is productive or unproductive. His principal care seems to be to accomplish just as little as possible. I have said that the slaves were without ingenuity—I must qualify that remark. I have been amused and astonished at their exceeding ingenuity in avoiding and slighting the work that was required of them. It has often seemed to me that their principal mental efforts were in this direction, and I think your correspondent will find universal testimony that they have decided talent in this line.   H. W. P."

In a volume entitled "Notes on Uncle Tom's Cabin; being a Logical Answer to its Allegations and Inferences against Slavery as an Institution," by the Rev. E. J. Stearns, of Maryland, (much the most thorough review of that work made from the Southern stand-point,) the author, who is a

New-Englander by birth, shows, by an elaborate calculation, that in Maryland, the cost of a negro, at twenty-one years of age, has been, to the man who raised him, eight hundred dollars. Six *per cent.* interest on this cost, with one and three-quarters per cent. for life insurance, per annum, makes the lowest wages of a negro, under the most favorable circumstances, sixty-two dollars a year, (or five dollars a month,) *paid in advance*, in the shape of food and clothing. The author, whose object is to prove that the slave-holder is not guilty, as Mrs. Stowe intimates, of *stealing* the negroes' labor, proceeds, as follows, to show that he pays a great deal more for it than Mrs. Stowe's neighbors in New England do, for the labor they hire:

"If now we add to this, (what every New-Englander who has lived at the South *knows*,) that Quashy does not do more than one-third, or, at the very utmost, one-half as much work as an able-bodied laborer on a farm at the North; and that, for this he receives, besides the five dollars above-mentioned, his food, clothing and shelter, with medical attendance and nursing when sick, and no deduction for lost time, even though he should be sick for years, while the 'farm-hand' at the North gets only ten or twelve dollars, and has to clothe himself out of it, and pay his own doctor's and nurse's bill in sickness, to say nothing of lost time, I think we shall come to the conclusion if there has been stealing anywhere, it has not been from Quashy."—p. 25.

"I recollect, the first time I saw Quashy at work in the field, I was struck by the lazy, listless manner in which he raised his hoe. It reminded me of the working-beam of the engine on the steam-boat that I had just landed from—fifteen strokes a minute; but there was this difference: that, whereas the working-beam kept steadily at it, Quashy, on the contrary, would stop about every five strokes and lean upon his hoe, and look around, apparently congratulating himself upon the amount of work he had accomplished.

"Mrs. Stowe may well call Quashy 'shiftless.' One of my father's hired men—who was with him.seven years—did more work in that time than an average negro would do in his whole life. Nay, I myself have done more work in a day,—and followed it up, too—than I ever saw a negro do, and I was considered remarkably lazy with the plow or hoe."—p. 142.

The *Journal of Commerce*, of April 21, has a communication from a slave-holder, urging an emigration of emigrant-laborers to Virginia and North Carolina, where, he says, the Irish and Germans are destined to drive out the negroes:

" The latter are too costly an article of Virginia luxury to be kept any longer. A good able-bodied negro costs now-a-days $1,000, and at this price is very unprofitable property. A mortgage on a flock of partridges is almost as certain. He may die, be maimed for life, or be induced by his philanthropic Northern friends to *vamose;* whereas, if ' Paddy or Hans' shuffles off his mortal coil, you suffer no pecuniary loss ; you don't even bury him, or pay his doctor's bill, but get another hand in his place.

" Hundreds of farmers and planters, mill owners, tobacconists, cotton factories, iron works, steam-boat owners, master builders, contractors, carpenters, stage proprietors, canal-boat owners, rail-road companies, and others are, and have been, short of hands these five years past, in Maryland, Virginia, and the Carolinas. They pay $150 or $200 per year, each hand, and his board and stealing, and if that hand be present or absent, sick or well, it is all the same. His clothes cost say $30 more, and in many cases the hirer has to pay his policy of life insurance. *A white man will do three times the work,* and will be five times better cared for, than in the Northern States in similar circumstances.

" White men are badly wanted in Maryland, Virginia, and North Carolina. Thousands of negroes have gone from there last year to Louisiana and Texas; their places must be filled. By all means let our Emigration Society encourage them to go South."

In another Condemnatory Review of "Uncle Tom's Cabin," by H. M. Brackenbridge, published in the *National Intelli-*

gencer, Dec., 1852, containing many very sensible observations on Slavery, resulting, as is announced, from ten years' personal observation of slaves, by the writer, and much reflection, it is stated that "the day's labor of the slave is notoriously not more than half that of the white man; and, if left to himself," (that is, not *driven*,) "not more than half that."

APPENDIX A.

THE statement that Georgia had disused the slave basis of representation for her own Legislature, was made upon information given me by a Georgia planter. Since the plate of page 531 was cast, I have endeavored, without success, to verify it; and am now inclined to think I had been misinformed. According to the latest authorities in the Astor and Law Libraries, in New York, it is strictly true with regard only to the election of the State Senate, which alone is representative of the citizens in their equality of political rights; in the lower house, thirty-seven counties, having the greatest population, counting all free white persons, and two-fifths of the people of color [not merely the slaves], have two votes each, which, however, represent the interests only of the whites; the remaining fifty-six poorer counties, but one each. By this arrangement, five hundred slaveholding citizens might exercise double the power of five thousand non-slaveholding citizens in the House, while the latter might have ten times more power than they in the Senate. This is evidently one of those absurd arrangements, based on no principle at all, which are hatched by compromises. The slave-basis has not been given up, if this arrangement still holds; but, on the other hand, it has not been honestly sustained. In more than one of the post-revolutionary Slave States, the slave-basis of representation, for their internal legislation, is entirely discarded, and there is no doubt it soon would be in all, but for the argument *ad hominem*, repeated by Mr. Howison. For consistency's sake, the slave-owners are, in some States, still allowed this entirely unnecessary advantage, for maintaining their control of legislation